W9-BZB-899

The Exuberant Garden
and the
Controlling Hand

The Exuberant Garden and the Controlling Hand

Plant Combinations for North American Gardens

William H. Frederick, Jr.

 Little, Brown and Company   *Boston · Toronto · London*

Library of Congress Cataloging-in-Publication Data

Frederick, William H. (William Heisler), 1926–
    The exuberant garden and the controlling hand : plant combinations for North American gardens / William H. Frederick, Jr. — 1st ed.
        p.   cm.
    Includes index.
    ISBN 0-316-29255-9
    1. Gardens—Design.   2. Plants, Ornamental. 3. Gardens—Pictorial works.   4. Gardens— United States—Design.   5. Plants, Ornamental— United States.   6. Gardens—United States— Pictorial works.
    I. Title.
    SB473.F828   1991
    712'.6'097—dc20   91-19655

10 9 8 7 6 5 4 3 2 1

TWP

Published simultaneously in Canada by Little, Brown & Company (Canada) Limited

Printed in Singapore

Also by William H. Frederick, Jr.
100 Great Garden Plants

Designed by Susan Marsh

Drawings on pp. 2, 26, and 31 by Barbara Seymour
Drawings in the Appendices are by
Nancy G. Frederick

Photograph Acknowledgments:
Larry Albee: p. x; p. 1; p. 9; p. 12; p. 13; p. 14; p. 20; p. 33; p. 59, figure 6; p. 62; p. 64; p. 70, top; p. 78; p. 81; p. 85; p. 87; p. 88; p. 103; p. 107; p. 109; p. 110; p. 111; p. 115; p. 116; p. 127, top right; p. 142; p. 144.
Brookside Gardens: p. 121, figure 2.
Charles O. Cresson: p. 7, figure 11; p. 60, figure 3.
Rick Darke: p. 125, figure 5.
Michael H. Dodge: p. 127, top left; p. 150.
John E. Elsley: p. 6, figure 3; p. 23, figure 3; p. 27, figure 1; p. 28, bottom inset; p. 38, bottom; p. 42, figure 3; p. 59, figures 3 and 5; p. 73, figure 8; p. 75, top inset; p. 77, figure 1; p. 124, bottom; p. 125, figure 3; p. 128; p. 129.
William M. Flook, Jr.: p. 106.
Crawford H. Greenewalt: p. 100, figure 2.
Gottlieb Hampfler: p. 141, bottom; p. 146, bottom; p. 147.
Pamela Harper: p. 23, figure 1; p. 28, top inset; p. 41, figure 2; p. 60, figure 2; p. 73, figure 6; p. 76, bottom; p. 77, bottom inset; p. 99, bottom inset.
Robert Hyland: p. 3, top inset; p. 53; p. 72, figure 2; p. 123, figure 2; p. 125, figure 1.
Robin Karson: p. 131.
Richard Keen: p. 59, figure 4; p. 134, top; p. 146, top.
Clarence E. Lewis: p. 46, figure 2.
Richard W. Lighty: p. 7, figure 10; p. 29; p. 58, figure 2; p. 59, figure 8; p. 75, bottom background and inset; p. 99, top background and inset.
Paul W. Meyer: p. 124, top.
Joanna Reed: p. 27, figure 4.
Claire Sawyers: p. 44, figure 3.
The Henry Francis duPont Winterthur Museum: p. 136, bottom (Gottlieb Hampfler, photographer).
Barry Yinger: p. 6, figure 2; p. 46, figure 1.
Photographs not otherwise credited are by the author.

Contents

1   Entrance Gardens   1

ASHFORD ENTRANCE GARDEN · DELDEO ENTRANCE GARDEN

Fragrance · Color and Textural Relationship Between House and Garden · Geometric Versus Curvilinear Ground Plans · Structuring a Plant Composition · Tubbed or Potted Plants · Comparison of the Two Gardens

2   Gardens to Be Viewed   21

WARD VIEW GARDENS · NEHOC VIEW GARDEN · SINGER VIEW GARDEN

Three Important Design Considerations (Shape of Lowest Ground Cover, Depth, and Center of Interest) · Texture · Winter Plant Palette

3   Gardens to Live In   53

E.H. FREDERICK LIVE-IN GARDEN · HINSLEY LIVE-IN GARDEN

Capitalizing on the Personality of the Site and the Owner · Ground Covers · Studied Abandon

Appendices Contents

Acknowledgments

I am indebted to John Elsley and Thomas Buchter for encouraging me to undertake this project.

Nancy G. Frederick, Richard W. Lighty, and Thomas Buchter provided steadfast support during a long gestation and had a major impact on the final product as readers.

Robert Herald was of continuous help on nomenclatural questions. He is not, however, responsible for any of the arbitrary decisions I have personally made in that regard.

Paul Skibinski was likewise of constant help, on questions of plant culture.

Photographic credits appear on the copyright page. All twenty sources involved helpful friends whose patience and understanding were remarkable.

Charles L. Gray, Jr., was responsible for introducing us to the world of computers, designing a brilliant and tailor-made set of programs needed for the creation of the Appendices, and dealing with a myriad of questions promptly and with the greatest cheer. It is my great regret that his untimely death has prevented him from seeing the finished product.

Suzanne Winkler, friend, secretary, and administrative assistant, has lived with the book's creation as intimately as myself. Starting from base zero, she has mastered two computer programs and numerous nomenclatural realignments, and has persevered patiently through the upheavals involved in several reorganizations.

Clients have been the testing ground for most of the ideas expressed in this book. My relationships with all of them have been memorable and valued. The following have generously permitted their gardens to be used as case studies: Mr. and Mrs. Theodore H. Ashford, Mr. and Mrs. Anthony J. Cardinal, Mr. and Mrs. Salvatore Deldeo, Mr. and Mrs. Curtis M. Hinsley, Mr. and Mrs. Horace L. Hotchkiss, Mr. and Mrs. Nelson T. Shields III, Mr. and Mrs. Alain R. Singer, Mr. and Mrs. Rodman Ward, Jr.

The author wishes to express deep appreciation to all of the above for their assistance.

Introduction

This book results from my strong conviction that Americans are ready for a close relationship with highly personalized gardens based on a uniquely American design philosophy.

This need to make gardens an important part of everyday living is expressed in the increasing number of visitors at our public gardens and historical garden restorations; by greater attendance at short courses on gardening topics; in the rapid jump in circulation of quality gardening periodicals; in the recent, somewhat emotional hug-a-plant response of the younger generation and the equally emotional enthusiasm of their parents for "instant" meadows; in the sudden turnaround and acceptance of herbaceous perennials (banished from the American scene for more than fifty years for being "too high-maintenance") as the in thing; in a burgeoning urge for Japanese gardens (these have much to teach us about how to enjoy a garden—because of differences in cultural background we often, unfortunately, miss the point and settle for copying superficial details); in the overzealous worship and subsequent rejection of British authors and visiting British garden dignitaries as oracles on gardening (their enthusiasm for ornamental plants is contagious; the difference between their climate and American ones makes their recommendations technically unreliable); and, finally, in the skyrocketing sales and expanding range of woody and herbaceous plants (by such innovative merchandisers as

Wayside Gardens, White Flower Farm, and Bluemel Nurseries) and annual and perennial flower seeds (Park Seed Company, Thompson & Morgan).

It is easy to document this yearning for a greater involvement with gardens and the reasons for it. Expansion in population, movement of people from small towns to cities, and general deprivation of contact with scenic beauty have left an enormous gap. People are out of personal touch with nature.

It is less easy to understand why it has taken so long for uniquely American gardens to come into being. The evolutionary process has involved several side trips.

There are some early landmarks that augured well and that continue to be standards worthy of emulation. The Danish-born midwestern landscape architect Jens Jensen (1860–1951) opened our eyes to the virtues of American plants by perfecting their use in man-made compositions and taught us to design with reverence and respect for the local landscape. Frank Lloyd Wright (1867–1959) shared this viewpoint, advocating the reduction of barriers between house and garden and stressing our responsibility for siting buildings not only harmoniously with the site but so as to capitalize and focus on the virtues of these sites. Unfortunately, both designers were ahead of their time.

The truly significant activity in the development of American gardens in the early part of the twentieth century came about in the design and building of large estate gardens. There was little uniquely American about them, other than the lavish expenditures involved and the speed with which they were created. They generally competed, each trying to outdo the other's interpretation of various forms of European neoclassicism. The movement toward large estate gardens did encourage the expansion of an industry supplying a wide range of both woody and herbaceous plants and the development of professional gardeners. This boom was brought to a halt by the combination of the progressive income tax of 1913 (which quickly became prohibitive), the stock market crash of 1929, the Depression, and the further increase in taxes in 1937. The demise of these heavily herbaceous, labor-intensive gardens left all of gardening with the taint of being available to none but the super-rich and ushered in the dark ages of American garden design, which were to last until 1980.

The effect on professional design offices was devastating. The training and practice of most landscape architects had focused almost exclusively on estate garden design. After the late thirties these architects found it so difficult to make a living that the field of residential garden design got a bad name, which has lasted until quite recently. More important, by the time economic conditions improved, the profession of landscape architecture was locked into the fields of regional and subdivision planning, highway development, and masonry-dominated corporate campuses and cityscapes. The new technical knowledge needed for these fields took educational precedence over art and horticulture, and landscape architects were no longer equipped for residential garden design.

During the sixties and seventies an awareness of ecological implications involved in massive planning processes came to the fore. This put plants back on the map again, but unfortunately only native plants. The native-plant movement rolled forward with religious fervor, and any plants other than native plants were damned. The argument that native plants "performed better" than alien plants was scientifically without basis. The argument that native plants were "aesthetically more appropriate" had some merit in non-garden landscape restoration; in other applications it was specious. To be sure, our total aesthetic would be unbalanced without the native landscape, but the idea that nature should take the place of art would be for civilization to go backward. Garden art without both natives and happily sited alien plants would deprive gardens of some of their greatest magic. It is a strong stretch of the imagination to say that the average city or subdivision backyard can contribute to the community well-being by planting only native plants. Advocates of this view have done tremendous good in many areas, but they have generally had a negative effect on residential garden design. The amorphous qualities of man-made native wildflower gardens and inaccurately described "maintenance-free meadows" at residential scale do little to fulfill the practical and emotional needs of the average homeowner.

Amid these dark ages there have, however, been three luminaries who have shed considerable light. All three designers have been specialists in residential garden design; all three have tested the waters of modernism and contributed to a uniquely American version of twentieth-century garden design; all three have known that the worldwide cornucopia of ornamental plants is one of the designer's greatest assets.

Fletcher Steele (1885–1971) managed to merge the bisymmetrical layouts of neoclassicism and the free-form asymmetrical layouts of modernism with great style and flair. Thomas Church (1902–1978), primarily on the West Coast, and James Rose (from 1910), on the East Coast, for the first time made the functional needs of clients a priority and emphasized the importance of indoor-outdoor relationships (an established custom of Japanese gardens, made possible in twentieth-century America largely by the increasingly common use of glass walls in domestic architecture). Rose in particular celebrates the effect of light, shadow, texture, sound, and space in the garden. The legacy of these three men leaves us with the best of design bases for contemporary gardens.

The contraction of the plant palette during the dark ages was tragic. Landscape architects came out of school familiar with at most five or six kinds of trees, at the most ten shrubs, and no herbaceous plants. From 1930 to 1980 the use of herbaceous perennials was perceived to be high-maintenance and high-cost, and therefore undesirable. Nursery inventories were slashed; many of the largest and best went out of business (Andorra Nurseries near Philadelphia; Henry Kohankie in Ohio). When economic conditions improved, competition among the survivors was stiff, mass production methods were adopted, and, as usual in such cases, the objective became large quantities of a few varieties rather than smaller quantities of many.

For some time the growing number of informed gardeners has questioned the lack of commercial availability of many fine plants thriving in our public gardens and arboreta. Likewise, these gardeners have envied the exuberance seen in British gardens and lacking in ours. Many home gardeners have come to realize what they have been missing by not growing herbaceous plants (perennial and annual). They find that the small-scale use of these plants is not very time-consuming and that the results are pleasurable and well worth the effort. Equally important, garden designers are coming to recognize that certain kinds of perennials (I like to call them survivors) are not high-maintenance and, in fact, as ground covers are very useful in cutting maintenance costs.

Plant merchandisers have responded to the need for a broad palette of both native and alien plants. It is time for us all, amateurs and professionals, to seize the opportunity of this wonderful moment in the history of American gardens.

The current clearly manifested need and desire for plant-rich, man-made, artistically designed gardens in no way runs counter to our American gardening tradition. We must, by all means, feel a reverence for our site, share a responsibility for harmonious siting of buildings and gardens within the local landscape, emphasize the importance of the indoor-outdoor relationship as a key to the greatest garden pleasure, and consider the rich plant palette available a resource for achieving the intended visual and choreographic effect. While striving for designs that are fresh and unfettered by the traditions of bilateral symmetry and Asiatic asceticism, we should capitalize on the delightful geometric discipline of the former and the deeply satisfying occult balance of the latter ("occult" is a term used in garden design to describe the use of asymmetry, not obvious to the untrained eye, to balance successfully different parts of a composition).

My own practice, specializing in residential garden design (starting in 1952), has uniquely experienced this exciting change. There has been an unprecedented demand for not just decoration but for a rich and relevant garden experience.

Because I believe that it is not just the presence of plants but their careful selection and use in combinations that make a garden a work of art, I have adhered strictly to a number of guidelines. It seems appropriate here to write down some of what I have been practicing. The guidelines below must be taken as basic assumptions to what follows:

1. The open spaces (negative space: lawn, low ground cover, pasture, et cetera) in gardens should be strong, eye-pleasing forms. Therefore, although plantings should often have a quality of froth and exuberance, each should have a quality of order to its edges so that these forms may remain strong and crisp.

2. A palette of plants should first be developed that can be trusted to thrive in the particular garden involved.

3. These plants should be chosen from the aristocrats (very best performers) of the ornamental plant world, regardless of whether they are native or alien. The roughly six hundred plants that are given in the Master Lists (Appendices 1A and 1B) and that compose the basic palette referred to throughout the book are those that I feel warrant this description.

4. The list should include herbaceous plants as well as woody plants (deciduous and evergreen) in order to give us the richest palette and the opportunity to completely clothe the ground with foliage and leave no bare earth, no mulched areas, available for the growth of weeds. (The tradition of separating woody and herbaceous plants for purposes of classification has regrettably carried over into the design area, where the distinction has tended to minimize the usefulness and magic of the latter.)

5. The following maintenance commitments are, I feel, a reasonable minimum. Anyone not willing to assume this degree of responsibility should, in my opinion, settle for an apartment with a nice view, stroll in the local public gardens for exercise and contact with nature, and visit gardens of friends who are more ardent for horticultural stimulation. Gardening, like any other activity in life, involves some commitment.
· Areas to be planted should first be cleared of all growth. Some gardeners may wish to do this manually. I prefer to use

Yellow-Groove Bamboo (*Phyllostachys aureosulcata*) and Blue Maid ® Holly (*Ilex x meserveae* Blue Maid ® 'Mesid') form the background for this terrace.

pest- and maintenance-free. In the few instances where I have included a plant in the Appendices because of some special quality of design magic that it has to offer despite a more burdensome maintenance requirement, this requirement should be understood and accepted.

· Woody plants will need some pruning. "Cut back" shrubs will need to be cut to the ground once a year (April). Thinning many shrubs by "depth pruning" (just after flowering) will be necessary every three to five years, depending on variety. Summer thinning of trees to improve air circulation and removing lower branches to keep views open will be periodic tasks.

· Herbaceous plants will need deadheading after flowers are spent. In some cases cutting the entire plant back after first bloom will yield a second round of color. These plants will all need to be cut back to ground level after frost (or later in the winter or early spring if their winter silhouette is effective or their seed heads attractive to birds). For the most part, herbaceous plants included in the basic palette do not need to be staked and do not need to be divided more often than once in five years. When dividing is done, the plants are lifted, the soil refurbished, and lively young pieces from the edge of the old clumps replanted and mulched. Deadheading and staking become unimportant in less tailored areas, such as meadows, woodlands, and marshes, and the plant selection can be expanded accordingly. However, the maintenance in these areas is not as light, it should be noted, as is often touted, since discipline is needed to maintain a balance between shy plants and the aggressors. Especially important is the yearly battle that must be fought keeping out such undesirables as Canadian Thistle (*Cirsium arvense*), Japanese Honeysuckle (*Lonicera japonica*), and Japanese Bittersweet (*Celastrus orbiculatus*).

appropriate herbicides to ensure the removal of noxious plants, such as Quack Grass and Bindweed, that are sure to reappear for years to come after hand weeding and/or cultivating. These areas should then be prepared as beds with emphasis on creating good soil structure adequately supplied with nutrients and organic matter. Covering exposed soil with such mulches as crushed bark will be necessary to start the ball rolling. A commitment to weeding and, optionally, spot herbicide treatment during the first two years will be required in order to allow the ornamental plants to cover and dominate unwanted growth.

· Plants should be used that are "survivors" in your area, provided they are properly sited and have adequate soil preparation. By definition a survivor has a wide tolerance of conditions and is relatively

For those who are only able or willing to make a modest time commitment to gardening, I would recommend staying away from:

Traditional beds of annuals (bedding plants)
Tulips and any other bulb that, to provide the best display, must be replaced every year
The traditional herbaceous border
Beds of hybrid Tea Roses, with their weekly spray requirements

This book will give examples of more permanent, lower-maintenance plants that will continue to give pleasure for many years.

For those who are bitten by the gardening bug, a progressively greater time commitment is inevitable. The hues added to the color palette by certain Tulips and annuals cannot be resisted. The texture of Scotch Thistle (*Onopordum acanthium*) and Giant Hogweed (*Heracleum mantegazzianum*) makes annual summer sowing of these biennials a must. The sine qua non of a stylish espalier or topiary often outweighs the necessary chores of training and pruning.

The plant palette presented in this book is limited in two ways:

First, it represents only those plants I have encountered in my fifty years of gardening in the same area (three gardens). I am approximately thirty miles southwest of Philadelphia (latitude 39 degrees, 45 minutes north; longitude 75 degrees, 40 minutes west). The terrain of my present garden is rolling piedmont 350 to 400 feet above sea level. The average annual rainfall is forty inches. The soil is clay loam and is predominantly acid. A large proportion of the gardens I have designed have similar mid-Atlantic conditions. I speak with greatest experience about plants thriving under these circumstances.

Second, this is a very personal book. It is not meant to be encyclopedic. Therefore, the plants recommended include only my favorites (after fifty years of growing or observing them). The combinations likewise are ones that I have used or would like to use.

It is my hope that these limitations will be a help rather than a hindrance in boiling down what is often an overabundance of choice and in helping the reader to sharpen his or her own critical faculties in deciding what is most satisfying in his or her garden.

The reader should understand clearly that my enthusiasm for the use of ornamental plants is not unbridled; that my particular preference (based on what I perceive as the needs of gardeners of the twentieth–twenty-first centuries) is to create gardens of exuberance; that exuberance in the garden, as in the best architecture, is only successful within a (perhaps concealed) framework of strong discipline.

The text that follows is intended to demonstrate both the need to balance exuberance and discipline and the ways in which it can be done. The five chapters are meant to be read sequentially, because the case is constructed like a building, starting with foundation stones and culminating in a full-blown structure.

Because it is easier to think about this balance between exuberance and discipline with relevance to specific types of gardens, the book has been subdivided into five chapters on that basis.

And because it is easier to understand the points I wish to make by actual examples, there are thirteen case studies (gardens I have designed, including plans and photographs) distributed throughout the text as follows:

Chapter 1. Entrance Gardens
    two examples
Chapter 2. Gardens to Be Viewed
    three examples
Chapter 3. Gardens to Live In
    two examples
Chapter 4. Swimming Pool Gardens
    two examples
Chapter 5. Gardens to Stroll In
    four examples

In addition, each chapter contains a series of commentaries (see Contents) that elaborate on subjects raised by the examples considered.

The extensive appendices (thirty-eight in total) follow the text.

My very strong hope is that the reader will not follow in a slavish way any plant combinations discussed, but will rather be stimulated with the help of these appendices to put together combinations especially appropriate to his or her own site and tastes.

Overleaf: Narcissus 'Trevithian' (left) and Hardy Fountain Grass (Pennisetum alopecuroides).

The Exuberant Garden
and the
Controlling Hand

ASHFORD ENTRANCE GARDEN

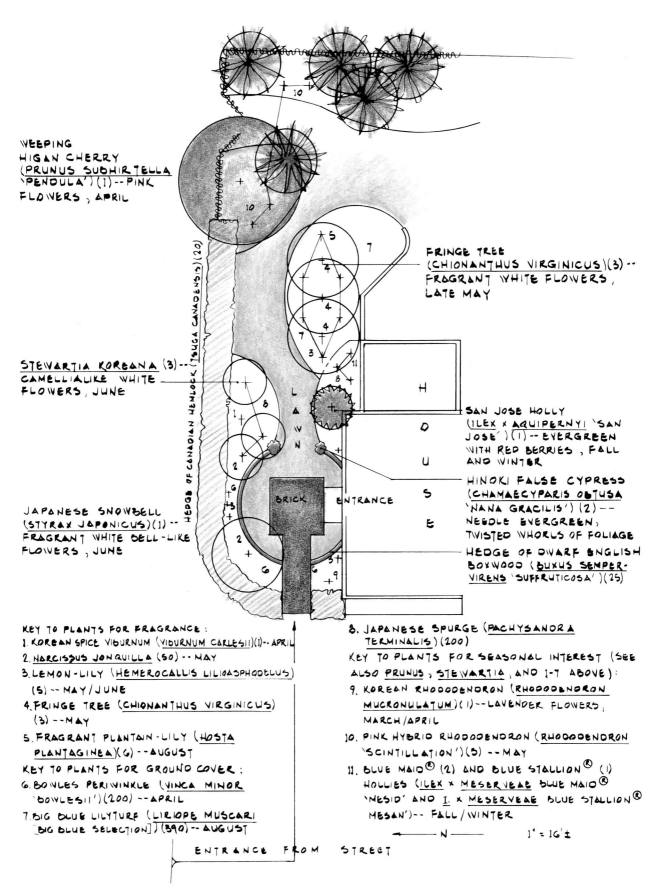

WEEPING
HIGAN CHERRY
(PRUNUS SUBHIRTELLA
'PENDULA') (1) -- PINK
FLOWERS, APRIL

HEDGE OF CANADIAN HEMLOCK (TSUGA CANADENSIS) (20)

STEWARTIA KOREANA (3) --
CAMELLIALIKE WHITE
FLOWERS, JUNE

JAPANESE SNOWBELL
(STYRAX JAPONICUS) (1) --
FRAGRANT WHITE BELL-LIKE
FLOWERS, JUNE

FRINGE TREE
(CHIONANTHUS VIRGINICUS) (3) --
FRAGRANT WHITE FLOWERS,
LATE MAY

LAWN

BRICK   ENTRANCE

HOUSE

SAN JOSE HOLLY
(ILEX × AQUIPERNYI 'SAN
JOSE') (1) -- EVERGREEN
WITH RED BERRIES, FALL
AND WINTER

HINOKI FALSE CYPRESS
(CHAMAECYPARIS OBTUSA
'NANA GRACILIS') (2) --
NEEDLE EVERGREEN,
TWISTED WHORLS OF FOLIAGE

HEDGE OF DWARF ENGLISH
BOXWOOD (BUXUS SEMPER-
VIRENS 'SUFFRUTICOSA') (25)

KEY TO PLANTS FOR FRAGRANCE:
1. KOREAN SPICE VIBURNUM (VIBURNUM CARLESII) (1) -- APRIL
2. NARCISSUS JONQUILLA (50) -- MAY
3. LEMON-LILY (HEMEROCALLIS LILIOASPHODELUS)
   (5) -- MAY/JUNE
4. FRINGE TREE (CHIONANTHUS VIRGINICUS)
   (3) -- MAY
5. FRAGRANT PLANTAIN-LILY (HOSTA
   PLANTAGINEA) (6) -- AUGUST
KEY TO PLANTS FOR GROUND COVER:
6. BOWLES PERIWINKLE (VINCA MINOR
   'BOWLESII') (200) -- APRIL
7. BIG BLUE LILYTURF (LIRIOPE MUSCARI
   [BIG BLUE SELECTION]) (390) -- AUGUST

8. JAPANESE SPURGE (PACHYSANDRA
   TERMINALIS) (200)
KEY TO PLANTS FOR SEASONAL INTEREST (SEE
ALSO PRUNUS, STEWARTIA, AND 1-7 ABOVE):
9. KOREAN RHODODENDRON (RHODODENDRON
   MUCRONULATUM) (1) -- LAVENDER FLOWERS,
   MARCH/APRIL
10. PINK HYBRID RHODODENDRON (RHODODENDRON
    'SCINTILLATION') (5) -- MAY
11. BLUE MAID® (2) AND BLUE STALLION® (1)
    HOLLIES (ILEX × MESERVEAE BLUE MAID®
    'MESID' AND I. × MESERVEAE BLUE STALLION®
    'MESAN') -- FALL/WINTER

← —— N —————   1" = 16'±

ENTRANCE FROM STREET

1 Entrance Gardens

What happens in the way of a garden opportunity between the door of your car and the door of your house can be a very important matter. Here, in an entrance garden, is the chance to provide a pleasant experience that starts the process of wiping out the hustle-bustle of the world, slowing the tempo of the viewer, serving as a transition between the scale of the highway and the scale of your living room, and setting the mood for a great house-and-garden experience. This is where garden magic first comes into play.

In some instances the trip from car to door may be made on foot. In others, visitors may drive their car directly to the door. The significant difference between walking and driving is that one moves more slowly on foot and has a greater opportunity to observe detail and enjoy such sensory stimulants as fragrance.

Let's examine two examples of entrance gardens, the Ashford and the Deldeo gardens.

Ashford Entrance Garden

The Ashford Garden occupies a narrow space between house and street and involves walking. The front door is approached from a driveway to the side rather than head-on. It was decided to retain an aged and handsome Weeping Higan Cherry (*Prunus subhirtella* 'Pendula') as part of a composition that would attract the viewer through the narrow opening in the tall Canadian Hemlock (*Tsuga canadensis*) hedge into the circular garden, edged by Dwarf English Boxwood (*Buxus sempervirens* 'Suffruticosa'), which is centered on and turns the viewer toward the front door.

The pyramidal small-leaf San Jose Holly

(*Ilex* x *aquipernyi* 'San Jose') at the corner of the house and the three *Stewartia koreana* opposite it give form to the circular garden and frame the view of the Cherry. The Cherry's pendulous branches lead the eye down to a carefully shaped patch of green turf. This lawn shape provides the pleasant hint that an informal garden lies beyond.

Plants were selected for this garden that would produce interesting details and attractive scents for the passerby to enjoy; see the charts on pages 2 and 4. (For additional plants providing fragrance, see Appendix 16.)

Interest in the Ashford Garden starts in March and April with the lavender blossoms

of the Korean Rhododendron (*Rhododendron mucronulatum*) (1 plant) and ends with the red berries on the two sorts of holly in the late fall and includes the other actors already mentioned. (See "Key to Plants for Seasonal Interest" on the Ashford Entrance Garden plan, page xviii.)

Such diversity of interest in a small space could be a hodgepodge if appropriate attention was not given at the outset to careful overall structuring of the garden and good tie-together with ground covers. In essence, one is displaying attractive jewels, and the jewel box must be of strong form.

Furthermore, to be aesthetically successful every garden must have a dominant center of interest, and in the case of entrance gardens this is necessarily the front door. In the Ashford Garden the bricked square in a green circle provides a strong architectural base for and relationship with the front door. The diverse detailing here falls into place around the circle-and-square design.

Ground covers are used to hold this all together. The bottom chart on page 4 describes some of them. (For an extensive listing of other ground covers, see Appendix 27.)

ASHFORD ENTRANCE GARDEN—PLANTS FOR DETAIL INTEREST

	J	F	M	A	MAY	J	JUL	AUG	SEP	O	N	D
The intriguing dark-green needle foliage of 2 Hinoki False Cypresses (*Chamaecyparis obtusa* 'Nana Gracilis'). This foliage is arranged in twisted whirls.												
Flaking bark in shades of tan, brown, and green on the *Stewartia koreana* (3 plants).												
White bell-shaped flowers on the Japanese Snowbell (*Styrax japonicus*) (1 plant) and white, pendulous, antlerlike blossoms on the Fringe Trees (*Chionanthus virginicus*) (3 plants).												

ASHFORD ENTRANCE GARDEN — PLANTS FOR FRAGRANCE

Numbers are keyed to garden plan
Dotted rules indicate time of flowering

	J	F	M	A	MAY	J	JUL	AUG	SEP	O	N	D
1.				•••••								
2.				•••••								
3.					•••••							
4.					••••							
5.								••••••••				

1. Korean Spice Viburnum (*Viburnum carlesii*) (1 plant), with its "tantalizing blend of carnation and gardenia"[1] (April).

2. *Narcissus jonquilla* (50 bulbs) (from Southern Europe and Algeria) in April and early May—the wild source of the powerful fragrance in subsequent jonquil hybrids.

3. The scented Lemon-Lily (*Hemerocallis lilioasphodelus*) (5 plants), which provides "a rich honeysuckle scent"[2] on May evenings.

4. Fringe Tree (*Chionanthus virginicus*) (3 plants) in late May ("the sweetness of white clover or the first cut of alfalfa"[3]).

5. Fragrant Plantain-Lily (*Hosta plantaginea*) (6 plants) in late August–early September ("a cosmetic quality like violet sachet"[4]).

1

2

ASHFORD ENTRANCE GARDEN — PLANTS FOR GROUND COVER

Numbers are keyed to garden plan
Dotted rules indicate time of flowering

	J	F	M	A	MAY	J	JUL	AUG	SEP	O	N	D
6.					••••							
					••••							
7.							•••••					
								•••••••				
8.												

6. Bowles Periwinkle (*Vinca minor* 'Bowlesii') (200 plants) in the circle garden. Small-scale broadleaf evergreen foliage; blue blossoms in early May through which the diminutive *Narcissus jonquilla* peek.

7. Big Blue Lilyturf (*Liriope muscari* [Big Blue Selection]) (390 plants) under the Fringe Trees. Strap-shaped evergreen leaves and lavender-blue blossoms complement the white-flowered Fragrant Plantain-Lilies (*Hosta plantaginea*) in late summer.

8. Japanese Spurge (*Pachysandra terminalis*) (200 plants), tying the above two together. This has symmetrically shaped, light-reflective evergreen leaves.

In the Ashford Entrance Garden, visitors (on foot) experience a variety of scents, depending on the season: **(1)** Korean Spice Viburnum (*Viburnum carlesii*) — beginning in April; **(2)** scented Lemon-Lily (*Hemerocallis lilioasphodelus*) — May; **(3)** *Narcissus jonquilla* — April; scented Lemon-Lily (*Hemerocallis lilioasphodelus*) — May; and **(4)** Fringe Tree (*Chionanthus virginicus*) — May.

1

2

3

7

8

9

Fragrance

One important form of exuberance is fragrance. Let's examine the opportunities for enhancing entrance gardens with fragrance. Although scent is useful in all parts of the garden, it seems particularly appropriate here. Susceptibility to fragrance certainly varies from individual to individual, but I suspect most of us are vulnerable to the effects of scent, for instance, long before we react to the most stimulating textural or color combination. Certainly the gardener needs a strong tool to switch visitors from the mind-set of the shopping center, business world, and highway to one that is receptive to the many other charms of home and garden.

My favorite scent-producing plants include the following (for a complete listing of plants providing scent, see Appendix 16):

For Long-Season Foliage Scent

Sweet-Fern (*Comptonia peregrina*)—"Redolent of bay leaves"[5]

Sweet Woodruff (*Galium odoratum*)—"New mown hay"[6]

Bigroot Cranesbill (*Geranium macrorrhizum*)—Retsina wine

Houttuynia cordata 'Chameleon'—"The leaves have the smell of Seville oranges, refreshing and pungent"[7]

Eglantine Rose (*Rosa eglanteria*)—Foliage has the fragrance of green apples; this is especially strong when the leaves first emerge in the spring

Thymes—Most sorts have a very seductive fragrance ("a combination of warm balsamic oils"[8]), many "redolent of lemon"[9]

Wooly Thyme (*Thymus pseudolanuginosus*)—Incenselike scent

For Seasonal Flower Fragrance

JANUARY AND FEBRUARY

Wintersweet (*Chimonanthus praecox*)—Yellow blossoms with the "fragrance of Jonquil and Violet"[10]

4

5

6

10

11

One of the plants providing long-season foliage scent is **(1)** Sweet-Fern (*Comptonia peregrina*). Seasonal flower fragrance is provided by **(2)** Wintersweet (*Chimonanthus praecox*) — January/February; **(3)** Winter Hazel (*Corylopsis platypetala*) — March/April; **(4)** Clove Currant (*Ribes odoratum*) — April; **(5)** Piedmont Azalea (*Rhododendron canescens*) — May; **(6)** Lily-of-the-Valley (*Convallaria majalis*) — May/June; **(7)** Plum Tart Iris (*Iris graminea*) — May/June; **(8)** Asphodel (*Asphodeline lutea*) — May/June; **(9)** Lilium 'Black Dragon' — June; **(10, 11)** Harlequin Glory Bower (*Clerodendrum trichotomum*) — blossoms in August/September are followed by highly ornamental fruit in September/October.

FEBRUARY AND MARCH

Chinese Witch-hazel (*Hamamelis mollis* 'Pallida')—"Pure delicious perfume of jonquil"[11]

Winter Aconite (*Eranthis hyemalis*)—Sweet peas

MARCH

Fragrant (shrub) Honeysuckle (*Lonicera fragrantissima*)

Winter Hazel (particularly *Corylopsis platypetala*)—"Cowslip scented"[12]

Diminutive bulbs suitable for naturalizing:
Crocus tomasinianus—Sweet-scented
Snowdrops (*Galanthus nivalis* and *G. elwesii*)—"Spring, honey, and moss"[13]
Spring Snowflake (*Leucojum vernum*)— "Vaguely violet scented"[14]
Siberian Squill (*Scilla siberica* 'Spring Beauty')

APRIL

Daphne x *burkwoodii* 'Carol Mackie'— Gardenia

Daphne caucasica—Clove and gardenia
Magnolias in variety, most especially Yulan Magnolia (*M. denudata* [syn. *M. heptapeta*])—Gentle scent of violets
Leatherleaf Mahonia (*Mahonia bealei*)— "Roses and Lily of the Valley"[15]
Hardy-Orange (*Poncirus trifoliata*)—Orange blossom scent
Yoshino Cherry (*Prunus yedoensis*)—A fine, sweet scent
Clove Currant (*Ribes odoratum*)—Clove scent
Winter Hazel (*Corylopsis*)

Fragrant Viburnums, especially:
V. farreri 'Candidissimum'—"Wisteria and cloves"[16]
V. farreri 'Nanum'
V. carlesii—"Tantalizing blend of carnation and gardenia"[17]

More spring bulbs, especially:
Grape-Hyacinths (*Muscari botryoides* 'Album' and *M. tubergenianum*)— "Mellow honey fragrance"[18]
Narcissus jonquilla and *N.* 'Trevithian'— Jonquil fragrance

Rosa (Gallica) 'Charles de Mills' provides fragrance in May and June.

MAY

Sweet Shrub (*Calycanthus floridus* 'Edith Wilder')—Described variously as strawberries, bananas, ripe apples
Sweet Mockorange (*Philadelphus coronarius*)—"A blend of orange fruit and jasmine"[19]

Various deciduous Azaleas, especially:
Coast Azalea (*Rhododendron atlanticum*)—"Gardenia and clove"[20]
Piedmont Azalea (*Rhododendron canescens*)—"Spice and honeysuckle"[21]
Royal Azalea (*Rhododendron schlippenbachii*)

Lilacs, particularly the highly scented old-fashioned white (*Syringa vulgaris* 'Alba')
Japanese Wisteria (*Wisteria floribunda*)—"Frail sweetness"[22]

Three fine herbaceous plants:
Lily-of-the-Valley (*Convallaria majalis*)
Lemon-Lily (*Hemerocallis lilioasphodelus*)—"Rich honeysuckle scent"[23] in the evening
Plum Tart Iris (*Iris graminea*)—"Hot stewed plums or apricots"[24]; Paul Skibinski says "Concord Grapes"

JUNE

American Yellowwood (*Cladrastis lutea*)
Virginia Sweetspire (*Itea virginica* 'Henry's Garnet')—"Sweetly fragrant"[25]; "very like that of the ordinary pond lily"[26]
Swamp Magnolia (*Magnolia virginiana*)—"Cool and fruity and sweet"[27]

More deciduous Azaleas (and hybrids thereof):
Sweet Azalea (*Rhododendron arborescens*)—"Sweet version of clove like *Clethra* or *Heliotrope*"[28]
Roseshell Azalea (*Rhododendron prinophyllum* [syn. *R. roseum*])—"Intensely clove"[29]
Swamp Azalea (*Rhododendron viscosum*)—"Smell . . . richly of clove"[30]

Old Shrub Roses take the highest prize for fragrance. Only those that maintain satisfactory summer foliage and are "well dressed" shrubs should be selected for such a prominent position as an entrance garden. A good example would be my favorite Gallica hybrid, *R.* 'Charles de Mills,' a beautiful, highly scented mauve, which is also fragrant in May.

Bulbous Lilies in great variety. Louise Beebe Wilder refers to the scent of Gold-Banded Lily (*Lilium auratum*) as "heavy and languorous."[31] *Lilium* 'Black Dragon' provides strong night scent for several weeks and has attractive seed pods for the balance of the summer.

Two herbaceous charmers:
Asphodel (*Asphodeline lutea*)—Also fragrant in May
Garden Heliotrope (*Valeriana officinalis*)

JULY

Sweet Pepperbush (*Clethra alnifolia*)—"Strong sweetness almost like Heliotrope"[32] carrying for long distances, especially over water

AUGUST

Butterfly Bush (*Buddleia davidii*)—Many attractive cultivars; my favorites are 'Black Knight' and 'Opera' ("honey scented"[33])
Tube Clematis (*Clematis heracleifolia* var. *Davidiana*)—Blossoms: "lemon and spices"[34]; foliage when drying: "new mown hay"[35]
Fragrant Plantain-Lily (*Hosta plantaginea*)—"Cosmetic quality–like violet sachet"[36]

SEPTEMBER

Sweet Autumn Clematis (*Clematis maximowicziana*)—"The sweetness of a well flavored vanilla layer cake"[37]
Harlequin Glory Bower (*Clerodendrum trichotomum*)—"Lily and *Nicotiana*,"[38] also fragrant in August
Daphne caucasica—Highly perfumed; blooms in fall and spring
Fragrant Elaeagnus (*Elaeagnus pungens* 'Fruitlandii')—"Musty grape-jonquil fragrance"[39]

OCTOBER

Common Witch-hazel (*Hamamelis virginiana*)—"Sweet musty scent"[40]

Deldeo Entrance Garden

By contrast with the Ashford entrance, where arrival is on foot, one arrives at the Deldeo front door by car. In such an instance, interesting detail would normally be lost because of the speed of movement. Instead, impact is achieved by massing plants in multilevel ground-covering drifts that are strongly structured.

This house is in a woodland setting, with the arrival area the major sunny spot. Because views of the house from many different angles occur from the approach drive, the planting composition must take its key from the house, enhance the architecture of the house, and focus attention on the front entrance (again the entrance is the center of interest).

Evergreen structure is provided to this planting by six Canadian Hemlocks (*Tsuga canadensis*) and one Nordmann Fir (*Abies nordmanniana*), which dominates. A curvilinear hedge of Dwarf Japanese Yew (*Taxus cuspidata* 'Nana') (47 plants) and three San Jose Hollies (*Ilex* x *aquipernyi* 'San Jose') serve to welcome the visitor to a right-handed turn around the circle, give a feeling of enclosure once one arrives within the garden, and help feature an interesting, twisted Black Cherry, which was saved from the bulldozer. River Birch (*Betula nigra*) and a grove (3 plants) of Paperbark Maples (*Acer griseum*) frame the entrance landing and front door.

Arrival in the Deldeo Garden is by car. Hence, color massing is more effective than detail plants. Note massing of Yellow-Twig Dogwood (*Cornus sericea* 'Flaviramea').

Numbers are keyed to garden plan
Dotted rules indicate time of flowering

	J	F	M	A	MAY	J	JUL	AUG	SEP	O	N	D
1. Canadian Hemlock (*Tsuga canadensis*)												
2. San Jose Holly (*Ilex* x *aquipernyi* 'San Jose')												
3. Blue Maid® and Blue Stallion® Hollies (*Ilex* x *meserveae* Blue Maid ® 'Mesid' and *I.* x *meserveae* Blue Stallion® 'Mesan')												
Paperbark Maple (*Acer griseum*)												
Fountain Leucothoe (*Leucothoe fontanesiana*)					•••••							
Nordmann Fir (*Abies nordmanniana*)												
River Birch (*Betula nigra*)												
Yellow-Twig Dogwood (*Cornus sericea* 'Flaviramea')												
Dwarf Japanese Yew (*Taxus cuspidata* 'Nana')												
Spring Glory Forsythia (*Forsythia* x *intermedia* 'Spring Glory')				•••								
Flowering Dogwood (*Cornus florida*)					••••							
Exbury Hybrid Azalea (Yellow) (*Rhododendron* [Exbury Hybrid] 'Golden Peace')					••••							
Crimson Pygmy Barberry (*Berberis thunbergii* 'Crimson Pygmy')												
Hyperion Daylily (*Hemerocallis* 'Hyperion')—Yellow							••••					
Lilyturf (Yellow Variegated) (*Liriope muscari* 'Variegata')—Strap-shaped leaves striped gold and green; lavender-blue flowers in August								••••••••				

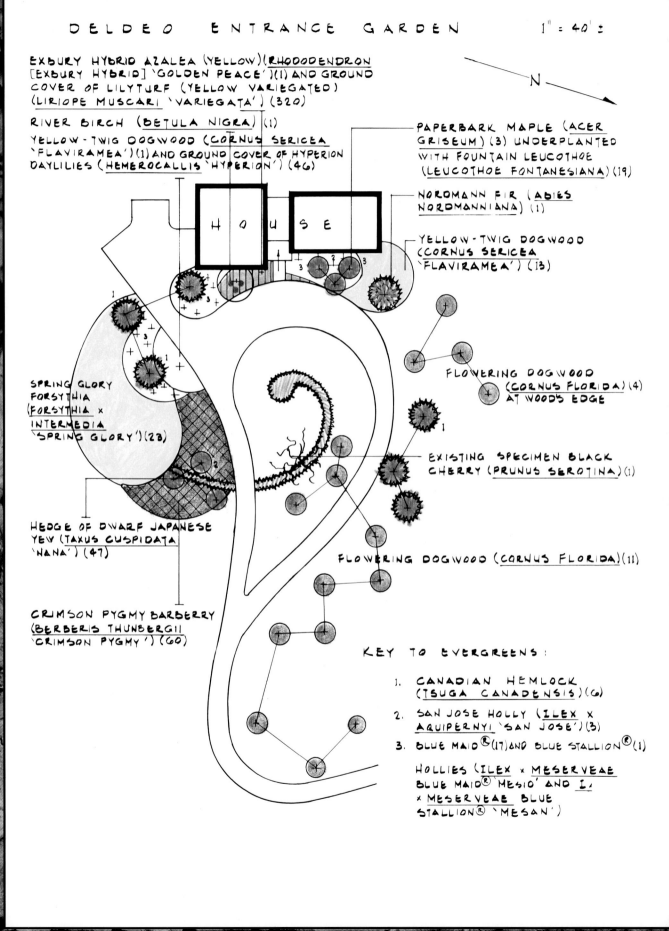

DELDEO ENTRANCE GARDEN   1" = 40' ±

N

EXBURY HYBRID AZALEA (YELLOW) (RHODODENDRON
[EXBURY HYBRID] 'GOLDEN PEACE') (1) AND GROUND
COVER OF LILYTURF (YELLOW VARIEGATED)
(LIRIOPE MUSCARI 'VARIEGATA') (320)

RIVER BIRCH (BETULA NIGRA) (1)

YELLOW-TWIG DOGWOOD (CORNUS SERICEA
'FLAVIRAMEA') (1) AND GROUND COVER OF HYPERION
DAYLILIES (HEMEROCALLIS 'HYPERION') (46)

PAPERBARK MAPLE (ACER
GRISEUM) (3) UNDERPLANTED
WITH FOUNTAIN LEUCOTHOE
(LEUCOTHOE FONTANESIANA) (19)

NORDMANN FIR (ABIES
NORDMANNIANA) (1)

YELLOW-TWIG DOGWOOD
(CORNUS SERICEA
'FLAVIRAMEA') (13)

HOUSE

FLOWERING DOGWOOD
(CORNUS FLORIDA) (4)
AT WOOD'S EDGE

SPRING GLORY
FORSYTHIA
(FORSYTHIA ×
INTERMEDIA
'SPRING GLORY') (23)

EXISTING SPECIMEN BLACK
CHERRY (PRUNUS SEROTINA) (1)

HEDGE OF DWARF JAPANESE
YEW (TAXUS CUSPIDATA
'NANA') (47)

FLOWERING DOGWOOD (CORNUS FLORIDA) (11)

CRIMSON PYGMY BARBERRY
(BERBERIS THUNBERGII
'CRIMSON PYGMY') (60)

KEY TO EVERGREENS:

1. CANADIAN HEMLOCK
    (TSUGA CANADENSIS) (6)

2. SAN JOSE HOLLY (ILEX ×
    AQUIPERNYI 'SAN JOSE') (3)

3. BLUE MAID® (17) AND BLUE STALLION® (1)

    HOLLIES (ILEX × MESERVEAE
    BLUE MAID® 'MESID' AND I.
    × MESERVEAE BLUE
    STALLION® 'MESAN')

Color and Textural Relationship Between House and Garden

The River Birch and Paperbark Maples were selected because of their texturally interesting exfoliating bark and the cherry, pink, bronze, and apricot colors thereof. The bark provides a strong all-year relationship with the rich tan, brown, and cherry colors in the stone and stained wooden siding of the house. The effect of the featured bark is enhanced by a backing of dark green hollies planted tightly together: *Ilex* x *aquipernyi* 'San Jose' (3 plants) and *Ilex* x *meserveae* Blue Maid® 'Mesid' and Blue Stallion® 'Mesan' (18 plants).

Low ground cover of golden-variegated Lilyturf (*Liriope muscari* 'Variegata') (320 plants) on both sides of the path highlights the entrance with its narrow, straplike texture. The evergreen bronzed-leaved Fountain Leucothoe (*Leucothoe fontanesiana*) (19 plants) grows below the grove of Paperbark Maples and picks up some of the color in their bark. Farther along the drive a ground cover planting of Crimson Pygmy Barberry (*Berberis thunbergii* 'Crimson Pygmy') (60 plants) echoes this color theme also during the warm months of the year and is equally effective in winter with its walnut-colored twigginess.

The yellow in the *Liriope* is repeated in the rest of the planting and gives a lightening contrast to the more sober colors of the composition. A large sweep (13 plants) of the Yellow-Twig Dogwood (*Cornus sericea* 'Flaviramea') sparkles in winter light; twenty-three Spring Glory Forsythia (*Forsythia* x *intermedia* 'Spring Glory') take center stage in April; a single sculptural deciduous yellow Exbury Hybrid Azalea (*Rhododendron* [Exbury Hybrid] 'Golden Peace') holds forth left of the entrance in May; and the tough ground cover Hyperion Daylily (*Hemerocallis* 'Hyperion') (46 plants) puts on a great show in July. (See the chart on page 10 for a listing of plants in the Deldeo Garden by seasonal interest.)

1

2

Other examples of massing in the Deldeo Garden are **(1)** Spring Glory Forsythia (*Forsythia* x *intermedia* 'Spring Glory') (*center rear*) and Crimson Pygmy Barberry (*Berberis thunbergii* 'Crimson Pygmy') (*left center*) and **(2)** yellow Hyperion Daylilies (*Hemerocallis* 'Hyperion') (*center*).

Opposite page: The massing of yellows in this planting scheme elaborates on the details near the door, where Exbury Hybrid Azalea (*Rhododendron* [Exbury Hybrid] 'Golden Peace') grows in a sea of golden-variegated Lilyturf (*Liriope muscari* 'Variegata').

Geometric forms generally produce strong messages more easily in small gardens than curvilinear forms.

Geometric Versus Curvilinear Ground Plans

A strong ground plan is essential to the successful control of the exuberant use of color and texture. An important point is that whereas the Ashford Garden uses geometric forms as its basis, the Deldeo Garden uses curvilinear form. The Ashford Garden is small and on level ground. The Deldeo Garden is large and on a hillside (the driveway rises as it approaches the house; the *Forsythia* bank rises even higher). Geometric forms generally produce strong messages more easily in small gardens than do curvilinear forms. Either curvilinear or rectilinear forms are satisfying in larger areas. Rectilinear forms work only on level sites. Curvilinear forms are particularly effective where they enhance the occult balance of an undulating site.

Structuring a Plant Composition

Control, however, does not result from a strong ground plan alone. There must be three-dimensional structure to reinforce the interest of the design. In the Ashford Garden we see how the eye is manipulated by a framed view of the Weeping Higan Cherry, whose pendulous habit then brings the eye down to the strong curvilinear turf shape and the highly organized circle garden. There, the horizontal line of the Boxwood hedge ties diverse elements together and creates repose for the eye.

In the Deldeo Garden we see how the conical dark green forms of Canadian Hemlocks and Nordmann Fir extend the form of the house on either side and add stability to the moundlike shrub plantings. In the same garden the **V** shape of the River Birch forms a space below which sparkles the narrow-textured chartreuse effect of variegated *Liriope* and makes certain that our eye rests on the front door. These are good examples of the roles certain types of plants play in providing structure to a total plant grouping. (For a listing of plants with outstanding qualities for structuring a composition, see Appendix 15.)

The overall objective of structuring is to add stability to a design and produce a picture in which all elements resolve into repose and harmony.

The great majority of plants and plant groupings produce round, mounded, even amorphous outlines. In my own garden design practice I rely particularly on vertical, conical, weeping, multistemmed, vase-shaped, and horizontal forms to do my structuring.

Verticals make very strong statements. Unless used appropriately, they tend to lead the eye up and out of the picture. Too many leave one feeling jumpy. In the mid-Atlantic United States we are familiar with hillsides of old field growth where the narrow, native Eastern Red Cedar (*Juniperus virginiana*) is abundant and successfully structures the landscape scene because of sufficient contrast with the horizontality of native Dogwoods and Hawthorns. The dramatic difference between these two forms is a particular source of richness in designing gardens.

Pendulous plants are mostly garden forms that do not occur in nature. As such it is

The rich contrast of vertical and horizontal forms is seen here (*above, left*) in an Eastern Shore of Maryland "old field," where Eastern Red Cedar (*Juniperus virginiana*) provides the vertical element, and (*above, right*) in a garden setting, where Slender Miscanthus (*Miscanthus sinensis* 'Gracillimus') echoes the vertical lines of the Eastern Red Cedars in the background and contrasts with the horizontality of Bird's Nest Spruce (*Picea abies* 'Nidiformis') and a ground cover planting of Creeping Cotoneaster (*Cotoneaster adpressus* var. *praecox*).

safest to use them only when it is desirable to direct eye movement for a specific purpose, such as down to a body of water or a piece of sculpture, or in any situation where the land rises from the viewer and it is desirable to bring the eye down to a focal point near at hand rather than have it rise away toward the slope.

Plants with horizontal branching habit rate highest because their form does most to create a feeling of repose. As will be seen from Appendix 15, they are surprisingly few in number, and these few must be cherished very highly. Among my favorites are:

Japanese Cornelian-Cherry (*Cornus officinalis*)
Burning Bush (*Euonymus alata*)
Pagoda Dogwood (*Cornus alternifolia*)
Flowering Dogwood (*Cornus florida*)
Blackhaw (*Viburnum prunifolium*)
Double-File Viburnum (*Viburnum plicatum* forma *tomentosum*)
Sargent Crabapple (*Malus sargentii*)

Hedges, and particularly clipped hedges, make very useful horizontals in the landscape as well (see Appendix 32).

1

(1) Incense-Cedar (*Calocedrus decurrens*), a garden aristocrat from the western United States, is another handsome vertical. Useful plants with contrasting horizontal form are (2) Pagoda Dogwood (*Cornus alternifolia*), an eastern U. S. native; (3) Burning Bush (*Euonymus alata*); and (4) Double-File Viburnum (*Viburnum plicatum* forma *tomentosum*).

2

3

4

Tubbed or Potted Plants

An optional form of exuberance that can be added to any garden and seems especially appropriate for entrance gardens is high-performance seasonal or tender plants in tubs or pots. So far the specific plants discussed for the two dooryard gardens we've examined have been relatively maintenance-free, in the sense that, once established, they essentially can be left alone. For more avid gardeners who want an extra touch of magic, additional color and fragrance can be added with tubbed or potted plants. The following are some examples that enhance the garden in summer.

Angel's-Trumpet (*Datura inoxia* subsp. *quinquecuspida*) (tender annual) provides a new set of blossoms each day. Tight buds each morning unfold in a spiral fashion during the afternoon, welcoming the family home in the evening.

High-quality evening fragrance can be provided by a tubbed specimen of Night

Jessamine (*Cestrum nocturnum*), a great joy not only as you pass by but pervasive enough that it floats in through the windows of the house on summer evenings. (This must be overwintered in a frost-free building.)

Tuberoses (*Polianthes tuberosa*) (tender bulb), depending on when they are potted, can be brought into bloom all during July and August. The scent is thoroughly worthy of celebration.

My favorite of all is the Peacock-Orchid (*Acidanthera bicolor*) (tender bulb). It is not an orchid but a bulbous relative of *Gladiolus*. It has gladioluslike foliage and slightly pendulous, starlike white flowers (resembling *Miltonias*) with chocolate-maroon throats. We put twelve or fifteen corms in a twelve- to fourteen-inch pot in June. The flowers display gracefully in September and early October, and weep out above the foliage on graceful stems. The fragrance is elegant close up but also moves around the garden on warm fall days, delighting us when we least expect it.

Comparison of the Two Gardens

The Ashford and Deldeo entrance gardens provide an interesting contrast in terms of viewer participation, a contrast that we will continue to discuss in the balance of the book.

To be effective, plant combinations seen from a distance from a moving car need to be bold statements, using large numbers of a single plant to make a color or textural im-pact. The Yellow-Twig Dogwood (*Cornus sericea* 'Flaviramea') (13 plants) and Spring Glory Forsythia (*Forsythia* x *intermedia* 'Spring Glory') (23 plants) plantings in the Deldeo Garden serve as good examples.

But, if a viewer is walking through a garden and becomes more intimately involved, an increase in richness of detail is most pleasant. The small, fragrant blossoms on the single Korean Spice Viburnum (*Viburnum carlesii*), underplanted with fifty of the diminutive, highly scented *Narcissus jonquilla*, illustrate such detail in the Ashford Garden.

By contrast, the mass of Yellow-Twig Dogwoods when seen close up would be relatively boring, and the effect of the Viburnum-*Narcissus* combination would fail to reach a person in a moving vehicle.

Hence, we have seen garden exuberance provided by the use of fragrant plants in conjunction with the footpath in the Ashford Garden and by color massing in the Deldeo Garden. Both plantings avail themselves of selections suitable to the objectives involved.

These two richly planted gardens have the common denominator of control. Each garden has a strong ground plan (one predominantly geometric, one curvilinear). Each planting demonstrates the use of various plant forms to structure the total planting, move the eye around, and bring the entire composition into repose. Finally, the two gardens have the same center of interest: the front door.

Additional summer interest can be provided in entrance gardens by the use of tender plants in tubs. This requires a small commitment of additional maintenance time by the owner. Shown on the opposite page are two favorites. *Top:* The Peacock-Orchid (*Acidanthera bicolor*) has foliage resembling a gladiolus and starlike white flowers with chocolate throats and an elegant fragrance. *Bottom:* Angel's-Trumpet (*Datura inoxia* subsp. *quinquecuspida*) produces a new set of blossoms each day. The tight buds it displays in the morning unfold in a spiral fashion during the afternoon, welcoming the family home in the evening.

NOTES

1. Helen Van Pelt Wilson and Leonie Bell, *The Fragrant Year* (New York: M. Barrows, 1967), p. 36.
2. Rosemary Verey, *The Scented Garden* (London: Michael Joseph, 1981), p. 140.
3. Wilson and Bell, p. 98.
4. Ibid., p. 171.
5. Thomas H. Everitt, *Encyclopedia of Horticulture* (New York: Garland Publishing, 1981), vol. 3, p. 849.
6. Ibid., vol. 5, p. 1428.
7. Graham Stuart Thomas, *Perennial Garden Plants or the Modern Florilegium* (London: J. M. Dent and Sons, 1976), p. 185.
8. Wilson and Bell, p. 224.
9. Ibid., p. 223.
10. Verey, p. 125.
11. Wilson and Bell, p. 19.
12. Louise Beebe Wilder, *The Fragrant Path* (New York: Macmillan, 1932), p. 120.
13. Verey, p. 79.
14. Wilson and Bell, p. 30.
15. Ibid., p. 25.
16. Ibid., p. 24.
17. Ibid., p. 36.
18. Verey, p. 82.
19. Wilson and Bell, p. 86.
20. Ibid., p. 81.
21. Ibid., p. 80.
22. Ibid., p. 100.
23. Verey, p. 140.
24. Thomas, p. 193.
25. Wilson and Bell, p. 185.
26. Wilder, p. 293.
27. Ibid., p. 125.
28. Wilson and Bell, p. 82.
29. Ibid., p. 80.
30. Ibid., p. 82.
31. Wilder, p. 106.
32. Wilson and Bell, p. 185.
33. Wilder, p. 118.
34. Ibid., p. 109.
35. Ibid., p. 108.
36. Wilson and Bell, p. 171.
37. Ibid., p. 103.
38. Ibid., p. 252.
39. Ibid., p. 250.
40. Ibid., p. 17.

2 Gardens to Be Viewed

Experiencing a garden is very much a sequential event and, at its best, one that is closely integrated with living in the associated house. The successful handling of the entrance garden prepares us for the downward shift in scale to the rooms of the house and makes us receptive to the mood that will be created by the interior decoration and the further relationship with the garden proper. This relationship often involves a view from a window or glass room into the garden itself.

Subsequent chapters will continue the sequential experience and consider situations where we are literally living in the garden and, finally, where we enjoy it as a series of events through which we stroll.

Views from the house to the garden are important because of the many months when we cannot live in the garden in my part of the world, the mid-Atlantic United States. With such views we can, in complete comfort, witness the drama of changing weather, lighting, garden interest, and birds during the eight months of the year we wouldn't want to sit in a chair outside.

Views of this sort, seen from a fixed viewpoint, present an opportunity for making immensely satisfying compositions. Let us look at three examples—the Ward View Gardens, the Nehoc View Garden, and the Singer View Garden—and discuss some guidelines that particularly apply to view gardens.

Ward View Gardens

The glass walls of the Ward living room and dining room look panoramically into a mature forest of handsome Oak, Tulip Poplar, and Beech. It was imperative that nothing be done to distract from this experience. Hence we established that no foreground planting would be high enough to interfere with the view of the forest. Before the garden was built the land fell away precipitously starting just below the windows. Construction of

timber-retaining walls provided level terraces on which to create transition plantings.

Because the owners spent part of their early married life in Japan, they have an abiding love of oriental art, furnishings, and gardens. The furnishings of the rooms show an oriental influence. We decided that it would be appropriate to repeat this influence in the gardens. Therefore the two window gardens have occultly balanced, curvilinear

Opposite page: The Ward living room garden has an occultly balanced, curvilinear plan, reflecting the Japanese influence on the architecture and decor of the house. Height of planting is limited to prevent competition with the view into the forest. Seen here is a "puddle" of moss that leads the viewer's eye to the focal point, a single plant of the yellow-and-green-striped *Acorus gramineus* 'Ogon.'

plans. No effort was made to copy Japanese gardens, but we did try to capture their minimalist spirit. The flowers are incidental to the attempt to combine shades and textures of green in a satisfying way.

Four large rocks and one flat stone were buried to one half to two thirds of their depth, and the designs of the two gardens were composed around them.

The living room garden features a carefully studied "puddle" of moss, which leads the viewer's eye to the focal point, a single plant of the yellow-and-green-striped Grassy-Leaved Sweet Flag (*Acorus gramineus* 'Ogon'). Behind this plant and its rock background is a sweep of the broad foliage of Hybrid Pigsqueak (*Bergenia* 'Perfecta') (30 plants), with large massings of the straplike dark green foliage of blue-flowered Big Blue Lilyturf (*Liriope muscari* [Big Blue Selection]) (125 plants) on either side. The only other plant used is European Wild-Ginger (*Asarum europaeum*) (24 plants), with its shiny dark green foliage one-half the scale of the *Bergenia*. With the exception of the *Bergenia*, whose winter foliage is "persistent," all of the other actors in this scene are evergreen.

It should be noted that the success of this particular textural combination depends on the moss. Moss will not thrive under all conditions. The combination of this shady northeastern location and devoted, persistent care from the owners turned the trick here. (For other plants with mosslike texture, see Appendix 29.)

The dining room garden features a single handsome rock surrounded by the small, dark green, oval foliage of Partridgeberry (*Mitchella repens*) (50 plants). The coarse, fingered foliage of Christmas-Rose (*Helleborus niger*) (14 plants) presents a strong contrast in the background. A single broadleaf evergreen with pendulous branches, Fountain Leucothoe (*Leucothoe fontanesiana*), and four gray-leaved (white-variegated) Solomon's Seal (*Polygonatum odoratum* 'Variegatum') provide a little more height close to the base of the house and are surrounded by our native Crested Iris (*Iris cristata*) (28 plants).

Two different foreground pictures reflect the moods of the two different rooms. Each, like the rooms, is minimalist and controlled but rich in texture. Because the coloration is subtle and responds to the forest colors, there is a happy transition between the house and the forest.

WARD VIEW GARDENS—SEASONAL INTEREST

Numbers are keyed to garden plan
Dotted rules indicate time of flowering

	J	F	M	A	MAY	J	JUL	AUG	SEP	O	N	D
1. Christmas-Rose (*Helleborus niger*)—Clustered, broad, dark evergreen leaves. White blossoms in March.		⋯	⋯									
2. Solomon's Seal (White Variegated) (*Polygonatum odoratum* 'Variegatum')—Green-and-white-variegated leaves. Pendulous white blossoms in May.					⋯							
3. Fountain Leucothoe (*Leucothoe fontanesiana*)—Evergreen wedge-shaped leaves, bronzing in winter.						⋯						
4. Partridgeberry (*Mitchella repens*)—Small, oval, leathery evergreen leaves. Red fruits in fall and winter.												
5. Big Blue Lilyturf (*Liriope muscari* [Big Blue Selection])—Narrow, strapshaped evergreen leaves. Lavender-blue flowers in August.								⋯				
6. Hybrid Pigsqueak (*Bergenia* 'Perfecta')—Cabbagelike persistent foliage, bronzing in winter. Pink blossoms in April.												
7. European Wild-Ginger (*Asarum europaeum*)—Shiny, oval, evergreen foliage.												
8. Crested Iris (*Iris cristata*)—Wedge-shaped leaves. Blue flowers in May.					⋯							

1

2

3

The Ward dining room garden (see garden plan, page 24) features a single handsome rock in a puddle of **(1)** Partridgeberry (*Mitchella repens*). The surrounding planting is structured by **(2)** one evergreen Fountain Leucothoe (*Leucothoe fontanesiana*) and **(3)** four white-variegated Solomon's Seal (*Polygonatum odoratum* 'Variegatum'). Ground covers (higher than the Partridgeberry) of contrasting textures complete the picture — Christmas-Rose (*Helleborus niger*) (*opposite page*) and Crested Iris (*Iris cristata*) (page 28, *bottom inset*).

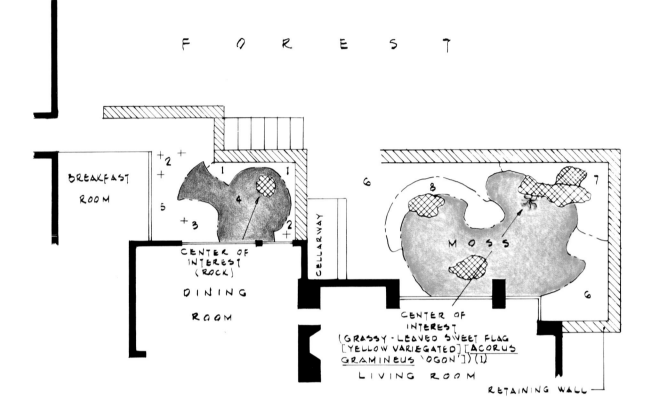

F O R E S T

BREAKFAST
ROOM

CENTER OF
INTEREST
(ROCK)

D I N I N G

R O O M

CELLARWAY

MOSS

CENTER OF
INTEREST
(GRASSY-LEAVED SWEET FLAG
[YELLOW VARIEGATED][ACORUS
GRAMINEUS 'OGON'])(1)

L I V I N G   R O O M

RETAINING WALL

KEY:

1. CHRISTMAS-ROSE (HELLEBORUS NIGER)
   (14)--CLUSTERED BROAD DARK EVER-
   GREEN LEAVES

2. SOLOMON'S SEAL (POLYGONATUM
   ODORATUM 'VARIEGATUM') (4)--BROAD
   WHITE-VARIEGATED LEAVES

3. FOUNTAIN LEUCOTHOE (LEUCOTHOE
   FONTANESIANA)(1)--EVERGREEN
   WEDGE-SHAPED LEAVES, BRONZING IN WINTER

4. PARTRIDGEBERRY (MITCHELLA REPENS)
   (50)--SMALL OVAL LEATHERY
   EVERGREEN LEAVES

5. CRESTED IRIS (IRIS CRISTATA)(28)

6. BIG BLUE LILYTURF (BLUE-FLOWERED)
   (LIRIOPE MUSCARI [BIG BLUE
   SELECTION]) (125)--STRAP-SHAPED
   LEAVES (EVERGREEN)

7. HYBRID PIGSQUEAK (BERGENIA
   'PERFECTA') (30)--CABBAGELIKE, PERSISTENT
   FOLIAGE BRONZING IN WINTER

8. EUROPEAN WILD-GINGER (ASARUM
   EUROPAEUM) (24)--SHINY OVAL
   EVERGREEN FOLIAGE

W A R D   V I E W   G A R D E N S

N

1" = 8' ±

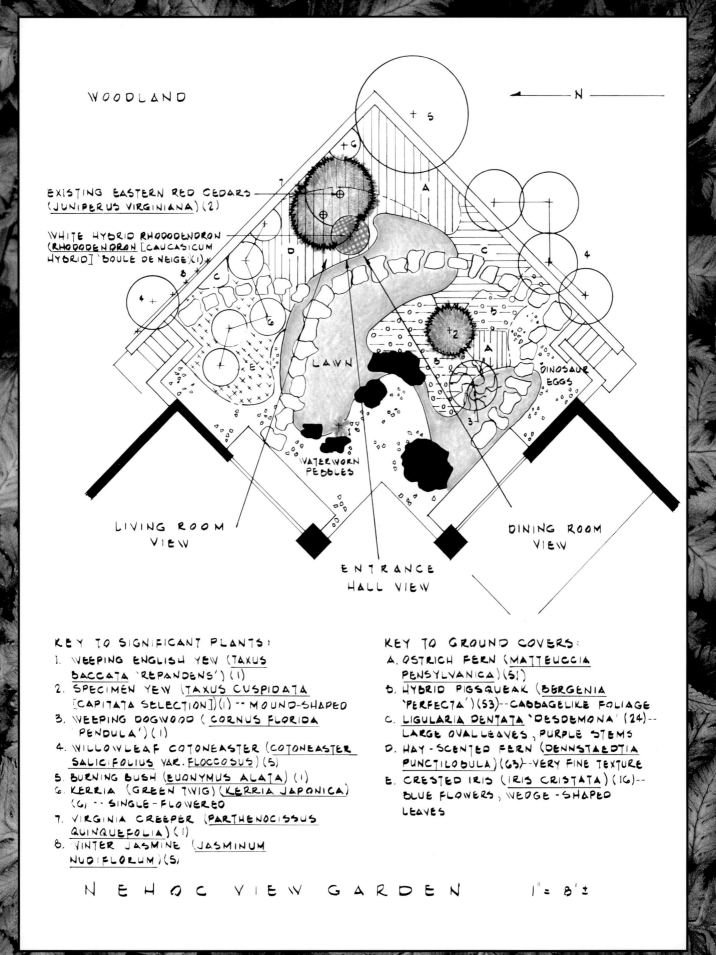

WOODLAND

N

EXISTING EASTERN RED CEDARS
(JUNIPERUS VIRGINIANA) (2)

WHITE HYBRID RHODODENDRON
(RHODODENDRON [CAUCASICUM
HYBRID] 'BOULE DE NEIGE)(1)

LAWN

DINOSAUR
EGGS

WATERWORN
PEBBLES

LIVING ROOM
VIEW

DINING ROOM
VIEW

ENTRANCE
HALL VIEW

KEY TO SIGNIFICANT PLANTS:
1. WEEPING ENGLISH YEW (TAXUS
   BACCATA 'REPANDENS') (1)
2. SPECIMEN YEW (TAXUS CUSPIDATA
   [CAPITATA SELECTION]) (1) -- MOUND-SHAPED
3. WEEPING DOGWOOD (CORNUS FLORIDA
   'PENDULA') (1)
4. WILLOWLEAF COTONEASTER (COTONEASTER
   SALICIFOLIUS VAR. FLOCCOSUS) (5)
5. BURNING BUSH (EUONYMUS ALATA) (1)
6. KERRIA (GREEN TWIG) (KERRIA JAPONICA)
   (6) -- SINGLE-FLOWERED
7. VIRGINIA CREEPER (PARTHENOCISSUS
   QUINQUEFOLIA) (1)
8. WINTER JASMINE (JASMINUM
   NUDIFLORUM) (5)

KEY TO GROUND COVERS:
A. OSTRICH FERN (MATTEUCCIA
   PENSYLVANICA) (51)
B. HYBRID PIGSQUEAK (BERGENIA
   'PERFECTA') (53) -- CABBAGELIKE FOLIAGE
C. LIGULARIA DENTATA 'DESDEMONA' (24) --
   LARGE OVAL LEAVES, PURPLE STEMS
D. HAY-SCENTED FERN (DENNSTAEDTIA
   PUNCTILOBULA) (63) -- VERY FINE TEXTURE
E. CRESTED IRIS (IRIS CRISTATA) (16) --
   BLUE FLOWERS, WEDGE-SHAPED
   LEAVES

NEHOC VIEW GARDEN   1" = 8'±

Nehoc View Garden

The Nehoc Garden, like the Ward gardens, is also seen from two rooms, as well as from the entrance hall connecting them: Both rooms and the hall have glass walls, which together wrap around two sides of a single square garden. In contrast to the Ward view, this garden, which is sunken into a rising hillside, is itself the main point of the view, and the forest beyond is secondary. Two handsome Eastern Red Cedars (*Juniperus virginiana*), thoroughly grown together, were preserved during construction, and their trunks, with the subsequently associated planting, became the garden's focal point.

Because this garden would be seen from several different angles and because its enclosure was rigidly rectilinear, it was decided early on that a curvilinear ground plan, occultly balanced in its third dimension, would be of considerably greater interest than a rectilinear composition.

A lawn panel of finely tuned shape leads the eye to the Eastern Red Cedars. A single broadleaf evergreen (*Rhododendron* [Caucasicum Hybrid] 'Boule de Neige') has been placed at their base. The dramatic foliage contrast leaves no doubt that this is the center of interest for all three views.

The flowing feeling of the lawn shape is enriched by contrast with the sweeps of small waterworn pebbles, larger rounded "dinosaur eggs," and strategically placed rocks.

Depth is added to the picture by repeating the needle evergreen texture of the Cedars with two Yews of different sizes and by placing a Weeping Dogwood (*Cornus florida* 'Pendula') in the foreground of one view. The green of the needle evergreens is echoed in winter by the bright green twigs of the Kerria (*Kerria japonica*) (6 plants).

The verticals of the cedars contrast strongly with the horizontal of the five-foot wall. This horizontality is reemphasized by the horizontal branching of the Burning Bush (*Euonymus alata*) (1 plant) in the background and the single strand of the five-fingered foliage of Virginia Creeper (*Parthenocissus quinquefolia*) (1 plant) just two feet down from the top of the wall. The pendulous habit of Winter Jasmine (*Jasminum nudiflorum*) (5 plants) and Willowleaf Cotoneaster (*Cotoneaster salicifolius* var. *floccosus*) (5 plants) echoes the form of the Weeping Dogwood and serves to direct the viewer's eye down into the strong pattern and texture of the garden floor.

The Nehoc View Garden (see plan on previous page) is seen from two rooms as well as the entrance hall connecting them. All have glass walls, which together wrap around two sides of a square garden. The ground plan is curvilinear with two existing (clustered) Eastern Red Cedars (*Juniperus virginiana*) as the focal point. Year-round interest is created by sharp textural contrast of rocks, pebbles, and a variety of foliage shapes.

1

2

The planting of the Nehoc View Garden is structured by the vertical green stems of **(1)** Kerria (*Kerria japonica*), horizontal habit of **(2)** Burning Bush (*Euonymus alata*), and Virginia Creeper (*Parthenocissus quinquefolia*) (page 29), trained on a horizontal wire, and the pendulous habit of **(3)** Willowleaf Cotoneaster (*Cotoneaster salicifolius* var. *floccosus*) and **(4)** Winter Jasmine (*Jasminum nudiflorum*).

3

4

Besides the texture of rocks and pebbles, the fine foliage of Ostrich Fern (*Matteuccia pensylvanica*) (*background, top*) and Hay-Scented Fern (*Dennstaedtia punctilobula*) (*background, bottom*) is contrasted with the oval foliage of Hybrid Pigsqueak (*Bergenia* 'Perfecta') (*inset, top*) and the wedge-shaped foliage of Crested Iris (*Iris cristata*) (*inset, bottom*).

In addition to the textures of the supporting cast of pebbles, stones, and rocks, interlocking ground cover plantings provide a background richness. Pointed wedgelike leaves of Crested Iris (*Iris cristata*) (16 plants) contrast with its large, oval-leaved neighbor *Ligularia dentata* 'Desdemona' (24 plants) and the exceedingly fine texture of Hay-Scented Fern (*Dennstaedtia punctilobula*) (63 plants). The taller Ostrich Fern (*Matteuccia pensylvanica*) (51 plants) contrasts with larger plantings of the *Ligularia,* and both are brought to earth by the shiny, smaller, cabbagelike foliage of Hybrid Pigsqueak (*Bergenia* 'Perfecta') (53 plants) in the foreground.

A garden like this, continually on display, must not only be of interest at all times but should reflect the passing of the seasons. To be sure, the changing light as leaves come and go on the surrounding trees accomplishes this to some extent. In addition, however, we have yellow blossoms on the Jasmine in February and March, the excitement of emerging fern fronds in April, and blossoms on the Crested Iris (light blue), Kerria (yellow), and Rhododendron and Weeping Dogwood (both white) in May. The *Ligularias* give us orange-yellow blossoms in summer. The Virginia Creeper and *Euonymus* provide red and pink foliage and the *Cotoneaster* matte-red berries, all in the fall.

NEHOC VIEW GARDEN—SEASONAL INTEREST

Numbers and letters are keyed to garden plan
Dotted rules indicate time of flowering

	J	F	M	A	MAY	J	JUL	AUG	SEP	O	N	D
Eastern Red Cedar (*Juniperus virginiana*)												
White Hybrid Rhododendron (*Rhododendron* [Caucasicum Hybrid] 'Boule de Neige')—White flowers in May.					·····							
1. Weeping English Yew (*Taxus baccata* 'Repandens')												
2. Pyramidal Japanese Yew (*Taxus cuspidata* [Capitata Selection])												
3. Weeping Dogwood (*Cornus florida* 'Pendula')—White flowers in May.					····							
4. Willowleaf Cotoneaster (*Cotoneaster salicifolius* var. *floccosus*)—Weeping form, leathery leaves (apple green in summer, bronze in fall and winter), red fruits in fall and winter.												
5. Burning Bush (*Euonymus alata*)—Horizontal habit, pink-to-red foliage in fall, as well as red berries; winged bark.												
6. Kerria (Single-Flowered) (*Kerria japonica*)—Green twigs in winter, yellow flowers in May.					······							
7. Virginia Creeper (*Parthenocissus quinquefolia*)—Scarlet foliage in fall.												
8. Winter Jasmine (*Jasminum nudiflorum*)—Yellow flowers February-March.		······										
A. Ostrich Fern (*Matteuccia pensylvanica*)												
B. Hybrid Pigsqueak (*Bergenia* 'Perfecta')—Cabbagelike foliage, pink flowers in April.												
C. *Ligularia dentata* 'Desdemona'—Large oval leaves, purple stems, orange-yellow flowers in July.							·····					
D. Hay-Scented Fern (*Dennstaedtia punctilobula*)—Very fine foliage texture.												
E. Crested Iris (*Iris cristata*)—Wedge-shaped leaves, blue flowers in May.					····							

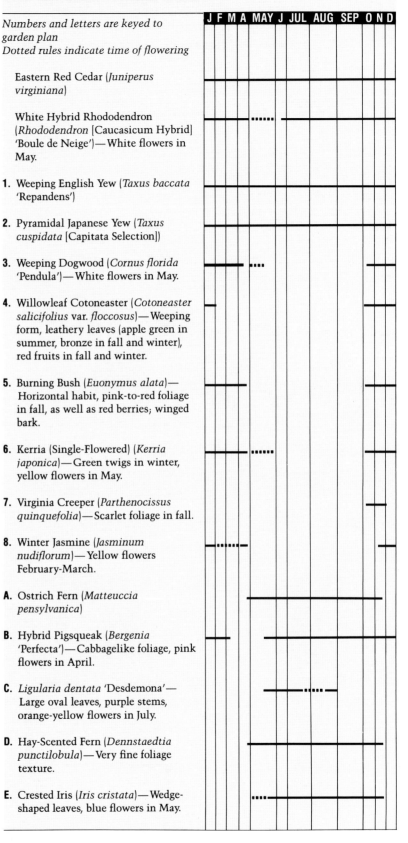

Virginia Creeper (*Parthenocissus quinquefolia*) in fall color. This plant, trained on a horizontal wire against a wall, provides part of the structure of the design. See pages 26 and 27 for its relationship to other structural elements involved.

SINGER VIEW GARDEN   1" = 16'±

KEY:
1. SEA BUCKTHORN (HIPPOPHAE RHAMNOIDES) (2)
2. SKYROCKET ROCKY MOUNTAIN JUNIPER (JUNIPERUS SCOPULORUM 'SKY ROCKET') (4) UNDERPLANTED WITH SEDUM 'AUTUMN JOY' (12)
3. THUNDERCLOUD PLUM (PRUNUS CERASIFERA 'THUNDERCLOUD') (2)
4. HEDGE OF AMERICAN ARBORVITAE (THUJA OCCIDENTALIS 'NIGRA') (23)

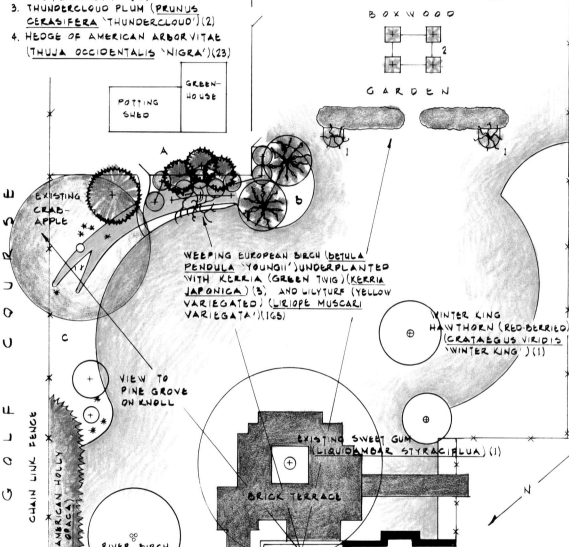

GREEN-HOUSE

POTTING SHED

BOXWOOD

GARDEN

A

EXISTING CRAB-APPLE

b

GOLF COURSE

CHAIN LINK FENCE

C

EXISTING AMERICAN HOLLY (ILEX OPACA)

WEEPING EUROPEAN BIRCH (BETULA PENDULA 'YOUNGII') UNDERPLANTED WITH KERRIA (GREEN TWIG) (KERRIA JAPONICA) (3), AND LILYTURF (YELLOW VARIEGATED) (LIRIOPE MUSCARI 'VARIEGATA') (165)

VIEW TO PINE GROVE ON KNOLL

RIVER BIRCH (BETULA NIGRA) (1)

WINTER KING HAWTHORN (RED-BERRIED) (CRATAEGUS VIRIDIS 'WINTER KING') (1)

PICKET FENCE

EXISTING SWEET GUM (LIQUIDAMBAR STYRACIFLUA) (1)

BRICK TERRACE

N

GLASS ROOM

A. CHINA GIRL® (7) AND CHINA BOY® (1) HOLLIES (ILEX CHINA GIRL® 'MESOG' AND I. CHINA BOY® 'MESDOB') BELOW TREE-FORM AMERICAN HOLLIES (I. OPACA) (3) AND EXISTING PLUM

YEW (CEPHALOTAXUS HARRINGTONIA VAR. PEDUNCULATA) (1)
b. JAPANESE BLACK PINE (PINUS THUNBERGIANA) (2), RED-TWIG DOGWOOD (CORNUS SERICEA) (3), HARDY FOUNTAIN GRASS (PENNISETUM ALOPECUROIDES) (8)
C. BOWLES PERIWINKLE (VINCA MINOR 'BOWLESII') (2000) UNDERPLANTED WITH SPRING BULBS AND ADAMS-NEEDLE (YUCCA SMALLIANA) (12)

Singer View Garden

The viewing point into the Singer Garden is an elegant room that is glass on two sides (converted from a screened porch). The view is panoramic, and one has the feeling of being in a garden all year but with all the comforts of home. It is a second-generation garden that needed reevaluation. We started with a major problem—three distinctly different views competing for the viewer's interest—which we were able to convert into a major asset—a view with one dominant center of interest and two secondary points of interest. The head-on view was of a relatively uninteresting potting shed and greenhouse in the corner. There was a charming view to the left of a rolling golf course lawn and a distant grove of Pines, all framed by a low limb of a beautiful aged Crabapple. The latter was backed up by, of all things, the handsome, dark green needle foliage of a large existing Plum Yew (*Cephalotaxus harringtonia* var. *pedunculata*). To the right rear was a view of the remnants of the previous owner's formal Boxwood garden.

To capitalize on the golf course view, all that was necessary was to trim the Crabapple to emphasize its character shape, remove a few miscellaneous shrubs along the fence line, and "purify" the existing Bowles Periwinkle (*Vinca minor* 'Bowlesii') ground cover by removing *Pachysandra*, English Ivy, and assorted perennials growing with it.

The formal Boxwood garden to the right was cleared and put in turf (to reduce maintenance), and only the two front hedges and two specimen Boxwoods farther back were saved. The owner's fondness for the extremely narrow, blue Skyrocket Rocky Mountain Juniper (*Juniperus scopulorum* 'Sky Rocket') was the key to restructuring this garden along low-maintenance lines. Four of these verticals were squared around a center pad of brick, with *Sedum* 'Autumn Joy' (12 plants) planted at their bases for textural contrast. A hedge of pyramidal American Arborvitae (*Thuja occidentalis* 'Nigra') (23 plants) was planted as a screen and background; it would be kept trimmed as a horizontal line. Against this hedge, and positioned to represent the back corners of the rectangle of the garden, were added two redleaf Thundercloud Plums (*Prunus cerasifera* 'Thundercloud'), whose red foliage would contrast with the blue of the Skyrocket Junipers. We used two plants of Sea Buckthorn (*Hippophae rhamnoides*), one at either end of the Boxwood hedge (on the house side), so that their gray needle foliage could provide a contrast with the broader leaf of the Boxwood and subtly pick up the gray of the Junipers.

The Singer Garden provides an all-year panoramic experience from a glass room. To the left is "borrowed scenery." To the right (shown on page 33) are the bones of a former formal Boxwood garden. Developing a focal point in the center section proved a challenge.

*Letters are keyed to garden plan
Dotted rules indicate time of flowering*

	J	F	M	A	MAY	J	JUL	AUG	SEP	O	N	D

Sweet Gum (*Liquidambar styraciflua*)—Star-shaped leaves turning orange, yellow, and red in fall. Winged twig bark attractive in winter.

River Birch (*Betula nigra*)— Attractive bark in winter.

Crabapple (*Malus* species)—Pink blossoms in May.

Winter King Hawthorn (*Crataegus viridis* 'Winter King')—Red berries in winter, white blossoms in May.

A. China Girl and China Boy Hollies (*Ilex* China Girl ® 'Mesog' and *I.* China Boy ® 'Mesdob')—Shiny evergreen horned leaves; red berries in fall.

A. American Holly (*Ilex opaca*)— Evergreen foliage; red berries in fall.

A. Plum Yew (*Cephalotaxus harringtonia* var. *pendunculata*)— Needle evergreen foliage.

B. Japanese Black Pine (*Pinus thunbergiana*)—Character plant form. Needle evergreen.

B. Red-Twig Dogwood (*Cornus sericea*)

B. Hardy Fountain Grass (*Pennisetum alopecuroides*)

C. Bowles Periwinkle (*Vinca minor* 'Bowlesii')—Evergreen ground cover. Blue flowers in April.

C. Adam's-Needle (*Yucca smalliana*)— Spiky evergreen foliage. Six-foot spikes of white flowers in June-July.

Weeping European Birch (*Betula pendula* 'Youngii')—Character plant form. White bark.

Kerria (Single-Flowered) (*Kerria japonica*)—Green twigs in winter, yellow flowers in May.

Lilyturf (Yellow Variegated) (*Liriope muscari* 'Variegata')—Strap-shaped leaves, striped gold and green; lavender-blue flowers in August.

continued on page 34

Opposite page, top: The "tease view" of the Boxwood garden as seen from the glass room. *Opposite page, bottom:* High-maintenance herbaceous borders were replaced with sod. This central feature provides all of the interest needed for a nongardening owner.

Specimens similar to those shown here were used in the Singer View Garden. **(1)** A single specimen Weeping European Birch (*Betula pendula* 'Youngii') provides a focus for the panoramic view. Framed on the left by an existing Plum Yew (*Cephalotaxus harringtonia* var. *pendunculata*) and on the right by **(2)** two Japanese Black Pine (*Pinus thunbergiana*) underplanted with **(3)** Red-Twig Dogwood (*Cornus sericea*) (shown with *C. sericea* 'Flaviramea') and **(4)** Hardy Fountain Grass (*Pennisetum alopecuroides*), this sculptural specimen is underplanted with Kerria (*Kerria japonica*) (vertical green twigs) (page 27, *top left*) and a horizontal line of the gold and green foliage of **(5)** variegated Lilyturf (*Liriope muscari* 'Variegata').

1

SINGER VIEW GARDEN—SEASONAL INTEREST *continued*

Numbers are keyed to garden plan

	J	F	M	A	MAY	J	JUL	AUG	SEP	O	N	D
1. Sea Buckthorn (*Hippophae rhamnoides*)—Small gray leaves; orange fruits in midsummer.					██	██	██	██	██			
2. Skyrocket Rocky Mountain Juniper (*Juniperus scopulorum* 'Sky Rocket')—Very narrow form, blue needle foliage.	██	██	██	██	██	██	██	██	██	██	██	██
3. Thundercloud Plum (*Prunus cerasifera* 'Thundercloud')				██	██	██	██	██	██			
4. American Arborvitae (*Thuja occidentalis* 'Nigra')—Narrow form, needle foliage remaining dark green in winter.	██	██	██	██	██	██	██	██	██	██	██	██

The view of the greenhouse complex, with its eye-grabbing white picket fence, remained dominant. One was disconcerted by a choice of three views from the glass room (represented on the garden plan by the three arrows), the most prominent one unattractive. The position of the fence meant that if any screening planting were to be done, the planting must move forward toward the glass room and be sufficiently rich in interest to qualify as the primary view. A planting was laid on that provided high screening: three American Hollies (*Ilex opaca*), relocated from other parts of the property (and trained into tree form), and two Japanese Black Pine (*Pinus thunbergiana*), to pick up the dark needle foliage of the Plum Yew. Below these and against the fence, eight hybrid China Girl and China Boy Hollies—*Ilex* China Girl ® 'Mesog' (7 plants) and China Boy® 'Mesdob' (1 plant)—with their shiny, light-reflective, horned leaves, were planted. For the focal point a character specimen of the graceful form of Weeping European Birch (*Betula pendula* 'Youngii') was used (in landscaping parlance a "character specimen" is a plant with a strong sculptural quality, often emphasized by pruning). Enriching detail fol-

2

3

lowed with the planting of three Kerria (*Kerria japonica*) (behind the Birch and in front of the China Girl ® Hollies) for their green stems in winter and their single yellow blossoms in May, both enhancements to the Birch in these seasons. Some froth was added to the Black Pine planting with a foreground grouping of Hardy Fountain Grass (*Pennisetum alopecuroides*) (8 plants) and Red-Twig Dogwood (*Cornus sericea*) (3 plants). This contrasts with the tightly organized two-fingered sweep of green and yellow foliage provided by golden-variegated Lilyturf (*Liriope muscari* 'Variegata') (165 plants) just in front of the Birch. The *Liriope* links the Weeping Birch to the aged Crabapple (*Malus* species), with its existing scattered underplanting of *Yucca smalliana*.

Because of its forward position and calculated richness of detail, the Birch planting dominates, causing the greenhouse complex to disappear and the other two views to recede into secondary positions. Wherever you sit in the glass room there is a genuine garden experience. (A detailed listing of seasonal interest in the Singer Garden is given in the chart on pages 32 and 34.)

4

5

1

Three Important Design Considerations

The exuberant plantings in these three gardens could have resulted in chaos without a strong degree of control. Three guidelines for maintaining control are particularly worthy of comment.

First, the distinctive shape and happy proportions of the lowest ground cover planting in any composition have a great deal to do with the success of the whole. Almost inevitably such ground cover occupies a relatively large, centrally positioned area in the picture. In a great many gardens the ground cover is lawn grass and, unfortunately, is frequently thought of simply as space that is left over, with all effort concentrated on the composition of the surrounding plantings and their flower, foliage, and fruiting interest. To dismiss ground cover in this way is to miss a great opportunity for not only pulling the whole composition together but giving it great strength of character.

Just as the human eye goes first to the

smooth, level surface of a body of water in any landscape scene, so the eye seeks the lowest, most noticeable ground cover in any garden composition, whether it be the fine texture of lawn grass or (in the absence of a finer texture) a large sweep of light-reflective ground cover such as *Pachysandra.* If this strong attractor is amorphous, uninteresting, or unsatisfying in shape, so is the entire picture. If, on the other hand, the shape involves nicely proportioned rectilinear and related geometric forms or pleasing, carefully refined curvilinear forms, and these shapes are crisply defined, the whole composition will sing. For clear examples of such strong design, see the plans for moss and Partridgeberry (*Mitchella repens*) in the Ward View Gardens (page 24) and for the lawn in the Nehoc View Garden (page 25) and the Cardinal Stroll Garden (page 119). For an extensive listing of ground covers, see Appendix 27.

2

The distinctive shape
and happy proportions
of the lowest ground
cover in any composi-
tion have a great deal to
do with the success of
the picture. Just as the
eye goes first to the
smooth, level surface of
a body of water **(1)** in
any garden scene, in the
absence of water the eye
goes to the lowest, most
noticeable ground cover.
Seen here are **(2)** Blue
Rug Juniper (*Juniperus
horizontalis* 'Wiltonii')
and **(3)** *Sedum ellacombianum*, used in
attractive free-form
shapes to pull two com-
positions together and
provide them with great
strength of character.

3

A second essential consideration when planning a landscape picture is to decide what is the center of interest and then consistently build the planting composition to enhance that objective. We've all read books that we dubbed failures because there were too many themes or plots without one that was dominant, or too many characters given equal importance. In the same sense, presumably we've all seen plantings involving one each of a number of varieties of plants and realized that the result was unsatisfying. Any area within your garden can suffer from this fault. When featuring a particular tree, you must arrange the plantings and structures to show it off and to emphasize its dominant positioning and its color and textural relationship with other plants in the garden. As soon as you also try to feature other single trees in the same area, you will have dissipated the dominant effect of the first tree.

I have worked with clients who possessed three garden ornaments from "Grandmother's garden" that they wanted to feature in the same area, and I had to explain that it was better to put two in storage and give one a chance to assume full sway in pulling the picture together. Of course, this is not to say that the center of interest cannot be more than one object, for a clump of three trees of one kind or even a small grove can occasionally be a very special feature. Likewise, several pieces of sculpture, if they appear successfully as a group, could come off very well. The important challenge is to create a point of emphasis, so that regardless of where you look in the garden, the eye is subtly led back to that point.

We have seen in Chapter 1 how plant forms assume an important role in moving the eye toward this point of emphasis and

It is essential when planning a landscape picture first to decide what is the center of interest and then to consistently build the planting composition to enhance that objective. *Top:* An uninterrupted sweep of Plumbago (*Ceratostigma plumbaginoides*), backed by a higher-level massing of Chinese Beautyberry (*Callicarpa dichotoma*), brings the eye to rest on a single plant of the light-gathering Firebush (*Kochia scoparia* forma *trichophylla* 'Childsii'). *Bottom:* The noncompeting horizontal of massed Bloody Cranesbill (*Geranium sanguineum*) helps to clearly establish the triad of Siberian Iris (*Iris sibirica*) as the focal point of the composition.

Garden scenes, like landscape paintings, often depend for their success on a feeling of depth. Foreground and middle-ground measuring points for the eye are part of the trick. *Opposite page, top:* The two vertical Eastern Red Cedars (*Juniperus virginiana*) were added as a middle-ground measuring point and echo a similar plant in the background. *Opposite page, bottom:* The branch of an ancient Tamarisk (*Tamarix ramosissima*) provides foreground framing for a view of a diving rock at the edge of a pool, while background is provided by a Dogwood and Conifers. Without such view structuring, the composition of both of these scenes would be much weaker.

how the relationship of plant colors to the colors of the house serves to establish the front door as the center of interest in those compositions. Later in this chapter we will discuss grouping different plant textures together as a tool to similarly focus attention where we want it.

The third guideline for maintaining control of a garden design is to establish a feeling of depth. Most landscape paintings depend for their success on this feeling. It is usually achieved by having foreground, middle-ground, and background interest, and the effect is equally important in planning landscape scenes. The eye uses the first two in measuring the distance to the background.

We have seen how a feeling of depth was created in the four gardens just described. The chart on page 40 outlines how it was achieved.

	WARD VIEW GARDENS		NEHOC VIEW GARDEN	SINGER VIEW GARDEN		
	Living Room Garden	*Dining Room Garden*		*Left-hand View*	*Middle View*	*Right-hand View*
Foreground	Flat rock	• Rock	Rock and small *Taxus baccata* 'Repandens' and *Taxus cuspidata* (Capitata Selection) specimens	*Liquidambar styraciflua*	*Liquidambar styraciflua*	*Liquidambar styraciflua*
Middle Ground	• *Acorus gramineus* 'Ogon,' rock, and *Bergenia* 'Perfecta'	*Helleborus niger*	• *Juniperus virginiana* • *Rhododendron* (Caucasicum Hybrid) 'Boule de Neige'	*Malus*	• *Betula pendula* 'Youngii' and • *Liriope muscari* 'Variegata'	*Buxus* hedge
Background	Forest	Forest	Wall	• Golf course lawn	Screen of *Ilex opaca, I.* China Girl® 'Mesog,' and *I.* China Boy® 'Mesdob'	• *Juniperus scopulorum* 'Sky Rocket' and • background of *Prunus cerasifera* 'Thundercloud' and *Thuja occidentalis* 'Nigra' hedge

Bullet indicates center of interest

Texture

The bulleted items indicate the center of interest in each composition. Please note that, as in landscape paintings, the center of interest can be located at any depth.

Texture

In looking at these four gardens we have seen plant textures and colors playing an important role in creating garden magic, as they do in all gardens. But it should be noted that this form of successful exuberance does not occur by chance. Both texture and color are actually significant tools for accomplishing varying design objectives in each garden.

Frequently a single plant will have both color and texture of significance, and it is difficult to evaluate the impact of each separately. (We will see how true this is in the concluding paragraphs of this chapter, when we deal with the palette of plants for winter interest.) However, we should consider texture alone for a moment, and by *texture* I mean in this instance primarily leaf shape (see Appendix 19). Bark texture can be studied by referring to Appendix 21; texture created by flower shape can be studied by referring to Appendix 20.

Generally speaking, although it is true that like textures create a feeling of quiet and harmony, if carried to an extreme they result in boredom. Contrasting textures provide interest and richness, but when carried to an extreme create chaos. The trick is to mesh these opposing forces in a harmonious balance aimed at turning or returning the eye to the center of interest. The eye normally goes to finer textures first when broad and fine are used together. For this reason the finest textures are usually used closest to the center of interest. (For a listing of plants with fine foliage texture and another of those with broad foliage texture, see Appendix 19.)

We have seen how the single narrow-leaf *Acorus* contrasted with the velvet texture of moss in the foreground and how the broad, cabbagelike texture of *Bergenia* behind the *Acorus* set up the highest textural contrast in the Ward living room garden. Textural contrast on a slightly larger scale between a rock, the small, oval foliage of Partridge-berry, and the coarse texture of Christmas-Roses similarly structured the picture from the Ward dining room. These high contrasts, surprisingly, caused a forest of giant trees in the rear to temporarily become simply attractive background.

The needle texture of the Eastern Red Cedars in the Nehoc Garden was contrasted with the broadest foliage in the garden, a Rhododendron. These textures were echoed in the ground pattern below, with fine-textured ferns and Iris contrasting with the broader foliage of *Ligularia* and *Bergenia.* The highest contrast remained, however, with the Red Cedars and Rhododendron as center of interest.

Although there were three separate areas of interest in the Singer Garden, it was interesting to see how the central one came to dominate with the help of the most dramatic textural contrast in the whole composition. There the narrow *Liriope* leaves and fine twigs of the European Weeping Birch and Kerria were sharply contrasted with the broader leaves of the two kinds of Hollies (the broadest textures in the picture).

The role of textural contrasts was also important in a larger garden project in which I was involved, where a sizable piece of sculpture had been placed in an irregularly shaped "bed" of river pebbles, all in a large lawn area. The garden was viewed from an elevation of eight to ten feet. Unfortunately, the vertical dominance of a row of large Eastern White Pines (*Pinus strobus*) on a neighbor's boundary in the background distracted the viewer from the intended center of interest.

To counteract this distraction, I recommended additional planting of high textural contrast. The background of this planting was five Empress Trees (*Paulownia tomentosa*) (eighteen-inch rounded to heart-shaped leaves) contrasted with three Cutleaf Staghorn Sumac (*Rhus typhina* 'Laciniata') (twenty-seven-inch-long compound leaves, as many as thirteen pairs, each finely divided,

1

2

Not only can manipulation of contrasting textures add interest to a garden, but it can also be a significant factor in bringing the eye to rest on the center of interest. As described in the text (pages 41–42), a gradual reduction in the scale of the contrasting foliages accomplishes just this: **(1)** Empress Tree (*Paulownia tomentosa*) in the background contrasted with **(2)** Cutleaf Staghorn Sumac (*Rhus typhina* 'Laciniata').

1

2

3

4

Additional variations in texture are provided by **(1)** Ornamental Rhubarb (*Rheum palmatum* 'Rubrum') contrasted with ornamental grasses and **(2)** Hyperion Daylily foliage (*Hemerocallis* 'Hyperion') in the middle ground; and **(3)** Hybrid Pigsqueak (*Bergenia* 'Sunningdale') contrasted with the **(4)** native Broomsedge (*Andropogon virginicus*) in the foreground.

or "cut"), underplanted with a mass planting of Ornamental Rhubarb (*Rheum palmatum* 'Rubrum') (leaves bluntly heart-shaped and eighteen inches long). By contrast, in front of this background on the right side of the pebble area and continuing partway behind the sculpture, drifts of narrow-leaved plants, including Hyperion Daylilies (*Hemerocallis* 'Hyperion') and two ornamental grasses (Prairie Cordgrass [*Spartina pectinata* 'Aureomarginata'] and Hardy Fountain Grass [*Pennisetum alopecuroides*]), were used. Two multiplant clumps of Hybrid Pigsqueak (*Bergenia* 'Sunningdale'), in the pebbles near the sculpture picked up the broadleaf texture from the background on a smaller scale. By a serendipitous occurrence, the picture was

completed by some Broomsedge (*Andropogon virginicus*), which seeded itself in random clumps in the pebbles.

The great contrast between the giant *Paulownia* leaves and the fine texture of the grasses grabbed the show away from the three-hundred-foot-long row of mature Eastern White Pines. By keeping the finest textures (grasses and pebbles) nearest the sculpture, we were able to make the eye rest there.

The point is that textural contrasts, though stimulating in themselves, are most successful when thought of and used as tools to carry out the objective of the design. In this case they were essential to moving the eye toward the center of interest.

Winter Plant Palette

One of the special opportunities associated with view gardens is the creation of stimulating winter pictures. Prime time for views from the house into the garden are the months of December, January, February, and March. Let's take a serious look at the plant palette for these months, with particular reference to combinations that will be effective when the viewing distance is on the indoor-outdoor scale. Form, texture, and color all play a role.

Although evergreens are basic to such a winter picture, a composition is of even greater textural interest when evergreens are mixed with deciduous woody plants. Therefore, both evergreen and deciduous plants must be considered.

When selecting evergreens it is important to note that those with gray-green foliage tend to only emphasize the depressing effects of tan lawn and field grasses, and that blue-greens seem more artificial than ever without the lushness of summer foliage around them. It is the black-green and bright green evergreens that are most useful in winter compositions. Some of my favorites are:

Nordmann Fir (*Abies nordmanniana*)—Dark green, pyramidal

Hinoki False Cypress (Semi-Dwarf) (*Chamaecyparis obtusa* 'Nana Gracilis')—Dark green, of irregular, dense habit

San Jose Holly (*Ilex* x *aquipernyi* 'San Jose')—Dark green, pyramidal; regular pruning advised to keep it dense

Blue Maid® and Blue Stallion® Hollies (*Ilex* x *meserveae* Blue Maid® 'Mesid' and *I.* x *meserveae* Blue Stallion® 'Mesan')—Dark green, irregular shrub; regular pruning advised to keep it dense

Eastern Red Cedar (*Juniperus virginiana*)—Black-green with lighter overtones, narrow, cigar-shaped, more irregular with age

Prime time for views from the house into the garden are the months of December, January, February, and March. There is a wide palette of plants to choose from for this period. Here Winterberry (*Ilex verticillata* 'Scarlett O'Hara') frames a view of River Birch (*Betula nigra*) with Yellow-Twig Dogwood (*Cornus sericea* 'Flaviramea') and Arden American Holly (*Ilex opaca* 'Arden') in the background.

1

2

3

4

Plants with foliage variegation can add cheer to winter plantings, especially as part of a consistent color scheme (otherwise they may "scream" at the viewer). Examples are **(1)** golden-variegated Cripps Hinoki False Cypress (*Chamaecyparis obtusa* 'Crippsii'), **(2)** golden-variegated Elaeagnus (*Elaeagnus pungens* 'Maculata'), **(3)** Adam's Needle (*Yucca flaccida* 'Golden Sword'), whose variegation becomes more distinct and dramatic in lower-temperature months, and **(4)** Veitch Bamboo (*Sasa veitchii*), whose foliage is solid green during warmer months and develops a tan variegation, which becomes wider as winter progresses.

Oriental Spruce (*Picea orientalis*)—Black-green, pyramidal
Canadian Hemlock (*Tsuga canadensis*)—Dark green, pyramidal

The following evergreens also add richness when used in combination with the dark greens:

Willowleaf Cotoneaster (*Cotoneaster salicifolius* var. *floccosus*)—Maroon-bronze foliage, apple green in summer, matte-red berries in fall; pendulous
Fountain Leucothoe (*Leucothoe fontanesiana*)—Maroon-bronze foliage, wedge-shaped leaves, arching stems
Veitch Bamboo (*Sasa veitchii*)—Light tan winter variegation, most effective in late winter

When very carefully placed, plants with golden foliage can add a highlight or pick up on yellow twigs or yellow blossoms in the composition. Among the best are:

Cripps Hinoki False Cypress (Gold-Plumed) (*Chamaecyparis obtusa* 'Crippsii')—Vertical needle evergreen
Elaeagnus (Yellow Variegated) (*Elaeagnus pungens* 'Maculata')—Broadleaf, green and gold
Adam's Needle (Yellow Variegated) (*Yucca flaccida* 'Golden Sword')—Yellow centers to leaves become more vivid in winter

5

6

Many deciduous plants have buds of special interest that are visible at short range during winter. Two favorites of mine are **(5)** *Ginkgo biloba*, with its spurlike buds, and **(6)** Star Magnolia (*Magnolia tomentosa*), whose fat, fuzzy buds tickle one's anticipation of spring.

For deciduous companions I like the following for their striking forms:

Pagoda Dogwood (*Cornus alternifolia*)— Horizontal branching habit
Redvein Enkianthus (*Enkianthus campanulatus*)—Vertical stems with sympodial branching
Maidenhair Tree (*Ginkgo biloba*, staminate) —Irregular habit, branches lined with dome-shaped spurs
Kentucky Coffeetree (*Gymnocladus dioica*) —Vase-shaped, suggests muscled strength

and those whose fat buds tickle our anticipation for spring:

Shadbush (*Amelanchier arborea* [syn. *A. canadensis*])
Flowering Dogwood (*Cornus florida*)
Star Magnolia (*Magnolia tomentosa*)
Royal Azalea (*Rhododendron schlippenbachii*)

The greatest opportunity of all comes in choosing from that wonderful group of plants with bark that is of color and/or textural interest (see Appendix 21 for a listing of plants by bark texture and Appendix 26 for a listing by bark color). Special favorites include:

Trees with light-reflective gray bark

American Yellowwood (*Cladrastis lutea*)
American Beech (*Fagus grandifolia*)

Trees, shrubs, and vines with highly textured bark

Paperbark Maple (*Acer griseum*)—Curling strips of orange- and cherry-colored bark
Shagbark Hickory (*Carya ovata*)—Extremely long (two to three feet and sometimes longer) narrow strips of beautiful gray bark shred off the trunk, starting at the bottom, where they curl, and retain a hold at the top
Japanese Cornelian-Cherry (*Cornus officinalis*)—Longitudinally flaking gray bark reveals underbark in orange-bronze shades
Turkish Filbert (*Corylus colurna*)—Speckled flakiness, in shades of gray
Climbing Hydrangea (*Hydrangea anomala* subsp. *petiolaris* 'Skylands Giant')— Rough grayed-tan exfoliation reveals lighter orange-tan underbark
Oakleaf Hydrangea (*Hydrangea quercifolia*) —Rough grayed-tan exfoliation reveals lighter orange-tan underbark
Beauty-Bush (*Kolkwitzia amabilis*)— Vertically exfoliating bark, shades of tan
Dawn Redwood (*Metasequoia glyptostroboides*)—Gnarled, musclelike bark, brown with orange-brown overtones, dramatized by widely flaring form of trunk as it meets the ground
Tanyosho Pine (*Pinus densiflora* 'Umbraculifera')—Layered, vertically exfoliating silver-gray bark reveals rough orange-brown underbark
Chestnut Rose (*Rosa roxburghii*)—Gray exfoliating strips of bark reveal smooth tan bark below

2

Trees and shrubs with textured and colored bark are extremely useful in planning winter landscapes. Shown here are **(1)** Dawn Redwood (*Metasequoia glyptostroboides*), **(2)** Paperbark Maple (*Acer griseum*), **(3)** River Birch (*Betula nigra*), **(4)** Yellow-Twig and Red-Twig Dogwood (*Cornus sericea* 'Flaviramea' and *C. sericea*), and **(5)** a white-stemmed Raspberry (*Rubus cockburnianus*).

1

3

4

5

Trees with textured bark patterned in more than one color

River Birch (*Betula nigra*)—Light peach, amber brown, under rough gray exfoliation
Korean Dogwood (*Cornus kousa*)—Lenticeled light gray and dark gray flaking bark reveals light greenish-tan underbark
Lacebark Pine (*Pinus bungeana*)—Curvilinear patches of dark gray, olive green (in several shades), and light gray
Sycamore (*Platanus occidentalis*)—Trunk irregularly speckled with patches of ivory, light and dark olive green, light brown, and gray; the lighter colors predominate at the top of the tree
Stewartia koreana—Speckled, flaking gray bark reveals orange-tan and green-tan underbark

Plants with "winged" bark on their twigs or branches

Burning Bush (*Euonymus alata*)
Sweet Gum (*Liquidambar styraciflua*)
Mossy-Cup Oak (*Quercus macrocarpa*)

Plants with red twigs

Redtwig Japanese Maple (*Acer palmatum* 'Sangokaku')
Red-Twig Dogwood (*Cornus sericea*)—Most effective in late winter

Plants with yellow twigs

Yellow-Twig Dogwood (*Cornus sericea* 'Flaviramea')—Most effective in late winter
Weeping Willow (Yellow Twig) (*Salix alba* var. *tristis*)—Most effective in late winter

Plants with bright green twigs

Winter Jasmine (*Jasminum nudiflorum*)
Kerria (Single Flowered) (*Kerria japonica*)
Hardy-Orange (*Poncirus trifoliata*)—Also has green thorns

Plants with white bark or twigs

Paper Birch (*Betula papyrifera*)
Cutleaf European Birch (*Betula pendula* 'Gracilis')
Weeping European Birch (*Betula pendula* 'Youngii')
Raspberry (White Stem) (*Rubus cockburnianus*)—White "bloom" over red bark

This list would be incomplete without our only hardy tall Bamboo, Yellow-Groove Bamboo (*Phyllostachys aureosulcata*). (In low-temperature years even it may kill to the ground.) Its winter form and beauty are so distinctive that the plant deserves special mention. The effect of multiple vertically noded stems delicately moving in winter breezes and reflecting light from green and yellow-green surfaces is a joy to the eye. (The fact that the foliage may wither to a gray-green is no disadvantage.) A strong contrasting dark evergreen foliage will enhance the effect. In a naturalistic situation this could be Rhododendron foliage; in a more organized setting a hedge of Blue Maid® Holly (*Ilex* x *meserveae* Blue Maid® 'Mesid') or Dwarf English Boxwood (*Buxus sempervirens* 'Suffruticosa') works well. (Note: In all instances *Phyllostachys* should be contained by a thirty-inch-deep barrier to control the invasive tendency of its roots.)

Winter fruit, flowers, and birds provide the potential, moreover, for even greater dynamics in the winter landscape. Fruits are generally at their best in early winter, flowers in mid- to late winter, and birds (where adequate cover is available and a regular food supply maintained) just about all of the time. (For additional information on months in which specific blossoms occur, see Appendix 13; for additional information on months in which specific fruits are at their best, see Appendix 14; for plants useful in attracting birds, see Appendix 17.)

The season of some of my favorite winter-flowering and winter-fruiting plants progresses like this (an asterisk denotes a bird attractor):

DECEMBER

Fruits (All Red)

Red Chokeberry (*Aronia arbutifolia* 'Brilliantissima')*
Glossy Hawthorn (*Crataegus nitida*)*
Washington Hawthorn (*Crataegus phaenopyrum*)*
Winterberry (*Ilex verticillata*)*
Winter Red Winterberry (Hybrid) (*Ilex verticillata* 'Winter Red')*
Arden American Holly (*Ilex opaca* 'Arden')*

Blossoms

Higan Cherry (Autumn Flowering) (*Prunus subhirtella* 'Autumnalis')—Pink

Generally speaking, fruits are at their best in early winter and flowers in mid to late winter. The fruits of Winterberries — see (1) *Ilex verticillata* 'Winter Red' — usually remain in good condition through Christmas; those of (2) Winter King Hawthorn (*Crataegus viridis* 'Winter King') often remain in showy condition considerably longer.

1

2

In mild winters the Hybrid Witch-hazels (*Hamamelis* x *intermedia*) and early *Crocus* may start flowering in February. In more severe years they can be counted on in March. **(1)** *Crocus tomasinianus* is shown planted under American Beech (*Fagus grandifolia*) with **(2)** *Hamamelis* x *intermedia* 'Diane,' while **(3)** *Hamamelis* x *intermedia* 'Jelena' is paired with **(4)** *Crocus ancyrensis* 'Golden Bunch.'

JANUARY

Fruits (All Red)

Washington Hawthorn (*Crataegus phaen-opyrum*)*
Winter King Hawthorn (*Crataegus viridis* 'Winter King')*
Arden American Holly (*Ilex opaca* 'Arden')*

Blossoms

Wintersweet (*Chimonanthus praecox*)—Yellow
Chinese Witch-hazel (*Hamamelis mollis* 'Pallida')—Yellow

FEBRUARY

Fruits (All Red)

Winter King Hawthorn (*Crataegus viridis* 'Winter King')*

Blossoms

Harry Lauder's Walking Stick (*Corylus avellana* 'Contorta')
Weeping European Filbert (*Corylus avellana* 'Pendula')
Turkish Filbert (*Corylus colurna*)
Crocus ancyrensis 'Golden Bunch'
Chinese Witch-hazel (*Hamamelis mollis* 'Pallida')—Yellow
Hybrid Witch-hazel (*Hamamelis* x *inter-media*—'Diane') Wine
Hybrid Witch-hazel (*Hamamelis* x *inter-media* 'Jelena')—Amber
Hybrid Witch-hazel (*Hamamelis* x *inter-media* 'Primavera')—Yellow
Japanese-Andromeda (*Pieris japonica*)—White

MARCH

Blossoms

Cornelian-Cherry (*Cornus mas*)
Japanese Cornelian-Cherry (*Cornus offi-cinalis*)—Yellow
Harry Lauder's Walking Stick (*Corylus avellana* 'Contorta')
Weeping European Filbert (*Corylus avellana* 'Pendula')
Turkish Filbert (*Corylus colurna*)
Crocus ancyrensis 'Golden Bunch'
Crocus tomasinianus—Flowers stay closed on cloudy days, emphasizing silvery outside of petals; flowers open on sunny days to a beautiful clear lavender

Winter Aconite (*Eranthis hyemalis*)—Bright
  yellow
Snowdrops (*Galanthus nivalis* for shady lo-
  cations; *Galanthus elwesii* for sun)—
  White
Hybrid Witch-hazel (*Hamamelis* x *inter-
  media* 'Diane')—Wine
Hybrid Witch-hazel (*Hamamelis* x *inter-
  media* 'Jelena')—Amber
Hybrid Witch-hazel (*Hamamelis* x *inter-
  media* 'Primavera')—Yellow
Winter Jasmine (*Jasminum nudiflorum*)—
  Yellow

Because of the distance involved from
window to planting, those plants whose interesting winter characteristics are more
finely detailed would not be effective.

Many of the plants discussed in this
section, to have any impact, must either
be used in substantial numbers—i.e., *Cornus sericea, C. sericea* 'Flaviramea,' *Crocus
tomasinianus, Eranthis hyemalis,
Galanthus elwesii, G. nivalis, Jasminum
nudiflorum, Kerria japonica*—or they should
be used close to the window as view framers
—i.e., *Acer griseum, Chimonanthus praecox, Cornus kousa, Corylus avellana*
'Contorta,' *Euonymus alata, Hamamelis
mollis* 'Pallida,' *Stewartia koreana.*

There is, for instance, very special charm
to snow accumulating on the "wings" of *Euonymus alata*; to individual florets opening
on *Chimonanthus praecox* on warm winter
days, to be followed (after the first florets
have frozen) by other individual florets the
next warm day; to all of the fingerlike blossoms on *Hamamelis mollis* 'Pallida' closing
tight as the temperature drops and staying
closed until the next warm spell, when they
all open. Add to this the changing light on
bark and buds and berries and the movement
of songbirds onstage and offstage, and a winter view of a garden can be anything but
dull.

The exuberance of the four gardens and
the winter plant palette described in this
chapter but hint at the possibilities for your
own garden. It is worthwhile to reiterate the
three design considerations already discussed
that ensure the creation of a successful
picture:
· choosing a distinctive shape and pleasing
  proportions for the lowest ground cover
· establishing a structured feeling of depth
· using color and texture to build to a single,
  strong center of interest.

3

4

Gardens that we live and dine in can most appropriately exhibit strong and distinct character based on the personality of the owner and the site. The craft approach to gardening is particularly fitting under such conditions. Examples are: *Left,* an embroiderie made from Helleri Dwarf Japanese Hollies (*Ilex crenata* 'Helleri'), surrounding Weeping English Yew (*Taxus baccata* 'Repandens'); *above,* a Yew (*Taxus*) topiary; and, *opposite page,* a peach espalier.

3 Gardens to Live In

Gardens that we actually live and dine in during the five warmest months of the year (May through September) provide an opportunity for the most intense of experiences and become a rich part of the fabric of our lives. In such gardens we are not just passing through, as in an entrance garden, or limited to merely looking out, as is the case in view gardens. Here we have a room in which we live out-of-doors, usually in close relationship to a room of the house.

The outdoor space, though normally larger than the adjoining room of the house, must be defined and have vertical and horizontal dimensions harmonious with it. As such it will have walls, which, if not real, may be formed by hedges (plants useful as hedges are listed in Appendix 32) and less organized plant groupings. These need not necessarily be room height. A bare suggestion from a low hedge, tree trunk, or planting will do. The outdoor room will have a ceiling or the suggestion thereof. This may be provided by overhanging branches, awnings, umbrellas, or arbors. Likewise, it will have a floor. This may be lawn, pebbles, or paving, such as exposed aggregate concrete, brick, or flagstone.

As a space to live in, the garden can most appropriately come to represent some aspect of the owner's personality and hence exhibit a strong and distinct character of its own. This special character may mean a garden designed around a plant (or group of plants) that has a certain significance for the owner.

It may take the form of more labor-intensive gardening, involving the use of decorative espaliers (see Appendix 34), topiaries (see Appendices 33 and 35), or embroideries (tiny clipped hedges usually made with herbaceous plants; see the lowest size ranges in Appendix 27, which lists recommended ground covers). Or it may result in a garden that reflects a particular interest in or enchantment with hummingbirds (see Appendix 17) or butterflies (Appendix 18).

In such a garden, because it is easy and convenient for the owner to inspect what is happening on a daily basis, we must demand especially rich results of the plant choreography. Emphasis should be placed on those plants that add interest during the months of heaviest use.

Because of both personality expression and close relationship to the interior decoration of the adjoining room of the house, it is in the live-in garden that the development of a color theme, whether constant or changing with the seasons, may be desirable. For the interested gardener, working with color can become an exercise that is constantly intriguing and continually challenging as its use is refined. (Appendix 24, which lists flowering plants by color and by month of bloom, and Appendix 22, which lists spring and summer foliage colors, may be useful in this pursuit.)

Strong personality involvement is the very essence of the exuberant garden. The following two gardens—the E. H. Frederick and the Hinsley gardens—will serve as examples.

E. H. Frederick Live-in Garden

When my mother selected a retirement community, the opportunity to have a garden was a strong influence on her choice. In the community she decided upon, one-story cottages faced rectangular greens and opened from the back onto another large space, where small gardens could be created adjacent to the cottages. An informal large lawn served as the background.

Her space—810 square feet, 27 by 30 feet —was partially defined by a storage room wall and the attractive, windowless brick end of an adjoining cottage. A wooden fence, stained silver-gray to match her cottage walls, was added to the west, and a Nellie R. Stevens Holly (*Ilex* 'Nellie R. Stevens') and Umbrella-Pine (*Sciadopitys verticillata*) were planted to partially close off the opening to the north and east, still allowing a piece of the large lawn at the rear to flow into the enclosure. The "room" was thus defined by boundaries, which made it a pleasant repetition in shape (square) of the living room, although larger. The ceiling was provided by the branches of a delightfully shaped Japanese Snowbell (*Styrax japonicus*).

A Weeping Higan Cherry (*Prunus subhirtella* 'Pendula') was placed in the highest corner, its pendulous branches bringing the eye down to the garden and drawing attention to the small flower bed. This bed was for treasures brought from my mother's previous garden. A yellow-berried Firethorn (*Pyracantha coccinea* 'Aurea') was espaliered on the brick wall of the adjoining cottage and was the focal point of the garden.

My mother had a penchant for white, yellow, and blue, so in addition to the four Dwarf Japanese Yews (*Taxus cuspidata* 'Nana'), four Littleleaf Japanese Hollies (*Ilex crenata* 'Microphylla'), which were used as background, and the herbaceous treasures that also followed this color scheme, we chose white Azaleas (*Rhododendron* [Mucronatum Hybrid] 'Delaware Valley White') (6 plants), blue-flowered Bowles Periwinkle (*Vinca minor* 'Bowlesii') (64 plants), and the white fragrant-flowered *Daphne caucasica* as the basic plantings. In addition, we saved a prominent location next to the terrace for her very much cherished white Tree Peony (*Paeonia suffruticosa*).

The range of seasonal interest is shown in the chart on page 56.

Such a garden, after the first year, is relatively maintenance-free. My mother very much wanted a flower bed, and the labor involved she considered a delight rather than a chore. It was here that her artist's love of color came into play.

The garden's seasonal interest was expanded by the herbaceous palette shown in the chart on page 58. Those plants marked with an asterisk in the chart were those my mother treasured too much to leave behind when she moved from her former home.

The 27-by-30-foot E. H. Frederick Live-in Garden, in a retirement community, is in size a proportional expansion of the living room adjoining it. *Opposite page, top:* The small tree, Japanese Snowbell (*Styrax japonicus*), serves as a ceiling. *Opposite page, bottom:* The informal espalier of yellow-berried Firethorn (*Pyracantha coccinea* 'Aurea') provides all-year interest from the living room and library windows. The color of the fruit reinforces the white-yellow-blue color scheme.

Numbers are keyed to garden plan
Dotted rules indicate time of flowering

	J	F	M	A	MAY	J	JUL	AUG	SEP	O	N	D
Nellie R. Stevens Holly (*Ilex* 'Nellie R. Stevens') (1 plant)—Shiny green foliage and red berries												
Umbrella-Pine (*Sciadopitys verticillata*) (1 plant)—Needle evergreen with needle pattern resembling ribs of an umbrella												
yellow-berried Firethorn (*Pyracantha coccinea* 'Aurea') (1 plant)—Pattern on the wall, plus yellow berries									—			
Weeping Higan Cherry (*Prunus subhirtella* 'Pendula') (1 plant)—Pink flowers			...									
1. Dwarf Japanese Yew (*Taxus cuspidata* 'Nana') (4 plants)—Needle evergreen												
2. Littleleaf Japanese Holly (*Ilex crenata* 'Microphylla') (4 plants)—Shrub with narrow dark evergreen leaves and dense habit												
3. white Azalea (*Rhododendron* [Mucronatum Hybrid] 'Delaware Valley White') (6 plants)					.....							
4. Bowles Periwinkle (*Vinca minor* 'Bowlesii') (64 plants)—Blue flowers					.....							
5. *Daphne caucasica* (1 plant)—Fragrant white flowers, blooming first in April and again in fall						..					....	
Tree Peony (*Paeonia suffruticosa*) (1 plant)—Crepe paper–like white flowers					....							
Japanese Snowbell (*Styrax japonicus*) (1 plant)—Pendulous, fragrant white blossoms							...					

E. H. FREDERICK LIVE-IN GARDEN

1" = 8' ±

KEY:
1. DWARF JAPANESE YEW (TAXUS CUSPIDATA 'NANA') (4)
2. LITTLELEAF JAPANESE HOLLY (ILEX CRENATA 'MICROPHYLLA') (4)
3. WHITE AZALEA (RHODODENDRON [MUCRONATUM HYBRID] 'DELAWARE VALLEY WHITE') (6)
4. BOWLES PERIWINKLE (VINCA MINOR 'BOWLESII') (64)
5. DAPHNE CAUCASICA (1)

ESPALIERED FIRETHORN (PYRACANTHA COCCINEA 'AUREA') (1) -- YELLOW-BERRIED

WEEPING HIGAN CHERRY (PRUNUS SUBHIRTELLA 'PENDULA') (1)

A. FLOWER BED
OXLIP (PRIMULA ELATIOR) (12) -- YELLOW
HERBACEOUS PEONY (PAEONIA LACTIFLORA 'FESTIVA MAXIMA') (1) -- WHITE
GERMAN IRIS (IRIS GERMANICA 'SOUTH PACIFIC') (3) -- LIGHT BLUE
BLUESTAR (AMSONIA HUBRICHTII) (3) -- LIGHT BLUE
COREOPSIS 'MOONBEAM' (6) -- LIGHT YELLOW
BORDER PHLOX (PHLOX PANICULATA 'MOUNT FUJI') (1) -- WHITE
HYPERION DAYLILY (HEMEROCALLIS 'HYPERION') (1) -- LEMON YELLOW
ASTER x FRIKARTII 'MONCH' (3) -- LAVENDER-BLUE
HARDY AGERATUM (EUPATORIUM COELESTINUM) (5)
GARLIC CHIVES (ALLIUM TUBEROSUM) (1) -- WHITE

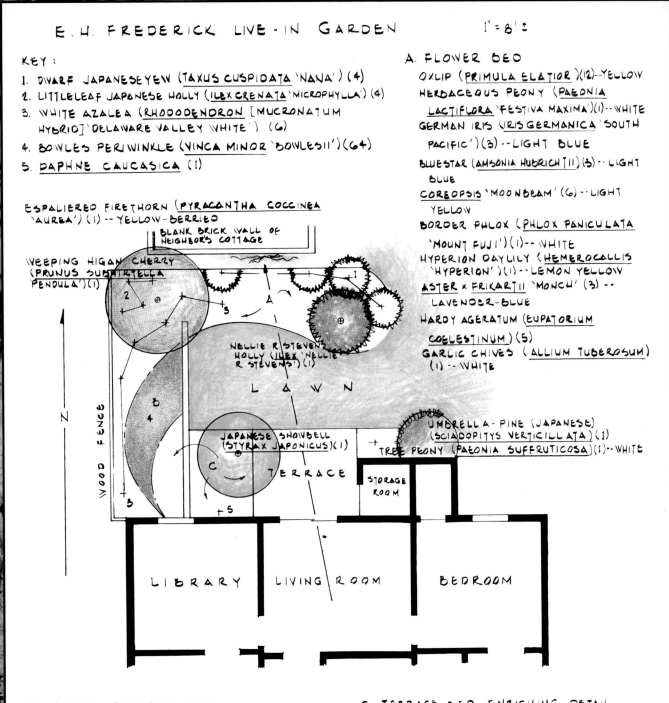

Labels within plan:
BLANK BRICK WALL OF NEIGHBOR'S COTTAGE
NELLIE R. STEVENS HOLLY (ILEX 'NELLIE R. STEVENS') (1)
L A W N
JAPANESE SNOWBELL (STYRAX JAPONICUS) (1)
WOOD FENCE
N
TERRACE
UMBRELLA-PINE (JAPANESE) (SCIADOPITYS VERTICILLATA) (1)
TREE PEONY (PAEONIA SUFFRUTICOSA) (1) -- WHITE
STORAGE ROOM
LIBRARY   LIVING ROOM   BEDROOM

B. SPRING-FLOWERING BULBS
SPRING STARFLOWER (IPHEION UNIFLORUM) (25)
TROUT LILY (ERYTHRONIUM 'PAGODA') (6) -- YELLOW
COMMON GRAPE-HYACINTH (MUSCARI BOTRYOIDES 'ALBUM') (12) -- WHITE
GLORY-OF-THE-SNOW (CHIONODOXA LUCILLAE) (25)
WINTER ACONITE (ERANTHIS HYEMALIS) (50)

C. TERRACE BED, ENRICHING DETAIL
VIOLA LABRADORICA (12) -- PURPLE BLOSSOMS, WINE-COLORED FOLIAGE
CRESTED IRIS (IRIS CRISTATA) (9) -- BLUE
SOLOMON'S SEAL (POLYGONATUM ODORATUM 'VARIEGATUM') (1)
LILY-OF-THE-VALLEY (CONVALLARIA MAJALIS) (24)
HYBRID CRANESBILL (GERANIUM 'JOHNSON'S BLUE') (3)
HARDY BEGONIA (BEGONIA GRANDIS) (3)

1

2

Both because of personality expression and close relationship to the interior decoration of the house, live-in gardens provide the perfect opportunity for development of a color theme. The artist-owner of the E. H. Frederick Live-in Garden has an obvious passion for white, yellow, and blue. Spring: **(1)** Bluestar (*Amsonia hubrichtii*) and **(2)** German Iris (*Iris germanica* 'South Pacific'). Summer: **(3)** Border Phlox (*Phlox paniculata* 'Mount Fuji'), **(4)** *Coreopsis* 'Moonbeam, **(5)** *Aster* x *frikartii* 'Monch' on left (showing its superiority to *Aster* x *frikartii* 'Wunder von Staffa'), and **(6)** lemon yellow Hyperion Daylily (*Hemerocallis* 'Hyperion'). Fall: **(7)** Garlic Chive (*Allium tuberosum*) and **(8)** Hardy Ageratum (*Eupatorium coelestinum*).

E. H. FREDERICK LIVE-IN GARDEN—EXPANDED HERBACEOUS PALETTE

Dotted rules indicate time of flowering	J	F	M	A	MAY	J	JUL	AUG	SEP	O	N	D
* Oxlip (*Primula elatior*) (12 plants)— Yellow					••••							
* Herbaceous Peony (*Paeonia lactiflora* 'Festiva Maxima') (1 plant) —White					••••							
* German Iris (*Iris germanica* 'South Pacific') (3 plants)—Light blue					••••							
Bluestar (Narrowleaf) (*Amsonia hubrichtii*) (3 plants)—Light blue					••••							
Coreopsis 'Moonbeam' (6 plants)— Fine dark green foliage, light yellow flowers						••••••••••••••••••••						
* summer Border Phlox (*Phlox paniculata* 'Mount Fuji') (1 plant)— White							•••••					
Aster x *frikartii* 'Monch' (3 plants)— Lavender-blue								••••••••				
* Hyperion Daylily (*Hemerocallis* 'Hyperion') (1 plant)—Lemon-yellow flowers							•••••					
Garlic Chives (*Allium tuberosum*) (1 plant)—White									••••••••••			
* Hardy Ageratum (*Eupatorium coelestinum*) (5 plants)—Blue									••••••••••			

3

4

5

6

7

8

1

2

3

4

5

In such an intimate garden, further enrichment could be provided (in the planting of Bowles Periwinkle [*Vinca minor* 'Bowlesii']) by the addition of diminutive early-spring-flowering bulbs selected to offer contrasts of flower form: **(1)** Winter Aconite (*Eranthis hyemalis*), **(2)** Glory-of-the-Snow (*Chionodoxa luciliae*), **(3)** yellow hybrid Trout Lily (*Erythronium* 'Pagoda'), **(4)** Spring Starflower (*Ipheion uniflorum*), and **(5)** white Common Grape-Hyacinth (*Muscari botryoides* 'Album').

With a younger, more ardent gardener, the richness of such a garden could be further expanded, in two ways. First, diminutive spring-flowering bulbs could be planted below the *Vinca* in the raised bed. Interesting contrasts in flower form could be achieved with the following selection:

Winter Aconite (*Eranthis hyemalis*) (50 plants)—Yellow blossoms like single roses, February-March

Glory-of-the-Snow (*Chionodoxa luciliae*) (25 plants)—Light blue starlike blossoms, March

Trout Lily (*Erythronium* 'Pagoda') (6 plants) —Large yellow dogtooth blossoms, April

Spring Starflower (*Ipheion uniflorum*) (25 plants)—Pale blue starlike blossoms, early May

Common Grape-Hyacinth (*Muscari botryoides* 'Album') (12 plants)—White "bottles," April

6

7

8

9

The blooms on these five plants would be in full view from the library window during March and April.

The second way to increase the drama of this garden would be to enrich the area under and adjacent to the *Styrax* with the following treasures, providing rich color and textural detail for those using the terrace:

Viola labradorica (12 plants)—Dramatic purple blossoms in April, wine-colored foliage April-October
Crested Iris (*Iris cristata*) (9 plants)—Above and below the wall; light blue flowers in May, with the Azaleas; yellow fall foliage
Solomon's Seal (White Variegated) (*Polygonatum odoratum* 'Variegatum') (1 plant) —Green-and-white-variegated foliage, white bell-like blossoms in May
Lily-of-the-Valley (*Convallaria majalis*) (24 plants)—Fragrant white blossoms, late May–early June

Hybrid Cranesbill (Blue) (*Geranium* 'Johnson's Blue') (3 plants)—True blue, late May
Hardy Begonia (*Begonia grandis*) (3 plants)— Pendulous pink blossoms, August- September

With the enrichment suggested in the two previous lists, the resulting garden provides the annual anticipation of early blossoms from spring bulbs, fragrance from the *Daphne* and *Convallaria*, and color from an extended choreography throughout the year. There are endless considerations in watching and perfecting the blue-yellow-white color scheme and deciding when and how much the espalier should be pruned to maximize design and minimize loss of fruit. This garden becomes a totally engrossing delight.

The richness of such a small garden could be further enhanced by a planting close by the terrace (at the base of the Japanese Snowbell [*Styrax japonicus*]) of plants with the charm of good detail, such as **(6)** *Viola labradorica*, **(7)** Solomon's Seal (*Polygonatum odoratum* 'Variegatum'), **(8)** Hardy Begonia (*Begonia grandis*), and **(9)** true-blue Hybrid Cranesbill (*Geranium* 'Johnson's Blue').

Hinsley Live-in Garden

Behind a row house in an attractive small town, this garden is an important part of the lives of a working couple both contemplating retirement in the near future.

The garden is 464 square feet (17.5 by 26.5 feet) and is enclosed by four-and-a-half-foot-high brick walls topped by wooden fences (to just about eye level) on both sides and a taller clapboard garage wall to the rear.

The owners pass through the garden daily on their way to and from the garage. In this respect it is a sort of entrance garden. On the other hand, the garden is intimately connected to the living-dining room of the house by a large and attractive window. In this sense it is a view garden. But because the garden is on the same elevation with the living-dining room and moving back and forth between the two spaces is easy, it is predominantly a garden to live in, a garden room.

The walls have been described. The feeling of a ceiling is achieved by the merest suggestion: an awning just outside the window, high arching branches from a large Hybrid Witch-hazel shrub (*Hamamelis* x *intermedia* 'Arnold Promise'), and overhanging horizontal-ascendant branches from a semi-espaliered Burning Bush (*Euonymus alata*). The structure of this outdoor room very closely echoes the furnishing of the first floor of the house, where one large space is subtly divided to reflect different functions (dining and living).

The circular brick-on-concrete terrace is for sunning. The owners enjoy reclining in deck chairs here on warm winter, spring, and fall days. It is a sunpocket. The nearer flagstone terrace is shaded by the row of three-story houses (of which this is one) from late-afternoon sun. Chairs and a table here provide the opportunity for tea or cocktails in the garden on warm days.

Because the garden and the house read very much as one long narrow space, the subdivision of house and garden into four areas—living room, dining room, flagstone terrace, and sunning terrace—adds a real feeling of spaciousness and changing interest. The garden itself as seen from the house is planned to have a great feeling of depth.

Delightfully textured herbaceous plants fill pockets in the blue-stone paving, providing foreground interest (for a listing of additional plants for this purpose, see Appendix 28):

Hybrid Pigsqueak (*Bergenia* 'Perfecta')—
    Cabbagelike leaves
Hybrid Thyme (*Thymus* 'Clear Gold')—
    Chartreuse needlelike foliage
Mountain Stonecrop (*Sedum ternatum*)—
    Fleshy gray-green oval foliage
Hen-and-Chicks (*Sempervivum* [Red Cultivar])—Red cactuslike rosette

The diminutive bulbs placed beneath the herbaceous plants in the blue-stone terrace are preceded by a *B* in the chart on page 67.

The fat buds on sympodially branched twigs of the Piedmont Azalea (*Rhododendron canescens*) produce fragrant pink flowers in May. It is also in the foreground, on the right.

A low hedge of clipped Dwarf Japanese Yew (*Taxus cuspidata* 'Nana') and a single San Jose Holly (*Ilex* x *aquipernyi* 'San Jose') subtly separate the two areas (just as furniture groupings define the two separate areas in the house) and provide a frame for the winter-flowering Witch-hazel (*Hamamelis* x *intermedia* 'Arnold Promise'), which is the center of interest.

The Boxwood hedge at the back trips the eye just enough to give extra depth to the background planting. This consists of a large plant of *Euonymus alata*, which has had branches removed from its back side and been planted tight against the garage wall. This is, in essence, a deep espalier. Enough branches are pruned back each year to keep the *Euonymus* from interfering with the sunning area, but it is not severely flattened as in typical espalier work. Because it has a rigid structure of its own and is self-supporting, it does not have to be fastened to the wall. It is, of course, green in the summer. In the fall its foliage is glorious shades of pink and its branches sparkle with diminutive red berries. In the winter its marvelous winged bark catches the changing light and picks up ridges of white when snows come. In early spring the fiddlelike leaves of the Cinnamon Fern (*Osmunda cinnamomea*)

The Hinsley Garden (only 17.5 by 26.5 feet) is a combination of live-in garden, entrance garden, and view garden. As an extension of the living-dining room of the house, it is also subtly divided into a sunning terrace (brick) and a late-afternoon shady terrace (blue stone). This structuring enhances the depth of the view from the house.

uncurl beneath the *Euonymus* as its own leaves unfold and small greenish blossoms appear.

The owners had lived on a good-sized country property previously and were tired of mowing grass. They were delighted when they discovered that in addition to not having grass they could have ground cover that provided a relatively low-maintenance garden *and* a long season of blossom and foliage interest. Most of the plants used in the Hinsley Garden for ground cover are not traditional ground covers but what I like to call survival perennials. (They are preceded by *SP* in the chart on pages 67–68.) (For an extensive listing of ground covers, see Appendix 27.)

The plant choreography in the Hinsley Garden is outlined in the chart on pages 65 and 67–68. As can be seen by studying this chart, yellows, whites, bronzes, and dark green predominate in the Hinsley Garden from winter through mid-March, when blues and purples start to move in. In May blue,

pale pink, and white hold forth, while June is lavender-blue and white until the yellows start. Yellows continue until frost, with orange, apricot, and lavender as summer partners, and white, blue, and rust as fall companions. The flowers themselves change with the seasons, and so does the overall color scheme.

There is a wonderful rhythm to the use of this garden: One may stay inside for warmth in the dead of winter (with continued visual connection with the garden), go out to the circular sunning terrace on warmish days in winter and spring, stay near the house for shade on warm spring, summer, and early fall afternoons, move into the air-conditioned house on really hot summer days, and return to the sunning terrace on cool, sunny fall afternoons. Weaving in and out of this rhythm is the exuberant choreography of blossoms and textures contrasted with the structure of walls, hedges, and paving.

With a winter-blooming Witch-hazel (*Hamamelis* x *intermedia* 'Arnold Promise') (*this page*) as the center of interest, the planting in the Hinsley Garden is relatively maintenance-free. There is no grass to mow, and survival perennials have been selected as ground covers. In this view (*opposite page*) taken from the window, the large leaves of Hybrid Pigsqueak (*Bergenia* 'Perfecta') in the right foreground contrast with the minute foliage of a chartreuse Hybrid Thyme (*Thymus* 'Clear Gold'). On the left a medium-size grass (*Calamagrostis acutiflora* 'Stricta') has blue-flowered Plumbago (*Ceratostigma plumbaginoides*) and yellow *Coreopsis* 'Moonbeam' at its base, tumbling onto the brick.

HINSLEY LIVE-IN GARDEN—SEASONAL INTEREST

Dotted rules indicate time of flowering	J	F	M	A	MAY	J	JUL	AUG	SEP	O	N	D
Dwarf Japanese Yew (*Taxus cuspidata* 'Nana') (6 plants)— Needle evergreen hedge												
Dwarf English Boxwood (*Buxus sempervirens* 'Suffruticosa') (13 plants)—Oval evergreen leaves												
San Jose Holly (*Ilex* x *aquipernyi* 'San Jose') (1 plant)—Small dark green leaves, red berries												
Burning Bush (*Euonymus alata*) (1 plant)—Fall: pink foliage, red berries; winter: winged bark; highly detailed chartreuse blossoms in May					······							
Hybrid Witch-hazel (*Hamamelis* x *intermedia* 'Arnold Promise') (1 plant) —Yellow blossoms uncurling on warm days, January, February, March	······											

continued on pages 67–68

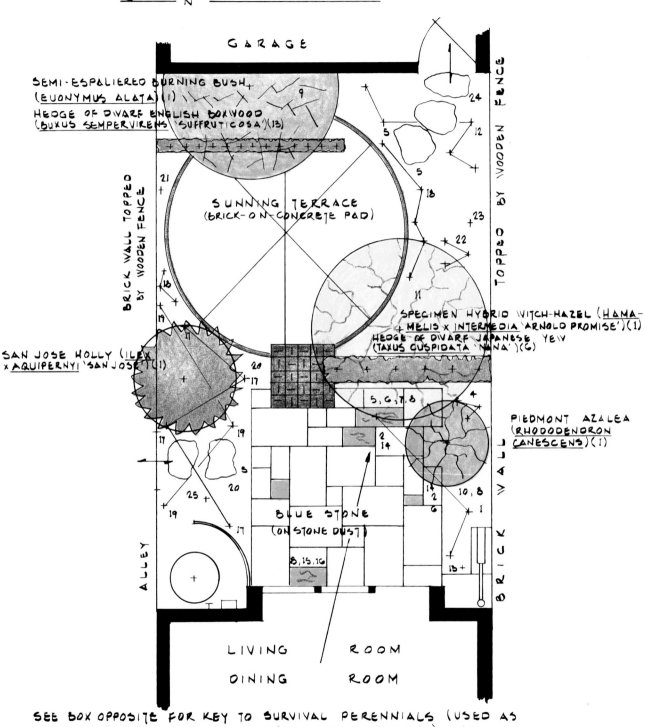

HINSLEY LIVE-IN GARDEN   1"= 4' ±

N

GARAGE

SEMI-ESPALIERED BURNING BUSH
(EUONYMUS ALATA) (1)
HEDGE OF DWARF ENGLISH BOXWOOD
(BUXUS SEMPERVIRENS 'SUFFRUTICOSA') (13)

SUNNING TERRACE
(BRICK-ON-CONCRETE PAD)

SPECIMEN HYBRID WITCH-HAZEL (HAMA-
MELIS × INTERMEDIA 'ARNOLD PROMISE') (1)
HEDGE OF DWARF JAPANESE YEW
(TAXUS CUSPIDATA 'NANA') (6)

SAN JOSE HOLLY (ILEX
× AQUIPERNYI 'SAN JOSE') (1)

PIEDMONT AZALEA
(RHODODENDRON
CANESCENS) (1)

5, 6, 7, 8

BLUE STONE
(ON STONE DUST)

LIVING   ROOM

DINING   ROOM

BRICK WALL TOPPED BY WOODEN FENCE

TOPPED BY WOODEN FENCE

ALLEY

BRICK WALL

SEE BOX OPPOSITE FOR KEY TO SURVIVAL PERENNIALS (USED AS
GROUND COVERS AND BETWEEN STEPPING-STONES) AND
SPRING BULBS

KEY TO SURVIVAL PERENNIALS AND SPRING BULBS IN HINSLEY LIVE-IN GARDEN PLAN

1. Hybrid Pigsqueak (*Bergenia* 'Perfecta') (3)

2. Winter Aconite (*Eranthis hyemalis*) (25)

3. Common Snowdrop (*Galanthus nivalis*) (25)

4. Christmas-Rose (*Helleborus niger*) (3)

5. Siberian Squill (*Scilla siberica* 'Spring Beauty') (25)

6. *Crocus* 'Purple Beauty' (12)

7. Carpet Bugleweed (*Ajuga reptans* 'Bronze Beauty') (36)

8. *Narcissus* 'Hawera' (25)

9. Cinnamon Fern (*Osmunda cinnamomea*) (11)

10. Sweet Woodruff (*Galium odoratum*) (10)

11. Lily-of-the-Valley (*Convallaria majalis*) (25)

12. Siberian Iris (*Iris sibirica* 'Flight of Butterflies') (5)

13. Meadow Rue (*Thalictrum rochebrunianum*) (1)

14. Hybrid Thyme (*Thymus* 'Clear Gold') (10)

15. Mountain Stonecrop (*Sedum ternatum*) (2)

16. Hen-and-Chicks (*Sempervivum* [Red Cultivar]) (3)

17. *Coreopsis* 'Moonbeam' (4)

18. Daylily (*Hemerocallis* 'Stella de Oro') (8)

19. Feather-Reed Grass (*Calamagrostis* x *acutiflora* 'Karl Foerster') (3)

20. Plumbago (*Ceratostigma plumbaginoides*) (8)

21. Sweet Autumn Clematis (*Clematis maximowicziana*) (1)

22. *Aster* 'Professor Anton Kippenberg' (3)

23. *Boltonia asteroides* 'Snowbank' (1)

24. Hardy Ageratum (*Eupatorium coelestinum*) (3)

25. *Sedum* 'Autumn Joy' (1)

Numbers are keyed to garden plan
Dotted rules indicate time of flowering
SP indicates a survival perennial,
B a spring bulb

	J	F	M	A	MAY	J	JUL	AUG	SEP	O	N	D
1. Hybrid Pigsqueak (*Bergenia* SP 'Perfecta') (3 plants)—Cabbagelike leaves, bronze in winter												
2. Winter Aconite (*Eranthis hyemalis*) B (25 bulbs)—Yellow blossoms like single roses		·····										
3. Common Snowdrop (*Galanthus* B *nivalis*) (25 bulbs)—White pendulous blossoms shaped like teardrops		········										
4. Christmas-Rose (*Helleborus niger*) SP (3 plants)—White blossoms, yellow centers	····											
5. Siberian Squill (*Scilla siberica* B 'Spring Beauty') (25 bulbs)—Nodding, true-blue blossoms			···									
6. *Crocus* 'Purple Beauty' (12 bulbs) B Piedmont Azalea (*Rhododendron canescens*) (1 plant)—Fragrant pink flowers, shaped like honeysuckle blossoms			···		···							
7. Carpet Bugleweed (*Ajuga reptans* SP 'Bronze Beauty') (36 plants)—Bronze-red leaves, lavender-blue flowers					····							
8. *Narcissus* 'Hawera' (25 bulbs)— B Delicate yellow blossoms clustered on wiry stems					·■··							
9. Cinnamon Fern (*Osmunda* SP *cinnamomea*) (11 plants)—Fiddleheads												
10. Sweet Woodruff (*Galium odoratum*) SP (10 plants)—Sharply pointed narrow green leaves, foamy white flowers						·····						
11. Lily-of-the-Valley (*Convallaria* SP *majalis*) (25 plants)—Fragrant white bell flowers arranged vertically on thin stalks						····						
12. Siberian Iris (*Iris sibirica* 'Flight of SP Butterflies') (5 plants)—Delicate, airy flowers, blue and white (with blue veins)						··						
13. Meadow Rue (*Thalictrum* SP *rochebrunianum*) (1 plant)—Delicate lavender blossoms on 6- to 8-foot stalks, charming hazy effect								·············				

continued on page 68

Numbers are keyed to garden plan Dotted rules indicate time of flowering SP indicates a survival perennial	J	F	M	A	MAY	J	JUL	AUG	SEP	O	N	D
14. Hybrid Thyme (*Thymus* 'Clear **SP** Gold') (10 plants)—Needle-y chartreuse foliage												
15. Mountain Stonecrop (*Sedum* **SP** *ternatum*) (2 plants)—Gray-green fleshy oval foliage												
16. Hen-and-Chicks (*Sempervivum* **SP** [Red Cultivar]) (3 plants)—Red cactuslike rosette												
17. *Coreopsis* 'Moonbeam' (4 plants)— **SP** Single light yellow daisies, frothy dark green needle foliage												
18. dwarf Daylily (*Hemerocallis* 'Stella **SP** de Oro') (8 plants)—Miniature orange Daylily												
19. Feather-Reed Grass (*Calamagrostis* **SP** x *acutiflora* 'Karl Foerster') (3 plants)—Upright ornamental grass with tan-apricot blossoms												
20. Plumbago (*Ceratostigma* **SP** *plumbaginoides*) (8 plants)—Clear cobalt blue blossoms												
21. Sweet Autumn Clematis (*Clematis* *maximowicziana*) (1 plant)— Clambering vine with frothy white blossoms												
22. *Aster* 'Professor Anton Kippenberg' **SP** (3 plants)—Dwarf, compact, lavender-blue daisylike blossoms												
23. *Boltonia asteroides* 'Snowbank' (1 plant)—Clustered small white daisies on 5-foot stalks, providing a billow of froth												
24. Hardy Ageratum (*Eupatorium* **SP** *coelestinum*) (3 plants)— Ageratumlike blue blossoms												
25. *Sedum* 'Autumn Joy' (1 plant)— **SP** Thick, fleshy foliage, flat heads of pink turning rust color												
San Jose Holly (*Ilex* x *aquipernyi* 'San Jose')—Small dark green leaves, red berries												

Capitalizing on the Personality of the Site and the Owner

In each of these gardens we have seen the interaction of the site personality with the garden's development. With the addition of a fence on one side, the E. H. Frederick Garden emphasized snug privacy. However, a tempting connection was left with an important asset of the site, the large lawn, giving this garden a very different character from that of the Hinsley Garden and its total separation from any other world.

The unique character of the Hinsley site, considering house and garden together, is the long, narrow shape. This given quality, combined with the owners' penchant for a movable feast, contributed to a subdividing of the garden and provided great variety and a considerable feeling of space to a small area.

The owners' personalities have affected the designs as well. My mother's interest in featuring treasures from a previous garden was a keystone in the development of her garden, and her willingness to become involved in the craft of training an espalier certainly added character. The fact that the Hinsleys were intrigued by the idea of a ballet of winter blossoms on the Witch-hazel (*Hamamelis* x *intermedia* 'Arnold Promise') meant that it could be featured as an abstract piece of sculpture contrasting with the crisp rectilinear hedge below it.

Many examples can be given of owner-plant relationships around which the garden's personality subsequently develops. The possibility of scented blossoms in December and January makes Wintersweet (*Chimonanthus praecox*) an example of a plant that is sufficiently interesting to provide the theme for a small garden. Sentiment is often a strong influence. The owner may have fond memories of a Weeping Willow (*Salix alba* var. *tristis*) or a gnarled old apple tree from his or her childhood. A seedling American Holly (*Ilex opaca*) that appeared in a former garden or a seedling Eastern Red Cedar (*Juniperus virginiana*) brought back from a picnic and nurtured to maturity are also possible themes.

Scientifically oriented garden owners may be intrigued by the primitive appearance of a monocotyledonous plant like Yellow-Groove Bamboo (*Phyllostachys aureosulcata*); a conifer that loses its needles in the winter, such as Bald Cypress (*Taxodium distichum*); the

1

2

3

See text on pages 68 and 70 for intriguing owner-plant relationships around which a garden's personality can develop. Examples are: **(1)** golden-twig Weeping Willow (*Salix alba* var. *tristis*), **(2)** Yellow-Groove Bamboo (*Phyllostachys aureosulcata*), and **(3)** Hardy-Orange (*Poncirus trifoliata*).

Plants with a story: *top,* Franklin Tree (*Franklinia alatamaha*), and *bottom,* Scouring Rush (*Equisetum hyemale*).

remarkable conifer that has broad deciduous foliage, *Ginkgo biloba;* and the northern version of an orange tree, Hardy-Orange (*Poncirus trifoliata*).

I am particularly fond of gardens whose personality rests on a plant with a story. *Equisetum hyemale,* for example, with its black-banded vertical green stems, is often referred to as Scouring Rush, because the stems have a high silica content, making them very handy for polishing. Seldom exceeding a height of twenty-four to thirty inches, it is a decadent member of the family Equisetaceae, which reached its climax in the late Paleozoic Era as a plant thirty feet tall with stems thirteen inches in diameter.

Cedar-of-Lebanon (*Cedrus libani* var. *stenocoma*) is a native of Asia Minor introduced into this country in colonial times. There are frequent references to it in the Bible. Solomon's temple is supposed to have been built with its massive timbers.

Dawn Redwood (*Metasequoia glyptostroboides*), shown on page 46, was known only as a Mesozoic paleobotanical record before 1945. In that year a stand of these Dawn Redwoods was found growing in a remote valley of western China. Three years later seeds were sent to America, where the tree now thrives, sometimes growing as much as five feet in one year.

Franklin Tree (*Franklinia alatamaha*) is the subject of a most intriguing tale. It was discovered by John Bartram, a colonial botanist, in 1770, growing along the Altamaha River, in Georgia. He named it after his friend Benjamin Franklin. Between 1770 and 1790 plants and seeds were collected and taken to Bartram's garden in Philadelphia. Since 1790 no plants have ever been found growing in the wild. This means that all existing descendants of this August-blooming plant, whose flowers are reminiscent of single white Camellias, have been grown directly or indirectly from seed from the trees in Bartram's Philadelphia garden. Incidentally, this plant, like Camellias and Tea, is a member of the family Theaceae.

Additional examples of capitalizing on the personality of site and owner will be seen in the chapters that follow.

Ground Covers

The phrase "ground covers," in the sense that I use it, needs to be redefined.

Japanese Spurge (*Pachysandra terminalis*), Bowles Periwinkle (*Vinca minor* 'Bowlesii'), and Baltic Ivy (*Hedera helix* 'Baltica') are indeed useful evergreen ground covers. However, in the broadest sense, ground covers can range in height from moss to any shrub that works well in mass plantings, and from those plants that are herbaceous in nature to those woody plants that are both deciduous and evergreen. I like to think of ground covers as a flow of paint on a canvas that ties together other elements in a painting. Small-scale ground covers are in order if the garden is small, just as larger-scale ground covers are needed to give bolder effects in a large garden. We are talking, of course, only about selected herbaceous plants and selected woody plants that possess certain characteristics. As will be seen from the extent of the lists in Appendix 27, the subject of ground covers has become a special interest of mine.

The herbaceous plants that I prefer to use as ground covers—and that are therefore given in Appendix 27—come from the following categories:

· Clump forming, planted closely enough that their foliage touches
· Mat forming
· Rampers
· Invaders

Woody plants that I recommend as ground covers, also found in Appendix 27, come from these categories:

· Rounded, spaced in such a way that foliage will touch and overlap slightly at maturity
· Horizontal branchers
· Carpet forming
· Sprawlers
· Shrubs that spread by underground stem or root

With herbaceous plants, I like to stick with those that are tough and that are what I call survival perennials.

As the different categories listed for selected herbaceous plants indicate, some survival perennials will spread together more quickly than others. The most aggressive spreading is done by underground stems or roots, such as Lungwort (*Pulmonaria angustifolia*); the least aggressive are clumps that can be planted closely together in a mulched bed, such as Fragrant Plantain-Lily (*Hosta plantaginea*). (See Appendix 27 for more information.)

Likewise, woody plants can be similarly divided according to ability to spread, habit of growth, et cetera. The most aggressive are those that are called invasive but that under difficult growing conditions are actually very useful, such as Yellowroot (*Xanthorhiza simplicissima*). Those that are horizontal in branching habit, on the other hand, such as Burning Bush (*Euonymus alata*), are especially useful because of their natural ability to starve lower-growing plants (i.e., weeds) of light. (See Appendix 27 for more information.)

Survival perennials were used as ground covers in the two gardens discussed in this chapter:

Carpet Bugleweed (*Ajuga reptans* 'Bronze Beauty')
Aster 'Professor Anton Kippenberg'
Hybrid Pigsqueak (*Bergenia* 'Perfecta')
Plumbago (*Ceratostigma plumbaginoides*)
Lily-of-the-Valley (*Convallaria majalis*)
Coreopsis 'Moonbeam'
Hardy Ageratum (*Eupatorium coelestinum*)
Sweet Woodruff (*Galium odoratum*)
Hybrid Cranesbill (Blue) (*Geranium* 'Johnson's Blue')
Christmas-Rose (*Helleborus niger*)
dwarf Daylily (*Hemerocallis* 'Stella de Oro')
Crested Iris (*Iris cristata*)
Cinnamon Fern (*Osmunda cinnamomea*)
Sedum 'Autumn Joy'
Mountain Stonecrop (*Sedum ternatum*)
Hybrid Thyme (*Thymus* 'Clear Gold')
Viola labradorica

Why this strong interest in a vastly expanded group of ground covers? Because of the two extremely important roles they play in contemporary American gardens.

First, ground covers are justly touted as labor-saving. This is true in the sense that bare soil and even mulched soil host weeds more readily than a dense mat of plants. It is, therefore, a worthwhile objective to plan plantings where trees, shrubs, and ground covers form a solid mass of foliage.

Second, ground covers in this expanded sense are an extremely valuable design tool. In the types of gardens that I advocate, ground covers provide a flow of paint that can be used to give sharp definition to shapes (rectilinear or curvilinear; see page 36); structure a design by use of color (see the Frederick Swimming Pool Garden at Ashland Hollow, pages 85–88) or texture; provide varying layers of height and consequent depth to a picture; and create planes on which taller plants of seasonal interest can be choreographed (see the Cardinal Stroll Garden, pages 114–117) or on which a plant of high sculptural quality can be displayed as a focal point (page 97).

We should therefore look upon the use of ground covers as one of our most valuable tools for creating controlled exuberance.

Studied Abandon

To live in a garden means a close association with all of its elements and a close observation of all that is happening.

In observing the seasonal changes involving textural contrasts and color combinations, we also become aware of our ability to control and manage nature, and this has the corollary result that we become less afraid to let nature have her way—to a certain extent. I like to call this studied abandon. With it comes a contagious feeling of being at one with nature, of lushness, of flowing with and enjoying the process.

In a garden that reflects studied abandon, we find mosses and plants with mosslike textures—such as Chamomile (*Chamaemelum nobile*), Creeping Nailwort (*Paronychia kapela* subsp. *serpyllifolia*), and Thymes in variety—occurring "at random." (See Appendix 29 for other plants with a mosslike effect.)

We also see plantings "happening" to come up between paving stones: In the shade, such gems as the white-spotted Bethlehem Lungwort (*Pulmonaria saccharata* 'Sissinghurst White') (green foliage, spotted with silver, and white flowers in April) combined with Japanese Silver Fern (*Athyrium goeringianum* 'Pictum'); in sun, the broad, bronze-leaved Carpet Bugleweed (*Ajuga reptans* 'Bronze Beauty') combined with fine-foliaged Korean Goat's Beard (*Aruncus aethusifolius*). (See Appendix 28 for other plants to use between stepping-stones.)

1

The close people-plant associations involved in live-in gardens provide the special opportunity for studied abandon, in which detail plantings (within the broader framework) appear to have their own way: **(1)** Moss and mosslike plants — **(2)** Chamomile (*Chamaemelum nobile*), **(3)** Creeping Nailwort (*Paronychia kapela* subsp. *serpyllifolia*), and **(4)** Hybrid Thyme (*Thymus* 'Clear Gold') — occur at random. Other plants happen to come up between stepping-stones, such as **(5)** green-and-white-spotted Bethlehem Lungwort (*Pulmonaria saccharata* 'Sissinghurst White') and **(6)** Japanese Silver Fern (*Athyrium goeringianum* 'Pictum') in a shady garden, and by **(7)** bronze-leaved Carpet Bugleweed (*Ajuga reptans* 'Bronze Beauty') and **(8)** Korean Goat's Beard (*Aruncus aethusifolius*) in a sunny one.

2

3

4

5

6

7

8

1

2

Some bulb–ground cover combinations: **(1)** *Narcissus* 'Trevithian' and **(2)** blue Lungwort (*Pulmonaria angustifolia*); and **(3)** Spanish Bluebells (*Endymion hispanicus* 'Excelsior') and **(4)** *Hosta* 'Kabitan.'

3

4

Opposite page: Other pairings of bulbs and ground covers are: *Crocosmia* 'Lucifer' (*inset, top*) and Hay-Scented Fern (*Dennstaedtia punctilobula*) (*background, top*); and Autumn-Crocus (*Colchicum* 'Autumn Queen') (*inset, bottom*) and blue Plumbago (*Ceratostigma plumbaginoides*) (*background, bottom*).

Another example is diminutive bulbs coming through ground covers as though from seed scattered by birds. (For suitable plants over spring-flowering bulbs, see Appendix 30.)

We have seen how *Vinca minor* 'Bowlesii' in the E. H. Frederick Garden and *Thymus* 'Clear Gold' in the Hinsley Garden, both underplanted with bulbs, were used to create studied abandon.

By way of further example, the following would be attractive combinations.

LATE APRIL

Narcissus 'Trevithian' (yellow) coming through a ground cover of blue Lungwort (*Pulmonaria angustifolia*).

MID-MAY

Spanish Bluebells (*Endymion hispanicus* 'Ex-

celsior') blooming with the chartreuse young foliage of Plantain-Lily (*Hosta* 'Kabitan'), which would subsequently cover the dying foliage of the bulbs.

JUNE

Crocosmia 'Lucifer' (scarlet flowers) in a sea of the light green Hay-Scented Fern (*Dennstaedtia punctilobula*).

SEPTEMBER

Autumn-Crocus (*Colchicum* 'Autumn Queen') (lavender-pink) overplanted with Plumbago (*Ceratostigma plumbaginoides*) (cobalt blue). The broad spring-only foliage of the *Colchicum* would add cheer to the location left drab by the late sprouting of the Plumbago foliage.

In addition, some plants of the type called lax by botanists (see "Weeping" section of Appendix 15) will result in a feeling of studied abandon as they hang over walls: Winter Jasmine (*Jasminum nudiflorum*), green-and-white-variegated Wintercreeper (*Euonymus fortunei* 'Gracilis'), and Cross Vine (*Bignonia capreolata*). Others spill out of beds onto terraces and paths: In the shade, such plants as Spotted-Dead-Nettle (*Lamium maculatum* 'White Nancy') combined with white Wild Bleeding-Heart (*Dicentra eximia* 'Purity'); in the sun, apricot-flowered Sun Rose (*Helianthemum apenninum* var. *Roseum*) with the creeping Pussy Willow (*Salix repens* var. *argentea*) and blue-flowered Sand Phlox (*Phlox bifida*). Also effective are vines (see "Climbing" section of Appendix 15) allowed to clamber almost where they will. This may occur on trellises and arbors or even through shrubs, such as *Clematis* x *jackmanii* (purple-blue flowers) in Sea Buckthorn (*Hippophae rhamnoides*) (narrow gray foliage), and trees (Sweet Autumn Clematis [*Clematis maximowicziana*] in an apple tree).

All the above examples make it appear that nature is on the move, but this apparent abandonment is really very studied, illustrating again the close relationship between exuberance and control. The fact that the effect of "abandonment" is most successful when there *is* control emphasizes the closeness of these two apparent opposites.

To sum up, the development of the E. H. Frederick and Hinsley gardens involved:

· capitalizing on the personality of the sites and the owners
· using ground covers as design tools
· employing designs that are strong enough to complement the exuberant effects of abandonment.

Studied abandon further involves "lax" plants like Cross Vine (*Bignonia capreolata*) (*top*), hanging over walls, while vines are allowed to clamber almost where they will. Sweet Autumn Clematis (*Clematis maximowicziana*) (*left*) is shown here on a stump. Other lax plants, like *Clematis* x *jackmanii* (*inset, opposite page*), might wander through Sea Buckthorn (*Hippophae rhamnoides*) (*background, opposite page*).

1

2

3

4

The effect of studied abandon can also be created by plants spilling out of beds onto terraces and paths, such as **(1)** white Wild Bleeding-Heart (*Dicentra eximia* 'Purity') and **(2)** green-and-white-variegated Spotted-Dead-Nettle (*Lamium maculatum* 'White Nancy') in the shade, and **(3)** apricot Sun Rose (*Helianthemum apenninum* var. *Roseum*) with **(4)** the creeping Pussy Willow (*Salix repens* var. *argentea*) in the sun.

77

4 Swimming Pool Gardens

A specialized sort of live-in garden peculiar to this country and the latter part of the twentieth century is the swimming pool garden. The combination of advanced technology, which has reduced the cost of swimming pools, and a generally more affluent society has made them an important feature of our landscape scene. Their popularity has had the positive effect of exposing sun worshipers and athletes to the charms of gardens and has provided an opportunity for progress in what is a truly American style of gardening.

This and the preceding chapter are meant to be read together, since they are both about the very essence of the contemporary American garden. Swimming pool gardens are simply a specialized kind of live-in garden, but the relaxed social life that is associated with them emphasizes the potential for subtly structured exuberance.

Principles already discussed involving structure, texture, and working toward a center of interest apply to swimming pool gardens as well. There are, however, some things about this type of garden that are truly unique.

First, the shape of the pool has a significant impact on the garden. The level plane of the water is always going to be by far the most eye-attracting part of such a composition. We have already observed the dominant effect of the lowest ground cover (often lawn grass) in any scheme without water, and we have likewise seen the importance of the shape of such a plane; the shape is equally important in the case of water. If the pool is geometric in form, the shape should be pleasantly proportioned and appropriate in size and shape to adjacent rooms of the house, the contours of the land, and the form of the part of the garden in which it is sited. Likewise, a curvilinear pool should meet these tests and should be a strong art form in itself. If the shape is successful aesthetically, it will have a major impact on the success of the planted garden.

Second, in a swimming pool garden the plant palette is focused on the summer months. With notable exceptions, most people do not get interested in their pool on a regular basis until late May or early June, when the weather is reasonably warm. That interest intensifies during June and July, levels off in August, and declines rapidly in September, due to shorter days and less consistently warm weather. (For plants that blossom between late May and September, consult Appendices 13 and 24; for those that fruit during this period, see Appendices 14 and 25; for those that provide colored foliage, see Appendix 22.)

Aside from the period of late May through mid-September, there is little to draw us to the pool area. The water is too cool to swim in between September and May and the pool is usually covered (more or less attractively) during that time.

Therefore, we have a highly seasonal specialty garden—an echo of those multiroom

The close-up of the Hotchkiss Swimming Pool Garden on the opposite page shows the Feather-Reed Grass (*Calamagrostis* x *acutiflora* 'Karl Foerster') carrying its apricot inflorescences and surrounded by Hyperion Daylilies (*Hemerocallis* 'Hyperion').

79

gardens on large estates in England and America earlier in this century. We have the opportunity, therefore, to concentrate on a plant palette that focuses on the summer months and to do something very special with it.

The third unique aspect of swimming pool gardens is their great need for exuberance. Although in a minority of cases pool plantings will need to be severe and stylized in some way, the vast majority of pool gardens reflect the casual, informal life-style currently associated with them. It is this atmosphere that especially suggests plantings of great exuberance based on a strong design. We will see elements of this exuberance in the two swimming pool gardens that follow, the Hotchkiss and the Frederick gardens.

Watch for the use of plants that are by their very nature exuberant, such as vines, grasses, plants with pendulous characteristics, and meadow plants.

Watch for the design tools described in Chapter 3 to be used with more emphasis:

· The brushstrokes (sweeping masses) of ground covers become stronger
· Sculptural plants are featured to provide especially rich effects
· Textural contrasts are intensified by greater use of extremes
· The effect of studied abandon is expanded by the dynamics of growth movement and wind movement

Hotchkiss Swimming Pool Garden

This garden is located in a rural town of strong historic heritage and is situated in a most unusual way. The house faces a residential street and lines up in an orderly way with the other dwellings. One reaches its entrance through a formal, oval, box-edged entrance garden.

By contrast, the back of the house obliquely overlooks an enviable view of pasture and extremely beautiful river's-edge marshland, part grasses, part shrubs, all structured with a few dark green spires of native Eastern Red Cedars (*Juniperus virginiana*). The principal rooms of the house are located in such a way as to take advantage of this view.

The swimming pool garden was placed in the north corner of the property, as far as possible from the line of view to the marsh. The overall planting scheme was designed to echo the free spirit of the marsh view and to relate the swimming pool garden to the house without distracting from this view.

The pool garden planting is structured by a native River Birch (*Betula nigra*), which is on axis with the entrance hall of the house; an orchard of dwarf fruit trees to the left (adding to the bucolic nature of the scene); and three single-stem Hetz' Wintergreen Arborvitae (*Thuja occidentalis* 'Hetz' Wintergreen') to pick up the vertical aspect of the marsh landscape. (We refrained from using native Eastern Red Cedars, since cedar-apple rust disease would almost assuredly result from the proximity of the Cedars to the dwarf orchard.) This latter triad is echoed by three plants of the most dramatic grass we can grow in our climate—Ravenna Grass (*Erianthus ravennae*). These plants are treated as pieces of sculpture in the heavy planting of herbaceous ground covers.

These four elements—the Birch, the fruit trees, the Arborvitae, and the Ravenna Grass—plus a single specimen winter-flowering Hybrid Witch-hazel (*Hamamelis* x *intermedia* 'Arnold Promise') and a background planting of Leatherleaf Mahonia (*Mahonia bealei*) (12 plants), provide a planting of all-year interest when seen from windows of the house.

The terrace sunning area and its furniture are discreetly tucked behind the River Birch. No diving board and no ladders were used.

From the principal approach to the pool, the patio, one's eye passes over the shimmering water surface to a chimney pot used as sculpture on the far side.

A brick path on the near side of the pool connects diving and sunning areas. The planting comes right up to the water's edge

The Hotchkiss Swimming Pool Garden jumps the fence from small-town backyard to rural landscape. The River Birch (*Betula nigra*) (*left of center*), native to this area, is the center of interest and is on axis from the main hallway of the house. The planting of predominantly herbaceous ground covers around is structured by three plants of Ravenna Grass (*Erianthus ravennae*) (tallest grasses pictured), suggesting the marsh grasses beyond, and is backed by three vertical evergreens, Hetz' Wintergreen Arborvitae (*Thuja occidentalis* 'Hetz' Wintergreen'). These in turn echo the native Eastern Red Cedars (*Juniperus virginiana*) in the distant landscape and help to pull in the "borrowed" scenery.

Plants have been used that have special interest during the swimming season. A feeling of exuberance is produced both by the array of butterflies, attracted by the Butterfly Bushes (*Buddleia davidii* cultivars) (*right rear*) and the *Sedum* 'Autumn Joy' (*foreground*), and the movement (wind and rapid growth) of ornamental grasses: Ravenna Grass (*Erianthus ravennae*) (*tall, center*) and Feather-Reed Grass (*Calamagrostis* x *acutiflora* 'Karl Foerster') (*lower, left of center*).

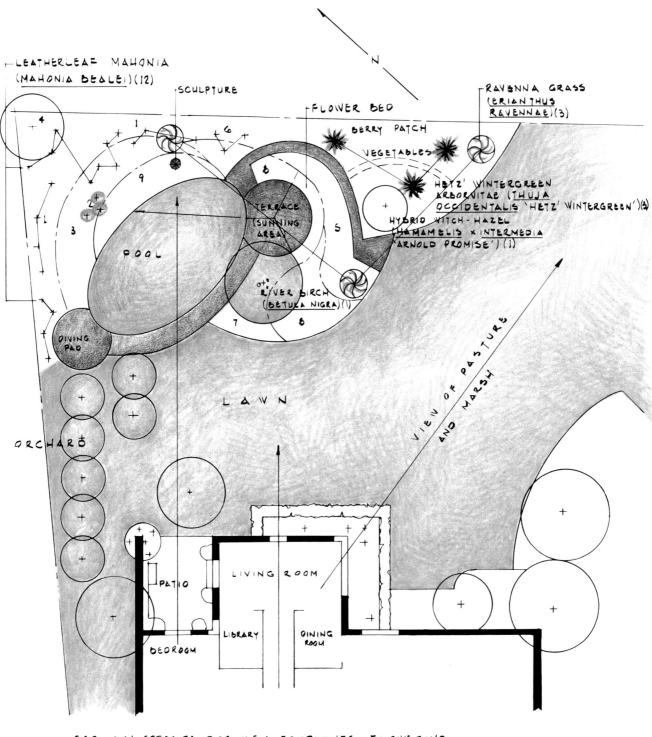

HOTCHKISS SWIMMING POOL GARDEN   1" = 16't

N

LEATHERLEAF MAHONIA
(MAHONIA BEALEI)(12)

SCULPTURE

FLOWER BED

RAVENNA GRASS
(ERIANTHUS
RAVENNAE)(3)

BERRY PATCH

VEGETABLES

HETZ' WINTERGREEN
ARBORVITAE (THUJA
OCCIDENTALIS 'HETZ' WINTERGREEN')(2)

HYBRID WITCH-HAZEL
(HAMAMELIS X INTERMEDIA
'ARNOLD PROMISE')(1)

TERRACE
(SUNNING
AREA)

POOL

S

RIVER BIRCH
(BETULA NIGRA)(1)

DINING
PAD

VIEW OF PASTURE
AND MARSH

LAWN

ORCHARD

LIVING ROOM

PATIO

LIBRARY

DINING
ROOM

BEDROOM

SEE BOX OPPOSITE FOR KEY TO PLANTS FLOWERING
DURING SWIMMING SEASON

on the far side of the pool. Once seated in the sunning area, one is in the heart of the garden and feels very much in a separate and exuberant world. From here the focal point has become the three clumps of the vertical, apricot-flowered (June) Feather-Reed Grass (*Calamagrostis* x *acutiflora* 'Karl Foerster').

Immediately to the southeast of the sunning terrace is the colorful detail of Mrs. Hotchkiss's summer flower border. A little farther beyond, hidden discreetly downhill and reached by a curvilinear path of dark-brick-colored crushed stone, is Mr. Hotchkiss's berry patch and vegetable garden.

The gentle slope from the Birch clump down to the lawn and down to the crushed-stone path is planted in large sweeps of the fragrant white Plantain-Lily (*Hosta* 'Royal Standard') (26 plants), Hardy Fountain Grass (*Pennisetum alopecuroides*) (27 plants), and the Garden Black-eyed-Susan (*Rudbeckia fulgida* var. *Sullivantii* 'Goldsturm') (44 plants), with their strongly contrasting textures.

Looking toward the *Calamagrostis* focal point, we also see a picture of strong textural contrasts. Large, dramatic foliage dominates the background. There are two patches of the blue-green (evergreen) compound foliage of *Mahonia bealei* (individual leaflets shaped somewhat like an American Holly leaf) and two patches of Oakleaf Hydrangea (*Hydrangea quercifolia*) (7 plants). Behind these and towering above them in the far corner is

the foliage of Cutleaf Staghorn Sumac (*Rhus typhina* 'Laciniata') (1 plant). This yellow-green foliage is enormous (eighteen inches) and composed of four-and-a-half-inch leaflets, but because the individual leaflets are finely cut it has the textural quality of a large fern.

Immediately in front of these shrubs is a large sweep of the ever-reliable lemon-yellow Hyperion Daylily (*Hemerocallis* 'Hyperion') (20 plants), with its narrow grasslike foliage. Overlapping with it and immediately adjacent to the pool edge is another large sweep, of *Sedum* 'Autumn Joy' (28 plants) and its very fleshy broad leaves.

What we have described so far in terms of textural contrast, although a stimulant to the eye, is relatively static. There are, by contrast, a number of dynamics to a garden such as this. First, a special effort has been made to attract butterflies (see Appendix 18 for a listing of plants that attract butterflies). Looking across the pool from the swimming pool terrace one sees a grouping of three Butterfly Bushes (*Buddleia davidii*) immediately to the right. The high, arching branches, with their spikelike flower heads nodding in the breeze, are well positioned to allow viewers on the terrace to observe the constantly changing drama of arriving and departing butterflies. These insects are also supported and attracted by *Rudbeckia* and *Sedum*.

The plant choreography for June, July, August, and September—if studied carefully—shows changing color and rapidly changing heights in most of the herbaceous plants (see the chart on page 84). In addition, the glorious effect of the grasses moving in the breezes as they mature is a constant source of pleasure. (For additional recommended grasses, see the "Fine Detail" section of Appendix 19.)

KEY FOR HOTCHKISS SWIMMING POOL GARDEN PLAN

1. Oakleaf Hydrangea (*Hydrangea quercifolia*) (7)

2. Feather-Reed Grass (*Calamagrostis* x *acutiflora* 'Karl Foerster') (3)

3. Hyperion Daylily (*Hemerocallis* 'Hyperion') (20)

4. Cutleaf Staghorn Sumac (*Rhus typhina* 'Laciniata') (1)

5. Garden Black-eyed-Susan (*Rudbeckia fulgida* var. *Sullivantii* 'Goldsturm') (44)

6. Butterfly Bush (*Buddleia davidii*) (3)

7. Plantain-Lily (*Hosta* 'Royal Standard') (26)

8. Hardy Fountain Grass (*Pennisetum alopecuroides*) (27)

9. *Sedum* 'Autumn Joy' (28)

HOTCHKISS SWIMMING POOL GARDEN—INTEREST DURING SWIMMING SEASON

Numbers are keyed to garden plan
Dotted rules indicate time of flowering

J F M A MAY J JUL AUG SEP O N D

1. Oakleaf Hydrangea (*Hydrangea quercifolia*) (7 plants)—Pure white snowflakelike blossoms in cone-shaped heads turn chartreuse in July, then tan-brown. Leaves turn shades of burgundy and peach in fall.

Ravenna Grass (*Erianthus ravennae*) (3 plants)—A grass providing a mound of pendulous foliage from June until mid-August, when 12- to 15-foot spikes suddenly shoot up to be crowned with fluffy cream-white heads in September-October.

2. Feather-Reed Grass (*Calamagrostis* x *acutiflora* 'Karl Foerster') (3 plants)— A grass of vertical habit, gracefully weeping leaves, narrow apricot-tan flower spikes in June, turning tan in July-August.

3. Hyperion Daylily (*Hemerocallis* 'Hyperion') (20 plants)—Lemon-yellow blossoms on 4-foot stems.

4. Cutleaf Staghorn Sumac (*Rhus typhina* 'Laciniata') (1 plant)— Yellow-green fernlike foliage on a rugged frame. Conelike rusty red fruits in August become walnut-colored. Foliage is rosy apricot in fall.

5. Garden Black-eyed-Susan (*Rudbeckia fulgida* var. *Sullivantii* 'Goldsturm') (44 plants)—Orange-yellow "Black-eyed Susan" Daisies, followed by black-brown ball-shaped seed heads.

6. Butterfly Bush (*Buddleia davidii*) (3 plants)—Spikes of color on arching stems attract butterflies. 'Black Knight'—very dark purple; 'Purple Prince'—purple; 'Fortune'— lavender, orange eye; 'Opera'— sparkling mauve.

7. Plantain-Lily (*Hosta* 'Royal Standard') (26 plants)—Spikes of white fragrant blossoms held well above the bright green foliage.

8. Hardy Fountain Grass (*Pennisetum alopecuroides*) (27 plants)—A grass with narrow brushlike blossoms, which nod on wiry stems. Strong lavender-pink cast when fresh.

9. *Sedum* 'Autumn Joy' (28 plants)— Flat heads of pink blossoms attractive to butterflies gradually turn a handsome rust color. Effective until crushed by heavy snow.

Frederick Swimming Pool Garden at Ashland Hollow

In this garden the pool is located some distance from the house but is intimately associated with a two-story Delaware springhouse (first story, fieldstone; second story, board and batten) built in the 1850s. The location is at the head of a stream valley with rather steep hillsides.

The owners wished to have the choice of sun or shade when using the pool, shade being especially desirable at mealtime. This, plus a nostalgic attachment to the idea of a grape arbor remembered from childhood, led to the construction of such an arbor immediately adjacent to the springhouse.

The steep hillside to the northwest of the pool has an attractive amphitheaterlike form and is well established in attractive Broom-

sedge (*Andropogon virginicus*). It was inevitable that this should dominate the scene from both the sunny and shady sitting areas and that the focal point would be the diving board virtually at the base of this slope.

The hillside to the north and northeast is wooded and tends to tie in with the volume of the springhouse. It was decided to use a large specimen Weeping European Beech (*Fagus sylvatica* 'Pendula') on the opposite side of the pool to balance the volume of the springhouse and help frame the view to the diving board–Broomsedge hillside. Another objective was to allow the Beech's pendulous nature to direct the eye back to the water surface.

The Frederick Swimming Pool Garden nestles at the base of an amphitheaterlike hillside. A Weeping European Beech (*Fagus sylvatica* 'Pendula') has been used to balance the volume of the springhouse and its associated patch of woods. The wine color of Crimson Pygmy Barberry (*Berberis thunbergii* 'Crimson Pygmy') serves as structure to tie the two together.

The Beech, the arbor, and the projecting branches from the hillside forest suggest the roof of this garden room. Walls are provided by the springhouse, the arbor, and a low retaining wall next to the game lawn but also, most especially, by the steep enfolding bank running from southwest to northeast, planted solidly with Crimson Pygmy Barberry (*Berberis thunbergii* 'Crimson Pygmy'). This ground cover planting of deep wine color ties the Beech solidly to the volume of the springhouse–forest and brings repose to a very complex scene. It provides a stable panoramic foreground to the meadow view and becomes the perfect background for more detailed planting immediately next to the pool.

When we have discussed structuring plantings before we have mainly dwelt on the use of plant forms or textural combinations. As in this case, color can provide an equally strong structural element.

The country atmosphere of the land forms, springhouse, and grape arbor suggested an exuberant meadowlike plant palette with strong textural contrasts. Grasslike textures were used near the water and in increasing tempo nearest the diving board, the center of interest. Larger-scale grasslike textures were used in a restrained way to structure background plantings, which are predominantly broadleaf.

Next to the water's edge, growing out of pockets let into the stone paving, are two grasses of contrasting form: Hardy Fountain Grass (*Pennisetum alopecuroides*), which forms a low mound, with angled inflorescences fanning out in all directions; and Feather-Reed Grass (*Calamagrostis* x *acutiflora* 'Karl Foerster'), which is taller and very vertical in habit. Their silhouettes are dramatized by the wine-red background of the Crimson Pygmy Barberry.

In plantings slightly farther away from the water, grasslike plantings of the two-and-a-half-foot-high golden-variegated Bamboo (*Arundinaria viridistriata*) and lower white-flowered Lilyturf (*Liriope muscari* 'Monroe White') are used.

Broadleaf background plantings include the yellow-flowered *Magnolia* 'Elizabeth' and the following large shrubs: Bottlebrush Buckeye (*Aesculus parviflora*), *Hydrangea paniculata* 'Tardiva,' and Chaste Tree (*Vitex agnus-castus* 'Latifolia'). These plantings are structured by a single, well-confined clump of Yellow-Groove Bamboo (*Phyllostachys aureosulcata*), a single clump of the Giant Reed (*Arundo donax*), and, grouped together, multiple clumps of the Giant Miscanthus (*Miscanthus* 'Giganteus').

This very rich planting is kept focused on the diving board area by a sequence of color choreography, which starts in that area in June with the woolly spires of the yellow-blossoming Olympic Mullein (*Verbascum olympicum*) and is followed shortly by the long-flowering, thoroughly satisfactory *Heliopsis helianthoides* subsp. *scabra* 'Karat,' with its single golden yellow daisies. The *Heliopsis* continue through July, soon overlapping with the orange-yellow daisies of Garden Black-eyed-Susan (*Rudbeckia fulgida* var. *Sullivantii* 'Goldsturm'). All of these are also dramatized by the wine-red background of the Crimson Pygmy Barberry.

During this same time period the two sweeps of lemon-yellow Hyperion Daylily (*Hemerocallis* 'Hyperion') on the hillside above have been framing a strong and appealing relationship between the diving board and its background meadow of Broomsedge.

White blossoms in pyramids decorate the *Aesculus parviflora* at the base of the forested slope in June. White blossoms suggesting snowflakes set as jewels appear in dramatic panicles on the *Hydrangea paniculata* 'Tardiva' in late summer. The magic of grapes in fruit concludes the season. The predominant planting is *Vitis* 'Concord,' which is dark blue with a lovely gray-blue bloom on the skin. The grapes present a most relaxed and bacchanalian scene. They are followed by lovely turquoise-blue fruit on the Porcelain Ampelopsis (*Ampelopsis brevipedunculata*).

Right: A nostalgic attachment to the idea of a grape arbor remembered from childhood made this the choice for providing shade adjacent to the pool. The bacchanalian quality of the fruit on a late August day adds to the exuberance of the scene. *Above:* The diving board, as the center of interest, has been surrounded by the richest part of the plant palette. Pictured here are giant Olympic Mulleins (*Verbascum olympicum*), which put on a great show in June.

Clearly there is strong organization to all of this, but it is well concealed by the overall exuberance and by special attention to achieving an atmosphere of studied abandon. In addition to clumps of herbaceous plants popping through the paving and vines clambering about the arbor in abundance, there are two other details that contribute to this atmosphere.

Grapes were omitted from the arbor planting just to the south of the springhouse door (above the pocket of golden-variegated Bamboo) to allow a patch of light to come through. A Madame Galen Trumpet Vine (*Campsis* x *tagliabuana* 'Madame Galen') was planted here. The result is that during July and part of August, branches hang down, presenting lovely large orange-apricot trumpets below the shade of the grapes and just above the pocket of Bamboo, with its chartreuse foliage longitudinally striped in various shades of yellow and green. Hummingbirds are often attracted to these tubular blossoms, thus enhancing the scene.

To the east of the diving board, near the pump house and at the base of the Barberry bank, another pocket was designated for an annual August seeding of the Giant Hogweed (*Heracleum mantegazzianum*). During the following June this monarch of the biennial world holds forth as a giant piece of sculpture between six and eight feet tall, with broad leaves and an inflorescence resembling a giant Queen-Anne's-lace.

The chart on pages 91–92 summarizes the choreography of this garden look.

These examples of studied abandon are part of the conscious effort made to create a feeling of exuberance. *Left:* The grape theme was interrupted in the arbor planting to enable a Madame Galen Trumpet Vine (*Campsis* x *tagliabuana* 'Madame Galen') room to drape apricot-orange blossoms above a clump of golden-variegated Bamboo (*Arundinaria viridistriata*). *Opposite page, top:* Stones have been left out of the paving around the pool to allow two forms of ornamental grass — Hardy Fountain Grass (*Pennisetum alopecuroides*) (low) and Feather-Reed Grass (*Calamagrostis* x *acutiflora* 'Karl Foerster') (taller) — to be placed casually at water's edge. *Opposite page, bottom:* The biennial Giant Hogweed (*Heracleum mantegazzianum*), with its enormous foliage and Queen-Anne's-lace-like flower, is seeded annually into a pocket to the right of the diving board.

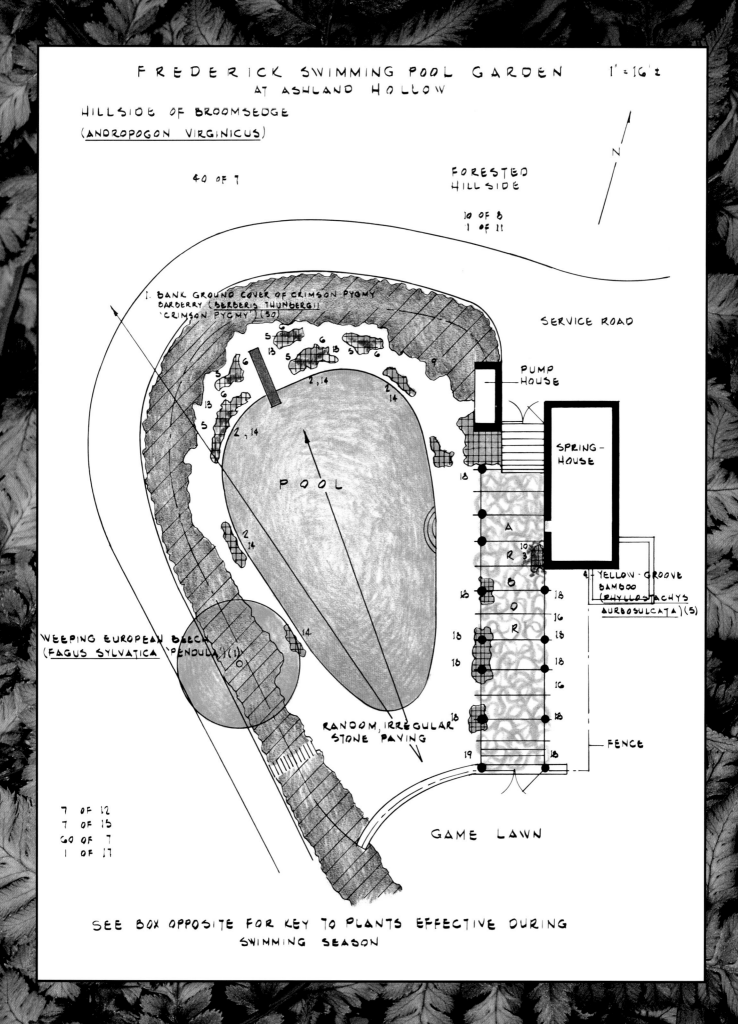

FREDERICK SWIMMING POOL GARDEN
AT ASHLAND HOLLOW   1" = 16' ±

HILLSIDE OF BROOMSEDGE
(ANDROPOGON VIRGINICUS)

40 OF 9

FORESTED
HILLSIDE

10 OF 8
1 OF 11

N

1. BANK GROUND COVER OF CRIMSON PYGMY
BARBERRY (BERBERIS THUNBERGII
'CRIMSON PYGMY') (50)

SERVICE ROAD

PUMP
HOUSE

SPRING-
HOUSE

POOL

A
R
B
O
R

4. YELLOW-GROOVE
BAMBOO
(PHYLLOSTACHYS
AUREOSULCATA) (5)

WEEPING EUROPEAN BEECH
(FAGUS SYLVATICA 'PENDULA') (1)

RANDOM, IRREGULAR
STONE PAVING

FENCE

7 OF 12
7 OF 15
60 OF 7
1 OF 17

GAME LAWN

SEE BOX OPPOSITE FOR KEY TO PLANTS EFFECTIVE DURING
SWIMMING SEASON

KEY FOR FREDERICK SWIMMING POOL GARDEN PLAN

1. Crimson Pygmy Barberry (*Berberis thunbergii* 'Crimson Pygmy') (50)

2. Feather-Reed Grass (*Calamagrostis* x *acutiflora* 'Karl Foerster') (10)

3. Bamboo (Yellow Variegated) (*Arundinaria viridistriata*) (5)

4. Yellow-Groove Bamboo (*Phyllostachys aureosulcata*) (5)

5. *Heliopsis helianthoides* subsp. *scabra* 'Karat' (6)

6. Olympic Mullein (*Verbascum olympicum*) (6)

7. Hyperion Daylily (*Hemerocallis* 'Hyperion') (100)

8. Bottlebrush Buckeye (*Aesculus parviflora*) (10)

9. Giant Hogweed (*Heracleum mantegazzianum*) (1)

10. Madame Galen Trumpet Vine (*Campsis* x *tagliabuana* 'Madame Galen') (1)

11. Giant Reed (*Arundo donax*) (1)

12. Giant Miscanthus (*Miscanthus* 'Giganteus') (7)

13. Garden Black-eyed-Susan (*Rudbeckia fulgida* var. *Sullivantii* 'Goldsturm') (25)

14. Hardy Fountain Grass (*Pennisetum alopecuroides*) (8)

15. *Hydrangea paniculata* 'Tardiva' (7)

16. White-flowered Lilyturf (*Liriope muscari* 'Monroe White') (25)

17. Chaste Tree (*Vitex agnus-castus* 'Latifolia') (1)

18. Grape (*Vitis* 'Concord') (10)

19. Porcelain Ampelopsis (*Ampelopsis brevipedunculata*) (2)

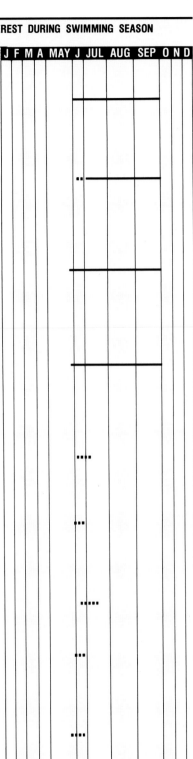

Numbers are keyed to garden plan
Dotted rules indicate time of flowering

1. Crimson Pygmy Barberry (*Berberis thunbergii* 'Crimson Pygmy') (50 plants, 4 feet on center)—Compact ground cover shrub with rich burgundy-colored foliage.

2. Feather-Reed Grass (*Calamagrostis* x *acutiflora* 'Karl Foerster') (10 plants)—A grass of vertical habit, gracefully weeping leaves, narrow apricot-tan flower spikes in June, turning tan in July-August.

3. Bamboo (Yellow Variegated) (*Arundinaria viridistriata*) (5 plants) —2.5-foot-high Bamboo. Long narrow leaves are longitudinally divided into stripes varying in shades of green and yellow.

4. Yellow-Groove Bamboo (*Phyllostachys aureosulcata*) (5 plants)—12 to 20 feet high. Stems dark green to yellow-green, with clearly marked nodes. Very graceful, fine-textured foliage.

5. *Heliopsis helianthoides* subsp. *scabra* 'Karat' (6 plants)—Single golden yellow daisies continue for a long flowering season.

6. Olympic Mullein (*Verbascum olympicum*) (6 plants)—Spikes to 8 feet with soft yellow flowers. Rosettes of gray-green foliage at base.

7. Hyperion Daylily (*Hemerocallis* 'Hyperion') (100 plants)—Lemon-yellow blossoms on 4-foot stems.

8. Bottlebrush Buckeye (*Aesculus parviflora*) (10 plants)—Shrubs to 12 feet, broad-spreading. Handsome dark green foliage. Pyramidal flower clusters of shimmering white.

9. Giant Hogweed (*Heracleum mantegazzianum*) (1 plant)—Highly sculptural plant growing to 8 feet; resembles a giant Queen-Anne's-lace except for its large broad leaves.

10. Madame Galen Trumpet Vine (*Campsis* x *tagliabuana* 'Madame Galen') (1 plant)—Vine with attractive coarse leaves and trumpetlike blossoms in a beautiful shade of apricot-orange.

continued on page 92

Numbers are keyed to garden plan
Dotted rules indicate time of flowering

	J	F	M	A	MAY	J	JUL	AUG	SEP	O	N	D

11. Giant Reed (*Arundo donax*) (1 plant) —Tallest grass we can grow in this area (15 to 20 feet). Resembles corn except for the greater grace to the pendulous gray-green leaves and large attractive silvery seed head.

12. Giant Miscanthus (*Miscanthus* 'Giganteus') (7 plants)—Large grass growing to between 10 and 12 feet, seed heads purple-brown.

13. Garden Black-eyed-Susan (*Rudbeckia fulgida* var. *Sullivantii* 'Goldsturm') (25 plants)—Orange-yellow "Black-eyed Susan" Daisies, followed by black-brown ball-shaped seed heads.

14. Hardy Fountain Grass (*Pennisetum alopecuroides*) (8 plants)—A grass with narrow brushlike blossoms that nod on wiry stems. Strong lavender-pink cast when fresh.

15. *Hydrangea paniculata* 'Tardiva' (7 plants)—Large shrub with cones of handsome white flowers much more gracefully displayed than the common *Hydrangea paniculata* 'Grandiflora.'

16. white-flowered Lilyturf (*Liriope muscari* 'Monroe White') (25 plants) —Evergreen ground cover. Strap-shaped leaves. Spikes of fresh, almost waxy white flowers.

17. Chaste Tree (*Vitex agnus-castus* 'Latifolia') (1 plant)—Large shrub, narrow pointed gray-green leaves. Spikes of lavender-blue flowers. Treated as a cut-back shrub here.

18. Grape (*Vitis* 'Concord') (10 plants)— Commonly used, old-fashioned blue grape. Eaten out of hand and used in jams and pies.

19. Porcelain Ampelopsis (*Ampelopsis brevipedunculata*) (2 plants)— Aggressive vine with clusters of berries that go through various color stages: white, green, turquoise blue, robin's egg blue.

Plant Selection to Emphasize Exuberance

Certain types of plants seem to possess the essence of a relaxed and ebullient atmosphere. The following are examples.

Vines (see "Climbing" section of Appendix 15) such as:
Ampelopsis brevipedunculata
Bignonia capreolata
Campsis x *tagliabuana* 'Madame Galen'
Clematis maximowicziana
Vitis 'Concord'
Wisteria floribunda

Grasses and grasslike plants (see "Fine Detail" section of Appendix 19) such as:
Arundinaria viridistriata
Calamagrostis x *acutiflora* 'Karl Foerster'
Erianthis ravennae
Liriope muscari 'Monroe White'
Miscanthus 'Giganteus'
Pennisetum alopecuroides
Phyllostachys aureosulcata

Plants with pendulous characteristics (see "Weeping" section of Appendix 15) such as:
Arundo donax
Fagus sylvatica 'Pendula'
Salix alba var. *tristis*

Meadow plants such as:
Heliopsis helianthoides subsp. *scabra* 'Karat'
Heracleum mantegazzianum
Rudbeckia fulgida var. *Sullivantii* 'Goldsturm'
Verbascum olympicum

The relaxed social life associated with swimming pools emphasizes the potential for subtly structured exuberance. Certain types of plants seem to carry the essence of a relaxed and ebullient atmosphere, such as the meadow plants Mullein (*Verbascum thapsus*) (*opposite page, top*) and Garden Black-eyed-Susan (*Rudbeckia fulgida* var. *Sullivantii* 'Goldsturm') (*opposite page, bottom*).

Other good choices for swimming pool gardens are vines (*Rosa* 'Dr. W. VanFleet') (*left*); plants with pendulous characteristics (yellow-twig Weeping Willow [*Salix alba* var. *tristis*]) (*above*); and grasses and grasslike plants (Hardy Fountain Grass [*Pennisetum alopecuroides*]) (*right*).

Ground Covers

As did the live-in gardens in Chapter 3, the two swimming pool gardens rely on heavier-than-usual use of plants as ground covers (for extensive listing of ground covers, see Appendix 27); that is, used in mass. *Berberis thunbergii* 'Crimson Pygmy,' *Aesculus parviflora, Hydrangea paniculata* 'Tardiva' (all in the Frederick Swimming Pool Garden), and *Hydrangea quercifolia* (in the Hotchkiss Swimming Pool Garden) are good examples of woody plants used in this way.

Recall the extensive herbaceous plantings of *Hemerocallis* 'Hyperion,' *Sedum* 'Autumn Joy,' *Hosta* 'Royal Standard,' *Pennisetum alopecuroides,* and *Rudbeckia fulgida* var. *Sullivantii* 'Goldsturm' radiating out from the hub of the Hotchkiss sunning terrace and the similar use of *Hemerocallis* 'Hyperion' in the Frederick Garden.

When seen in plan view (that is, when looking down on a garden plan), such strong brushstrokes (large massings of one kind of plant) are recognized for their purpose in structuring a design with texture and/or color, a system carried to perfection by the Brazilian landscape architect Roberto Burle Marx. Such massing naturally occurs in meadow sites in late summer and fall, when interlocking masses of wildflowers create exuberantly colored and textured compositions. Often a few "rogues"—other kinds of flowers—will be scattered through each such mass of wildflowers. In garden design we borrow this technique of massing but leave out the rogues, thus producing a dramatic effect by "purification."

We also find ground covers used to feature one or more sculptural plants in the swimming pool gardens (see the "Irregular, Sculptural" section of Appendix 15). The three *Erianthus ravennae* rising regally above masses of *Rudbeckia fulgida* var. *Sullivantii* 'Goldsturm,' *Pennisetum alopecuroides,* and *Sedum* 'Autumn Joy' in the Hotchkiss Garden, and the single *Heracleum mantegazzianum* taking on a dramatic stance against a mass planting of *Berberis thunbergii* 'Crimson Pygmy' in the Frederick Garden, are good examples.

As pointed out above, masses of wildflowers are seldom pure; one or more rogues from outside frequently invade a neighboring patch. The use of ground covers to feature one or more sculptural plants is a refined echo of this effect that helps with that exaggeration which is exuberance.

The element of studied abandon can take many forms. Here we see sculptural plants that, when featured in a sea of a single ground cover, provide delightful drama. This technique is a purification of the meadow syndrome in which a taller rogue invades a pure patch of meadow flowers. Examples of plants with good sculptural qualities are the biennial Scotch Thistle (*Onopordum acanthium*) (*opposite page, top*); the hybrid biennial Mullein (*Verbascum* 'Harkness Hybrid') (*opposite page, bottom*); and the woody Adam's Needle (*Yucca flaccida* 'Golden Sword') (*above*).

Stronger-than-usual textural contrasts, in which the broadest textures are more often contrasted with the finest textures, add the enrichment of excitement. *Top,* Staghorn Sumac (*Rhus typhina*) (*left*) with *Spiraea thunbergii* (*right*); *bottom,* Tamarisk (*Tamarix ramosissima* 'Summer Glow') (*left*) with Siebold Plantain-Lily (*Hosta sieboldiana* 'Elegans') (*right*); *opposite page, top,* Devil's-Walking Stick (*Aralia spinosa*) (*inset*) with Japanese Butterbur (*Petasites japonicus*); and *opposite page, bottom,* Plume-Poppy (*Macleaya cordata*) (*inset*) with Blue Lyme Grass (*Elymus racemosus* 'Glaucus').

Textural Contrasts

You will also notice stronger-than-usual textural contrasts in the swimming pool gardens. The broadest textures are more often contrasted with the finest textures in this kind of garden, adding enrichment and excitement. Examples of each follow:

BROADEST TEXTURES

Aesculus parviflora
Aralia spinosa
Catalpa bignonioides
Datura inoxia subsp. *quinquecuspida* (annual)
Hedera colchica 'Dentata'
Hosta plantaginea
Hosta sieboldiana 'Elegans'
Macleaya cordata
Magnolia macrophylla
Paulownia tomentosa
Peltiphyllum peltatum
Petasites japonicus

Rheum palmatum 'Rubrum'
Rheum rhabarbarum
Rhus typhina
Ricinus communis (annual)

FINEST TEXTURES

Albizia julibrissin 'Rosea'
Bamboos in variety
Cytisus scoparius
Equisetum hyemale
Grasses in variety
Helianthus salicifolius
Hemerocallis in variety
Iris sibirica
Kochia scoparia forma *trichophylla* 'Childsii' (annual)
Liriope in variety
Metasequoia glyptostroboides
Moss and ground covers providing mosslike texture (see Appendix 29)
Paeonia officinalis
Spiraea thunbergii
Tamarix ramosissima

1

2

The mesmerizing dynamics of movement enhance the exuberance of a garden. Butterflies are particularly entrancing as they come and go to the blossoms of **(1)** *Buddleia davidii* 'Black Knight,' the branches of which themselves nod in the breeze; **(2)** birds such as Ruby-Throated Hummingbirds love trumpet-shaped flowers; and **(3)** ornamental grasses move both vertically, with swift seasonal growth, and horizontally, with the wind.

The Dynamics of Movement

The plants that are selected for a garden and the way they are used contribute to the dynamics of movement, a special kind of dynamics that should be mentioned.

Birds come (because we have supplied conditions they enjoy) and go. A mockingbird frequently disputes the ownership of my garden with me. Of special charm are the hummingbirds, which love trumpet-shaped flowers and come regularly to *Campsis* x *tagliabuana* 'Madame Galen' and most of the *Salvias*. (They come just as readily to blue flowers as to red ones, despite the myth that they are attracted only by red.) (For bird-attracting plants, see Appendix 17.)

Ornamental grasses (see the "Fine Detail" section of Appendix 19) move both vertically and horizontally.

In a single season grasses start from ground level and reach mature height. With the tallest, *Arundo donax*, this height can be between fifteen and twenty feet. With this sort of vertical movement during June, July, August, and September the garden scene changes daily. (Note: For this reason ornamental grasses are especially satisfying for immediate effect in a newly planted garden; design objectives are achieved in one season if soil and moisture conditions are right.)

With grasses reaching well out of the ground, especially in July, August, and September, there is sufficient foliage to catch the passing breezes. The way this foliage responds can easily set the daily mood of the garden: emphasizing calm on a windless day, rustling benevolently in gentle breezes, and dramatizing the occasional howling storm. All of the *Panicums* and *Miscanthus* react well. I particularly like the shimmering effect of *Miscanthus* 'Giganteus' (the tallest *Miscanthus*) foliage on a sunny day in a strong breeze.

Most delightful of all are the butterflies (for plants attractive to butterflies, see Appendix 18), which appear for a long period from midsummer to early fall. There are a number of plants that will attract them, but I like Butterfly Bush (*Buddleia davidii*) best of all. Not only do the insects like the plant's nectar, but the structure of the *Buddleia* displays them beautifully when they visit. If *Buddleias* are cut to the ground regularly in mid-April, they will send up light, gracefully arching branches, which move lightly in the breeze and respond ever so slightly to the weight of the butterflies. The attracting blossoms occur at the end of six- to eight-foot-long branches, putting their visitors slightly above eye level and in most instances silhouetting them against the summer sky. The resulting array of butterfly colors against the purple, blue, lavender, and mauve of the blossoms is a delightful ballet to behold.

The Exuberant Garden

I firmly believe that gardens have a vital role to play in our contemporary lives. They are probably even more important than such other art forms as painting, sculpture, dance, theater, and music, simply because they are the art form that most keeps us in touch with the natural world. I sense particularly the need for gardens of strong exuberance, gardens that represent a celebration of the merging of art and nature. The garden as art form is in essence a controlled exaggeration of that which touches us most deeply in nature.

The four gardens described in this chapter and the preceding one illustrate basic design principles, such as the importance of a strong ground plan (geometric versus curvilinear) and the need for structure in plant combinations, as well as depth structuring of views (foreground, middle ground, and background) and the importance of working toward a center of interest.

They also make the point that if our gardens are to be emotionally responsive to the needs of twentieth-century American

life there are certain other tools that we must learn to use; exuberance doesn't simply happen.

Some of the tools are:

· Capitalizing on the personality of the site
· Developing the plan around the interests and personality of the owner
· Selecting plants with especially exuberant characteristics
· Stretching the possibility of textural contrasts to the extreme
· Expanding our concept of ground covers and their uses
· Taking advantage of the opportunities that controlled designs give for studied abandon

The possibility of each of us achieving such a personally meaningful garden is strong. The plants we select, the combinations we use, the overall plan we develop, are limited only by our own imagination.

5 Gardens to Stroll In

A multiplicity of experiences in a garden, as opposed to a single one, in itself provides enrichment and exuberance. We can be delighted by the cumulative effect of arriving via an entrance garden, enjoying the house-garden relationship as part of a view garden, and finally settling into the comfort of a live-in garden.

If we take the concept of multiple experiences further in a garden where space permits, we can have several different experiences occurring in the same garden: functional (athletic, horticultural, et cetera) and aesthetic. What's more, the connecting links become pleasant experiences in themselves. I like to think of such a garden as a "stroll garden," a term borrowed from Japan, where it means exactly what it says. The visitor there strolls about a certain type of garden, enjoying a series of experiences, primarily aesthetic. The route taken is usually a circuit, with the same view or activity never repeated.

Although very stylized in Japan, this same experience is perfectly well known to many American families. I remember clearly that after a heavy Sunday dinner at my grandparents' it was quite customary in salubrious weather to "take a walk around the yard." We would always walk in a circuit, and great interest would be taken in the flowers, fruits, and fragrances of the season; recollections would be savored about events associated with the planting of certain plants and the donors of others. And, under the influence of

the garden mood, the stage was set for conversations with guests one hadn't had a chance to speak to at dinner, stimulating discussions, and encouraging exchanges of confidences and feelings of affection.

Such gardens have always brought pleasure to my life, and many of my clients have responded to them with similar enthusiasm. "A stroll in the garden before dinner" has frequently been cited as a very significant use of the garden, an important element in switching gears from the high-pressure everyday world to the relaxation that is "home."

The parts of a contemporary American stroll garden assort themselves into two broad categories: assets of the site, and special interests of the owners.

Site assets include a bog, a stream, a pond, a great view; a particularly interesting piece of architecture, such as an old barn or springhouse; or a magnificent specimen tree or grove of trees to be specially featured.

Special interests of the owners include athletic activities, such as swimming, tennis, badminton, croquet, lawn bowling, and archery; horticultural activities, such as maintaining a kitchen garden, fruit garden, herb garden, garden work area (comprising seedling beds, propagation frames, nursery, compost bins, trash storage, et cetera), perennial border, hybrid Tea Rose garden, dwarf conifer collection, *Clematis* garden, *Camellia* garden, Alpine garden (with troughs and rock garden) or arboretum; the display of sculp-

An American stroll garden involves passing through a series of experiences, each different. Some of these experiences may be based on assets of the site. The existing Bamboo grove in the Lennihan Garden (*opposite page*), when shaped and edged with Blue Maid ® Holly (*Ilex x meserveae* Blue Maid ® 'Mesid'), becomes a special backdrop for a terrace overlooking a meadow garden.

ture or topiary (see Appendices 33 and 35 for plants suitable for the latter purpose); or animals in the garden, such as attracting wild birds or animals, housing ornamental birds like doves and peacocks, and keeping breeding ponds for fish, ornamental or otherwise.

The owners' interest in aesthetics may be limited to simply providing a mood or atmosphere, e.g., a country mood. The latter would involve creating or preserving the following: hedgerows; orchards, with naturalized bulbs (see Appendix 36); meadows (see Appendix 37 for ornamental plants adaptable for this purpose); groves—using natives such as Persimmon (*Diospyros virginiana*), Kentucky Coffeetree (*Gymnocladus dioica*), and American Holly (*Ilex opaca*), and aliens such as *Ginkgo biloba* and Dawn Redwood (*Metasequoia glyptostroboides*); copses, formed by massings of a single kind of shrub; i.e., Witch-hazels (*Hamamelis* x *intermedia* cultivars, *H. mollis* and its cultivars), Winter Hazel (*Corylopsis* species), hybrid Lilacs (*Syringa vulgaris* hybrids), and Double-File Viburnum (*Viburnum plicatum* forma *tomentosum*); and woodlands, with associated native wildflowers or wildflower effects produced with a combination of aliens and natives.

On the other hand, the owners' aesthetic interest may involve seeing the garden as an art form. This may take a geometric approach (classical bisymmetry or contemporary occult balance, using geometric forms*) or a curvilinear approach (English landscape school, Japanese gardens, and highly studied and controlled curvilinear forms, as in gardens by Fletcher Steele, Thomas Church, and Roberto Burle Marx†).

Whatever the form, the stroll garden provides especially broad scope for any owner's interest in playing the color game. Each sec-

tion of the garden can have a different color scheme.

Most important of all, the stroll garden is a natural setup for any owner who enjoys horticultural happenings seasonally choreographed to provide multiple acts in the year-long drama (i.e., spring walk, wildflower meadow, fall *Cyclamen* walk, winter garden).

Just as every garden site and the personal interests of every owner will be different, so the occurrence of these elements and their mix in any one garden will be infinitely varied.

Although some of the examples that follow are fairly high in maintenance requirements, not all elements of a stroll garden need necessarily fall into this category. A single grapevine trellised and shading a portion of a paved courtyard, a grove of small trees atop a rise in the lawn, a single apple tree next to an old stone farmhouse, an existing meadow preserved and mown only once a year, can hardly be called demanding. Each, however, invests a part of a garden with a distinct and charming mood.

Capitalizing on the Assets of the Site

Two good examples of taking advantage of site assets are shown in pictures on pages 102 and 105.

First is the meadowlike site of the Lennihan Garden, which ensured ideal growing conditions for the Bamboo that is hardiest in our area, Yellow-Groove Bamboo (*Phyllostachys aureosulcata*). A sizable clump from an early planting had become well established by the time a garden design was started. We decided to cut an entrance path into the garden from the street (via a driveway) through the center of the grove. This path gives visitors a close look at the striking details of the Bamboo stalks—dark green accented by nodes, darker green above the nodes, and a whitish blush below produce an experience of exotic mystery.

On the far side of this grove the path comes out on a circular stone terrace, which provides a starting point for a circulation path through the garden, as well as a sitting area from which to look. The terrace has been snuggled against the Bamboo so that visitors can enjoy its sense of protection and shelter, but it is separated from it by a neat dark green hedge of Blue Maid® Holly (*Ilex* x *meserveae* Blue Maid® 'Mesid'). The hedge is kept informally clipped at a height of be-

* See William H. Frederick, Jr., "The Gardens of Northern Europe," *Garden Design* 7 (Winter 1988/1989): 40–43, 86 (published by the American Society of Landscape Architects, Washington, D.C.).

† For more information about Fletcher Steele, see Robin Karson, *Fletcher Steele, Landscape Architect: An Account of the Gardenmaker's Life 1885–1971* (New York: Abrams, 1989). For more about Thomas Church, see Thomas D. Church et al., *Gardens Are for People*, 2nd ed. (New York: McGraw-Hill, 1983). For more about Roberto Burle Marx, see P. M. Bardi, *The Tropical Gardens of Burle Marx* (New York: Reinhold, 1964), and Flavio L. Motta, *Roberto Burle Marx, e a nova visão da paisagem* (São Paulo, Brazil: Nobel, 1984).

tween two and a half and three feet. The broad dark green leaves of the Holly contrast handsomely with the narrow lighter green leaves of the Bamboo. The horizontal line created by the Blue Maid® Holly hedge contrasts with the verticality of the Bamboo, and the two together form a very strong architectural relationship with the stone terrace. By capitalizing on this existing asset of the site, we were able to provide both an event within a stroll garden and an intriguing connection between events. (Note: A thirty-inch barrier of stainless steel was placed around the Bamboo to prevent it from spreading once the new configuration was decided upon.)

The second example is the great Oak in the Rockefeller Garden, which sits on a rocky knoll a short stroll above the house. From the base one can enjoy a delightful view of rolling countryside with leafy protection from the summer sun overhead. Minimal, careful regrading to create a level spot at its base and placement of a few paving stones provided a surface for iron furniture. Note that nothing was "planted"—

there are times when it is just as important not to plant as to plant. Restraint was the order of the day in capitalizing on a natural asset of the site. Other aspects of this garden might be more developed, thus providing variety and change of mood to the stroll.

Capitalizing on the Owner's Interests

Specialized Horticultural Activities

A sampling of the variety of horticultural activities that may occur in a stroll garden are shown in pictures on pages 106 and 107.

The kitchen garden designed for the Van Horn Ely family filled a long, narrow space that was left over between the house and the greenhouse. It was an area the owners saw daily because they passed through it going from house to garage. Since it was handy to the kitchen and had a cheery, sunny exposure, it seemed an ideal spot in which to grow salad fixings and other small vegetables. To give it textural excitement, we included the perennial vegetables rhubarb (large broad leaves) and asparagus (fine

In the Rockefeller Garden, the large Oak, on a hillside above the house, provides a destination to which one strolls and where one can relax on a hot day.

needle-y foliage). To provide all-year structure, apples were espaliered on frames (screening the greenhouse), grapes were trained on a tall vertical trellis, and dwarf peaches (underplanted with that highly pungent tender mint, *Mentha requienii*) were used to carry out the pattern of the garden. A ceramic bas-relief of the Babylonian symbol for the word "seed" was created as a focal point.

Lovers of Alpine plants are a special breed who know that these plants are both demanding in their soil and drainage requirements and needful of special attention to be displayed to best advantage. The plant palette of the Flook Garden, on the opposite page, consists of both very small dwarf conifers and high-elevation Alpine rock plants. These plants can be divided by soil and culture requirements into three categories. Those in each category have been grouped together

in separate troughs, or boxes, raised to bring the treasures closer to eye level. As can be seen, the elevation of the beds varies to dramatize the different qualities of the three groups.

The blossoms and fragrance of Old Shrub Roses provide an intoxication that cannot be resisted; once hooked on them, one is "gone." In the mid-Atlantic states their moment is very fleeting—no more than two weeks at the end of May and the beginning of June. Therefore, they are another horticultural specialty. Along the Old Shrub Rose Path at Ashland Hollow, Purpleleaf Sand Cherry (*Prunus* x *cistena*) and bronze-leaf Carpet Bugleweed (*Ajuga reptans* 'Bronze Beauty') provide a perfect foil for the wondrous shades of pink, mauve, and lavender roses (see Appendix 31 for a selection of recommended Old Shrub Roses).

A specialty garden within a stroll garden may derive from the owner's interest in a particular group of plants; i.e., salad fixings (the Van Horn Ely Garden) (*opposite page, top*), Alpines (Flook Garden) (*opposite page, bottom*), and Old Shrub Roses (Ashland Hollow) (*above*).

An entire area of a garden may be designed around a single piece of sculpture. *Above*, a contemplative section of the Bancroft Garden, which takes its cue from Vera Eberstadt Kuffner's marble sculpture.

Topiary is a form of sculpture particularly appropriate to gardens. This may take traditional forms, such as the spiral Pyramidal Japanese Yew (*Taxus cuspidata*) (Capitata Selection) (*right*).

Sculpture Display

Garden owners' interest in fine sculpture as a garden ornament is part of an ancient garden tradition and is exemplified by a section of the Bancroft Garden, on the opposite page. This contemplative garden of plants, pebbles, and water was designed specifically to display a very beautiful marble sculpture by Vera Eberstadt Kuffner. The artist's training with Jean Arp (1887–1966), the French sculptor known for his pioneering work in abstract forms, is apparent and suggested the Mondrian-influenced rectilinear ground plan for the garden. The garden is a secret spot enclosed by hedges. The photograph is taken from a viewing bench. The patterns of Shore Juniper (*Juniperus conferta*), white pebbles, and olive green water connect the sculpture to the viewer and the site. The weeping Red Jade Crabapple (*Malus* 'Red Jade') always causes the eye to return to the sculpture.

A form of sculpture particularly appropriate to gardens is topiary (for plants that make appropriate topiary subjects, see Appendices 33 and 35). The owner may be entertained by traditional forms, such as the spiral Pyramidal Japanese Yew (*Taxus cuspidata*) (Capitata Selection) illustrated on the opposite page. Or he or she may be intrigued by training a flowering and/or fruiting plant into a form in which it does not naturally occur, such as making a small "orange tree" out of a Hardy-Orange (*Poncirus trifoliata*).

My own interest in long-flowered Japanese Wisteria (*Wisteria floribunda*) trained as trees has provided subject matter for a most interesting section of my own garden. Over the years I have trained single vines as trees twelve feet or more in height. The system used is to train the vine vertically, on a pipe well set in concrete, allowing it to establish side branches only in whorls at intervals of no less than thirty-six inches. The advantage of this method is that the blossoms hang free and unencumbered and are well displayed in the interstices between branches. Pruning and tying up need be done only once a year. The benefits, in my opinion, are definitely worth the effort.

Such horticultural activities are examples of the diversity that may occur in a stroll garden, depending on the interests of the owners.

Topiary may also involve training a flowering and/or fruiting plant into a form in which it does not naturally occur, such as the Japanese Wisteria vine (*Wisteria floribunda*) pictured above. The branches of the Wisteria are purposely spaced no closer together than thirty-six inches in order to provide uninterrupted display of individual flower clusters.

Changing moods are the key to successful variety in a stroll garden. A country mood is established with this "designed" orchard.

Varieties of Aesthetic Moods

Even more important, stroll gardens provide the opportunity to create a variety of aesthetic experiences. Moods can be consciously controlled and varied. Stroll gardens may take the unstudied form of country atmosphere or highly studied artistic forms that are either geometric or curvilinear in nature. It is possible for such highly studied forms to be so severe that barrenness and sterility result. The following discussion and examples will make it clear that this need not be the case. On the contrary, strong form is essential to the successful and exuberant use of color, texture, and imaginatively planned seasonal choreography.

COUNTRY ATMOSPHERE

The country mood is relatively easy to visualize—it is part of our farm heritage. The picture on this page shows an orchard that has been created from whole cloth. It was planted primarily for the effect of its spring blossoms. As such, artistic liberties were taken. Alternating trees are Japanese Flowering Crabapple (*Malus floribunda*), grown

entirely for their blossoms rather than edible fruit. Because this ornamental crab flowers very heavily and has blossoms of a slightly deeper pink than those of most apple trees that produce eating apples, it beefs up the country orchard effect. A further bit of artistry includes the addition of such late-flowering *Narcissus* cultivars as 'Hera' (small cup, white), 'Trevithian' (very fragrant, yellow), 'Loch Fyne' (large cup, bicolor), and 'Pomona' (small cup, bicolor) (for other bulbs useful for naturalizing, see Appendix 36). These blossom with the trees. Because they are properly naturalized (the bulbs are hand strewn and planted where they fall), the effect is as though they were seeded by birds, and they look quite at home. The mood of country is enhanced, and the memory of two weeks in the spring lasts all year.

GEOMETRIC AND CURVILINEAR FORMS

Many different and exciting experiences can be created by the use of more highly studied design forms. These can generally be divided into geometric and curvilinear.

Studio Garden at Ashland Hollow

The flower garden surrounding the studio at Ashland Hollow illustrates the use of a geometric design. It is a square space surrounded by a low wall and is paved in a basket-weave brick pattern according to an asymmetrical rectilinear layout. All lines are straight and orderly, but the feeling is very relaxed. It is the perfect structure for a rich and exuberant planting that can spill out over the paths, strengthening the design impact by partially concealing the wonderful pattern. There are more than 100 permanent residents of these beds (woody plants and herbaceous perennials); more than 700 Tulips (in twelve cultivars) are planted every fall; and 685 bedding plants in fifty varieties go in every May.

The choreography of rich color combinations changes constantly during the growing season. A good example is Tulip time, when the ground is covered with solid sweeps of light and dark blue Pansies (*Viola* x *wittrockiana* subsp. *tricolor*) and dwarf Forget-me-nots (*Myosotis sylvatica* 'Indigo Com-

Some portions of a stroll garden may involve very controlled art form design. Examples of both rectilinear and curvilinear art form layouts will be seen on the following pages. The rectilinear pattern of the Studio Garden at Ashland Hollow provides strong bones for an exuberance of all-season plantings.

111

1

2

3

4

The May palette of the studio garden, in addition to Tulips and **(1)** Forget-me-nots (*Myosotis sylvatica* 'Indigo Compacta'), includes **(2)** Spring Vetchling (*Lathyrus vernus*), **(3)** Flowering Quince (*Chaenomeles* x *superba* 'Rowallane') (*background*), **(4)** the fresh chartreuse Plantain-Lily (*Hosta* 'Kabitan'), and **(5)** Guinea-Hen Flower (*Fritillaria meleagris*).

pacta'), the miniature Solomon's Seal (*Polygonatum falcatum*) and just-emerging chartreuse leaves of Plantain-Lily (*Hosta* 'Kabitan'), with occasional clumps of Guinea-Hen Flower (*Fritillaria meleagris*) and the blue-lavender (with mauve overtones) of Spring Vetchling (*Lathyrus vernus*). From this carpet emerge solid-color "circles" and "rectangles" of orange, apricot, peach, yellow, maroon, and lavender Tulips.

The air is pervaded by the spicy fragrance of the nearby Clove Currant (*Ribes odoratum*), and the sun backlights the carmine flowers of Flowering Quince (*Chaenomeles* x *superba* 'Rowallane') growing over a wall.

This is obviously a high-maintenance garden in some ways, but the necessity for maintaining grass paths and sharp edges is nonexistent. The more important need is to keep this immense diversity from looking like a zoo. The presence of the strong geometric structure is an important element in accomplishing this and in setting a mood that strikes a happy balance between control and exuberance.

5

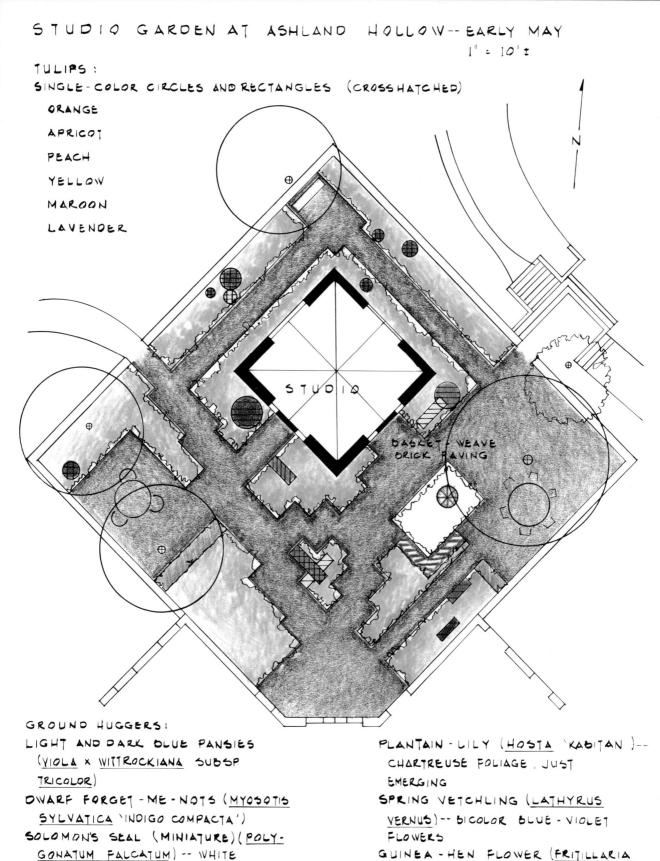

STUDIO GARDEN AT ASHLAND HOLLOW -- EARLY MAY
1" = 10' ±

TULIPS:
SINGLE-COLOR CIRCLES AND RECTANGLES (CROSSHATCHED)
ORANGE
APRICOT
PEACH
YELLOW
MAROON
LAVENDER

STUDIO

BASKET-WEAVE
BRICK PAVING

GROUND HUGGERS:
LIGHT AND DARK BLUE PANSIES
  (VIOLA x WITTROCKIANA SUBSP
  TRICOLOR)
DWARF FORGET-ME-NOTS (MYOSOTIS
  SYLVATICA 'INDIGO COMPACTA')
SOLOMON'S SEAL (MINIATURE) (POLY-
  GONATUM FALCATUM) -- WHITE
  FLOWERS, 6" TALL

PLANTAIN-LILY (HOSTA 'KABITAN') --
  CHARTREUSE FOLIAGE, JUST
  EMERGING
SPRING VETCHLING (LATHYRUS
  VERNUS) -- BICOLOR BLUE-VIOLET
  FLOWERS
GUINEA-HEN FLOWER (FRITILLARIA
  MELEAGRIS) -- PURPLE AND MAROON

Cardinal Stroll Garden

A contrasting aesthetic experience is involved in the strong curvilinear form of the Cardinal Stroll Garden. This garden is on a wooded site sloping from northeast to southwest. Two holes have been made in the woodland canopy for the two principal parts of the garden.

The northeastern section was cleared to provide light enough for what was initially thought of as a view garden and is now more of an invitation to stroll. The strength and character of this design depend on a strongly shaped curvilinear patch of lawn. In the southwestern section three interrelated ponds of dynamic form provide the central feature and cohesive element.

From the point of view of plant combinations, this garden is important in demonstrating the value of ground covers as important design tools. They are used extensively both to reinforce the basic structure of each area and to change moods as one strolls through the garden.

In the northeastern section of the garden the point of greatest winter interest—Winterberry (*Ilex verticillata*) (6 plants) and San Jose Holly (*Ilex* x *aquipernyi* 'San Jose') (4 plants)—is featured and reinforced by the evergreen ground cover Japanese Spurge (*Pachysandra terminalis*) (*H* on the garden plan). A ground cover of lemon-yellow Hyperion Daylilies (*Hemerocallis* 'Hyperion') (38 plants) (*G*) in late June–early July is found both near the house, where it surrounds a planting of yellow deciduous Exbury Hybrid Azaleas (*Rhododendron* [Exbury Hybrid] 'Golden Peace') (8 plants) (*G*), and at a distance (9 plants), where it serves as a base for a specimen golden-margined ornamental grass, Cordgrass (*Spartina pectinata* 'Aureomarginata') (*K*).

Sedum ellacombianum is used in three areas where the soil is poorest and driest: once as a ground cover (225 plants) around golden-variegated red-twig Tartarian Dogwood shrubs (*Cornus alba* 'Spaethii') (4 plants) (*I*); second, as a base (192 plants) for twelve clumps of the slightly taller and darker green lavender-blue-flowered Big Blue

Lilyturf (*Liriope muscari* [Big Blue Selection] (*L*); and finally as a tie-together (100 plants) for six clumps of the mint-green Lady's-Mantle (*Alchemilla vulgaris*) and ten clumps of the July-flowering Garden Black-eyed-Susan (*Rudbeckia fulgida* var. *Sullivantii* 'Goldsturm') (*M*). The darkest corner, the northeast, is lightened by the white (and, in the wrong location, dangerously invasive) Variegated Goutweed (*Aegopodium podagraria* 'Variegatum') (100 plants). This is enlivened with three clumps of Big Blue Lilyturf. Together they serve as an underplanting for four Mapleleaf Viburnums (*Viburnum acerifolium*) (*V*). A visually strong mass planting of the broadleaved, fragrant, white-flowered Plantain-Lily (*Hosta* 'Royal Standard') (125 plants) (*A*) occupies the entire west side of this northeast section, hopping a path in the process.

The *Hemerocallis, Sedum, Aegopodium,* and *Hosta* provide structural bones to the design and definition for the extremely important lawn shape. The other inclusions described provide enrichment and changing moods as one strolls through the area.

The layout of the ponds in the water garden was largely dictated by the location of an existing stream. Because the view from the house and approach to the ponds was at right angles to the stream valley, it was visually desirable to establish a strong cross axis (southeast to northwest) (see dock and arrow pointing northwest on garden plan). This axis was stretched between an existing clump of Beech trees near the house and a new grouping of rocks backed by existing Swamp Maples (*Acer rubrum*), which were underplanted with Royal Azaleas (*Rhododendron schlippenbachii*) (10 plants). On the far side of the great pond the rocks serve as the focal point.

The curvilinear forms
of the Cardinal Stroll
Garden are reinforced
by heavy use of ground
covers. The ground
cover used varies,
depending on soil and
light conditions; enrich-
ment is achieved by the
occasional insertion of
taller ground covers in
patches of ground hug-
gers. *Above:* Plantain-
Lily (*Hosta* 'Royal Standard') defines the lawn
shape.

Right: The yellow-green
of *Sedum ellacombi-
anum* provides a fine foil
for the golden-variegated
foliage of Tartarian Dog-
wood (*Cornus alba*
'Spaethii') in heavy clay
and full sun.

The Beech grove was underplanted with
the gray-green foliage of Yellow-Archangel
(Lamiastrum galeobdolon 'Variegatum') (290
plants) (N); both banks of the great pond
with Bowles Periwinkle (Vinca minor 'Bowlesii') (239 plants) (O); and the Swamp
Maple–Royal Azalea cluster with Bigroot
Cranesbill (Geranium macrorrhizum) (300
plants) (J). This picture was further enriched
in the following ways: The transition from
Lamiastrum to Vinca was enlivened with
scattered clumps of lavender-blue Big Blue
Lilyturf (Liriope muscari [Big Blue Selection])
(27 plants) (N), with its contrasting strap-
shaped leaves. At the northwestern side of
the great pond, Marsh Marigolds (Caltha palustris) (45 plants) (C) were planted at water's
edge. Lightly on the house side of the great
pond and heavily on the northwestern side,
blue Siberian Iris (Iris sibirica 'Dreaming
Spires') (60 plants) (O) were planted in the
Vinca; they were omitted in those spots on
the northwest side where their foliage would
interrupt the view of the rock cluster. In this
area Autumn-Crocus (Colchicum 'Autumn
Queen') (9 plants) (P) was tucked in for fall
bloom. The rock cluster was further visually
strengthened by the addition of three Yellow
Water Iris (Iris pseudacorus) (O), whose foliage is considerably taller than that of the
Siberians.

As one proceeds past the great pond to the
westernmost pond, ground covers reinforce
the design relationship between the stream
crossing and the circular terrace. The foliage
shape of European Wild-Ginger (Asarum europaeum) (75 plants) is echoed in larger size
by Japanese Butterbur (Petasites japonicus)
(3 plants) (Q) on the northern side of the
path and Ligularia stenocephala 'The Rocket'
(3 plants) (X) on the southern side. The
Ligularia is surrounded by the native New
York Fern (Thelypteris noveboracensis) (60
plants) (X).

Immediately around the circular water's-
edge landing is a planting of the chartreuse-
leaved Plantain-Lily (Hosta 'Kabitan') (25
plants), which reinforces this circular shape
and from which spring the sculptured form
and orange blossoms of Turk's-Cap Lily (Lilium superbum) (6 plants) (R). Just across the
stream Bee Balm (Monarda didyma) (6
plants) (D) has been spotted and is naturalizing itself.

A planting of Rosebay Rhododendron
(Rhododendron maximum) (8 plants) (W)
helps to emphasize the conclusive nature of

the terrace as a point at which to pause and
then continue along the far shore. Between
the Rhododendron and the terrace occurs a
ground cover planting of strong textural contrast. The blue-gray foliage of Siebold
Plantain-Lily (Hosta sieboldiana 'Elegans')
(35 plants) is enlivened by a foreground planting of golden-variegated Lilyturf (Liriope
muscari 'Variegata') (108 plants) and clumps
of Maidenhair Fern (Adiantum pedatum) (35
plants) (W).

The return path along the northwestern
side of the ponds is yet another mood. It
passes through the Siberian Iris–Bowles Periwinkle (O) and Bigroot Cranesbill (Geranium
macrorrhizum) (J) plantings. There is a
strong fabric of Lily-of-the-Valley (Convallaria majalis) (175 plants) and Hardy
Begonia (Begonia grandis) (36 plants) (S), a
colony of red Cardinal Flower (Lobelia cardinalis) (24 plants) (F) in an especially damp
spot, and another of the lovely pale-blue-
flowered Blue Star (Amsonia tabernaemontana) (20 plants) (E). There are also extensive
plantings of Wild Ginger (Asarum canadense) (115 plants), in one instance as a base
for the richly pink-flowered Purple Loosestrife (Lythrum salicaria 'Dropmore Purple')
(3 plants) (T), and in another as a companion
for the charming white-variegated Solomon's
Seal (Polygonatum odoratum 'Variegatum')
(11 plants) (U).

In the Cardinal Stroll Garden, a curvilinear form is the theme appropriate to the
site and the one to which these owners are
responsive. The planting technique for carrying out such a design has involved extensive
use of ground covers. Sometimes ground covers have been used alone, in masses; sometimes they have been combined for richness
with secondary ground cover–type plants or
larger woody plants; and occasionally they
have been used together with both secondary
ground covers and woody shrubs and trees.
(For an extensive listing of ground covers,
see Appendix 27.)

This garden is in itself a true "stroll garden," as I use the phrase. The experience
starts from the house, where the view
tempts the visitor outside, and continues
with a choice of lawn and paved path, which
immediately gets the visitor on the move
into a series of plant and water experiences
that change at every turning.

KEY TO CARDINAL STROLL GARDEN PLAN

Ground Covers Solo

A. fragrant white Plantain-Lily (*Hosta* 'Royal Standard') (98 plants)

B. Bowles Periwinkle (*Vinca minor* 'Bowlesii') (715 plants)

C. Marsh Marigold (*Caltha palustris*) (45 plants)

D. Bee Balm (*Monarda didyma*) (6 plants)

E. Blue Star (*Amsonia tabernaemontana*) (20 plants)

F. Cardinal Flower (*Lobelia cardinalis*) (24 plants)

Ground Covers with Woody Shrubs and Trees

G. yellow Hyperion Daylily (*Hemerocallis* 'Hyperion') (38 plants) plus yellow deciduous Exbury Hybrid Azaleas (*Rhododendron* [Exbury Hybrid] 'Golden Peace') (8 plants)

H. Japanese Spurge (*Pachysandra terminalis*) (530 plants) plus Winterberry (*Ilex verticillata*) (6 plants) and San Jose Holly (*Ilex* x *aquipernyi* 'San Jose') (4 plants)

I. *Sedum ellacombianum* (225 plants) plus golden-variegated red-twig Tartarian Dogwood (*Cornus alba* 'Spaethii') (4 plants)

J. Bigroot Cranesbill (*Geranium macrorrhizum*) (300 plants) plus Royal Azalea (*Rhododendron schlippenbachii*) (10 plants)

Ground Covers with Insertions of Taller Ground Covers

K. yellow Hyperion Daylily (*Hemerocallis* 'Hyperion') (9 plants) plus the golden-variegated Cordgrass (*Spartina pectinata* 'Aureomarginata') (1 plant)

L. *Sedum ellacombianum* (192 plants) plus lavender-blue-flowered Big Blue Lilyturf (*Liriope muscari* [Big Blue Selection]) (12 plants)

M. *Sedum ellacombianum* (100 plants) plus Garden Black-eyed-Susan (*Rudbeckia fulgida* var. *Sullivantii* 'Goldsturm') (10 plants) and Lady's-Mantle (*Alchemilla vulgaris*) (6 plants)

N. white-variegated Yellow-Archangel (*Lamiastrum galeobdolon* 'Variegatum') (290 plants) plus lavender-blue-flowered Big Blue Lilyturf (*Liriope muscari* [Big Blue Selection]) (27 plants)

O. Bowles Periwinkle (*Vinca minor* 'Bowlesii") (239 plants) plus dark blue Siberian Iris (*Iris sibirica* 'Dreaming Spires') (60 plants) and Yellow Water Iris (*Iris pseudacorus*) (3 plants)

P. Bowles Periwinkle (*Vinca minor* 'Bowlesii') (27 plants) and Autumn-Crocus (*Colchicum* 'Autumn Queen') (19 plants)

Q. European Wild-Ginger (*Asarum europaeum*) (75 plants) and Japanese Butterbur (*Petasites japonicus*) (3 plants)

R. yellow-variegated Plantain-Lily (*Hosta* 'Kabitan') (25 plants) and orange Turk's-Cap Lily (*Lilium superbum*) (6 plants)

S. Lily-of-the-Valley (*Convallaria majalis*) (175 plants) and Hardy Begonia (*Begonia grandis*) (36 plants)

T. Wild Ginger (*Asarum canadense*) (115 plants) plus Purple Loosestrife (*Lythrum salicaria* 'Dropmore Purple') (3 plants)

U. Wild Ginger (*Asarum canadense*) (72 plants) plus white-variegated Solomon's Seal (*Polygonatum odoratum* 'Variegatum') (11 plants)

Ground Covers with Insertions of Taller Ground Covers and Woody Shrubs and Trees

V. white Variegated Goutweed (*Aegopodium podagraria* 'Variegatum') (100 plants) plus lavender-blue-flowered Big Blue Liriope (*Liriope muscari* [Big Blue Selection]) (3 plants) plus Mapleleaf Viburnum (*Viburnum acerifolium*) (4 plants)

W. yellow-variegated Lilyturf (*Liriope muscari* 'Variegata') (108 plants) plus blue-gray Siebold Plantain-Lily (*Hosta sieboldiana* 'Elegans') (35 plants) and Maidenhair Fern (*Adiantum pedatum*) (35 plants) plus Rosebay Rhododendron (*Rhododendron maximum*) (8 plants)

X. New York Fern (*Thelypteris noveboracensis*) (60 plants) plus Sweet Azalea (*Rhododendron arborescens*) (1 plant) plus *Ligularia stenocephala* 'The Rocket' (3 plants)

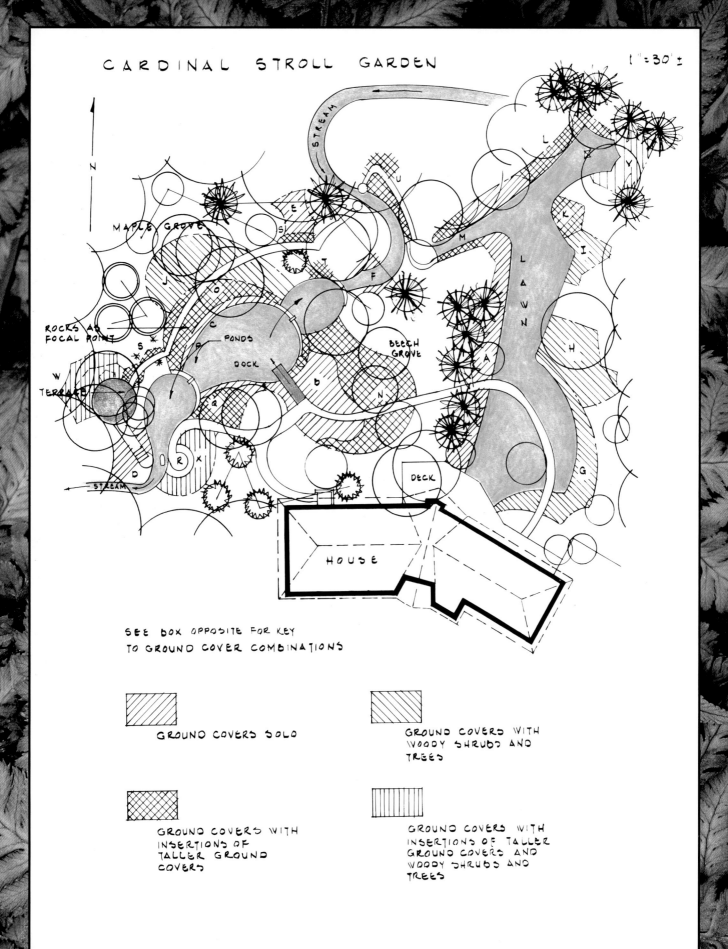

CARDINAL STROLL GARDEN

1"=30'±

STREAM

MAPLE GROVE

ROCKS AS
FOCAL POINT

W
TERRACE

STREAM

PONDS

DOCK

BEECH
GROVE

LAWN

DECK

HOUSE

SEE BOX OPPOSITE FOR KEY
TO GROUND COVER COMBINATIONS

GROUND COVERS SOLO

GROUND COVERS WITH
WOODY SHRUBS AND
TREES

GROUND COVERS WITH
INSERTIONS OF
TALLER GROUND
COVERS

GROUND COVERS WITH
INSERTIONS OF TALLER
GROUND COVERS AND
WOODY SHRUBS AND
TREES

The Cardinal Garden and the two that are discussed next (the Shields and Frederick stroll gardens) provide good examples of a design characteristic that has special significance in planning stroll gardens: The center of interest changes as one strolls. For instance, in the Cardinal Garden, when we stand on the deck, our eye moves first across the lawn to a view onto a neighbor's pond; as we walk down the path to the pond garden our eye becomes involved with the cross-pond view of the rock cluster and its surrounding composition; as we stand on the circular terrace our eye focuses on a view of the dock framed by an American Hornbeam (*Carpinus caroliniana*) of great character. Arrows on the plan for the Shields Garden (page 122) indicate the significant viewing points as one strolls through that garden. The descriptions that follow give some idea of focal points in the plant compositions, which may vary with changing seasonal display.

PLAYING GAMES WITH COLOR

A major aesthetic consideration in any garden is the matter of color. Stroll gardens provide unlimited opportunity for this form of expression because they have space for more than one color experience. (The following appendices should be helpful in working on color composition: Appendix 22, "Color of Foliage—Spring and Summer"; Appendix 23, "Color of Foliage—Fall"; Appendix 24, "Color of Flower"; Appendix 25, "Color of Fruit or Seed Head"; and Appendix 26, "Color of Bark.")

Shields Stroll Garden

The most frequently used part of this garden is a sunpocket deck just off the kitchen, a perfect place for meals and loafing all year, and especially for late breakfasts and lunches on borderline days in spring and fall, and even sometimes in winter. Because of this timetable and because other parts of the garden are readily usable from May through August, the strongest planting emphasis here has been placed on the September-through-April period.

A rich palette of yellow-green and dark green evergreens—American Holly (*Ilex opaca*) (6 plants) (broadleaf), Eastern Red Cedar (*Juniperus virginiana*) (3 plants) (needle), and Canadian Hemlock (*Tsuga canadensis*) (needle)—provides background for the principal structural plants, the River Birches (*Betula nigra*) (3 plants), with their mood-setting bark colors, including bronze with violet overtones, peach, apricot, and off-white. These colors have been reflected by and contrasted with shrub plantings of the blue-green evergreen Leatherleaf Mahonia (*Mahonia bealei*) (12 plants), underplanted with the green to wine-bronze cabbagelike foliage of both the Hybrid Pigsqueak (*Bergenia* 'Perfecta') (36 plants) and the Fountain Leucothoe (*Leucothoe fontanesiana*) (12 plants), with its wedge-shaped leaves, and with large sweeps of the purple-tan foliage and seed heads of Hardy Fountain Grass (*Pennisetum alopecuroides*) (14 plants). The subtleties of this basic color scheme evolve and permutate with every change in the weather, length of day, angle of the sun, and hours of the day. A bit of sparkle is added by the yellow threadlike blossoms of Chinese Witch-hazel (*Hamamelis mollis* 'Pallida') (3 plants) in January and February, the light-catching lavender of *Crocus tomasinianus* (350 plants), under the Birches, in March, and April's pink shower of Weeping Higan Cherry blossoms (*Prunus subhirtella* 'Pendula').

The Shields Stroll Garden provides a series of distinctly different color experiences. The sunpocket deck is especially popular on borderline days in spring and fall. Featured there are three specimens of (1) River Birch (*Betula nigra*). Their bronze tones are picked up by the foliage of (2) Fountain Leucothoe (*Leucothoe fontanesiana*). Accompanying the Birches are evergreens of winter interest: (3) Leatherleaf Mahonia (*Mahonia bealei*) and (4)American Holly (*Ilex opaca*). The Birches' lavender tones are repeated by the blossoms of (5) *Crocus tomasinianus*, and (6) a winter-flowering Chinese Witch-hazel (*Hamamelis mollis* 'Pallida') adds sparkle to the scene.

1

2

3

4

5

6

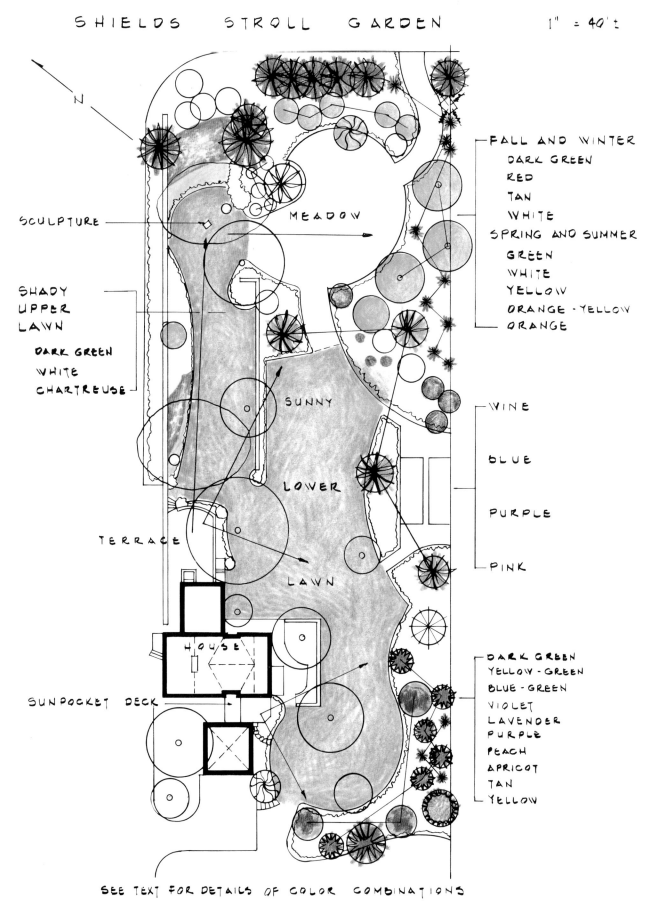

SHIELDS STROLL GARDEN   1" = 40'±

N

FALL AND WINTER
    DARK GREEN
    RED
    TAN
    WHITE
SPRING AND SUMMER
    GREEN
    WHITE
    YELLOW
    ORANGE-YELLOW
    ORANGE

SCULPTURE

MEADOW

SHADY
UPPER
LAWN

    DARK GREEN
    WHITE
    CHARTREUSE

WINE

BLUE

PURPLE

PINK

SUNNY

LOWER

TERRACE

LAWN

HOUSE

DARK GREEN
YELLOW-GREEN
BLUE-GREEN
VIOLET
LAVENDER
PURPLE
PEACH
APRICOT
TAN
YELLOW

SUNPOCKET DECK

SEE TEXT FOR DETAILS OF COLOR COMBINATIONS

1

2

3

Warmer spring and fall days encourage strolls to the meadow, an area where mowing is limited to once or twice a year in order that the form of the grasses and the blossoms of wildflowers can be enjoyed. The palette in fall and winter is largely dark green, red, tan, and white. Here three young native Sycamores (*Platanus occidentalis*), reflecting the glory of an ancient specimen on a higher level, exhibit patches of white bark, which are dramatized by the contrast with olive tan and dark brown. Dark green Dwarf Inkberry Holly (*Ilex glabra* 'Densa') (10 plants) and Eastern Red Cedars (10 plants) provide a nicely structured background. The red berries of Winter King Hawthorn (*Crataegus viridis* 'Winter King') (3 plants) and Winter Red Winterberry (*Ilex verticillata* 'Winter Red') (11 plants) sparkle in the foreground above the tan of winter grasses.

A winter stroll to the Shields meadow is a red and white experience. Plantings include (1) Winter Red Winterberry (*Ilex verticillata* 'Winter Red') and (2) Winter King Hawthorn (*Crataegus viridis* 'Winter King'), as well as (3) several Sycamores (*Platanus occidentalis*).

Among the meadow grasses of summer is an orange and yellow scheme. *Top:* Garden Black-eyed-Susan (*Rudbeckia fulgida* var. *Sullivantii* 'Goldsturm'). *Bottom:* Butterfly-Weed (*Asclepias tuberosa*) (see text on page 129).

As soon as spring breaks, the idea of strolls in the garden becomes inviting, and when consistent warmth is assured, outdoor living shifts to the terrace. It is from this point that gardens on two levels of distinctly different moods and color palettes—the shady upper lawn and sunny lower lawn—invite the viewer to closer inspection.

The palette of the sunny lower lawn is a color tour de force involving wine, blue, purple, and pink. Blue Atlas Cedars (*Cedrus atlantica* 'Glauca') (4 plants) and one existing Colorado Blue Spruce (*Picea pungens* cultivar) structure this area and are contrasted with the rich wine foliages of the red-leaf Thundercloud Plum (*Prunus cerasifera* 'Thundercloud') (4 plants) and Purpleleaf Smoke Bush (*Cotinus coggygria* 'Purpureus') (3 plants).

The season starts in April with the blue-lavender blossoms of Korean Rhododendron (*Rhododendron mucronulatum*) (6 plants), the pink of an older existing *Magnolia soulangiana*, and a ground cover of the true-blue Lungwort (*Pulmonaria angustifolia*) (260 plants). All are enriched by the contrast with the view toward the meadow, where yellow-green blossoms on a *Magnolia* 'Elizabeth' and Japanese Cornelian-Cherry (*Cornus officinalis*) (5 plants) frame a view of naturalized white and yellow *Narcissus*.

French Hybrid Lilacs (*Syringa vulgaris* hybrids) (14 plants) in shades of blue, lavender, and wine follow in May, contrasted with a sweep of the platterlike white blossoms of Double-File Viburnum (*Viburnum plicatum* forma *tomentosum*) (6 plants) (see page 126).

In June the wine-colored foliages are going strong, and spikes of Siberian Iris (*Iris sibirica* 'Flight of Butterflies') (3 plants) are sparkling with blossoms, blue and white with blue veins. The clumps of Blue Oat Grass (*Helictotrichon sempervirens*) (4 plants) and a dash of gray-foliaged Beach Wormwood (*Artemesia stelleriana*) (3 plants) bring the Blue Atlas Cedar colors into the foreground.

Opposite page: The palette of the sunny lower lawn in the Shields Garden is a color tour de force. The background is wine foliage: **(1)** Thundercloud Plum (*Prunus cerasifera* 'Thundercloud'), seen here with pink Dogwood (*Cornus florida* 'Rubra') in the foreground, and **(2)** Purpleleaf Smoke Bush (*Cotinus coggygria* 'Purpureus'). Used as blenders are gray and gray-blue foliages — **(3)** Blue Atlas Cedar (*Cedrus atlantica* 'Glauca'), **(4)** Beach Wormwood (*Artemesia stelleriana*), and **(5)** Blue Oat Grass (*Helictotrichon sempervirens*).

1

2

3

In the Shields Garden, pink, purple, and blue flowers — hybrid Lilacs **(1)** *Syringa vulgaris* 'Ludwig Spaeth,' **(2)** *S. vulgaris* 'Congo,' and **(3)** *S. vulgaris* 'Firmament' — appear with the white blossoms of **(4)** Double-File Viburnum (*Viburnum plicatum* forma *tomentosum*).

Opposite page, top: The June-blooming Siberian Iris (*Iris sibirica* 'Flight of Butterflies') (*background*) flowers just a month before the elegant combination of Butterfly Bush (*Buddleia davidii* 'Opera') (*top inset*) and Bishop's Crest Daylily (*Hemerocallis* 'Bishop's Crest') (*bottom inset*). *Opposite page, bottom:* Variegated Miscanthus (*Miscanthus sinensis* 'Variegatus') (*background*) contrasts with pink Loosestrife (*Lythrum virgatum* 'Morden Pink') (*inset*).

4

July and August are probably the richest moments here. Spikes of blue, purple, and wine, alive with butterflies in myriad colors, bob on the Butterfly Bushes (*Buddleia davidii* cultivars) (3 plants) against a ground cover background of lavender-peach Daylilies (*Hemerocallis* 'Bishop's Crest') (15 plants). The strong vertical pink of Loosestrife (*Lythrum virgatum* 'Morden Pink') (1 plant), contrasted with the white Variegated Miscanthus (*Miscanthus sinensis* 'Variegatus') (3 plants), steals the show.

The color strength of the tree, shrub, and herbaceous foliages continues into the fall, and a new act emerges with the pink of *Sedum* 'Autumn Joy' (20 plants) and the cobalt blue of Plumbago (*Ceratostigma plumbaginoides*) (100 plants) against a background of bright purple Chinese Beautyberry (*Callicarpa dichotoma*) (7 plants).

1

2

3

GARDENS TO STROLL IN

4

The shady upper lawn, by contrast, has a palette engaging in the subtleties of dark green (Dwarf English Boxwood [*Buxus sempervirens* 'Suffruticosa'] and Canadian Hemlocks [*Tsuga canadensis*]), white, and chartreuse.

The white blossoms are entirely a May-June matter: Hohman's golden-variegated Flowering Dogwood (*Cornus florida* 'Hohman's Golden') (1 plant), Azaleas, golden-leaf Sweet Mockorange (*Philadelphus coronarius* 'Aureus') (3 plants), Oakleaf Hydrangea (*Hydrangea quercifolia*) (9 plants), and Korean Dogwood (*Cornus kousa*) (3 plants).

The chartreuse element is more of an all-season affair. It provides a stimulating contrast with the whites in May and June and enlivens and provides a cooling effect in the deep shade of summer. The earliest contributors are the young shoots of Plantain-Lily (*Hosta* 'Kabitan') (144 plants), which are quickly followed by the flat yellow-green blossoms of Cushion Spurge (*Euphorbia epithymoides*) (50 plants).

In early May the uncurling leaves of both the Hohman's golden-variegated Flowering Dogwood and golden-leaf Sweet Mockorange

are displaying their variegation at its finest. Later in the month the straplike foliage of golden-variegated Lilyturf (*Liriope muscari* 'Variegata') (168 plants) is in fine form for journeyman's service the rest of the season, and by July the seed heads of Oakleaf Hydrangea have taken on lime-green-chartreuse coloration.

There is, moreover, a color relationship between this upper lawn and the meadow in its summer phase. The white blossoms of Swamp Magnolia (*Magnolia virginiana*) (5 plants), Buttonbush (*Cephalanthus occidentalis*) (5 plants), and Sweet Pepperbush (*Clethra alnifolia*) (3 plants) are in full spate. The eye is pleased to move from a moment of restful chartreuse to the sparkle of orange-yellow Garden Black-eyed-Susan (*Rudbeckia fulgida* var. *Sullivantii* 'Goldsturm') (36 plants) and rich orange Butterfly-Weed (*Asclepias tuberosa*) (48 plants), pictured on page 124, among the meadow grass.

The five distinct areas of this stroll garden —sunpocket deck, shady upper lawn, sunny lower lawn, meadow, and terrace—provide rich and varied experiences for the color-sensitive owners throughout the year.

The shady upper lawn adjacent to the Shieldses' terrace is a restful combination of dark greens, whites, and chartreuse. From here are seen (among others) the yellow-green blossoms of **(1)** Cushion Spurge (*Euphorbia epithymoides*) and the lively foliage of **(2)** Sweet Mockorange (*Philadelphus coronarius* 'Aureus' [Golden]), along with **(3)** *Magnolia* 'Elizabeth' and **(4)** Plantain-Lily (*Hosta* 'Kabitan').

Color is a very personal and emotional matter. (The following appendices should be helpful in determining color composition: Appendix 22, "Color of Foliage—Spring and Summer"; Appendix 23, "Color of Foliage—Fall"; Appendix 24, "Color of Flower"; Appendix 25, "Color of Fruit or Seed Head"; and Appendix 26, "Color of Bark.") I, for one, am not interested in it simply as a decorative element. For me it is a biological necessity and a prime reason for gardening. As enjoyable as the native landscape is (and my life would be diminished in a major way without it), the emotional richness provided by color as produced in a designed garden is essential. It is here that the full palette of plants now available to us from all over the world can be tapped, arranged to please our eye, suit our site, and create the moods and atmospheres that strengthen our lives.

There have been many articles written about color combinations, many attempts to analyze what makes successful combinations, and many recommendations as to what gardeners should do. I get bogged down in such intellectualizing, am bored with the preoccupation with avoiding clashes, and think of many exceptions to every rule.

Most of these recommendations were made in England, where there is less sunshine. In the North American climate, where days are usually either sunny or smoggy, courageous color statements are more appropriate and the preoccupation with pastels has less meaning.

Similarly, this English style of guidelines is too small in scope. A broad brushstroke is more often needed where combinations are composed of generous masses of single colors.

My own feeling is that when making gardens with a color experience as the objective, the plant combinations should be as responsive to our time as our contemporary art. I believe that any group of colors that please you can be used together if the relative proportions are happy together. With experience your eye will tell you what proportions are best.

The colors of associated architecture have an effect on the combination of flower and foliage colors the gardener chooses. The earth colors of silvery gray textured wood (with purple Loosestrife [*Lythrum salicaria* 'Dropmore Purple']) (*top*) and of stone (with Chinese Lilac [*Syringa* x *chinensis*]) (*bottom*) are backgrounds against which a wide variation of color combinations will succeed.

For the richest experiences I generally like to use plants whose flowers literally cover the plant, that is, as much color per square inch as possible. Because foliage provides 100 percent color and usually is effective much longer than the blossoms on any one plant, colored foliage is especially useful. Plants for highlight or accent may be less color-saturated and more delicate, e.g., Meadow Rue (*Thalictrum rochebrunianum*).

I try to be very conscious of the colors of associated architecture. They usually influence the color combination I choose, since they certainly will have an effect on it. The earth colors of stone walls (either in the gray or tan-brown direction), silvery gray textured wood, and sand-tan stucco are backgrounds against which a wide variation of color combinations will work well. Many brick colors work well with only a small palette of colors. White siding sucks the strength out of all but the most vibrant combinations.

In daring hands the colors used in garden architecture can provide major enhancement to the planting scheme. At the great American garden designed by Fletcher Steele at Naumkeag, in Stockbridge, Massachusetts, there is a wonderful color tour de force involving steps leading through a Birch grove to a cutting garden on a lower level. Rather classical double stairs connect a series of landings, leading one comfortably down a steep hillside. The railings are made of a single two-inch pipe curving sinuously downward in counterpoint to the geometry of the stairs. They are painted a slightly pinkish-white, picking up on the trunks of the pure white Birch in the grove through which one passes. The steps and landings themselves are the gray of concrete block. Under each landing are half-circle pools below half-dome indentations. Water drops from the back of each half-dome into its pool, adding sound to the "deep woods" charm. Each half-dome is painted cobalt blue. As one descends, glimpses are visible of the great valley floor below with mountains beyond. At the bottom, when one turns around and looks back, the eye is stunned by the pattern of blue semicircles and sinuous railings ascending the hillside.

Designed by the landscape architect Fletcher Steele, this stairway at Naumkeag, in Stockbridge, Massachusetts, with its cobalt blue fountain backs, is a good example of the successful use of a daring architectural color in a garden setting.

Unlike our native landscape, where saturated color occurs only in the fall, art form gardens and the worldwide cornucopia of plants available to us provide the opportunity for rich color experiences at other seasons. This is most successful where generous masses of the same color are used together. Shown above are eight plants of Azalea Herbert (*left*) and thirteen plants of Azalea Stewartstonian (*right*), both *Rhododendron* Gable hybrids.

Color as it exists in the native landscape in which I live, on the East Coast of the United States, is mostly shades of medium green during the gardening season. The showiest blossoms of the spring season are white and belong to our native Flowering Dogwood (*Cornus florida*). Essentially all woodland wildflowers are spring-blooming and are both subtle in color and, because of scale, visible only on close inspection. Examples are Spring Beauty (*Claytonia virginica*), White Wake-Robin (*Trillium grandiflorum*), Virginia Bluebells (*Mertensia virginica*), Bloodroot (*Sanguinaria canadensis*), and Wild Honeysuckle (*Rhododendron periclymenoides*).

Most meadow wildflowers, many of which are actually aliens escaped here, don't turn up until summer. Although very colorful in themselves, such plants as Black Snakeroot (*Cimicifuga racemosa*), Cardinal Flower (*Lobelia cardinalis*), and Black-eyed-Susan (*Rudbeckia hirta*), have the subtle effect of a Botticelli painting because of their mixture with other greens (grasses et cetera), except in the rare instances when they occur in solid masses.

Our only display of truly saturated color comes in the fall, when meadows and marshes become rich with lavish masses of purple such as Ironweed (*Vernonia noveboracensis*), true blue such as Swamp Aster (*Aster puniceus*), and yellows such as Goldenrod (*Solidago juncea*) and Beggar-Tick (*Bidens polylepis*). At the same time our forests turn into a symphony of orange, burgundy, scarlet, and yellow, with Swamp Maple (*Acer rubrum*), Flowering Dogwood (*Cornus florida*), Sour Gum (*Nyssa sylvatica*), Tulip Poplar (*Liriodendron tulipifera*), and others.

Where no walls, fences, or buildings are involved, the green of our native landscape is not always the asset it might seem at first. It can be amorphous and absorbing, draining all of the life from the color picture we are trying to paint. The addition of very dark green or wine-maroon foliages in such instances may be desirable to provide structure, definition, form, to what we are trying to create.

Chartreuse, shown at left with Loosestrife (*Lythrum salicaria* 'Dropmore Purple'); maroon-wine (Crimson Pygmy Barberry [*Berberis thunbergii* 'Crimson Pygmy']), shown below with *Heliopsis helianthoides* subsp. *scabra* 'Karat' and Feather-Reed Grass (*Calamagrostis* x *acutiflora* 'Karl Foerster') in the foreground; and blue are recommended as blenders and background colors. White is best reserved for use with yellows and/or grays.

I am cautious about the use of pure white. It stands out in any composition, poking holes in the attempted combination. Unless you want to reserve it for a single focal point or for structuring a composition, it is best saved for use with yellows and grays. Particularly in the case of multicolored plantings of "evergreen" Azaleas (such as *Rhododendron* [Kurume hybrids]) and hybrid Rhododendrons, it produces a jumpy, disconcerting sensation. For some reason book after book touts white as a blender. I cannot agree. I have found masses of blue, chartreuse, and maroon-wine much more successful for this purpose. Palettes in the yellow-orange-red direction or, equally, those in the purple-blue-pink direction respond just as well to these three treasured hues.

My advice is to regularly visit other gardens that have color as an objective of importance, study what you see, take notes on the ideas you like, and, in your mind's eye, test these ideas in your own garden, under your own lighting conditions. Then, if you like what you've visualized, put the plan into action. Think of color as a game you play with yourself. Don't be afraid to try what may seem unconventional. Strike a bargain with yourself: You can make changes next year if you are not satisfied. Such changes can often be minor—a larger proportion of this, a smaller proportion of that.

Because we are talking about stroll gardens, where there is the opportunity to have more than one color experience, it is important to think about the sequence in which color combinations are seen in terms of their effect on the viewer.

Gertrude Jekyll (who is often too studied and dogmatic for me) tells about an experience that is certainly germane. It occurred as she approached a section of a garden that was very lively: blood red, yellow, purple, ivory,

buff yellow, and yellow (all Wallflowers). She emphasizes that the approach was through a narrow, dark area: black-green evergreens, shade, the only colors white and purple. This approach contributed to the "big bang" experience of entering an area of vibrant color. The same effect can be seen in the Abby Aldrich Rockefeller Garden (designed by Beatrix Jones Farrand), in Seal Harbor, Maine. This sunny summer garden of brilliant hues is approached by way of the "Spirit Path," all in shades and textures of green, structured by trunks of large shade-producing conifers. The visitor is calmed; children quiet down. As the transition occurs through a narrow opening in an evergreen hedge, visitors gasp with pleasure. Gertrude Jekyll notes, moreover, that the reverse of this process has its pleasurable effect: "I am not sure the return journey would not present the more brilliant picture of the two, for I have often observed in passing from warm coloring to cold, that the eye receives a kind of delightful shock of surprise that color can be so strong and so pure and so altogether satisfying."*

As a repeat visitor to Sissinghurst, a remarkable garden created in the mid-1900s by V. Sackville-West and her husband, Harold Nicolson, in Kent, England, I usually follow the "room to room" sequence, which starts with purple and blues, moves through pinks and mauves, and culminates with the sunset colors of the Cottage Garden. This sequence very closely mirrors the way the light of morning leads us into the brilliance of mid-day, and the effect is so rich and wonderful that all thoughts of the world beyond are totally obliterated. The highest drama for me is what happens next. One is led across the garden on a narrow path bordered by high Yew hedges of dark green. The recent color experiences are savored in the eye's memory and gradually resolved into peacefulness and unencumbered receptivity. This is apt preparation for the final great choreography: From a narrow opening in the hedge one enters into the marvelous subtleties of the dark green, white, and gray garden. V. Sackville-West often recorded enjoying this garden at dusk or on moonlit nights and observed the importance of these colors under such conditions. In the brief periods I have spent in this garden, I have felt as if I have experienced the changing light of a full day.

* Gertrude Jekyll, *Home and Garden* (London: Longmans, Green, 1900), 38.

The variations that can be made on color sequence are endless and provide a delightful challenge and unlimited pleasure for anyone developing a stroll garden.

The following are a few commentaries about and descriptions of color combinations that to me are notable.

· A herbaceous combination that once stopped me in my tracks consisted of a saturated, deep orange-scarlet background, almost transparent light-reflective soft apricot-pink in the middle ground, and tall spikes of soft greenish-yellow in the foreground. (Courtesy Christopher Lloyd, Great Dixter, Kent, England.)

· Pink alone or with shades of pink can be fairly characterless. Add some crimson and purple. It will take away the chocolate box look. (A recommendation from Lanning Roper, an American garden designer who practiced in England.)

· A large solid planting of "evergreen" Azaleas seen from above had carmine pinks in the foreground, orange-red in the background. Lavender, orange-red, and passionate pink occurred in drifts in between. The viewer felt as though his eye were running over velvet. (Wendy Heckert Azalea bowl, in Wilmington, Delaware.)

· A few samples of H. F. duPont's genius at Winterthur:

The "cool" yellow of Winter Hazels (*Corylopsis*) combined with the "warm" lavender of Korean Rhododendron (*Rhododendron*

Learning by daring experimentation in your own garden is a lot of fun and the key to success with color. *Above:* In the great summer garden at Great Dixter, Christopher Lloyd has backed yellow Mulleins (*Verbascum*) with pink and peach *Alstroemerias* and the orange-scarlet-flowered Maltese-Cross plant (*Lychnis chalcedonica*).

The sequence of events is a very important part of a color experience. *Opposite page:* At the Abby Aldrich Rockefeller Garden, in Seal Harbor, Maine, the visitor first travels down a path of quiet green (mosses and other native ground covers) (*top*), which prepares him for a riotous color experience (*bottom*).

mucronulatum) produces an unforgettable early spring richness.

A planting of hybrid flowering Quince (*Chaenomeles*) produces rose, wine, carmine, brick, scarlet, salmon, white, and salmon-yellow blossoms. The touch of genius in this scene is Chinese Snowball Viburnum (*Viburnum macrocephalum* forma *macrocephalum*), whose large snowball-like blossoms are a lively chartreuse at Quince time.

Asiatic Candelabra Primroses in the quarry are peach, pink, lavender, and yellow. The touch that makes it all work is a few dashes of tangerine, adding just the right amount of lively highlight.

In Winterthur's Azalea woods, in a sea of the blue Spanish Bluebell (*Endymion hispanicus*) are extensive plantings of evergreen Azaleas in shades of pink. In the midst of this a lavender grouping is highlighted by one or two plants of a rather shocking cherry red. H. F. duPont's friend Sylvia Saunders admired the vitality of the combination. When she asked what made him decide to add those few "discordant" plants to the grouping, he replied that the additions were meant to "chic it up." They do!

It should be noted that duPont's outstanding success with color is not the result of single inspirations at single moments in time, but of a long-term interest and commitment; success involved successive refinements over a long period of time. Relying on trial and error, and making changes, are things that the most experienced gardeners are prepared to do.

The work of another great gardener attests to the value of experimentation. At Winterthur, in the April garden, H. F. duPont has combined the warm lavender of Korean Rhododendron (*Rhododendron mucronulatum*) and cool yellow of Winter Hazel (*Corylopsis platypetala*) (*top*); tangerine and apricot are used with mauve and pink in the planting of Asiatic Candelabra Primroses in the quarry (*bottom*).

In Winterthur's predominantly pink Azalea woods (May) a lavender grouping is highlighted by a touch of cherry red to "chic it up."

SEASONAL CHOREOGRAPHY

As has been apparent with the gardens we have touched on already, it is possible to compose moments of great beauty for every month of the year, and many alternative combinations are possible at certain points in the year. (See Appendix 13, "Seasonal Interest—Flower"; Appendix 14, "Seasonal Interest—Fruit and Seed Heads"; Appendix 24, "Color of Flower"; Appendix 25, "Color of Fruit or Seed Head"; and Appendix 38, "Some Favorite Plant Combinations.") The opportunity for such combinations is especially strong in a stroll garden, where different activities, different lighting, and different growing conditions suggest a wide range of choice.

These possibilities start building in December, reach a fever pitch of richness in April and May, and gradually wind down from June through November. Not all garden owners will want such a continuous succession of events, for they may find that resting points between events provide a time for savoring what has passed, anticipating what is to come, or engaging in other activities. Cer-

tainly the richness of plant choreography should correspond to the times of year when one is most likely to use the garden. For some, spring and fall are the high points of garden use, and summer is time away on vacation. For others, spring and fall are too hectic, and summer is the moment to savor the garden. Others retreat to an air-conditioned interior in July and August and look forward to crisp fall days in the garden. And for some, winter is a vacation time, while their opposites find the garden important during this season for bracing strolls and the moment when garden views from inside produce the assurance that spring will come yet again.

Choreography for seasonal interest has been of special interest and provided great pleasure in my own garden, a description of which follows.

Frederick Stroll Garden at Ashland Hollow

The accompanying plan of the Frederick Stroll Garden at Ashland Hollow and the chart showing seasonal interest by garden area (see below) serve the purposes of showing the diverse elements that can occur in a stroll garden, explaining how they can be linked together, and revealing the variation and overlapping of interest produced by plant combinations at different times of the year. The chart also emphasizes the fact that many plantings are of interest at more than one season, for extended periods of time, and even all year.

This garden is located in a steep-sided stream valley that falls gently from west to east. There are essentially two circuits: One is on a lower level and has a close association with the house and stream, and the other is on an upper level of the valley sides.

From examining the chart it will be readily apparent that the Quince (*Chaenomeles*) hillside, the orchard (see page 110), and the Old Shrub Rose path (see page 107) peak for brief moments only. Those moments are so special that the memories linger all year. The richness and vibrance of the Quince colors (soft pink, dark pink, salmon, brick, and near yellow) are pure joy to an eye starved by winter. The thoroughly satisfying combination of apple blossoms and naturalized *Narcissus* in the orchard is the essence of May. What V. Sackville-West called the Ancien Regime colors of the Shrub Roses, plus their ethereal fragrance pervading the whole valley, are anticipated with pleasure for a full year.

The swimming pool garden (see page 85, page 87, page 89, and page 133), the game lawn, and the vegetable garden are planted to correspond to their time of functional use.

The winter garden (see page 43) and hillside meadow are intimately related, and each has a long season. The former takes advantage of the wide palette of plants with berries, bark color and texture, foliage texture and color, and blossoms, which are all part of the long and wonderful cycle leading to spring. The hillside meadow is a naturally occurring and carefully preserved stand of Broomsedge (*Andropogon virginicus*).

The dark green, gray, and white shrub path is predominantly of summer interest. It is specifically designed for viewing on summer evenings at dusk or even in the moonlight.

The studio garden (see page 14; page 37, top; and page 111) plays an important role in spring, summer, and fall.

The Tree Wisteria walk (see page 109) and the *Calocedrus* steps (see page 142) are good examples of plantings that are designed for two or more distinct seasons.

FREDERICK STROLL GARDEN AT ASHLAND HOLLOW—SEASONAL INTEREST

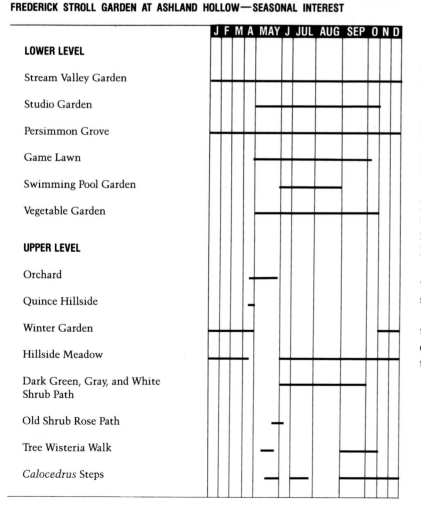

	J	F	M	A	MAY	J	JUL	AUG	SEP	O	N	D
LOWER LEVEL												
Stream Valley Garden												
Studio Garden												
Persimmon Grove												
Game Lawn												
Swimming Pool Garden												
Vegetable Garden												
UPPER LEVEL												
Orchard												
Quince Hillside												
Winter Garden												
Hillside Meadow												
Dark Green, Gray, and White Shrub Path												
Old Shrub Rose Path												
Tree Wisteria Walk												
Calocedrus Steps												

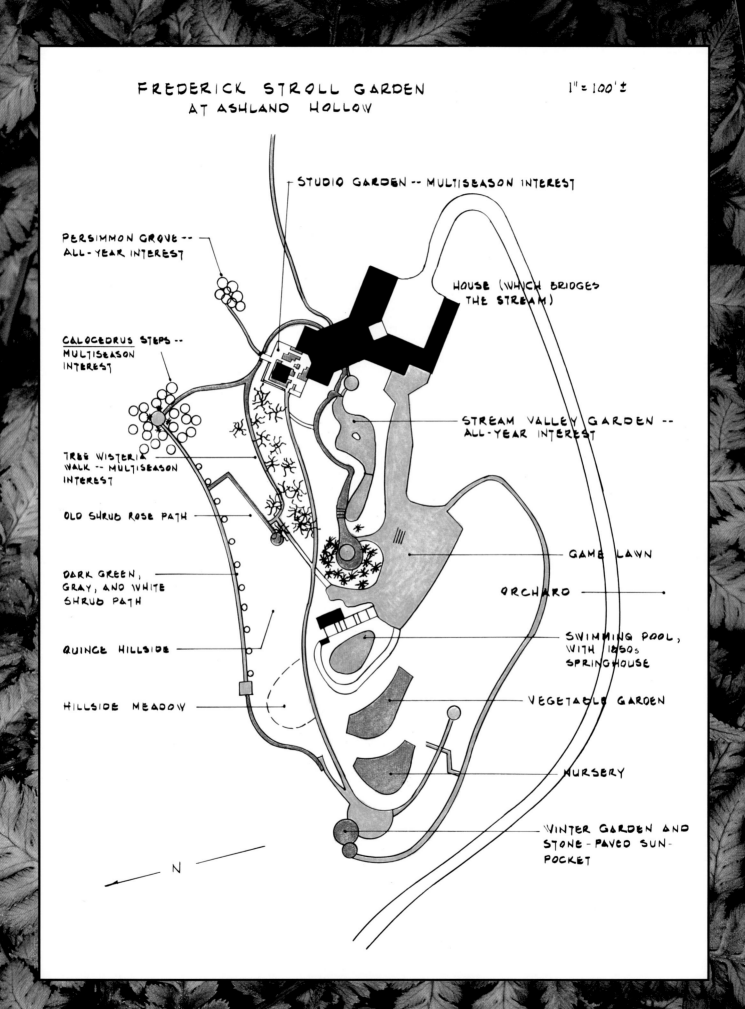

FREDERICK STROLL GARDEN
AT ASHLAND HOLLOW

1" = 100' ±

STUDIO GARDEN -- MULTISEASON INTEREST

PERSIMMON GROVE --
ALL-YEAR INTEREST

HOUSE (WHICH BRIDGES
THE STREAM)

CALOCEDRUS STEPS --
MULTISEASON
INTEREST

STREAM VALLEY GARDEN --
ALL-YEAR INTEREST

TREE WISTERIA
WALK -- MULTISEASON
INTEREST

OLD SHRUB ROSE PATH

GAME LAWN

DARK GREEN,
GRAY, AND WHITE
SHRUB PATH

ORCHARD

QUINCE HILLSIDE

SWIMMING POOL,
WITH 1850s
SPRINGHOUSE

HILLSIDE MEADOW

VEGETABLE GARDEN

NURSERY

WINTER GARDEN AND
STONE-PAVED SUN-
POCKET

N

During May, Wisteria vines trained as trees display their white, pink, and lavender blossoms. *Left: Wisteria floribunda* 'Alba' is seen in combination with the dwarf Lilac (*Syringa patula*).

The Tree Wisteria walk features vines of long-flowered Japanese Wisteria (*Wisteria floribunda*) trained as trees. These flower around May 20 and are accompanied by a large planting of the soft blue narrow-leaf Bluestar (*Amsonia hubrichtii*), the wine-colored foliage of Purpleleaf Smoke Bush (*Cotinus coggygria* 'Purple Supreme'), and the pale lavender blossoms of the dwarf Lilac (*Syringa patula*). In September this same area sparkles with the mauve-pink blossoms of Gibraltar Bush Clover (*Lespedeza thunbergii* 'Gibraltar') and the soft blue of *Aster* 'Dwarf Opal' against the wine-maroon foliage of Purpleleaf Sand Cherry (*Prunus* x *cistena*) and Purpleleaf Smoke Bush. All are backed by three Golden-Larch (*Pseudolarix kaempferi*), whose foliage seems to glow from within on sunny days.

The mauve-pink blossoms of Gibraltar Bush Clover (*Lespedeza thunbergii* 'Gibraltar') (*above right*) are combined with (*opposite page*) *Aster* 'Dwarf Opal' (*foreground*) against the wine-maroon foliage of Purpleleaf Smoke Bush (*Cotinus coggygria* 'Purple Supreme') (*right center*) for a second season of interest on the Tree Wisteria walk in the Frederick Stroll Garden. Just behind the Aster is the fine foliage of Bluestar (*Amsonia hubrichtii*), whose star-shaped blue flowers are an important part of the May composition.

The Frederick Stroll Garden at Ashland Hollow is designed in such a way that separate areas of the garden are of interest (varying in duration) at different times of the year. (See the chart on page 138 demonstrating this choreography.) May on the *Calocedrus* steps finds the orange-red of Ghent Hybrid Azalea (*Rhododendron* x *gandavense* 'Coccinea Speciosa') and the chartreuse (green-and-gold-variegated) foliage of Flowering Dogwood (*Cornus florida* 'Hohman's Golden') against a background of purpleleaf Rivers European Beech (*Fagus sylvatica* 'Riversii'). The *Calocedrus* steps also provide a second act in July and a third in the fall (see text below).

The *Calocedrus* steps have three different seasons. They first pull together in late May, when the orange-red of the deciduous Ghent Hybrid Azalea (*Rhododendron* x *gandavense* 'Coccinea Speciosa') sings under the chartreuse foliage of Hohman's golden-variegated Flowering Dogwood (*Cornus florida* 'Hohman's Golden') and the bisecting path focuses on the lavender candelabralike blossoms of a specimen Empress Tree (*Paulownia tomentosa*). In early July a ground cover of the deep apricot Daylily 'Aten' (*Hemerocallis* 'Aten') brings the area to life again, with Dogwood foliage that has become a darker gold and green. Various *Sedums* and *Euphorbias* in yellows and bronzes enrich the scene. Finally, in the fall, red fruits on Creeping Cotoneaster (*Cotoneaster adpressus* var. *praecox*) and Tea Viburnum (*Viburnum setigerum*) contrast with a striking display of purple fruits on a large patch of Chinese Beautyberry (*Callicarpa dichotoma*). These are played against large specimens of horizontally branching Burning Bush (*Euonymus alata*), whose foliage is soft glowing carmine and pink. Ornamental grasses add to the picture, with

five clumps of Slender Miscanthus (*Miscanthus sinensis* 'Gracillimus') in the background and three clumps of Purple Moor Grass (*Molina caerulea* subsp. *arundinacea*) highlighting the foreground. Bowles Periwinkle (*Vinca minor* 'Bowlesii')—underplanted with the yellow-flowered bulbous Fall-Daffodil (*Sternbergia lutea*)—and cobalt-blue-flowered Plumbago (*Ceratostigma plumbaginoides*)—underplanted with lavender Autumn-Crocus (*Colchicum* 'Autumn Queen')—tie this symphony together.

Lastly, two parts of the lower level garden—the Persimmon grove and the stream valley garden—with which we live more intimately, are of all-year interest.

The Persimmon grove we see daily from our bedroom and bathroom windows. It is a deceit in the sense that it appears to be a continuation of the existing farm hedgerow along a contour of a steep hillside (visually connecting the patio and hillside). It and its background planting are totally contrived out of both exotic and native plants with strong ornamental characteristics at different seasons of the year.

The yellow-green of Virginia Pine (*Pinus virginiana*) contrasts with the dark green of Japanese Torreya (*Torreya nucifera*) in the background. Late winter finds attractive pendulous blossoms on *Corylus colurna*, the Turkish Filbert.

Early spring produces a spectacle of white and yellow blossoms, Yulan Magnolia (*Magnolia denudata*) and Japanese Cornelian-Cherry (*Cornus officinalis* 'Kintoki') respectively.

Midspring brings carmine pink "apple blossoms" on long stems on the Parkman Flowering Crabapple (*Malus halliana* 'Parkmanii').

Vibrant orange blossoms on a hybrid Daylily (*Hemerocallis* 'Rocket City') sparkle in the field grass in July and are followed by attractive fruits on the Staghorn Sumac (*Rhus typhina*) in August.

Fall is a time of particular intensity that carries right through to Christmas. A cluster of Persimmon trees (*Diospyros virginiana*) is dazzling not only because of the fruit but also because of the wonderfully subtle colors of the foliage and the Japanesque branching habit that is exposed when the leaves fall. A secondary feature is a fruiting specimen of the old-fashioned Osage Orange (*Maclura pomifera*), with its large corrugated apple-green orbs. This is backed by *Euonymus* shrubs, valuable for their foliage and fruit colors (*Euonymus europaea* 'Red Cascade,' *E. hamiltoniana*, and *E. sachalinensis*). Late October provides the brilliant yellow of four Maidenhair Trees (*Ginkgo biloba*) and the drama involved as they all drop their leaves in concert. The show is carried through December and beyond by the persistent shiny red fruits on Winter King Hawthorn (*Crataegus viridis* 'Winter King').

The stream valley garden (see page 144), designed by Conrad Hamerman, is an especially intimate part of our lives, since the house is built like a bridge across the stream itself and most rooms have views up and down the valley. The stream has been dammed, creating four ponds and five waterfalls. The banks have been planted with curvilinear masses of ground covers and shrubs that will tolerate the shade of existing Beech and Tulip Poplars. The theme is essentially shades and textures of greens.

In the fall, the dramatic foliage of Staghorn Sumac (*Rhus typhina*) (*background*) provides a color riot beneath the grove of native Persimmons (*Diospyros virginiana*). The fruits of this Persimmon (*inset*) are a table delicacy when picked after the first frost.

In the Frederick Stroll Garden at Ashland Hollow, the stream valley garden, intimately associated with the house, is of all-year interest. The landforms, the forms of the trees, and the strong ground plan (water and ground covers) combine into a site-specific sculpture that changes with the light variations of each day of the year and each hour of the day (design by Conrad Hamerman).

The varying green tones of the stream valley garden are interrupted by three displays: evergreen-type Azaleas (brick red, salmon pink, mauve, purple, and true soft pink) in mid-May; sparkling red Cardinal Flowers (*Lobelia cardinalis*) in a bay of the main pond in August; and the wonderful foliage colors of Azaleas and deciduous forest in the fall. The forms of the trees and the strong forms of the ground plan (water and ground covers) compose a sculpture that changes in its effect with the light variations of each day of the year and each hour of the day.

This is, to be sure, an extreme example of a stroll garden. Few gardeners are so ardent; few residential gardens have this much space. The choreographic principles involved in planning for a single season, multiple seasons, or all year are, however, applicable to any garden and particularly to any with the opportunity for more than one experience.

In summary, larger gardens provide the chance for multiple experiences based on assets of the site, varied social and athletic activities, specialized horticultural interests, and aesthetic preferences and interests.

In addition to stroll gardens, we have discussed entrance gardens, view gardens, live-in gardens, and swimming pool gardens. Any single garden in reality probably has elements from two or more of these categories. In this sense most gardens are multiple-experience gardens, and the opportunities discussed in this chapter clearly apply.

This book will have been a success if the reader is stimulated to put together plant combinations appropriate for his or her own garden. For that reason, a series of appendices follows that, it is hoped, will offer assistance in this regard.

In the final analysis, the strength of character of each garden will depend on the fullest expression therein of the owner's personality.

The stream valley garden is largely composed of shades and textures of green. There are, however, three exceptional blasts of color from: evergreen-type Azaleas in mid-May (*top*); Cardinal Flower (*Lobelia cardinalis*) (*bottom*) in early August; and the wonderful foliage colors of Azaleas and forest trees in the fall. The garden in winter is shown on the opposite page.

U.S.D.A. Plant Hardiness Zone Map, 1990

Range of average annual minimum temperatures for each zone

	Zone	Temperature
	Zone 1	Below −50°F
	Zone 2	−50° to −40°
	Zone 3	−40° to −30°
	Zone 4	−30° to −20°
	Zone 5	−20° to −10°
	Zone 6	−10° to 0°
	Zone 7	0° to 10°
	Zone 8	10° to 20°
	Zone 9	20° to 30°
	Zone 10	30° to 40°
	Zone 11	Above 40°

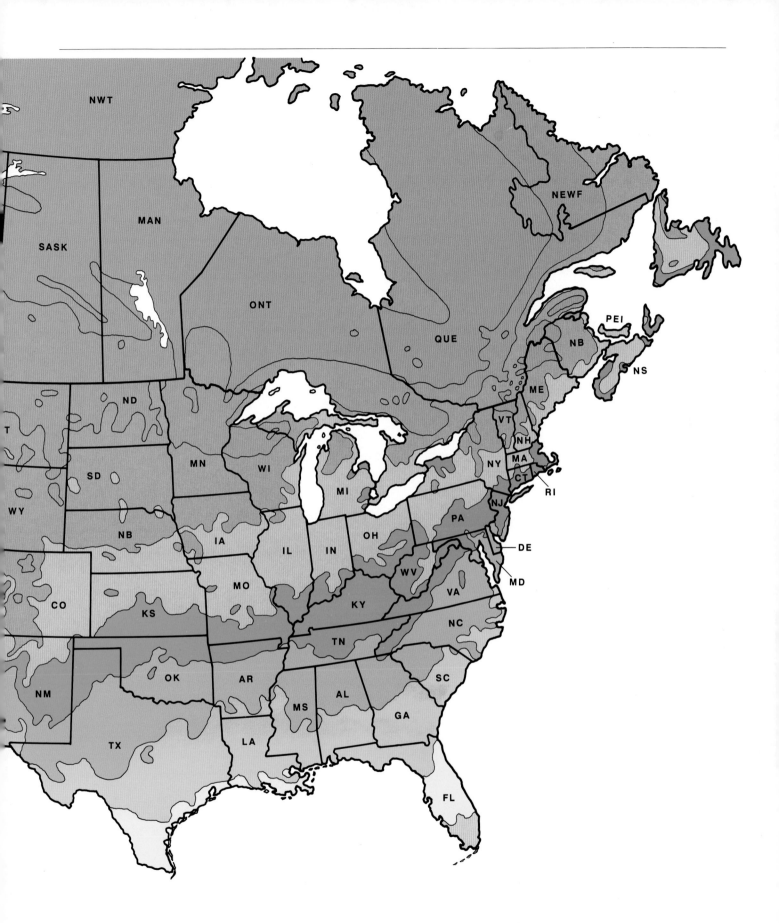

Appendices

Introduction to the Appendices

It is the fervent hope of the author that plant combinations in the text will have inspired readers to put together their own designs suited to their own conditions and tastes, rather than to slavishly follow what others have done. To this end, more than forty plant lists have been assembled in the following appendices in an attempt to help with cultural and design considerations.

The basic palette of approximately six hundred plants is not an exhaustive list and is both extremely catholic and, for the following reasons, highly personal in nature.

As I mentioned in the Introduction, I have spent fifty years gardening in the same area, in three different gardens. My location is roughly thirty miles southwest of Philadelphia (latitude 39 degrees, 45 minutes north; longitude 75 degrees, 40 minutes west). The terrain of my present garden is rolling piedmont 350 to 400 feet above sea level, and the average annual rainfall is forty inches. The soil, clay loam, is predominantly acid. Since many of the gardens I have designed have similar mid-Atlantic conditions, I speak with greatest experience about plants thriving under these circumstances.

Second, *The Exuberant Garden and the Controlling Hand* is not meant to be encyclopedic but to reflect my own viewpoint. Therefore, the plants recommended include only those that I, after fifty years of growing or observing them, consider the best performers. I hope these limitations will help rather than hinder the reader in boiling down what is often an overwhelming choice and in deciding what works best in his or her garden.

The lists in the Appendices are composed of both woody (evergreen and deciduous) and herbaceous plants (including bulbs for naturalizing). For the most part, these are the very best performers available when planted within the recommended hardiness zones and under the soil, moisture, and light conditions recommended.

There is a heavy representation of woody and herbaceous plants useful as ground covers (see Appendix 27) because of the importance I attach to ground covers from both a design and maintenance viewpoint (see Chapter 3, pages 71–72). Followers of the current trend to revive traditional herbaceous borders may be disappointed to see that some of their favorites are not included. Omission of such plants is very likely due to the fact that they are not sufficiently self-maintaining to meet my standards.

On the other hand, there are a small number of entries that, because they provide some very special element of magic to garden design, have been included in spite of somewhat higher maintenance requirements. Among these are plants with a hardiness zone listed as *T* (my symbol, meaning that they are tender, not tolerant of frost), and those in Appendix 1A showing special requirements under the column heading "Notes." (For an explanation of the meaning of the figures used in the "Notes" column, see the introductory material in Appendix 1A, page 153.) Readers wishing to avoid more intensive maintenance should avoid these plants.

For example, *Cestrum nocturnum* (Night Jessamine) provides such outstanding fragrance that I have included it, even though it is tender and must be kept in a tub and housed in a frost-free place in the wintertime.

Equisetum hyemale (Scouring Rush) has been included in spite of its invasive nature—which requires the placement of eighteen-inch barriers in the soil around it to prevent its spread—because its striking vertical habit, primitive appearance, and black-banded tubular stems simply have no equal from a design viewpoint.

Another plant whose design characteristics for me outweigh its maintenance requirements is *Ricinus communis* 'Zanzibarensis' (Castor Bean), which is an annual and must be reseeded each year. This plant is of special value for its bold texture. It grows more than twelve feet in height in a single season and is clothed with dramatic large red leaves during the summer.

Use of Plant Lists

The following abbreviations are used with some Latin plant names and are found throughout the Appendices: *subsp.* stands for subspecies, *var.* for variety.

Some Latin names are followed by synonyms that, although no longer considered botanically correct, are commonly used in the horticultural community. The synonyms are given in parentheses and preceded by the abbreviation *syn.*; e.g., "*Magnolia denudata* (syn. *M. heptapeta*)."

Appendix 1A and Appendices 3–12 largely apply to site conditions under which you garden. These include soil composition, soil moisture, available light, and various adverse conditions that may occur; Appendices 6–12 particularly address tolerances to such conditions. All of these lists are subdivided by hardiness zones.

If the lists that make up the Appendices are to be helpful, you must know the relevant facts about your own site. Most especially you must know what hardiness zone your garden is in. You can determine your hardiness zone by acquainting yourself with the lowest winter temperatures in the area during the last ten-year period. This can be done by checking with the nearest U. S. Government (Department of Commerce) National Weather Service office. With this information, you can establish the hardiness zone by studying the U.S.D.A. Plant Hardiness Zone Map on page 148. In lists arranged by hardiness zone, plants should not be considered with hardiness zones higher than your own.

Appendices 1B, 2, and 13–38 pertain to plant uses from a design viewpoint. The most important items of information are summarized in Appendix 1B.

If you have begun using the Appendices by first finding plants with design characteristics useful to you, then you must:

1. Make sure the plants will be hardy in your location. In lists where plants are not grouped by hardiness zones, the zone for individual plants can be found in Appendix 1A.
2. Determine whether the soil, light, and moisture requirements of the plants correspond to those you can provide. This also can be determined by consulting Appendix 1A.

Appendix 1B is equally useful, in that it provides information about design characteristics when you have selected a plant because it fulfills a special cultural requirement; i.e., tolerance of wind, alkaline soils.

Because of my strong interest in plants as ground covers, the appendix devoted to the subject (Appendix 27) includes separate lists on these critical preferences:

Hardiness Zone
Soil Preference
Moisture Preference
Light Preference

and design characteristics:

Size
Plant Type

Appendices 16–18 and 28–37 are specialty lists that should be helpful.

Appendix 38 is a list designed to demonstrate the potential for interesting plant choreography during every month of the year and is entitled "Some Favorite Plant Combinations."

For a complete listing of the Appendices and what they cover, please see the Appendices Contents, pages vii–viii.

APPENDIX 1A
Master List:
Summary of Cultural Preferences and Tolerances

This listing presents, in alphabetical order by Latin name (common name follows Latin name), all of the roughly six hundred plants contained in the basic palette and provides standard cultural information about each. For lists of plants by individual cultural preference or tolerance, see Appendices 3–12.

Notes

The "Notes" column provides information about plants that have special requirements. The figures in this column are keyed as follows:

1. Tender annual. Start from seed each spring.
2. Tender bulb or tuber. Lift bulbs in fall and replant each spring after winter storage in a frost-free location.
3. Biennial. Start seed in summer for bloom the following spring.
4. Short-lived.
5. Tender woody plant. Best handled in a tub kept in a frost-free place during winter. Annual cut-back and repotting recommended.
6. Cut back shrub in northern part of range.
7. Extremely invasive. Provide root barriers.
8. Moderately invasive. Provide root barriers or be prepared for annual discipline with the spade.
9. Suckers from roots.
10. Narrow tolerance:
    a. Sharp drainage required. Gritty or sandy, well-drained soil needed.
    b. Adequate supply of moisture required during entire growing season.
    c. Light shade is beneficial.
    d. Regular fertilization is beneficial.
    e. Does best with only moderate fertility.
    f. Sharp drainage required, especially during dormancy.

11. Winter protection needed in northern part of range.
12. Susceptible to damage in heavy snow unless foliage is tied in each fall.
13. In northern part of range, foliage burns in late winter, creating an eyesore in the garden in May (until new growth covers old) unless foliage is cut off.
14. Thin or cut plant back totally in very early spring to encourage young growth,
    a. which will have brightest colored bark.
    b. which will produce lushest foliage.
15. Frequent division needed for best performance.
16. Requires staking.
17. Needs an exceptionally strong support, annual pruning, and tying in.
18. Spraying necessary in some areas to control
    a. lace fly.
    b. fungal diseases.
19. Slugs are attracted to foliage of this plant. Be prepared to use slug bait or other controls.
20. Must be protected from rabbits, which find it especially attractive.
21. Stem canker can be a problem. Best controlled by cutting out infected branches as they occur.
22. First flush of foliage often destroyed by *anthracnose*. Not fatal to tree. Second flush of foliage survives.
23. Hard-to-control woolly adelgid and scale plague mature specimens of these trees in some parts of eastern United States. Check with the Cooperative Extension Service, School of Agriculture, at your nearest land grant university.

The figures under the column heading "Size (Feet)" represent the lower end of the size range for each plant. The measurement "0.0" signifies a plant less than 6 inches tall.

A key to all other abbreviations used is given with each page.

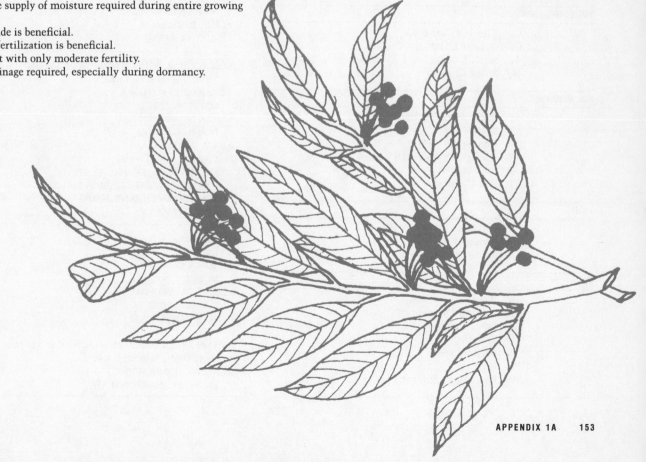

APPENDIX 1A
Master List:
Summary of Cultural Preferences and Tolerances

KEY TO ABBREVIATIONS

ZONE

Plant hardiness zones adapted from U.S.D.A. Plant Hardiness Zone Map, 1990 (page 148).

Range of Average Annual Minimum Temperatures

1	Below −50° F.
2	−50° to −40° F.
3	−40° to −30° F.
4	−30° to −20° F.
5	−20° to −10° F.
6	−10° to 0° F.
7	0° to 10° F.
8	10° to 20° F.
9	20° to 30° F.
10	30° to 40° F.
11	Above 40° F.
T	Tender in the Mid-Atlantic Region

TYPE

W   Woody
P   Perennial
I   Biennial
A   Annual
B   Bulb
E   Evergreen

SOIL COMPOSITION

CL   Clay and Clay Loam
OL   Organic Loam
SL   Sandy Loam
SG   Stony, Gravelly

SOIL MOISTURE

B   Bog or Standing Water
WE   Water's Edge
CM   Consistently Moist, Not Boggy
AV   Average, Dry Between Rains
D   Dry
F   Fast-Draining

LIGHT

F   Full Sun
P   Partial Shade
S   Shade

TOLERANCE

W   Wind
PA   Poor Air Drainage
LF   Low Fertility
D   Drought
SS   Shallow Soil
HPH   High pH
HMS   Hot, Muggy Summers

NAME

ABELIA X GRANDIFLORA
    GLOSSY ABELIA
ABIES NORDMANNIANA
    NORDMANN FIR
ACANTHOPANAX SIEBOLDIANUS
    FIVELEAF-ARALIA
ACER GRISEUM
    PAPERBARK MAPLE
ACER PALMATUM 'BLOODGOOD'
    REDLEAF JAPANESE MAPLE
ACER PALMATUM 'EVER RED'
    RED CUTLEAF JAPANESE MAPLE

ACER PALMATUM 'SANGOKAKU'
    REDTWIG JAPANESE MAPLE
ACER PALMATUM VAR. DISSECTUM OR A. P. 'WATERFALL'
    GREEN CUTLEAF JAPANESE MAPLE
ACER PLATANOIDES 'CRIMSON KING'
    CRIMSON KING NORWAY MAPLE
ACER RUBRUM
    SWAMP MAPLE
ACER SACCHARUM
    SUGAR MAPLE
ACHILLEA 'CORONATION GOLD'
    HYBRID YARROW

ACHILLEA 'MOONSHINE'
    HYBRID YARROW
ACHILLEA MILLEFOLIUM 'ROSEA'
    PINK COMMON YARROW
ACIDANTHERA BICOLOR
    PEACOCK-ORCHID
ACORUS GRAMINEUS 'OGON'
    GRASSY-LEAVED SWEET FLAG
ADIANTUM PEDATUM
    MAIDENHAIR FERN
ADINA RUBELLA
    GLOSSY ADINA

AEGOPODIUM PODAGRARIA 'VARIEGATUM'
    VARIEGATED GOUTWEED
AESCULUS PARVIFLORA
    BOTTLEBRUSH BUCKEYE
AESCULUS SPLENDENS
    FLAME BUCKEYE
AJUGA REPTANS
    CARPET BUGLEWEED
AJUGA REPTANS 'BRONZE BEAUTY'
    CARPET BUGLEWEED (BRONZE FOLIAGE)
AJUGA REPTANS (GIANT FORM)
    BUGLEWEED

ALCHEMILLA VULGARIS
    LADY'S-MANTLE
ALLIUM CERNUUM
    NODDING ONION
ALLIUM TUBEROSUM
    GARLIC CHIVE
ALLIUM ZEBDANENSE

AMELANCHIER ARBOREA (SYN. A. CANADENSIS)
    SHADBUSH, SERVICEBERRY
AMSONIA HUBRICHTII
    BLUESTAR (NARROWLEAF)

FAMILY	ZONE*	TYPE	SIZE (FEET)	SOIL COMPOSITION	SOIL MOISTURE	LIGHT	TOLERANCE	NOTES†
CAPRIFOLIACEAE	6	W	3.0	OL	AV, F	F, P	HMS	6
PINACEAE	5	W, E	52.0	OL	AV	F	W	
ARALIACEAE	4	W	6.5	CL, OL, SL, SG	AV, D, F	F, P, S	W, PA, LF, D, SS, HMS	
ACERACEAE	5	W	13.0	CL, OL, SL	AV	F	PA, HPH, HMS	
ACERACEAE	5	W	13.0	OL	AV, F	F, P	HPH	
ACERACEAE	6	W	6.5	OL	AV, F	F, P	HPH	
ACERACEAE	5	W	13.0	OL	AV	F		
ACERACEAE	6	W	6.5	OL	AV, F	F, P	HPH	
ACERACEAE	4	W	26.0	CL, OL	AV	F	HPH	
ACERACEAE	4	W	26.0	CL, OL	CM, AV, D, F	F	PA, HMS	
ACERACEAE	3	W	52.0	OL	AV, F	F	W	
COMPOSITAE	3	P	1.5	OL, SL	AV, F	F	D	
COMPOSITAE	3	P	0.5	CL, OL, SL, SG	AV, D, F	F	LF, D	
COMPOSITAE	2	P	1.5	CL, OL, SL	AV, D, F	F	W, PA, LF, D, SS, H	
IRIDACEAE	T	A	3.0			F	PA, HMS	2
ARACEAE	6	P	1.0	OL	WE, CM	F, P		
POLYPODIACEAE	3	P	1.5	OL	CM, F	S	HPH	
RUBIACEAE	6	W	3.0	OL	AV	F, P		6
UMBELLIFERAE	3	P	0.5	CL, OL, SL	CM, AV, D, F	P, S	PA, LF, D, HMS	
HIPPOCASTANACEAE	5	W	6.5	OL	AV	F, P	D, HPH	
HIPPOCASTANACEAE	6	W	13.0	OL	AV	F		
LABIATAE	4	P	0.0	OL, SL	AV	F, P	LF, D	
LABIATAE	4	P	0.0	OL, SL	AV	F, P	PA, LF, D, HMS	
LABIATAE	4	P	0.0	OL, SL	AV	F, P	PA, LF, D, HMS	
ROSACEAE	3	P	1.0	OL	CM, AV	P	PA, HMS	
AMARYLLIDACEAE	5	B	0.5	CL, OL, SG	AV, D, FD	F	W, PA, D, HMS	
AMARYLLIDACEAE	4	B	1.0	CL, OL, SL	AV, D, FD	F	PA, LF, D, HMS	
AMARYLLIDACEAE	5	B	0.0	OL	AV, D	F, P	PA, D, HMS	
ROSACEAE	3	W	26.0	CL, OL, SL, SG	CM, AV	F, P	HPH	
APOCYNACEAE	5	P	1.5	CL, OL	AV, D	F	W, PA, LF, D, HMS	

* See "Use of Plant Lists," page 152.
† See page 153.

Master List:
Summary of Cultural Preferences and Tolerances

KEY TO ABBREVIATIONS

ZONE

Plant hardiness zones adapted from U.S.D.A. Plant Hardiness Zone Map, 1990 (page 148).

Range of Average Annual Minimum Temperatures

1	Below −50° F.
2	−50° to −40° F.
3	−40° to −30° F.
4	−30° to −20° F.
5	−20° to −10° F.
6	−10° to 0° F.
7	0° to 10° F.
8	10° to 20° F.
9	20° to 30° F.
10	30° to 40° F.
11	Above 40° F.
T	Tender in the Mid-Atlantic Region

TYPE

W	Woody
P	Perennial
I	Biennial
A	Annual
B	Bulb
E	Evergreen

SOIL COMPOSITION

CL	Clay and Clay Loam
OL	Organic Loam
SL	Sandy Loam
SG	Stony, Gravelly

SOIL MOISTURE

B	Bog or Standing Water
WE	Water's Edge
CM	Consistently Moist, Not Boggy
AV	Average, Dry Between Rains
D	Dry
F	Fast-Draining

LIGHT

F	Full Sun
P	Partial Shade
S	Shade

TOLERANCE

W	Wind
PA	Poor Air Drainage
LF	Low Fertility
D	Drought
SS	Shallow Soil
HPH	High pH
HMS	Hot, Muggy Summers

NAME

AMSONIA TABERNAEMONTANA
  BLUE STAR
ANEMONE BLANDA 'ATROCAERULEA'
  WINDFLOWER
ANEMONE VITIFOLIA 'ROBUSTISSIMA'

ANEMONE X HYBRIDA 'QUEEN CHARLOTTE'
  JAPANESE ANEMONE (HYBRID, PINK)
ARABIS PROCURRENS
  ROCKCRESS
ARALIA SPINOSA
  DEVIL'S-WALKING STICK

ARENARIA VERNA
  IRISH MOSS
ARONIA ARBUTIFOLIA 'BRILLIANTISSIMA'
  RED CHOKEBERRY
ARTEMESIA ABSINTHIUM 'LAMBROOK SILVER'

ARTEMESIA LUDOVICIANA 'SILVER QUEEN'

ARTEMESIA STELLERIANA
  BEACH WORMWOOD
ARTEMESIA VERSICOLOR
  MUGWORT

ARUM ITALICUM 'PICTUM'

ARUNCUS AETHUSIFOLIUS
  GOAT'S BEARD (KOREAN)
ARUNCUS DIOICUS
  GOAT'S BEARD
ARUNDINARIA VIRIDISTRIATA
  BAMBOO (YELLOW VARIEGATED)
ARUNDO DONAX
  GIANT REED
ASARUM EUROPAEUM
  EUROPEAN WILD-GINGER

ASCLEPIAS TUBEROSA
  BUTTERFLY-WEED
ASPHODELINE LUTEA
  ASPHODEL
ASTER AMELLUS 'NOCTURNE'
  ITALIAN ASTER
ASTER CORDIFOLIUS
  BLUE WOOD ASTER
ASTER NOVAE-ANGLIAE 'HARRINGTON'S PINK'
  NEW ENGLAND ASTER
ASTER PUNICEUS
  SWAMP ASTER

ASTER TATARICUS
  TARTARIAN ASTER
ASTER X FRIKARTII 'MONCH'

ASTILBE X ARENDSII CULTIVARS

ATHYRIUM GOERINGIANUM 'PICTUM'
  JAPANESE SILVER FERN
BACCHARIS HALIMIFOLIA, PISTILLATE
  GROUNDSELBUSH (SEED-BEARING)
BAPTISIA AUSTRALIS
  BLUE FALSE INDIGO

FAMILY	ZONE*	TYPE	SIZE (FEET)	SOIL COMPOSITION	SOIL MOISTURE	LIGHT	TOLERANCE	NOTES†
APOCYNACEAE	3	P	3.0	CL, OL	AV, D	F, P	PA, HMS	
RANUNCULACEAE	5	B	0.0	OL	AV	P	PA, HMS	
RANUNCULACEAE	4	P	1.5	OL	AV	F, P	D	
RANUNCULACEAE	5	P	3.0	OL	CM, F	F, P		
CRUCIFERAE	4	P, E	0.5	OL, SL	CM, AV, F	F, P		
ARALIACEAE	4	W	26.0	CL, OL, SL, SG	CM, AV, F	F, P	PA, LF, D, HMS	
CARYOPHYLLACEAE	4	P	0.0	SL, SG	CM	P	10a, b, c, d	
ROSACEAE	4	W	6.5	OL	CM, AV	F		
COMPOSITAE	3	P	3.0	OL, SL	AV, D, F	F	LF, D, HMS	
COMPOSITAE	4	P	1.5	OL, SL	AV, D, F	F	W, PA, LF, D, SS, HMS	
COMPOSITAE	2	P	0.5	SL	AV, D, F	F	W, LF, D, HMS	
COMPOSITAE	5	P	0.0	OL, SL	AV, D, F	F	W, PA, LF, D, SS, HMS	
ARACEAE	6	P, E	1.5	OL	CM, AV	F, P	PA, HMS	
ROSACEAE	4	P	0.5	OL	CM, AV	F, P	PA, D, HMS	
ROSACEAE	3	P	3.0	OL	CM	P		
GRAMINEAE	5	W	1.5	CL, OL	CM, AV, D, F	F, P	W, PA, LF, D, HMS	6
GRAMINEAE	6	P	13.0	OL, SL	AV	F		
ARISTOLOCHIACEAE	5	P, E	0.0	OL	CM, AV	P, S	PA, D, HMS	
ASCLEPIADACEAE	3	P	1.5	CL, OL, SL, SG	AV, F	F	W, PA, LF, D, HMS	
LILIACEAE	5	P	1.5	CL, OL, SL	AV, F	F	PA, D, HMS	
COMPOSITAE	3	P	1.0	OL	AV, D, F	F	D, HMS	4
COMPOSITAE	5	P	3.0	CL, OL, SG	AV, F	P	D	
COMPOSITAE	5	P	3.0	OL	OL	CM	FS	
COMPOSITAE	2	P	3.0	OL, SL	CM	F, P		
COMPOSITAE	3	P	6.5	CL, OL, SL, SG	CM, AV, D, F	F	D, HMS	
COMPOSITAE	5	P	1.5	CL, OL, SL	AV, F	F, P		10f, 11
SAXIFRAGACEAE	4	P	1.5	OL	WE, CM	F, P	PA, HMS	
POLYPODIACEAE	5	P	0.5	OL	CM, AV	P, S	PA, HMS	
COMPOSITAE	4	W	6.5	OL, SL	WE, CM, AV	F	PA, D, HPH, HMS	
LEGUMINOSAE	3	P	3.0	CL, SL, SG	AV, D, F	F	W, LF, D, HMS	

* See "Use of Plant Lists," page 152.
† See page 153.

Master List:
Summary of Cultural Preferences and Tolerances

KEY TO ABBREVIATIONS

ZONE

Plant hardiness zones adapted from U.S.D.A. Plant Hardiness Zone Map, 1990 (page 148).

Range of Average Annual Minimum Temperatures

1	Below −50° F.
2	−50° to −40° F.
3	−40° to −30° F.
4	−30° to −20° F.
5	−20° to −10° F.
6	−10° to 0° F.
7	0° to 10° F.
8	10° to 20° F.
9	20° to 30° F.
10	30° to 40° F.
11	Above 40° F.
T	Tender in the Mid-Atlantic Region

TYPE

W	Woody
P	Perennial
I	Biennial
A	Annual
B	Bulb
E	Evergreen

SOIL COMPOSITION

CL	Clay and Clay Loam
OL	Organic Loam
SL	Sandy Loam
SG	Stony, Gravelly

SOIL MOISTURE

B	Bog or Standing Water
WE	Water's Edge
CM	Consistently Moist, Not Boggy
AV	Average, Dry Between Rains
D	Dry
F	Fast-Draining

LIGHT

F	Full Sun
P	Partial Shade
S	Shade

TOLERANCE

W	Wind
PA	Poor Air Drainage
LF	Low Fertility
D	Drought
SS	Shallow Soil
HPH	High pH
HMS	Hot, Muggy Summers

NAME

BEGONIA GRANDIS
  HARDY BEGONIA
BERBERIS JULIANAE 'NANA'
  WINTERGREEN BARBERRY (COMPACT)
BERBERIS THUNBERGII 'ATROPURPUREA'
  REDLEAF JAPANESE BARBERRY
BERBERIS THUNBERGII 'CRIMSON PYGMY'
  CRIMSON PYGMY BARBERRY
BERBERIS WILSONIAE VAR. STAPFIANA
  WILSON'S BARBERRY
BERBERIS WISLEYENSIS (SYN. B. TRIACANTHOPHORA)
  THREESPINE BARBERRY

BERGENIA 'PERFECTA'
  HYBRID PIGSQUEAK
BERGENIA 'SUNNINGDALE'
  HYBRID PIGSQUEAK
BETULA LENTA
  SWEET BIRCH
BETULA NIGRA
  RIVER BIRCH
BETULA PAPYRIFERA
  PAPER BIRCH
BETULA PENDULA 'GRACILIS'
  CUTLEAF EUROPEAN BIRCH

BETULA PENDULA 'YOUNGII'
  WEEPING EUROPEAN BIRCH
BIGNONIA CAPREOLATA
  CROSS VINE
BOLTONIA ASTEROIDES 'SNOWBANK'

BRUNNERA MACROPHYLLA
  SIBERIAN BUGLOSS
BUDDLEIA ALTERNIFOLIA
  FOUNTAIN BUDDLEIA
BUDDLEIA DAVIDII 'BLACK KNIGHT'
  BUTTERFLY BUSH (DARK PURPLE)

BUDDLEIA DAVIDII 'OPERA'
  BUTTERFLY BUSH (ELECTRIC MAUVE)
BUDDLEIA DAVIDII 'PURPLE PRINCE'
  BUTTERFLY BUSH (LAVENDER)
BUPHTHALUM SALICIFOLIUM
  WILLOWLEAF OXEYE
BUXUS 'GREEN GEM'
  GREEN GEM BOXWOOD
BUXUS MICROPHYLLA 'COMPACTA'
  KINGSVILLE LITTLELEAF BOXWOOD
BUXUS SEMPERVIRENS 'SUFFRUTICOSA'
  DWARF ENGLISH BOXWOOD

BUXUS SINICA VAR. INSULARIS 'TIDE HILL'
  TIDE HILL KOREAN BOXWOOD
BUXUS SINICA VAR. INSULARIS
    'WINTERGREEN' (OHIO CULTIVAR)
  WINTERGREEN KOREAN BOXWOOD
CALAMAGROSTIS X ACUTIFLORA 'KARL FOERSTER'
    (SYN. C. EPIGEOUS 'HORTORUM')
  FEATHER-REED GRASS
CALLICARPA DICHOTOMA
  CHINESE BEAUTYBERRY
CALLICARPA JAPONICA
  JAPANESE BEAUTYBERRY

FAMILY	ZONE*	TYPE	SIZE (FEET)	SOIL COMPOSITION	SOIL MOISTURE	LIGHT	TOLERANCE	NOTES†
BEGONIACEAE	6	P	1.5	OL	CM, AV	P, S	PA	
BERBERIDACEAE	6	W, E	3.0	OL	AV	F, P		
BERBERIDACEAE	4	W	3.0	OL	AV	F	W, LF, D, HPH	
BERBERIDACEAE	4	W	1.5	CL, OL, SL, SG	AV, D, F	F	PA, LF, D, HMS	
BERBERIDACEAE	7	W	3.0	CL, OL, SL	AV	F		
BERBERIDACEAE	6	W, E	3.0	OL	AV	F		
SAXIFRAGACEAE	2	P, E	1.0	CL, OL, SL, SG	CM, AV	P	HPH	19
SAXIFRAGACEAE	2	P, E	1.0	CL, OL, SL, SG	CM, AV	P	HPH	19
BETULACEAE	4	W	26.0	OL, SL	WE, CM, AV, D, F	F	PA, HMS	
BETULACEAE	4	W	52.0	OL, SL	WE, CM, AV, D, F	F	PA, HMS	
BETULACEAE	2	W	52.0	OL	WE, CM, AV	F		
BETULACEAE	3	W	26.0	OL	WE, CM, AV	F, P		
BETULACEAE	3	W	13.0	OL	WE, CM, AV	F, P		
BIGNONIACEAE	6	W, E	52.0	OL	AV, D	F	PA, D, HMS	
COMPOSITAE	3	P	3.0	OL	CM, AV	F		
BORAGINACEAE	3	P	1.0	OL	CM, AV, D	P	PA, HMS	
LOGANIACEAE	4	W	6.5	OL	AV	F	LF	
LOGANIACEAE	5	W	3.0	CL, OL, SG	AV, D, F	F	PA, D, HMS	6
LOGANIACEAE	5	W	3.0	CL, OL, SG	AV, D, F	F	PA, D, HMS	6
LOGANIACEAE	5	W	3.0	CL, OL, SG	AV, D, F	F	PA, D, HMS	6
COMPOSITAE	3	P	1.5	CL, OL, SL	WE, CM	F, P	LF, HPH	
BUXACEAE	5	W, E	1.5	OL	AV, FD	F, P		
BUXACEAE	7	W, E	0.5	OL	AV, FD	F, P		
BUXACEAE	6	W, E	3.0	OL	CM, AV, F	F, P		
BUXACEAE	5	W, E	1.0	CL, OL, SL	AV, D, F	F, P		
BUXACEAE	5	W, E	1.5	OL, SL	AV	F, P		
GRAMINEAE	5	P	3.0	CL, OL	CM, AV	F	W, PA, HMS	
VERBENACEAE	6	W	3.0	CL, OL, SL, SG	AV, D, F	F	PA, D, HMS	6
VERBENACEAE	5	W	6.5	CL, OL, SL	CM, AV	F		6

* See "Use of Plant Lists," page 152.
† See page 153.

Master List:
Summary of Cultural Preferences and Tolerances

KEY TO ABBREVIATIONS

ZONE

Plant hardiness zones adapted from U.S.D.A. Plant Hardiness Zone Map, 1990 (page 148).

Range of Average Annual Minimum Temperatures

1	Below −50° F.
2	−50° to −40° F.
3	−40° to −30° F.
4	−30° to −20° F.
5	−20° to −10° F.
6	−10° to 0° F.
7	0° to 10° F.
8	10° to 20° F.
9	20° to 30° F.
10	30° to 40° F.
11	Above 40° F.
T	Tender in the Mid-Atlantic Region

TYPE

W	Woody
P	Perennial
I	Biennial
A	Annual
B	Bulb
E	Evergreen

SOIL COMPOSITION

CL	Clay and Clay Loam
OL	Organic Loam
SL	Sandy Loam
SG	Stony, Gravelly

SOIL MOISTURE

B	Bog or Standing Water
WE	Water's Edge
CM	Consistently Moist, Not Boggy
AV	Average, Dry Between Rains
D	Dry
F	Fast-Draining

LIGHT

F	Full Sun
P	Partial Shade
S	Shade

TOLERANCE

W	Wind
PA	Poor Air Drainage
LF	Low Fertility
D	Drought
SS	Shallow Soil
HPH	High pH
HMS	Hot, Muggy Summers

NAME

CALOCEDRUS DECURRENS
  INCENSE-CEDAR
CALYCANTHUS FLORIDUS 'EDITH WILDER'
  SWEET SHRUB
CAMPANULA RAPUNCULOIDES
  CREEPING BELLFLOWER
CAMPSIS X TAGLIABUANA 'MADAME GALEN'
  MADAME GALEN TRUMPET VINE
CANNA X GENERALIS 'MOHAWK'

CARPINUS BETULUS
  EUROPEAN HORNBEAM

CARYA OVATA
  SHAGBARK HICKORY
CARYOPTERIS X CLANDONENSIS 'BLUE MIST'
  BLUEBEARD
CATALPA BIGNONIOIDES
  SOUTHERN CATALPA
CEDRUS ATLANTICA 'GLAUCA'
  BLUE ATLAS CEDAR
CEDRUS LIBANI VAR. STENOCOMA
  CEDAR-OF-LEBANON
CEPHALANTHUS OCCIDENTALIS
  BUTTONBUSH

CEPHALOTAXUS HARRINGTONIA VAR. PEDUNCULATA
  PLUM YEW (SPREADING)
CERATOSTIGMA PLUMBAGINOIDES
  PLUMBAGO
CERCIDIPHYLLUM JAPONICUM
  KATSURA TREE
CERCIS CANADENSIS 'FOREST PANSY'
  FOREST PANSY REDBUD
CERCIS CHINENSIS
  CHINESE REDBUD
CESTRUM NOCTURNUM
  NIGHT JESSAMINE

CHAENOMELES JAPONICA VAR. ALPINA
  ALPINE JAPANESE FLOWERING QUINCE
CHAENOMELES SPECIOSA CULTIVARS
  FLOWERING QUINCE
CHAENOMELES X SUPERBA 'JET TRAIL'
  HYBRID FLOWERING QUINCE (SPREADING, WHITE-FLOWERED)
CHAENOMELES X SUPERBA CULTIVARS
  HYBRID FLOWERING QUINCE
CHAMAECYPARIS OBTUSA 'CRIPPSII'
  CRIPPS HINOKI FALSE CYPRESS (GOLD-PLUMED)
CHAMAECYPARIS OBTUSA 'FILICOIDES'
  FERNSPRAY HINOKI FALSE CYPRESS

CHAMAECYPARIS OBTUSA 'NANA GRACILIS'
  HINOKI FALSE CYPRESS (SEMI-DWARF)
CHAMAECYPARIS OBTUSA 'NANA'
  DWARF HINOKI FALSE CYPRESS
CHAMAECYPARIS OBTUSA VAR. BREVIRAMEA
  HINOKI FALSE CYPRESS (VERTICAL)
CHAMAECYPARIS PISIFERA 'GOLD SPANGLE'
  SAWARA FALSE CYPRESS
CHAMAECYPARIS PISIFERA 'SQUARROSA'
  MOSS SAWARA FALSE CYPRESS
CHAMAEMELUM NOBILE
  CHAMOMILE

FAMILY	ZONE*	TYPE	SIZE (FEET)	SOIL COMPOSITION	SOIL MOISTURE	LIGHT	TOLERANCE	NOTES†
CUPRESSACEAE	6	W, E	26.0	OL	CM, AV, F	F		
CALYCANTHACEAE	5	W	6.5	OL, SL	AV	F, P		
CAMPANULACEAE	3	P	1.5	OL, SL	CM	P		
BIGNONIACEAE	5	W	6.5	CL, OL, SL	AV, D, F	F	PA, D, HPH, HMS	
CANNACEAE	T	A	3.0	OL	CM, AV	F	PA, HMS	2
BETULACEAE	5	W	26.0	OL	AV	F		
JUGLANDACEAE	4	W	52.0	OL	AV, D, F	F	W, PA, D, HPH, HMS	
VERBENACEAE	4	W	1.5	OL, SL, SG	AV, F	F	W, HPH	6
BIGNONIACEAE	5	W	26.0	CL, OL, SL	CM, AV, D, F	F	W, PA, LF, D, HPH, HMS	
PINACEAE	7	W, E	52.0	OL	CM, AV	F		
PINACEAE	5	W, E	52.0	OL	AV	F	W, PA, HMS	
RUBIACEAE	4	W	13.0	OL	WE, CM	F, P	W, HPH	
CEPHALOTAXACEAE	5	W, E	3.0	OL, SL	CM, AV, F	P		
PLUMBAGINACEAE	6	P	0.5	OL, SL	AV, F	F, P	W, PA, D, HMS	
CERIDIPHYLLACEAE	5	W	26.0	OL	CM	F	HPH	
LEGUMINOSAE	5	W	13.0	OL, SG	AV, D, F	F	W, LF, HPH	21
LEGUMINOSAE	6	W	26.0	OL	F	F	HPH	
SOLANACEAE	T	W	3.0	OL	AV	F, P	PA, HMS	5
ROSACEAE	4	W	1.5	CL, OL, SG	AV, D, F	F	W, D	
ROSACEAE	4	W	3.0	CL, OL, SL	AV, D, F	F		
ROSACEAE	4	W	1.5	CL, OL, SG	AV, D, F	F	W, D	
ROSACEAE	5	W	3.0	CL, OL, SG	AV, D, F	F	W, D	
CUPRESSACEAE	6	W, E	13.0	OL	AV	F, P		
CUPRESSACEAE	5	W, E	6.5	OL, SL	AV	F		
CUPRESSACEAE	5	W, E	6.5	OL, SL	AV	F	PA, HMS	
CUPRESSACEAE	5	W, E	1.5	OL	AV	F		
CUPRESSACEAE	5	W, E	13.0	OL	AV	F		
CUPRESSACEAE	5	W, E	6.5	OL	AV	F		
CUPRESSACEAE	5	W, E	52.0	OL	CM	F		
COMPOSITAE	4	P	0.0	OL	AV, F	F	D	

* See "Use of Plant Lists," page 152.
† See page 153.

Master List:
Summary of Cultural Preferences and Tolerances

KEY TO ABBREVIATIONS

ZONE

Plant hardiness zones adapted from U.S.D.A. Plant Hardiness Zone Map, 1990 (page 148).

Range of Average Annual Minimum Temperatures

1	Below −50° F.
2	−50° to −40° F.
3	−40° to −30° F.
4	−30° to −20° F.
5	−20° to −10° F.
6	−10° to 0° F.
7	0° to 10° F.
8	10° to 20° F.
9	20° to 30° F.
10	30° to 40° F.
11	Above 40° F.
T	Tender in the Mid-Atlantic Region

TYPE

W	Woody
P	Perennial
I	Biennial
A	Annual
B	Bulb
E	Evergreen

SOIL COMPOSITION

CL	Clay and Clay Loam
OL	Organic Loam
SL	Sandy Loam
SG	Stony, Gravelly

SOIL MOISTURE

B	Bog or Standing Water
WE	Water's Edge
CM	Consistently Moist, Not Boggy
AV	Average, Dry Between Rains
D	Dry
F	Fast-Draining

LIGHT

F	Full Sun
P	Partial Shade
S	Shade

TOLERANCE

W	Wind
PA	Poor Air Drainage
LF	Low Fertility
D	Drought
SS	Shallow Soil
HPH	High pH
HMS	Hot, Muggy Summers

NAME

CHELONE LYONII
    TURTLEHEAD
CHIMONANTHUS PRAECOX
    WINTERSWEET
CHIONANTHUS VIRGINICUS
    FRINGE TREE
CHIONODOXA GIGANTEA 'ALBA'
    GLORY-OF-THE-SNOW (WHITE)
CHIONODOXA LUCILIAE
    GLORY-OF-THE-SNOW (BLUE)
CHIONODOXA SARDENSIS
    GLORY-OF-THE-SNOW (BLUE)

CHRYSANTHEMUM WEYRICHII 'WHITE BOMB'

CIMICIFUGA RACEMOSA
    BLACK SNAKEROOT
CLADRASTIS LUTEA
    AMERICAN YELLOWWOOD
CLEMATIS 'MRS. CHOLMONDELEY'

CLEMATIS 'PRINS HENDRIK'

CLEMATIS 'RAMONA'

CLEMATIS HERACLEIFOLIA VAR. DAVIDIANA
    TUBE CLEMATIS
CLEMATIS MAXIMOWICZIANA
    SWEET AUTUMN CLEMATIS
CLEMATIS X JACKMANII

CLERODENDRUM TRICHOTOMUM
    HARLEQUIN GLORY BOWER
CLETHRA ALNIFOLIA
    SWEET PEPPERBUSH
CLETHRA BARBINERVIS
    JAPANESE CLETHRA

COLCHICUM 'AUTUMN QUEEN'
    AUTUMN-CROCUS
COLCHICUM 'THE GIANT'
    AUTUMN-CROCUS
COLUTEA X MEDIA
    BLADDER SENNA (HYBRID)
COMPTONIA PEREGRINA
    SWEET-FERN
CONVALLARIA MAJALIS
    LILY-OF-THE-VALLEY
COREOPSIS 'MOONBEAM'

CORNUS ALBA 'ELEGANTISSIMA'
    TARTARIAN DOGWOOD (WHITE VARIEGATED)
CORNUS ALBA 'SPAETHII'
    TARTARIAN DOGWOOD (YELLOW VARIEGATED)
CORNUS ALTERNIFOLIA
    PAGODA DOGWOOD
CORNUS FLORIDA
    FLOWERING DOGWOOD
CORNUS FLORIDA 'HOHMAN'S GOLDEN'
    FLOWERING DOGWOOD (YELLOW VARIEGATED)
CORNUS KOUSA
    KOREAN DOGWOOD

FAMILY	ZONE*	TYPE	SIZE (FEET)	SOIL COMPOSITION	SOIL MOISTURE	LIGHT	TOLERANCE	NOTES†
SCROPHULARIACEAE	3	P	1.5	OL, SL	B, WE, CM	F, P	HPH	
CALYCANTHACEAE	7	W	6.5	OL, SL	CM, AV, D, F	F, P	PA, HMS	
OLEACEAE	5	W	13.0	OL	WE, CM, AV, F	F	PA, HPH, HMS	
LILIACEAE	5	B	0.5	OL, SL	AV	P	PA, HMS	
LILIACEAE	5	B	0.5	OL, SL	AV	P	PA, HMS	
LILIACEAE	5	B	0.5	OL, SL	AV	P	PA, HMS	
COMPOSITAE	5	P	0.5	OL	AV	F		
RANUNCULACEAE	3	P	6.5	OL	CM, AV	P, S		
LEGUMINOSAE	4	W	26.0	OL	AV, D, F	F	HPH	
RANUNCULACEAE	4	W	6.5	OL	CM, AV, F	F, P	HPH	
RANUNCULACEAE	4	W	6.5	OL	CM, AV, F	F, P	HPH	
RANUNCULACEAE	4	W	6.5	OL	CM, AV, F	F, P	HPH	
RANUNCULACEAE	3	P	3.0	OL	CM	P		
RANUNCULACEAE	4	W	6.5	OL	F	F	HPH	
RANUNCULACEAE	4	W	6.5	OL	CM, AV, F	F, P	HPH	
VERBENACEAE	7	W	13.0	OL	CM, AV	F		
CLETHRACEAE	5	W	6.5	CL, OL	B, WE, CM, AV	F	PA, LF, HMS	
CLETHRACEAE	6	W	6.5	OL	WE, CM, AV	F	PA, HMS	
LILIACEAE	5	B	0.5	OL, SL	CM, AV	F, P	PA, HMS	
LILIACEAE	5	B	0.5	OL, SL	CM, AV	F, P	PA, HMS	
LEGUMINOSAE	5	W	6.5	CL, OL, SL	AV, D, F	F	W, PA, LF, D, HMS	
MYRICACEAE	4	W	3.0	OL, SL	AV, D, F	F	LF, D	
LILIACEAE	4	P	0.5	OL	CM, AV	P, S		
COMPOSITAE	3	P	1.0	OL, SL	AV, D, F	F	W, PA, LF, D, HMS	
CORNACEAE	3	W	3.0	OL	CM, AV	F, P		
CORNACEAE	3	W	3.0	OL	CM, AV	F, P		
CORNACEAE	4	W	13.0	OL	CM, AV	F, P		
CORNACEAE	5	W	13.0	OL	AV, F	F, P	W, PA, HMS	
CORNACEAE	5	W	13.0	OL	AV, F	F, P	W, PA, HMS	
CORNACEAE	5	W	13.0	OL	CM, AV, F	F		

* See "Use of Plant Lists," page 152.
† See page 153.

Master List:
Summary of Cultural Preferences and Tolerances

KEY TO ABBREVIATIONS

ZONE

Plant hardiness zones adapted from U.S.D.A. Plant Hardiness Zone Map, 1990 (page 148).

Range of Average Annual Minimum Temperatures

1	Below −50° F.
2	−50° to −40° F.
3	−40° to −30° F.
4	−30° to −20° F.
5	−20° to −10° F.
6	−10° to 0° F.
7	0° to 10° F.
8	10° to 20° F.
9	20° to 30° F.
10	30° to 40° F.
11	Above 40° F.
T	Tender in the Mid-Atlantic Region

TYPE

W	Woody
P	Perennial
I	Biennial
A	Annual
B	Bulb
E	Evergreen

SOIL COMPOSITION

CL	Clay and Clay Loam
OL	Organic Loam
SL	Sandy Loam
SG	Stony, Gravelly

SOIL MOISTURE

B	Bog or Standing Water
WE	Water's Edge
CM	Consistently Moist, Not Boggy
AV	Average, Dry Between Rains
D	Dry
F	Fast-Draining

LIGHT

F	Full Sun
P	Partial Shade
S	Shade

TOLERANCE

W	Wind
PA	Poor Air Drainage
LF	Low Fertility
D	Drought
SS	Shallow Soil
HPH	High pH
HMS	Hot, Muggy Summers

NAME

CORNUS MAS
  CORNELIAN-CHERRY
CORNUS OFFICINALIS
  JAPANESE CORNELIAN-CHERRY
CORNUS RACEMOSA
  GRAY DOGWOOD
CORNUS RACEMOSA (DWARF)
  DWARF GRAY DOGWOOD
CORNUS SERICEA
  RED-TWIG DOGWOOD
CORNUS SERICEA 'FLAVIRAMEA'
  YELLOW-TWIG DOGWOOD

CORYLOPSIS PLATYPETALA
  WINTER HAZEL
CORYLUS AVELLANA 'CONTORTA'
  HARRY LAUDER'S WALKING STICK
CORYLUS AVELLANA 'PENDULA'
  WEEPING EUROPEAN FILBERT
CORYLUS COLURNA
  TURKISH FILBERT
COTINUS COGGYGRIA 'PURPUREUS'
  PURPLELEAF SMOKE BUSH
COTONEASTER ADPRESSUS 'LITTLE GEM'
  CREEPING COTONEASTER (DWARF)

COTONEASTER ADPRESSUS VAR. PRAECOX
  CREEPING COTONEASTER
COTONEASTER APICULATUS
  CRANBERRY COTONEASTER
COTONEASTER HORIZONTALIS
  ROCKSPRAY COTONEASTER
COTONEASTER SALICIFOLIUS VAR. FLOCCOSUS
  WILLOWLEAF COTONEASTER
COTULA SQUALIDA
  NEW ZEALAND BRASS-BUTTONS
CRAMBE CORDIFOLIA
  COLEWORT

CRATAEGUS NITIDA
  GLOSSY HAWTHORN
CRATAEGUS PHAENOPYRUM
  WASHINGTON HAWTHORN
CRATAEGUS VIRIDIS 'WINTER KING'
  WINTER KING HAWTHORN
CROCOSMIA 'LUCIFER'

CROCOSMIA POTTSII

CROCOSMIA X CROCOSMIIFLORA

CROCUS ANCYRENSIS 'GOLDEN BUNCH'

CROCUS SIEBERI

CROCUS TOMASINIANUS

CRUCIANELLA STYLOSA
  CROSSWORT
CYCLAMEN HEDERIFOLIUM
  BABY CYCLAMEN
CYTISUS SCOPARIUS
  SCOTCH BROOM

FAMILY	ZONE*	TYPE	SIZE (FEET)	SOIL COMPOSITION	SOIL MOISTURE	LIGHT	TOLERANCE	NOTES†
CORNACEAE	5	W	13.0	CL, OL	AV, F	F, P	W, PA, D, HMS	
CORNACEAE	5	W	13.0	CL, OL	AV, F	F, P	W, PA, D, HPH, HMS	
CORNACEAE	3	W	6.5	OL, SG	WE, CM, AV, D, F	F, P	W, PA, D, SS, HPH, HMS	
CORNACEAE	3	W	1.0	OL, SG	WE, CM, AV, F	F, P	W, PA, D, SS, HPH, HMS	
CORNACEAE	3	W	3.0	OL	WE, CM, AV	F	W, PA, HMS	14a
CORNACEAE	3	W	3.0	OL	WE, CM, AV	F	W, PA, HMS	14a
HAMAMELIDACEAE	5	W	6.5	OL	AV	F, P		
BETULACEAE	4	W	3.0	CL, OL	AV, D, F	F	PA, LF, D, HMS	
BETULACEAE	4	W	6.5	CL, OL	AV, D, F	F	PA, LF, D, HMS	
BETULACEAE	5	W	26.0	OL	AV, D, F	F	D, HPH	
ANACARDIACEAE	5	W	6.5	OL, SL, SG	AV, D, F	F	PA, LF, D, HMS	14b
ROSACEAE	5	W	0.0	OL	AV, D, F	F	D	
ROSACEAE	6	W	1.5	OL	AV, D, F	F	W, PA, D, HMS	
ROSACEAE	5	W	1.5	OL	AV, D, F	F		
ROSACEAE	5	W	1.5	OL, SG	AV, D, F	F		
ROSACEAE	6	W, E	13.0	OL	CM, AV	F		
COMPOSITAE	8	P	0.0	OL	CM, AV	F, P		
CRUCIFERAE	5	P	3.0	CL, OL	AV	F, P	PA, D, HMS	
ROSACEAE	4	W	13.0	CL, OL, SG	AV, D, F	F	W, PA, LF, D, HPH, HMS	
ROSACEAE	4	W	13.0	CL, OL, SG	AV, D, F	F	W, PA, LF, D, HPH, HMS	
ROSACEAE	5	W	13.0	CL, OL, SG	CM, AV, D, F	F	W, PA, LF, D, HPH, HMS	
IRIDACEAE	6	B	1.5	OL, SL	AV, FD	F	PA, HMS	
IRIDACEAE	6	B	1.0	OL, SL	AV, FD	F	PA, HMS	
IRIDACEAE	6	B	1.5	OL, SL	AV, FD	F	PA, HMS	
IRIDACEAE	5	B	0.0	OL, SL, SG	AV, FD	F, P	PA, HMS	
IRIDACEAE	5	B	0.0	OL, SL, SG	AV, FD	F, P	PA, HMS	
IRIDACEAE	5	B	0.0	OL, SL, SG	AV, FD	F, P	PA, HMS	
RUBIACEAE	6	P	1.5	OL	AV, F	F, P		
PRIMULACEAE	5	B	0.0	OL	CM, AV	P		
LEGUMINOSAE	6	W	3.0	CL, OL, SL, SG	AV, F	F	W, PA, D, HMS	4

* See "Use of Plant Lists," page 152.
† See page 153.

Master List:
Summary of Cultural Preferences and Tolerances

KEY TO ABBREVIATIONS

ZONE

Plant hardiness zones adapted from U.S.D.A. Plant Hardiness Zone Map, 1990 (page 148).

Range of Average Annual Minimum Temperatures

1	Below −50° F.
2	−50° to −40° F.
3	−40° to −30° F.
4	−30° to −20° F.
5	−20° to −10° F.
6	−10° to 0° F.
7	0° to 10° F.
8	10° to 20° F.
9	20° to 30° F.
10	30° to 40° F.
11	Above 40° F.
T	Tender in the Mid-Atlantic Region

TYPE

W	Woody
P	Perennial
I	Biennial
A	Annual
B	Bulb
E	Evergreen

SOIL COMPOSITION

CL	Clay and Clay Loam
OL	Organic Loam
SL	Sandy Loam
SG	Stony, Gravelly

SOIL MOISTURE

B	Bog or Standing Water
WE	Water's Edge
CM	Consistently Moist, Not Boggy
AV	Average, Dry Between Rains
D	Dry
F	Fast-Draining

LIGHT

F	Full Sun
P	Partial Shade
S	Shade

TOLERANCE

W	Wind
PA	Poor Air Drainage
LF	Low Fertility
D	Drought
SS	Shallow Soil
HPH	High pH
HMS	Hot, Muggy Summers

NAME

CYTISUS X PRAECOX 'LUTEUS'
  WARMINSTER BROOM
DAPHNE CAUCASICA

DAPHNE X BURKWOODII 'CAROL MACKIE'

DATURA INOXIA SUBSP. QUINQUECUSPIDA
  ANGEL'S-TRUMPET
DENNSTAEDTIA PUNCTILOBULA
  HAY-SCENTED FERN
DEUTZIA GRACILIS
  SLENDER DEUTZIA

DIANTHUS DELTOIDES
  MAIDEN PINK
DICENTRA 'LUXURIANT'
  BLEEDING-HEART (HYBRID)
DICENTRA EXIMIA 'PURITY'
  WILD BLEEDING-HEART (WHITE)
DICENTRA SPECTABILIS
  BLEEDING-HEART
DIERVILLA SESSILIFOLIA
  SOUTHERN BUSH-HONEYSUCKLE
DIOSPYROS KAKI
  ORIENTAL PERSIMMON

DIOSPYROS VIRGINIANA
  PERSIMMON
DIPLAZIUM CONILII

ECHINACEA PURPUREA
  PURPLE CONEFLOWER
ECHINOPS RITRO
  GLOBE THISTLE
ELAEAGNUS PUNGENS 'FRUITLANDII'
  FRAGRANT ELAEAGNUS
ELAEAGNUS PUNGENS 'MACULATA'
  ELAEAGNUS (YELLOW VARIEGATED)

ENDYMION HISPANICUS 'EXCELSIOR'
    (SYN. SCILLA CAMPANULATA 'EXCELSIOR')
  SPANISH BLUEBELL
ENKIANTHUS CAMPANULATUS
  REDVEIN ENKIANTHUS
ENKIANTHUS PERULATUS
  WHITE ENKIANTHUS
EPIMEDIUM PINNATUM SUBSP. COLCHICUM

EPIMEDIUM X YOUNGIANUM 'NIVEUM'

EQUISETUM HYEMALE
  SCOURING RUSH
ERANTHIS HYEMALIS
  WINTER ACONITE
ERANTHIS X TUBERGENII
  WINTER ACONITE (HYBRID)
ERIANTHUS RAVENNAE
  RAVENNA GRASS
EUONYMUS ALATA
  WINGED EUONYMUS, BURNING BUSH
EUONYMUS FORTUNEI 'COLORATA'
  PURPLELEAF WINTERCREEPER

FAMILY	ZONE*	TYPE	SIZE (FEET)	SOIL COMPOSITION	SOIL MOISTURE	LIGHT	TOLERANCE	NOTES†
LEGUMINOSAE	6	W	3.0	CL, OL	AV, F	F		4
THYMELAEACEAE	5	W	3.0	OL	AV, D, F	F, P	PA	
THYMELAEACEAE	5	W	3.0	OL, SL	AV, F	F	LF	
SOLANACEAE	T	A	3.0	OL, SL	AV, F	F	PA, HMS	1
POLYPODIACEAE	3	P	1.5	CL, OL, SL	CM, AV, F	F, P, S		
SAXIFRAGACEAE	5	W	1.5	OL	AV	F, P	PA, HMS	
CARYOPHYLLACEAE	3	P	0.0	SL	AV, F	F	HPH	
FUMARIACEAE	3	P	1.0	OL	CM, AV	P	PA, D, HMS	
FUMARIACEAE	3	P	1.0	OL	CM, AV	P, S	PA	
FUMARIACEAE	2	P	1.5	OL	AV	P, S		
CAPRIFOLIACEAE	4	W	3.0	CL, OL, SL	AV, F	F	W, D, HPH	
EBENACEAE	7	W	13.0	OL	AV	F	HPH	
EBENACEAE	5	W	26.0	CL, OL	AV, D	F	D, HPH	
POLYPODIACEAE	5	P	1.0	OL	AV	P, S		
COMPOSITAE	3	P	1.5	CL, OL, SL	AV	F, P	D, HMS	
COMPOSITAE	3	P	3.0	OL	CM, AV	F		
ELAEAGNACEAE	7	W, E	13.0	OL	AV, D	F	W, PA, D, HPH, HMS	
ELAEAGNACEAE	7	W, E	6.5	OL	AV, D	F	W, PA, D, HPH, HMS	
LILIACEAE	5	B	0.5	OL	CM, AV	P	PA, HMS	
ERICACEAE	5	W	6.5	OL	WE, CM, AV	F, P		
ERICACEAE	6	W	3.0	OL	WE, CM, AV	F, P		
BERBERIDACEAE	5	P	0.5	OL	CM, AV, D	P, S	PA, LF, D, HMS	
BERBERIDACEAE	5	P	0.5	OL	CM, AV, D	P, S	PA, LF, D, HMS	
EQUISITACEAE	5	P	1.5	OL, SL, SG	B, WE, CM, AV	F		8
RANUNCULACEAE	5	B	0.0	OL, SL	CM, AV	P	PA, HPH, HMS	
RANUNCULACEAE	5	B	0.0	OL, SL	CM, AV	P	PA, HPH, HMS	
GRAMINEAE	5	P	6.5	CL, OL	AV	F		
CELASTRACEAE	4	W	6.5	CL, OL	AV, D, F	F, P	W, PA, LF, D, SS, HMS	
CELASTRACEAE	4	W, E	0.5	CL, OL	AV, D, F	F		

* See "Use of Plant Lists," page 152.
† See page 153.

Master List:
Summary of Cultural Preferences and Tolerances

KEY TO ABBREVIATIONS

ZONE

Plant hardiness zones adapted from U.S.D.A. Plant Hardiness Zone Map, 1990 (page 148).

Range of Average Annual Minimum Temperatures

1	Below −50° F.
2	−50° to −40° F.
3	−40° to −30° F.
4	−30° to −20° F.
5	−20° to −10° F.
6	−10° to 0° F.
7	0° to 10° F.
8	10° to 20° F.
9	20° to 30° F.
10	30° to 40° F.
11	Above 40° F.
T	Tender in the Mid-Atlantic Region

TYPE

W	Woody
P	Perennial
I	Biennial
A	Annual
B	Bulb
E	Evergreen

SOIL COMPOSITION

CL	Clay and Clay Loam
OL	Organic Loam
SL	Sandy Loam
SG	Stony, Gravelly

SOIL MOISTURE

B	Bog or Standing Water
WE	Water's Edge
CM	Consistently Moist, Not Boggy
AV	Average, Dry Between Rains
D	Dry
F	Fast-Draining

LIGHT

F	Full Sun
P	Partial Shade
S	Shade

TOLERANCE

W	Wind
PA	Poor Air Drainage
LF	Low Fertility
D	Drought
SS	Shallow Soil
HPH	High pH
HMS	Hot, Muggy Summers

NAME

EUONYMUS FORTUNEI 'GRACILIS'
  WINTERCREEPER (WHITE VARIEGATED)
EUONYMUS FORTUNEI 'MINIMA'
  LITTLELEAF WINTERCREEPER
EUONYMUS FORTUNEI 'SILVER QUEEN'
  SILVER QUEEN WINTERCREEPER
EUONYMUS FORTUNEI VAR. RADICANS
  WINTERCREEPER (SPREADING)
EUPATORIUM COELESTINUM
  HARDY AGERATUM
EUPHORBIA COROLLATA
  FLOWERING SPURGE

EUPHORBIA CYPARISSIAS
  CYPRESS SPURGE
EUPHORBIA EPITHYMOIDES
  CUSHION SPURGE
EXOCHORDA GIRALDII VAR. WILSONII
  WILSON PEARLBUSH
FAGUS GRANDIFOLIA
  AMERICAN BEECH
FAGUS SYLVATICA 'LACINIATA'
  CUTLEAF EUROPEAN BEECH
FAGUS SYLVATICA 'PENDULA'
  WEEPING EUROPEAN BEECH

FAGUS SYLVATICA 'RIVERSII'
  RIVERS EUROPEAN BEECH (PURPLELEAF)
FILIPENDULA PURPUREA 'ELEGANS'
  SHOWY JAPANESE MEADOWSWEET
FILIPENDULA PURPUREA 'NANA'
  DWARF JAPANESE MEADOWSWEET
FILIPENDULA ULMARIA 'AUREA'
  GOLDEN QUEEN OF THE MEADOW
FORSYTHIA SUSPENSA
  WEEPING FORSYTHIA
FORSYTHIA VIRIDISSIMA 'BRONXENSIS'
  DWARF GREENSTEM FORSYTHIA

FORSYTHIA X INTERMEDIA 'SPRING GLORY'
  SPRING GLORY FORSYTHIA
FOTHERGILLA GARDENII
  DWARF FOTHERGILLA
FRANKLINIA ALATAMAHA
  FRANKLIN TREE
GALANTHUS ELWESII
  GIANT SNOWDROP
GALANTHUS NIVALIS
  COMMON SNOWDROP
GALIUM ODORATUM
  SWEET WOODRUFF

GALTONIA CANDICANS
  SUMMER-HYACINTH
GAULTHERIA PROCUMBENS
  WINTERGREEN
GENISTA SYLVESTRIS 'LYDIA'
  SPREADING BROOM
GERANIUM 'JOHNSON'S BLUE'
  HYBRID CRANESBILL (BLUE)
GERANIUM MACRORRHIZUM
  BIGROOT CRANESBILL
GERANIUM SANGUINEUM
  BLOODY CRANESBILL

FAMILY	ZONE*	TYPE	SIZE (FEET)	SOIL COMPOSITION	SOIL MOISTURE	LIGHT	TOLERANCE	NOTES†
CELASTRACEAE	5	W, E	0.5	CL, OL	AV, D, F	F, P		
CELASTRACEAE	5	W, E	0.0	CL, OL	AV, D, F	F		
CELASTRACEAE	6	W	1.5	CL, OL, SG	AV, D, F	F, P	D	
CELASTRACEAE	4	W, E	0.5	OL	AV	F	HPH	
COMPOSITAE	6	P	1.0	CL, OL	CM, AV, D, F	F, P	W, PA, D, HMS	
EUPHORBIACEAE	3	P	1.5	CL, OL, SL, SG	D, F	F, P	PA, LF, D, HMS	
EUPHORBIACEAE	4	P	0.5	CL, SG	AV, D, F	F	LF, D	8
EUPHORBIACEAE	4	P	1.0	SL, SG	D, F		LF	
ROSACEAE	5	W	6.5	OL	AV	F		
FAGACEAE	4	W	52.0	OL	CM, F	F		
FAGACEAE	5	W	52.0	OL	CM, F	F		
FAGACEAE	5	W	52.0	OL	CM, AV	F		
FAGACEAE	5	W	52.0	OL	CM, AV	F		
ROSACEAE	6	P	3.0	OL	WE, CM	P		
ROSACEAE	5	P	1.0	OL	WE, CM, AV	F, P		
ROSACEAE	3	P	0.5	OL	WE, CM	P, S		
OLEACEAE	5	W	6.5	CL, OL	AV, D, F	F	W, PA, LF, D, HMS	
OLEACEAE	6	W	1.0	CL, OL	AV, D, F	F		
OLEACEAE	6	W	6.5	CL, OL, SL	AV, D, F	F	PA, LF, D, HMS	
HAMAMELIDACEAE	5	W	3.0	OL	CM, AV	F, P	PA, HMS	
THEACEAE	6	W	13.0	OL, SL	CM, AV	F		
AMARYLLIDACEAE	5	B	0.0	CL, OL	AV	F	PA, HPH, HMS	
AMARYLLIDACEAE	5	B	0.0	CL, OL	AV	P	PA, HPH, HMS	
RUBIACEAE	5	P	0.5	OL	CM, F	F, P, S		
LILIACEAE	6	B	1.5	OL	CM, AV, FD	F	PA, HMS	
ERICACEAE	4	W	0.0	OL, SL	WE, CM, F	P, S		10b
LEGUMINOSAE	7	W	1.5	OL, SL, SG	AV, D, F	F	D, HMS	
GERANIACEAE	3	P	1.0	OL	CM, AV	P	PA, HMS	
GERANIACEAE	3	P	1.0	CL, OL	CM, AV, D, F	P, S	PA, HMS	
GERANIACEAE	3	P	0.5	OL	CM, AV, F	F, P	HPH	

* See "Use of Plant Lists," page 152.
† See page 153.

Master List:
Summary of Cultural Preferences and Tolerances

KEY TO ABBREVIATIONS

ZONE

Plant hardiness zones adapted from U.S.D.A. Plant Hardiness Zone Map, 1990 (page 148).

Range of Average Annual Minimum Temperatures

1	Below −50° F.
2	−50° to −40° F.
3	−40° to −30° F.
4	−30° to −20° F.
5	−20° to −10° F.
6	−10° to 0° F.
7	0° to 10° F.
8	10° to 20° F.
9	20° to 30° F.
10	30° to 40° F.
11	Above 40° F.
T	Tender in the Mid-Atlantic Region

TYPE

W	Woody
P	Perennial
I	Biennial
A	Annual
B	Bulb
E	Evergreen

SOIL COMPOSITION

CL	Clay and Clay Loam
OL	Organic Loam
SL	Sandy Loam
SG	Stony, Gravelly

SOIL MOISTURE

B	Bog or Standing Water
WE	Water's Edge
CM	Consistently Moist, Not Boggy
AV	Average, Dry Between Rains
D	Dry
F	Fast-Draining

LIGHT

F	Full Sun
P	Partial Shade
S	Shade

TOLERANCE

W	Wind
PA	Poor Air Drainage
LF	Low Fertility
D	Drought
SS	Shallow Soil
HPH	High pH
HMS	Hot, Muggy Summers

NAME

GINKGO BILOBA, STAMINATE
  MAIDENHAIR TREE
GLEDITSIA TRIACANTHOS VAR. INERMIS 'SHADEMASTER'
  THORNLESS HONEY-LOCUST
GYMNOCLADUS DIOICA
  KENTUCKY COFFEETREE
HALESIA TETRAPTERA
  CAROLINA SILVER-BELL
HAMAMELIS MOLLIS 'PALLIDA'
  CHINESE WITCH-HAZEL (SOFT YELLOW)
HAMAMELIS VIRGINIANA
  COMMON WITCH-HAZEL (LATE AUTUMN)

HAMAMELIS X INTERMEDIA 'DIANE'
  HYBRID WITCH-HAZEL (RED)
HAMAMELIS X INTERMEDIA 'JELENA'
  HYBRID WITCH-HAZEL (ORANGE)
HAMAMELIS X INTERMEDIA 'PRIMAVERA'
  HYBRID WITCH-HAZEL (BRIGHT YELLOW)
HEDERA COLCHICA 'DENTATA'
  PERSIAN IVY
HEDERA HELIX 'BALTICA'
  BALTIC IVY
HEDERA HELIX 'BULGARIA'
  BULGARIAN IVY

HEDERA HELIX 'BUTTERCUP'
  BUTTERCUP ENGLISH IVY (YELLOW VARIEGATED)
HEDERA HELIX 'ERECTA'
  ENGLISH IVY (UPRIGHT)
HEDERA HELIX 'GOLD HEART'
  GOLD HEART ENGLISH IVY (YELLOW VARIEGATED)
HEDERA HELIX 'OGALALLA'
  OGALALLA ENGLISH IVY
HEDYOTIS CAERULEA
  QUAKER LADIES, BLUETS
HELIANTHEMUM APENNINUM VAR. ROSEUM
  SUN ROSE

HELIANTHUS SALICIFOLIUS
  SUNFLOWER (NARROWLEAF)
HELICTOTRICHON SEMPERVIRENS
  BLUE OAT GRASS
HELIOPSIS HELIANTHOIDES SUBSP. SCABRA 'KARAT'

HELLEBORUS NIGER
  CHRISTMAS-ROSE
HELLEBORUS ORIENTALIS HYBRIDS
  LENTEN-ROSE
HEMEROCALLIS 'HYPERION'
  HYPERION DAYLILY

HEMEROCALLIS FULVA 'EUROPA'
  ORANGE DAYLILY
HEMEROCALLIS LILIOASPHODELUS
  LEMON-LILY
HERACLEUM MANTEGAZZIANUM
  GIANT HOGWEED
HEUCHERA 'PALACE PURPLE' STRAIN
  ALUMROOT (PURPLELEAF)
HIBISCUS SYRIACUS 'BLUEBIRD'
  ROSE OF SHARON (BLUE)
HIBISCUS SYRIACUS 'DIANA'
  ROSE OF SHARON (TRIPLOID WHITE)

FAMILY	ZONE*	TYPE	SIZE (FEET)	SOIL COMPOSITION	SOIL MOISTURE	LIGHT	TOLERANCE	NOTES†
GINKGOACEAE	4	W	52.0	CL, OL	AV, D, F	F	W, D, HPH	
LEGUMINOSAE	4	W	52.0	CL, OL, SG	AV, D, F	F	W, PA, D, HPH, HMS	
LEGUMINOSAE	4	W	52.0	CL, OL, SG	AV, D, F	F	W, PA, D, HPH, HMS	
STYRACACEAE	5	W	26.0	OL	CM, AV	F, P		
HAMAMELIDACEAE	5	W	13.0	OL	AV	F, P		
HAMAMELIDACEAE	4	W	13.0	CL, OL	CM, AV, D, F	P	W, PA, D, HPH, HMS	
HAMAMELIDACEAE	5	W	13.0	OL	AV	F, P		
HAMAMELIDACEAE	5	W	13.0	OL	AV	F, P		
HAMAMELIDACEAE	5	W	13.0	OL	AV	F, P		
ARALIACEAE	7	W, E	6.5	OL	AV	F, P		
ARALIACEAE	6	W, E	0.0	OL, SG	AV, F	F, P	PA, HMS	
ARALIACEAE	5	W, E	0.0	OL	AV	F, P	PA, HMS	
ARALIACEAE	6	W	6.5	OL	CM, AV	F, P	HPH	
ARALIACEAE	7	W, E	1.5	OL	AV	F, P		
ARALIACEAE	6	W	6.5	OL	CM, AV	F, P	HPH	
ARALIACEAE	5	W, E	0.0	OL	AV	F, P	PA, HMS	
RUBIACEAE	4	P	0.0	OL	CM, AV	F		4
CISTACEAE	5	P	0.5	SL, SG	AV, F	F	HPH	4
COMPOSITAE	5	P	3.0	OL, SL	CM, AV, F	F		
GRAMINEAE	5	P	1.0	OL	CM, AV	F, P		
COMPOSITAE	4	P	3.0	CL, OL, SL, SG	AV, D, F	F, P	PA, LF, D, HMS	
RANUNCULACEAE	3	P, E	0.5	OL	CM, AV	P	PA, HMS	
RANUNCULACEAE	4	P, E	1.0	OL	CM, AV	P	PA, HMS	
LILIACEAE	5	P	3.0	CL, OL, SL	AV, F	F, P	W, PA, D, HMS	
LILIACEAE	5	P	3.0	CL, OL	CM, AV, D	F, P	LF	
LILIACEAE	3	P	1.5	OL	CM	F, P		
UMBELLIFERAE	5	I	3.0	CL, OL, SL	WE, CM, AV, F	F		3
SAXIFRAGACEAE	4	P	1.0	OL	CM, AV, F	P		
MALVACEAE	5	W	6.5	OL	AV	F	PA, HMS	
MALVACEAE	5	W	6.5	OL	AV	F	PA, HMS	

* See "Use of Plant Lists," page 152.
† See page 153.

Master List:
Summary of Cultural Preferences and Tolerances

KEY TO ABBREVIATIONS

ZONE

Plant hardiness zones adapted from U.S.D.A. Plant Hardiness Zone Map, 1990 (page 148).

Range of Average Annual Minimum Temperatures

1	Below −50° F.
2	−50° to −40° F.
3	−40° to −30° F.
4	−30° to −20° F.
5	−20° to −10° F.
6	−10° to 0° F.
7	0° to 10° F.
8	10° to 20° F.
9	20° to 30° F.
10	30° to 40° F.
11	Above 40° F.
T	Tender in the Mid-Atlantic Region

TYPE

W	Woody
P	Perennial
I	Biennial
A	Annual
B	Bulb
E	Evergreen

SOIL COMPOSITION

CL	Clay and Clay Loam
OL	Organic Loam
SL	Sandy Loam
SG	Stony, Gravelly

SOIL MOISTURE

B	Bog or Standing Water
WE	Water's Edge
CM	Consistently Moist, Not Boggy
AV	Average, Dry Between Rains
D	Dry
F	Fast-Draining

LIGHT

F	Full Sun
P	Partial Shade
S	Shade

TOLERANCE

W	Wind
PA	Poor Air Drainage
LF	Low Fertility
D	Drought
SS	Shallow Soil
HPH	High pH
HMS	Hot, Muggy Summers

NAME

HIPPOPHAE RHAMNOIDES
  SEA BUCKTHORN
HOSTA 'KABITAN'
  PLANTAIN-LILY (YELLOW VARIEGATED)
HOSTA PLANTAGINEA
  FRAGRANT PLANTAIN-LILY
HOSTA SIEBOLDIANA 'ELEGANS'
  SIEBOLD PLANTAIN-LILY (BLUE, SEERSUCKER LEAVES)
HOSTA UNDULATA
  WAVY-LEAVED PLANTAIN-LILY
HOSTA VENTRICOSA
  BLUE PLANTAIN-LILY

HOUTTUYNIA CORDATA 'CHAMELEON'

HYDRANGEA ANOMALA SUBSP. PETIOLARIS 'SKYLANDS GIANT'
  CLIMBING HYDRANGEA
HYDRANGEA ASPERA SUBSP. SARGENTIANA

HYDRANGEA MACROPHYLLA 'BLUE BILLOW'
  BLUE LACECAP HYDRANGEA
HYDRANGEA PANICULATA
  PANICLE HYDRANGEA
HYDRANGEA QUERCIFOLIA
  OAKLEAF HYDRANGEA

HYPERICUM FRONDOSUM
  GOLDEN ST.-JOHN'S-WORT
HYPERICUM KALMIANUM
  KALM ST.-JOHN'S-WORT
ILEX CHINA BOY ® 'MESDOB'
  CHINA BOY ® HOLLY
ILEX CHINA GIRL ® 'MESOG'
  CHINA GIRL ® HOLLY
ILEX CRENATA 'HELLERI'
  HELLERI DWARF JAPANESE HOLLY
ILEX CRENATA 'MICROPHYLLA'
  LITTLELEAF JAPANESE HOLLY

ILEX GLABRA 'DENSA'
  DWARF INKBERRY HOLLY
ILEX OPACA 'ARDEN'
  ARDEN AMERICAN HOLLY
ILEX OPACA 'XANTHOCARPA'
  YELLOW-BERRIED AMERICAN HOLLY
ILEX VERTICILLATA
  WINTERBERRY
ILEX VERTICILLATA 'WINTER RED'
  WINTER RED WINTERBERRY (HYBRID)
ILEX X AQUIPERNYI 'SAN JOSE'
  SAN JOSE HOLLY

ILEX X MESERVEAE BLUE MAID ® 'MESID'
  BLUE MAID ® HOLLY
ILEX X MESERVEAE BLUE STALLION ® 'MESAN'
  BLUE STALLION ® HOLLY
IMPERATA CYLINDRICA 'RED BARON'
  JAPANESE BLOOD GRASS
INDIGOFERA INCARNATA 'ALBA'
  CHINESE INDIGO (WHITE)
INULA HELENIUM
  ELECAMPANE
IRIS CRISTATA
  CRESTED IRIS

FAMILY	ZONE*	TYPE	SIZE (FEET)	SOIL COMPOSITION	SOIL MOISTURE	LIGHT	TOLERANCE	NOTES†
ELAEAGNACEAE	3	W	13.0	CL, OL, SL, SG	AV, D, F	F	W, PA, LF, D, HMS	9
LILIACEAE	3	P	1.0	OL	CM, AV	P, S	PA, HMS	19
LILIACEAE	3	P	1.5	OL	CM, AV	P, S	PA, HMS	
LILIACEAE	3	P	1.5	OL	CM, AV	P, S		
LILIACEAE	3	P	0.5	OL	CM, AV	P, S	PA, HMS	19
LILIACEAE	3	P	1.5	OL	CM, AV	P, S	PA, HMS	
SAURURACEAE	5	P	1.0	OL, SL	BG, WE, CM	P, S		7
SAXIFRAGACEAE	5	W	6.5	OL	CM, AV	F, P	HPH	
SAXIFRAGACEAE	7	W	3.0	OL	CM, AV, F	P		
SAXIFRAGACEAE	6	W	1.5	OL	CM	F, P		
SAXIFRAGACEAE	4	W	6.5	OL	AV	F	PA, D, HPH, HMS	
SAXIFRAGACEAE	5	W	6.5	CL, OL	AV	F, P	PA, HMS	
HYPERICACEAE	5	W	3.0	CL, OL	AV, D, F	F	D	
HYPERICACEAE	4	W	1.5	CL, OL, SL, SG	AV, D, F	F	D	
AQUIFOLIACEAE	5	W, E	3.0	OL	AV	F	PA, HMS	
AQUIFOLIACEAE	5	W, E	3.0	OL	AV	F	PA, HMS	
AQUIFOLIACEAE	6	W, E	3.0	OL	AV	F, P	PA, HMS	
AQUIFOLIACEAE	6	W, E	6.5	OL	AV	F, P	PA, HMS	
AQUIFOLIACEAE	5	W, E	6.5	CL, OL	CM, AV, D, F	F	PA, HMS	
AQUIFOLIACEAE	6	W, E	13.0	OL	CM, AV	F	W, PA, D, HMS	
AQUIFOLIACEAE	6	W, E	13.0	OL	CM, AV	F	W, PA, D, HMS	
AQUIFOLIACEAE	4	W	6.5	OL	WE, CM, AV	F	PA, HMS	
AQUIFOLIACEAE	4	W	6.5	OL	WE, CM, AV	F	PA, HMS	
AQUIFOLIACEAE	5	W, E	13.0	OL	CM, AV, F	F, P	PA, D, HMS	
AQUIFOLIACEAE	5	W, E	3.0	OL	AV	F	W, PA, HMS	
AQUIFOLIACEAE	5	W, E	3.0	OL	AV	F	W, PA, HMS	
GRAMINEAE	6	P	1.5	CL, OL	CM, AV	F	HPH, HMS	
LEGUMINOSAE	5	W	1.0	OL	AV	F, P, S	PA, D, HMS	6
COMPOSITAE	3	P	6.5	OL	CM, AV	F, P		
IRIDACEAE	5	P	0.5	OL	CM, AV	P	PA, D, HMS	

Master List:
Summary of Cultural Preferences and Tolerances

KEY TO ABBREVIATIONS

ZONE

Plant hardiness zones adapted from U.S.D.A. Plant Hardiness Zone Map, 1990 (page 148).

Range of Average Annual Minimum Temperatures

1	Below −50° F.
2	−50° to −40° F.
3	−40° to −30° F.
4	−30° to −20° F.
5	−20° to −10° F.
6	−10° to 0° F.
7	0° to 10° F.
8	10° to 20° F.
9	20° to 30° F.
10	30° to 40° F.
11	Above 40° F.
T	Tender in the Mid-Atlantic Region

TYPE

W Woody
P Perennial
I Biennial
A Annual
B Bulb
E Evergreen

SOIL COMPOSITION

CL Clay and Clay Loam
OL Organic Loam
SL Sandy Loam
SG Stony, Gravelly

SOIL MOISTURE

B Bog or Standing Water
WE Water's Edge
CM Consistently Moist, Not Boggy
AV Average, Dry Between Rains
D Dry
F Fast-Draining

LIGHT

F Full Sun
P Partial Shade
S Shade

TOLERANCE

W Wind
PA Poor Air Drainage
LF Low Fertility
D Drought
SS Shallow Soil
HPH High pH
HMS Hot, Muggy Summers

NAME

IRIS GRAMINEA
  PLUM TART IRIS
IRIS PSEUDACORUS
  YELLOW WATER IRIS
IRIS SIBIRICA CULTIVARS
  SIBERIAN IRIS
IRIS TECTORUM
  ROOF IRIS
ITEA VIRGINICA 'HENRY'S GARNET'
  VIRGINIA SWEETSPIRE
JASMINUM NUDIFLORUM
  WINTER JASMINE

JUNIPERUS CHINENSIS 'KAIZUKA'
  HOLLYWOOD JUNIPER
JUNIPERUS HORIZONTALIS 'WILTONII'
  BLUE RUG JUNIPER
JUNIPERUS SABINA 'TAMARISCIFOLIA'
  TAMARIX JUNIPER
JUNIPERUS SCOPULORUM 'SKY ROCKET'
  SKYROCKET ROCKY MOUNTAIN JUNIPER
JUNIPERUS VIRGINIANA
  EASTERN RED CEDAR
JUNIPERUS X MEDIA 'OLD GOLD'
  OLD GOLD JUNIPER

JUNIPERUS X MEDIA 'PFITZERIANA COMPACTA'
  NICK'S COMPACT JUNIPER
KALMIA LATIFOLIA
  MOUNTAIN-LAUREL
KERRIA JAPONICA
  KERRIA (SINGLE-FLOWERED)
KIRENGESHOMA PALMATA

KOCHIA SCOPARIA FORMA TRICHOPHYLLA 'CHILDSII'
  FIREBUSH, RED SUMMER-CYPRESS
KOELREUTERIA PANICULATA
  GOLDEN-RAIN TREE

KOLKWITZIA AMABILIS
  BEAUTY-BUSH
LAMIASTRUM GALEOBDOLON 'VARIEGATUM'
  YELLOW-ARCHANGEL (WHITE VARIEGATED)
LAMIUM MACULATUM 'WHITE NANCY'
  SPOTTED-DEAD-NETTLE (WHITE)
LATHYRUS VERNUS
  SPRING VETCHLING
LESPEDEZA THUNBERGII
  THUNBERG BUSH CLOVER
LESPEDEZA THUNBERGII 'ALBIFLORA'
  THUNBERG BUSH CLOVER (WHITE)

LEUCOJUM VERNUM
  SPRING SNOWFLAKE
LEUCOTHOE FONTANESIANA
  FOUNTAIN LEUCOTHOE
LEUCOTHOE FONTANESIANA 'NANA'
  DWARF FOUNTAIN LEUCOTHOE
LIATRIS SCARIOSA 'WHITE SPIRE'
  GAY-FEATHER (WHITE)
LIATRIS SPICATA 'KOBOLD'
  GAY-FEATHER (LAVENDER)
LIGUSTRUM QUIHOUI
  PRIVET (CHINESE)

FAMILY	ZONE*	TYPE	SIZE (FEET)	SOIL COMPOSITION	SOIL MOISTURE	LIGHT	TOLERANCE	NOTES†
IRIDACEAE	5	P	0.5	OL, SL	CM, AV	F		
IRIDACEAE	5	P	3.0	OL	B, WE	F		
IRIDACEAE	3	P	1.5	CL, OL	CM, AV	F	PA, D, HMS	
IRIDACEAE	5	P	0.5	SL, SG	CM	F, P	LF	
SAXIFRAGACEAE	6	W	3.0	OL	WE, CM, AV	F, P	PA, HMS	
OLEACEAE	6	W	1.5	OL	AV	F		
CUPRESSACEAE	6	W, E	3.0	CL, OL, SL, SG	AV, D, F	F	W, PA, D, HPH, HMS	
CUPRESSACEAE	3	W, E	0.5	CL, OL, SL, SG	AV, D, F	F	W, PA, D, HPH, HMS	
CUPRESSACEAE	4	W, E	1.0	CL, OL	AV, D, F	F	W, LF, D	
CUPRESSACEAE	5	W, E	6.5	OL	AV, D	F	W, PA, D, HPH, HMS	12
CUPRESSACEAE	3	W, E	52.0	CL, OL, SL, SG	AV, D, F	F	W, PA, LF, D, HPH, HMS	
CUPRESSACEAE	5	W, E	1.5	CL, OL, SL, SG	AV, D, F	F	W, PA, D, HPH, HMS	
CUPRESSACEAE	4	W, E	1.5	CL, OL, SL, SG	AV, D, F	F	W, PA, D, HMS	
ERICACEAE	5	W, E	13.0	OL	WE, CM	F, P		
ROSACEAE	5	W	3.0	OL	AV	F, P	PA, HPH, HMS	
SAXIFRAGACEAE	5	P	3.0	OL	CM, AV	P		
CHENOPODIACEAE	T	A	1.5	CL, OL, SL	CM, AV, D	F	PA, D, HMS	1
SAPINDACEAE	5	W	13.0	OL, SL	AV, D, F	F	PA, D, HPH, HMS	
CAPRIFOLIACEAE	5	W	6.5	OL	CM, AV, D, F	F	PA, D, HPH, HMS	
LABIATAE	5	P	1.5	CL, OL, SG	AV, D, F	P, S	PA, LF, D, HMS	
LABIATAE	5	P	0.5	OL	CM, AV	F, P, S		
LEGUMINOSAE	5	P	1.5	OL	AV	P		
LEGUMINOSAE	5	W	3.0	CL, OL, SL	AV, D, F	F	W, PA, LF, D, HPH, HMS	6
LEGUMINOSAE	6	W	0.0	OL	AV	F	PA, D, HMS	6
AMARYLLIDACEAE	5	B	0.5	OL	CM, AV	P	PA, HMS	
ERICACEAE	5	W, E	3.0	OL	WE, CM, AV, F	F, P, S		
ERICACEAE	5	W, E	3.0	OL	WE, CM, AV	F, P, S		
COMPOSITAE	3	P	1.5	OL, SL	AV, F	F	D	
COMPOSITAE	3	P	1.5	SL	CM, AV	F	LF, D	
OLEACEAE	5	W	6.5	CL, OL	CM, AV, D, F	F, P	W, PA, D, HPH, HMS	

* See "Use of Plant Lists," page 152.
† See page 153.

Master List:
Summary of Cultural Preferences and Tolerances

KEY TO ABBREVIATIONS

ZONE

Plant hardiness zones adapted from U.S.D.A. Plant Hardiness Zone Map, 1990 (page 148).

Range of Average Annual Minimum Temperatures

1	Below −50° F.
2	−50° to −40° F.
3	−40° to −30° F.
4	−30° to −20° F.
5	−20° to −10° F.
6	−10° to 0° F.
7	0° to 10° F.
8	10° to 20° F.
9	20° to 30° F.
10	30° to 40° F.
11	Above 40° F.
T	Tender in the Mid-Atlantic Region

TYPE

W	Woody
P	Perennial
I	Biennial
A	Annual
B	Bulb
E	Evergreen

SOIL COMPOSITION

CL	Clay and Clay Loam
OL	Organic Loam
SL	Sandy Loam
SG	Stony, Gravelly

SOIL MOISTURE

B	Bog or Standing Water
WE	Water's Edge
CM	Consistently Moist, Not Boggy
AV	Average, Dry Between Rains
D	Dry
F	Fast-Draining

LIGHT

F	Full Sun
P	Partial Shade
S	Shade

TOLERANCE

W	Wind
PA	Poor Air Drainage
LF	Low Fertility
D	Drought
SS	Shallow Soil
HPH	High pH
HMS	Hot, Muggy Summers

NAME

LILIUM 'BLACK DRAGON'
  HYBRID TRUMPET LILY (WHITE, FRAGRANT)
LILIUM SPECIES AND HYBRIDS

LIQUIDAMBAR STYRACIFLUA
  SWEET GUM
LIRIOPE MUSCARI (BIG BLUE SELECTION)
  BIG BLUE LILYTURF
LIRIOPE MUSCARI 'MONROE WHITE'
  LILYTURF (WHITE)
LIRIOPE MUSCARI 'VARIEGATA'
  LILYTURF (YELLOW VARIEGATED)

LONICERA FRAGRANTISSIMA
  FRAGRANT HONEYSUCKLE
LUZULA SYLVATICA 'MARGINATA'
  GREATER WOOD RUSH
LYCORIS SPRENGERI

LYCORIS SQUAMIGERA
  RESURRECTION LILY
LYSICHITON AMERICANUM
  YELLOW SKUNK-CABBAGE (WESTERN AMERICAN)
LYSICHITON CAMTSCHATCENSE
  WHITE SKUNK-CABBAGE (ASIATIC)

LYSIMACHIA CLETHROIDES
  GOOSENECK LOOSESTRIFE
LYSIMACHIA PUNCTATA
  GARDEN LOOSESTRIFE
LYTHRUM SALICARIA 'DROPMORE PURPLE'
  PURPLE LOOSESTRIFE
MACLEAYA CORDATA
  PLUME-POPPY
MAGNOLIA 'ELIZABETH'
  MAGNOLIA (YELLOW)
MAGNOLIA 'SUSAN'
  MAGNOLIA (COMPACT, PINK)

MAGNOLIA DENUDATA (SYN. M. HEPTAPETA)
  YULAN MAGNOLIA
MAGNOLIA MACROPHYLLA
  LARGE-LEAVED CUCUMBER TREE
MAGNOLIA VIRGINIANA
  SWAMP MAGNOLIA
MAGNOLIA X LOEBNERI
  MAGNOLIA (LOEBNERI HYBRID)
MAGNOLIA X SOULANGIANA 'VERBANICA'
  SAUCER MAGNOLIA (PINK)
MAHONIA BEALEI
  LEATHERLEAF MAHONIA

MALUS 'RED JADE'
  RED JADE CRABAPPLE
MALUS FLORIBUNDA
  JAPANESE FLOWERING CRABAPPLE
MALUS HUPEHENSIS
  TEA CRABAPPLE
MALUS SARGENTII
  SARGENT CRABAPPLE
MERTENSIA VIRGINICA
  VIRGINIA BLUEBELLS
METASEQUOIA GLYPTOSTROBOIDES
  DAWN REDWOOD

FAMILY	ZONE*	TYPE	SIZE (FEET)	SOIL COMPOSITION	SOIL MOISTURE	LIGHT	TOLERANCE	NOTES†
LILIACEAE	5	B	6.5	OL	AV	F, P	PA, HMS	
LILIACEAE	5	B	3.0	OL, SL	AV	F, P		
HAMAMELIDACEAE	5	W	52.0	OL	CM, AV	F	PA, HMS	
LILIACEAE	6	W, E	0.5	OL	AV	P	PA, HMS	13
LILIACEAE	6	W, E	0.5	OL	AV	P	PA, HMS	13
LILIACEAE	6	W, E	0.5	OL	AV	P	PA, HMS	13
CAPRIFOLIACEAE	5	W	6.5	CL, OL	CM, AV, D, F	F	PA, D, HPH, HMS	
JUNCACEAE	6	P, E	1.5	OL	CM, AV, F	P, S	D	
AMARYLLIDACEAE	5	B	1.5	OL	CM, AV, F	F, P	PA, HMS	
AMARYLLIDACEAE	5	B	1.5	OL	CM, AV, FD	F, P	PA, HMS	
ARACEAE	5	P	1.5	OL, SL	B, WE	F, P		
ARACEAE	5	P	1.5	OL, SL	B, WE	F, P		
PRIMULACEAE	3	P	1.5	OL	WE, CM, AV	F, P		
PRIMULACEAE	5	P	1.5	OL	WE, CM, AV	F, P	D	
LYTHRACEAE	3	P	3.0	CL, OL, SL	B, WE, CM, AV, D	F, P	PA, LF, HMS	
PAPAVERACEAE	3	P	6.5	OL, SL	AV	P		8
MAGNOLIACEAE	5	W	26.0	OL	AV	F	PA, HPH, HMS	
MAGNOLIACEAE	6	W	13.0	OL	AV	F	HPH	
MAGNOLIACEAE	6	W	26.0	OL	AV	F	HPH	
MAGNOLIACEAE	6	W	26.0	OL	CM, AV	F	HPH	
MAGNOLIACEAE	5	W	26.0	OL, SL	WE, CM, AV	F	PA, HPH, HMS	
MAGNOLIACEAE	5	W	26.0	OL	AV	F	HPH	
MAGNOLIACEAE	5	W	13.0	OL	AV	F	HPH	
BERBERIDACEAE	6	W, E	3.0	OL	AV	F, P	PA, HPH, HMS	
ROSACEAE	3	W	13.0	OL	AV	F	PA, HPH, HMS	
ROSACEAE	4	W	13.0	OL	AV	F	W, PA, HPH, HMS	
ROSACEAE	4	W	13.0	OL	AV	F	HPH	
ROSACEAE	4	W	6.5	OL	AV	F	W, PA, HPH, HMS	
BORAGINACEAE	5	B	0.5	OL, SL, SG	CM, AV	P	PA, HMS	
TAXODIACEAE	5	W	52.0	OL	CM, AV	F	HPH	

* See "Use of Plant Lists," page 152.
† See page 153.

Master List:
Summary of Cultural Preferences and Tolerances

KEY TO ABBREVIATIONS

ZONE

Plant hardiness zones adapted from U.S.D.A. Plant Hardiness Zone Map, 1990 (page 148).

Range of Average Annual Minimum Temperatures

1	Below −50° F.
2	−50° to −40° F.
3	−40° to −30° F.
4	−30° to −20° F.
5	−20° to −10° F.
6	−10° to 0° F.
7	0° to 10° F.
8	10° to 20° F.
9	20° to 30° F.
10	30° to 40° F.
11	Above 40° F.
T	Tender in the Mid-Atlantic Region

TYPE

W	Woody
P	Perennial
I	Biennial
A	Annual
B	Bulb
E	Evergreen

SOIL COMPOSITION

CL	Clay and Clay Loam
OL	Organic Loam
SL	Sandy Loam
SG	Stony, Gravelly

SOIL MOISTURE

B	Bog or Standing Water
WE	Water's Edge
CM	Consistently Moist, Not Boggy
AV	Average, Dry Between Rains
D	Dry
F	Fast-Draining

LIGHT

F	Full Sun
P	Partial Shade
S	Shade

TOLERANCE

W	Wind
PA	Poor Air Drainage
LF	Low Fertility
D	Drought
SS	Shallow Soil
HPH	High pH
HMS	Hot, Muggy Summers

NAME

MICROBIOTA DECUSSATA
  SIBERIAN-CYPRESS
MISCANTHUS 'GIGANTEUS'
  GIANT MISCANTHUS
MISCANTHUS SINENSIS 'CABARET'
  MISCANTHUS (WHITE VARIEGATED)
MISCANTHUS SINENSIS 'GRACILLIMUS'
  SLENDER MISCANTHUS
MISCANTHUS SINENSIS 'MORNING LIGHT'
  SLENDER VARIEGATED MISCANTHUS
MISCANTHUS SINENSIS 'SILVER FEATHER' (='SILBERFEDER')
  SILVER FEATHER MISCANTHUS

MISCANTHUS SINENSIS 'STRICTUS'
  PORCUPINE GRASS
MISCANTHUS SINENSIS 'VARIEGATUS'
  VARIEGATED MISCANTHUS
MOLINIA CAERULEA SUBSP. ARUNDINACEA
  PURPLE MOOR GRASS
MONARDA DIDYMA
  BEE BALM
MUSCARI AZUREUM 'ALBUM'
  GRAPE-HYACINTH (WHITE)
MUSCARI BOTRYOIDES 'ALBUM'
  COMMON GRAPE-HYACINTH (WHITE)

MUSCARI TUBERGENIANUM
  GRAPE-HYACINTH (BLUE)
MYRICA PENSYLVANICA
  BAYBERRY
NARCISSUS 'CARLTON'

NARCISSUS 'FORTUNE'

NARCISSUS 'HERA'

NARCISSUS 'LOCH FYNE'

NARCISSUS 'MOONMIST'

NARCISSUS 'MRS. ERNST H. KRELAGE'

NARCISSUS 'PEEPING TOM'

NARCISSUS 'POMONA'

NARCISSUS 'QUEEN OF SPAIN'

NARCISSUS 'TREVITHIAN'

NARCISSUS JONQUILLA
  JONQUIL
NARCISSUS PSEUDONARCISSUS SUBSP. OBVALLARIS
  TENBY DAFFODIL
NEPETA X FAASSENII

NYSSA SYLVATICA
  SOUR GUM
OMPHALODES VERNA
  BLUE-EYED MARY
ONOPORDUM ACANTHIUM
  SCOTCH THISTLE

FAMILY	ZONE*	TYPE	SIZE (FEET)	SOIL COMPOSITION	SOIL MOISTURE	LIGHT	TOLERANCE	NOTES†
CUPRESSACEAE	4	W, E	0.5	CL, OL	AV, D, F	F, P, S		
GRAMINEAE	5	P	6.5	OL, SL	WE, CM	F	PA, HMS	
GRAMINEAE	5	P	3.0	CL, OL, SL, SG	CM, AV, D, F	F, P	PA, D, HMS	
GRAMINEAE	5	P	3.0	CL, OL, SL	CM, AV, D, F	F, P	W, PA, D, HMS	
GRAMINEAE	5	P	3.0	CL, OL, SL	CM, AV, D, F	F, P	PA, D, HMS	
GRAMINEAE	5	P	3.0	CL, OL, SL	CM, AV, D	F	PA, D, HMS	
GRAMINEAE	5	P	3.0	CL, OL, SL	CM, AV, D	F, P	PA, D, HMS	
GRAMINEAE	5	P	3.0	CL, OL, SL	CM, AV, D, F	F, P	PA, D, HMS	
GRAMINEAE	5	P	3.0	OL	AV	F	PA, HMS	
LABIATAE	4	P	1.5	OL	WE, CM	F, P	PA, HMS	15
LILIACEAE	5	B	0.0	OL	CM, AV, FD	P	PA, HMS	
LILIACEAE	5	B	0.0	OL	CM, AV, FD	P	PA, HMS	
LILIACEAE	5	B	0.0	OL	CM, AV, FD	P	PA, HMS	
MYRICACEAE	4	W	6.5	CL, OL, SL, SG	WE, CM, AV, D, F	F	W, PA, LF, D, SS, HMS	
AMARYLLIDACEAE	5	B	0.5	CL, OL, SL	CM, AV	F, P	W, HMS	
AMARYLLIDACEAE	5	B	0.5	CL, OL, SL	CM, AV	F, P	PA, HMS	
AMARYLLIDACEAE	5	B	0.5	CL, OL, SL	CM, AV	F, P	PA, HMS	
AMARYLLIDACEAE	5	B	0.5	CL, OL, SL	CM, AV	F, P	PA, LF, HMS	
AMARYLLIDACEAE	5	B	0.5	CL, OL, SL	CM, AV	F, P	PA, HMS	
AMARYLLIDACEAE	5	B	0.5	CL, OL, SL	CM, AV	F, P	PA, HMS	
AMARYLLIDACEAE	5	B	0.5	CL, OL, SL	CM, AV	F, P	PA, HMS	
AMARYLLIDACEAE	5	B	0.5	CL, OL, SL	CM, AV	F, P	PA, HMS	
AMARYLLIDACEAE	5	B	0.5	CL, OL, SL	CM, AV	F, P	PA, HMS	
AMARYLLIDACEAE	5	B	0.5	CL, OL, SL	CM, AV	F, P	PA, HMS	
AMARYLLIDACEAE	5	B	0.5	OL, SL	CM, AV	F, P	W, HMS	
AMARYLLIDACEAE	5	B	0.5	CL, OL, SL	CM, AV	F, P	PA, HMS	
LABIATAE	3	P	1.0	OL	CM, AV, D, F	F	LF, D, HMS	
NYSSACEAE	5	W	52.0	OL, SL	WE, CM, AV	F	PA, HMS	
BORAGINACEAE	5	P	0.5	OL	CM, AV	P		
COMPOSITAE	5	I	6.5	CL, OL, SL	AV, D	F	D	3

* See "Use of Plant Lists," page 152.
† See page 153.

Master List:
Summary of Cultural Preferences and Tolerances

KEY TO ABBREVIATIONS

ZONE

Plant hardiness zones adapted from U.S.D.A. Plant Hardiness Zone Map, 1990 (page 148).

Range of Average Annual Minimum Temperatures

1	Below −50° F.
2	−50° to −40° F.
3	−40° to −30° F.
4	−30° to −20° F.
5	−20° to −10° F.
6	−10° to 0° F.
7	0° to 10° F.
8	10° to 20° F.
9	20° to 30° F.
10	30° to 40° F.
11	Above 40° F.
T	Tender in the Mid-Atlantic Region

TYPE

W	Woody
P	Perennial
I	Biennial
A	Annual
B	Bulb
E	Evergreen

SOIL COMPOSITION

CL	Clay and Clay Loam
OL	Organic Loam
SL	Sandy Loam
SG	Stony, Gravelly

SOIL MOISTURE

B	Bog or Standing Water
WE	Water's Edge
CM	Consistently Moist, Not Boggy
AV	Average, Dry Between Rains
D	Dry
F	Fast-Draining

LIGHT

F	Full Sun
P	Partial Shade
S	Shade

TOLERANCE

W	Wind
PA	Poor Air Drainage
LF	Low Fertility
D	Drought
SS	Shallow Soil
HPH	High pH
HMS	Hot, Muggy Summers

NAME

OPHIOPOGON JAPONICUS 'NANUS'
    DWARF MONDO GRASS
OSMUNDA CINNAMOMEA
    CINNAMON FERN
OSMUNDA CLAYTONIANA
    INTERRUPTED FERN
OSMUNDA REGALIS
    ROYAL FERN
OXYDENDRUM ARBOREUM
    SOURWOOD
PACHYSANDRA PROCUMBENS
    ALLEGHANY SPURGE

PACHYSANDRA TERMINALIS
    JAPANESE SPURGE
PACHYSANDRA TERMINALIS 'GREEN CARPET'
    GREEN CARPET JAPANESE SPURGE
PACHYSANDRA TERMINALIS 'VARIEGATA' OR 'SILVER EDGE'
    JAPANESE SPURGE (WHITE VARIEGATED)
PAEONIA 'BLACK PIRATE'
    HYBRID TREE PEONY (MAROON)
PAEONIA—HERBACEOUS HYBRIDS
    HYBRID HERBACEOUS PEONY
PAEONIA—WOODY HYBRIDS
    HYBRID TREE PEONY

PAEONIA TENUIFOLIA
    FERN-LEAVED PEONY
PANICUM VIRGATUM 'STRICTUM'
    TALL SWITCH GRASS
PAPAVER ORIENTALE
    ORIENTAL POPPY
PARONYCHIA KAPELA SUBSP. SERPYLLIFOLIA
    CREEPING NAILWORT
PAULOWNIA TOMENTOSA
    EMPRESS TREE
PAXISTIMA CANBYI

PELTIPHYLLUM PELTATUM
    UMBRELLA PLANT
PENNISETUM ALOPECUROIDES
    HARDY FOUNTAIN GRASS
PEROVSKIA ABROTANOIDES X P. ATRIPLICIFOLIA
    HYBRID PEROVSKIA
PETASITES FRAGRANS
    WINTER HELIOTROPE
PETASITES JAPONICUS
    JAPANESE BUTTERBUR
PHALARIS ARUNDINACEA VAR. PICTA
    RIBBON GRASS (WHITE VARIEGATED)

PHELLODENDRON AMURENSE
    AMUR CORKTREE
PHILADELPHUS CORONARIUS
    SWEET MOCKORANGE
PHILADELPHUS X FALCONERI
    FALCONER HYBRID MOCKORANGE
PHLOMIS RUSSELIANA
    JERUSALEM-SAGE
PHLOX BIFIDA
    SAND PHLOX
PHLOX PILOSA SUBSP. OZARKANA
    OZARK DOWNY PHLOX

FAMILY	ZONE*	TYPE	SIZE (FEET)	SOIL COMPOSITION	SOIL MOISTURE	LIGHT	TOLERANCE	NOTES†
LILIACEAE	7	W, E	0.0	OL	AV	P		
OSMUNDACEAE	4	P	3.0	OL	WE, CM, AV	P, S	PA, HMS	
OSMUNDACEAE	4	P	3.0	OL	WE, CM	P, S	PA, HMS	
OSMUNDACEAE	3	P	3.0	OL	WE, CM	S	PA, HMS	
ERICACEAE	5	W	26.0	OL	CM, AV, F	F		
BUXACEAE	4	P	0.5	OL	CM, AV	P, S	D	
BUXACEAE	5	W, E	0.5	OL	AV	P, S	W, PA, LF, D, HMS	
BUXACEAE	5	W, E	0.5	OL	AV	S	W, PA, D, HMS	
BUXACEAE	5	W, E	0.5	OL	AV	S	W, PA, D, HMS	
PAEONIACEAE	6	W	3.0	OL	AV, D, F	F, P	D	
PAEONIACEAE	2	P	1.5	OL	AV, F	F, P		
PAEONIACEAE	6	W	3.0	OL	AV, D, F	F, P	D	
PAEONIACEAE	4	P	1.0	OL	AV, F	F, P		
GRAMINEAE	5	P	1.5	CL, OL, SL	CM, AV	F	PA, HMS	
PAPAVERACEAE	3	P	3.0	CL, OL, SL	AV, D, F	F	PA, D, HMS	
CARYOPHYLLACEAE	6	P	0.0	OL, SL, SG	AV, F	F		
BIGNONIACEAE	6	W	26.0	OL	AV	F	HPH	
CELASTRACEAE	4	W, E	0.5	OL	AV, F	P		
SAXIFRAGACEAE	6	P	1.5	OL	B, WE			
GRAMINEAE	5	P	1.5	OL	AV	F	W, PA, HMS	
LABIATAE	5	P	3.0	CL, OL, SL, SG	AV	F		
COMPOSITAE	5	P	0.5	CL	WE, CM, AV	F, P, S		
COMPOSITAE	4	P	1.5	OL	WE, CM	P, S		
GRAMINEAE	4	P	3.0	CL, OL, SL	WE, CM, AV	F, P	HPH	7
RUTACEAE	4	W	26.0	OL	AV, D, F	F	D, HPH	
SAXIFRAGACEAE	5	W	6.5	CL, OL	AV, D, F	F, P	PA, LF, D, HMS	
SAXIFRAGACEAE	5	W	6.5	CL, OL	AV, D, F	F, P	PA, D, HMS	
LABIATAE	5	P	1.5	OL	D, F	F	D, HMS	
POLEMONIACEAE	4	P, E	0.5	SL, SG	AV, F	F	W, PA, D, SS, HMS	
POLEMONIACEAE	5	P, E	0.5	OL	CM, AV	F, P	PA, D, HPH, HMS	

* See "Use of Plant Lists," page 152.
† See page 153.

Master List:
Summary of Cultural Preferences and Tolerances

KEY TO ABBREVIATIONS

ZONE

Plant hardiness zones adapted from U.S.D.A. Plant Hardiness Zone Map, 1990 (page 148).

Range of Average Annual Minimum Temperatures

1	Below −50° F.
2	−50° to −40° F.
3	−40° to −30° F.
4	−30° to −20° F.
5	−20° to −10° F.
6	−10° to 0° F.
7	0° to 10° F.
8	10° to 20° F.
9	20° to 30° F.
10	30° to 40° F.
11	Above 40° F.
T	Tender in the Mid-Atlantic Region

TYPE

W	Woody
P	Perennial
I	Biennial
A	Annual
B	Bulb
E	Evergreen

SOIL COMPOSITION

CL	Clay and Clay Loam
OL	Organic Loam
SL	Sandy Loam
SG	Stony, Gravelly

SOIL MOISTURE

B	Bog or Standing Water
WE	Water's Edge
CM	Consistently Moist, Not Boggy
AV	Average, Dry Between Rains
D	Dry
F	Fast-Draining

LIGHT

F	Full Sun
P	Partial Shade
S	Shade

TOLERANCE

W	Wind
PA	Poor Air Drainage
LF	Low Fertility
D	Drought
SS	Shallow Soil
HPH	High pH
HMS	Hot, Muggy Summers

NAME

PHLOX STOLONIFERA 'ALBA'
  CREEPING PHLOX
PHLOX STOLONIFERA 'BLUE RIDGE'
  CREEPING PHLOX
PHLOX STOLONIFERA 'SHERWOOD PURPLE'
  CREEPING PHLOX
PHLOX SUBULATA
  MOSS PHLOX
PHYLLOSTACHYS AUREOSULCATA
  YELLOW-GROOVE BAMBOO
PHYSOSTEGIA VIRGINIANA
  FALSE DRAGONHEAD

PHYSOSTEGIA VIRGINIANA 'SUMMER SNOW'
  FALSE DRAGONHEAD (WHITE)
PICEA ABIES 'NIDIFORMIS'
  BIRD'S NEST SPRUCE
PICEA ORIENTALIS
  ORIENTAL SPRUCE
PICEA PUNGENS 'HOOPSII'
  HOOPS COLORADO SPRUCE (BLUE)
PIERIS JAPONICA
  JAPANESE-ANDROMEDA
PINUS BUNGEANA
  LACEBARK PINE

PINUS DENSIFLORA 'UMBRACULIFERA'
  TANYOSHO PINE
PINUS FLEXILIS
  LIMBER PINE
PINUS KORAIENSIS
  KOREAN PINE
PINUS MUGO VAR. MUGO
  SWISS MOUNTAIN PINE
PINUS PARVIFLORA 'GLAUCA'
  JAPANESE WHITE PINE (BLUE)
PINUS STROBUS
  EASTERN WHITE PINE

PINUS STROBUS 'FASTIGIATA'
  FASTIGIATE EASTERN WHITE PINE
PINUS THUNBERGIANA
  JAPANESE BLACK PINE
PINUS THUNBERGIANA 'OCULUS-DRACONIS'
  DRAGON'S-EYE JAPANESE BLACK PINE
PINUS VIRGINIANA
  VIRGINIA PINE
PLATANUS OCCIDENTALIS
  SYCAMORE
POLIANTHES TUBEROSA
  TUBEROSE

POLYGONATUM ODORATUM 'VARIEGATUM'
  SOLOMON'S SEAL (WHITE VARIEGATED)
POLYSTICHUM ACROSTICHOIDES
  CHRISTMAS FERN
POLYSTICHUM TRIPTERON

PONCIRUS TRIFOLIATA
  HARDY-ORANGE
POTENTILLA TRIDENTATA
  THREE-TOOTHED CINQUEFOIL
PRUNUS 'HALLY JOLIVETTE'
  FLOWERING CHERRY (PINK HYBRID)

FAMILY	ZONE*	TYPE	SIZE (FEET)	SOIL COMPOSITION	SOIL MOISTURE	LIGHT	TOLERANCE	NOTES†
POLEMONIACEAE	5	P	0.0	OL	CM, AV, F	P, S	HPH	
POLEMONIACEAE	5	P	0.0	OL	CM, AV, F	P, S	HPH	
POLEMONIACEAE	5	P	0.0	OL	CM, AV, F	P, S	HPH	
POLEMONIACEAE	3	P, E	0.0	SL	AV, F	F	W, PA, LF, D, HMS	
GRAMINEAE	6	W	13.0	OL	WE, CM, AV	F		7
LABIATAE	3	P	3.0	CL, OL, SL	CM, AV, F	F, P	PA, D, HMS	
LABIATAE	3	P	3.0	CL, OL, SL	CM, AV, F	F, P	PA, D, HMS	
PINACEAE	3	W, E	3.0	CL, OL	AV	F	W, PA, HMS	
PINACEAE	5	W, E	52.0	OL	AV	F	PA, HPH, HMS	
PINACEAE	3	W, E	52.0	OL	AV, D, F	F	W, HPH	
ERICACEAE	6	W, E	3.0	OL	WE, CM, AV	P		18a
PINACEAE	5	W, E	26.0	OL	AV, D, F	F	W, D, HPH	
PINACEAE	5	W, E	13.0	OL	AV	F		
PINACEAE	4	W, E	26.0	OL	AV, D, F	F	W, PA, D, HPH, HMS	
PINACEAE	4	W, E	26.0	OL	AV, D, F	F	W, PA, D, HPH, HMS	
PINACEAE	3	W, E	3.0	OL, SG	AV, D, F	F	W, D, HPH	
PINACEAE	5	W, E	26.0	OL	AV	F	PA, HPH, HMS	
PINACEAE	3	W, E	52.0	OL	CM, AV	F	HPH	
PINACEAE	3	W, E	26.0	OL	CM, AV	F	HPH	
PINACEAE	6	W, E	26.0	OL, SL, SG	AV, F	F	W, HPH	
PINACEAE	6	W, E	13.0	OL, SL	AV, F	F	HPH	
PINACEAE	5	W, E	26.0	CL, OL, SL	AV, D, F	F	W, PA, LF, D, HPH, HMS	
PLATANACEAE	5	W	52.0	OL	CM, AV	F	PA, HPH, HMS	22
AGAVACEAE	T	A	1.0	OL, SL	CM, AV	F		2
LILIACEAE	4	P	1.5	OL	CM, AV, F	P, S	PA, D, HMS	
POLYPODIACEAE	3	P, E	1.0	OL	AV	P, S	PA, D, HMS	
POLYPODIACEAE	5	P	1.0	OL	CM, AV	P, S	PA, HMS	
RUTACEAE	6	W	6.5	OL	AV, D, F	F	D	
ROSACEAE	2	P, E	0.5	OL, SL	D, F	F	LF, D, SS, HMS	
ROSACEAE	5	W	13.0	OL	AV	F		

* See "Use of Plant Lists," page 152.
† See page 153.

Master List:
Summary of Cultural Preferences and Tolerances

KEY TO ABBREVIATIONS

ZONE

Plant hardiness zones adapted from U.S.D.A. Plant Hardiness Zone Map, 1990 (page 148).

Range of Average Annual Minimum Temperatures

1	Below −50° F.	
2	−50° to −40° F.	
3	−40° to −30° F.	
4	−30° to −20° F.	
5	−20° to −10° F.	
6	−10° to 0° F.	
7	0° to 10° F.	
8	10° to 20° F.	
9	20° to 30° F.	
10	30° to 40° F.	
11	Above 40° F.	
T	Tender in the Mid-Atlantic Region	

TYPE

W   Woody
P   Perennial
I   Biennial
A   Annual
B   Bulb
E   Evergreen

SOIL COMPOSITION

CL   Clay and Clay Loam
OL   Organic Loam
SL   Sandy Loam
SG   Stony, Gravelly

SOIL MOISTURE

B   Bog or Standing Water
WE   Water's Edge
CM   Consistently Moist, Not Boggy
AV   Average, Dry Between Rains
D   Dry
F   Fast-Draining

LIGHT

F   Full Sun
P   Partial Shade
S   Shade

TOLERANCE

W   Wind
PA   Poor Air Drainage
LF   Low Fertility
D   Drought
SS   Shallow Soil
HPH   High pH
HMS   Hot, Muggy Summers

NAME

PRUNUS CERASIFERA 'THUNDERCLOUD'
  THUNDERCLOUD PLUM
PRUNUS SUBHIRTELLA 'AUTUMNALIS'
  HIGAN CHERRY (AUTUMN-FLOWERING)
PRUNUS SUBHIRTELLA 'PENDULA'
  WEEPING HIGAN CHERRY
PRUNUS X CISTENA
  PURPLELEAF SAND CHERRY
PRUNUS YEDOENSIS
  YOSHINO CHERRY
PSEUDOLARIX KAEMPFERI
  GOLDEN-LARCH

PSEUDOTSUGA MENZIESII
  DOUGLAS-FIR
PTERIDIUM AQUILINUM VAR. LATIUSCULUM
  BRACKEN
PULMONARIA ANGUSTIFOLIA
  LUNGWORT
PULMONARIA SACCHARATA 'MARGERY FISH'
  BETHLEHEM LUNGWORT
PULMONARIA SACCHARATA 'SISSINGHURST WHITE'
  BETHLEHEM LUNGWORT (WHITE)
PYRACANTHA COCCINEA 'AUREA'
  FIRETHORN (YELLOW FRUIT)

QUERCUS ALBA
  WHITE OAK
QUERCUS MACROCARPA
  MOSSY-CUP OAK
QUERCUS PHELLOS
  WILLOW OAK
QUERCUS RUBRA
  RED OAK
RHEUM PALMATUM 'RUBRUM'
  ORNAMENTAL RHUBARB
RHODODENDRON (CATAWBIENSE HYBRIDS)

RHODODENDRON (GABLE HYBRIDS)
  GABLE HYBRID AZALEAS
RHODODENDRON (GLENN DALE HYBRIDS)
  GLENN DALE HYBRID AZALEAS
RHODODENDRON (KAEMPFERI HYBRIDS)
  TORCH HYBRID AZALEAS
RHODODENDRON (KNAP HILL HYBRID) 'TUNIS'
  KNAP HILL HYBRID AZALEA (ORANGE-BRICK)
RHODODENDRON (KURUME HYBRIDS)
  KURUME HYBRID AZALEAS
RHODODENDRON ARBORESCENS
  SWEET AZALEA

RHODODENDRON ATLANTICUM
  COAST AZALEA
RHODODENDRON CANESCENS
  PIEDMONT AZALEA
RHODODENDRON MAXIMUM
  ROSEBAY RHODODENDRON
RHODODENDRON MUCRONULATUM
  KOREAN RHODODENDRON
RHODODENDRON PRINOPHYLLUM
  ROSESHELL AZALEA
RHODODENDRON SCHLIPPENBACHII
  ROYAL AZALEA

FAMILY	ZONE*	TYPE	SIZE (FEET)	SOIL COMPOSITION	SOIL MOISTURE	LIGHT	TOLERANCE	NOTES†
ROSACEAE	5	W	13.0	OL	AV	F	PA, D, HPH, HMS	
ROSACEAE	5	W	13.0	OL	AV	F		
ROSACEAE	6	W	13.0	OL	AV	F		
ROSACEAE	3	W	3.0	OL	AV, D, F	F	D, HPH, HMS	
ROSACEAE	6	W	13.0	OL	AV	F		
PINACEAE	6	W	26.0	OL	CM, AV	F		
PINACEAE	3	W, E	52.0	OL	AV	F	W, HPH	
POLYPODIACEAE	3	P	3.0	SL, SG	CM, AV, D, F	F, P	D	
BORAGINACEAE	3	P	0.5	OL	CM, AV	P, S	PA, D, HMS	
BORAGINACEAE	3	P	0.5	OL	CM, AV	P, S		
BORAGINACEAE	3	P	0.5	OL	AV	P, S		
ROSACEAE	7	W	6.5	CL, OL, SL	AV	F	PA, D, HMS	
FAGACEAE	4	W	52.0	OL	CM, AV	F	W, PA, HPH, HMS	
FAGACEAE	4	W	52.0	OL	AV, D	F	W, D, HPH	
FAGACEAE	6	W	26.0	OL	CM, AV	F		
FAGACEAE	3	W	26.0	OL	AV, D, F	F	PA, D, HPH, HMS	
POLYGONACEAE	5	P	3.0	OL, SL	WE, CM	F, P		4
ERICACEAE	4	W, E	6.5	OL	CM, AV	F, P		
ERICACEAE	5	W	3.0	OL	AV	F, P	PA, HMS	
ERICACEAE	6	W	3.0	OL	AV	F, P		
ERICACEAE	6	W	6.5	OL	AV	P	PA, HMS	
ERICACEAE	6	W	3.0	OL	AV	F, P		
ERICACEAE	6	W	3.0	OL	AV	F, P	PA, HMS	
ERICACEAE	5	W	6.5	OL	CM, AV	F, P	PA, HMS	
ERICACEAE	5	W	1.5	OL, SL	CM, AV, F	F		
ERICACEAE	7	W	6.5	OL	CM, AV	P		
ERICACEAE	4	W, E	6.5	OL	WE, CM, AV	P, S	PA, HMS	
ERICACEAE	5	W	3.0	OL	AV	P	PA, HMS	
ERICACEAE	3	W	6.5	OL	AV	F		
ERICACEAE	5	W	3.0	OL	AV, F	F, P	PA, HMS	

* See "Use of Plant Lists," page 152.
† See page 153.

Master List:
Summary of Cultural Preferences and Tolerances

KEY TO ABBREVIATIONS

ZONE

Plant hardiness zones adapted from U.S.D.A. Plant Hardiness Zone Map, 1990 (page 148).

Range of Average Annual Minimum Temperatures

1	Below −50° F.
2	−50° to −40° F.
3	−40° to −30° F.
4	−30° to −20° F.
5	−20° to −10° F.
6	−10° to 0° F.
7	0° to 10° F.
8	10° to 20° F.
9	20° to 30° F.
10	30° to 40° F.
11	Above 40° F.
T	Tender in the Mid-Atlantic Region

TYPE

W	Woody
P	Perennial
I	Biennial
A	Annual
B	Bulb
E	Evergreen

SOIL COMPOSITION

CL	Clay and Clay Loam
OL	Organic Loam
SL	Sandy Loam
SG	Stony, Gravelly

SOIL MOISTURE

B	Bog or Standing Water
WE	Water's Edge
CM	Consistently Moist, Not Boggy
AV	Average, Dry Between Rains
D	Dry
F	Fast-Draining

LIGHT

F	Full Sun
P	Partial Shade
S	Shade

TOLERANCE

W	Wind
PA	Poor Air Drainage
LF	Low Fertility
D	Drought
SS	Shallow Soil
HPH	High pH
HMS	Hot, Muggy Summers

NAME

RHODODENDRON VASEYI
  PINK-SHELL AZALEA
RHODODENDRON VISCOSUM
  SWAMP AZALEA
RHODODENDRON X ERIOCARPUM AND R. X NAKAHARAI
  CULTIVARS AND HYBRIDS
RHODODENDRON X GANDAVENSE 'COCCINEA SPECIOSA'
  GHENT HYBRID AZALEA (ORANGE)
RHODODENDRON X GANDAVENSE 'DAVIESII'
  GHENT HYBRID AZALEA (WHITE-YELLOW, FRAGRANT)
RHODOTYPOS SCANDENS
  JETBEAD

RHUS AROMATICA 'GRO-LOW'
  FRAGRANT SUMAC (DWARF)
RHUS TYPHINA
  STAGHORN SUMAC
RHUS TYPHINA 'LACINIATA'
  CUTLEAF STAGHORN SUMAC
RIBES ODORATUM
  CLOVE CURRANT
RICINUS COMMUNIS
  CASTOR BEAN
RICINUS COMMUNIS 'ZANZIBARENSIS'
  CASTOR BEAN

ROBINIA HISPIDA
  ROSE-ACACIA
RODGERSIA AESCULIFOLIA
  RODGERSIA
RODGERSIA PODOPHYLLA
  BRONZELEAF RODGERSIA
RODGERSIA TABULARIS
  SHIELDLEAF RODGERSIA
ROSA 'DOORENBOS SELECTION'
  HYBRID SPINOSISSIMA ROSE
ROSA (GALLICA) 'CHARLES DE MILLS'

ROSA (POLYANTHA) 'THE FAIRY'

ROSA (SHRUB) 'LILLIAN GIBSON'

ROSA (SHRUB) 'SEA FOAM'

ROSA CAROLINA
  PASTURE ROSE
ROSA EGLANTERIA
  EGLANTINE ROSE
ROSA NITIDA
  SHINING ROSE

ROSA ROXBURGHII
  CHESTNUT ROSE
ROSA RUGOSA AND HYBRIDS

ROSA VIRGINIANA
  VIRGINIA ROSE
RUBUS COCKBURNIANUS
  RASPBERRY (WHITE STEM)
RUBUS IDAEUS 'AUREUS'
  RASPBERRY (CREEPING, GOLDLEAF)
RUDBECKIA FULGIDA VAR. SULLIVANTII 'GOLDSTURM'
  GARDEN BLACK-EYED-SUSAN

FAMILY	ZONE*	TYPE	SIZE (FEET)	SOIL COMPOSITION	SOIL MOISTURE	LIGHT	TOLERANCE	NOTES†
ERICACEAE	5	W	6.5	OL	CM, AV, F	F, P	PA, HMS	
ERICACEAE	4	W	6.5	OL, SL	WE, CM, AV	F, P	PA, HMS	
ERICACEAE	6	W, E	1.0	OL	AV	F, P		20
ERICACEAE	5	W	3.0	OL	AV	F, P	PA, HMS	
ERICACEAE	5	W	3.0	OL	AV	F, P	PA, HMS	
ROSACEAE	5	W	3.0	CL, OL	AV, D, F	F, P, S	PA, D, HMS	
ANACARDIACEAE	3	W	1.5	CL, OL, SG	AV, D, F	F	PA, LF, D, HMS	
ANACARDIACEAE	3	W	6.5	CL, OL, SL, SG	AV, D, F	F	W, PA, LF, D, HMS	
ANACARDIACEAE	3	W	6.5	CL, OL, SL, SG	AV, D, F	F	W, PA, LF, D, SS, HMS	
SAXIFRAGACEAE	5	W	3.0	OL	AV	F		
EUPHORBIACEAE	T	A	6.5	OL	AV	F	PA, HMS	1
EUPHORBIACEAE	T	A	13.0	OL	AV	F	PA, HMS	1
LEGUMINOSAE	4	W	3.0	CL, OL, SL, SG	AV, D, F	F	PA, LF, D, HPH, HMS	8
SAXIFRAGACEAE	4	P	1.5	OL	B, WE, CM	P, S		
SAXIFRAGACEAE	4	P	1.5	OL	B, WE, CM	F, P		
SAXIFRAGACEAE	4	P	1.5	OL	B, WE, CM	F, P		
ROSACEAE	5	W	1.5	CL, OL, SL	AV, D, F	F	D	
ROSACEAE	5	W	3.0	CL, OL	AV	F		18b
ROSACEAE	5	W	1.5	CL, OL, SG	AV, D, F	F	D, SS	
ROSACEAE	5	W	6.5	CL, OL	AV	F	PA, HMS	18b
ROSACEAE	5	W	1.5	OL, SG	AV, D, F	F	SS	
ROSACEAE	5	W	3.0	CL, OL, SL, SG	AV, D, F	F	W, PA, LF, D, SS, HMS	
ROSACEAE	5	W	3.0	CL, OL	AV	F	W	
ROSACEAE	4	W	3.0	CL, OL, SL	AV, D, F	F	W, PA, LF, D, HMS	
ROSACEAE	6	W	6.5	CL, OL	AV	F	PA, HMS	
ROSACEAE	3	W	3.0	CL, OL, SL, SG	AV, D, F	F	W, D	
ROSACEAE	5	W	3.0	CL, OL, SL	WE, CM, AV, D, F	F	PA, D, HMS	
ROSACEAE	5	W	6.5	CL, OL	CM, AV	F	PA, D, HMS	6
ROSACEAE	6	W	0.5	OL	AV	F		
COMPOSITAE	3	P	1.5	CL, OL, SL	CM, AV	F	LF	

* See "Use of Plant Lists," page 152.
† See page 153.

Master List: Summary of Cultural Preferences and Tolerances

KEY TO ABBREVIATIONS

ZONE

Plant hardiness zones adapted from U.S.D.A. Plant Hardiness Zone Map, 1990 (page 148).

Range of Average Annual Minimum Temperatures

1	Below −50° F.
2	−50° to −40° F.
3	−40° to −30° F.
4	−30° to −20° F.
5	−20° to −10° F.
6	−10° to 0° F.
7	0° to 10° F.
8	10° to 20° F.
9	20° to 30° F.
10	30° to 40° F.
11	Above 40° F.
T	Tender in the Mid-Atlantic Region

TYPE

W	Woody
P	Perennial
I	Biennial
A	Annual
B	Bulb
E	Evergreen

SOIL COMPOSITION

CL	Clay and Clay Loam
OL	Organic Loam
SL	Sandy Loam
SG	Stony, Gravelly

SOIL MOISTURE

B	Bog or Standing Water
WE	Water's Edge
CM	Consistently Moist, Not Boggy
AV	Average, Dry Between Rains
D	Dry
F	Fast-Draining

LIGHT

F	Full Sun
P	Partial Shade
S	Shade

TOLERANCE

W	Wind
PA	Poor Air Drainage
LF	Low Fertility
D	Drought
SS	Shallow Soil
HPH	High pH
HMS	Hot, Muggy Summers

NAME

SAGINA SUBULATA
    CORSICAN PEARLWORT
SALIX 'HAKURO'
    WILLOW (YELLOW VARIEGATED)
SALIX ACUTIFOLIA 'LONGIFOLIA'
    SHARPLEAF PUSSY WILLOW
SALIX ALBA 'KALMTHOUT'
    WHITE WILLOW (YELLOW TWIG)
SALIX ALBA 'REGALIS'
    WHITE WILLOW (COLUMNAR, GRAY LEAF)
SALIX ALBA 'SERICEA'
    WHITE WILLOW (GRAY LEAF)

SALIX ALBA VAR. TRISTIS
    WEEPING WILLOW (YELLOW TWIG)
SALIX CHAENOMELOIDES
    PUSSY WILLOW (PURPLE STEM)
SALIX DAPHNOIDES 'AGLAIA'
    PUSSY WILLOW
SALIX ELAEAGNOS
    ROSEMARY-LEAVED WILLOW (NARROW, GRAY LEAF)
SALIX GRACILISTYLA
    BIG-CATKIN WILLOW
SALIX GRACILISTYLA 'MELANOSTACHYS'
    PUSSY WILLOW (BLACK)

SALIX REPENS VAR. ARGENTEA
    PUSSY WILLOW (CREEPING)
SALIX X RUBRA 'EUGENEI'
    RED PUSSY WILLOW (COLUMNAR)
SALVIA ARGENTEA
    SILVER SAGE
SAPONARIA OFFICINALIS
    BOUNCING BET
SASA VEITCHII
    VEITCH BAMBOO
SASSAFRAS ALBIDUM

SAXIFRAGA STOLONIFERA
    STRAWBERRY-BEGONIA
SCIADOPITYS VERTICILLATA
    UMBRELLA-PINE
SCILLA SIBERICA 'SPRING BEAUTY'
    SIBERIAN SQUILL
SEDUM 'AUTUMN JOY'

SEDUM 'VERA JAMISON'

SEDUM ELLACOMBIANUM

SEDUM FLORIFERUM 'WEIHANSTEPHANER GOLD'

SEDUM POPULIFOLIUM
    POPLAR STONECROP
SEDUM SARMENTOSUM
    STRINGY STONECROP
SEDUM SPURIUM
    TWO ROW STONECROP
SEDUM SPURIUM 'BRONZE CARPET'
    TWO ROW STONECROP (BRONZE FOLIAGE)
SEDUM TERNATUM
    MOUNTAIN STONECROP

FAMILY	ZONE*	TYPE	SIZE (FEET)	SOIL COMPOSITION	SOIL MOISTURE	LIGHT	TOLERANCE	NOTES†
CARYOPHYLLACEAE	5	P, E	0.0	SL, SG	CM, AV	F, P	LF	
SALICACEAE	5	W	6.5	OL	CM, AV	F		
SALICACEAE	5	W	13.0	OL, SL	WE, CM, AV	F	W	
SALICACEAE	3	W	3.0	CL, OL, SL	WE, CM, AV	F		
SALICACEAE	3	W	26.0	OL, SL	WE, CM, AV	F		
SALICACEAE	3	W	6.5	CL, OL, SL	WE, CM, AV	F		
SALICACEAE	4	W	52.0	OL	WE, CM, AV	F	HPH	
SALICACEAE	5	W	6.5	OL	CM, AV	F		
SALICACEAE	5	W	26.0	CL, OL	WE, CM, AV	F		
SALICACEAE	4	W	6.5	OL, SL	WE, CM, AV	F		
SALICACEAE	5	W	6.5	OL	CM, AV	F		
SALICACEAE	5	W	6.5	OL	CM, AV	F		
SALICACEAE	4	W	3.0	OL, SL	WE, CM, AV	F	W	
SALICACEAE	5	W	13.0	CL, OL, SL	WE, CM, AV	F		
LABIATAE	6	P	1.5	SL	AV, D, F	F	LF, D	4
CARYOPHYLLACEAE	2	P	1.5	OL, SL	F	F, P	LF	8
GRAMINEAE	7	W, E	1.5	OL	AV	F, P	PA, HMS	8
LAURACEAE	5	W	52.0	CL, OL	AV, D, F	F	W, PA, LF, D, HPH, HMS	
SAXIFRAGACEAE	6	P	0.0	OL	CM, AV	P		
TAXODIACEAE	6	W, E	26.0	OL	CM, AV, F	F		
LILIACEAE	5	B	0.0	OL, SL	CM, AV, FD	P	PA, HMS	
CRASSULACEAE	3	P	1.5	OL, SL	AV, F	F, P	LF, D, HMS	
CRASSULACEAE	5	P	0.0	CL, OL, SL	AV, D	F	W, PA, LF, D, HMS	
CRASSULACEAE	3	P	0.0	CL, OL, SL, SG	AV, D, F	F, P	W, PA, LF, D, HMS	
CRASSULACEAE	5	P	0.0	CL, OL, SL, SG	AV, D, F	F, P	W, PA, LF, D, HMS	
CRASSULACEAE	4	W	0.5	OL, SL	AV	F, P	LF, D, HMS	
CRASSULACEAE	3	P, E	0.0	CL, OL, SL, SG	AV, D, F	F, P	W, PA, LF, D, HMS	
CRASSULACEAE	3	P	0.0	CL, OL, SL, SG	AV, D, F	F, P	W, PA, LF, D, HMS	
CRASSULACEAE	3	P	0.5	CL, OL, SL, SG	AV, D, F	F, P	W, PA, LF, D, HMS	
CRASSULACEAE	4	P	0.0	OL, SG	CM, AV	P, S		

* See "Use of Plant Lists," page 152.
† See page 153.

Master List:
Summary of Cultural Preferences and Tolerances

KEY TO ABBREVIATIONS

ZONE

Plant hardiness zones adapted from U.S.D.A. Plant Hardiness Zone Map, 1990 (page 148).

Range of Average Annual Minimum Temperatures

1	Below −50° F.
2	−50° to −40° F.
3	−40° to −30° F.
4	−30° to −20° F.
5	−20° to −10° F.
6	−10° to 0° F.
7	0° to 10° F.
8	10° to 20° F.
9	20° to 30° F.
10	30° to 40° F.
11	Above 40° F.
T	Tender in the Mid-Atlantic Region

TYPE

W	Woody
P	Perennial
I	Biennial
A	Annual
B	Bulb
E	Evergreen

SOIL COMPOSITION

CL	Clay and Clay Loam
OL	Organic Loam
SL	Sandy Loam
SG	Stony, Gravelly

SOIL MOISTURE

B	Bog or Standing Water
WE	Water's Edge
CM	Consistently Moist, Not Boggy
AV	Average, Dry Between Rains
D	Dry
F	Fast-Draining

LIGHT

F	Full Sun
P	Partial Shade
S	Shade

TOLERANCE

W	Wind
PA	Poor Air Drainage
LF	Low Fertility
D	Drought
SS	Shallow Soil
HPH	High pH
HMS	Hot, Muggy Summers

NAME

SKIMMIA REEVESIANA

SOPHORA JAPONICA 'REGENT'
   JAPANESE PAGODA TREE
SORBARIA SORBIFOLIA
   URAL FALSE SPIRAEA
SPIRAEA PRUNIFOLIA
   BRIDAL-WREATH
SPIRAEA THUNBERGII

SPIRAEA X VANHOUTTEI

STACHYS BYZANTINA
   LAMB'S-EARS
STEPHANANDRA INCISA 'CRISPA'
   STEPHANANDRA (COMPACT CUTLEAF)
STERNBERGIA LUTEA
   FALL-DAFFODIL
STEWARTIA KOREANA

STOKESIA LAEVIS 'BLUE DANUBE'
   STOKES-ASTER
STRANVAESIA DAVIDIANA VAR. UNDULATA 'PROSTRATA'

STYRAX JAPONICUS
   JAPANESE SNOWBELL
STYRAX JAPONICUS 'CARILLON'
   JAPANESE SNOWBELL (WEEPING)
SYMPHORICARPOS X CHENAULTII 'HANCOCK'
   HANCOCK CORALBERRY
SYMPHYTUM X UPLANDICUM
   RUSSIAN COMFREY
SYRINGA LACINIATA
   CUT-LEAF LILAC

SYRINGA PATULA (SYN. S. PALIBINIANA,
   S. MICROPHYLLA 'INGWERSEN'S DWARF')
   LILAC (DWARF)
SYRINGA RETICULATA
   JAPANESE TREE LILAC
SYRINGA VULGARIS 'ALBA'
   LILAC (COMMON WHITE)
SYRINGA VULGARIS HYBRIDS
   HYBRID LILACS
SYRINGA X CHINENSIS
   CHINESE LILAC

TAMARIX RAMOSISSIMA
   TAMARISK
TAXODIUM DISTICHUM VAR. NUTANS 'PRAIRIE SENTINEL'
   PRAIRIE SENTINEL POND CYPRESS
TAXUS BACCATA 'ADPRESSA FOWLE'
   MIDGET BOXLEAF YEW
TAXUS BACCATA 'REPANDENS'
   WEEPING ENGLISH YEW
TAXUS CUSPIDATA 'NANA'
   DWARF JAPANESE YEW
TAXUS CUSPIDATA (CAPITATA SELECTION)
   PYRAMIDAL JAPANESE YEW

FAMILY	ZONE*	TYPE	SIZE (FEET)	SOIL COMPOSITION	SOIL MOISTURE	LIGHT	TOLERANCE	NOTES†
RUTACEAE	7	W, E	3.0	OL	CM, AV	P		
LEGUMINOSAE	6	W	52.0	OL	AV, D, F	F	PA, D, HPH, HMS	
ROSACEAE	3	W	3.0	OL	AV	F, P	LF, HPH	
ROSACEAE	5	W	3.0	OL	AV, D	F, P	PA, D, HMS	
ROSACEAE	4	W	3.0	CL, OL	AV, F	F		
ROSACEAE	3	W	3.0	OL	AV, D	F	D, HPH	
LABIATAE	4	P	1.0	SL	AV, D, F	F	W, LF, D, HMS	
ROSACEAE	5	W	1.5	CL, OL	AV, D, F	F, P	W	
AMARYLLIDACEAE	5	B	0.0	OL, SL	AV, D, FD	F	D, HPH	
THEACEAE	6	W	13.0	OL	CM, AV	F		
COMPOSITAE	5	P	1.0	OL, SL	F	F	D	10a, e
ROSACEAE	6	W, E	3.0	CL, OL	AV	F		
STYRACEAE	6	W	26.0	OL	CM, AV	F		
STYRACACEAE	6	W	6.5	OL	CM, AV	F		
CAPRIFOLIACEAE	5	W	3.0	CL, OL, SG	AV, D, F	F, P	PA, LF, D, SS, HPH, HMS	
BORAGINACEAE	5	P	3.0	CL, OL, SL	CM, AV	F, P	PA, D, HMS	16
OLEACEAE	5	W	3.0	CL, OL	AV, D, F	F	W, HPH	
OLEACEAE	4	W	3.0	CL, OL	AV, D, F	F	W, PA, D, HMS	
OLEACEAE	5	W	13.0	OL	AV, F	F	W, PA, D, HMS	
OLEACEAE	3	W	6.5	CL, OL	AV	F	HPH	
OLEACEAE	3	W	6.5	CL, OL	AV	F	HPH	
OLEACEAE	4	W	6.5	CL, OL	AV, D, F	F	W, PA, D, HPH, HMS	
TAMARICACEAE	4	W	13.0	OL, SL	AV, D	F	W, HPH	21
TAXODIACEAE	6	W	52.0	OL, SL	B, WE, CM	F	HPH	
TAXACEAE	5	W, E	1.5	OL	AV, F	F	PA, HMS	
TAXACEAE	5	W, E	3.0	OL	AV, F	F, P		
TAXACEAE	4	W, E	6.5	OL	AV, F	F, P	PA, HMS	
TAXACEAE	4	W, E	6.5	OL	CM, AV, F	F, P	PA, HMS	

* See "Use of Plant Lists," page 152.
† See page 153.

Master List:
Summary of Cultural Preferences and Tolerances

KEY TO ABBREVIATIONS

ZONE

Plant hardiness zones adapted from U.S.D.A. Plant Hardiness Zone Map, 1990 (page 148).

Range of Average Annual Minimum Temperatures

1	Below −50° F.
2	−50° to −40° F.
3	−40° to −30° F.
4	−30° to −20° F.
5	−20° to −10° F.
6	−10° to 0° F.
7	0° to 10° F.
8	10° to 20° F.
9	20° to 30° F.
10	30° to 40° F.
11	Above 40° F.
T	Tender in the Mid-Atlantic Region

TYPE

W Woody
P Perennial
I Biennial
A Annual
B Bulb
E Evergreen

SOIL COMPOSITION

CL Clay and Clay Loam
OL Organic Loam
SL Sandy Loam
SG Stony, Gravelly

SOIL MOISTURE

B Bog or Standing Water
WE Water's Edge
CM Consistently Moist, Not Boggy
AV Average, Dry Between Rains
D Dry
F Fast-Draining

LIGHT

F Full Sun
P Partial Shade
S Shade

TOLERANCE

W Wind
PA Poor Air Drainage
LF Low Fertility
D Drought
SS Shallow Soil
HPH High pH
HMS Hot, Muggy Summers

NAME

TAXUS X MEDIA 'SENTINALIS'
  SENTINAL YEW
TELEKIA SPECIOSA
  HEARTLEAF OXEYE
THALICTRUM ROCHEBRUNIANUM
  MEADOW RUE
THELYPTERIS HEXAGONOPTERA
  BROAD BEECH FERN
THELYPTERIS NOVEBORACENSIS
  NEW YORK FERN
THELYPTERIS PHEGOPTERIS
  NARROW BEECHFERN

THERMOPSIS CAROLINIANA
  CAROLINA LUPINE
THUJA OCCIDENTALIS 'HETZ' WINTERGREEN'
  'HETZ' WINTERGREEN ARBORVITAE
THUJA OCCIDENTALIS 'NIGRA'
  AMERICAN ARBORVITAE (DARK GREEN)
THUJA PLICATA 'ATROVIRENS'
  GIANT ARBORVITAE (BRIGHT GREEN)
THYMUS 'CLEAR GOLD'
  HYBRID THYME (YELLOW LEAF)
THYMUS PSEUDOLANUGINOSUS
  WOOLY THYME

THYMUS SERPYLLUM
  WILD THYME
TIARELLA CORDIFOLIA VAR. COLLINA
  WHERRY'S FOAM FLOWER
TILIA CORDATA
  LITTLELEAF LINDEN
TRACHYSTEMON ORIENTALIS

TSUGA CANADENSIS
  CANADIAN HEMLOCK
TSUGA CANADENSIS 'BENNETT'
  BENNETT'S DWARF HEMLOCK

TSUGA CANADENSIS 'COLE'S PROSTRATE'
  COLE'S PROSTRATE HEMLOCK
TSUGA CANADENSIS 'PENDULA'
  SARGENT'S WEEPING HEMLOCK
TYPHA ANGUSTIFOLIA
  NARROWLEAVED CATTAIL
VACCINIUM CORYMBOSUM
  HIGHBUSH BLUEBERRY
VALERIANA OFFICINALIS
  GARDEN HELIOTROPE
VERBASCUM OLYMPICUM
  OLYMPIC MULLEIN

VERNONIA NOVEBORACENSIS
  IRONWEED
VERONICA 'SUNNY BORDER BLUE'
  SPEEDWELL
VERONICA INCANA
  WOOLY SPEEDWELL
VERONICA LONGIFOLIA 'SUBSESSILIS'
  SPEEDWELL (BLUE)
VERONICASTRUM VIRGINICUM
  CULVER'S ROOT
VIBURNUM ACERIFOLIUM
  MAPLELEAF VIBURNUM

FAMILY	ZONE*	TYPE	SIZE (FEET)	SOIL COMPOSITION	SOIL MOISTURE	LIGHT	TOLERANCE	NOTES†
TAXACEAE	5	W, E	6.5	OL	AV, F	F	PA, HMS	12
COMPOSITAE	3	P	3.0	OL	WE, CM, AV	F	HPH	
RANUNCULACEAE	5	P	3.0	OL	CM, AV	P		
POLYPODIACEAE	5	P	1.0	OL	CM, F	P, S	D	
POLYPODIACEAE	5	P	1.0	OL	CM, F	P		
POLYPODIACEAE	5	P	1.0	OL	CM, F	P, S	D	
LEGUMINOSAE	3	P	3.0	OL, SL	AV, D, F	F	D	
CUPRESSACEAE	4	W, E	26.0	OL	CM, AV	F	HPH	
CUPRESSACEAE	3	W, E	26.0	CL, OL	AV	F	PA, D, HMS	
CUPRESSACEAE	5	W, E	52.0	OL	CM, AV	F		
LABIATAE	5	P	0.0	OL, SL, SG	AV, D, F	F, P	PA, LF, D, SS, HMS	
LABIATAE	5	P	0.0	OL, SL, SG	AV, D, F	F, P	PA, LF, D, SS, HMS	
LABIATAE	3	P	0.0	OL, SL, SG	D, F	F, P	PA, LF, D, SS, HMS	
SAXIFRAGACEAE	3	P	0.5	OL	CM, AV	P		
TILIACEAE	3	W	52.0	OL	AV	F	HPH	
BORAGINACEAE	6	P	1.5	CL, OL	CM, AV	P, S	PA, HMS	19
PINACEAE	3	W, E	52.0	OL	CM, AV	F, P		23
PINACEAE	3	W, E	3.0	CL, OL	AV	F, P		23
PINACEAE	3	W, E	3.0	CL, OL	AV	F, P	PA, HMS	23
PINACEAE	3	W, E	6.5	CL, OL	AV	F, P		23
TYPHACEAE	4	P	3.0	OL, SL	B, WE	F, P	PA, HMS	
ERICACEAE	4	W	6.5	OL, SL, SG	AV, D, F	F, P	W, PA, SS, HMS	
VALERIANACEAE	5	P	3.0	OL	CM	F		
SCROPHULARIACEAE	5	I	3.0	CL, OL, SL	AV, D, F	F	W, PA, LF, D, HMS	3
COMPOSITAE	4	P	3.0	OL	CM, AV	F	PA, HMS	
SCROPHULARIACEAE	4	P	1.5	OL	CM, AV, F	F, P		
SCROPHULARIACEAE	3	P	0.5	OL	AV, F	F, P		
SCROPHULARIACEAE	4	P	1.5	OL	CM, AV, F	F, P		
SCROPHULARIACEAE	3	P	3.0	OL	CM, AV	F	HPH	
CAPRIFOLIACEAE	3	W	3.0	OL, SG	AV, D, F	P, S	PA, D, HMS	

* See "Use of Plant Lists," page 152.
† See page 153.

Master List:
Summary of Cultural Preferences and Tolerances

KEY TO ABBREVIATIONS

ZONE

Plant hardiness zones adapted from U.S.D.A. Plant Hardiness Zone Map, 1990 (page 148).

Range of Average Annual Minimum Temperatures

1	Below −50° F.
2	−50° to −40° F.
3	−40° to −30° F.
4	−30° to −20° F.
5	−20° to −10° F.
6	−10° to 0° F.
7	0° to 10° F.
8	10° to 20° F.
9	20° to 30° F.
10	30° to 40° F.
11	Above 40° F.
T	Tender in the Mid-Atlantic Region

TYPE

W	Woody
P	Perennial
I	Biennial
A	Annual
B	Bulb
E	Evergreen

SOIL COMPOSITION

CL	Clay and Clay Loam
OL	Organic Loam
SL	Sandy Loam
SG	Stony, Gravelly

SOIL MOISTURE

B	Bog or Standing Water
WE	Water's Edge
CM	Consistently Moist, Not Boggy
AV	Average, Dry Between Rains
D	Dry
F	Fast-Draining

LIGHT

F	Full Sun
P	Partial Shade
S	Shade

TOLERANCE

W	Wind
PA	Poor Air Drainage
LF	Low Fertility
D	Drought
SS	Shallow Soil
HPH	High pH
HMS	Hot, Muggy Summers

NAME

VIBURNUM CARLESII
  KOREAN SPICE VIBURNUM
VIBURNUM DILATATUM 'MICHAEL DODGE'
  LINDEN VIBURNUM (YELLOW FRUIT)
VIBURNUM FARRERI 'CANDIDISSIMUM'
  FRAGRANT VIBURNUM (WHITE-FLOWERED)
VIBURNUM FARRERI 'NANUM'
  DWARF FRAGRANT VIBURNUM
VIBURNUM ICHANGENSE

VIBURNUM MACROCEPHALUM FORMA MACROCEPHALUM
  CHINESE SNOWBALL VIBURNUM

VIBURNUM NUDUM 'WINTERTHUR'
  SMOOTH WITHE-ROD (SUPERIOR SELECTION)
VIBURNUM PLICATUM FORMA TOMENTOSUM
  DOUBLE-FILE VIBURNUM
VIBURNUM PRUNIFOLIUM
  BLACKHAW
VIBURNUM RHYTIDOPHYLLUM
  LEATHERLEAF VIBURNUM
VIBURNUM SETIGERUM
  TEA VIBURNUM
VIBURNUM SIEBOLDII 'SENECA'

VINCA MINOR 'BOWLESII'
  BOWLES PERIWINKLE
VINCA MINOR 'VARIEGATA'
  PERIWINKLE (GREEN AND YELLOW)
VIOLA LABRADORICA

VITEX AGNUS-CASTUS 'LATIFOLIA'
  MONK'S PEPPER, CHASTE TREE (BLUE)
VITEX AGNUS-CASTUS 'SILVER SPIRE'
  MONK'S PEPPER, CHASTE TREE (WHITE)
WALDSTEINIA TERNATA

WISTERIA FLORIBUNDA
  JAPANESE WISTERIA
XANTHORHIZA SIMPLICISSIMA
  YELLOWROOT
YUCCA FLACCIDA 'GOLDEN SWORD'
  ADAM'S NEEDLE (YELLOW VARIEGATED)
YUCCA GLAUCA
  SOAPWEED
YUCCA SMALLIANA
  ADAM'S-NEEDLE
ZELKOVA SERRATA 'GREEN VASE'

FAMILY	ZONE*	TYPE	SIZE (FEET)	SOIL COMPOSITION	SOIL MOISTURE	LIGHT	TOLERANCE	NOTES†
CAPRIFOLIACEAE	4	W	3.0	OL	AV	F	HPH	
CAPRIFOLIACEAE	5	W	6.5	OL	AV	F, P		
CAPRIFOLIACEAE	5	W	6.5	OL	AV	F, P	HPH	
CAPRIFOLIACEAE	5	W	3.0	OL	AV	F, P		
CAPRIFOLIACEAE	6	W	6.5	OL	AV	F		
CAPRIFOLIACEAE	7	W	13.0	OL	CM, AV, D, F	F	PA, HMS	
CAPRIFOLIACEAE	6	W	6.5	OL	CM, AV	F		
CAPRIFOLIACEAE	5	W	6.5	CL, OL	CM, AV, F	F, P	PA, HMS	
CAPRIFOLIACEAE	3	W	13.0	CL, OL	AV, D	F, P	D, HPH	
CAPRIFOLIACEAE	6	W, E	6.5	OL	AV	P	HPH	
CAPRIFOLIACEAE	6	W	6.5	OL	AV	F		
CAPRIFOLIACEAE	5	W	13.0	CL, OL	AV, D, F	F	W, PA, D, HPH, HMS	
APOCYNACEAE	4	W, E	0.0	OL	AV	F, P, S	PA, D, HMS	18b
APOCYNACEAE	4	W, E	0.0	OL	AV	F, P, S	PA, HMS	
VIOLACEAE	4	P	0.0	OL	AV	P		
VERBENACEAE	6	W	3.0	OL	AV, D, F	F	PA, LF, D, HMS	6
VERBENACEAE	6	W	3.0	OL	AV, D, F	F	PA, LF, D, HMS	6
ROSACEAE	4	P, E	0.0	OL	CM, AV, D, F	F, P		
LEGUMINOSAE	5	W	13.0	CL, OL, SL	AV, D, F	F	W, PA, D, HMS	17
RANUNCULACEAE	5	W	1.0	OL, SL	CM, AV	F, P	PA, HMS	
AGAVACEAE	4	W, E	3.0	CL, OL, SL	AV, D, F	F	W, PA, LF, D, HMS	
AGAVACEAE	4	W, E	3.0	CL, OL, SL	AV, D, F	F	W, PA, LF, D, HMS	
AGAVACEAE	4	W, E	3.0	CL, OL, SL	AV, D, F	F	W, PA, LF, D, HMS	
ULMACEAE	6	W	52.0	OL	AV	F	HPH	

APPENDIX 1B
Master List:
Summary of Design Characteristics

This listing presents, in alphabetical order by Latin name (common name follows Latin name), all of the roughly six hundred plants contained in the basic palette and provides standard design characteristics about each. For lists of plants with the specific design characteristics covered here, see Appendices 13-15 and 19-26. The figures listed under the heading "Size (Feet)" represent the lower end of the size range for each plant. A key to abbreviations is on each page.

KEY TO ABBREVIATIONS

TYPE

W	Woody	A	Annual
P	Perennial	B	Bulb
I	Biennial	E	Evergreen

STRUCTURE

VT	Vertical
H	Horizontal
MO	Mound
BS	Ball on a Stick
VS	Vase
W	Weeping
I	Irregular, Sculptural
MS	Multistemmed
C	Climbing

COLOR: FOLIAGE, SPRING & SUMMER

BG	Blue-Green
GR	Gray-Green
GW	Green and White Variegated
YG	Yellow-Green
GG	Green and Gold Variegated
PR	Pink and Red

COLOR: FOLIAGE, FALL

O	Orange	R	Red
Y	Yellow	W	Wine

COLOR: FLOWER

Y	Yellow	PU	Purple
O	Orange	V	Violet
A	Apricot	B	Blue
R	Red	C	Chartreuse
PK	Pink	W	White

FLOWER COLOR: BY MONTH

1	January	7	July
2	February	8	August
3	March	9	September
4	April	10	October
5	May	11	November
6	June	12	December

COLOR: FRUIT & SEED HEAD

Y	Yellow
O	Orange, Brown
R	Red
PB	Purple-Black
B	Blue
W	White-Silver

FRUIT & SEED HEAD COLOR BY MONTH

1	January	7	July
2	February	8	August
3	March	9	September
4	April	10	October
5	May	11	November
6	June	12	December

COLOR: BARK

Y	Yellow	PU	Purple
OC	Orange-Cherry	GN	Green
		GR	Gray
R	Red	W	White

TEXTURE: FOLIAGE

FN	Fine Detail—Narrow, Linear—Needle
FB	Fine Detail—Narrow, Linear—Blade
FR	Fine Detail—Small, Rounded
FO	Fine Detail—Other Leaf Shapes
BS	Broad—Strong Design Impact
BM	Broad—For Ground Cover Massing

TEXTURE: FLOWER

S	Spikes, Cones, Wands, and Spraylike Heads
P	Pendulous
FD	Daisylike
FT	Flat Top
BL	Ball-like
I	Irregular and/or Complex

TEXTURE: BARK

BK	Interesting Bark Texture

NAME

ABELIA X GRANDIFLORA
  GLOSSY ABELIA
ABIES NORDMANNIANA
  NORDMANN FIR
ACANTHOPANAX SIEBOLDIANUS
  FIVELEAF-ARALIA
ACER GRISEUM
  PAPERBARK MAPLE
ACER PALMATUM 'BLOODGOOD'
  REDLEAF JAPANESE MAPLE

ACER PALMATUM 'EVER RED'
  RED CUTLEAF JAPANESE MAPLE
ACER PALMATUM 'SANGOKAKU'
  REDTWIG JAPANESE MAPLE
ACER PALMATUM VAR. DISSECTUM OR A. P. 'WATERFALL'
  GREEN CUTLEAF JAPANESE MAPLE
ACER PLATANOIDES 'CRIMSON KING'
  CRIMSON KING NORWAY MAPLE
ACER RUBRUM
  SWAMP MAPLE
ACER SACCHARUM
  SUGAR MAPLE

ACHILLEA 'CORONATION GOLD'
  HYBRID YARROW
ACHILLEA 'MOONSHINE'
  HYBRID YARROW
ACHILLEA MILLEFOLIUM 'ROSEA'
  PINK COMMON YARROW
ACIDANTHERA BICOLOR
  PEACOCK-ORCHID
ACORUS GRAMINEUS 'OGON'
  GRASSY-LEAVED SWEET FLAG
ADIANTUM PEDATUM
  MAIDENHAIR FERN

ADINA RUBELLA
  GLOSSY ADINA
AEGOPODIUM PODAGRARIA 'VARIEGATUM'
  VARIEGATED GOUTWEED
AESCULUS PARVIFLORA
  BOTTLEBRUSH BUCKEYE
AESCULUS SPLENDENS
  FLAME BUCKEYE
AJUGA REPTANS
  CARPET BUGLEWEED
AJUGA REPTANS 'BRONZE BEAUTY'
  CARPET BUGLEWEED (BRONZE FOLIAGE)

AJUGA REPTANS (GIANT FORM)
  BUGLEWEED
ALCHEMILLA VULGARIS
  LADY'S-MANTLE
ALLIUM CERNUUM
  NODDING ONION
ALLIUM TUBEROSUM
  GARLIC CHIVE
ALLIUM ZEBDANENSE

AMELANCHIER ARBOREA (SYN. A. CANADENSIS)
  SHADBUSH, SERVICEBERRY

| GENERAL DESIGN | | | COLOR | | | | | | | TEXTURE | | |
TYPE	SIZE (FEET)	STRUCTURE	FOLIAGE SPRING & SUMMER	FALL	FLOWER COLOR	MONTH	FRUIT & SEED HEAD COLOR	MONTH	BARK	FOLIAGE	FLOWER	BARK
W	3.0	MO		W	PK, W	7, 8, 9				P		
W, E	52.0	VT							GR	FN		
W	6.5	MO	YG		C	5				FO		BK
W	13.0	BS, I		O, Y, R					OC, PU			BK
W	13.0	H	PR	R					R, PU, GR	FO		
W	6.5	MO, I	PR	W					R, PU, GR	FO		
W	13.0	VS, I							R			
W	6.5	MO, I	YG	O, Y					GN, GR	FO		
W	26.0	BS	PR		R	5				BS	BL	
W	26.0	BS		Y, R	R	4			GR			
W	52.0	BS		O, Y, R								
P	1.5				Y	6, 7				FO	FT	
P	0.5	H	GR		Y	6, 7				FO	FT	
P	1.5	H, MO			PK	6				FO	FT	
A	3.0	VT			W	8, 9					P	
P	1.0		GG							FB		
P	1.5	H	BG							FR		
W	3.0	MO	PR		W	8						BK
P	0.5	H	GW									
W	6.5				W	6				BS	S	
W	13.0	BS			PK	6				BS	S	
P	0.0	H			V, B	5				BM	S	
P	0.0	H	PR	R	B	5				BM	S	
P	0.0	H			B	5				BM	S	
P	1.0	H, MO	GR		C	5, 6					I	
B	0.5	W			PK	6				FB	BL	
B	1.0	MO			W	8, 9				FB	BL	
B	0.0	H			W	4, 5				FB	BL	
W	26.0	BS, I, MS		Y, R	W	4, 5	R, PB	6, 7	PU, GR		I, P	

Master List:
Summary of Design Characteristics

KEY TO ABBREVIATIONS

TYPE

W	Woody	A	Annual
P	Perennial	B	Bulb
I	Biennial	E	Evergreen

STRUCTURE

VT	Vertical
H	Horizontal
MO	Mound
BS	Ball on a Stick
VS	Vase
W	Weeping
I	Irregular, Sculptural
MS	Multistemmed
C	Climbing

COLOR: FOLIAGE, SPRING & SUMMER

BG	Blue-Green
GR	Gray-Green
GW	Green and White Variegated
YG	Yellow-Green
GG	Green and Gold Variegated
PR	Pink and Red

COLOR: FOLIAGE, FALL

O	Orange	R	Red
Y	Yellow	W	Wine

COLOR: FLOWER

Y	Yellow	PU	Purple
O	Orange	V	Violet
A	Apricot	B	Blue
R	Red	C	Chartreuse
PK	Pink	W	White

FLOWER COLOR: BY MONTH

1	January	7	July
2	February	8	August
3	March	9	September
4	April	10	October
5	May	11	November
6	June	12	December

COLOR: FRUIT & SEED HEAD

Y	Yellow
O	Orange, Brown
R	Red
PB	Purple-Black
B	Blue
W	White-Silver

FRUIT & SEED HEAD COLOR BY MONTH

1	January	7	July
2	February	8	August
3	March	9	September
4	April	10	October
5	May	11	November
6	June	12	December

COLOR: BARK

Y	Yellow	PU	Purple
OC	Orange-Cherry	GN	Green
		GR	Gray
R	Red	W	White

TEXTURE: FOLIAGE

FN	Fine Detail—Narrow, Linear—Needle
FB	Fine Detail—Narrow, Linear—Blade
FR	Fine Detail—Small, Rounded
FO	Fine Detail—Other Leaf Shapes
BS	Broad—Strong Design Impact
BM	Broad—For Ground Cover Massing

TEXTURE: FLOWER

S	Spikes, Cones, Wands, and Spraylike Heads
P	Pendulous
FD	Daisylike
FT	Flat Top
BL	Ball-like
I	Irregular and/or Complex

TEXTURE: BARK

BK	Interesting Bark Texture

NAME

AMSONIA HUBRICHTII
  BLUESTAR (NARROWLEAF)
AMSONIA TABERNAEMONTANA
  BLUE STAR
ANEMONE BLANDA 'ATROCAERULEA'
  WINDFLOWER
ANEMONE VITIFOLIA 'ROBUSTISSIMA'

ANEMONE X HYBRIDA 'QUEEN CHARLOTTE'
  JAPANESE ANEMONE (HYBRID, PINK)

ARABIS PROCURRENS
  ROCKCRESS
ARALIA SPINOSA
  DEVIL'S-WALKING STICK
ARENARIA VERNA
  IRISH MOSS
ARONIA ARBUTIFOLIA 'BRILLIANTISSIMA'
  RED CHOKEBERRY
ARTEMESIA ABSINTHIUM 'LAMBROOK SILVER'

ARTEMESIA LUDOVICIANA 'SILVER QUEEN'

ARTEMESIA STELLERIANA
  BEACH WORMWOOD
ARTEMESIA VERSICOLOR
  MUGWORT
ARUM ITALICUM 'PICTUM'

ARUNCUS AETHUSIFOLIUS
  GOAT'S BEARD (KOREAN)
ARUNCUS DIOICUS
  GOAT'S BEARD
ARUNDINARIA VIRIDISTRIATA
  BAMBOO (YELLOW VARIEGATED)

ARUNDO DONAX
  GIANT REED
ASARUM EUROPAEUM
  EUROPEAN WILD-GINGER
ASCLEPIAS TUBEROSA
  BUTTERFLY-WEED
ASPHODELINE LUTEA
  ASPHODEL
ASTER AMELLUS 'NOCTURNE'
  ITALIAN ASTER
ASTER CORDIFOLIUS
  BLUE WOOD ASTER

ASTER NOVAE-ANGLIAE 'HARRINGTON'S PINK'
  NEW ENGLAND ASTER
ASTER PUNICEUS
  SWAMP ASTER
ASTER TATARICUS
  TARTARIAN ASTER
ASTER X FRIKARTII 'MONCH'

ASTILBE X ARENDSII CULTIVARS

ATHYRIUM GOERINGIANUM 'PICTUM'
  JAPANESE SILVER FERN

GENERAL DESIGN   COLOR   TEXTURE

TYPE	SIZE (FEET)	STRUCTURE	FOLIAGE SPRING & SUMMER	FALL	FLOWER COLOR	FLOWER MONTH	FRUIT & SEED HEAD COLOR	MONTH	BARK	TEXTURE FOLIAGE	FLOWER	BARK
P	1.5		YG	Y	B	5				FN	I	
P	3.0				B	5					I	
B	0.0	H			B	4					FD	
P	1.5				PK	8					FD	
P	3.0				PK	8, 9					FD	
P, E	0.5	H			W	5					FD	
W	26.0	H, VS, MS		R	W	7, 8	R, PB	8, 9		BS	S	
P	0.0	H			W							
W	6.5			R	W		R	10, 11, 12			FT, P	
P	3.0		GR									
P	1.5		GR							FO		
P	0.5	H	GR							FO		
P	0.0		GR							FO		
P, E	1.5				Y, C	5, 6	R	7		BM, BS	S	
P	0.5	H			W	5				FO	S	
P	3.0				W	6				FO	S	
W	1.5	H	GG							BM, BS		
P	13.0	VT, I	GR		W	9, 10	W	10, 11		BS	S	
P, E	0.0	H								BM		
P	1.5	MO			Y, O	7, 8					FT	
P	1.5	VT, I	GR		Y	5, 6				FB	S	
P	1.0				V, B	7, 8					FD	
P	3.0				V, B, W	8, 9, 10					FD	
P	3.0				PK	9, 10					FD	
P	3.0				V, B	9, 10					FD	
P	6.5	I			PU, V, B	9, 10					FD	
P	1.5	MO			V, B	8, 9					FD	
P	1.5	MO			A, R, P, PU, V, W	6				FO	S	
P	0.5	H	GR							FO		

Master List:
Summary of Design Characteristics

KEY TO ABBREVIATIONS

TYPE

W	Woody	A	Annual
P	Perennial	B	Bulb
I	Biennial	E	Evergreen

STRUCTURE

VT	Vertical
H	Horizontal
MO	Mound
BS	Ball on a Stick
VS	Vase
W	Weeping
I	Irregular, Sculptural
MS	Multistemmed
C	Climbing

COLOR: FOLIAGE, SPRING & SUMMER

BG	Blue-Green
GR	Gray-Green
GW	Green and White Variegated
YG	Yellow-Green
GG	Green and Gold Variegated
PR	Pink and Red

COLOR: FOLIAGE, FALL

O	Orange	R	Red
Y	Yellow	W	Wine

COLOR: FLOWER

Y	Yellow	PU	Purple
O	Orange	V	Violet
A	Apricot	B	Blue
R	Red	C	Chartreuse
PK	Pink	W	White

FLOWER COLOR: BY MONTH

1	January	7	July
2	February	8	August
3	March	9	September
4	April	10	October
5	May	11	November
6	June	12	December

COLOR: FRUIT & SEED HEAD

Y	Yellow
O	Orange, Brown
R	Red
PB	Purple-Black
B	Blue
W	White-Silver

FRUIT & SEED HEAD COLOR BY MONTH

1	January	7	July
2	February	8	August
3	March	9	September
4	April	10	October
5	May	11	November
6	June	12	December

COLOR: BARK

Y	Yellow	PU	Purple
OC	Orange-Cherry	GN	Green
		GR	Gray
R	Red	W	White

TEXTURE: FOLIAGE

FN	Fine Detail—Narrow, Linear—Needle
FB	Fine Detail—Narrow, Linear—Blade
FR	Fine Detail—Small, Rounded
FO	Fine Detail—Other Leaf Shapes
BS	Broad—Strong Design Impact
BM	Broad—For Ground Cover Massing

TEXTURE: FLOWER

S	Spikes, Cones, Wands, and Spraylike Heads
P	Pendulous
FD	Daisylike
FT	Flat Top
BL	Ball-like
I	Irregular and/or Complex

TEXTURE: BARK

BK	Interesting Bark Texture

NAME

BACCHARIS HALIMIFOLIA, PISTILLATE
GROUNDSELBUSH (SEED-BEARING)
BAPTISIA AUSTRALIS
BLUE FALSE INDIGO
BEGONIA GRANDIS
HARDY BEGONIA
BERBERIS JULIANAE 'NANA'
WINTERGREEN BARBERRY (COMPACT)
BERBERIS THUNBERGII 'ATROPURPUREA'
REDLEAF JAPANESE BARBERRY

BERBERIS THUNBERGII 'CRIMSON PYGMY'
CRIMSON PYGMY BARBERRY
BERBERIS WILSONIAE VAR. STAPFIANA
WILSON'S BARBERRY
BERBERIS WISLEYENSIS (SYN. B. TRIACANTHOPHORA)
THREESPINE BARBERRY
BERGENIA 'PERFECTA'
HYBRID PIGSQUEAK
BERGENIA 'SUNNINGDALE'
HYBRID PIGSQUEAK
BETULA LENTA
SWEET BIRCH

BETULA NIGRA
RIVER BIRCH
BETULA PAPYRIFERA
PAPER BIRCH
BETULA PENDULA 'GRACILIS'
CUTLEAF EUROPEAN BIRCH
BETULA PENDULA 'YOUNGII'
WEEPING EUROPEAN BIRCH
BIGNONIA CAPREOLATA
CROSS VINE
BOLTONIA ASTEROIDES 'SNOWBANK'

BRUNNERA MACROPHYLLA
SIBERIAN BUGLOSS
BUDDLEIA ALTERNIFOLIA
FOUNTAIN BUDDLEIA
BUDDLEIA DAVIDII 'BLACK KNIGHT'
BUTTERFLY BUSH (DARK PURPLE)
BUDDLEIA DAVIDII 'OPERA'
BUTTERFLY BUSH (ELECTRIC MAUVE)
BUDDLEIA DAVIDII 'PURPLE PRINCE'
BUTTERFLY BUSH (LAVENDER)
BUPHTHALUM SALICIFOLIUM
WILLOWLEAF OXEYE

BUXUS 'GREEN GEM'
GREEN GEM BOXWOOD
BUXUS MICROPHYLLA 'COMPACTA'
KINGSVILLE LITTLELEAF BOXWOOD
BUXUS SEMPERVIRENS 'SUFFRUTICOSA'
DWARF ENGLISH BOXWOOD
BUXUS SINICA VAR. INSULARIS 'TIDE HILL'
TIDE HILL KOREAN BOXWOOD

BUXUS SINICA VAR. INSULARIS
'WINTERGREEN' (OHIO CULTIVAR)
WINTERGREEN KOREAN BOXWOOD

GENERAL DESIGN			COLOR							TEXTURE		
TYPE	SIZE (FEET)	STRUCTURE	FOLIAGE SPRING & SUMMER	FALL	FLOWER COLOR	MONTH	FRUIT & SEED HEAD COLOR	MONTH	BARK	FOLIAGE	FLOWER	BARK
W	6.5	MO			W	9	W	9, 10, 11				
P	3.0	MO	BG		V, B	5, 6					S	
P	1.5	H, W			PK	8, 9					P	
W, E	3.0		YG	O, R	Y	5						
W	3.0	MO	PR	R	Y	4						
W	1.5	H, MO	PR		Y	4						
W	3.0	MO	BG	R						FR		
W, E	3.0		YG	O, Y	Y					FN		
P, E	1.0	MO		W	PK	4, 5				BS, BM	I	
P, E	1.0	MO		W	PK	4, 5				BS, BM	I	
W	26.0	BS		Y					R, PU			BK
W	52.0	VS, MS		Y					OC, R			BK
W	52.0	VS, MS		Y					W			
W	26.0	W		Y					W	FO		
W	13.0	W, IS		Y					W			
W, E	52.0	C		Y, R, W	Y, O, R	5, 6					I	
P	3.0				W	9, 10					FD	
P	1.0	H, MO			B	4, 5				BM	I	
W	6.5	MO, BS, W			V	5					S, P	
W	3.0			O	PU	7, 8					S	
W	3.0			O	PK, PU						S	
W	3.0			O	PU	7, 8					S	
P	1.5				Y	6, 7				FN	FD	
W, E	1.5	MO										
W, E	0.5											
W, E	3.0	MO										
W, E	1.0	MO								FR		
W, E	1.5	MO										

Master List:
Summary of Design Characteristics

KEY TO ABBREVIATIONS

TYPE

W	Woody	A	Annual
P	Perennial	B	Bulb
I	Biennial	E	Evergreen

STRUCTURE

VT	Vertical
H	Horizontal
MO	Mound
BS	Ball on a Stick
VS	Vase
W	Weeping
I	Irregular, Sculptural
MS	Multistemmed
C	Climbing

COLOR: FOLIAGE, SPRING & SUMMER

BG	Blue-Green
GR	Gray-Green
GW	Green and White Variegated
YG	Yellow-Green
GG	Green and Gold Variegated
PR	Pink and Red

COLOR: FOLIAGE, FALL

O	Orange	R	Red
Y	Yellow	W	Wine

COLOR: FLOWER

Y	Yellow	PU	Purple
O	Orange	V	Violet
A	Apricot	B	Blue
R	Red	C	Chartreuse
PK	Pink	W	White

FLOWER COLOR: BY MONTH

1	January	7	July
2	February	8	August
3	March	9	September
4	April	10	October
5	May	11	November
6	June	12	December

COLOR: FRUIT & SEED HEAD

Y	Yellow
O	Orange, Brown
R	Red
PB	Purple-Black
B	Blue
W	White-Silver

FRUIT & SEED HEAD COLOR BY MONTH

1	January	7	July
2	February	8	August
3	March	9	September
4	April	10	October
5	May	11	November
6	June	12	December

COLOR: BARK

Y	Yellow	PU	Purple
OC	Orange-Cherry	GN	Green
		GR	Gray
R	Red	W	White

TEXTURE: FOLIAGE

FN	Fine Detail—Narrow, Linear—Needle
FB	Fine Detail—Narrow, Linear—Blade
FR	Fine Detail—Small, Rounded
FO	Fine Detail—Other Leaf Shapes
BS	Broad—Strong Design Impact
BM	Broad—For Ground Cover Massing

TEXTURE: FLOWER

S	Spikes, Cones, Wands, and Spraylike Heads
P	Pendulous
FD	Daisylike
FT	Flat Top
BL	Ball-like
I	Irregular and/or Complex

TEXTURE: BARK

BK	Interesting Bark Texture

NAME

CALAMAGROSTIS X ACUTIFLORA 'KARL FOERSTER'
    (SYN. C. EPIGEOUS 'HORTORUM')
    FEATHER-REED GRASS
CALLICARPA DICHOTOMA
    CHINESE BEAUTYBERRY
CALLICARPA JAPONICA
    JAPANESE BEAUTYBERRY
CALOCEDRUS DECURRENS
    INCENSE-CEDAR

CALYCANTHUS FLORIDUS 'EDITH WILDER'
    SWEET SHRUB
CAMPANULA RAPUNCULOIDES
    CREEPING BELLFLOWER
CAMPSIS X TAGLIABUANA 'MADAME GALEN'
    MADAME GALEN TRUMPET VINE
CANNA X GENERALIS 'MOHAWK'

CARPINUS BETULUS
    EUROPEAN HORNBEAM
CARYA OVATA
    SHAGBARK HICKORY

CARYOPTERIS X CLANDONENSIS 'BLUE MIST'
    BLUEBEARD
CATALPA BIGNONIOIDES
    SOUTHERN CATALPA
CEDRUS ATLANTICA 'GLAUCA'
    BLUE ATLAS CEDAR
CEDRUS LIBANI VAR. STENOCOMA
    CEDAR-OF-LEBANON
CEPHALANTHUS OCCIDENTALIS
    BUTTONBUSH
CEPHALOTAXUS HARRINGTONIA VAR. PEDUNCULATA
    PLUM YEW (SPREADING)

CERATOSTIGMA PLUMBAGINOIDES
    PLUMBAGO
CERCIDIPHYLLUM JAPONICUM
    KATSURA TREE
CERCIS CANADENSIS 'FOREST PANSY'
    FOREST PANSY REDBUD
CERCIS CHINENSIS
    CHINESE REDBUD
CESTRUM NOCTURNUM
    NIGHT JESSAMINE
CHAENOMELES JAPONICA VAR. ALPINA
    ALPINE JAPANESE FLOWERING QUINCE

CHAENOMELES SPECIOSA CULTIVARS
    FLOWERING QUINCE
CHAENOMELES X SUPERBA 'JET TRAIL'
    HYBRID FLOWERING QUINCE (SPREADING, WHITE-FLOWERED)
CHAENOMELES X SUPERBA CULTIVARS
    HYBRID FLOWERING QUINCE
CHAMAECYPARIS OBTUSA 'CRIPPSII'
    CRIPPS HINOKI FALSE CYPRESS (GOLD-PLUMED)
CHAMAECYPARIS OBTUSA 'FILICOIDES'
    FERNSPRAY HINOKI FALSE CYPRESS

TYPE	SIZE (FEET)	STRUCTURE	FOLIAGE SPRING & SUMMER	FALL	FLOWER COLOR	MONTH	FRUIT & SEED HEAD COLOR	MONTH	BARK	FOLIAGE	FLOWER	BARK
P	3.0	VT	YG	O	A	6	O	7, 8, 9, 10		FB	S	
W	3.0						PB	10, 11, 12				
W	6.5			Y			PB	9, 10, 11				
W, E	26.0	VT							OC	FN		
W	6.5			Y	R, PU	5					I	
P	1.5				B	6, 7					P	
W	6.5	C, I			O	7, 8			GR	BS	I	BK
A	3.0	VT, I	PR		A	7, 8, 9				BS	S	
W	26.0	H, BS							GR			BK
W	52.0	VS, IS		O					GR	BS		BK
W	1.5	MO	GR		B	8, 9				FB	I	
W	26.0	H	YG		W	6				BS	S	
W, E	52.0	VT, I	BG				W	10, 11, 12		FN		
W, E	52.0	VT								FN		
W	13.0	MO			W	6, 7	R					
W, E	3.0	H								FN		
P	0.5	H		W	B	8, 9, 10					I	
W	26.0	MS		Y, R, W								
W	13.0	VS, I	PR		PU	4, 5					I	
W	26.0	MS		Y	PK, PU	5					I	
W	3.0											
W	1.5	H			O	4	Y	10, 11			FD	
W	3.0	I			O, A, R, PK, W	4	Y	10, 11			FD	
W	1.5	H			W	4	Y	10, 11				
W	3.0				O, A, R, PK, W	4	Y	10, 11				
W, E	13.0	VT	GG							FN		
W, E	6.5									FN		

Master List:
Summary of Design Characteristics

KEY TO ABBREVIATIONS

TYPE

W	Woody	A	Annual
P	Perennial	B	Bulb
I	Biennial	E	Evergreen

STRUCTURE

VT	Vertical
H	Horizontal
MO	Mound
BS	Ball on a Stick
VS	Vase
W	Weeping
I	Irregular, Sculptural
MS	Multistemmed
C	Climbing

COLOR: FOLIAGE, SPRING & SUMMER

BG	Blue-Green
GR	Gray-Green
GW	Green and White Variegated
YG	Yellow-Green
GG	Green and Gold Variegated
PR	Pink and Red

COLOR: FOLIAGE, FALL

O	Orange	R	Red
Y	Yellow	W	Wine

COLOR: FLOWER

Y	Yellow	PU	Purple
O	Orange	V	Violet
A	Apricot	B	Blue
R	Red	C	Chartreuse
PK	Pink	W	White

FLOWER COLOR: BY MONTH

1	January	7	July
2	February	8	August
3	March	9	September
4	April	10	October
5	May	11	November
6	June	12	December

COLOR: FRUIT & SEED HEAD

Y	Yellow
O	Orange, Brown
R	Red
PB	Purple-Black
B	Blue
W	White-Silver

FRUIT & SEED HEAD COLOR BY MONTH

1	January	7	July
2	February	8	August
3	March	9	September
4	April	10	October
5	May	11	November
6	June	12	December

COLOR: BARK

Y	Yellow	PU	Purple
OC	Orange-Cherry	GN	Green
		GR	Gray
R	Red	W	White

TEXTURE: FOLIAGE

FN	Fine Detail—Narrow, Linear—Needle
FB	Fine Detail—Narrow, Linear—Blade
FR	Fine Detail—Small, Rounded
FO	Fine Detail—Other Leaf Shapes
BS	Broad—Strong Design Impact
BM	Broad—For Ground Cover Massing

TEXTURE: FLOWER

S	Spikes, Cones, Wands, and Spraylike Heads
P	Pendulous
FD	Daisylike
FT	Flat Top
BL	Ball-like
I	Irregular and/or Complex

TEXTURE: BARK

BK	Interesting Bark Texture

NAME

CHAMAECYPARIS OBTUSA 'NANA GRACILIS'
   HINOKI FALSE CYPRESS (SEMI-DWARF)
CHAMAECYPARIS OBTUSA 'NANA'
   DWARF HINOKI FALSE CYPRESS
CHAMAECYPARIS OBTUSA VAR. BREVIRAMEA
   HINOKI FALSE CYPRESS (VERTICAL)
CHAMAECYPARIS PISIFERA 'GOLD SPANGLE'
   SAWARA FALSE CYPRESS
CHAMAECYPARIS PISIFERA 'SQUARROSA'
   MOSS SAWARA FALSE CYPRESS

CHAMAEMELUM NOBILE
   CHAMOMILE
CHELONE LYONII
   TURTLEHEAD
CHIMONANTHUS PRAECOX
   WINTERSWEET
CHIONANTHUS VIRGINICUS
   FRINGE TREE
CHIONODOXA GIGANTEA 'ALBA'
   GLORY-OF-THE-SNOW (WHITE)
CHIONODOXA LUCILIAE
   GLORY-OF-THE-SNOW (BLUE)

CHIONODOXA SARDENSIS
   GLORY-OF-THE-SNOW (BLUE)
CHRYSANTHEMUM WEYRICHII 'WHITE BOMB'

CIMICIFUGA RACEMOSA
   BLACK SNAKEROOT
CLADRASTIS LUTEA
   AMERICAN YELLOWWOOD
CLEMATIS 'MRS. CHOLMONDELEY'

CLEMATIS 'PRINS HENDRIK'

CLEMATIS 'RAMONA'

CLEMATIS HERACLEIFOLIA VAR. DAVIDIANA
   TUBE CLEMATIS
CLEMATIS MAXIMOWICZIANA
   SWEET AUTUMN CLEMATIS
CLEMATIS X JACKMANII

CLERODENDRUM TRICHOTOMUM
   HARLEQUIN GLORY BOWER
CLETHRA ALNIFOLIA
   SWEET PEPPERBUSH

CLETHRA BARBINERVIS
   JAPANESE CLETHRA
COLCHICUM 'AUTUMN QUEEN'
   AUTUMN-CROCUS
COLCHICUM 'THE GIANT'
   AUTUMN-CROCUS
COLUTEA X MEDIA
   BLADDER SENNA (HYBRID)
COMPTONIA PEREGRINA
   SWEET-FERN
CONVALLARIA MAJALIS
   LILY-OF-THE-VALLEY

TYPE	SIZE (FEET)	STRUCTURE	FOLIAGE SPRING & SUMMER	FALL	FLOWER COLOR	MONTH	FRUIT & SEED HEAD COLOR	MONTH	BARK	TEXTURE FOLIAGE	FLOWER	BARK
W, E	6.5	I								FN		
W, E	1.5	MO								FN		
W, E	13.0	I								FN		BK
W, E	6.5	MO	GG	Y						FN		
W, E	52.0	I	GR							FN		
P	0.0	H			W	8, 9				FN		
P	1.5				PK, PU	8, 9					S	
W	6.5				Y	1, 2					FD	
W	13.0	MS		Y	W	5	PB	6, 7	GR		P	
B	0.5	H			W	4					FD	
B	0.5	H			B	4					FD	
B	0.5	H			B, W	4					FD	
P	0.5	H			W	9, 0					FD	
P	6.5	VT			W	6, 7					S	
W	26.0			O, Y	W	6			GR		P	BK
W	6.5	C			B	6					FD	
W	6.5	C			B	6					FD	
W	6.5	C			PU, B	6					FD	
P	3.0	I			B	7, 8, 9	W				S	
W	6.5	C			W	8, 9	W				FD	
W	6.5	C			PU	6					FD	
W	13.0	YG			R, W	8, 9	B	9, 10		BS	FT	
W	6.5	MS		O, Y	W	7, 8	PB	9			S	
W	6.5	MS			W	7, 8			OC		P	
B	0.5				PU, V	9, 10					BL	
B	0.5				PU, V	9, 10					BL	
W	6.5		BG		A	7					I	
W	3.0	H, MO									FO	
P	0.5	H		Y	W	5					P	

Master List:
Summary of Design Characteristics

KEY TO ABBREVIATIONS

TYPE

W	Woody	A	Annual
P	Perennial	B	Bulb
I	Biennial	E	Evergreen

STRUCTURE

VT	Vertical
H	Horizontal
MO	Mound
BS	Ball on a Stick
VS	Vase
W	Weeping
I	Irregular, Sculptural
MS	Multistemmed
C	Climbing

COLOR: FOLIAGE, SPRING & SUMMER

BG	Blue-Green
GR	Gray-Green
GW	Green and White Variegated
YG	Yellow-Green
GG	Green and Gold Variegated
PR	Pink and Red

COLOR: FOLIAGE, FALL

O	Orange	R	Red
Y	Yellow	W	Wine

COLOR: FLOWER

Y	Yellow	PU	Purple
O	Orange	V	Violet
A	Apricot	B	Blue
R	Red	C	Chartreuse
PK	Pink	W	White

FLOWER COLOR: BY MONTH

1	January	7	July
2	February	8	August
3	March	9	September
4	April	10	October
5	May	11	November
6	June	12	December

COLOR: FRUIT & SEED HEAD

Y	Yellow
O	Orange, Brown
R	Red
PB	Purple-Black
B	Blue
W	White-Silver

FRUIT & SEED HEAD COLOR BY MONTH

1	January	7	July
2	February	8	August
3	March	9	September
4	April	10	October
5	May	11	November
6	June	12	December

COLOR: BARK

Y	Yellow	PU	Purple
OC	Orange-Cherry	GN	Green
		GR	Gray
R	Red	W	White

TEXTURE: FOLIAGE

FN	Fine Detail—Narrow, Linear—Needle
FB	Fine Detail—Narrow, Linear—Blade
FR	Fine Detail—Small, Rounded
FO	Fine Detail—Other Leaf Shapes
BS	Broad—Strong Design Impact
BM	Broad—For Ground Cover Massing

TEXTURE: FLOWER

S	Spikes, Cones, Wands, and Spraylike Heads
P	Pendulous
FD	Daisylike
FT	Flat Top
BL	Ball-like
I	Irregular and/or Complex

TEXTURE: BARK

BK	Interesting Bark Texture

NAME

COREOPSIS 'MOONBEAM'

CORNUS ALBA 'ELEGANTISSIMA'
   TARTARIAN DOGWOOD (WHITE VARIEGATED)
CORNUS ALBA 'SPAETHII'
   TARTARIAN DOGWOOD (YELLOW VARIEGATED)
CORNUS ALTERNIFOLIA
   PAGODA DOGWOOD
CORNUS FLORIDA
   FLOWERING DOGWOOD

CORNUS FLORIDA 'HOHMAN'S GOLDEN'
   FLOWERING DOGWOOD (YELLOW VARIEGATED)
CORNUS KOUSA
   KOREAN DOGWOOD
CORNUS MAS
   CORNELIAN-CHERRY
CORNUS OFFICINALIS
   JAPANESE CORNELIAN-CHERRY
CORNUS RACEMOSA
   GRAY DOGWOOD
CORNUS RACEMOSA (DWARF)
   DWARF GRAY DOGWOOD

CORNUS SERICEA
   RED-TWIG DOGWOOD
CORNUS SERICEA 'FLAVIRAMEA'
   YELLOW-TWIG DOGWOOD
CORYLOPSIS PLATYPETALA
   WINTER HAZEL
CORYLUS AVELLANA 'CONTORTA'
   HARRY LAUDER'S WALKING STICK
CORYLUS AVELLANA 'PENDULA'
   WEEPING EUROPEAN FILBERT
CORYLUS COLURNA
   TURKISH FILBERT

COTINUS COGGYGRIA 'PURPUREUS'
   PURPLELEAF SMOKE BUSH
COTONEASTER ADPRESSUS 'LITTLE GEM'
   CREEPING COTONEASTER (DWARF)
COTONEASTER ADPRESSUS VAR. PRAECOX
   CREEPING COTONEASTER
COTONEASTER APICULATUS
   CRANBERRY COTONEASTER
COTONEASTER HORIZONTALIS
   ROCKSPRAY COTONEASTER
COTONEASTER SALICIFOLIUS VAR. FLOCCOSUS
   WILLOWLEAF COTONEASTER

COTULA SQUALIDA
   NEW ZEALAND BRASS-BUTTONS
CRAMBE CORDIFOLIA
   COLEWORT
CRATAEGUS NITIDA
   GLOSSY HAWTHORN
CRATAEGUS PHAENOPYRUM
   WASHINGTON HAWTHORN
CRATAEGUS VIRIDIS 'WINTER KING'
   WINTER KING HAWTHORN
CROCOSMIA 'LUCIFER'

| GENERAL DESIGN | | | COLOR | | | | | | | TEXTURE | | |
TYPE	SIZE (FEET)	STRUCTURE	FOLIAGE SPRING & SUMMER	FOLIAGE FALL	FLOWER COLOR	FLOWER MONTH	FRUIT & SEED HEAD COLOR	FRUIT & SEED HEAD MONTH	BARK	FOLIAGE	FLOWER	BARK
P	1.0	MO			Y	6, 7, 8, 9 10				FN	FD	
W	3.0		GW						R			
W	3.0		GW						R			
W	13.0	H			W	5	R, PB, B	9, 10	GN		FT	
W	13.0	H		R	W	5	R	9, 10	GR		FD	
W	13.0	H	GG	Y, R, W	W	5	R	9, 10	GR		FD	
W	13.0	H, VS		R	W	5, 6	R	9	GR, W		FD	
W	13.0	H, MO			Y	3, 4	R	8, 9	OC		BL	
W	13.0	H, MO			Y	3, 4	R	8, 9	OC		BL	BK
W	6.5	MO		W	W		R, W	7, 8	R, GR			
W	1.0	MO		W	W		R, W	7, 8	R			
W	3.0	MO			W		B, W	7, 8	R		FT	
W	3.0	MO			W		B, W	7, 8	Y		FT	
W	6.5	MO			Y	4					P	
W	3.0	I			C	1, 2, 3, 4					P	
W	6.5	W, I			C	1, 2, 3, 4					P	
W	26.0				Y, C	1, 2, 3, 4			GR			BK
W	6.5	MO, I	PR	R, W	PK							
W	0.0	H, MO										
W	1.5	MO			PK	5	R	8, 9				
W	1.5	MO			PK	5	R	8, 9				
W	1.5	H			PK	5		9, 10				
W, E	13.0	MO, W		W	W		R	10, 11, 12			P	
P	0.0	H	PR	O	Y					FO		
P	3.0	I			W	5, 6				BS	I	
W	13.0	H		O	W	5	R	1, 2, 3, 11 12	GR		FT	
W	13.0	H		O	W	5	R	1, 2, 11, 12	GR		FT	
W	13.0	H, BS			W	5	O, R	1, 2, 11, 12	GR		FT	
B	1.5				R	6					S	

Master List:
Summary of Design Characteristics

KEY TO ABBREVIATIONS

TYPE

W	Woody	A	Annual
P	Perennial	B	Bulb
I	Biennial	E	Evergreen

STRUCTURE

VT	Vertical
H	Horizontal
MO	Mound
BS	Ball on a Stick
VS	Vase
W	Weeping
I	Irregular, Sculptural
MS	Multistemmed
C	Climbing

COLOR: FOLIAGE, SPRING & SUMMER

BG	Blue-Green
GR	Gray-Green
GW	Green and White Variegated
YG	Yellow-Green
GG	Green and Gold Variegated
PR	Pink and Red

COLOR: FOLIAGE, FALL

O	Orange	R	Red
Y	Yellow	W	Wine

COLOR: FLOWER

Y	Yellow	PU	Purple
O	Orange	V	Violet
A	Apricot	B	Blue
R	Red	C	Chartreuse
PK	Pink	W	White

FLOWER COLOR: BY MONTH

1	January	7	July
2	February	8	August
3	March	9	September
4	April	10	October
5	May	11	November
6	June	12	December

COLOR: FRUIT & SEED HEAD

Y	Yellow
O	Orange, Brown
R	Red
PB	Purple-Black
B	Blue
W	White-Silver

FRUIT & SEED HEAD COLOR BY MONTH

1	January	7	July
2	February	8	August
3	March	9	September
4	April	10	October
5	May	11	November
6	June	12	December

COLOR: BARK

Y	Yellow	PU	Purple
OC	Orange-Cherry	GN	Green
		GR	Gray
R	Red	W	White

TEXTURE: FOLIAGE

FN	Fine Detail—Narrow, Linear—Needle
FB	Fine Detail—Narrow, Linear—Blade
FR	Fine Detail—Small, Rounded
FO	Fine Detail—Other Leaf Shapes
BS	Broad—Strong Design Impact
BM	Broad—For Ground Cover Massing

TEXTURE: FLOWER

S	Spikes, Cones, Wands, and Spraylike Heads
P	Pendulous
FD	Daisylike
FT	Flat Top
BL	Ball-like
I	Irregular and/or Complex

TEXTURE: BARK

BK	Interesting Bark Texture

NAME

CROCOSMIA POTTSII

CROCOSMIA X CROCOSMIIFLORA

CROCUS ANCYRENSIS 'GOLDEN BUNCH'

CROCUS SIEBERI

CROCUS TOMASINIANUS

CRUCIANELLA STYLOSA
   CROSSWORT
CYCLAMEN HEDERIFOLIUM
   BABY CYCLAMEN
CYTISUS SCOPARIUS
   SCOTCH BROOM
CYTISUS X PRAECOX 'LUTEUS'
   WARMINSTER BROOM
DAPHNE CAUCASICA

DAPHNE X BURKWOODII 'CAROL MACKIE'

DATURA INOXIA SUBSP. QUINQUECUSPIDA
   ANGEL'S-TRUMPET
DENNSTAEDTIA PUNCTILOBULA
   HAY-SCENTED FERN
DEUTZIA GRACILIS
   SLENDER DEUTZIA
DIANTHUS DELTOIDES
   MAIDEN PINK
DICENTRA 'LUXURIANT'
   BLEEDING-HEART (HYBRID)
DICENTRA EXIMIA 'PURITY'
   WILD BLEEDING-HEART (WHITE)

DICENTRA SPECTABILIS
   BLEEDING-HEART
DIERVILLA SESSILIFOLIA
   SOUTHERN BUSH-HONEYSUCKLE
DIOSPYROS KAKI
   ORIENTAL PERSIMMON
DIOSPYROS VIRGINIANA
   PERSIMMON
DIPLAZIUM CONILII

ECHINACEA PURPUREA
   PURPLE CONEFLOWER

ECHINOPS RITRO
   GLOBE THISTLE
ELAEAGNUS PUNGENS 'FRUITLANDII'
   FRAGRANT ELAEAGNUS
ELAEAGNUS PUNGENS 'MACULATA'
   ELAEAGNUS (YELLOW VARIEGATED)
ENDYMION HISPANICUS 'EXCELSIOR'
     (SYN. SCILLA CAMPANULATA 'EXCELSIOR')
   SPANISH BLUEBELL
ENKIANTHUS CAMPANULATUS
   REDVEIN ENKIANTHUS

	GENERAL DESIGN		COLOR				FRUIT & SEED HEAD		BARK	TEXTURE		
TYPE	SIZE (FEET)	STRUCTURE	FOLIAGE SPRING & SUMMER	FALL	FLOWER COLOR	MONTH	COLOR	MONTH		FOLIAGE	FLOWER	BARK
B	1.0			O	Y, O	7					S	
B	1.5			O	O	8					S	
B	0.0				Y	3						
B	0.0				PU, V	3						
B	0.0				V	3, 4						
P	1.5		YG		PK	5, 6				FN	BL	
B	0.0				PK	10				FR		
W	3.0				Y	6			GN	FR	I	
W	3.0				Y	5			GN	FR	I	
W	3.0	MO			W						BL	
W	3.0	MO	GW		W	4, 5				FN		
A	3.0				W	6, 7, 8						
P	1.5	H	YG							FO		
W	1.5	MO			W	5					I	
P	0.0	H, MO			R, P	5, 6				FN	FD	
P	1.0	H, MO	GR		R, P	5				FO	S, P	
P	1.0	H, MO	GR		W	5				FO	S, P	
P	1.5				PK	5					P	
W	3.0	MO		R	Y	6						
W	13.0	W, I		R			O	10, 11				
W	26.0	I		O, Y			Y, O					BK
P	1.0	H								FO		
P	1.5	MO			O, PK, V	6, 7, 8					FD	
P	3.0	I	GR		B	7, 8					BL	
W, E	13.0	MO	GR		W	9, 10					I	
W, E	6.5	MO	GG		W							
B	0.5				B	5					S	
W	6.5	I, MS		R	Y, R, PK	5					P	

Master List:
Summary of Design Characteristics

NAME

ENKIANTHUS PERULATUS
WHITE ENKIANTHUS
EPIMEDIUM PINNATUM SUBSP. COLCHICUM

EPIMEDIUM X YOUNGIANUM 'NIVEUM'

EQUISETUM HYEMALE
SCOURING RUSH
ERANTHIS HYEMALIS
WINTER ACONITE

ERANTHIS X TUBERGENII
WINTER ACONITE (HYBRID)
ERIANTHUS RAVENNAE
RAVENNA GRASS
EUONYMUS ALATA
WINGED EUONYMUS, BURNING BUSH
EUONYMUS FORTUNEI 'COLORATA'
PURPLELEAF WINTERCREEPER
EUONYMUS FORTUNEI 'GRACILIS'
WINTERCREEPER (WHITE VARIEGATED)
EUONYMUS FORTUNEI 'MINIMA'
LITTLELEAF WINTERCREEPER

EUONYMUS FORTUNEI 'SILVER QUEEN'
SILVER QUEEN WINTERCREEPER
EUONYMUS FORTUNEI VAR. RADICANS
WINTERCREEPER (SPREADING)
EUPATORIUM COELESTINUM
HARDY AGERATUM
EUPHORBIA COROLLATA
FLOWERING SPURGE
EUPHORBIA CYPARISSIAS
CYPRESS SPURGE
EUPHORBIA EPITHYMOIDES
CUSHION SPURGE

EXOCHORDA GIRALDII VAR. WILSONII
WILSON PEARLBUSH
FAGUS GRANDIFOLIA
AMERICAN BEECH
FAGUS SYLVATICA 'LACINIATA'
CUTLEAF EUROPEAN BEECH
FAGUS SYLVATICA 'PENDULA'
WEEPING EUROPEAN BEECH
FAGUS SYLVATICA 'RIVERSII'
RIVERS EUROPEAN BEECH (PURPLELEAF)
FILIPENDULA PURPUREA 'ELEGANS'
SHOWY JAPANESE MEADOWSWEET

FILIPENDULA PURPUREA 'NANA'
DWARF JAPANESE MEADOWSWEET
FILIPENDULA ULMARIA 'AUREA'
GOLDEN QUEEN OF THE MEADOW
FORSYTHIA SUSPENSA
WEEPING FORSYTHIA
FORSYTHIA VIRIDISSIMA 'BRONXENSIS'
DWARF GREENSTEM FORSYTHIA
FORSYTHIA X INTERMEDIA 'SPRING GLORY'
SPRING GLORY FORSYTHIA
FOTHERGILLA GARDENII
DWARF FOTHERGILLA

KEY TO ABBREVIATIONS

TYPE

W	Woody	A	Annual
P	Perennial	B	Bulb
I	Biennial	E	Evergreen

STRUCTURE

VT	Vertical
H	Horizontal
MO	Mound
BS	Ball on a Stick
VS	Vase
W	Weeping
I	Irregular, Sculptural
MS	Multistemmed
C	Climbing

COLOR: FOLIAGE, SPRING & SUMMER

BG	Blue-Green
GR	Gray-Green
GW	Green and White Variegated
YG	Yellow-Green
GG	Green and Gold Variegated
PR	Pink and Red

COLOR: FOLIAGE, FALL

O	Orange	R	Red
Y	Yellow	W	Wine

COLOR: FLOWER

Y	Yellow	PU	Purple
O	Orange	V	Violet
A	Apricot	B	Blue
R	Red	C	Chartreuse
PK	Pink	W	White

FLOWER COLOR: BY MONTH

1	January	7	July
2	February	8	August
3	March	9	September
4	April	10	October
5	May	11	November
6	June	12	December

COLOR: FRUIT & SEED HEAD

Y	Yellow
O	Orange, Brown
R	Red
PB	Purple-Black
B	Blue
W	White-Silver

FRUIT & SEED HEAD COLOR BY MONTH

1	January	7	July
2	February	8	August
3	March	9	September
4	April	10	October
5	May	11	November
6	June	12	December

COLOR: BARK

Y	Yellow	PU	Purple
OC	Orange-Cherry	GN	Green
		GR	Gray
R	Red	W	White

TEXTURE: FOLIAGE

FN	Fine Detail—Narrow, Linear—Needle
FB	Fine Detail—Narrow, Linear—Blade
FR	Fine Detail—Small, Rounded
FO	Fine Detail—Other Leaf Shapes
BS	Broad—Strong Design Impact
BM	Broad—For Ground Cover Massing

TEXTURE: FLOWER

S	Spikes, Cones, Wands, and Spraylike Heads
P	Pendulous
FD	Daisylike
FT	Flat Top
BL	Ball-like
I	Irregular and/or Complex

TEXTURE: BARK

BK	Interesting Bark Texture

TYPE	SIZE (FEET)	STRUCTURE	FOLIAGE SPRING & SUMMER	FALL	FLOWER COLOR	MONTH	FRUIT & SEED HEAD COLOR	MONTH	BARK	FOLIAGE	FLOWER	BARK
W	3.0	MO		O, R	W	4						
P	0.5	H	BG		Y	4				BM	I	
P	0.5	H	YG		W	4				FB	I	
P	1.5	VT, I	YG						GN	FB		BK
B	0.0	H			Y	3					FD	
B	0.0	H			Y	3					FD	
P	6.5	VT, MO, I	GR		W	9, 10	W	10, 11, 12		FB	S	
W	6.5	H		R				11, 12	GR			BK
W, E	0.5	H		R						BM		
W, E	0.5	H	GW							BM		
W, E	0.0	H								FR		
W	1.5	H	GW							BM		
W, E	0.5	H								BM		
P	1.0		YG		B	9, 10					FT	
P	1.5		BG		W	7, 8				FN	FD	
P	0.5		BG		Y	4				FN	FT	
P	1.0	MO	BG		Y, CH	4, 5				FB	FT	
W	6.5		BG		W	5					P	
W	52.0	H, MO		Y					GR			BK
W	52.0	H, MO							GR		FO	BK
W	52.0	W, I							GR			BK
W	52.0	MO	PR						GR			BK
P	3.0			W		6					I	
P	1.0				PK	7, 8				BM	I	
P	0.5	MO	GG		W							
W	6.5	W			Y	4						
W	1.0	H, MO	YG	W	Y	4						
W	6.5	MO			Y	4					I	
W	3.0			O, Y	W	4, 5					S	

Master List: Summary of Design Characteristics

KEY TO ABBREVIATIONS

TYPE

W	Woody	A	Annual
P	Perennial	B	Bulb
I	Biennial	E	Evergreen

STRUCTURE

VT	Vertical
H	Horizontal
MO	Mound
BS	Ball on a Stick
VS	Vase
W	Weeping
I	Irregular, Sculptural
MS	Multistemmed
C	Climbing

COLOR: FOLIAGE, SPRING & SUMMER

BG	Blue-Green
GR	Gray-Green
GW	Green and White Variegated
YG	Yellow-Green
GG	Green and Gold Variegated
PR	Pink and Red

COLOR: FOLIAGE, FALL

O	Orange	R	Red
Y	Yellow	W	Wine

COLOR: FLOWER

Y	Yellow	PU	Purple
O	Orange	V	Violet
A	Apricot	B	Blue
R	Red	C	Chartreuse
PK	Pink	W	White

FLOWER COLOR: BY MONTH

1	January	7	July
2	February	8	August
3	March	9	September
4	April	10	October
5	May	11	November
6	June	12	December

COLOR: FRUIT & SEED HEAD

Y	Yellow
O	Orange, Brown
R	Red
PB	Purple-Black
B	Blue
W	White-Silver

FRUIT & SEED HEAD COLOR BY MONTH

1	January	7	July
2	February	8	August
3	March	9	September
4	April	10	October
5	May	11	November
6	June	12	December

COLOR: BARK

Y	Yellow	PU	Purple
OC	Orange-Cherry	GN	Green
		GR	Gray
R	Red	W	White

TEXTURE: FOLIAGE

FN	Fine Detail—Narrow, Linear—Needle
FB	Fine Detail—Narrow, Linear—Blade
FR	Fine Detail—Small, Rounded
FO	Fine Detail—Other Leaf Shapes
BS	Broad—Strong Design Impact
BM	Broad—For Ground Cover Massing

TEXTURE: FLOWER

S	Spikes, Cones, Wands, and Spraylike Heads
P	Pendulous
FD	Daisylike
FT	Flat Top
BL	Ball-like
I	Irregular and/or Complex

TEXTURE: BARK

BK	Interesting Bark Texture

NAME

FRANKLINIA ALATAMAHA
  FRANKLIN TREE
GALANTHUS ELWESII
  GIANT SNOWDROP
GALANTHUS NIVALIS
  COMMON SNOWDROP
GALIUM ODORATUM
  SWEET WOODRUFF
GALTONIA CANDICANS
  SUMMER-HYACINTH

GAULTHERIA PROCUMBENS
  WINTERGREEN
GENISTA SYLVESTRIS 'LYDIA'
  SPREADING BROOM
GERANIUM 'JOHNSON'S BLUE'
  HYBRID CRANESBILL (BLUE)
GERANIUM MACRORRHIZUM
  BIGROOT CRANESBILL
GERANIUM SANGUINEUM
  BLOODY CRANESBILL
GINKGO BILOBA, STAMINATE
  MAIDENHAIR TREE

GLEDITSIA TRIACANTHOS VAR. INERMIS 'SHADEMASTER'
  THORNLESS HONEY-LOCUST
GYMNOCLADUS DIOICA
  KENTUCKY COFFEETREE
HALESIA TETRAPTERA
  CAROLINA SILVER-BELL
HAMAMELIS MOLLIS 'PALLIDA'
  CHINESE WITCH-HAZEL (SOFT YELLOW)
HAMAMELIS VIRGINIANA
  COMMON WITCH-HAZEL (LATE AUTUMN)
HAMAMELIS X INTERMEDIA 'DIANE'
  HYBRID WITCH-HAZEL (RED)

HAMAMELIS X INTERMEDIA 'JELENA'
  HYBRID WITCH-HAZEL (ORANGE)
HAMAMELIS X INTERMEDIA 'PRIMAVERA'
  HYBRID WITCH-HAZEL (BRIGHT YELLOW)
HEDERA COLCHICA 'DENTATA'
  PERSIAN IVY
HEDERA HELIX 'BALTICA'
  BALTIC IVY
HEDERA HELIX 'BULGARIA'
  BULGARIAN IVY
HEDERA HELIX 'BUTTERCUP'
  BUTTERCUP ENGLISH IVY (YELLOW VARIEGATED)

HEDERA HELIX 'ERECTA'
  ENGLISH IVY (UPRIGHT)
HEDERA HELIX 'GOLD HEART'
  GOLD HEART ENGLISH IVY (YELLOW VARIEGATED)
HEDERA HELIX 'OGALALLA'
  OGALALLA ENGLISH IVY
HEDYOTIS CAERULEA
  QUAKER LADIES, BLUETS
HELIANTHEMUM APENNINUM VAR. ROSEUM
  SUN ROSE
HELIANTHUS SALICIFOLIUS
  SUNFLOWER (NARROWLEAF)

TYPE	SIZE (FEET)	STRUCTURE	FOLIAGE SPRING & SUMMER	FALL	FLOWER COLOR	MONTH	FRUIT & SEED HEAD COLOR	MONTH	BARK	FOLIAGE	FLOWER	BARK
W	13.0	BS, I		W	W	8, 9			GR		FD	
B	0.0	H			W	3					P	
B	0.0	H			W	3					P	
P	0.5	H			W	5				FN		
B	1.5	VT			W	6, 7					S	
W	0.0	H		R	W	5	R	9, 10		BM		
W	1.5	H, MO			Y	6			GN	FR		
P	1.0			B		5						
P	1.0	H, MO	BG	O, Y, R	PK	5, 6				BM	FD	
P	0.5	H, MO			PK, PU	5, 6				FO	FD	
W	52.0	I		Y					OC			BK
W	52.0	VS		Y						FR		
W	52.0	VS, I	BG			6	PB	8, 9, 10, 11, 12	GR	BS	P	BK
W	26.0	H		Y	W	5	O		GR, W		P	
W	13.0	VS		Y	Y	1, 2, 3, 4					I	
W	13.0	H, VS		Y	Y	10, 11					I	
W	13.0	VS		Y	R	2, 3, 4					I	
W	13.0	VS		Y	O	2, 3, 4					I	
W	13.0	VS		Y	Y	2, 3, 4					I	
W, E	6.5	C, H								BM, BS		
W, E	0.0	H								BM		
W, E	0.0	H								BM		
W	6.5	C, I	GG							BM		
W, E	1.5	H, I								BM		
W	6.5	C	GG							BM		
W, E	0.0	H								BM		
P	0.0	H			V, B	5						
P	0.5	H	GR		A	6				FR	FD	
P	3.0	I			Y	9, 10				FB	FD	

Master List:
Summary of Design Characteristics

KEY TO ABBREVIATIONS

TYPE

W	Woody	A	Annual
P	Perennial	B	Bulb
I	Biennial	E	Evergreen

STRUCTURE

VT	Vertical
H	Horizontal
MO	Mound
BS	Ball on a Stick
VS	Vase
W	Weeping
I	Irregular, Sculptural
MS	Multistemmed
C	Climbing

COLOR: FOLIAGE, SPRING & SUMMER

BG	Blue-Green
GR	Gray-Green
GW	Green and White Variegated
YG	Yellow-Green
GG	Green and Gold Variegated
PR	Pink and Red

COLOR: FOLIAGE, FALL

O	Orange	R	Red
Y	Yellow	W	Wine

COLOR: FLOWER

Y	Yellow	PU	Purple
O	Orange	V	Violet
A	Apricot	B	Blue
R	Red	C	Chartreuse
PK	Pink	W	White

FLOWER COLOR: BY MONTH

1	January	7	July
2	February	8	August
3	March	9	September
4	April	10	October
5	May	11	November
6	June	12	December

COLOR: FRUIT & SEED HEAD

Y	Yellow
O	Orange, Brown
R	Red
PB	Purple-Black
B	Blue
W	White-Silver

FRUIT & SEED HEAD COLOR BY MONTH

1	January	7	July
2	February	8	August
3	March	9	September
4	April	10	October
5	May	11	November
6	June	12	December

COLOR: BARK

Y	Yellow	PU	Purple
OC	Orange-Cherry	GN	Green
		GR	Gray
R	Red	W	White

TEXTURE: FOLIAGE

FN	Fine Detail—Narrow, Linear—Needle
FB	Fine Detail—Narrow, Linear—Blade
FR	Fine Detail—Small, Rounded
FO	Fine Detail—Other Leaf Shapes
BS	Broad—Strong Design Impact
BM	Broad—For Ground Cover Massing

TEXTURE: FLOWER

S	Spikes, Cones, Wands, and Spraylike Heads
P	Pendulous
FD	Daisylike
FT	Flat Top
BL	Ball-like
I	Irregular and/or Complex

TEXTURE: BARK

BK	Interesting Bark Texture

NAME

HELICTOTRICHON SEMPERVIRENS
  BLUE OAT GRASS
HELIOPSIS HELIANTHOIDES SUBSP. SCABRA 'KARAT'

HELLEBORUS NIGER
  CHRISTMAS-ROSE
HELLEBORUS ORIENTALIS HYBRIDS
  LENTEN-ROSE
HEMEROCALLIS 'HYPERION'
  HYPERION DAYLILY

HEMEROCALLIS FULVA 'EUROPA'
  ORANGE DAYLILY
HEMEROCALLIS LILIOASPHODELUS
  LEMON-LILY
HERACLEUM MANTEGAZZIANUM
  GIANT HOGWEED
HEUCHERA 'PALACE PURPLE' STRAIN
  ALUMROOT (PURPLELEAF)
HIBISCUS SYRIACUS 'BLUEBIRD'
  ROSE OF SHARON (BLUE)
HIBISCUS SYRIACUS 'DIANA'
  ROSE OF SHARON (TRIPLOID WHITE)

HIPPOPHAE RHAMNOIDES
  SEA BUCKTHORN
HOSTA 'KABITAN'
  PLANTAIN-LILY (YELLOW VARIEGATED)
HOSTA PLANTAGINEA
  FRAGRANT PLANTAIN-LILY
HOSTA SIEBOLDIANA 'ELEGANS'
  SIEBOLD PLANTAIN-LILY (BLUE, SEERSUCKER LEAVES)
HOSTA UNDULATA
  WAVY-LEAVED PLANTAIN-LILY
HOSTA VENTRICOSA
  BLUE PLANTAIN-LILY

HOUTTUYNIA CORDATA 'CHAMELEON'

HYDRANGEA ANOMALA SUBSP. PETIOLARIS 'SKYLANDS GIANT'
  CLIMBING HYDRANGEA
HYDRANGEA ASPERA SUBSP. SARGENTIANA

HYDRANGEA MACROPHYLLA 'BLUE BILLOW'
  BLUE LACECAP HYDRANGEA
HYDRANGEA PANICULATA
  PANICLE HYDRANGEA
HYDRANGEA QUERCIFOLIA
  OAKLEAF HYDRANGEA

HYPERICUM FRONDOSUM
  GOLDEN ST.-JOHN'S-WORT
HYPERICUM KALMIANUM
  KALM ST.-JOHN'S-WORT
ILEX CHINA BOY ® 'MESDOB'
  CHINA BOY ® HOLLY
ILEX CHINA GIRL ® 'MESOG'
  CHINA GIRL ® HOLLY
ILEX CRENATA 'HELLERI'
  HELLERI DWARF JAPANESE HOLLY
ILEX CRENATA 'MICROPHYLLA'
  LITTLELEAF JAPANESE HOLLY

GENERAL DESIGN			COLOR								TEXTURE		
TYPE	SIZE	STRUCTURE	FOLIAGE		FLOWER		FRUIT & SEED HEAD		BARK		FOLIAGE	FLOWER	BARK
	(FEET)		SPRING & SUMMER	FALL	COLOR	MONTH	COLOR	MONTH					
P	1.0	MO	BG		O	6					FB	S	
P	3.0	MO		Y		6, 7						FD	
P, E	0.5	H, MO			W	3, 4					BS, BM	FD	
P, E	1.0	H, MO			PK, C, W	3, 4					BM, BS	FD	
P	3.0	H			Y	6, 7					FB	I	
P	3.0	H	YG		O	6, 7					FB	I	
P	1.5				Y	5					FB	I	
I	3.0	I			W	6					BS	FT	
P	1.0		PR	W	W						BM		
W	6.5				B	8, 9						FD	
W	6.5				W	8, 9						FD	
W	13.0	I	GR				O	7, 8			FN		
P	1.0	H, MO	GG		V	8					BM	S	
P	1.5	H, MO	YG		W	8, 9					BM, BS	S	
P	1.5	H, MO	BG		W	5					BM, BS	S	
P	0.5	H, MO			PU, V	8					BM	S	
P	1.5	H, MO			PU, B	6, 7					BM, BS	S	
P	1.0	H	PR		W	6, 7					BM	FD	
W	6.5	C, I			W	6			OC			FT	BK
W	3.0				V, W	7					BS	FT	
W	1.5	MO			B	6, 7						FT	
W	6.5	MO			W	8, 9						S	
W	6.5	MO		O, W	W	6			OC			S	BK
W	3.0	MO			Y	7, 8			OC				BK
W	1.5	MO			Y	7, 8			OC				BK
W, E	3.0	MO	YG										
W, E	3.0	MO	YG				R						
W, E	3.0	MO											
W, E	6.5												

Master List:
Summary of Design Characteristics

KEY TO ABBREVIATIONS

TYPE

W	Woody	A	Annual
P	Perennial	B	Bulb
I	Biennial	E	Evergreen

STRUCTURE

VT	Vertical
H	Horizontal
MO	Mound
BS	Ball on a Stick
VS	Vase
W	Weeping
I	Irregular, Sculptural
MS	Multistemmed
C	Climbing

COLOR: FOLIAGE, SPRING & SUMMER

BG	Blue-Green
GR	Gray-Green
GW	Green and White Variegated
YG	Yellow-Green
GG	Green and Gold Variegated
PR	Pink and Red

COLOR: FOLIAGE, FALL

O	Orange	R	Red
Y	Yellow	W	Wine

COLOR: FLOWER

Y	Yellow	PU	Purple
O	Orange	V	Violet
A	Apricot	B	Blue
R	Red	C	Chartreuse
PK	Pink	W	White

FLOWER COLOR: BY MONTH

1	January	7	July
2	February	8	August
3	March	9	September
4	April	10	October
5	May	11	November
6	June	12	December

COLOR: FRUIT & SEED HEAD

Y	Yellow
O	Orange, Brown
R	Red
PB	Purple-Black
B	Blue
W	White-Silver

FRUIT & SEED HEAD COLOR BY MONTH

1	January	7	July
2	February	8	August
3	March	9	September
4	April	10	October
5	May	11	November
6	June	12	December

COLOR: BARK

Y	Yellow	PU	Purple
OC	Orange-Cherry	GN	Green
		GR	Gray
R	Red	W	White

TEXTURE: FOLIAGE

FN	Fine Detail—Narrow, Linear—Needle
FB	Fine Detail—Narrow, Linear—Blade
FR	Fine Detail—Small, Rounded
FO	Fine Detail—Other Leaf Shapes
BS	Broad—Strong Design Impact
BM	Broad—For Ground Cover Massing

TEXTURE: FLOWER

S	Spikes, Cones, Wands, and Spraylike Heads
P	Pendulous
FD	Daisylike
FT	Flat Top
BL	Ball-like
I	Irregular and/or Complex

TEXTURE: BARK

BK	Interesting Bark Texture

NAME

ILEX GLABRA 'DENSA'
  DWARF INKBERRY HOLLY
ILEX OPACA 'ARDEN'
  ARDEN AMERICAN HOLLY
ILEX OPACA 'XANTHOCARPA'
  YELLOW-BERRIED AMERICAN HOLLY
ILEX VERTICILLATA
  WINTERBERRY
ILEX VERTICILLATA 'WINTER RED'
  WINTER RED WINTERBERRY (HYBRID)

ILEX X AQUIPERNYI 'SAN JOSE'
  SAN JOSE HOLLY
ILEX X MESERVEAE BLUE MAID ® 'MESID'
  BLUE MAID ® HOLLY
ILEX X MESERVEAE BLUE STALLION ® 'MESAN'
  BLUE STALLION ® HOLLY
IMPERATA CYLINDRICA 'RED BARON'
  JAPANESE BLOOD GRASS
INDIGOFERA INCARNATA 'ALBA'
  CHINESE INDIGO (WHITE)
INULA HELENIUM
  ELECAMPANE

IRIS CRISTATA
  CRESTED IRIS
IRIS GRAMINEA
  PLUM TART IRIS
IRIS PSEUDACORUS
  YELLOW WATER IRIS
IRIS SIBIRICA CULTIVARS
  SIBERIAN IRIS
IRIS TECTORUM
  ROOF IRIS
ITEA VIRGINICA 'HENRY'S GARNET'
  VIRGINIA SWEETSPIRE

JASMINUM NUDIFLORUM
  WINTER JASMINE
JUNIPERUS CHINENSIS 'KAIZUKA'
  HOLLYWOOD JUNIPER
JUNIPERUS HORIZONTALIS 'WILTONII'
  BLUE RUG JUNIPER
JUNIPERUS SABINA 'TAMARISCIFOLIA'
  TAMARIX JUNIPER
JUNIPERUS SCOPULORUM 'SKY ROCKET'
  SKYROCKET ROCKY MOUNTAIN JUNIPER
JUNIPERUS VIRGINIANA
  EASTERN RED CEDAR

JUNIPERUS X MEDIA 'OLD GOLD'
  OLD GOLD JUNIPER
JUNIPERUS X MEDIA 'PFITZERIANA COMPACTA'
  NICK'S COMPACT JUNIPER
KALMIA LATIFOLIA
  MOUNTAIN-LAUREL
KERRIA JAPONICA
  KERRIA (SINGLE-FLOWERED)
KIRENGESHOMA PALMATA

KOCHIA SCOPARIA FORMA TRICHOPHYLLA 'CHILDSII'
  FIREBUSH; RED SUMMER-CYPRESS

GENERAL DESIGN			COLOR							TEXTURE		
TYPE	SIZE (FEET)	STRUCTURE	FOLIAGE SPRING & SUMMER	FALL	FLOWER COLOR	MONTH	FRUIT & SEED HEAD COLOR	MONTH	BARK	FOLIAGE	FLOWER	BARK
W, E	6.5	MO					PB	10, 11, 12				
W, E	13.0	VT					R	1, 2, 11, 12				
W, E	13.0	VT					Y	1, 2, 11, 12				
W	6.5			Y			R	1, 11, 12				
W	6.5			Y			R	1, 11, 12				
W, E	13.0	VT					R	1, 2, 3, 4, 11, 12				
W, E	3.0	MO					R			BS		
W, E	3.0	MO								BS		
P	1.5	VT	PR	R		9		10, 11, 12		FB		
W	1.0	H			W	6						S
P	6.5	I			Y	6, 7				FD		
P	0.5	H		Y	B	5				FB	I	
P	0.5	VT			PU	5						
P	3.0	VT, I			Y	5				FB	I	
P	1.5	VT, I			PU, V, B, W	6				FB	I	
P	0.5	H			B	5, 6				FB	I	
W	3.0	MO		R, W	W	6						S
W	1.5	W			Y	2, 3			GN	FR		
W, E	3.0	I	YG							FN		
W, E	0.5	H	BG							FN		
W, E	1.0		GR							FN		
W, E	6.5	VT	BG							FN		
W, E	52.0	VT					B	9, 10, 11, 12		FN		
W, E	1.5	H	GG							FN		
W, E	1.5	H								FN		
W, E	13.0	I, MS			PK, W	6					BL	
W	3.0	MO	YG	Y	Y	5			GN	FD		
P	3.0	W			Y	9				P		
A	1.5		YG	R						FN		

Master List:
Summary of Design Characteristics

KEY TO ABBREVIATIONS

TYPE

W	Woody	A	Annual
P	Perennial	B	Bulb
I	Biennial	E	Evergreen

STRUCTURE

VT	Vertical
H	Horizontal
MO	Mound
BS	Ball on a Stick
VS	Vase
W	Weeping
I	Irregular, Sculptural
MS	Multistemmed
C	Climbing

COLOR: FOLIAGE, SPRING & SUMMER

BG	Blue-Green
GR	Gray-Green
GW	Green and White Variegated
YG	Yellow-Green
GG	Green and Gold Variegated
PR	Pink and Red

COLOR: FOLIAGE, FALL

O	Orange	R	Red
Y	Yellow	W	Wine

COLOR: FLOWER

Y	Yellow	PU	Purple
O	Orange	V	Violet
A	Apricot	B	Blue
R	Red	C	Chartreuse
PK	Pink	W	White

FLOWER COLOR: BY MONTH

1	January	7	July
2	February	8	August
3	March	9	September
4	April	10	October
5	May	11	November
6	June	12	December

COLOR: FRUIT & SEED HEAD

Y	Yellow
O	Orange, Brown
R	Red
PB	Purple-Black
B	Blue
W	White-Silver

FRUIT & SEED HEAD COLOR BY MONTH

1	January	7	July
2	February	8	August
3	March	9	September
4	April	10	October
5	May	11	November
6	June	12	December

COLOR: BARK

Y	Yellow	PU	Purple
OC	Orange-Cherry	GN	Green
R	Red	GR	Gray
		W	White

TEXTURE: FOLIAGE

FN	Fine Detail—Narrow, Linear—Needle
FB	Fine Detail—Narrow, Linear—Blade
FR	Fine Detail—Small, Rounded
FO	Fine Detail—Other Leaf Shapes
BS	Broad—Strong Design Impact
BM	Broad—For Ground Cover Massing

TEXTURE: FLOWER

S	Spikes, Cones, Wands, and Spraylike Heads
P	Pendulous
FD	Daisylike
FT	Flat Top
BL	Ball-like
I	Irregular and/or Complex

TEXTURE: BARK

BK	Interesting Bark Texture

NAME

KOELREUTERIA PANICULATA
  GOLDEN-RAIN TREE
KOLKWITZIA AMABILIS
  BEAUTY-BUSH
LAMIASTRUM GALEOBDOLON 'VARIEGATUM'
  YELLOW-ARCHANGEL (WHITE VARIEGATED)
LAMIUM MACULATUM 'WHITE NANCY'
  SPOTTED-DEAD-NETTLE (WHITE)
LATHYRUS VERNUS
  SPRING VETCHLING

LESPEDEZA THUNBERGII
  THUNBERG BUSH CLOVER
LESPEDEZA THUNBERGII 'ALBIFLORA'
  THUNBERG BUSH CLOVER (WHITE)
LEUCOJUM VERNUM
  SPRING SNOWFLAKE
LEUCOTHOE FONTANESIANA
  FOUNTAIN LEUCOTHOE
LEUCOTHOE FONTANESIANA 'NANA'
  DWARF FOUNTAIN LEUCOTHOE
LIATRIS SCARIOSA 'WHITE SPIRE'
  GAY-FEATHER (WHITE)

LIATRIS SPICATA 'KOBOLD'
  GAY-FEATHER (LAVENDER)
LIGUSTRUM QUIHOUI
  PRIVET (CHINESE)
LILIUM 'BLACK DRAGON'
  HYBRID TRUMPET LILY (WHITE, FRAGRANT)
LILIUM SPECIES AND HYBRIDS

LIQUIDAMBAR STYRACIFLUA
  SWEET GUM

LIRIOPE MUSCARI (BIG BLUE SELECTION)
  BIG BLUE LILYTURF
LIRIOPE MUSCARI 'MONROE WHITE'
  LILYTURF (WHITE)
LIRIOPE MUSCARI 'VARIEGATA'
  LILYTURF (YELLOW VARIEGATED)
LONICERA FRAGRANTISSIMA
  FRAGRANT HONEYSUCKLE
LUZULA SYLVATICA 'MARGINATA'
  GREATER WOOD RUSH
LYCORIS SPRENGERI

LYCORIS SQUAMIGERA
  RESURRECTION LILY
LYSICHITON AMERICANUM
  YELLOW SKUNK-CABBAGE (WESTERN AMERICAN)
LYSICHITON CAMTSCHATCENSE
  WHITE SKUNK-CABBAGE (ASIATIC)
LYSIMACHIA CLETHROIDES
  GOOSENECK LOOSESTRIFE
LYSIMACHIA PUNCTATA
  GARDEN LOOSESTRIFE
LYTHRUM SALICARIA 'DROPMORE PURPLE'
  PURPLE LOOSESTRIFE

GENERAL DESIGN · COLOR · TEXTURE

TYPE	SIZE (FEET)	STRUCTURE	FOLIAGE SPRING & SUMMER	FOLIAGE FALL	FLOWER COLOR	FLOWER MONTH	FRUIT & SEED HEAD COLOR	FRUIT & SEED HEAD MONTH	BARK	TEXTURE FOLIAGE	TEXTURE FLOWER	TEXTURE BARK
W	13.0	BS		O	Y	6	Y	7, 8		BS		
W	6.5	VS		R	PK	5			OC		I	BK
P	1.5	H	GW		Y	5						
P	0.5	H	GW		W	5					S	
P	1.5				PK, PU	4, 5						
W	3.0				PK, PU, V	9				FR	I	
W	0.0				PK, PU	9					P	
B	0.5	H			C, W	3					P	
W, E	3.0	MO, W		R, W	W	5				BM		
W, E	3.0	MO, W		R, W	W	5				BM		
P	1.5	VT			W	6, 7				FN	S	
P	1.5	VT			PU	6, 7				FN	S	
W	6.5				W	7	PB	9, 10			S	
B	6.5	I			W	6, 7				FB	I	
B	3.0	I			Y, O, A, PK, PU, V, C, W	6, 7				FB	I	
W	52.0			Y, R, W		11, 12	PB		GR	BS	B	
W, E	0.5	H			V, B	8	PB	9, 10		FB	S	
W, E	0.5	H			W	8	PB	9, 10		FB	S	
W, E	0.5	H	GG		V, B	8				FB	S	
W	6.5	MO	BG		W	2, 3, 4					I	
P, E	1.5											
B	1.5				PK, PU, B	9					S, I	
B	1.5				P	9					S, I	
P	1.5		YG		Y, C	4, 5					S	
P	1.5						W	4, 5				S
P	1.5			Y	W	7, 8					P	
P	1.5				Y	6, 7					FD	
P	3.0				PK	6, 7					S	

Master List:
Summary of Design Characteristics

KEY TO ABBREVIATIONS

TYPE

W	Woody	A	Annual
P	Perennial	B	Bulb
I	Biennial	E	Evergreen

STRUCTURE

VT	Vertical
H	Horizontal
MO	Mound
BS	Ball on a Stick
VS	Vase
W	Weeping
I	Irregular, Sculptural
MS	Multistemmed
C	Climbing

COLOR: FOLIAGE, SPRING & SUMMER

BG	Blue-Green
GR	Gray-Green
GW	Green and White Variegated
YG	Yellow-Green
GG	Green and Gold Variegated
PR	Pink and Red

COLOR: FOLIAGE, FALL

O	Orange	R	Red
Y	Yellow	W	Wine

COLOR: FLOWER

Y	Yellow	PU	Purple
O	Orange	V	Violet
A	Apricot	B	Blue
R	Red	C	Chartreuse
PK	Pink	W	White

FLOWER COLOR: BY MONTH

1	January	7	July
2	February	8	August
3	March	9	September
4	April	10	October
5	May	11	November
6	June	12	December

COLOR: FRUIT & SEED HEAD

Y	Yellow
O	Orange, Brown
R	Red
PB	Purple-Black
B	Blue
W	White-Silver

FRUIT & SEED HEAD COLOR BY MONTH

1	January	7	July
2	February	8	August
3	March	9	September
4	April	10	October
5	May	11	November
6	June	12	December

COLOR: BARK

Y	Yellow	PU	Purple
OC	Orange-Cherry	GN	Green
		GR	Gray
R	Red	W	White

TEXTURE: FOLIAGE

FN	Fine Detail—Narrow, Linear—Needle
FB	Fine Detail—Narrow, Linear—Blade
FR	Fine Detail—Small, Rounded
FO	Fine Detail—Other Leaf Shapes
BS	Broad—Strong Design Impact
BM	Broad—For Ground Cover Massing

TEXTURE: FLOWER

S	Spikes, Cones, Wands, and Spraylike Heads
P	Pendulous
FD	Daisylike
FT	Flat Top
BL	Ball-like
I	Irregular and/or Complex

TEXTURE: BARK

BK	Interesting Bark Texture

NAME

MACLEAYA CORDATA
  PLUME-POPPY
MAGNOLIA 'ELIZABETH'
  MAGNOLIA (YELLOW)
MAGNOLIA 'SUSAN'
  MAGNOLIA (COMPACT, PINK)
MAGNOLIA DENUDATA (SYN. M. HEPTAPETA)
  YULAN MAGNOLIA
MAGNOLIA MACROPHYLLA
  LARGE-LEAVED CUCUMBER TREE

MAGNOLIA VIRGINIANA
  SWAMP MAGNOLIA
MAGNOLIA X LOEBNERI
  MAGNOLIA (LOEBNERI HYBRID)
MAGNOLIA X SOULANGIANA 'VERBANICA'
  SAUCER MAGNOLIA (PINK)
MAHONIA BEALEI
  LEATHERLEAF MAHONIA
MALUS 'RED JADE'
  RED JADE CRABAPPLE
MALUS FLORIBUNDA
  JAPANESE FLOWERING CRABAPPLE

MALUS HUPEHENSIS
  TEA CRABAPPLE
MALUS SARGENTII
  SARGENT CRABAPPLE
MERTENSIA VIRGINICA
  VIRGINIA BLUEBELLS
METASEQUOIA GLYPTOSTROBOIDES
  DAWN REDWOOD
MICROBIOTA DECUSSATA
  SIBERIAN-CYPRESS
MISCANTHUS 'GIGANTEUS'
  GIANT MISCANTHUS

MISCANTHUS SINENSIS 'CABARET'
  MISCANTHUS (WHITE VARIEGATED)
MISCANTHUS SINENSIS 'GRACILLIMUS'
  SLENDER MISCANTHUS
MISCANTHUS SINENSIS 'MORNING LIGHT'
  SLENDER VARIEGATED MISCANTHUS
MISCANTHUS SINENSIS 'SILVER FEATHER' (='SILBERFEDER')
  SILVER FEATHER MISCANTHUS
MISCANTHUS SINENSIS 'STRICTUS'
  PORCUPINE GRASS
MISCANTHUS SINENSIS 'VARIEGATUS'
  VARIEGATED MISCANTHUS

MOLINIA CAERULEA SUBSP. ARUNDINACEA
  PURPLE MOOR GRASS
MONARDA DIDYMA
  BEE BALM
MUSCARI AZUREUM 'ALBUM'
  GRAPE-HYACINTH (WHITE)
MUSCARI BOTRYOIDES 'ALBUM'
  COMMON GRAPE-HYACINTH (WHITE)
MUSCARI TUBERGENIANUM
  GRAPE-HYACINTH (BLUE)
MYRICA PENSYLVANICA
  BAYBERRY

TYPE	SIZE (FEET)	STRUCTURE	FOLIAGE SPRING & SUMMER	FALL	FLOWER COLOR	MONTH	FRUIT & SEED HEAD COLOR	MONTH	BARK	FOLIAGE	FLOWER	BARK
P	6.5	I	BG		A	6, 7		7, 8		BS	S	
W	26.0				Y	4, 5	R		GR		BL	
W	13.0				R, PU	4	R		GR		BL	
W	26.0	I			W	4	R		GR		BL	
W	26.0				W		O, R					
W	26.0	I, MS			W	6, 7	R	8, 9	GR		FD	
W	26.0				PK, W	4	R		GR		BL	
W	13.0	I			PK	4	R		GR		BL	
W, E	3.0	I	BG		Y	4	B	5		BS	S	
W	13.0	W, I			P, W	5	R	10, 11, 12			FD	
W	13.0	H, MO			PK, W	5	Y	10, 11				
W	13.0	VS			PK, W	5	Y, R	10, 11				
W	6.5	H, I			PK, W	5	R	10, 11, 12			FD	
B	0.5		BG		B	4, 5					P	
W	52.0	VT	YG	O, W					OC	FN		BK
W, E	0.5	H							OC	FN		
P	6.5	VT, W, I			C, W	9, 10	W	10, 11, 12		FB	S	
P	3.0	MO, I	GW		PK	9, 10		10, 11, 12			S	
P	3.0	MO			A, PK	9	O, PB	10, 11, 12		FB	S	
P	3.0	MO, I	GW		PK	9, 10		10, 11, 12			S	
P	3.0	VT, MO, I			W	9, 10	W	10, 11, 12		FB	S	
P	3.0	M, I	GG		W	9, 10		10, 11, 12		FB	S	
P	3.0	MO, I	GW		PK, W	9, 10		10, 11, 12		FB	S	
P	3.0	I				9, 10	PB	10, 11, 12		FB	S	
P	1.5	H			R	6, 7					I	
B	0.0				W	4					S	
B	0.0				W	4					S	
B	0.0				B	4					S	
W	6.5	MO, I					PB, BL, W	1, 2, 10, 11, 12				

Master List:
Summary of Design Characteristics

KEY TO ABBREVIATIONS

TYPE

W	Woody	A	Annual
P	Perennial	B	Bulb
I	Biennial	E	Evergreen

STRUCTURE

VT	Vertical
H	Horizontal
MO	Mound
BS	Ball on a Stick
VS	Vase
W	Weeping
I	Irregular, Sculptural
MS	Multistemmed
C	Climbing

COLOR: FOLIAGE, SPRING & SUMMER

BG	Blue-Green
GR	Gray-Green
GW	Green and White Variegated
YG	Yellow-Green
GG	Green and Gold Variegated
PR	Pink and Red

COLOR: FOLIAGE, FALL

O	Orange	R	Red
Y	Yellow	W	Wine

COLOR: FLOWER

Y	Yellow	PU	Purple
O	Orange	V	Violet
A	Apricot	B	Blue
R	Red	C	Chartreuse
PK	Pink	W	White

FLOWER COLOR: BY MONTH

1	January	7	July
2	February	8	August
3	March	9	September
4	April	10	October
5	May	11	November
6	June	12	December

COLOR: FRUIT & SEED HEAD

Y	Yellow
O	Orange, Brown
R	Red
PB	Purple-Black
B	Blue
W	White-Silver

FRUIT & SEED HEAD COLOR BY MONTH

1	January	7	July
2	February	8	August
3	March	9	September
4	April	10	October
5	May	11	November
6	June	12	December

COLOR: BARK

Y	Yellow	PU	Purple
OC	Orange-Cherry	GN	Green
		GR	Gray
R	Red	W	White

TEXTURE: FOLIAGE

FN	Fine Detail—Narrow, Linear—Needle
FB	Fine Detail—Narrow, Linear—Blade
FR	Fine Detail—Small, Rounded
FO	Fine Detail—Other Leaf Shapes
BS	Broad—Strong Design Impact
BM	Broad—For Ground Cover Massing

TEXTURE: FLOWER

S	Spikes, Cones, Wands, and Spraylike Heads
P	Pendulous
FD	Daisylike
FT	Flat Top
BL	Ball-like
I	Irregular and/or Complex

TEXTURE: BARK

BK	Interesting Bark Texture

NAME

NARCISSUS 'CARLTON'

NARCISSUS 'FORTUNE'

NARCISSUS 'HERA'

NARCISSUS 'LOCH FYNE'

NARCISSUS 'MOONMIST'

NARCISSUS 'MRS. ERNST H. KRELAGE'

NARCISSUS 'PEEPING TOM'

NARCISSUS 'POMONA'

NARCISSUS 'QUEEN OF SPAIN'

NARCISSUS 'TREVITHIAN'

NARCISSUS JONQUILLA
JONQUIL

NARCISSUS PSEUDONARCISSUS SUBSP. OBVALLARIS
TENBY DAFODIL
NEPETA X FAASSENII

NYSSA SYLVATICA
SOUR GUM
OMPHALODES VERNA
BLUE-EYED MARY
ONOPORDUM ACANTHIUM
SCOTCH THISTLE
OPHIOPOGON JAPONICUS 'NANUS'
DWARF MONDO GRASS

OSMUNDA CINNAMOMEA
CINNAMON FERN
OSMUNDA CLAYTONIANA
INTERRUPTED FERN
OSMUNDA REGALIS
ROYAL FERN
OXYDENDRUM ARBOREUM
SOURWOOD
PACHYSANDRA PROCUMBENS
ALLEGHANY SPURGE
PACHYSANDRA TERMINALIS
JAPANESE SPURGE

PACHYSANDRA TERMINALIS 'GREEN CARPET'
GREEN CARPET JAPANESE SPURGE
PACHYSANDRA TERMINALIS 'VARIEGATA' OR 'SILVER EDGE'
JAPANESE SPURGE (WHITE VARIEGATED)
PAEONIA 'BLACK PIRATE'
HYBRID TREE PEONY (MAROON)
PAEONIA—HERBACEOUS HYBRIDS
HYBRID HERBACEOUS PEONY
PAEONIA—WOODY HYBRIDS
HYBRID TREE PEONY
PAEONIA TENUIFOLIA
FERN-LEAVED PEONY

TYPE	SIZE (FEET)	STRUCTURE	FOLIAGE SPRING & SUMMER	FALL	FLOWER COLOR	MONTH	FRUIT & SEED HEAD COLOR	MONTH	BARK	FOLIAGE	FLOWER	BARK
B	0.5				Y	4					I	
B	0.5				Y, O	4					I	
B	0.5				W	4					I	
B	0.5				O, W	4					I	
B	0.5				Y	4					I	
B	0.5				W	4					I	
B	0.5				Y	4					I	
B	0.5				O, W	4					I	
B	0.5				Y	4					I	
B	0.5				Y	4, 5					I	
B	0.5				Y	4					I	
B	0.5				Y	4					I	
P	1.0	MO			B	6, 7					S	
W	52.0	H, I		O, R								BK
P	0.5	H, MO			B, W	4, 5						
I	6.5	VT, I	GR		PU	6, 7			GR, W		BL	BK
W, E	0.0											
P	3.0	VT				5				FO	S	
P	3.0	VT				5				FO	S	
P	3.0	VT, MO				5				FR	S	
W	26.0	W, I		R, W	C, W	7			GN		P	
P	0.5	H			PK, PU, W						S	
W, E	0.5	H								BM		
W, E	0.5	H								BM		
W, E	0.5	H	GW							BM		
W	3.0	MO	BG		R	5				BS		
P	1.5	MO			R, PK, W	5					BL	
W	3.0	MO			Y, A, R, W	5				BS		
P	1.0	MO			R	5				FN	FD	

Master List:
Summary of Design Characteristics

KEY TO ABBREVIATIONS

TYPE

W	Woody	A	Annual
P	Perennial	B	Bulb
I	Biennial	E	Evergreen

STRUCTURE

VT	Vertical
H	Horizontal
MO	Mound
BS	Ball on a Stick
VS	Vase
W	Weeping
I	Irregular, Sculptural
MS	Multistemmed
C	Climbing

COLOR: FOLIAGE, SPRING & SUMMER

BG	Blue-Green
GR	Gray-Green
GW	Green and White Variegated
YG	Yellow-Green
GG	Green and Gold Variegated
PR	Pink and Red

COLOR: FOLIAGE, FALL

O	Orange	R	Red
Y	Yellow	W	Wine

COLOR: FLOWER

Y	Yellow	PU	Purple
O	Orange	V	Violet
A	Apricot	B	Blue
R	Red	C	Chartreuse
PK	Pink	W	White

FLOWER COLOR: BY MONTH

1	January	7	July
2	February	8	August
3	March	9	September
4	April	10	October
5	May	11	November
6	June	12	December

COLOR: FRUIT & SEED HEAD

Y	Yellow
O	Orange, Brown
R	Red
PB	Purple-Black
B	Blue
W	White-Silver

FRUIT & SEED HEAD COLOR BY MONTH

1	January	7	July
2	February	8	August
3	March	9	September
4	April	10	October
5	May	11	November
6	June	12	December

COLOR: BARK

Y	Yellow	PU	Purple
OC	Orange-Cherry	GN	Green
		GR	Gray
R	Red	W	White

TEXTURE: FOLIAGE

FN	Fine Detail—Narrow, Linear—Needle
FB	Fine Detail—Narrow, Linear—Blade
FR	Fine Detail—Small, Rounded
FO	Fine Detail—Other Leaf Shapes
BS	Broad—Strong Design Impact
BM	Broad—For Ground Cover Massing

TEXTURE: FLOWER

S	Spikes, Cones, Wands, and Spraylike Heads
P	Pendulous
FD	Daisylike
FT	Flat Top
BL	Ball-like
I	Irregular and/or Complex

TEXTURE: BARK

BK	Interesting Bark Texture

NAME

PANICUM VIRGATUM 'STRICTUM'
    TALL SWITCH GRASS
PAPAVER ORIENTALE
    ORIENTAL POPPY
PARONYCHIA KAPELA SUBSP. SERPYLLIFOLIA
    CREEPING NAILWORT
PAULOWNIA TOMENTOSA
    EMPRESS TREE
PAXISTIMA CANBYI

PELTIPHYLLUM PELTATUM
    UMBRELLA PLANT
PENNISETUM ALOPECUROIDES
    HARDY FOUNTAIN GRASS
PEROVSKIA ABROTANOIDES X P. ATRIPLICIFOLIA
    HYBRID PEROVSKIA
PETASITES FRAGRANS
    WINTER HELIOTROPE
PETASITES JAPONICUS
    JAPANESE BUTTERBUR
PHALARIS ARUNDINACEA VAR. PICTA
    RIBBON GRASS (WHITE VARIEGATED)

PHELLODENDRON AMURENSE
    AMUR CORKTREE
PHILADELPHUS CORONARIUS
    SWEET MOCKORANGE
PHILADELPHUS X FALCONERI
    FALCONER HYBRID MOCKORANGE
PHLOMIS RUSSELIANA
    JERUSALEM-SAGE
PHLOX BIFIDA
    SAND PHLOX
PHLOX PILOSA SUBSP. OZARKANA
    OZARK DOWNY PHLOX

PHLOX STOLONIFERA 'ALBA'
    CREEPING PHLOX
PHLOX STOLONIFERA 'BLUE RIDGE'
    CREEPING PHLOX
PHLOX STOLONIFERA 'SHERWOOD PURPLE'
    CREEPING PHLOX
PHLOX SUBULATA
    MOSS PHLOX
PHYLLOSTACHYS AUREOSULCATA
    YELLOW-GROOVE BAMBOO
PHYSOSTEGIA VIRGINIANA
    FALSE DRAGONHEAD

PHYSOSTEGIA VIRGINIANA 'SUMMER SNOW'
    FALSE DRAGONHEAD (WHITE)
PICEA ABIES 'NIDIFORMIS'
    BIRD'S NEST SPRUCE
PICEA ORIENTALIS
    ORIENTAL SPRUCE
PICEA PUNGENS 'HOOPSII'
    HOOPS COLORADO SPRUCE (BLUE)
PIERIS JAPONICA
    JAPANESE-ANDROMEDA
PINUS BUNGEANA
    LACEBARK PINE

TYPE	SIZE (FEET)	STRUCTURE	FOLIAGE SPRING & SUMMER	FALL	FLOWER COLOR	MONTH	FRUIT & SEED HEAD COLOR	MONTH	BARK	FOLIAGE	FLOWER	BARK
P	1.5	I				8, 9	PB	9, 10		FB	S	
P	3.0	I			O, A, R, PK, V	5						
P	0.0	H								FN		
W	26.0	H, BS			PU, V	5				BS	S	
W, E	0.5	H								FN		
P	1.5	MO								BS		
P	1.5	MO			PK	8	PB	9, 10		FB	S, P	
P	3.0			GR	V, B	7, 8				FO	S	
P	0.5	MO			PU, V	4				BM, BS		
P	1.5	H			Y	4				BM, BS		
P	3.0	H, MO	GW							FB	S	
W	26.0	H		Y			PB	9, 10, 11		BS		BK
W	6.5	MO, W			Y, W						FD	
W	6.5	MO			W	5, 6					FD	
P	1.5	VT, I	YG		Y	6					S	
P, E	0.5	H			B	4, 5				FN		
P, E	0.5				PK	5, 6				FB	FD	
P	0.0	H			W	5				FR	FD	
P	0.0	H			B	5				FR	FD	
P	0.0	H			PU	5				FR	FD	
P, E	0.0	H			PK, PU, V, B	4				FN		
W	13.0	VT, MS	YG						GN	FB		
P	3.0				PK	8, 9					S	
P	3.0				W	8, 9					S	
W, E	3.0	H								FN		
W, E	52.0	VT								FN		
W, E	52.0	VT	BG							FN		
W, E	3.0				W	3, 4					P	
W, E	26.0	MS	YG						GN, GR, W	FN		BK

Master List:
Summary of Design Characteristics

KEY TO ABBREVIATIONS

TYPE

W	Woody	A	Annual
P	Perennial	B	Bulb
I	Biennial	E	Evergreen

STRUCTURE

VT	Vertical
H	Horizontal
MO	Mound
BS	Ball on a Stick
VS	Vase
W	Weeping
I	Irregular, Sculptural
MS	Multistemmed
C	Climbing

COLOR: FOLIAGE, SPRING & SUMMER

BG	Blue-Green
GR	Gray-Green
GW	Green and White Variegated
YG	Yellow-Green
GG	Green and Gold Variegated
PR	Pink and Red

COLOR: FOLIAGE, FALL

O	Orange	R	Red
Y	Yellow	W	Wine

COLOR: FLOWER

Y	Yellow	PU	Purple
O	Orange	V	Violet
A	Apricot	B	Blue
R	Red	C	Chartreuse
PK	Pink	W	White

FLOWER COLOR: BY MONTH

1	January	7	July
2	February	8	August
3	March	9	September
4	April	10	October
5	May	11	November
6	June	12	December

COLOR: FRUIT & SEED HEAD

Y	Yellow
O	Orange, Brown
R	Red
PB	Purple-Black
B	Blue
W	White-Silver

FRUIT & SEED HEAD COLOR BY MONTH

1	January	7	July
2	February	8	August
3	March	9	September
4	April	10	October
5	May	11	November
6	June	12	December

COLOR: BARK

Y	Yellow	PU	Purple
OC	Orange-Cherry	GN	Green
		GR	Gray
R	Red	W	White

TEXTURE: FOLIAGE

FN	Fine Detail—Narrow, Linear—Needle
FB	Fine Detail—Narrow, Linear—Blade
FR	Fine Detail—Small, Rounded
FO	Fine Detail—Other Leaf Shapes
BS	Broad—Strong Design Impact
BM	Broad—For Ground Cover Massing

TEXTURE: FLOWER

S	Spikes, Cones, Wands, and Spraylike Heads
P	Pendulous
FD	Daisylike
FT	Flat Top
BL	Ball-like
I	Irregular and/or Complex

TEXTURE: BARK

BK	Interesting Bark Texture

NAME

PINUS DENSIFLORA 'UMBRACULIFERA'
  TANYOSHO PINE
PINUS FLEXILIS
  LIMBER PINE
PINUS KORAIENSIS
  KOREAN PINE
PINUS MUGO VAR. MUGO
  SWISS MOUNTAIN PINE
PINUS PARVIFLORA 'GLAUCA'
  JAPANESE WHITE PINE (BLUE)

PINUS STROBUS
  EASTERN WHITE PINE
PINUS STROBUS 'FASTIGIATA'
  FASTIGIATE EASTERN WHITE PINE
PINUS THUNBERGIANA
  JAPANESE BLACK PINE
PINUS THUNBERGIANA 'OCULUS-DRACONIS'
  DRAGON'S-EYE JAPANESE BLACK PINE
PINUS VIRGINIANA
  VIRGINIA PINE
PLATANUS OCCIDENTALIS
  SYCAMORE

POLIANTHES TUBEROSA
  TUBEROSE
POLYGONATUM ODORATUM 'VARIEGATUM'
  SOLOMON'S SEAL (WHITE VARIEGATED)
POLYSTICHUM ACROSTICHOIDES
  CHRISTMAS FERN
POLYSTICHUM TRIPTERON

PONCIRUS TRIFOLIATA
  HARDY-ORANGE
POTENTILLA TRIDENTATA
  THREE-TOOTHED CINQUEFOIL

PRUNUS 'HALLY JOLIVETTE'
  FLOWERING CHERRY (PINK HYBRID)
PRUNUS CERASIFERA 'THUNDERCLOUD'
  THUNDERCLOUD PLUM
PRUNUS SUBHIRTELLA 'AUTUMNALIS'
  HIGAN CHERRY (AUTUMN-FLOWERING)
PRUNUS SUBHIRTELLA 'PENDULA'
  WEEPING HIGAN CHERRY
PRUNUS X CISTENA
  PURPLELEAF SAND CHERRY
PRUNUS YEDOENSIS
  YOSHINO CHERRY

PSEUDOLARIX KAEMPFERI
  GOLDEN-LARCH
PSEUDOTSUGA MENZIESII
  DOUGLAS-FIR
PTERIDIUM AQUILINUM VAR. LATIUSCULUM
  BRACKEN
PULMONARIA ANGUSTIFOLIA
  LUNGWORT
PULMONARIA SACCHARATA 'MARGERY FISH'
  BETHLEHEM LUNGWORT
PULMONARIA SACCHARATA 'SISSINGHURST WHITE'
  BETHLEHEM LUNGWORT (WHITE)

| GENERAL DESIGN | | | COLOR | | | | | | | TEXTURE | | |
| TYPE | SIZE | STRUCTURE | FOLIAGE | | FLOWER | | FRUIT & SEED HEAD | | BARK | FOLIAGE | FLOWER | BARK |
	(FEET)		SPRING & SUMMER	FALL	COLOR	MONTH	COLOR	MONTH				
W, E	13.0	H, VS, I, MS	YG						OC	FN		
W, E	26.0	I	BG						GN, GR	FN		
W, E	26.0		BG							FN		
W, E	3.0	H, MO								FN		
W, E	26.0	H, I	BG							FN		
W, E	52.0	H	BG						GR	FN		
W, E	26.0	VT	BG							FN		
W, E	26.0	I								FN		
W, E	13.0	I	GG							FN		
W, E	26.0	H, I	YG							FN		
W	52.0	BS							OC, GR, W			BK
A	1.0				W	7, 8					S	
P	1.5	W	GG		W	5					P	
P, E	1.0	H								BM		
P	1.0	H								FO		
W	6.5	I		Y	W	4	Y	10	GN		FD	BK
P, E	0.5	H			W	5				FO	FD	
W	13.0	VS			PK, W	4					I	
W	13.0	BS	PR	R, W	PK	5					I	
W	13.0	H			PK	4, 11, 12			OC		I	
W	13.0	W			PK	4			OC		I	
W	3.0	MO	PR	R	W	5					I	
W	13.0	H			PK, W	4			OC		I	
W	26.0	VT, H	YG	Y						FN		
W, E	52.0	VT	GR, BG							FN		
P	3.0	H								FO		
P	0.5	H			B	4				BM	I	
P	0.5	H	GW		PK, B	4				BM	I	
P	0.5	H			W	4						

Master List:
Summary of Design Characteristics

KEY TO ABBREVIATIONS

TYPE

W	Woody	A	Annual
P	Perennial	B	Bulb
I	Biennial	E	Evergreen

STRUCTURE

VT	Vertical
H	Horizontal
MO	Mound
BS	Ball on a Stick
VS	Vase
W	Weeping
I	Irregular, Sculptural
MS	Multistemmed
C	Climbing

COLOR: FOLIAGE, SPRING & SUMMER

BG	Blue-Green
GR	Gray-Green
GW	Green and White Variegated
YG	Yellow-Green
GG	Green and Gold Variegated
PR	Pink and Red

COLOR: FOLIAGE, FALL

O	Orange	R	Red
Y	Yellow	W	Wine

COLOR: FLOWER

Y	Yellow	PU	Purple
O	Orange	V	Violet
A	Apricot	B	Blue
R	Red	C	Chartreuse
PK	Pink	W	White

FLOWER COLOR: BY MONTH

1	January	7	July
2	February	8	August
3	March	9	September
4	April	10	October
5	May	11	November
6	June	12	December

COLOR: FRUIT & SEED HEAD

Y	Yellow
O	Orange, Brown
R	Red
PB	Purple-Black
B	Blue
W	White-Silver

FRUIT & SEED HEAD COLOR BY MONTH

1	January	7	July
2	February	8	August
3	March	9	September
4	April	10	October
5	May	11	November
6	June	12	December

COLOR: BARK

Y	Yellow	PU	Purple
OC	Orange-Cherry	GN	Green
		GR	Gray
R	Red	W	White

TEXTURE: FOLIAGE

FN	Fine Detail—Narrow, Linear—Needle
FB	Fine Detail—Narrow, Linear—Blade
FR	Fine Detail—Small, Rounded
FO	Fine Detail—Other Leaf Shapes
BS	Broad—Strong Design Impact
BM	Broad—For Ground Cover Massing

TEXTURE: FLOWER

S	Spikes, Cones, Wands, and Spraylike Heads
P	Pendulous
FD	Daisylike
FT	Flat Top
BL	Ball-like
I	Irregular and/or Complex

TEXTURE: BARK

BK	Interesting Bark Texture

NAME

PYRACANTHA COCCINEA 'AUREA'
  FIRETHORN (YELLOW FRUIT)
QUERCUS ALBA
  WHITE OAK
QUERCUS MACROCARPA
  MOSSY-CUP OAK
QUERCUS PHELLOS
  WILLOW OAK
QUERCUS RUBRA
  RED OAK

RHEUM PALMATUM 'RUBRUM'
  ORNAMENTAL RHUBARB
RHODODENDRON (CATAWBIENSE HYBRIDS)

RHODODENDRON (GABLE HYBRIDS)
  GABLE HYBRID AZALEAS
RHODODENDRON (GLENN DALE HYBRIDS)
  GLENN DALE HYBRID AZALEAS
RHODODENDRON (KAEMPFERI HYBRIDS)
  TORCH HYBRID AZALEAS
RHODODENDRON (KNAP HILL HYBRID) 'TUNIS'
  KNAP HILL HYBRID AZALEA (ORANGE-BRICK)

RHODODENDRON (KURUME HYBRIDS)
  KURUME HYBRID AZALEAS
RHODODENDRON ARBORESCENS
  SWEET AZALEA
RHODODENDRON ATLANTICUM
  COAST AZALEA
RHODODENDRON CANESCENS
  PIEDMONT AZALEA
RHODODENDRON MAXIMUM
  ROSEBAY RHODODENDRON
RHODODENDRON MUCRONULATUM
  KOREAN RHODODENDRON

RHODODENDRON PRINOPHYLLUM
  ROSESHELL AZALEA
RHODODENDRON SCHLIPPENBACHII
  ROYAL AZALEA
RHODODENDRON VASEYI
  PINK-SHELL AZALEA
RHODODENDRON VISCOSUM
  SWAMP AZALEA
RHODODENDRON X ERIOCARPUM AND R. X
  NAKAHARAI CULTIVARS AND HYBRIDS
RHODODENDRON X GANDAVENSE 'COCCINEA SPECIOSA'
  GHENT HYBRID AZALEA (ORANGE)

RHODODENDRON X GANDAVENSE 'DAVIESII'
  GHENT HYBRID AZALEA (WHITE-YELLOW, FRAGRANT)
RHODOTYPOS SCANDENS
  JETBEAD
RHUS AROMATICA 'GRO-LOW'
  FRAGRANT SUMAC (DWARF)
RHUS TYPHINA
  STAGHORN SUMAC
RHUS TYPHINA 'LACINIATA'
  CUTLEAF STAGHORN SUMAC
RIBES ODORATUM
  CLOVE CURRANT

| GENERAL DESIGN | | | COLOR | | | | | | | TEXTURE | | |
TYPE	SIZE (FEET)	STRUCTURE	FOLIAGE SPRING & SUMMER	FALL	FLOWER COLOR	MONTH	FRUIT & SEED HEAD COLOR	MONTH	BARK	FOLIAGE	FLOWER	BARK
W	6.5	MO					Y	9, 10, 11				
W	52.0	H							GR			BK
W	52.0	H, BS							GR			BK
W	26.0	BS		Y						FN		
W	26.0	BS		R								
P	3.0	I			PK	5, 6				BS	S	
W, E	6.5	MO			R, PK, PU, V, W	5				BS	BL	
W	3.0			O, Y	R, PK, PU, V, W	5					I	
W	3.0	MO			R, PK, PU, V	5					I	
W	6.5	MO, I		O, Y	A, R, PK	5					I	
W	3.0	I			O, R	5					I	
W	3.0	MO		R	R, PK, PU, V, W	5					I	
W	6.5	I		R	W	6					I	
W	1.5	H	BG		PK, W	5					I	
W	6.5	I			PK	5					I	
W, E	6.5	MO			PK, W	6				BS	BL	
W	3.0	I		Y, R, W	PU, V	4					I	
W	6.5		BG		PK	5, 6					I	
W	3.0	I		O, Y, R	PK, W	5					I	
W	6.5	I		R	PK, C	5					I	
W	6.5				W	6, 7					I	
W, E	1.0	H			R, PK, W	6					I	
W	3.0	I			O	5					I	
W	3.0	I			Y, W	5					I	
W	3.0				W	5	PB	9, 10				
W	1.5	H, MO		O, R	Y, C	4	R				S	
W	6.5	I, MS		O, Y, R	C	7	R	8, 9, 10, 11	R	BS	S	BK
W	6.5	I, MS		O, Y, R	C	7	R	8, 9, 10, 11	R	FO	S	BK
W	3.0	W		R	Y, R	4				FO	I	

Master List:
Summary of Design Characteristics

KEY TO ABBREVIATIONS

TYPE

W	Woody	A	Annual
P	Perennial	B	Bulb
I	Biennial	E	Evergreen

STRUCTURE

VT	Vertical
H	Horizontal
MO	Mound
BS	Ball on a Stick
VS	Vase
W	Weeping
I	Irregular, Sculptural
MS	Multistemmed
C	Climbing

COLOR: FOLIAGE, SPRING & SUMMER

BG	Blue-Green
GR	Gray-Green
GW	Green and White Variegated
YG	Yellow-Green
GG	Green and Gold Variegated
PR	Pink and Red

COLOR: FOLIAGE, FALL

O	Orange	R	Red
Y	Yellow	W	Wine

COLOR: FLOWER

Y	Yellow	PU	Purple
O	Orange	V	Violet
A	Apricot	B	Blue
R	Red	C	Chartreuse
PK	Pink	W	White

FLOWER COLOR: BY MONTH

1	January	7	July
2	February	8	August
3	March	9	September
4	April	10	October
5	May	11	November
6	June	12	December

COLOR: FRUIT & SEED HEAD

Y	Yellow
O	Orange, Brown
R	Red
PB	Purple-Black
B	Blue
W	White-Silver

FRUIT & SEED HEAD COLOR BY MONTH

1	January	7	July
2	February	8	August
3	March	9	September
4	April	10	October
5	May	11	November
6	June	12	December

COLOR: BARK

Y	Yellow	PU	Purple
OC	Orange-Cherry	GN	Green
		GR	Gray
R	Red	W	White

TEXTURE: FOLIAGE

FN	Fine Detail—Narrow, Linear—Needle
FB	Fine Detail—Narrow, Linear—Blade
FR	Fine Detail—Small, Rounded
FO	Fine Detail—Other Leaf Shapes
BS	Broad—Strong Design Impact
BM	Broad—For Ground Cover Massing

TEXTURE: FLOWER

S	Spikes, Cones, Wands, and Spraylike Heads
P	Pendulous
FD	Daisylike
FT	Flat Top
BL	Ball-like
I	Irregular and/or Complex

TEXTURE: BARK

BK	Interesting Bark Texture

NAME

RICINUS COMMUNIS
    CASTOR BEAN
RICINUS COMMUNIS 'ZANZIBARENSIS'
    CASTOR BEAN
ROBINIA HISPIDA
    ROSE-ACACIA
RODGERSIA AESCULIFOLIA
    RODGERSIA
RODGERSIA PODOPHYLLA
    BRONZELEAF RODGERSIA

RODGERSIA TABULARIS
    SHIELDLEAF RODGERSIA
ROSA 'DOORENBOS SELECTION'
    HYBRID SPINOSISSIMA ROSE
ROSA (GALLICA) 'CHARLES DE MILLS'

ROSA (POLYANTHA) 'THE FAIRY'

ROSA (SHRUB) 'LILLIAN GIBSON'

ROSA (SHRUB) 'SEA FOAM'

ROSA CAROLINA
    PASTURE ROSE
ROSA EGLANTERIA
    EGLANTINE ROSE
ROSA NITIDA
    SHINING ROSE
ROSA ROXBURGHII
    CHESTNUT ROSE
ROSA RUGOSA AND HYBRIDS

ROSA VIRGINIANA
    VIRGINIA ROSE

RUBUS COCKBURNIANUS
    RASPBERRY (WHITE STEM)
RUBUS IDAEUS 'AUREUS'
    RASPBERRY (CREEPING, GOLDLEAF)
RUDBECKIA FULGIDA VAR. SULLIVANTII 'GOLDSTURM'
    GARDEN BLACK-EYED-SUSAN
SAGINA SUBULATA
    CORSICAN PEARLWORT
SALIX 'HAKURO'
    WILLOW (YELLOW VARIEGATED)
SALIX ACUTIFOLIA 'LONGIFOLIA'
    SHARPLEAF PUSSY WILLOW

SALIX ALBA 'KALMTHOUT'
    WHITE WILLOW (YELLOW TWIG)
SALIX ALBA 'REGALIS'
    WHITE WILLOW (COLUMNAR, GRAY LEAF)
SALIX ALBA 'SERICEA'
    WHITE WILLOW (GRAY LEAF)
SALIX ALBA VAR. TRISTIS
    WEEPING WILLOW (YELLOW TWIG)
SALIX CHAENOMELOIDES
    PUSSY WILLOW (PURPLE STEM)
SALIX DAPHNOIDES 'AGLAIA'
    PUSSY WILLOW

TYPE	SIZE (FEET)	STRUCTURE	FOLIAGE SPRING & SUMMER	FALL	FLOWER COLOR	MONTH	FRUIT & SEED HEAD COLOR	MONTH	BARK	TEXTURE FOLIAGE	FLOWER	BARK
A	6.5	I										
A	13.0	I	PR	R						BS		
W	3.0	I			PK, V	5, 6			R		P	BK
P	1.5	MO	PR		PK, W	5				BM, BS	S	
P	1.5	MO	PR	O	W	5				BM, BS	S	
P	1.5	MO			W	5				BM, BS	S	
W	1.5	H			R	5, 6				FR	FD	
W	3.0				PK	6					FD	
W	1.5	H			PK	6, 7, 8					I	
W	6.5	W			PK	6					FD	
W	1.5				W	6, 7, 8					I	
W	3.0			O, R	PK, PU	6	R	1, 2, 3, 10, 11, 12	R			
W	3.0				PK	5, 6						
W	3.0			R	PK	6	R	8, 9, 10			FD	
W	6.5	MO			PK, V	6			OC, GR	FR	FD	BK
W	3.0	MO, I		O, Y	R, PK, PU, W	6	O, R	10, 11, 12			FD	
W	3.0			O, R	PK, PU	6	R	1, 2, 3, 11, 12	R		FD	
W	6.5	W	GR						W			BK
W	0.5	H	GG	Y								
P	1.5	MO			O	7, 8	PB	9, 10			FD	
P, E	0.0	H			W							
W	6.5		GG									
W	13.0	I			W	1, 2, 3, 4, 12			W			
W	3.0								Y			
W	26.0	VT	GR									
W	6.5	M	GR							FB		
W	52.0	W							Y	FB		
W	6.5	MO			PU, W	3, 4			PU			
W	26.0	I			W	1, 2, 3, 4, 12			PU, W			

Master List:
Summary of Design Characteristics

KEY TO ABBREVIATIONS

TYPE

W	Woody	A	Annual
P	Perennial	B	Bulb
I	Biennial	E	Evergreen

STRUCTURE

VT	Vertical
H	Horizontal
MO	Mound
BS	Ball on a Stick
VS	Vase
W	Weeping
I	Irregular, Sculptural
MS	Multistemmed
C	Climbing

COLOR: FOLIAGE, SPRING & SUMMER

BG	Blue-Green
GR	Gray-Green
GW	Green and White Variegated
YG	Yellow-Green
GG	Green and Gold Variegated
PR	Pink and Red

COLOR: FOLIAGE, FALL

O	Orange	R	Red
Y	Yellow	W	Wine

COLOR: FLOWER

Y	Yellow	PU	Purple
O	Orange	V	Violet
A	Apricot	B	Blue
R	Red	C	Chartreuse
PK	Pink	W	White

FLOWER COLOR: BY MONTH

1	January	7	July
2	February	8	August
3	March	9	September
4	April	10	October
5	May	11	November
6	June	12	December

COLOR: FRUIT & SEED HEAD

Y	Yellow
O	Orange, Brown
R	Red
PB	Purple-Black
B	Blue
W	White-Silver

FRUIT & SEED HEAD COLOR BY MONTH

1	January	7	July
2	February	8	August
3	March	9	September
4	April	10	October
5	May	11	November
6	June	12	December

COLOR: BARK

Y	Yellow	PU	Purple
OC	Orange-Cherry	GN	Green
		GR	Gray
R	Red	W	White

TEXTURE: FOLIAGE

FN	Fine Detail—Narrow, Linear—Needle
FB	Fine Detail—Narrow, Linear—Blade
FR	Fine Detail—Small, Rounded
FO	Fine Detail—Other Leaf Shapes
BS	Broad—Strong Design Impact
BM	Broad—For Ground Cover Massing

TEXTURE: FLOWER

S	Spikes, Cones, Wands, and Spraylike Heads
P	Pendulous
FD	Daisylike
FT	Flat Top
BL	Ball-like
I	Irregular and/or Complex

TEXTURE: BARK

BK	Interesting Bark Texture

NAME

SALIX ELAEAGNOS
  ROSEMARY-LEAVED WILLOW (NARROW, GRAY LEAF)
SALIX GRACILISTYLA
  BIG-CATKIN WILLOW
SALIX GRACILISTYLA 'MELANOSTACHYS'
  PUSSY WILLOW (BLACK)
SALIX REPENS VAR. ARGENTEA
  PUSSY WILLOW (CREEPING)
SALIX X RUBRA 'EUGENEI'
  RED PUSSY WILLOW (COLUMNAR)

SALVIA ARGENTEA
  SILVER SAGE
SAPONARIA OFFICINALIS
  BOUNCING BET
SASA VEITCHII
  VEITCH BAMBOO
SASSAFRAS ALBIDUM

SAXIFRAGA STOLONIFERA
  STRAWBERRY-BEGONIA
SCIADOPITYS VERTICILLATA
  UMBRELLA-PINE

SCILLA SIBERICA 'SPRING BEAUTY'
  SIBERIAN SQUILL
SEDUM 'AUTUMN JOY'

SEDUM 'VERA JAMISON'

SEDUM ELLACOMBIANUM

SEDUM FLORIFERUM 'WEIHANSTEPHANER GOLD'

SEDUM POPULIFOLIUM
  POPLAR STONECROP

SEDUM SARMENTOSUM
  STRINGY STONECROP
SEDUM SPURIUM
  TWO ROW STONECROP
SEDUM SPURIUM 'BRONZE CARPET'
  TWO ROW STONECROP (BRONZE FOLIAGE)
SEDUM TERNATUM
  MOUNTAIN STONECROP
SKIMMIA REEVESIANA

SOPHORA JAPONICA 'REGENT'
  JAPANESE PAGODA TREE

SORBARIA SORBIFOLIA
  URAL FALSE SPIRAEA
SPIRAEA PRUNIFOLIA
  BRIDAL-WREATH
SPIRAEA THUNBERGII

SPIRAEA X VANHOUTTEI

STACHYS BYZANTINA
  LAMB'S-EARS
STEPHANANDRA INCISA 'CRISPA'
  STEPHANANDRA (COMPACT CUTLEAF)

TYPE	SIZE (FEET)	STRUCTURE	FOLIAGE SPRING & SUMMER	FALL	FLOWER COLOR	MONTH	FRUIT & SEED HEAD COLOR	MONTH	BARK	FOLIAGE	FLOWER	BARK
GENERAL DESIGN			**COLOR**							**TEXTURE**		
W	6.5	MO	GR							FN		
W	6.5	MO			R, W	3, 4			GR			
W	6.5	MO			Y, R, PU	3, 4						
W	3.0	H	GR		V, W	4						
W	13.0	VT	BG		PK, W	4			GN			
P	1.5	I	GR		V	6, 7				BM	S	
P	1.5	H			PK, W	6, 7, 8						
W, E	1.5	H								BM, BS		
W	52.0	H, I		O, Y, R	C	4	R, PB, B	8, 9	GN			
P	0.0	H	GR		PK, W	6, 7				BM	I	
W, E	26.0	VT								FN		
B	0.0	H			B	3, 4					P	
P	1.5	MO	BG		PK	9	O, R	10		BM	FT	
P	0.0	M	GR		PK	8				BM	FT	
P	0.0	H	YG		Y	6				BM	FT	
P	0.0		YG		Y	5, 6				FO	FT	
W	0.5	H			PK					FO		
P, E	0.0	H	YG		Y	6				FN	FT	
P	0.0	H			PK, W	5, 6				BM	FT	
P	0.5	H	PR		PK, W	6				BM	FT	
P	0.0	H	YG		W	5						
W, E	3.0	MO			W	5	R	10, 11		BM		
W	52.0				Y	6, 7	Y	7, 8, 9	GN	FR		
W	3.0	MO, MS			W	6, 7				BS	S	
W	3.0			O, R	W	5					S	
W	3.0	MO	YG	O, Y	W	4			OC	FN		BK
W	3.0	MO, W	BG		W	5						
P	1.0	H	GR		V	6				BM		
W	1.5	MO		W	C	6			R	FO		BK

Master List:
Summary of Design Characteristics

KEY TO ABBREVIATIONS

TYPE

W	Woody	A	Annual
P	Perennial	B	Bulb
I	Biennial	E	Evergreen

STRUCTURE

VT	Vertical
H	Horizontal
MO	Mound
BS	Ball on a Stick
VS	Vase
W	Weeping
I	Irregular, Sculptural
MS	Multistemmed
C	Climbing

COLOR: FOLIAGE, SPRING & SUMMER

BG	Blue-Green
GR	Gray-Green
GW	Green and White Variegated
YG	Yellow-Green
GG	Green and Gold Variegated
PR	Pink and Red

COLOR: FOLIAGE, FALL

O	Orange	R	Red
Y	Yellow	W	Wine

COLOR: FLOWER

Y	Yellow	PU	Purple
O	Orange	V	Violet
A	Apricot	B	Blue
R	Red	C	Chartreuse
PK	Pink	W	White

FLOWER COLOR: BY MONTH

1	January	7	July
2	February	8	August
3	March	9	September
4	April	10	October
5	May	11	November
6	June	12	December

COLOR: FRUIT & SEED HEAD

Y	Yellow
O	Orange, Brown
R	Red
PB	Purple-Black
B	Blue
W	White-Silver

FRUIT & SEED HEAD COLOR BY MONTH

1	January	7	July
2	February	8	August
3	March	9	September
4	April	10	October
5	May	11	November
6	June	12	December

COLOR: BARK

Y	Yellow	PU	Purple
OC	Orange-Cherry	GN	Green
		GR	Gray
R	Red	W	White

TEXTURE: FOLIAGE

FN	Fine Detail—Narrow, Linear—Needle
FB	Fine Detail—Narrow, Linear—Blade
FR	Fine Detail—Small, Rounded
FO	Fine Detail—Other Leaf Shapes
BS	Broad—Strong Design Impact
BM	Broad—For Ground Cover Massing

TEXTURE: FLOWER

S	Spikes, Cones, Wands, and Spraylike Heads
P	Pendulous
FD	Daisylike
FT	Flat Top
BL	Ball-like
I	Irregular and/or Complex

TEXTURE: BARK

BK	Interesting Bark Texture

NAME

STERNBERGIA LUTEA
   FALL-DAFFODIL
STEWARTIA KOREANA

STOKESIA LAEVIS 'BLUE DANUBE'
   STOKES-ASTER
STRANVAESIA DAVIDIANA VAR. UNDULATA 'PROSTRATA'

STYRAX JAPONICUS
   JAPANESE SNOWBELL

STYRAX JAPONICUS 'CARILLON'
   JAPANESE SNOWBELL (WEEPING)
SYMPHORICARPOS X CHENAULTII 'HANCOCK'
   HANCOCK CORALBERRY
SYMPHYTUM X UPLANDICUM
   RUSSIAN COMFREY
SYRINGA LACINIATA
   CUT-LEAF LILAC
SYRINGA PATULA (SYN. S. PALIBINIANA, S. MICROPHYLLA
      'INGWERSEN'S DWARF')
   LILAC (DWARF)

SYRINGA RETICULATA
   JAPANESE TREE LILAC
SYRINGA VULGARIS 'ALBA'
   LILAC (COMMON WHITE)
SYRINGA VULGARIS HYBRIDS
   HYBRID LILACS
SYRINGA X CHINENSIS
   CHINESE LILAC
TAMARIX RAMOSISSIMA
   TAMARISK
TAXODIUM DISTICHUM VAR. NUTANS 'PRAIRIE SENTINEL'
   PRAIRIE SENTINEL POND CYPRESS

TAXUS BACCATA 'ADPRESSA FOWLE'
   MIDGET BOXLEAF YEW
TAXUS BACCATA 'REPANDENS'
   WEEPING ENGLISH YEW
TAXUS CUSPIDATA 'NANA'
   DWARF JAPANESE YEW
TAXUS CUSPIDATA (CAPITATA SELECTION)
   PYRAMIDAL JAPANESE YEW
TAXUS X MEDIA 'SENTINALIS'
   SENTINEL YEW
TELEKIA SPECIOSA
   HEARTLEAF OXEYE

THALICTRUM ROCHEBRUNIANUM
   MEADOW RUE
THELYPTERIS HEXAGONOPTERA
   BROAD BEECH FERN
THELYPTERIS NOVEBORACENSIS
   NEW YORK FERN
THELYPTERIS PHEGOPTERIS
   NARROW BEECHFERN
THERMOPSIS CAROLINIANA
   CAROLINA LUPINE
THUJA OCCIDENTALIS 'HETZ' WINTERGREEN'
   'HETZ' WINTERGREEN ARBORVITAE

TYPE	SIZE (FEET)	STRUCTURE	FOLIAGE SPRING & SUMMER	FALL	FLOWER COLOR	MONTH	FRUIT & SEED HEAD COLOR	MONTH	BARK	FOLIAGE	FLOWER	BARK
B	0.0	H			Y	10				FB	BL	
W	13.0	VT		O, Y, R	W	6			OC, GN, W		FD	
P	1.0	MO			B	7, 8					FD	
W, E	3.0	H			W	6	R	10, 11, 12				
W	26.0	H		Y	W	6			GR		P	
W	6.5	MO, W			W	6			GR		P	
W	3.0	H, W			PK	7, 8	R	9, 10, 11, 12		FB		
P	3.0				PK, B	5, 6					P	
W	3.0	MO			PU, V	5				FO	S	
W	3.0	MO			PU, V	5					S	
W	13.0	MS			W	6			OC			
W	6.5	MS	BG		W	5					S	
W	6.5	MS	BG		P, PU, V, B, W	5					S	
W	6.5	MO			V	5					S	
W	13.0	I	BG		PK	6, 7			OC	FN	S	
W	52.0	VT	YG	O						FN		BK
W, E	1.5									FN		
W, E	3.0	H, MO, W								FN		
W, E	6.5	H								FN		
W, E	6.5	VT					R			FN		
W, E	6.5	VT								FN		
P	3.0				Y	6					FD	
P	3.0	I	BG		PK, V	6, 7, 8				FR	S	
P	1.0	H	YG							FO		
P	1.0	H	YG	O, Y						FO		
P	1.0	H								FO		
P	3.0	MO, I	BG		Y	5, 6					S	
W, E	26.0	VT								FN		

Master List:
Summary of Design Characteristics

KEY TO ABBREVIATIONS

TYPE

W	Woody	A	Annual
P	Perennial	B	Bulb
I	Biennial	E	Evergreen

STRUCTURE

VT	Vertical
H	Horizontal
MO	Mound
BS	Ball on a Stick
VS	Vase
W	Weeping
I	Irregular, Sculptural
MS	Multistemmed
C	Climbing

COLOR: FOLIAGE, SPRING & SUMMER

BG	Blue-Green
GR	Gray-Green
GW	Green and White Variegated
YG	Yellow-Green
GG	Green and Gold Variegated
PR	Pink and Red

COLOR: FOLIAGE, FALL

O	Orange	R	Red
Y	Yellow	W	Wine

COLOR: FLOWER

Y	Yellow	PU	Purple
O	Orange	V	Violet
A	Apricot	B	Blue
R	Red	C	Chartreuse
PK	Pink	W	White

FLOWER COLOR: BY MONTH

1	January	7	July
2	February	8	August
3	March	9	September
4	April	10	October
5	May	11	November
6	June	12	December

COLOR: FRUIT & SEED HEAD

Y	Yellow
O	Orange, Brown
R	Red
PB	Purple-Black
B	Blue
W	White-Silver

FRUIT & SEED HEAD COLOR BY MONTH

1	January	7	July
2	February	8	August
3	March	9	September
4	April	10	October
5	May	11	November
6	June	12	December

COLOR: BARK

Y	Yellow	PU	Purple
OC	Orange-Cherry	GN	Green
		GR	Gray
R	Red	W	White

TEXTURE: FOLIAGE

FN	Fine Detail—Narrow, Linear—Needle
FB	Fine Detail—Narrow, Linear—Blade
FR	Fine Detail—Small, Rounded
FO	Fine Detail—Other Leaf Shapes
BS	Broad—Strong Design Impact
BM	Broad—For Ground Cover Massing

TEXTURE: FLOWER

S	Spikes, Cones, Wands, and Spraylike Heads
P	Pendulous
FD	Daisylike
FT	Flat Top
BL	Ball-like
I	Irregular and/or Complex

TEXTURE: BARK

BK	Interesting Bark Texture

NAME

THUJA OCCIDENTALIS 'NIGRA'
   AMERICAN ARBORVITAE (DARK GREEN)
THUJA PLICATA 'ATROVIRENS'
   GIANT ARBORVITAE (BRIGHT GREEN)
THYMUS 'CLEAR GOLD'
   HYBRID THYME (YELLOW LEAF)
THYMUS PSEUDOLANUGINOSUS
   WOOLY THYME
THYMUS SERPYLLUM
   WILD THYME

TIARELLA CORDIFOLIA VAR. COLLINA
   WHERRY'S FOAM FLOWER
TILIA CORDATA
   LITTLELEAF LINDEN
TRACHYSTEMON ORIENTALIS

TSUGA CANADENSIS
   CANADIAN HEMLOCK
TSUGA CANADENSIS 'BENNETT'
   BENNETT'S DWARF HEMLOCK
TSUGA CANADENSIS 'COLE'S PROSTRATE'
   COLE'S PROSTRATE HEMLOCK

TSUGA CANADENSIS 'PENDULA'
   SARGENT'S WEEPING HEMLOCK
TYPHA ANGUSTIFOLIA
   NARROWLEAVED CATTAIL
VACCINIUM CORYMBOSUM
   HIGHBUSH BLUEBERRY
VALERIANA OFFICINALIS
   GARDEN HELIOTROPE
VERBASCUM OLYMPICUM
   OLYMPIC MULLEIN
VERNONIA NOVEBORACENSIS
   IRONWEED

VERONICA 'SUNNY BORDER BLUE'
   SPEEDWELL
VERONICA INCANA
   WOOLY SPEEDWELL
VERONICA LONGIFOLIA 'SUBSESSILIS'
   SPEEDWELL (BLUE)
VERONICASTRUM VIRGINICUM
   CULVER'S ROOT
VIBURNUM ACERIFOLIUM
   MAPLELEAF VIBURNUM
VIBURNUM CARLESII
   KOREAN SPICE VIBURNUM

VIBURNUM DILATATUM 'MICHAEL DODGE'
   LINDEN VIBURNUM (YELLOW FRUIT)
VIBURNUM FARRERI 'CANDIDISSIMUM'
   FRAGRANT VIBURNUM (WHITE-FLOWERED)
VIBURNUM FARRERI 'NANUM'
   DWARF FRAGRANT VIBURNUM
VIBURNUM ICHANGENSE

VIBURNUM MACROCEPHALUM FORMA MACROCEPHALUM
   CHINESE SNOWBALL VIBURNUM
VIBURNUM NUDUM 'WINTERTHUR'
   SMOOTH WITHE-ROD (SUPERIOR SELECTION)

TYPE	SIZE (FEET)	STRUCTURE	FOLIAGE SPRING & SUMMER	FOLIAGE FALL	FLOWER COLOR	FLOWER MONTH	FRUIT & SEED HEAD COLOR	FRUIT & SEED HEAD MONTH	BARK	TEXTURE FOLIAGE	TEXTURE FLOWER	TEXTURE BARK
W, E	26.0	VT										
W, E	52.0	VT								FN		
P	0.0	H	GG		PK	6				FN		
P	0.0	H	BG		PU							
P	0.0	H	GR		PU	6				FN		
P	0.5	H	YG		W	5					S	
W	52.0	BS			Y							
P	1.5				V, B	4				BM	I	
W, E	52.0	VT								FN		
W, E	3.0	H								FN		
W, E	3.0	H, W								FN		
W, E	6.5	W								FN		
P	3.0	VT, I					O	7, 8, 9, 10, 11, 12		FB	S	
W	6.5	MO, I		O, R	P, W	5	B	7, 8	R		P	
P	3.0	I			PK, W	5, 6				FO	FT	
I	3.0	VT, I	GR	Y		6					S	
P	3.0				PU	8, 9					I	
P	1.5				B	7, 8					S	
P	0.5	H	GR		B	8					S	
P	1.5			B		7, 8					S	
P	3.0				PK, B, W	8					S	
W	3.0	MO, W		O, R, W	W		PB	10, 11			FT	
W	3.0	MO		O, Y	PK, W	4					FT	
W	6.5			R	W		Y	10, 11, 12			FT	
W	6.5	I		R	W	3, 4					FT	
W	3.0	MO		R	PK, W	3, 4						
W	6.5				W		R	10, 11			FT	
W	13.0				C, W	4, 5			GR			
W	6.5			W	W		R, B	9, 10, 11			FT	

Master List:
Summary of Design Characteristics

KEY TO ABBREVIATIONS

TYPE

W	Woody	A	Annual
P	Perennial	B	Bulb
I	Biennial	E	Evergreen

STRUCTURE

VT	Vertical
H	Horizontal
MO	Mound
BS	Ball on a Stick
VS	Vase
W	Weeping
I	Irregular, Sculptural
MS	Multistemmed
C	Climbing

COLOR: FOLIAGE, SPRING & SUMMER

BG	Blue-Green
GR	Gray-Green
GW	Green and White Variegated
YG	Yellow-Green
GG	Green and Gold Variegated
PR	Pink and Red

COLOR: FOLIAGE, FALL

O	Orange	R	Red
Y	Yellow	W	Wine

COLOR: FLOWER

Y	Yellow	PU	Purple
O	Orange	V	Violet
A	Apricot	B	Blue
R	Red	C	Chartreuse
PK	Pink	W	White

FLOWER COLOR: BY MONTH

1	January	7	July
2	February	8	August
3	March	9	September
4	April	10	October
5	May	11	November
6	June	12	December

COLOR: FRUIT & SEED HEAD

Y	Yellow
O	Orange, Brown
R	Red
PB	Purple-Black
B	Blue
W	White-Silver

FRUIT & SEED HEAD COLOR BY MONTH

1	January	7	July
2	February	8	August
3	March	9	September
4	April	10	October
5	May	11	November
6	June	12	December

COLOR: BARK

Y	Yellow	PU	Purple
OC	Orange-Cherry	GN	Green
		GR	Gray
R	Red	W	White

TEXTURE: FOLIAGE

FN	Fine Detail—Narrow, Linear—Needle
FB	Fine Detail—Narrow, Linear—Blade
FR	Fine Detail—Small, Rounded
FO	Fine Detail—Other Leaf Shapes
BS	Broad—Strong Design Impact
BM	Broad—For Ground Cover Massing

TEXTURE: FLOWER

S	Spikes, Cones, Wands, and Spraylike Heads
P	Pendulous
FD	Daisylike
FT	Flat Top
BL	Ball-like
I	Irregular and/or Complex

TEXTURE: BARK

BK	Interesting Bark Texture

NAME

VIBURNUM PLICATUM FORMA TOMENTOSUM
    DOUBLE-FILE VIBURNUM
VIBURNUM PRUNIFOLIUM
    BLACKHAW
VIBURNUM RHYTIDOPHYLLUM
    LEATHERLEAF VIBURNUM
VIBURNUM SETIGERUM
    TEA VIBURNUM
VIBURNUM SIEBOLDII 'SENECA'

VINCA MINOR 'BOWLESII'
    BOWLES PERIWINKLE
VINCA MINOR 'VARIEGATA'
    PERIWINKLE (GREEN AND YELLOW)
VIOLA LABRADORICA

VITEX AGNUS-CASTUS 'LATIFOLIA'
    MONK'S PEPPER, CHASTE TREE (BLUE)
VITEX AGNUS-CASTUS 'SILVER SPIRE'
    MONK'S PEPPER, CHASTE TREE (WHITE)
WALDSTEINIA TERNATA

WISTERIA FLORIBUNDA
    JAPANESE WISTERIA
XANTHORHIZA SIMPLICISSIMA
    YELLOWROOT
YUCCA FLACCIDA 'GOLDEN SWORD'
    ADAM'S NEEDLE (YELLOW VARIEGATED)
YUCCA GLAUCA
    SOAPWEED
YUCCA SMALLIANA
    ADAM'S-NEEDLE
ZELKOVA SERRATA 'GREEN VASE'

| GENERAL DESIGN | | | COLOR | | | | | | | | TEXTURE | | |
TYPE	SIZE (FEET)	STRUCTURE	FOLIAGE SPRING & SUMMER	FALL	FLOWER COLOR	MONTH	FRUIT & SEED HEAD COLOR	MONTH	BARK		FOLIAGE	FLOWER	BARK
W	6.5	H			W	5						FT	
W	13.0	H, MO		W	W	5	PB, B	9, 10, 11				FT	
W, E	6.5				W		R						
W	6.5	VS, W		W			O, R	9, 10, 11			P		
W	13.0				W	7	R	8			BS	FT	
W, E	0.0	H			B	5					BM	FD	
W, E	0.0	H	GG		B	5					BM	FD	
P	0.0		PR		PU								I
W	3.0				V, B	7, 8						S	
W	3.0				W	7, 8						S	
P, E	0.0	H			Y	5, 6					FO	FD	
W	13.0	I		Y	PK, PU, W	5			GR		BS	B, P	
W	1.0	H	YG	O, Y	R	4							
W, E	3.0	VT, I	GG		W	6					BM, BS	S, P	
W, E	3.0	VT, I	GR		W	6					FB	S, P	
W, E	3.0	VT, I	GR		W	6					BM, BS	S, P	
W	52.0	VS		O					OC				

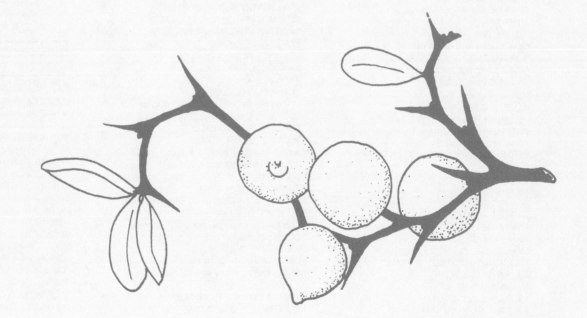

APPENDIX 2
Plant Listing by Mature Height

Plants in this list are divided as follows:

6 inches or less
6–12 inches
12–18 inches
18 inches–3 feet
3–6.5 feet
6.5–13 feet
13–26 feet
26–52 feet
More than 52 feet

Each of the above sections is subdivided by hardiness zone. The letter *T* under the heading "Zone" indicates a plant that is tender, not tolerant of frost.

Further information about all the following plants is summarized in the Master Lists, Appendices 1A and 1B.

6 INCHES OR LESS

ZONE	LATIN NAME
3	DIANTHUS DELTOIDES
	PHLOX SUBULATA
	SEDUM ELLACOMBIANUM
	SEDUM SARMENTOSUM
	SEDUM SPURIUM
	THYMUS SERPYLLUM
	TSUGA CANADENSIS 'COLE'S PROSTRATE'
4	AJUGA REPTANS
	AJUGA REPTANS 'BRONZE BEAUTY'
	AJUGA REPTANS (GIANT FORM)
	ARENARIA VERNA
	CHAMAEMELUM NOBILE
	GAULTHERIA PROCUMBENS
	HEDYOTIS CAERULEA
	SEDUM TERNATUM
	VINCA MINOR 'BOWLESII'
	VINCA MINOR 'VARIEGATA'
	VIOLA LABRADORICA
	WALDSTEINIA TERNATA
5	ALLIUM ZEBDANENSE
	ANEMONE BLANDA 'ATROCAERULEA'
	ARTEMESIA VERSICOLOR
	ASARUM EUROPAEUM
	COTONEASTER ADPRESSUS 'LITTLE GEM'
	CROCUS ANCYRENSIS 'GOLDEN BUNCH'
	CROCUS SIEBERI
	CROCUS TOMASINIANUS
	CYCLAMEN HEDERIFOLIUM
	ERANTHIS HYEMALIS
	ERANTHIS X TUBERGENII
	EUONYMUS FORTUNEI 'MINIMA'
	GALANTHUS ELWESII
	GALANTHUS NIVALIS
	HEDERA HELIX 'BULGARIA'
	HEDERA HELIX 'OGALALLA'
	MUSCARI AZUREUM 'ALBUM'

ZONE	LATIN NAME
	MUSCARI BOTRYOIDES 'ALBUM'
	MUSCARI TUBERGENIANUM
	PHLOX STOLONIFERA 'ALBA'
	PHLOX STOLONIFERA 'BLUE RIDGE'
	PHLOX STOLONIFERA 'SHERWOOD PURPLE'
	SAGINA SUBULATA
	SCILLA SIBERICA 'SPRING BEAUTY'
	SEDUM 'VERA JAMISON'
	SEDUM FLORIFERUM 'WEIHANSTEPHANER GOLD'
	STERNBERGIA LUTEA
	THYMUS 'CLEAR GOLD'
	THYMUS PSEUDOLANUGINOSUS
6	HEDERA HELIX 'BALTICA'
	LESPEDEZA THUNBERGII 'ALBIFLORA'
	PARONYCHIA KAPELA SUBSP. SERPYLLIFOLIA
	SAXIFRAGA STOLONIFERA
7	OPHIOPOGON JAPONICUS 'NANUS'
8	COTULA SQUALIDA

6-12 INCHES

ZONE	LATIN NAME
2	ARTEMESIA STELLERIANA
	POTENTILLA TRIDENTATA
3	ACHILLEA 'MOONSHINE'
	AEGOPODIUM PODAGRARIA 'VARIEGATUM'
	FILIPENDULA ULMARIA 'AUREA'
	GERANIUM SANGUINEUM
	HELLEBORUS NIGER
	HOSTA UNDULATA
	JUNIPERUS HORIZONTALIS 'WILTONII'
	PULMONARIA ANGUSTIFOLIA
	PULMONARIA SACCHARATA 'MARGERY FISH'
	PULMONARIA SACCHARATA 'SISSINGHURST WHITE'
	SEDUM SPURIUM 'BRONZE CARPET'
	TIARELLA CORDIFOLIA VAR. COLLINA
	VERONICA INCANA
4	ARABIS PROCURRENS
	ARUNCUS AETHUSIFOLIUS
	CONVALLARIA MAJALIS
	EUONYMUS FORTUNEI 'COLORATA'
	EUONYMUS FORTUNEI VAR. RADICANS
	EUPHORBIA CYPARISSIAS
	MICROBIOTA DECUSSATA
	PACHYSANDRA PROCUMBENS
	PAXISTIMA CANBYI
	PHLOX BIFIDA
	SEDUM POPULIFOLIUM
5	ALLIUM CERNUUM
	ATHYRIUM GOERINGIANUM 'PICTUM'
	CHIONODOXA GIGANTEA 'ALBA'
	CHIONODOXA LUCILIAE
	CHIONODOXA SARDENSIS
	CHRYSANTHEMUM WEYRICHII 'WHITE BOMB'
	COLCHICUM 'AUTUMN QUEEN'
	COLCHICUM 'THE GIANT'

ZONE	LATIN NAME
	ENDYMION HISPANICUS 'EXCELSIOR' (SYN. SCILLA CAMPANULATA 'EXCELSIOR')
	EPIMEDIUM PINNATUM SUBSP. COLCHICUM
	EPIMEDIUM X YOUNGIANUM 'NIVEUM'
	EUONYMUS FORTUNEI 'GRACILIS'
	GALIUM ODORATUM
	HELIANTHEMUM APENNINUM VAR. ROSEUM
	IRIS CRISTATA
	IRIS GRAMINEA
	IRIS TECTORUM
	LAMIUM MACULATUM 'WHITE NANCY'
	LEUCOJUM VERNUM
	MERTENSIA VIRGINICA
	NARCISSUS 'CARLTON'
	NARCISSUS 'FORTUNE'
	NARCISSUS 'HERA'
	NARCISSUS 'LOCH FYNE'
	NARCISSUS 'MOONMIST'
	NARCISSUS 'MRS. ERNST H. KRELAGE'
	NARCISSUS 'PEEPING TOM'
	NARCISSUS 'POMONA'
	NARCISSUS 'QUEEN OF SPAIN'
	NARCISSUS 'TREVITHIAN'
	NARCISSUS JONQUILLA
	NARCISSUS PSEUDONARCISSUS SUBSP. OBVALLARIS
	OMPHALODES VERNA
	PACHYSANDRA TERMINALIS
	PACHYSANDRA TERMINALIS 'GREEN CARPET'
	PACHYSANDRA TERMINALIS 'VARIEGATA' OR 'SILVER EDGE'
	PETASITES FRAGRANS
	PHLOX PILOSA SUBSP. OZARKANA
6	CERATOSTIGMA PLUMBAGINOIDES
	LIRIOPE MUSCARI (BIG BLUE SELECTION)
	LIRIOPE MUSCARI 'MONROE WHITE'
	LIRIOPE MUSCARI 'VARIEGATA'
	RUBUS IDAEUS 'AUREUS'
7	BUXUS MICROPHYLLA 'COMPACTA'

12–18 INCHES

ZONE	LATIN NAME
2	BERGENIA 'PERFECTA'
	BERGENIA 'SUNNINGDALE'
3	ALCHEMILLA VULGARIS
	ASTER AMELLUS 'NOCTURNE'
	BRUNNERA MACROPHYLLA
	COREOPSIS 'MOONBEAM'
	CORNUS RACEMOSA (DWARF)
	DICENTRA 'LUXURIANT'
	DICENTRA EXIMIA 'PURITY'
	GERANIUM 'JOHNSON'S BLUE'
	GERANIUM MACRORRHIZUM
	HOSTA 'KABITAN'
	NEPETA X FAASSENII
	POLYSTICHUM ACROSTICHOIDES
4	ALLIUM TUBEROSUM
	EUPHORBIA EPITHYMOIDES
	HELLEBORUS ORIENTALIS HYBRIDS

ZONE	LATIN NAME
	HEUCHERA 'PALACE PURPLE' STRAIN
	JUNIPERUS SABINA 'TAMARISCIFOLIA'
	PAEONIA TENUIFOLIA
	STACHYS BYZANTINA
5	BUXUS SINICA VAR. INSULARIS 'TIDE HILL'
	DIPLAZIUM CONILII
	FILIPENDULA PURPUREA 'NANA'
	HELICTOTRICHON SEMPERVIRENS
	HOUTTUYNIA CORDATA 'CHAMELEON'
	INDIGOFERA INCARNATA 'ALBA'
	POLYSTICHUM TRIPTERON
	STOKESIA LAEVIS 'BLUE DANUBE'
	THELYPTERIS HEXAGONOPTERA
	THELYPTERIS NOVEBORACENSIS
	THELYPTERIS PHEGOPTERIS
	XANTHORHIZA SIMPLICISSIMA
6	ACORUS GRAMINEUS 'OGON'
	CROCOSMIA POTTSII
	EUPATORIUM COELESTINUM
	FORSYTHIA VIRIDISSIMA 'BRONXENSIS'
	RHODODENDRON X ERIOCARPUM AND R. X NAKAHARAI CULTIVARS AND HYBRIDS
T	POLIANTHES TUBEROSA

18 INCHES–3 FEET

ZONE	LATIN NAME
2	ACHILLEA MILLEFOLIUM 'ROSEA'
	DICENTRA SPECTABILIS
	PAEONIA—HERBACEOUS HYBRIDS
	SAPONARIA OFFICINALIS
3	ACHILLEA 'CORONATION GOLD'
	ADIANTUM PEDATUM
	ASCLEPIAS TUBEROSA
	BUPHTHALUM SALICIFOLIUM
	CAMPANULA RAPUNCULOIDES
	CHELONE LYONII
	DENNSTAEDTIA PUNCTILOBULA
	ECHINACEA PURPUREA
	EUPHORBIA COROLLATA
	HEMEROCALLIS LILIOASPHODELUS
	HOSTA PLANTAGINEA
	HOSTA SIEBOLDIANA 'ELEGANS'
	HOSTA VENTRICOSA
	IRIS SIBIRICA CULTIVARS
	LIATRIS SCARIOSA 'WHITE SPIRE'
	LIATRIS SPICATA 'KOBOLD'
	LYSIMACHIA CLETHROIDES
	RHUS AROMATICA 'GRO-LOW'
	RUDBECKIA FULGIDA VAR. SULLIVANTII 'GOLDSTURM'
	SEDUM 'AUTUMN JOY'
4	ANEMONE VITIFOLIA 'ROBUSTISSIMA'
	ARTEMESIA LUDOVICIANA 'SILVER QUEEN'
	ASTILBE X ARENDSII CULTIVARS
	BERBERIS THUNBERGII 'CRIMSON PYGMY'
	CARYOPTERIS X CLANDONENSIS 'BLUE MIST'
	CHAENOMELES JAPONICA VAR. ALPINA
	CHAENOMELES X SUPERBA 'JET TRAIL'
	HYPERICUM KALMIANUM

ZONE	LATIN NAME
	JUNIPERUS X MEDIA 'PFITZERIANA COMPACTA'
	MONARDA DIDYMA
	PETASITES JAPONICUS
	POLYGONATUM ODORATUM 'VARIEGATUM'
	RODGERSIA AESCULIFOLIA
	RODGERSIA PODOPHYLLA
	RODGERSIA TABULARIS
	VERONICA 'SUNNY BORDER BLUE'
	VERONICA LONGIFOLIA 'SUBSESSILIS'
5	AMSONIA HUBRICHTII
	ARUNDINARIA VIRIDISTRIATA
	ASPHODELINE LUTEA
	ASTER X FRIKARTII 'MONCH'
	BUXUS 'GREEN GEM'
	BUXUS SINICA VAR. INSULARIS 'WINTERGREEN' (OHIO CULTIVAR)
	CHAMAECYPARIS OBTUSA 'NANA'
	COTONEASTER APICULATUS
	COTONEASTER HORIZONTALIS
	DEUTZIA GRACILIS
	EQUISETUM HYEMALE
	JUNIPERUS X MEDIA 'OLD GOLD'
	LAMIASTRUM GALEOBDOLON 'VARIEGATUM'
	LATHYRUS VERNUS
	LYCORIS SPRENGERI
	LYCORIS SQUAMIGERA
	LYSICHITON AMERICANUM
	LYSICHITON CAMTSCHATCENSE
	LYSIMACHIA PUNCTATA
	PANICUM VIRGATUM 'STRICTUM'
	PENNISETUM ALOPECUROIDES
	PHLOMIS RUSSELIANA
	RHODODENDRON ATLANTICUM
	ROSA 'DOORENBOS SELECTION'
	ROSA (POLYANTHA) 'THE FAIRY'
	ROSA (SHRUB) 'SEA FOAM'
	STEPHANANDRA INCISA 'CRISPA'
	TAXUS BACCATA 'ADPRESSA FOWLE'
6	ARUM ITALICUM 'PICTUM'
	BEGONIA GRANDIS
	COTONEASTER ADPRESSUS VAR. PRAECOX
	CROCOSMIA 'LUCIFER'
	CROCOSMIA X CROCOSMIIFLORA
	CRUCIANELLA STYLOSA
	EUONYMUS FORTUNEI 'SILVER QUEEN'
	GALTONIA CANDICANS
	HYDRANGEA MACROPHYLLA 'BLUE BILLOW'
	IMPERATA CYLINDRICA 'RED BARON'
	JASMINUM NUDIFLORUM
	LUZULA SYLVATICA 'MARGINATA'
	PELTIPHYLLUM PELTATUM
	SALVIA ARGENTEA
	TRACHYSTEMON ORIENTALIS
7	GENISTA SYLVESTRIS 'LYDIA'
	HEDERA HELIX 'ERECTA'
	SASA VEITCHII
T	KOCHIA SCOPARIA FORMA TRICHOPHYLLA 'CHILDSII'

3–6.5 FEET

ZONE	LATIN NAME
2	ASTER PUNICEUS
3	AMSONIA TABERNAEMONTANA
	ARTEMESIA ABSINTHIUM 'LAMBROOK SILVER'
	ARUNCUS DIOICUS
	BAPTISIA AUSTRALIS
	BOLTONIA ASTEROIDES 'SNOWBANK'
	CLEMATIS HERACLEIFOLIA VAR. DAVIDIANA
	CORNUS ALBA 'ELEGANTISSIMA'
	CORNUS ALBA 'SPAETHII'
	CORNUS SERICEA
	CORNUS SERICEA 'FLAVIRAMEA'
	ECHINOPS RITRO
	LYTHRUM SALICARIA 'DROPMORE PURPLE'
	OSMUNDA REGALIS
	PAPAVER ORIENTALE
	PHYSOSTEGIA VIRGINIANA
	PHYSOSTEGIA VIRGINIANA 'SUMMER SNOW'
	PICEA ABIES 'NIDIFORMIS'
	PINUS MUGO VAR. MUGO
	PRUNUS X CISTENA
	PTERIDIUM AQUILINUM VAR. LATIUSCULUM
	ROSA RUGOSA AND HYBRIDS
	SALIX ALBA 'KALMTHOUT'
	SORBARIA SORBIFOLIA
	SPIRAEA X VANHOUTTEI
	TELEKIA SPECIOSA
	THERMOPSIS CAROLINIANA
	TSUGA CANADENSIS 'BENNETT'
	VERONICASTRUM VIRGINICUM
	VIBURNUM ACERIFOLIUM
4	BERBERIS THUNBERGII 'ATROPURPUREA'
	CHAENOMELES SPECIOSA CULTIVARS
	COMPTONIA PEREGRINA
	CORYLUS AVELLANA 'CONTORTA'
	DIERVILLA SESSILIFOLIA
	HELIOPSIS HELIANTHOIDES SUBSP. SCABRA 'KARAT'
	OSMUNDA CINNAMOMEA
	OSMUNDA CLAYTONIANA
	PHALARIS ARUNDINACEA VAR. PICTA
	ROBINIA HISPIDA
	ROSA NITIDA
	SALIX REPENS VAR. ARGENTEA
	SPIRAEA THUNBERGII
	SYRINGA PATULA (SYN. S. PALIBINIANA, S. MICROPHYLLA 'INGWERSEN'S DWARF')
	TYPHA ANGUSTIFOLIA
	VERNONIA NOVEBORACENSIS
	VIBURNUM CARLESII
	YUCCA FLACCIDA 'GOLDEN SWORD'
	YUCCA GLAUCA
	YUCCA SMALLIANA
5	ANEMONE X HYBRIDA 'QUEEN CHARLOTTE'
	ASTER CORDIFOLIUS
	ASTER NOVAE-ANGLIAE 'HARRINGTON'S PINK'
	BUDDLEIA DAVIDII 'BLACK KNIGHT'
	BUDDLEIA DAVIDII 'OPERA'
	BUDDLEIA DAVIDII 'PURPLE PRINCE'

APPENDIX 3
Plant Listing by Soil Preference

Plants in this list are divided as follows:

Clay and Clay Loam
Organic Loam
Sandy Loam
Stony, Gravelly

Each of the above sections is subdivided by hardiness zone.

The letter *T* under the heading "Zone" indicates a plant that is tender, not tolerant of frost.

Further information about all the following plants is summarized in the Master Lists, Appendices 1A and 1B.

CLAY AND CLAY LOAM

ZONE	LATIN NAME
2	ACHILLEA MILLEFOLIUM 'ROSEA'
	BERGENIA 'PERFECTA'
	BERGENIA 'SUNNINGDALE'
3	ACHILLEA 'MOONSHINE'
	AEGOPODIUM PODAGRARIA 'VARIEGATUM'
	AMELANCHIER ARBOREA (SYN. A. CANADENSIS)
	AMSONIA TABERNAEMONTANA
	ASCLEPIAS TUBEROSA
	ASTER TATARICUS
	BAPTISIA AUSTRALIS
	BUPHTHALUM SALICIFOLIUM
	DENNSTAEDTIA PUNCTILOBULA
	ECHINACEA PURPUREA
	EUPHORBIA COROLLATA
	GERANIUM MACRORRHIZUM
	HIPPOPHAE RHAMNOIDES
	IRIS SIBIRICA CULTIVARS
	JUNIPERUS HORIZONTALIS 'WILTONII'
	JUNIPERUS VIRGINIANA
	LYTHRUM SALICARIA 'DROPMORE PURPLE'
	PAPAVER ORIENTALE
	PHYSOSTEGIA VIRGINIANA
	PHYSOSTEGIA VIRGINIANA 'SUMMER SNOW'
	PICEA ABIES 'NIDIFORMIS'
	RHUS AROMATICA 'GRO-LOW'
	RHUS TYPHINA
	RHUS TYPHINA 'LACINIATA'
	ROSA RUGOSA AND HYBRIDS
	RUDBECKIA FULGIDA VAR. SULLIVANTII 'GOLDSTURM'
	SALIX ALBA 'KALMTHOUT'
	SALIX ALBA 'SERICEA'
	SEDUM ELLACOMBIANUM
	SEDUM SARMENTOSUM
	SEDUM SPURIUM
	SEDUM SPURIUM 'BRONZE CARPET'
	SYRINGA VULGARIS 'ALBA'
	SYRINGA VULGARIS HYBRIDS
	THUJA OCCIDENTALIS 'NIGRA'
	TSUGA CANADENSIS 'BENNETT'
	TSUGA CANADENSIS 'COLE'S PROSTRATE'

ZONE	LATIN NAME
	TSUGA CANADENSIS 'PENDULA'
	VIBURNUM PRUNIFOLIUM
4	ACANTHOPANAX SIEBOLDIANUS
	ACER PLATANOIDES 'CRIMSON KING'
	ACER RUBRUM
	ALLIUM TUBEROSUM
	ARALIA SPINOSA
	BERBERIS THUNBERGII 'CRIMSON PYGMY'
	CHAENOMELES JAPONICA VAR. ALPINA
	CHAENOMELES SPECIOSA CULTIVARS
	CHAENOMELES X SUPERBA 'JET TRAIL'
	CORYLUS AVELLANA 'CONTORTA'
	CORYLUS AVELLANA 'PENDULA'
	CRATAEGUS NITIDA
	CRATAEGUS PHAENOPYRUM
	DIERVILLA SESSILIFOLIA
	EUONYMUS ALATA
	EUONYMUS FORTUNEI 'COLORATA'
	EUPHORBIA CYPARISSIAS
	GINKGO BILOBA, STAMINATE
	GLEDITSIA TRIACANTHOS VAR. INERMIS 'SHADEMASTER'
	GYMNOCLADUS DIOICA
	HAMAMELIS VIRGINIANA
	HELIOPSIS HELIANTHOIDES SUBSP. SCABRA 'KARAT'
	HYPERICUM KALMIANUM
	JUNIPERUS SABINA 'TAMARISCIFOLIA'
	JUNIPERUS X MEDIA 'PFITZERIANA COMPACTA'
	MICROBIOTA DECUSSATA
	MYRICA PENSYLVANICA
	PHALARIS ARUNDINACEA VAR. PICTA
	ROBINIA HISPIDA
	ROSA NITIDA
	SPIRAEA THUNBERGII
	SYRINGA PATULA (SYN. S. PALIBINIANA, S. MICROPHYLLA 'INGWERSEN'S DWARF')
	SYRINGA X CHINENSIS
	YUCCA FLACCIDA 'GOLDEN SWORD'
	YUCCA GLAUCA
	YUCCA SMALLIANA
5	ACER GRISEUM
	ALLIUM CERNUUM
	AMSONIA HUBRICHTII
	ARUNDINARIA VIRIDISTRIATA
	ASPHODELINE LUTEA
	ASTER CORDIFOLIUS
	ASTER X FRIKARTII 'MONCH'
	BUDDLEIA DAVIDII 'BLACK KNIGHT'
	BUDDLEIA DAVIDII 'OPERA'
	BUDDLEIA DAVIDII 'PURPLE PRINCE'
	BUXUS SINICA VAR. INSULARIS 'TIDE HILL'
	CALAMAGROSTIS X ACUTIFLORA 'KARL FOERSTER' (SYN. C. EPIGEOUS 'HORTORUM')
	CALLICARPA JAPONICA
	CAMPSIS X TAGLIABUANA 'MADAME GALEN'
	CATALPA BIGNONIOIDES
	CHAENOMELES X SUPERBA CULTIVARS
	CLETHRA ALNIFOLIA
	COLUTEA X MEDIA
	CORNUS MAS
	CORNUS OFFICINALIS
	CRAMBE CORDIFOLIA
	CRATAEGUS VIRIDIS 'WINTER KING'

ZONE	LATIN NAME
	DIOSPYROS VIRGINIANA
	ERIANTHUS RAVENNAE
	EUONYMUS FORTUNEI 'GRACILIS'
	EUONYMUS FORTUNEI 'MINIMA'
	FORSYTHIA SUSPENSA
	GALANTHUS ELWESII
	GALANTHUS NIVALIS
	HEMEROCALLIS 'HYPERION'
	HEMEROCALLIS FULVA 'EUROPA'
	HERACLEUM MANTEGAZZIANUM
	HYDRANGEA QUERCIFOLIA
	HYPERICUM FRONDOSUM
	ILEX GLABRA 'DENSA'
	JUNIPERUS X MEDIA 'OLD GOLD'
	LAMIASTRUM GALEOBDOLON 'VARIEGATUM'
	LESPEDEZA THUNBERGII
	LIGUSTRUM QUIHOUI
	LONICERA FRAGRANTISSIMA
	MISCANTHUS SINENSIS 'CABARET'
	MISCANTHUS SINENSIS 'GRACILLIMUS'
	MISCANTHUS SINENSIS 'MORNING LIGHT'
	MISCANTHUS SINENSIS 'SILVER FEATHER'(=SILBERFEDER)
	MISCANTHUS SINENSIS 'STRICTUS'
	MISCANTHUS SINENSIS 'VARIEGATUS'
	NARCISSUS 'CARLTON'
	NARCISSUS 'FORTUNE'
	NARCISSUS 'HERA'
	NARCISSUS 'LOCH FYNE'
	NARCISSUS 'MOONMIST'
	NARCISSUS 'MRS. ERNST H. KRELAGE'
	NARCISSUS 'PEEPING TOM'
	NARCISSUS 'POMONA'
	NARCISSUS 'QUEEN OF SPAIN'
	NARCISSUS 'TREVITHIAN'
	NARCISSUS PSEUDONARCISSUS SUBSP. OBVALLARIS
	ONOPORDUM ACANTHIUM
	PANICUM VIRGATUM 'STRICTUM'
	PEROVSKIA ABROTANOIDES X P. ATRIPLICIFOLIA
	PETASITES FRAGRANS
	PHILADELPHUS CORONARIUS
	PHILADELPHUS X FALCONERI
	PINUS VIRGINIANA
	RHODOTYPOS SCANDENS
	ROSA 'DOORENBOS SELECTION'
	ROSA (GALLICA) 'CHARLES DE MILLS'
	ROSA (POLYANTHA) 'THE FAIRY'
	ROSA (SHRUB) 'LILLIAN GIBSON'
	ROSA CAROLINA
	ROSA EGLANTERIA
	ROSA VIRGINIANA
	RUBUS COCKBURNIANUS
	SALIX DAPHNOIDES 'AGLAIA'
	SALIX X RUBRA 'EUGENEI'
	SASSAFRAS ALBIDUM
	SEDUM 'VERA JAMISON'
	SEDUM FLORIFERUM 'WEIHANSTEPHANER GOLD'
	STEPHANANDRA INCISA 'CRISPA'
	SYMPHORICARPOS X CHENAULTII 'HANCOCK'
	SYMPHYTUM X UPLANDICUM
	SYRINGA LACINIATA
	VERBASCUM OLYMPICUM
	VIBURNUM PLICATUM FORMA TOMENTOSUM
	VIBURNUM SIEBOLDII 'SENECA'
	WISTERIA FLORIBUNDA

ZONE	LATIN NAME
6	CALLICARPA DICHOTOMA
	CYTISUS SCOPARIUS
	CYTISUS X PRAECOX 'LUTEUS'
	EUONYMUS FORTUNEI 'SILVER QUEEN'
	EUPATORIUM COELESTINUM
	FORSYTHIA VIRIDISSIMA 'BRONXENSIS'
	FORSYTHIA X INTERMEDIA 'SPRING GLORY'
	IMPERATA CYLINDRICA 'RED BARON'
	JUNIPERUS CHINENSIS 'KAIZUKA'
	ROSA ROXBURGHII
	STRANVAESIA DAVIDIANA VAR. UNDULATA 'PROSTRATA'
	TRACHYSTEMON ORIENTALIS
7	BERBERIS WILSONIAE VAR. STAPFIANA
	PYRACANTHA COCCINEA 'AUREA'
T	KOCHIA SCOPARIA FORMA TRICHOPHYLLA 'CHILDSII'

ORGANIC LOAM

ZONE	LATIN NAME
2	ACHILLEA MILLEFOLIUM 'ROSEA'
	ASTER PUNICEUS
	BERGENIA 'PERFECTA'
	BERGENIA 'SUNNINGDALE'
	BETULA PAPYRIFERA
	DICENTRA SPECTABILIS
	PAEONIA—HERBACEOUS HYBRIDS
	POTENTILLA TRIDENTATA
	SAPONARIA OFFICINALIS
3	ACER SACCHARUM
	ACHILLEA 'CORONATION GOLD'
	ACHILLEA 'MOONSHINE'
	ADIANTUM PEDATUM
	AEGOPODIUM PODAGRARIA 'VARIEGATUM'
	ALCHEMILLA VULGARIS
	AMELANCHIER ARBOREA (SYN. A. CANADENSIS)
	AMSONIA TABERNAEMONTANA
	ARTEMESIA ABSINTHIUM 'LAMBROOK SILVER'
	ARUNCUS DIOICUS
	ASCLEPIAS TUBEROSA
	ASTER AMELLUS 'NOCTURNE'
	ASTER TATARICUS
	BETULA PENDULA 'GRACILIS'
	BETULA PENDULA 'YOUNGII'
	BOLTONIA ASTEROIDES 'SNOWBANK'
	BRUNNERA MACROPHYLLA
	BUPHTHALUM SALICIFOLIUM
	CAMPANULA RAPUNCULOIDES
	CHELONE LYONII
	CIMICIFUGA RACEMOSA
	CLEMATIS HERACLEIFOLIA VAR. DAVIDIANA
	COREOPSIS 'MOONBEAM'
	CORNUS ALBA 'ELEGANTISSIMA'
	CORNUS ALBA 'SPAETHII'
	CORNUS RACEMOSA
	CORNUS RACEMOSA (DWARF)
	CORNUS SERICEA
	CORNUS SERICEA 'FLAVIRAMEA'
	DENNSTAEDTIA PUNCTILOBULA
	DICENTRA 'LUXURIANT'
	DICENTRA EXIMIA 'PURITY'

ZONE	LATIN NAME
	ECHINACEA PURPUREA
	ECHINOPS RITRO
	EUPHORBIA COROLLATA
	FILIPENDULA ULMARIA 'AUREA'
	GERANIUM 'JOHNSON'S BLUE'
	GERANIUM MACRORRHIZUM
	GERANIUM SANGUINEUM
	HELLEBORUS NIGER
	HEMEROCALLIS LILIOASPHODELUS
	HIPPOPHAE RHAMNOIDES
	HOSTA 'KABITAN'
	HOSTA PLANTAGINEA
	HOSTA SIEBOLDIANA 'ELEGANS'
	HOSTA UNDULATA
	HOSTA VENTRICOSA
	INULA HELENIUM
	IRIS SIBIRICA CULTIVARS
	JUNIPERUS HORIZONTALIS 'WILTONII'
	JUNIPERUS VIRGINIANA
	LIATRIS SCARIOSA 'WHITE SPIRE'
	LYSIMACHIA CLETHROIDES
	LYTHRUM SALICARIA 'DROPMORE PURPLE'
	MACLEAYA CORDATA
	MALUS 'RED JADE'
	NEPETA X FAASSENII
	OSMUNDA REGALIS
	PAPAVER ORIENTALE
	PHYSOSTEGIA VIRGINIANA
	PHYSOSTEGIA VIRGINIANA 'SUMMER SNOW'
	PICEA ABIES 'NIDIFORMIS'
	PICEA PUNGENS 'HOOPSII'
	PINUS MUGO VAR. MUGO
	PINUS STROBUS
	PINUS STROBUS 'FASTIGIATA'
	POLYSTICHUM ACROSTICHOIDES
	PRUNUS X CISTENA
	PSEUDOTSUGA MENZIESII
	PULMONARIA ANGUSTIFOLIA
	PULMONARIA SACCHARATA 'MARGERY FISH'
	PULMONARIA SACCHARATA 'SISSINGHURST WHITE'
	RHODODENDRON PRINOPHYLLUM
	RHUS AROMATICA 'GRO-LOW'
	RHUS TYPHINA
	RHUS TYPHINA 'LACINIATA'
	ROSA RUGOSA AND HYBRIDS
	RUDBECKIA FULGIDA VAR. SULLIVANTII 'GOLDSTURM'
	SALIX ALBA 'KALMTHOUT'
	SALIX ALBA 'REGALIS'
	SALIX ALBA 'SERICEA'
	SEDUM 'AUTUMN JOY'
	SEDUM ELLACOMBIANUM
	SEDUM SARMENTOSUM
	SEDUM SPURIUM
	SEDUM SPURIUM 'BRONZE CARPET'
	SORBARIA SORBIFOLIA
	SPIRAEA X VANHOUTTEI
	SYRINGA VULGARIS 'ALBA'
	SYRINGA VULGARIS HYBRIDS
	TELEKIA SPECIOSA
	THERMOPSIS CAROLINIANA
	THUJA OCCIDENTALIS 'NIGRA'
	THYMUS SERPYLLUM
	TIARELLA CORDIFOLIA VAR. COLLINA
	TILIA CORDATA
	TSUGA CANADENSIS
	TSUGA CANADENSIS 'BENNETT'
	TSUGA CANADENSIS 'COLE'S PROSTRATE'

ZONE	LATIN NAME
	TSUGA CANADENSIS 'PENDULA'
	VERONICA INCANA
	VERONICASTRUM VIRGINICUM
	VIBURNUM ACERIFOLIUM
	VIBURNUM PRUNIFOLIUM
4	ACANTHOPANAX SIEBOLDIANUS
	ACER PLATANOIDES 'CRIMSON KING'
	ACER RUBRUM
	AJUGA REPTANS
	AJUGA REPTANS 'BRONZE BEAUTY'
	AJUGA REPTANS (GIANT FORM)
	ALLIUM TUBEROSUM
	ANEMONE VITIFOLIA 'ROBUSTISSIMA'
	ARABIS PROCURRENS
	ARALIA SPINOSA
	ARONIA ARBUTIFOLIA 'BRILLIANTISSIMA'
	ARTEMESIA LUDOVICIANA 'SILVER KING'
	ARUNCUS AETHUSIFOLIUS
	ASTILBE X ARENDSII CULTIVARS
	BACCHARIS HALIMIFOLIA, PISTILLATE
	BERBERIS THUNBERGII 'ATROPURPUREA'
	BERBERIS THUNBERGII 'CRIMSON PYGMY'
	BETULA LENTA
	BETULA NIGRA
	BUDDLEIA ALTERNIFOLIA
	CARYA OVATA
	CARYOPTERIS X CLANDONENSIS 'BLUE MIST'
	CEPHALANTHUS OCCIDENTALIS
	CHAENOMELES JAPONICA VAR. ALPINA
	CHAENOMELES SPECIOSA CULTIVARS
	CHAENOMELES X SUPERBA 'JET TRAIL'
	CHAMAEMELUM NOBILE
	CLADRASTIS LUTEA
	CLEMATIS 'MRS. CHOLMONDELEY'
	CLEMATIS 'PRINS HENDRIK'
	CLEMATIS 'RAMONA'
	CLEMATIS MAXIMOWICZIANA
	CLEMATIS X JACKMANII
	COMPTONIA PEREGRINA
	CONVALLARIA MAJALIS
	CORNUS ALTERNIFOLIA
	CORYLUS AVELLANA 'CONTORTA'
	CORYLUS AVELLANA 'PENDULA'
	CRATAEGUS NITIDA
	CRATAEGUS PHAENOPYRUM
	DIERVILLA SESSILIFOLIA
	EUONYMUS ALATA
	EUONYMUS FORTUNEI 'COLORATA'
	EUONYMUS FORTUNEI VAR. RADICANS
	FAGUS GRANDIFOLIA
	GAULTHERIA PROCUMBENS
	GINKGO BILOBA, STAMINATE
	GLEDITSIA TRIACANTHOS VAR. INERMIS 'SHADEMASTER'
	GYMNOCLADUS DIOICA
	HAMAMELIS VIRGINIANA
	HEDYOTIS CAERULEA
	HELIOPSIS HELIANTHOIDES SUBSP. SCABRA 'KARAT'
	HELLEBORUS ORIENTALIS HYBRIDS
	HEUCHERA 'PALACE PURPLE' STRAIN
	HYDRANGEA PANICULATA
	HYPERICUM KALMIANUM
	ILEX VERTICILLATA
	ILEX VERTICILLATA 'WINTER RED'
	JUNIPERUS SABINA 'TAMARISCIFOLIA'
	JUNIPERUS X MEDIA 'PFITZERIANA COMPACTA'

ZONE	LATIN NAME
	MALUS FLORIBUNDA
	MALUS HUPEHENSIS
	MALUS SARGENTII
	MICROBIOTA DECUSSATA
	MONARDA DIDYMA
	MYRICA PENSYLVANICA
	OSMUNDA CINNAMOMEA
	OSMUNDA CLAYTONIANA
	PACHYSANDRA PROCUMBENS
	PAEONIA TENUIFOLIA
	PAXISTIMA CANBYI
	PETASITES JAPONICUS
	PHALARIS ARUNDINACEA VAR. PICTA
	PHELLODENDRON AMURENSE
	PINUS FLEXILIS
	PINUS KORAIENSIS
	POLYGONATUM ODORATUM 'VARIEGATUM'
	QUERCUS ALBA
	QUERCUS MACROCARPA
	RHODODENDRON (CATAWBIENSE HYBRIDS)
	RHODODENDRON MAXIMUM
	RHODODENDRON VISCOSUM
	ROBINIA HISPIDA
	RODGERSIA AESCULIFOLIA
	RODGERSIA PODOPHYLLA
	RODGERSIA TABULARIS
	ROSA NITIDA
	SALIX ALBA VAR. TRISTIS
	SALIX ELAEAGNOS
	SALIX REPENS VAR. ARGENTEA
	SEDUM POPULIFOLIUM
	SEDUM TERNATUM
	SPIRAEA THUNBERGII
	SYRINGA PATULA (SYN. S. PALIBINIANA, S. MICROPHYLLA 'INGWERSEN'S DWARF')
	SYRINGA X CHINENSIS
	TAMARIX RAMOSISSIMA
	TAXUS CUSPIDATA 'NANA'
	TAXUS CUSPIDATA (CAPITATA SELECTION)
	THUJA OCCIDENTALIS 'HETZ' WINTERGREEN'
	TYPHA ANGUSTIFOLIA
	VACCINIUM CORYMBOSUM
	VERNONIA NOVEBORACENSIS
	VERONICA 'SUNNY BORDER BLUE'
	VERONICA LONGIFOLIA 'SUBSESSILIS'
	VIBURNUM CARLESII
	VINCA MINOR 'BOWLESII'
	VINCA MINOR 'VARIEGATA'
	VIOLA LABRADORICA
	WALDSTEINIA TERNATA
	YUCCA FLACCIDA 'GOLDEN SWORD'
	YUCCA GLAUCA
	YUCCA SMALLIANA
5	ABIES NORDMANNIANA
	ACER GRISEUM
	ACER PALMATUM 'BLOODGOOD'
	ACER PALMATUM 'SANGOKAKU'
	AESCULUS PARVIFLORA
	ALLIUM CERNUUM
	ALLIUM ZEBDANENSE
	AMSONIA HUBRICHTII
	ANEMONE BLANDA 'ATROCAERULEA'
	ANEMONE X HYBRIDA 'QUEEN CHARLOTTE'
	ARTEMESIA VERSICOLOR
	ARUNDINARIA VIRIDISTRIATA

ZONE	LATIN NAME
	ASARUM EUROPAEUM
	ASPHODELINE LUTEA
	ASTER CORDIFOLIUS
	ASTER X FRIKARTII 'MONCH'
	ATHYRIUM GOERINGIANUM 'PICTUM'
	BUDDLEIA DAVIDII 'BLACK KNIGHT'
	BUDDLEIA DAVIDII 'OPERA'
	BUDDLEIA DAVIDII 'PURPLE PRINCE'
	BUXUS 'GREEN GEM'
	BUXUS SINICA VAR. INSULARIS 'TIDE HILL'
	BUXUS SINICA VAR. INSULARIS 'WINTERGREEN' (OHIO CULTIVAR)
	CALAMAGROSTIS X ACUTIFLORA 'KARL FOERSTER' (SYN. C. EPIGEOUS 'HORTORUM')
	CALLICARPA JAPONICA
	CALYCANTHUS FLORIDUS 'EDITH WILDER'
	CAMPSIS X TAGLIABUANA 'MADAME GALEN'
	CARPINUS BETULUS
	CATALPA BIGNONIOIDES
	CEDRUS LIBANI VAR. STENOCOMA
	CEPHALOTAXUS HARRINGTONIA VAR. PEDUNCULATA
	CERCIDIPHYLLUM JAPONICUM
	CERCIS CANADENSIS 'FOREST PANSY'
	CHAENOMELES X SUPERBA CULTIVARS
	CHAMAECYPARIS OBTUSA 'FILICOIDES'
	CHAMAECYPARIS OBTUSA 'NANA GRACILIS'
	CHAMAECYPARIS OBTUSA 'NANA'
	CHAMAECYPARIS OBTUSA VAR. BREVIRAMEA
	CHAMAECYPARIS PISIFERA 'GOLD SPANGLE'
	CHAMAECYPARIS PISIFERA 'SQUARROSA'
	CHIONANTHUS VIRGINICUS
	CHIONODOXA GIGANTEA 'ALBA'
	CHIONODOXA LUCILIAE
	CHIONODOXA SARDENSIS
	CHRYSANTHEMUM WEYRICHII 'WHITE BOMB'
	CLETHRA ALNIFOLIA
	COLCHICUM 'AUTUMN QUEEN'
	COLCHICUM 'THE GIANT'
	COLUTEA X MEDIA
	CORNUS FLORIDA
	CORNUS FLORIDA 'HOHMAN'S GOLDEN'
	CORNUS KOUSA
	CORNUS MAS
	CORNUS OFFICINALIS
	CORYLOPSIS PLATYPETALA
	CORYLUS COLURNA
	COTINUS COGGYGRIA 'PURPUREUS'
	COTONEASTER ADPRESSUS 'LITTLE GEM'
	COTONEASTER APICULATUS
	COTONEASTER HORIZONTALIS
	CRAMBE CORDIFOLIA
	CRATAEGUS VIRIDIS 'WINTER KING'
	CROCUS ANCYRENSIS 'GOLDEN BUNCH'
	CROCUS SIEBERI
	CROCUS TOMASINIANUS
	CYCLAMEN HEDERIFOLIUM
	DAPHNE CAUCASICA
	DAPHNE X BURKWOODII 'CAROL MACKIE'
	DEUTZIA GRACILIS

ZONE	LATIN NAME
	DIOSPYROS VIRGINIANA
	DIPLAZIUM CONILII
	ENDYMION HISPANICUS 'EXCELSIOR' (SYN. SCILLA CAMPANULATA 'EXCELSIOR')
	ENKIANTHUS CAMPANULATUS
	EPIMEDIUM PINNATUM SUBSP. COLCHICUM
	EPIMEDIUM X YOUNGIANUM 'NIVEUM'
	EQUISETUM HYEMALE
	ERANTHIS HYEMALIS
	ERANTHIS X TUBERGENII
	ERIANTHUS RAVENNAE
	EUONYMUS FORTUNEI 'GRACILIS'
	EUONYMUS FORTUNEI 'MINIMA'
	EXOCHORDA GIRALDII VAR. WILSONII
	FAGUS SYLVATICA 'LACINIATA'
	FAGUS SYLVATICA 'PENDULA'
	FAGUS SYLVATICA 'RIVERSII'
	FILIPENDULA PURPUREA 'NANA'
	FORSYTHIA SUSPENSA
	FOTHERGILLA GARDENII
	GALANTHUS ELWESII
	GALANTHUS NIVALIS
	GALIUM ODORATUM
	HALESIA TETRAPTERA
	HAMAMELIS MOLLIS 'PALLIDA'
	HAMAMELIS X INTERMEDIA 'DIANE'
	HAMAMELIS X INTERMEDIA 'JELENA'
	HAMAMELIS X INTERMEDIA 'PRIMAVERA'
	HEDERA HELIX 'BULGARIA'
	HEDERA HELIX 'OGALALLA'
	HELIANTHUS SALICIFOLIUS
	HELICTOTRICHON SEMPERVIRENS
	HEMEROCALLIS 'HYPERION'
	HEMEROCALLIS FULVA 'EUROPA'
	HERACLEUM MANTEGAZZIANUM
	HIBISCUS SYRIACUS 'BLUEBIRD'
	HIBISCUS SYRIACUS 'DIANA'
	HOUTTUYNIA CORDATA 'CHAMELEON'
	HYDRANGEA ANOMALA SUBSP. PETIOLARIS 'SKYLANDS GIANT'
	HYDRANGEA QUERCIFOLIA
	HYPERICUM FRONDOSUM
	ILEX CHINA BOY ® 'MESDOB'
	ILEX CHINA GIRL ® 'MESOG'
	ILEX GLABRA 'DENSA'
	ILEX X AQUIPERNYI 'SAN JOSE'
	ILEX X MESERVEAE BLUE MAID ® 'MESID'
	ILEX X MESERVEAE BLUE STALLION ® 'MESAN'
	INDIGOFERA INCARNATA 'ALBA'
	IRIS CRISTATA
	IRIS GRAMINEA
	IRIS PSEUDACORUS
	JUNIPERUS SCOPULORUM 'SKY ROCKET'
	JUNIPERUS X MEDIA 'OLD GOLD'
	KALMIA LATIFOLIA
	KERRIA JAPONICA
	KIRENGESHOMA PALMATA
	KOELREUTERIA PANICULATA
	KOLKWITZIA AMABILIS
	LAMIASTRUM GALEOBDOLON 'VARIEGATUM'
	LAMIUM MACULATUM 'WHITE NANCY'
	LATHYRUS VERNUS
	LESPEDEZA THUNBERGII
	LEUCOJUM VERNUM
	LEUCOTHOE FONTANESIANA

ZONE	LATIN NAME
	LEUCOTHOE FONTANESIANA 'NANA'
	LIGUSTRUM QUIHOUI
	LILIUM 'BLACK DRAGON'
	LILIUM SPECIES AND HYBRIDS
	LIQUIDAMBAR STYRACIFLUA
	LONICERA FRAGRANTISSIMA
	LYCORIS SPRENGERI
	LYCORIS SQUAMIGERA
	LYSICHITON AMERICANUM
	LYSICHITON CAMTSCHATCENSE
	LYSIMACHIA PUNCTATA
	MAGNOLIA 'ELIZABETH'
	MAGNOLIA VIRGINIANA
	MAGNOLIA X LOEBNERI
	MAGNOLIA X SOULANGIANA 'VERBANICA'
	MERTENSIA VIRGINICA
	METASEQUOIA GLYPTOSTROBOIDES
	MISCANTHUS 'GIGANTEUS'
	MISCANTHUS SINENSIS 'CABARET'
	MISCANTHUS SINENSIS 'GRACILLIMUS'
	MISCANTHUS SINENSIS 'MORNING LIGHT'
	MISCANTHUS SINENSIS 'SILVER FEATHER' (='SILBERFEDER')
	MISCANTHUS SINENSIS 'STRICTUS'
	MISCANTHUS SINENSIS 'VARIEGATUS'
	MOLINIA CAERULEA SUBSP. ARUNDINACEA
	MUSCARI AZUREUM 'ALBUM'
	MUSCARI BOTRYOIDES 'ALBUM'
	MUSCARI TUBERGENIANUM
	NARCISSUS 'CARLTON'
	NARCISSUS 'FORTUNE'
	NARCISSUS 'HERA'
	NARCISSUS 'LOCH FYNE'
	NARCISSUS 'MOONMIST'
	NARCISSUS 'MRS. ERNST H. KRELAGE'
	NARCISSUS 'PEEPING TOM'
	NARCISSUS 'POMONA'
	NARCISSUS 'QUEEN OF SPAIN'
	NARCISSUS 'TREVITHIAN'
	NARCISSUS JONQUILLA
	NARCISSUS PSEUDONARCISSUS SUBSP. OBVALLARIS
	NYSSA SYLVATICA
	OMPHALODES VERNA
	ONOPORDUM ACANTHIUM
	OXYDENDRUM ARBOREUM
	PACHYSANDRA TERMINALIS
	PACHYSANDRA TERMINALIS 'GREEN CARPET'
	PACHYSANDRA TERMINALIS 'VARIEGATA' OR 'SILVER EDGE'
	PANICUM VIRGATUM 'STRICTUM'
	PENNISETUM ALOPECUROIDES
	PEROVSKIA ABROTANOIDES X P. ATRIPLICIFOLIA
	PHILADELPHUS CORONARIUS
	PHILADELPHUS X FALCONERI
	PHLOMIS RUSSELIANA
	PHLOX PILOSA SUBSP. OZARKANA
	PHLOX STOLONIFERA 'ALBA'
	PHLOX STOLONIFERA 'BLUE RIDGE'
	PHLOX STOLONIFERA 'SHERWOOD PURPLE'
	PICEA ORIENTALIS
	PINUS BUNGEANA
	PINUS DENSIFLORA 'UMBRACULIFERA'
	PINUS PARVIFLORA 'GLAUCA'
	PINUS VIRGINIANA
	PLATANUS OCCIDENTALIS
	POLYSTICHUM TRIPTERON

ZONE	LATIN NAME
	PRUNUS 'HALLY JOLIVETTE'
	PRUNUS CERASIFERA 'THUNDERCLOUD'
	PRUNUS SUBHIRTELLA 'AUTUMNALIS'
	RHEUM PALMATUM 'RUBRUM'
	RHODODENDRON (GABLE HYBRIDS)
	RHODODENDRON ARBORESCENS
	RHODODENDRON ATLANTICUM
	RHODODENDRON MUCRONULATUM
	RHODODENDRON SCHLIPPENBACHII
	RHODODENDRON VASEYI
	RHODODENDRON X GANDAVENSE 'COCCINEA SPECIOSA'
	RHODODENDRON X GANDAVENSE 'DAVIESII'
	RHODOTYPOS SCANDENS
	RIBES ODORATUM
	ROSA 'DOORENBOS SELECTION'
	ROSA (GALLICA) 'CHARLES DE MILLS'
	ROSA (POLYANTHA) 'THE FAIRY'
	ROSA (SHRUB) 'LILLIAN GIBSON'
	ROSA (SHRUB) 'SEA FOAM'
	ROSA CAROLINA
	ROSA EGLANTERIA
	ROSA VIRGINIANA
	RUBUS COCKBURNIANUS
	SALIX 'HAKURO'
	SALIX ACUTIFOLIA 'LONGIFOLIA'
	SALIX CHAENOMELOIDES
	SALIX DAPHNOIDES 'AGLAIA'
	SALIX GRACILISTYLA
	SALIX GRACILISTYLA 'MELANOSTACHYS'
	SALIX X RUBRA 'EUGENEI'
	SASSAFRAS ALBIDUM
	SCILLA SIBERICA 'SPRING BEAUTY'
	SEDUM 'VERA JAMISON'
	SEDUM FLORIFERUM 'WEIHANSTEPHANER GOLD'
	SPIRAEA PRUNIFOLIA
	STEPHANANDRA INCISA 'CRISPA'
	STERNBERGIA LUTEA
	STOKESIA LAEVIS 'BLUE DANUBE'
	SYMPHORICARPOS X CHENAULTII 'HANCOCK'
	SYMPHYTUM X UPLANDICUM
	SYRINGA LACINIATA
	SYRINGA RETICULATA
	TAXUS BACCATA 'ADPRESSA FOWLE'
	TAXUS BACCATA 'REPANDENS'
	TAXUS X MEDIA 'SENTINALIS'
	THALICTRUM ROCHEBRUNIANUM
	THELYPTERIS HEXAGONOPTERA
	THELYPTERIS NOVEBORACENSIS
	THELYPTERIS PHEGOPTERIS
	THUJA PLICATA 'ATROVIRENS'
	THYMUS 'CLEAR GOLD'
	THYMUS PSEUDOLANUGINOSUS
	VALERIANA OFFICINALIS
	VERBASCUM OLYMPICUM
	VIBURNUM DILATATUM 'MICHAEL DODGE'
	VIBURNUM FARRERI 'CANDIDISSIMUM'
	VIBURNUM FARRERI 'NANUM'
	VIBURNUM PLICATUM FORMA TOMENTOSUM
	VIBURNUM SIEBOLDII 'SENECA'
	WISTERIA FLORIBUNDA
	XANTHORHIZA SIMPLICISSIMA

ZONE	LATIN NAME
6	ABELIA X GRANDIFLORA
	ACER PALMATUM 'EVER RED'
	ACER PALMATUM VAR. DISSECTUM OR A. P. 'WATERFALL'
	ACORUS GRAMINEUS 'OGON'
	ADINA RUBELLA
	AESCULUS SPLENDENS
	ARUM ITALICUM 'PICTUM'
	ARUNDO DONAX
	BEGONIA GRANDIS
	BERBERIS JULIANAE 'NANA'
	BERBERIS WISLEYENSIS (SYN. B. TRIACANTHOPHORA)
	BIGNONIA CAPREOLATA
	BUXUS SEMPERVIRENS 'SUFFRUTICOSA'
	CALLICARPA DICHOTOMA
	CALOCEDRUS DECURRENS
	CERATOSTIGMA PLUMBAGINOIDES
	CERCIS CHINENSIS
	CHAMAECYPARIS OBTUSA 'CRIPPSII'
	CLETHRA BARBINERVIS
	COTONEASTER ADPRESSUS VAR. PRAECOX
	COTONEASTER SALICIFOLIUS VAR. FLOCCOSUS
	CROCOSMIA 'LUCIFER'
	CROCOSMIA POTTSII
	CROCOSMIA X CROCOSMIIFLORA
	CRUCIANELLA STYLOSA
	CYTISUS SCOPARIUS
	CYTISUS X PRAECOX 'LUTEUS'
	ENKIANTHUS PERULATUS
	EUONYMUS FORTUNEI 'SILVER QUEEN'
	EUPATORIUM COELESTINUM
	FILIPENDULA PURPUREA 'ELEGANS'
	FORSYTHIA VIRIDISSIMA 'BRONXENSIS'
	FORSYTHIA X INTERMEDIA 'SPRING GLORY'
	FRANKLINIA ALATAMAHA
	GALTONIA CANDICANS
	HEDERA HELIX 'BALTICA'
	HEDERA HELIX 'BUTTERCUP'
	HEDERA HELIX 'GOLD HEART'
	HYDRANGEA MACROPHYLLA 'BLUE BILLOW'
	ILEX CRENATA 'HELLERI'
	ILEX CRENATA 'MICROPHYLLA'
	ILEX OPACA 'ARDEN'
	ILEX OPACA 'XANTHOCARPA'
	IMPERATA CYLINDRICA 'RED BARON'
	ITEA VIRGINICA 'HENRY'S GARNET'
	JASMINUM NUDIFLORUM
	JUNIPERUS CHINENSIS 'KAIZUKA'
	LESPEDEZA THUNBERGII 'ALBIFLORA'
	LIRIOPE MUSCARI (BIG BLUE SELECTION)
	LIRIOPE MUSCARI 'MONROE WHITE'
	LIRIOPE MUSCARI 'VARIEGATA'
	LUZULA SYLVATICA 'MARGINATA'
	MAGNOLIA 'SUSAN'
	MAGNOLIA DENUDATA (SYN. M. HEPTAPETA)
	MAGNOLIA MACROPHYLLA
	MAHONIA BEALEI
	PAEONIA 'BLACK PIRATE'
	PAEONIA—WOODY HYBRIDS
	PARONYCHIA KAPELA SUBSP. SERPYLLIFOLIA
	PAULOWNIA TOMENTOSA
	PELTIPHYLLUM PELTATUM
	PHYLLOSTACHYS AUREOSULCATA
	PIERIS JAPONICA

ZONE	LATIN NAME
	PINUS THUNBERGIANA
	PINUS THUNBERGIANA 'OCULUS-DRACONIS'
	PONCIRUS TRIFOLIATA
	PRUNUS SUBHIRTELLA 'PENDULA'
	PRUNUS YEDOENSIS
	PSEUDOLARIX KAEMPFERI
	QUERCUS PHELLOS
	RHODODENDRON (GLENN DALE HYBRIDS)
	RHODODENDRON (KAEMPFERI HYBRIDS)
	RHODODENDRON (KNAP HILL HYBRID) 'TUNIS'
	RHODODENDRON (KURUME HYBRIDS)
	RHODODENDRON X ERIOCARPUM AND R. X NAKAHARAI CULTIVARS AND HYBRIDS
	ROSA ROXBURGHII
	RUBUS IDAEUS 'AUREUS'
	SAXIFRAGA STOLONIFERA
	SCIADOPITYS VERTICILLATA
	SOPHORA JAPONICA 'REGENT'
	STEWARTIA KOREANA
	STRANVAESIA DAVIDIANA VAR. UNDULATA 'PROSTRATA'
	STYRAX JAPONICUS
	STYRAX JAPONICUS 'CARILLON'
	TAXODIUM DISTICHUM VAR. NUTANS 'PRAIRIE SENTINEL'
	TRACHYSTEMON ORIENTALIS
	VIBURNUM ICHANGENSE
	VIBURNUM NUDUM 'WINTERTHUR'
	VIBURNUM RHYTIDOPHYLLUM
	VIBURNUM SETIGERUM
	VITEX AGNUS-CASTUS 'LATIFOLIA'
	VITEX AGNUS-CASTUS 'SILVER SPIRE'
	ZELKOVA SERRATA 'GREEN VASE'
7	BERBERIS WILSONIAE VAR. STAPFIANA
	BUXUS MICROPHYLLA 'COMPACTA'
	CEDRUS ATLANTICA 'GLAUCA'
	CHIMONANTHUS PRAECOX
	CLERODENDRUM TRICHOTOMUM
	DIOSPYROS KAKI
	ELAEAGNUS PUNGENS 'FRUITLANDII'
	ELAEAGNUS PUNGENS 'MACULATA'
	GENISTA SYLVESTRIS 'LYDIA'
	HEDERA COLCHICA 'DENTATA'
	HEDERA HELIX 'ERECTA'
	HYDRANGEA ASPERA SUBSP. SARGENTIANA
	OPHIOPOGON JAPONICUS 'NANUS'
	PYRACANTHA COCCINEA 'AUREA'
	RHODODENDRON CANESCENS
	SASA VEITCHII
	SKIMMIA REEVESIANA
	VIBURNUM MACROCEPHALUM FORMA MACROCEPHALUM
8	COTULA SQUALIDA
T	CANNA X GENERALIS 'MOHAWK'
	DATURA INOXIA SUBSP. QUINQUECUSPIDA
	KOCHIA SCOPARIA FORMA TRICHOPHYLLA 'CHILDSII'
	POLIANTHES TUBEROSA
	RICINUS COMMUNIS
	RICINUS COMMUNIS 'ZANZIBARENSIS'

SANDY LOAM

ZONE	LATIN NAME
2	ACHILLEA MILLEFOLIUM 'ROSEA'
	ARTEMESIA STELLERIANA
	ASTER PUNICEUS
	BERGENIA 'PERFECTA'
	BERGENIA 'SUNNINGDALE'
	POTENTILLA TRIDENTATA
	SAPONARIA OFFICINALIS
3	ACHILLEA 'CORONATION GOLD'
	ACHILLEA 'MOONSHINE'
	AEGOPODIUM PODAGRARIA 'VARIEGATUM'
	AMELANCHIER ARBOREA (SYN. A. CANADENSIS)
	ARTEMISIA ABSINTHIUM 'LAMBROOK SILVER'
	ASCLEPIAS TUBEROSA
	ASTER TATARICUS
	BAPTISIA AUSTRALIS
	BUPHTHALUM SALICIFOLIUM
	CAMPANULA RAPUNCULOIDES
	CHELONE LYONII
	COREOPSIS 'MOONBEAM'
	DENNSTAEDTIA PUNCTILOBULA
	DIANTHUS DELTOIDES
	ECHINACEA PURPUREA
	EUPHORBIA COROLLATA
	HIPPOPHAE RHAMNOIDES
	JUNIPERUS HORIZONTALIS 'WILTONII'
	JUNIPERUS VIRGINIANA
	LIATRIS SCARIOSA 'WHITE SPIRE'
	LIATRIS SPICATA 'KOBOLD'
	LYTHRUM SALICARIA 'DROPMORE PURPLE'
	MACLEAYA CORDATA
	PAPAVER ORIENTALE
	PHLOX SUBULATA
	PHYSOSTEGIA VIRGINIANA
	PHYSOSTEGIA VIRGINIANA 'SUMMER SNOW'
	PTERIDIUM AQUILINUM VAR. LATIUSCULUM
	RHUS TYPHINA
	RHUS TYPHINA 'LACINIATA'
	ROSA RUGOSA AND HYBRIDS
	RUDBECKIA FULGIDA VAR. SULLIVANTII 'GOLDSTURM'
	SALIX ALBA 'KALMTHOUT'
	SALIX ALBA 'REGALIS'
	SALIX ALBA 'SERICEA'
	SEDUM 'AUTUMN JOY'
	SEDUM ELLACOMBIANUM
	SEDUM SARMENTOSUM
	SEDUM SPURIUM
	SEDUM SPURIUM 'BRONZE CARPET'
	THERMOPSIS CAROLINIANA
	THYMUS SERPYLLUM
4	ACANTHOPANAX SIEBOLDIANUS
	AJUGA REPTANS
	AJUGA REPTANS 'BRONZE BEAUTY'
	AJUGA REPTANS (GIANT FORM)
	ALLIUM TUBEROSUM
	ARABIS PROCURRENS
	ARALIA SPINOSA
	ARENARIA VERNA
	ARTEMISIA LUDOVICIANA 'SILVER QUEEN'
	BACCHARIS HALIMIFOLIA, PISTILLATE

ZONE	LATIN NAME
	BERBERIS THUNBERGII 'CRIMSON PYGMY'
	BETULA LENTA
	BETULA NIGRA
	CARYOPTERIS X CLANDONENSIS 'BLUE MIST'
	CHAENOMELES SPECIOSA CULTIVARS
	COMPTONIA PEREGRINA
	DIERVILLA SESSILIFOLIA
	EUPHORBIA EPITHYMOIDES
	GAULTHERIA PROCUMBENS
	HELIOPSIS HELIANTHOIDES SUBSP. SCABRA 'KARAT'
	HYPERICUM KALMIANUM
	JUNIPERUS X MEDIA 'PFITZERIANA COMPACTA'
	MYRICA PENSYLVANICA
	PHALARIS ARUNDINACEA VAR. PICTA
	PHLOX BIFIDA
	RHODODENDRON VISCOSUM
	ROBINIA HISPIDA
	ROSA NITIDA
	SALIX ELAEAGNOS
	SALIX REPENS VAR. ARGENTEA
	SEDUM POPULIFOLIUM
	STACHYS BYZANTINA
	TAMARIX RAMOSISSIMA
	TYPHA ANGUSTIFOLIA
	VACCINIUM CORYMBOSUM
	YUCCA FLACCIDA 'GOLDEN SWORD'
	YUCCA GLAUCA
	YUCCA SMALLIANA
5	ACER GRISEUM
	ARTEMESIA VERSICOLOR
	ASPHODELINE LUTEA
	ASTER X FRIKARTII 'MONCH'
	BUXUS SINICA VAR. INSULARIS 'TIDE HILL'
	BUXUS SINICA VAR. INSULARIS 'WINTERGREEN' (OHIO CULTIVAR)
	CALLICARPA JAPONICA
	CALYCANTHUS FLORIDUS 'EDITH WILDER'
	CAMPSIS X TAGLIABUANA 'MADAME GALEN'
	CATALPA BIGNONIOIDES
	CEPHALOTAXUS HARRINGTONIA VAR. PEDUNCULATA
	CHAMAECYPARIS OBTUSA 'FILICOIDES'
	CHAMAECYPARIS OBTUSA 'NANA GRACILIS'
	CHIONODOXA GIGANTEA 'ALBA'
	CHIONODOXA LUCILIAE
	CHIONODOXA SARDENSIS
	COLCHICUM 'AUTUMN QUEEN'
	COLCHICUM 'THE GIANT'
	COLUTEA X MEDIA
	COTINUS COGGYGRIA 'PURPUREUS'
	CROCUS ANCYRENSIS 'GOLDEN BUNCH'
	CROCUS SIEBERI
	CROCUS TOMASINIANUS
	DAPHNE X BURKWOODII 'CAROL MACKIE'
	EQUISETUM HYEMALE
	ERANTHIS HYEMALIS
	ERANTHIS X TUBERGENII
	HELIANTHEMUM APENNINUM VAR. ROSEUM
	HELIANTHUS SALICIFOLIUS
	HEMEROCALLIS 'HYPERION'
	HERACLEUM MANTEGAZZIANUM

APPENDIX 4
Plant Listing by Soil Moisture Preference

Plants in this list are divided as follows:

Bog or Standing Water
Water's Edge
Consistently Moist, Not Boggy
Average, Dry Between Rains
Dry
Fast-Draining

Each of the above sections is subdivided by hardiness zone.

The letter *T* under the heading "Zone" indicates a plant that is tender, not tolerant of frost.

Further information about all the following plants is summarized in the Master Lists, Appendices 1A and 1B.

BOG OR STANDING WATER

ZONE	LATIN NAME
3	CHELONE LYONII
	LYTHRUM SALICARIA 'DROPMORE PURPLE'
4	RODGERSIA AESCULIFOLIA
	RODGERSIA PODOPHYLLA
	RODGERSIA TABULARIS
	TYPHA ANGUSTIFOLIA
5	CLETHRA ALNIFOLIA
	EQUISETUM HYEMALE
	HOUTTUYNIA CORDATA 'CHAMELEON'
	IRIS PSEUDACORUS
	LYSICHITON AMERICANUM
	LYSICHITON CAMTSCHATCENSE
6	PELTIPHYLLUM PELTATUM
	TAXODIUM DISTICHUM VAR. NUTANS 'PRAIRIE SENTINEL'

WATER'S EDGE

ZONE	LATIN NAME
2	BETULA PAPYRIFERA
3	BETULA PENDULA 'GRACILIS'
	BETULA PENDULA 'YOUNGII'
	BUPHTHALUM SALICIFOLIUM
	CHELONE LYONII
	CORNUS RACEMOSA
	CORNUS RACEMOSA (DWARF)
	CORNUS SERICEA
	CORNUS SERICEA 'FLAVIRAMEA'
	FILIPENDULA ULMARIA 'AUREA'
	LYSIMACHIA CLETHROIDES
	LYTHRUM SALICARIA 'DROPMORE PURPLE'
	OSMUNDA REGALIS
	SALIX ALBA 'KALMTHOUT'
	SALIX ALBA 'REGALIS'
	SALIX ALBA 'SERICEA'
	TELEKIA SPECIOSA

ZONE	LATIN NAME
4	ASTILBE X ARENDSII CULTIVARS
	BACCHARIS HALIMIFOLIA, PISTILLATE
	BETULA LENTA
	BETULA NIGRA
	CEPHALANTHUS OCCIDENTALIS
	GAULTHERIA PROCUMBENS
	ILEX VERTICILLATA
	ILEX VERTICILLATA 'WINTER RED'
	MONARDA DIDYMA
	MYRICA PENSYLVANICA
	OSMUNDA CINNAMOMEA
	OSMUNDA CLAYTONIANA
	PETASITES JAPONICUS
	PHALARIS ARUNDINACEA VAR. PICTA
	RHODODENDRON MAXIMUM
	RHODODENDRON VISCOSUM
	RODGERSIA AESCULIFOLIA
	RODGERSIA PODOPHYLLA
	RODGERSIA TABULARIS
	SALIX ALBA VAR. TRISTIS
	SALIX ELAEAGNOS
	SALIX REPENS VAR. ARGENTEA
	TYPHA ANGUSTIFOLIA
5	CHIONANTHUS VIRGINICUS
	CLETHRA ALNIFOLIA
	ENKIANTHUS CAMPANULATUS
	EQUISETUM HYEMALE
	FILIPENDULA PURPUREA 'NANA'
	HERACLEUM MANTEGAZZIANUM
	HOUTTUYNIA CORDATA 'CHAMELEON'
	IRIS PSEUDACORUS
	KALMIA LATIFOLIA
	LEUCOTHOE FONTANESIANA
	LEUCOTHOE FONTANESIANA 'NANA'
	LYSICHITON AMERICANUM
	LYSICHITON CAMTSCHATCENSE
	LYSIMACHIA PUNCTATA
	MAGNOLIA VIRGINIANA
	MISCANTHUS 'GIGANTEUS'
	NYSSA SYLVATICA
	PETASITES FRAGRANS
	RHEUM PALMATUM 'RUBRUM'
	ROSA VIRGINIANA
	SALIX ACUTIFOLIA 'LONGIFOLIA'
	SALIX DAPHNOIDES 'AGLAIA'
	SALIX X RUBRA 'EUGENEI'
6	ACORUS GRAMINEUS 'OGON'
	CLETHRA BARBINERVIS
	ENKIANTHUS PERULATUS
	FILIPENDULA PURPUREA 'ELEGANS'
	ITEA VIRGINICA 'HENRY'S GARNET'
	PELTIPHYLLUM PELTATUM
	PHYLLOSTACHYS AUREOSULCATA
	PIERIS JAPONICA
	TAXODIUM DISTICHUM VAR. NUTANS 'PRAIRIE SENTINEL'

CONSISTENTLY MOIST, NOT BOGGY

ZONE	LATIN NAME
2	ASTER PUNICEUS
	BERGENIA 'PERFECTA'
	BERGENIA 'SUNNINGDALE'
	BETULA PAPYRIFERA
3	ADIANTUM PEDATUM
	AEGOPODIUM PODAGRARIA 'VARIEGATUM'

ZONE	LATIN NAME
	ALCHEMILLA VULGARIS
	AMELANCHIER ARBOREA (SYN. A. CANADENSIS)
	ARUNCUS DIOICUS
	ASTER TATARICUS
	BETULA PENDULA 'GRACILIS'
	BETULA PENDULA 'YOUNGII'
	BOLTONIA ASTEROIDES 'SNOWBANK'
	BRUNNERA MACROPHYLLA
	BUPHTHALUM SALICIFOLIUM
	CAMPANULA RAPUNCULOIDES
	CHELONE LYONII
	CIMICIFUGA RACEMOSA
	CLEMATIS HERACLEIFOLIA VAR. DAVIDIANA
	CORNUS ALBA 'ELEGANTISSIMA'
	CORNUS ALBA 'SPAETHII'
	CORNUS RACEMOSA
	CORNUS RACEMOSA (DWARF)
	CORNUS SERICEA
	CORNUS SERICEA 'FLAVIRAMEA'
	DENNSTAEDTIA PUNCTILOBULA
	DICENTRA 'LUXURIANT'
	DICENTRA EXIMIA 'PURITY'
	ECHINOPS RITRO
	FILIPENDULA ULMARIA 'AUREA'
	GERANIUM 'JOHNSON'S BLUE'
	GERANIUM MACRORRHIZUM
	GERANIUM SANGUINEUM
	HELLEBORUS NIGER
	HEMEROCALLIS LILIOASPHODELUS
	HOSTA 'KABITAN'
	HOSTA PLANTAGINEA
	HOSTA SIEBOLDIANA 'ELEGANS'
	HOSTA UNDULATA
	HOSTA VENTRICOSA
	INULA HELENIUM
	IRIS SIBIRICA CULTIVARS
	LIATRIS SPICATA 'KOBOLD'
	LYSIMACHIA CLETHROIDES
	LYTHRUM SALICARIA 'DROPMORE PURPLE'
	NEPETA X FAASSENII
	OSMUNDA REGALIS
	PHYSOSTEGIA VIRGINIANA
	PHYSOSTEGIA VIRGINIANA 'SUMMER SNOW'
	PINUS STROBUS
	PINUS STROBUS 'FASTIGIATA'
	PTERIDIUM AQUILINUM VAR. LATIUSCULUM
	PULMONARIA ANGUSTIFOLIA
	PULMONARIA SACCHARATA 'MARGERY FISH'
	RUDBECKIA FULGIDA VAR. SULLIVANTII 'GOLDSTURM'
	SALIX ALBA 'KALMTHOUT'
	SALIX ALBA 'REGALIS'
	SALIX ALBA 'SERICEA'
	TELEKIA SPECIOSA
	TIARELLA CORDIFOLIA VAR. COLLINA
	TSUGA CANADENSIS
	VERONICASTRUM VIRGINICUM
4	ACER RUBRUM
	ARABIS PROCURRENS
	ARALIA SPINOSA
	ARENARIA VERNA
	ARONIA ARBUTIFOLIA 'BRILLIANTISSIMA'
	ARUNCUS AETHUSIFOLIUS
	ASTILBE X ARENDSII CULTIVARS
	BACCHARIS HALIMIFOLIA, PISTILLATE

BETULA LENTA
BETULA NIGRA
CEPHALANTHUS OCCIDENTALIS
CLEMATIS 'MRS. CHOLMONDELEY'
CLEMATIS 'PRINS HENDRIK'
CLEMATIS 'RAMONA'
CLEMATIS X JACKMANII
CONVALLARIA MAJALIS
CORNUS ALTERNIFOLIA
FAGUS GRANDIFOLIA
GAULTHERIA PROCUMBENS
HAMAMELIS VIRGINIANA
HEDYOTIS CAERULEA
HELLEBORUS ORIENTALIS HYBRIDS
HEUCHERA 'PALACE PURPLE' STRAIN
ILEX VERTICILLATA
ILEX VERTICILLATA 'WINTER RED'
MONARDA DIDYMA
MYRICA PENSYLVANICA
OSMUNDA CINNAMOMEA
OSMUNDA CLAYTONIANA
PACHYSANDRA PROCUMBENS
PETASITES JAPONICUS
PHALARIS ARUNDINACEA VAR. PICTA
POLYGONATUM ODORATUM 'VARIEGATUM'
QUERCUS ALBA
RHODODENDRON (CATAWBIENSE HYBRIDS)
RHODODENDRON MAXIMUM
RHODODENDRON VISCOSUM
RODGERSIA AESCULIFOLIA
RODGERSIA PODOPHYLLA
RODGERSIA TABULARIS
SALIX ALBA VAR. TRISTIS
SALIX ELAEAGNOS
SALIX REPENS VAR. ARGENTEA
SEDUM TERNATUM
TAXUS CUSPIDATA (CAPITATA SELECTION)
THUJA OCCIDENTALIS 'HETZ' WINTERGREEN'
VERNONIA NOVEBORACENSIS
VERONICA 'SUNNY BORDER BLUE'
VERONICA LONGIFOLIA 'SUBSESSILIS'
WALDSTEINIA TERNATA

5
ANEMONE X HYBRIDA 'QUEEN CHARLOTTE'
ARUNDINARIA VIRIDISTRIATA
ASARUM EUROPAEUM
ATHYRIUM GOERINGIANUM 'PICTUM'
CALAMAGROSTIS X ACUTIFLORA 'KARL FOERSTER' (SYN. C. EPIGEOUS 'HORTORUM')
CALLICARPA JAPONICA
CATALPA BIGNONIOIDES
CEPHALOTAXUS HARRINGTONIA VAR. PEDUNCULATA
CERCIDIPHYLLUM JAPONICUM
CHAMAECYPARIS PISIFERA 'SQUARROSA'
CHIONANTHUS VIRGINICUS
CLETHRA ALNIFOLIA
COLCHICUM 'AUTUMN QUEEN'
COLCHICUM 'THE GIANT'
CORNUS KOUSA
CRATAEGUS VIRIDIS 'WINTER KING'
CYCLAMEN HEDERIFOLIUM
ENDYMION HISPANICUS 'EXCELSIOR' (SYN. SCILLA CAMPANULATA 'EXCELSIOR')
ENKIANTHUS CAMPANULATUS

EPIMEDIUM PINNATUM SUBSP. COLCHICUM
EPIMEDIUM X YOUNGIANUM 'NIVEUM'
EQUISETUM HYEMALE
ERANTHIS HYEMALIS
ERANTHIS X TUBERGENII
FAGUS SYLVATICA 'LACINIATA'
FAGUS SYLVATICA 'PENDULA'
FAGUS SYLVATICA 'RIVERSII'
FILIPENDULA PURPUREA 'NANA'
FOTHERGILLA GARDENII
GALIUM ODORATUM
HALESIA TETRAPTERA
HELIANTHUS SALICIFOLIUS
HELICTOTRICHON SEMPERVIRENS
HEMEROCALLIS FULVA 'EUROPA'
HERACLEUM MANTEGAZZIANUM
HOUTTUYNIA CORDATA 'CHAMELEON'
HYDRANGEA ANOMALA SUBSP. PETIOLARIS 'SKYLANDS GIANT'
ILEX GLABRA 'DENSA'
ILEX X AQUIPERNYI 'SAN JOSE'
IRIS CRISTATA
IRIS GRAMINEA
IRIS TECTORUM
KALMIA LATIFOLIA
KIRENGESHOMA PALMATA
KOLKWITZIA AMABILIS
LAMIUM MACULATUM 'WHITE NANCY'
LEUCOJUM VERNUM
LEUCOTHOE FONTANESIANA
LEUCOTHOE FONTANESIANA 'NANA'
LIGUSTRUM QUIHOUI
LIQUIDAMBAR STYRACIFLUA
LONICERA FRAGRANTISSIMA
LYCORIS SPRENGERI
LYCORIS SQUAMIGERA
LYSIMACHIA PUNCTATA
MAGNOLIA VIRGINIANA
MERTENSIA VIRGINICA
METASEQUOIA GLYPTOSTROBOIDES
MISCANTHUS 'GIGANTEUS'
MISCANTHUS SINENSIS 'CABARET'
MISCANTHUS SINENSIS 'GRACILLIMUS'
MISCANTHUS SINENSIS 'MORNING LIGHT'
MISCANTHUS SINENSIS 'SILVER FEATHER' (='SILBERFEDER')
MISCANTHUS SINENSIS 'STRICTUS'
MISCANTHUS SINENSIS 'VARIEGATUS'
MUSCARI AZUREUM 'ALBUM'
MUSCARI BOTRYOIDES 'ALBUM'
MUSCARI TUBERGENIANUM
NARCISSUS 'CARLTON'
NARCISSUS 'FORTUNE'
NARCISSUS 'HERA'
NARCISSUS 'LOCH FYNE'
NARCISSUS 'MOONMIST'
NARCISSUS 'MRS. ERNST H. KRELAGE'
NARCISSUS 'PEEPING TOM'
NARCISSUS 'POMONA'
NARCISSUS 'QUEEN OF SPAIN'
NARCISSUS 'TREVITHIAN'
NARCISSUS JONQUILLA
NARCISSUS PSEUDONARCISSUS SUBSP. OBVALLARIS
NYSSA SYLVATICA
OXYDENDRUM ARBOREUM
PANICUM VIRGATUM 'STRICTUM'
PETASITES FRAGRANS
PHLOX PILOSA SUBSP. OZARKANA
PHLOX STOLONIFERA 'ALBA'

PHLOX STOLONIFERA 'BLUE RIDGE'
PHLOX STOLONIFERA 'SHERWOOD PURPLE'
PLATANUS OCCIDENTALIS
POLYSTICHUM TRIPTERON
RHEUM PALMATUM 'RUBRUM'
RHODODENDRON ARBORESCENS
RHODODENDRON ATLANTICUM
RHODODENDRON VASEYI
ROSA VIRGINIANA
RUBUS COCKBURNIANUS
SAGINA SUBULATA
SALIX 'HAKURO'
SALIX ACUTIFOLIA 'LONGIFOLIA'
SALIX CHAENOMELOIDES
SALIX DAPHNOIDES 'AGLAIA'
SALIX GRACILISTYLA
SALIX GRACILISTYLA 'MELANOSTACHYS'
SALIX X RUBRA 'EUGENEI'
SCILLA SIBERICA 'SPRING BEAUTY'
SYMPHYTUM X UPLANDICUM
THALICTRUM ROCHEBRUNIANUM
THELYPTERIS HEXAGONOPTERA
THELYPTERIS NOVEBORACENSIS
THELYPTERIS PHEGOPTERIS
THUJA PLICATA 'ATROVIRENS'
VALERIANA OFFICINALIS
VIBURNUM PLICATUM FORMA TOMENTOSUM
XANTHORHIZA SIMPLICISSIMA

6
ACORUS GRAMINEUS 'OGON'
ARUM ITALICUM 'PICTUM'
BEGONIA GRANDIS
BUXUS SEMPERVIRENS 'SUFFRUTICOSA'
CALOCEDRUS DECURRENS
CLETHRA BARBINERVIS
COTONEASTER SALICIFOLIUS VAR. FLOCCOSUS
ENKIANTHUS PERULATUS
EUPATORIUM COELESTINUM
FILIPENDULA PURPUREA 'ELEGANS'
FRANKLINIA ALATAMAHA
GALTONIA CANDICANS
HEDERA HELIX 'BUTTERCUP'
HEDERA HELIX 'GOLD HEART'
HYDRANGEA MACROPHYLLA 'BLUE BILLOW'
ILEX OPACA 'ARDEN'
ILEX OPACA 'XANTHOCARPA'
IMPERATA CYLINDRICA 'RED BARON'
ITEA VIRGINICA 'HENRY'S GARNET'
LUZULA SYLVATICA 'MARGINATA'
MAGNOLIA MACROPHYLLA
PHYLLOSTACHYS AUREOSULCATA
PIERIS JAPONICA
PSEUDOLARIX KAEMPFERI
QUERCUS PHELLOS
SAXIFRAGA STOLONIFERA
SCIADOPITYS VERTICILLATA
STEWARTIA KOREANA
STYRAX JAPONICUS
STYRAX JAPONICUS 'CARILLON'
TAXODIUM DISTICHUM VAR. NUTANS 'PRAIRIE SENTINEL'
TRACHYSTEMON ORIENTALIS
VIBURNUM NUDUM 'WINTERTHUR'

7
CEDRUS ATLANTICA 'GLAUCA'
CHIMONANTHUS PRAECOX
CLERODENDRUM TRICHOTOMUM

ZONE	LATIN NAME
	HYDRANGEA ASPERA SUBSP. SARGENTIANA
	RHODODENDRON CANESCENS
	SKIMMIA REEVESIANA
	VIBURNUM MACROCEPHALUM FORMA MACROCEPHALUM
8	COTULA SQUALIDA
T	CANNA X GENERALIS 'MOHAWK'
	KOCHIA SCOPARIA FORMA TRICHOPHYLLA 'CHILDSII'
	POLIANTHES TUBEROSA

AVERAGE, DRY BETWEEN RAINS

ZONE	LATIN NAME
2	ACHILLEA MILLEFOLIUM 'ROSEA'
	ARTEMESIA STELLERIANA
	BERGENIA 'PERFECTA'
	BERGENIA 'SUNNINGDALE'
	BETULA PAPYRIFERA
	DICENTRA SPECTABILIS
	PAEONIA—HERBACEOUS HYBRIDS
3	ACER SACCHARUM
	ACHILLEA 'CORONATION GOLD'
	ACHILLEA 'MOONSHINE'
	AEGOPODIUM PODAGRARIA 'VARIEGATUM'
	ALCHEMILLA VULGARIS
	AMELANCHIER ARBOREA (SYN. A. CANADENSIS)
	AMSONIA TABERNAEMONTANA
	ARTEMESIA ABSINTHIUM 'LAMBROOK SILVER'
	ASCLEPIAS TUBEROSA
	ASTER AMELLUS 'NOCTURNE'
	ASTER TATARICUS
	BAPTISIA AUSTRALIS
	BETULA PENDULA 'GRACILIS'
	BETULA PENDULA 'YOUNGII'
	BOLTONIA ASTEROIDES 'SNOWBANK'
	BRUNNERA MACROPHYLLA
	CIMICIFUGA RACEMOSA
	COREOPSIS 'MOONBEAM'
	CORNUS ALBA 'ELEGANTISSIMA'
	CORNUS ALBA 'SPAETHII'
	CORNUS RACEMOSA
	CORNUS RACEMOSA (DWARF)
	CORNUS SERICEA
	CORNUS SERICEA 'FLAVIRAMEA'
	DENNSTAEDTIA PUNCTILOBULA
	DIANTHUS DELTOIDES
	DICENTRA 'LUXURIANT'
	DICENTRA EXIMIA 'PURITY'
	ECHINACEA PURPUREA
	ECHINOPS RITRO
	GERANIUM 'JOHNSON'S BLUE'
	GERANIUM MACRORRHIZUM
	GERANIUM SANGUINEUM
	HELLEBORUS NIGER
	HIPPOPHAE RHAMNOIDES
	HOSTA 'KABITAN'
	HOSTA PLANTAGINEA
	HOSTA SIEBOLDIANA 'ELEGANS'
	HOSTA UNDULATA
	HOSTA VENTRICOSA
	INULA HELENIUM
	IRIS SIBIRICA CULTIVARS

ZONE	LATIN NAME
	JUNIPERUS HORIZONTALIS 'WILTONII'
	JUNIPERUS VIRGINIANA
	LIATRIS SCARIOSA 'WHITE SPIRE'
	LIATRIS SPICATA 'KOBOLD'
	LYSIMACHIA CLETHROIDES
	LYTHRUM SALICARIA 'DROPMORE PURPLE'
	MACLEAYA CORDATA
	MALUS 'RED JADE'
	NEPETA X FAASSENII
	PAPAVER ORIENTALE
	PHLOX SUBULATA
	PHYSOSTEGIA VIRGINIANA
	PHYSOSTEGIA VIRGINIANA 'SUMMER SNOW'
	PICEA ABIES 'NIDIFORMIS'
	PICEA PUNGENS 'HOOPSII'
	PINUS MUGO VAR. MUGO
	PINUS STROBUS
	PINUS STROBUS 'FASTIGIATA'
	POLYSTICHUM ACROSTICHOIDES
	PRUNUS X CISTENA
	PSEUDOTSUGA MENZIESII
	PTERIDIUM AQUILINUM VAR. LATIUSCULUM
	PULMONARIA ANGUSTIFOLIA
	PULMONARIA SACCHARATA 'MARGERY FISH'
	PULMONARIA SACCHARATA 'SISSINGHURST WHITE'
	QUERCUS RUBRA
	RHODODENDRON PRINOPHYLLUM
	RHUS AROMATICA 'GRO-LOW'
	RHUS TYPHINA
	RHUS TYPHINA 'LACINIATA'
	ROSA RUGOSA AND HYBRIDS
	RUDBECKIA FULGIDA VAR. SULLIVANTII 'GOLDSTURM'
	SALIX ALBA 'KALMTHOUT'
	SALIX ALBA 'REGALIS'
	SALIX ALBA 'SERICEA'
	SEDUM 'AUTUMN JOY'
	SEDUM ELLACOMBIANUM
	SEDUM SARMENTOSUM
	SEDUM SPURIUM
	SEDUM SPURIUM 'BRONZE CARPET'
	SORBARIA SORBIFOLIA
	SPIRAEA X VANHOUTTEI
	SYRINGA VULGARIS 'ALBA'
	SYRINGA VULGARIS HYBRIDS
	TELEKIA SPECIOSA
	THERMOPSIS CAROLINIANA
	THUJA OCCIDENTALIS 'NIGRA'
	TIARELLA CORDIFOLIA VAR. COLLINA
	TILIA CORDATA
	TSUGA CANADENSIS
	TSUGA CANADENSIS 'BENNETT'
	TSUGA CANADENSIS 'COLE'S PROSTRATE'
	TSUGA CANADENSIS 'PENDULA'
	VERONICA INCANA
	VERONICASTRUM VIRGINICUM
	VIBURNUM ACERIFOLIUM
	VIBURNUM PRUNIFOLIUM
4	ACANTHOPANAX SIEBOLDIANUS
	ACER PLATANOIDES 'CRIMSON KING'
	ACER RUBRUM
	AJUGA REPTANS
	AJUGA REPTANS 'BRONZE BEAUTY'
	AJUGA REPTANS (GIANT FORM)
	ALLIUM TUBEROSUM
	ANEMONE VITIFOLIA 'ROBUSTISSIMA'

ZONE	LATIN NAME
	ARABIS PROCURRENS
	ARALIA SPINOSA
	ARONIA ARBUTIFOLIA 'BRILLIANTISSIMA'
	ARTEMESIA LUDOVICIANA 'SILVER QUEEN'
	ARUNCUS AETHUSIFOLIUS
	BACCHARIS HALIMIFOLIA, PISTILLATE
	BERBERIS THUNBERGII 'ATROPURPUREA'
	BERBERIS THUNBERGII 'CRIMSON PYGMY'
	BETULA LENTA
	BETULA NIGRA
	BUDDLEIA ALTERNIFOLIA
	CARYA OVATA
	CARYOPTERIS X CLANDONENSIS 'BLUE MIST'
	CHAENOMELES JAPONICA VAR. ALPINA
	CHAENOMELES SPECIOSA CULTIVARS
	CHAENOMELES X SUPERBA 'JET TRAIL'
	CHAMAEMELUM NOBILE
	CLADRASTIS LUTEA
	CLEMATIS 'MRS. CHOLMONDELEY'
	CLEMATIS 'PRINS HENDRIK'
	CLEMATIS 'RAMONA'
	CLEMATIS X JACKMANII
	COMPTONIA PEREGRINA
	CONVALLARIA MAJALIS
	CORNUS ALTERNIFOLIA
	CORYLUS AVELLANA 'CONTORTA'
	CORYLUS AVELLANA 'PENDULA'
	CRATAEGUS NITIDA
	CRATAEGUS PHAENOPYRUM
	DIERVILLA SESSILIFOLIA
	EUONYMUS ALATA
	EUONYMUS FORTUNEI 'COLORATA'
	EUONYMUS FORTUNEI VAR. RADICANS
	EUPHORBIA CYPARISSIAS
	GINKGO BILOBA, STAMINATE
	GLEDITSIA TRIACANTHOS VAR. INERMIS 'SHADEMASTER'
	GYMNOCLADUS DIOICA
	HAMAMELIS VIRGINIANA
	HEDYOTIS CAERULEA
	HELIOPSIS HELIANTHOIDES SUBSP. SCABRA 'KARAT'
	HELLEBORUS ORIENTALIS HYBRIDS
	HEUCHERA 'PALACE PURPLE' STRAIN
	HYDRANGEA PANICULATA
	HYPERICUM KALMIANUM
	ILEX VERTICILLATA
	ILEX VERTICILLATA 'WINTER RED'
	JUNIPERUS SABINA 'TAMARISCIFOLIA'
	JUNIPERUS X MEDIA 'PFITZERIANA COMPACTA'
	MALUS FLORIBUNDA
	MALUS HUPEHENSIS
	MALUS SARGENTII
	MICROBIOTA DECUSSATA
	MYRICA PENSYLVANICA
	OSMUNDA CINNAMOMEA
	PACHYSANDRA PROCUMBENS
	PAEONIA TENUIFOLIA
	PAXISTIMA CANBYI
	PHALARIS ARUNDINACEA VAR. PICTA
	PHELLODENDRON AMURENSE
	PHLOX BIFIDA
	PINUS FLEXILIS
	PINUS KORAIENSIS
	POLYGONATUM ODORATUM 'VARIEGATUM'
	QUERCUS ALBA
	QUERCUS MACROCARPA

ZONE	LATIN NAME
	RHODODENDRON (CATAWBIENSE HYBRIDS)
	RHODODENDRON MAXIMUM
	RHODODENDRON VISCOSUM
	ROBINIA HISPIDA
	ROSA NITIDA
	SALIX ALBA VAR. TRISTIS
	SALIX ELAEAGNOS
	SALIX REPENS VAR. ARGENTEA
	SEDUM POPULIFOLIUM
	SEDUM TERNATUM
	SPIRAEA THUNBERGII
	STACHYS BYZANTINA
	SYRINGA PATULA
	(SYN. S. PALIBINIANA, S. MICROPHYLLA 'INGWERSEN'S DWARF')
	SYRINGA X CHINENSIS
	TAMARIX RAMOSISSIMA
	TAXUS CUSPIDATA 'NANA'
	TAXUS CUSPIDATA (CAPITATA SELECTION)
	THUJA OCCIDENTALIS 'HETZ' WINTERGREEN'
	VACCINIUM CORYMBOSUM
	VERNONIA NOVEBORACENSIS
	VERONICA 'SUNNY BORDER BLUE'
	VERONICA LONGIFOLIA 'SUBSESSILIS'
	VIBURNUM CARLESII
	VINCA MINOR 'BOWLESII'
	VINCA MINOR 'VARIEGATA'
	VIOLA LABRADORICA
	WALDSTEINIA TERNATA
	YUCCA FLACCIDA 'GOLDEN SWORD'
	YUCCA GLAUCA
	YUCCA SMALLIANA
5	ABIES NORDMANNIANA
	ACER GRISEUM
	ACER PALMATUM 'BLOODGOOD'
	ACER PALMATUM 'SANGOKAKU'
	AESCULUS PARVIFLORA
	ALLIUM CERNUUM
	ALLIUM ZEBDANENSE
	AMSONIA HUBRICHTII
	ANEMONE BLANDA 'ATROCAERULEA'
	ARTEMESIA VERSICOLOR
	ARUNDINARIA VIRIDISTRIATA
	ASARUM EUROPAEUM
	ASPHODELINE LUTEA
	ASTER CORDIFOLIUS
	ASTER X FRIKARTII 'MONCH'
	ATHYRIUM GOERINGIANUM 'PICTUM'
	BUDDLEIA DAVIDII 'BLACK KNIGHT'
	BUDDLEIA DAVIDII 'OPERA'
	BUDDLEIA DAVIDII 'PURPLE PRINCE'
	BUXUS 'GREEN GEM'
	BUXUS SINICA VAR. INSULARIS 'TIDE HILL'
	BUXUS SINICA VAR. INSULARIS 'WINTERGREEN' (OHIO CULTIVAR)
	CALAMAGROSTIS X ACUTIFLORA 'KARL FOERSTER' (SYN. C. EPIGEOUS 'HORTORUM')
	CALLICARPA JAPONICA
	CALYCANTHUS FLORIDUS 'EDITH WILDER'
	CAMPSIS X TAGLIABUANA 'MADAME GALEN'
	CARPINUS BETULUS
	CATALPA BIGNONIOIDES
	CEDRUS LIBANI VAR. STENOCOMA

ZONE	LATIN NAME
	CEPHALOTAXUS HARRINGTONIA VAR. PEDUNCULATA
	CERCIS CANADENSIS 'FOREST PANSY'
	CHAENOMELES X SUPERBA CULTIVARS
	CHAMAECYPARIS OBTUSA 'FILICOIDES'
	CHAMAECYPARIS OBTUSA 'NANA GRACILIS'
	CHAMAECYPARIS OBTUSA 'NANA'
	CHAMAECYPARIS OBTUSA VAR. BREVIRAMEA
	CHAMAECYPARIS PISIFERA 'GOLD SPANGLE'
	CHIONANTHUS VIRGINICUS
	CHIONODOXA GIGANTEA 'ALBA'
	CHIONODOXA LUCILIAE
	CHIONODOXA SARDENSIS
	CHRYSANTHEMUM WEYRICHII 'WHITE BOMB'
	CLETHRA ALNIFOLIA
	COLCHICUM 'AUTUMN QUEEN'
	COLCHICUM 'THE GIANT'
	COLUTEA X MEDIA
	CORNUS FLORIDA
	CORNUS FLORIDA 'HOHMAN'S GOLDEN'
	CORNUS KOUSA
	CORNUS MAS
	CORNUS OFFICINALIS
	CORYLOPSIS PLATYPETALA
	CORYLUS COLURNA
	COTINUS COGGYGRIA 'PURPUREUS'
	COTONEASTER ADPRESSUS 'LITTLE GEM'
	COTONEASTER APICULATUS
	COTONEASTER HORIZONTALIS
	CRAMBE CORDIFOLIA
	CRATAEGUS VIRIDIS 'WINTER KING'
	CROCUS ANCYRENSIS 'GOLDEN BUNCH'
	CROCUS SIEBERI
	CROCUS TOMASINIANUS
	CYCLAMEN HEDERIFOLIUM
	DAPHNE CAUCASICA
	DAPHNE X BURKWOODII 'CAROL MACKIE'
	DEUTZIA GRACILIS
	DIOSPYROS VIRGINIANA
	DIPLAZIUM CONILII
	ENDYMION HISPANICUS 'EXCELSIOR' (SYN. SCILLA CAMPANULATA 'EXCELSIOR')
	ENKIANTHUS CAMPANULATUS
	EPIMEDIUM PINNATUM SUBSP. COLCHICUM
	EPIMEDIUM X YOUNGIANUM 'NIVEUM'
	EQUISETUM HYEMALE
	ERANTHIS HYEMALIS
	ERANTHIS X TUBERGENII
	ERIANTHUS RAVENNAE
	EUONYMUS FORTUNEI 'GRACILIS'
	EUONYMUS FORTUNEI 'MINIMA'
	EXOCHORDA GIRALDII VAR. WILSONII
	FAGUS SYLVATICA 'LACINIATA'
	FAGUS SYLVATICA 'PENDULA'
	FAGUS SYLVATICA 'RIVERSII'
	FILIPENDULA PURPUREA 'NANA'
	FORSYTHIA SUSPENSA
	FOTHERGILLA GARDENII
	GALANTHUS ELWESII
	GALANTHUS NIVALIS
	HALESIA TETRAPTERA
	HAMAMELIS MOLLIS 'PALLIDA'
	HAMAMELIS X INTERMEDIA 'DIANE'

ZONE	LATIN NAME
	HAMAMELIS X INTERMEDIA 'JELENA'
	HAMAMELIS X INTERMEDIA 'PRIMAVERA'
	HEDERA HELIX 'BULGARIA'
	HEDERA HELIX 'OGALALLA'
	HELIANTHEMUM APENNINUM VAR. ROSEUM
	HELIANTHUS SALICIFOLIUS
	HELICTOTRICHON SEMPERVIRENS
	HEMEROCALLIS 'HYPERION'
	HEMEROCALLIS FULVA 'EUROPA'
	HERACLEUM MANTEGAZZIANUM
	HIBISCUS SYRIACUS 'BLUEBIRD'
	HIBISCUS SYRIACUS 'DIANA'
	HYDRANGEA ANOMALA SUBSP. PETIOLARIS 'SKYLANDS GIANT'
	HYDRANGEA QUERCIFOLIA
	HYPERICUM FRONDOSUM
	ILEX CHINA BOY ® 'MESDOB'
	ILEX CHINA GIRL ® 'MESOG'
	ILEX GLABRA 'DENSA'
	ILEX X AQUIPERNYI 'SAN JOSE'
	ILEX X MESERVEAE BLUE MAID ® 'MESID'
	ILEX X MESERVEAE BLUE STALLION ® 'MESAN'
	INDIGOFERA INCARNATA 'ALBA'
	IRIS CRISTATA
	IRIS GRAMINEA
	JUNIPERUS SCOPULORUM 'SKY ROCKET'
	JUNIPERUS X MEDIA 'OLD GOLD'
	KERRIA JAPONICA
	KIRENGESHOMA PALMATA
	KOELREUTERIA PANICULATA
	KOLKWITZIA AMABILIS
	LAMIASTRUM GALEOBDOLON 'VARIEGATUM'
	LAMIUM MACULATUM 'WHITE NANCY'
	LATHYRUS VERNUS
	LESPEDEZA THUNBERGII
	LEUCOJUM VERNUM
	LEUCOTHOE FONTANESIANA
	LEUCOTHOE FONTANESIANA 'NANA'
	LIGUSTRUM QUIHOUI
	LILIUM 'BLACK DRAGON'
	LILIUM SPECIES AND HYBRIDS
	LIQUIDAMBAR STYRACIFLUA
	LONICERA FRAGRANTISSIMA
	LYCORIS SPRENGERI
	LYCORIS SQUAMIGERA
	LYSIMACHIA PUNCTATA
	MAGNOLIA 'ELIZABETH'
	MAGNOLIA VIRGINIANA
	MAGNOLIA X LOEBNERI
	MAGNOLIA X SOULANGIANA 'VERBANICA'
	MERTENSIA VIRGINICA
	METASEQUOIA GLYPTOSTROBOIDES
	MISCANTHUS SINENSIS 'CABARET'
	MISCANTHUS SINENSIS 'GRACILLIMUS'
	MISCANTHUS SINENSIS 'MORNING LIGHT'
	MISCANTHUS SINENSIS 'SILVER FEATHER' (='SILBERFEDER')
	MISCANTHUS SINENSIS 'STRICTUS'
	MISCANTHUS SINENSIS 'VARIEGATUS'
	MOLINIA CAERULEA SUBSP. ARUNDINACEA
	MUSCARI AZUREUM 'ALBUM'
	MUSCARI BOTRYOIDES 'ALBUM'
	MUSCARI TUBERGENIANUM

ZONE	LATIN NAME

NARCISSUS 'CARLTON'
NARCISSUS 'FORTUNE'
NARCISSUS 'HERA'
NARCISSUS 'LOCH FYNE'
NARCISSUS 'MOONMIST'
NARCISSUS 'MRS. ERNST H. KRELAGE'
NARCISSUS 'PEEPING TOM'
NARCISSUS 'POMONA'
NARCISSUS 'QUEEN OF SPAIN'
NARCISSUS 'TREVITHIAN'
NARCISSUS JONQUILLA
NARCISSUS PSEUDONARCISSUS SUBSP.
   OBVALLARIS
NYSSA SYLVATICA
ONOPORDUM ACANTHIUM
OXYDENDRUM ARBOREUM
PACHYSANDRA TERMINALIS
PACHYSANDRA TERMINALIS 'GREEN
   CARPET'
PACHYSANDRA TERMINALIS
   'VARIEGATA' OR 'SILVER EDGE'
PANICUM VIRGATUM 'STRICTUM'
PENNISETUM ALOPECUROIDES
PEROVSKIA ABROTANOIDES X
   P.ATRIPLICIFOLIA
PETASITES FRAGRANS
PHILADELPHUS CORONARIUS
PHILADELPHUS X FALCONERI
PHLOX PILOSA SUBSP. OZARKANA
PHLOX STOLONIFERA 'ALBA'
PHLOX STOLONIFERA 'BLUE RIDGE'
PHLOX STOLONIFERA 'SHERWOOD
   PURPLE'
PICEA ORIENTALIS
PINUS BUNGEANA
PINUS DENSIFLORA 'UMBRACULIFERA'
PINUS PARVIFLORA 'GLAUCA'
PINUS VIRGINIANA
PLATANUS OCCIDENTALIS
POLYSTICHUM TRIPTERON
PRUNUS 'HALLY JOLIVETTE'
PRUNUS CERASIFERA
   'THUNDERCLOUD'
PRUNUS SUBHIRTELLA 'AUTUMNALIS'
RHODODENDRON (GABLE HYBRIDS)
RHODODENDRON ARBORESCENS
RHODODENDRON ATLANTICUM
RHODODENDRON MUCRONULATUM
RHODODENDRON SCHLIPPENBACHII
RHODODENDRON VASEYI
RHODODENDRON X GANDAVENSE
   'COCCINEA SPECIOSA'
RHODODENDRON X GANDAVENSE
   'DAVIESII'
RHODOTYPOS SCANDENS
RIBES ODORATUM
ROSA 'DOORENBOS SELECTION'
ROSA (GALLICA) 'CHARLES DE MILLS'
ROSA (POLYANTHA) 'THE FAIRY'
ROSA (SHRUB) 'LILLIAN GIBSON'
ROSA (SHRUB) 'SEA FOAM'
ROSA CAROLINA
ROSA EGLANTERIA
ROSA VIRGINIANA
RUBUS COCKBURNIANUS
SAGINA SUBULATA
SALIX 'HAKURO'
SALIX ACUTIFOLIA 'LONGIFOLIA'
SALIX CHAENOMELOIDES
SALIX DAPHNOIDES 'AGLAIA'
SALIX GRACILISTYLA
SALIX GRACILISTYLA
   'MELANOSTACHYS'

SALIX X RUBRA 'EUGENEI'
SASSAFRAS ALBIDUM
SCILLA SIBERICA 'SPRING BEAUTY'
SEDUM 'VERA JAMISON'
SEDUM FLORIFERUM
   'WEIHANSTEPHANER GOLD'
SPIRAEA PRUNIFOLIA
STEPHANANDRA INCISA 'CRISPA'
STERNBERGIA LUTEA
SYMPHORICARPOS X CHENAULTII
   'HANCOCK'
SYMPHYTUM X UPLANDICUM
SYRINGA LACINIATA
SYRINGA RETICULATA
TAXUS BACCATA 'ADPRESSA FOWLE'
TAXUS BACCATA 'REPANDENS'
TAXUS X MEDIA 'SENTINALIS'
THALICTRUM ROCHEBRUNIANUM
THUJA PLICATA 'ATROVIRENS'
THYMUS 'CLEAR GOLD'
THYMUS PSEUDOLANUGINOSUS
VERBASCUM OLYMPICUM
VIBURNUM DILATATUM 'MICHAEL
   DODGE'
VIBURNUM FARRERI 'CANDIDISSIMUM'
VIBURNUM FARRERI 'NANUM'
VIBURNUM PLICATUM FORMA
   TOMENTOSUM
VIBURNUM SIEBOLDII 'SENECA'
WISTERIA FLORIBUNDA
XANTHORHIZA SIMPLICISSIMA

6 ABELIA X GRANDIFLORA
ACER PALMATUM 'EVER RED'
ACER PALMATUM VAR. DISSECTUM OR
   A. P. 'WATERFALL'
ADINA RUBELLA
AESCULUS SPLENDENS
ARUM ITALICUM 'PICTUM'
ARUNDO DONAX
BEGONIA GRANDIS
BERBERIS JULIANAE 'NANA'
BERBERIS WISLEYENSIS
   (SYN. B. TRIACANTHOPHORA)
BIGNONIA CAPREOLATA
BUXUS SEMPERVIRENS 'SUFFRUTICOSA'
CALLICARPA DICHOTOMA
CALOCEDRUS DECURRENS
CERATOSTIGMA PLUMBAGINOIDES
CHAMAECYPARIS OBTUSA 'CRIPPSII'
CLETHRA BARBINERVIS
COTONEASTER ADPRESSUS VAR.
   PRAECOX
COTONEASTER SALICIFOLIUS VAR.
   FLOCCOSUS
CROCOSMIA 'LUCIFER'
CROCOSMIA POTTSII
CROCOSMIA X CROCOSMIIFLORA
CRUCIANELLA STYLOSA
CYTISUS SCOPARIUS
CYTISUS X PRAECOX 'LUTEUS'
ENKIANTHUS PERULATUS
EUONYMUS FORTUNEI 'SILVER QUEEN'
EUPATORIUM COELESTINUM
FORSYTHIA VIRIDISSIMA 'BRONXENSIS'
FORSYTHIA X INTERMEDIA 'SPRING
   GLORY'
FRANKLINIA ALATAMAHA
GALTONIA CANDICANS
HEDERA HELIX 'BALTICA'
HEDERA HELIX 'BUTTERCUP'
HEDERA HELIX 'GOLD HEART'
ILEX CRENATA 'HELLERI'

ILEX CRENATA 'MICROPHYLLA'
ILEX OPACA 'ARDEN'
ILEX OPACA 'XANTHOCARPA'
IMPERATA CYLINDRICA 'RED BARON'
ITEA VIRGINICA 'HENRY'S GARNET'
JASMINUM NUDIFLORUM
JUNIPERUS CHINENSIS 'KAIZUKA'
LESPEDEZA THUNBERGII 'ALBIFLORA'
LIRIOPE MUSCARI (BIG BLUE
   SELECTION)
LIRIOPE MUSCARI 'MONROE WHITE'
LIRIOPE MUSCARI 'VARIEGATA'
LUZULA SYLVATICA 'MARGINATA'
MAGNOLIA 'SUSAN'
MAGNOLIA DENUDATA
   (SYN. M. HEPTAPETA)
MAGNOLIA MACROPHYLLA
MAHONIA BEALEI
PAEONIA 'BLACK PIRATE'
PAEONIA—WOODY HYBRIDS
PARONYCHIA KAPELA SUBSP.
   SERPYLLIFOLIA
PAULOWNIA TOMENTOSA
PHYLLOSTACHYS AUREOSULCATA
PIERIS JAPONICA
PINUS THUNBERGIANA
PINUS THUNBERGIANA 'OCULUS-
   DRACONIS'
PONCIRUS TRIFOLIATA
PRUNUS SUBHIRTELLA 'PENDULA'
PRUNUS YEDOENSIS
PSEUDOLARIX KAEMPFERI
QUERCUS PHELLOS
RHODODENDRON (GLENN DALE
   HYBRIDS)
RHODODENDRON (KAEMPFERI
   HYBRIDS)
RHODODENDRON (KNAP HILL HYBRID)
   'TUNIS'
RHODODENDRON (KURUME HYBRIDS)
RHODODENDRON X ERIOCARPUM
   AND R. X NAKAHARAI CULTIVARS
   AND HYBRIDS
ROSA ROXBURGHII
RUBUS IDAEUS 'AUREUS'
SALVIA ARGENTEA
SAXIFRAGA STOLONIFERA
SCIADOPITYS VERTICILLATA
SOPHORA JAPONICA 'REGENT'
STEWARTIA KOREANA
STRANVAESIA DAVIDIANA VAR.
   UNDULATA 'PROSTRATA'
STYRAX JAPONICUS
STYRAX JAPONICUS 'CARILLON'
TRACHYSTEMON ORIENTALIS
VIBURNUM ICHANGENSE
VIBURNUM NUDUM 'WINTERTHUR'
VIBURNUM RHYTIDOPHYLLUM
VIBURNUM SETIGERUM
VITEX AGNUS-CASTUS 'LATIFOLIA'
VITEX AGNUS-CASTUS 'SILVER SPIRE'
ZELKOVA SERRATA 'GREEN VASE'

7 BERBERIS WILSONIAE VAR. STAPFIANA
BUXUS MICROPHYLLA 'COMPACTA'
CEDRUS ATLANTICA 'GLAUCA'
CHIMONANTHUS PRAECOX
CLERODENDRUM TRICHOTOMUM
DIOSPYROS KAKI
ELAEAGNUS PUNGENS 'FRUITLANDII'
ELAEAGNUS PUNGENS 'MACULATA'
GENISTA SYLVESTRIS 'LYDIA'
HEDERA COLCHICA 'DENTATA'

ZONE	LATIN NAME
	HEDERA HELIX 'ERECTA'
	HYDRANGEA ASPERA SUBSP. SARGENTIANA
	OPHIOPOGON JAPONICUS 'NANUS'
	PYRACANTHA COCCINEA 'AUREA'
	RHODODENDRON CANESCENS
	SASA VEITCHII
	SKIMMIA REEVESIANA
	VIBURNUM MACROCEPHALUM FORMA MACROCEPHALUM
8	COTULA SQUALIDA
T	CANNA X GENERALIS 'MOHAWK'
	CESTRUM NOCTURNUM
	DATURA INOXIA SUBSP. QUINQUECUSPIDA
	KOCHIA SCOPARIA FORMA TRICHOPHYLLA 'CHILDSII'
	POLIANTHES TUBEROSA
	RICINUS COMMUNIS
	RICINUS COMMUNIS 'ZANZIBARENSIS'

DRY

ZONE	LATIN NAME
2	ACHILLEA MILLEFOLIUM 'ROSEA'
	ARTEMESIA STELLERIANA
	POTENTILLA TRIDENTATA
3	ACHILLEA 'MOONSHINE'
	AEGOPODIUM PODAGRARIA 'VARIEGATUM'
	AMSONIA TABERNAEMONTANA
	ARTEMESIA ABSINTHIUM 'LAMBROOK SILVER'
	ASTER AMELLUS 'NOCTURNE'
	ASTER TATARICUS
	BAPTISIA AUSTRALIS
	BRUNNERA MACROPHYLLA
	COREOPSIS 'MOONBEAM'
	CORNUS RACEMOSA
	EUPHORBIA COROLLATA
	GERANIUM MACRORRHIZUM
	HIPPOPHAE RHAMNOIDES
	JUNIPERUS HORIZONTALIS 'WILTONII'
	JUNIPERUS VIRGINIANA
	LYTHRUM SALICARIA 'DROPMORE PURPLE'
	NEPETA X FAASSENII
	PAPAVER ORIENTALE
	PICEA PUNGENS 'HOOPSII'
	PINUS MUGO VAR. MUGO
	PRUNUS X CISTENA
	PTERIDIUM AQUILINUM VAR. LATIUSCULUM
	QUERCUS RUBRA
	RHUS AROMATICA 'GRO-LOW'
	RHUS TYPHINA
	RHUS TYPHINA 'LACINIATA'
	ROSA RUGOSA AND HYBRIDS
	SEDUM ELLACOMBIANUM
	SEDUM SARMENTOSUM
	SEDUM SPURIUM
	SEDUM SPURIUM 'BRONZE CARPET'
	SPIRAEA X VANHOUTTEI
	THERMOPSIS CAROLINIANA
	THYMUS SERPYLLUM
	VIBURNUM ACERIFOLIUM
	VIBURNUM PRUNIFOLIUM

ZONE	LATIN NAME
4	ACANTHOPANAX SIEBOLDIANUS
	ACER RUBRUM
	ALLIUM TUBEROSUM
	ARTEMISIA LUDOVICIANA 'SILVER QUEEN'
	BERBERIS THUNBERGII 'CRIMSON PYGMY'
	BETULA LENTA
	BETULA NIGRA
	CARYA OVATA
	CHAENOMELES JAPONICA VAR. ALPINA
	CHAENOMELES SPECIOSA CULTIVARS
	CHAENOMELES X SUPERBA 'JET TRAIL'
	CLADRASTIS LUTEA
	COMPTONIA PEREGRINA
	CORYLUS AVELLANA 'CONTORTA'
	CORYLUS AVELLANA 'PENDULA'
	CRATAEGUS NITIDA
	CRATAEGUS PHAENOPYRUM
	EUONYMUS ALATA
	EUONYMUS FORTUNEI 'COLORATA'
	EUPHORBIA CYPARISSIAS
	EUPHORBIA EPITHYMOIDES
	GINKGO BILOBA, STAMINATE
	GLEDITSIA TRIACANTHOS VAR. INERMIS 'SHADEMASTER'
	GYMNOCLADUS DIOICA
	HAMAMELIS VIRGINIANA
	HELIOPSIS HELIANTHOIDES SUBSP. SCABRA 'KARAT'
	HYPERICUM KALMIANUM
	JUNIPERUS SABINA 'TAMARISCIFOLIA'
	JUNIPERUS X MEDIA 'PFITZERIANA COMPACTA'
	MICROBIOTA DECUSSATA
	MYRICA PENSYLVANICA
	PHELLODENDRON AMURENSE
	PINUS FLEXILIS
	PINUS KORAIENSIS
	QUERCUS MACROCARPA
	ROBINIA HISPIDA
	ROSA NITIDA
	STACHYS BYZANTINA
	SYRINGA PATULA (SYN. S. PALIBINIANA, S. MICROPHYLLA 'INGWERSEN'S DWARF')
	SYRINGA X CHINENSIS
	TAMARIX RAMOSISSIMA
	VACCINIUM CORYMBOSUM
	WALDSTEINIA TERNATA
	YUCCA FLACCIDA 'GOLDEN SWORD'
	YUCCA GLAUCA
	YUCCA SMALLIANA
5	ALLIUM CERNUUM
	ALLIUM ZEBDANENSE
	AMSONIA HUBRICHTII
	ARTEMESIA VERSICOLOR
	ARUNDINARIA VIRIDISTRIATA
	BUDDLEIA DAVIDII 'BLACK KNIGHT'
	BUDDLEIA DAVIDII 'OPERA'
	BUDDLEIA DAVIDII 'PURPLE PRINCE'
	BUXUS 'GREEN GEM'
	BUXUS SINICA VAR. INSULARIS 'TIDE HILL'
	CAMPSIS X TAGLIABUANA 'MADAME GALEN'
	CATALPA BIGNONIOIDES
	CERCIS CANADENSIS 'FOREST PANSY'
	CHAENOMELES X SUPERBA CULTIVARS
	COLUTEA X MEDIA

ZONE	LATIN NAME
	CORYLUS COLURNA
	COTINUS COGGYGRIA 'PURPUREUS'
	COTONEASTER ADPRESSUS 'LITTLE GEM'
	COTONEASTER APICULATUS
	COTONEASTER HORIZONTALIS
	CRATAEGUS VIRIDIS 'WINTER KING'
	CROCUS ANCYRENSIS 'GOLDEN BUNCH'
	CROCUS SIEBERI
	CROCUS TOMASINIANUS
	DAPHNE CAUCASICA
	DIOSPYROS VIRGINIANA
	EPIMEDIUM PINNATUM SUBSP. COLCHICUM
	EPIMEDIUM X YOUNGIANUM 'NIVEUM'
	EUONYMUS FORTUNEI 'GRACILIS'
	EUONYMUS FORTUNEI 'MINIMA'
	FORSYTHIA SUSPENSA
	HEMEROCALLIS FULVA 'EUROPA'
	HYPERICUM FRONDOSUM
	ILEX GLABRA 'DENSA'
	JUNIPERUS SCOPULORUM 'SKY ROCKET'
	JUNIPERUS X MEDIA 'OLD GOLD'
	KOELREUTERIA PANICULATA
	KOLKWITZIA AMABILIS
	LAMIASTRUM GALEOBDOLON 'VARIEGATUM'
	LESPEDEZA THUNBERGII
	LIGUSTRUM QUIHOUI
	LONICERA FRAGRANTISSIMA
	LYCORIS SQUAMIGERA
	MISCANTHUS SINENSIS 'CABARET'
	MISCANTHUS SINENSIS 'GRACILLIMUS'
	MISCANTHUS SINENSIS 'MORNING LIGHT'
	MISCANTHUS SINENSIS 'SILVER FEATHER' (='SILBERFEDER')
	MISCANTHUS SINENSIS 'STRICTUS'
	MISCANTHUS SINENSIS 'VARIEGATUS'
	MUSCARI AZUREUM 'ALBUM'
	MUSCARI BOTRYOIDES 'ALBUM'
	MUSCARI TUBERGENIANUM
	ONOPORDUM ACANTHIUM
	PHILADELPHUS CORONARIUS
	PHILADELPHUS X FALCONERI
	PHLOMIS RUSSELIANA
	PINUS BUNGEANA
	PINUS VIRGINIANA
	RHODOTYPOS SCANDENS
	ROSA 'DOORENBOS SELECTION'
	ROSA (POLYANTHA) 'THE FAIRY'
	ROSA (SHRUB) 'SEA FOAM'
	ROSA CAROLINA
	ROSA VIRGINIANA
	SASSAFRAS ALBIDUM
	SCILLA SIBERICA 'SPRING BEAUTY'
	SEDUM 'VERA JAMISON'
	SEDUM FLORIFERUM 'WEIHANSTEPHANER GOLD'
	SPIRAEA PRUNIFOLIA
	STEPHANANDRA INCISA 'CRISPA'
	STERNBERGIA LUTEA
	SYMPHORICARPOS X CHENAULTII 'HANCOCK'
	SYRINGA LACINIATA
	THYMUS 'CLEAR GOLD'
	THYMUS PSEUDOLANUGINOSUS
	VERBASCUM OLYMPICUM
	VIBURNUM SIEBOLDII 'SENECA'
	WISTERIA FLORIBUNDA

ZONE	LATIN NAME
6	BIGNONIA CAPREOLATA
	CALLICARPA DICHOTOMA
	COTONEASTER ADPRESSUS VAR. PRAECOX
	CROCOSMIA 'LUCIFER'
	CROCOSMIA POTTSII
	CROCOSMIA X CROCOSMIIFLORA
	EUONYMUS FORTUNEI 'SILVER QUEEN'
	EUPATORIUM COELESTINUM
	FORSYTHIA VIRIDISSIMA 'BRONXENSIS'
	FORSYTHIA X INTERMEDIA 'SPRING GLORY'
	GALTONIA CANDICANS
	JUNIPERUS CHINENSIS 'KAIZUKA'
	PAEONIA 'BLACK PIRATE'
	PAEONIA—WOODY HYBRIDS
	PONCIRUS TRIFOLIATA
	SALVIA ARGENTEA
	SOPHORA JAPONICA 'REGENT'
	VITEX AGNUS-CASTUS 'LATIFOLIA'
	VITEX AGNUS-CASTUS 'SILVER SPIRE'
7	BUXUS MICROPHYLLA 'COMPACTA'
	CHIMONANTHUS PRAECOX
	ELAEAGNUS PUNGENS 'FRUITLANDII'
	ELAEAGNUS PUNGENS 'MACULATA'
	GENISTA SYLVESTRIS 'LYDIA'
	VIBURNUM MACROCEPHALUM FORMA MACROCEPHALUM
T	KOCHIA SCOPARIA FORMA TRICHOPHYLLA 'CHILDSII'

FAST-DRAINING

ZONE	LATIN NAME
2	ACHILLEA MILLEFOLIUM 'ROSEA'
	ARTEMESIA STELLERIANA
	PAEONIA—HERBACEOUS HYBRIDS
	POTENTILLA TRIDENTATA
	SAPONARIA OFFICINALIS
3	ACER SACCHARUM
	ACHILLEA 'CORONATION GOLD'
	ACHILLEA 'MOONSHINE'
	ADIANTUM PEDATUM
	AEGOPODIUM PODAGRARIA 'VARIEGATUM'
	ARTEMESIA ABSINTHIUM 'LAMBROOK SILVER'
	ASCLEPIAS TUBEROSA
	ASTER AMELLUS 'NOCTURNE'
	ASTER TATARICUS
	BAPTISIA AUSTRALIS
	COREOPSIS 'MOONBEAM'
	CORNUS RACEMOSA
	CORNUS RACEMOSA (DWARF)
	DENNSTAEDTIA PUNCTILOBULA
	DIANTHUS DELTOIDES
	EUPHORBIA COROLLATA
	GERANIUM MACRORRHIZUM
	GERANIUM SANGUINEUM
	HIPPOPHAE RHAMNOIDES
	JUNIPERUS HORIZONTALIS 'WILTONII'
	JUNIPERUS VIRGINIANA
	LIATRIS SCARIOSA 'WHITE SPIRE'
	NEPETA X FAASSENII
	PAPAVER ORIENTALE
	PHLOX SUBULATA
	PHYSOSTEGIA VIRGINIANA

ZONE	LATIN NAME
	PHYSOSTEGIA VIRGINIANA 'SUMMER SNOW'
	PICEA PUNGENS 'HOOPSII'
	PINUS MUGO VAR. MUGO
	PRUNUS X CISTENA
	PTERIDIUM AQUILINUM VAR. LATIUSCULUM
	QUERCUS RUBRA
	RHUS AROMATICA 'GRO-LOW'
	RHUS TYPHINA
	RHUS TYPHINA 'LACINIATA'
	ROSA RUGOSA AND HYBRIDS
	SEDUM 'AUTUMN JOY'
	SEDUM ELLACOMBIANUM
	SEDUM SARMENTOSUM
	SEDUM SPURIUM
	SEDUM SPURIUM 'BRONZE CARPET'
	THERMOPSIS CAROLINIANA
	THYMUS SERPYLLUM
	VERONICA INCANA
	VIBURNUM ACERIFOLIUM
4	ACANTHOPANAX SIEBOLDIANUS
	ACER RUBRUM
	ALLIUM TUBEROSUM
	ARABIS PROCURRENS
	ARALIA SPINOSA
	ARTEMESIA LUDOVICIANA 'SILVER QUEEN'
	BERBERIS THUNBERGII 'CRIMSON PYGMY'
	BETULA LENTA
	BETULA NIGRA
	CARYA OVATA
	CARYOPTERIS X CLANDONENSIS 'BLUE MIST'
	CHAENOMELES JAPONICA VAR. ALPINA
	CHAENOMELES SPECIOSA CULTIVARS
	CHAENOMELES X SUPERBA 'JET TRAIL'
	CHAMAEMELUM NOBILE
	CLADRASTIS LUTEA
	CLEMATIS 'MRS. CHOLMONDELEY'
	CLEMATIS 'PRINS HENDRIK'
	CLEMATIS 'RAMONA'
	CLEMATIS MAXIMOWICZIANA
	CLEMATIS X JACKMANII
	COMPTONIA PEREGRINA
	CORYLUS AVELLANA 'CONTORTA'
	CORYLUS AVELLANA 'PENDULA'
	CRATAEGUS NITIDA
	CRATAEGUS PHAENOPYRUM
	DIERVILLA SESSILIFOLIA
	EUONYMUS ALATA
	EUONYMUS FORTUNEI 'COLORATA'
	EUPHORBIA CYPARISSIAS
	EUPHORBIA EPITHYMOIDES
	FAGUS GRANDIFOLIA
	GAULTHERIA PROCUMBENS
	GINKGO BILOBA, STAMINATE
	GLEDITSIA TRIACANTHOS VAR. INERMIS 'SHADEMASTER'
	GYMNOCLADUS DIOICA
	HAMAMELIS VIRGINIANA
	HELIOPSIS HELIANTHOIDES SUBSP. SCABRA 'KARAT'
	HEUCHERA 'PALACE PURPLE' STRAIN
	HYPERICUM KALMIANUM
	JUNIPERUS SABINA 'TAMARISCIFOLIA'
	JUNIPERUS X MEDIA 'PFITZERIANA COMPACTA'
	MICROBIOTA DECUSSATA
	MYRICA PENSYLVANICA
	PAEONIA TENUIFOLIA

ZONE	LATIN NAME
	PAXISTIMA CANBYI
	PHELLODENDRON AMURENSE
	PHLOX BIFIDA
	PINUS FLEXILIS
	PINUS KORAIENSIS
	POLYGONATUM ODORATUM 'VARIEGATUM'
	ROBINIA HISPIDA
	ROSA NITIDA
	SPIRAEA THUNBERGII
	STACHYS BYZANTINA
	SYRINGA PATULA (SYN. S. PALIBINIANA, S. MICROPHYLLA 'INGWERSEN'S DWARF')
	SYRINGA X CHINENSIS
	TAXUS CUSPIDATA 'NANA'
	TAXUS CUSPIDATA (CAPITATA SELECTION)
	VACCINIUM CORYMBOSUM
	VERONICA 'SUNNY BORDER BLUE'
	VERONICA LONGIFOLIA 'SUBSESSILIS'
	WALDSTEINIA TERNATA
	YUCCA FLACCIDA 'GOLDEN SWORD'
	YUCCA GLAUCA
	YUCCA SMALLIANA
5	ACER PALMATUM 'BLOODGOOD'
	ALLIUM CERNUUM
	ANEMONE X HYBRIDA 'QUEEN CHARLOTTE'
	ARTEMESIA VERSICOLOR
	ARUNDINARIA VIRIDISTRIATA
	ASPHODELINE LUTEA
	ASTER CORDIFOLIUS
	ASTER X FRIKARTII 'MONCH'
	BUDDLEIA DAVIDII 'BLACK KNIGHT'
	BUDDLEIA DAVIDII 'OPERA'
	BUDDLEIA DAVIDII 'PURPLE PRINCE'
	BUXUS 'GREEN GEM'
	BUXUS SINICA VAR. INSULARIS 'TIDE HILL'
	CAMPSIS X TAGLIABUANA 'MADAME GALEN'
	CATALPA BIGNONIOIDES
	CEPHALOTAXUS HARRINGTONIA VAR. PEDUNCULATA
	CERCIS CANADENSIS 'FOREST PANSY'
	CHAENOMELES X SUPERBA CULTIVARS
	CHIONANTHUS VIRGINICUS
	COLUTEA X MEDIA
	CORNUS FLORIDA
	CORNUS FLORIDA 'HOHMAN'S GOLDEN'
	CORNUS KOUSA
	CORNUS MAS
	CORNUS OFFICINALIS
	CORYLUS COLURNA
	COTINUS COGGYGRIA 'PURPUREUS'
	COTONEASTER ADPRESSUS 'LITTLE GEM'
	COTONEASTER APICULATUS
	COTONEASTER HORIZONTALIS
	CRATAEGUS VIRIDIS 'WINTER KING'
	CROCUS ANCYRENSIS 'GOLDEN BUNCH'
	CROCUS SIEBERI
	CROCUS TOMASINIANUS
	DAPHNE CAUCASICA
	DAPHNE X BURKWOODII 'CAROL MACKIE'
	EUONYMUS FORTUNEI 'GRACILIS'
	EUONYMUS FORTUNEI 'MINIMA'

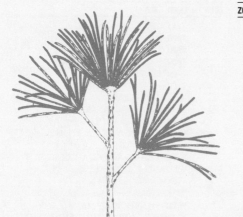

ZONE	LATIN NAME
	FORSYTHIA SUSPENSA
	GALIUM ODORATUM
	HELIANTHEMUM APENNINUM VAR. ROSEUM
	HELIANTHUS SALICIFOLIUS
	HEMEROCALLIS 'HYPERION'
	HERACLEUM MANTEGAZZIANUM
	HYPERICUM FRONDOSUM
	ILEX GLABRA 'DENSA'
	ILEX X AQUIPERNYI 'SAN JOSE'
	JUNIPERUS X MEDIA 'OLD GOLD'
	KOELREUTERIA PANICULATA
	KOLKWITZIA AMABILIS
	LAMIASTRUM GALEOBDOLON 'VARIEGATUM'
	LESPEDEZA THUNBERGII
	LEUCOTHOE FONTANESIANA
	LIGUSTRUM QUIHOUI
	LONICERA FRAGRANTISSIMA
	LYCORIS SPRENGERI
	LYCORIS SQUAMIGERA
	MISCANTHUS SINENSIS 'CABARET'
	MISCANTHUS SINENSIS 'GRACILLIMUS'
	MISCANTHUS SINENSIS 'MORNING LIGHT'
	MISCANTHUS SINENSIS 'VARIEGATUS'
	MUSCARI AZUREUM 'ALBUM'
	MUSCARI BOTRYOIDES 'ALBUM'
	MUSCARI TUBERGENIANUM
	OXYDENDRUM ARBOREUM
	PHILADELPHUS CORONARIUS
	PHILADELPHUS X FALCONERI
	PHLOMIS RUSSELIANA
	PHLOX STOLONIFERA 'ALBA'
	PHLOX STOLONIFERA 'BLUE RIDGE'
	PHLOX STOLONIFERA 'SHERWOOD PURPLE'
	PINUS BUNGEANA
	PINUS VIRGINIANA
	RHODODENDRON ATLANTICUM
	RHODODENDRON SCHLIPPENBACHII
	RHODODENDRON VASEYI
	RHODOTYPOS SCANDENS
	ROSA 'DOORENBOS SELECTION'
	ROSA (POLYANTHA) 'THE FAIRY'
	ROSA (SHRUB) 'SEA FOAM'
	ROSA CAROLINA
	ROSA VIRGINIANA
	SASSAFRAS ALBIDUM
	SCILLA SIBERICA 'SPRING BEAUTY'
	SEDUM FLORIFERUM 'WEIHANSTEPHANER GOLD'
	STEPHANANDRA INCISA 'CRISPA'

ZONE	LATIN NAME
	STERNBERGIA LUTEA
	STOKESIA LAEVIS 'BLUE DANUBE'
	SYMPHORICARPOS X CHENAULTII 'HANCOCK'
	SYRINGA LACINIATA
	SYRINGA RETICULATA
	TAXUS BACCATA 'ADPRESSA FOWLE'
	TAXUS BACCATA 'REPANDENS'
	TAXUS X MEDIA 'SENTINALIS'
	THELYPTERIS HEXAGONOPTERA
	THELYPTERIS NOVEBORACENSIS
	THELYPTERIS PHEGOPTERIS
	THYMUS 'CLEAR GOLD'
	THYMUS PSEUDOLANUGINOSUS
	VERBASCUM OLYMPICUM
	VIBURNUM PLICATUM FORMA TOMENTOSUM
	VIBURNUM SIEBOLDII 'SENECA'
	WISTERIA FLORIBUNDA
6	ABELIA X GRANDIFLORA
	ACER PALMATUM 'EVER RED'
	ACER PALMATUM VAR. DISSECTUM OR A. P. 'WATERFALL'
	BUXUS SEMPERVIRENS 'SUFFRUTICOSA'
	CALLICARPA DICHOTOMA
	CALOCEDRUS DECURRENS
	CERATOSTIGMA PLUMBAGINOIDES
	CERCIS CHINENSIS
	COTONEASTER ADPRESSUS VAR. PRAECOX
	CROCOSMIA 'LUCIFER'
	CROCOSMIA POTTSII
	CROCOSMIA X CROCOSMIIFLORA
	CRUCIANELLA STYLOSA
	CYTISUS SCOPARIUS
	CYTISUS X PRAECOX 'LUTEUS'
	EUONYMUS FORTUNEI 'SILVER QUEEN'
	EUPATORIUM COELESTINUM
	FORSYTHIA VIRIDISSIMA 'BRONXENSIS'
	FORSYTHIA X INTERMEDIA 'SPRING GLORY'
	GALTONIA CANDICANS
	HEDERA HELIX 'BALTICA'
	JUNIPERUS CHINENSIS 'KAIZUKA'
	LUZULA SYLVATICA 'MARGINATA'
	PAEONIA 'BLACK PIRATE'
	PAEONIA—WOODY HYBRIDS
	PARONYCHIA KAPELA SUBSP. SERPYLLIFOLIA
	PINUS THUNBERGIANA
	PINUS THUNBERGIANA 'OCULUS-DRACONIS'
	PONCIRUS TRIFOLIATA
	SALVIA ARGENTEA
	SCIADOPITYS VERTICILLATA
	SOPHORA JAPONICA 'REGENT'
	VITEX AGNUS-CASTUS 'LATIFOLIA'
	VITEX AGNUS-CASTUS 'SILVER SPIRE'
7	BUXUS MICROPHYLLA 'COMPACTA'
	CHIMONANTHUS PRAECOX
	GENISTA SYLVESTRIS 'LYDIA'
	HYDRANGEA ASPERA SUBSP. SARGENTIANA
	VIBURNUM MACROCEPHALUM FORMA MACROCEPHALUM
T	DATURA INOXIA SUBSP. QUINQUECUSPIDA

APPENDIX 5
Plant Listing by Light Preference

Plants in this list are divided as follows:

Full Sun
Partial Shade
Shade

Each of the above sections is subdivided by hardiness zone.

The letter *T* under the heading "Zone" indicates a plant that is tender, not tolerant of frost.

Further information about all the following plants can be found in the Master Lists, Appendices 1A and 1B.

FULL SUN

ZONE	LATIN NAME
2	ACHILLEA MILLEFOLIUM 'ROSEA'
	ARTEMESIA STELLERIANA
	ASTER PUNICEUS
	BETULA PAPYRIFERA
	PAEONIA—HERBACEOUS HYBRIDS
	POTENTILLA TRIDENTATA
	SAPONARIA OFFICINALIS
3	ACER SACCHARUM
	ACHILLEA 'CORONATION GOLD'
	ACHILLEA 'MOONSHINE'
	AMELANCHIER ARBOREA (SYN. A. CANADENSIS)
	AMSONIA TABERNAEMONTANA
	ARTEMESIA ABSINTHIUM 'LAMBROOK SILVER'
	ASCLEPIAS TUBEROSA
	ASTER AMELLUS 'NOCTURNE'
	ASTER TATARICUS
	BAPTISIA AUSTRALIS
	BETULA PENDULA 'GRACILIS'
	BETULA PENDULA 'YOUNGII'
	BOLTONIA ASTEROIDES 'SNOWBANK'
	BUPHTHALUM SALICIFOLIUM
	CHELONE LYONII
	COREOPSIS 'MOONBEAM'
	CORNUS ALBA 'ELEGANTISSIMA'
	CORNUS ALBA 'SPAETHII'
	CORNUS RACEMOSA
	CORNUS RACEMOSA (DWARF)
	CORNUS SERICEA
	CORNUS SERICEA 'FLAVIRAMEA'
	DENNSTAEDTIA PUNCTILOBULA
	DIANTHUS DELTOIDES
	ECHINACEA PURPUREA
	ECHINOPS RITRO
	EUPHORBIA COROLLATA
	GERANIUM SANGUINEUM
	HEMEROCALLIS LILIOASPHODELUS
	HIPPOPHAE RHAMNOIDES
	INULA HELENIUM
	IRIS SIBIRICA CULTIVARS
	JUNIPERUS HORIZONTALIS 'WILTONII'
	JUNIPERUS VIRGINIANA
	LIATRIS SCARIOSA 'WHITE SPIRE'
	LIATRIS SPICATA 'KOBOLD'
	LYSIMACHIA CLETHROIDES

ZONE	LATIN NAME
	LYTHRUM SALICARIA 'DROPMORE PURPLE'
	MALUS 'RED JADE'
	NEPETA X FAASSENII
	PAPAVER ORIENTALE
	PHLOX SUBULATA
	PHYSOSTEGIA VIRGINIANA
	PHYSOSTEGIA VIRGINIANA 'SUMMER SNOW'
	PICEA ABIES 'NIDIFORMIS'
	PICEA PUNGENS 'HOOPSII'
	PINUS MUGO VAR. MUGO
	PINUS STROBUS
	PINUS STROBUS 'FASTIGIATA'
	PRUNUS X CISTENA
	PSEUDOTSUGA MENZIESII
	PTERIDIUM AQUILINUM VAR. LATIUSCULUM
	QUERCUS RUBRA
	RHODODENDRON PRINOPHYLLUM
	RHUS AROMATICA 'GRO-LOW'
	RHUS TYPHINA
	RHUS TYPHINA 'LACINIATA'
	ROSA RUGOSA AND HYBRIDS
	RUDBECKIA FULGIDA VAR. SULLIVANTII 'GOLDSTURM'
	SALIX ALBA 'KALMTHOUT'
	SALIX ALBA 'REGALIS'
	SALIX ALBA 'SERICEA'
	SEDUM 'AUTUMN JOY'
	SEDUM ELLACOMBIANUM
	SEDUM SARMENTOSUM
	SEDUM SPURIUM
	SEDUM SPURIUM 'BRONZE CARPET'
	SORBARIA SORBIFOLIA
	SPIRAEA X VANHOUTTEI
	SYRINGA VULGARIS 'ALBA'
	SYRINGA VULGARIS HYBRIDS
	TELEKIA SPECIOSA
	THERMOPSIS CAROLINIANA
	THUJA OCCIDENTALIS 'NIGRA'
	THYMUS SERPYLLUM
	TILIA CORDATA
	TSUGA CANADENSIS
	TSUGA CANADENSIS 'BENNETT'
	TSUGA CANADENSIS 'COLE'S PROSTRATE'
	TSUGA CANADENSIS 'PENDULA'
	VERONICA INCANA
	VERONICASTRUM VIRGINICUM
	VIBURNUM PRUNIFOLIUM
4	ACANTHOPANAX SIEBOLDIANUS
	ACER PLATANOIDES 'CRIMSON KING'
	ACER RUBRUM
	AJUGA REPTANS
	AJUGA REPTANS 'BRONZE BEAUTY'
	AJUGA REPTANS (GIANT FORM)
	ALLIUM TUBEROSUM
	ANEMONE VITIFOLIA 'ROBUSTISSIMA'
	ARABIS PROCURRENS
	ARALIA SPINOSA
	ARONIA ARBUTIFOLIA 'BRILLIANTISSIMA'
	ARTEMESIA LUDOVICIANA 'SILVER QUEEN'
	ARUNCUS AETHUSIFOLIUS
	ASTILBE X ARENDSII CULTIVARS
	BACCHARIS HALIMIFOLIA, PISTILLATE
	BERBERIS THUNBERGII 'ATROPURPUREA'
	BERBERIS THUNBERGII 'CRIMSON PYGMY'
	BETULA LENTA

ZONE	LATIN NAME
	BETULA NIGRA
	BUDDLEIA ALTERNIFOLIA
	CARYA OVATA
	CARYOPTERIS X CLANDONENSIS 'BLUE MIST'
	CEPHALANTHUS OCCIDENTALIS
	CHAENOMELES JAPONICA VAR. ALPINA
	CHAENOMELES SPECIOSA CULTIVARS
	CHAENOMELES X SUPERBA 'JET TRAIL'
	CHAMAEMELUM NOBILE
	CLADRASTIS LUTEA
	CLEMATIS 'MRS. CHOLMONDELEY'
	CLEMATIS 'PRINS HENDRIK'
	CLEMATIS 'RAMONA'
	CLEMATIS MAXIMOWICZIANA
	CLEMATIS X JACKMANII
	COMPTONIA PEREGRINA
	CORNUS ALTERNIFOLIA
	CORYLUS AVELLANA 'CONTORTA'
	CORYLUS AVELLANA 'PENDULA'
	CRATAEGUS NITIDA
	CRATAEGUS PHAENOPYRUM
	DIERVILLA SESSILIFOLIA
	EUONYMUS ALATA
	EUONYMUS FORTUNEI 'COLORATA'
	EUONYMUS FORTUNEI VAR. RADICANS
	EUPHORBIA CYPARISSIAS
	FAGUS GRANDIFOLIA
	GINKGO BILOBA, STAMINATE
	GLEDITSIA TRIACANTHOS VAR. INERMIS 'SHADEMASTER'
	GYMNOCLADUS DIOICA
	HEDYOTIS CAERULEA
	HELIOPSIS HELIANTHOIDES SUBSP. SCABRA 'KARAT'
	HYDRANGEA PANICULATA
	HYPERICUM KALMIANUM
	ILEX VERTICILLATA
	ILEX VERTICILLATA 'WINTER RED'
	JUNIPERUS SABINA 'TAMARISCIFOLIA'
	JUNIPERUS X MEDIA 'PFITZERIANA COMPACTA'
	MALUS FLORIBUNDA
	MALUS HUPEHENSIS
	MALUS SARGENTII
	MICROBIOTA DECUSSATA
	MONARDA DIDYMA
	MYRICA PENSYLVANICA
	PAEONIA TENUIFOLIA
	PHALARIS ARUNDINACEA VAR. PICTA
	PHELLODENDRON AMURENSE
	PHLOX BIFIDA
	PINUS FLEXILIS
	PINUS KORAIENSIS
	QUERCUS ALBA
	QUERCUS MACROCARPA
	RHODODENDRON (CATAWBIENSE HYBRIDS)
	RHODODENDRON VISCOSUM
	ROBINIA HISPIDA
	RODGERSIA PODOPHYLLA
	RODGERSIA TABULARIS
	ROSA NITIDA
	SALIX ALBA VAR. TRISTIS
	SALIX ELAEAGNOS
	SALIX REPENS VAR. ARGENTEA
	SEDUM POPULIFOLIUM
	SPIRAEA THUNBERGII
	STACHYS BYZANTINA
	SYRINGA PATULA (SYN. S. PALIBINIANA, S. MICROPHYLLA 'INGWERSEN'S DWARF')

ZONE	LATIN NAME
	SYRINGA X CHINENSIS
	TAMARIX RAMOSISSIMA
	TAXUS CUSPIDATA 'NANA'
	TAXUS CUSPIDATA (CAPITATA SELECTION)
	THUJA OCCIDENTALIS 'HETZ' WINTERGREEN'
	TYPHA ANGUSTIFOLIA
	VACCINIUM CORYMBOSUM
	VERNONIA NOVEBORACENSIS
	VERONICA 'SUNNY BORDER BLUE'
	VERONICA LONGIFOLIA 'SUBSESSILIS'
	VIBURNUM CARLESII
	VINCA MINOR 'BOWLESII'
	VINCA MINOR 'VARIEGATA'
	WALDSTEINIA TERNATA
	YUCCA FLACCIDA 'GOLDEN SWORD'
	YUCCA GLAUCA
	YUCCA SMALLIANA
5	ABIES NORDMANNIANA
	ACER GRISEUM
	ACER PALMATUM 'BLOODGOOD'
	ACER PALMATUM 'SANGOKAKU'
	AESCULUS PARVIFLORA
	ALLIUM CERNUUM
	ALLIUM ZEBDANENSE
	AMSONIA HUBRICHTII
	ANEMONE X HYBRIDA 'QUEEN CHARLOTTE'
	ARTEMESIA VERSICOLOR
	ARUNDINARIA VIRIDISTRIATA
	ASPHODELINE LUTEA
	ASTER X FRIKARTII 'MONCH'
	BUDDLEIA DAVIDII 'BLACK KNIGHT'
	BUDDLEIA DAVIDII 'OPERA'
	BUDDLEIA DAVIDII 'PURPLE PRINCE'
	BUXUS 'GREEN GEM'
	BUXUS SINICA VAR. INSULARIS 'TIDE HILL'
	BUXUS SINICA VAR. INSULARIS 'WINTERGREEN' (OHIO CULTIVAR)
	CALAMAGROSTIS X ACUTIFLORA 'KARL FOERSTER' (SYN. C. EPIGEOUS 'HORTORUM')
	CALLICARPA JAPONICA
	CALYCANTHUS FLORIDUS 'EDITH WILDER'
	CAMPSIS X TAGLIABUANA 'MADAME GALEN'
	CARPINUS BETULUS
	CATALPA BIGNONIOIDES
	CEDRUS LIBANI VAR. STENOCOMA
	CERCIDIPHYLLUM JAPONICUM
	CERCIS CANADENSIS 'FOREST PANSY'
	CHAENOMELES X SUPERBA CULTIVARS
	CHAMAECYPARIS OBTUSA 'FILICOIDES'
	CHAMAECYPARIS OBTUSA 'NANA GRACILIS'
	CHAMAECYPARIS OBTUSA 'NANA'
	CHAMAECYPARIS OBTUSA VAR. BREVIRAMEA
	CHAMAECYPARIS PISIFERA 'GOLD SPANGLE'
	CHAMAECYPARIS PISIFERA 'SQUARROSA'
	CHIONANTHUS VIRGINICUS
	CHRYSANTHEMUM WEYRICHII 'WHITE BOMB'
	CLETHRA ALNIFOLIA
	COLCHICUM 'AUTUMN QUEEN'
	COLCHICUM 'THE GIANT'
	COLUTEA X MEDIA

ZONE	LATIN NAME

CORNUS FLORIDA
CORNUS FLORIDA 'HOHMAN'S GOLDEN'
CORNUS KOUSA
CORNUS MAS
CORNUS OFFICINALIS
CORYLOPSIS PLATYPETALA
CORYLUS COLURNA
COTINUS COGGYGRIA 'PURPUREUS'
COTONEASTER ADPRESSUS 'LITTLE GEM'
COTONEASTER APICULATUS
COTONEASTER HORIZONTALIS
CRAMBE CORDIFOLIA
CRATAEGUS VIRIDIS 'WINTER KING'
CROCUS ANCYRENSIS 'GOLDEN BUNCH'
CROCUS SIEBERI
CROCUS TOMASINIANUS
DAPHNE CAUCASICA
DAPHNE X BURKWOODII 'CAROL MACKIE'
DEUTZIA GRACILIS
DIOSPYROS VIRGINIANA
ENKIANTHUS CAMPANULATUS
EQUISETUM HYEMALE
ERIANTHUS RAVENNAE
EUONYMUS FORTUNEI 'GRACILIS'
EUONYMUS FORTUNEI 'MINIMA'
EXOCHORDA GIRALDII VAR. WILSONII
FAGUS SYLVATICA 'LACINIATA'
FAGUS SYLVATICA 'PENDULA'
FAGUS SYLVATICA 'RIVERSII'
FILIPENDULA PURPUREA 'NANA'
FORSYTHIA SUSPENSA
FOTHERGILLA GARDENII
GALANTHUS ELWESII
GALIUM ODORATUM
HALESIA TETRAPTERA
HAMAMELIS MOLLIS 'PALLIDA'
HAMAMELIS X INTERMEDIA 'DIANE'
HAMAMELIS X INTERMEDIA 'JELENA'
HAMAMELIS X INTERMEDIA 'PRIMAVERA'
HEDERA HELIX 'BULGARIA'
HEDERA HELIX 'OGALALLA'
HELIANTHEMUM APENNINUM VAR. ROSEUM
HELIANTHUS SALICIFOLIUS
HELICTOTRICHON SEMPERVIRENS
HEMEROCALLIS 'HYPERION'
HEMEROCALLIS FULVA 'EUROPA'
HERACLEUM MANTEGAZZIANUM
HIBISCUS SYRIACUS 'BLUEBIRD'
HIBISCUS SYRIACUS 'DIANA'
HYDRANGEA ANOMALA SUBSP. PETIOLARIS 'SKYLANDS GIANT'
HYDRANGEA QUERCIFOLIA
HYPERICUM FRONDOSUM
ILEX CHINA BOY ® 'MESDOB'
ILEX CHINA GIRL ® 'MESOG'
ILEX GLABRA 'DENSA'
ILEX X AQUIPERNYI 'SAN JOSE'
ILEX X MESERVEAE BLUE MAID ® 'MESID'
ILEX X MESERVEAE BLUE STALLION ® 'MESAN'
INDIGOFERA INCARNATA 'ALBA'
IRIS GRAMINEA
IRIS PSEUDACORUS
IRIS TECTORUM
JUNIPERUS SCOPULORUM 'SKY ROCKET'

JUNIPERUS X MEDIA 'OLD GOLD'
KALMIA LATIFOLIA
KERRIA JAPONICA
KOELREUTERIA PANICULATA
KOLKWITZIA AMABILIS
LAMIUM MACULATUM 'WHITE NANCY'
LESPEDEZA THUNBERGII
LIGUSTRUM QUIHOUI
LILIUM 'BLACK DRAGON'
LILIUM SPECIES AND HYBRIDS
LIQUIDAMBAR STYRACIFLUA
LONICERA FRAGRANTISSIMA
LYCORIS SPRENGERI
LYCORIS SQUAMIGERA
LYSICHITON AMERICANUM
LYSICHITON CAMTSCHATCENSE
LYSIMACHIA PUNCTATA
MAGNOLIA 'ELIZABETH'
MAGNOLIA VIRGINIANA
MAGNOLIA X LOEBNERI
MAGNOLIA X SOULANGIANA 'VERBANICA'
METASEQUOIA GLYPTOSTROBOIDES
MISCANTHUS 'GIGANTEUS'
MISCANTHUS SINENSIS 'CABARET'
MISCANTHUS SINENSIS 'GRACILLIMUS'
MISCANTHUS SINENSIS 'MORNING LIGHT'
MISCANTHUS SINENSIS 'SILVER FEATHER' (='SILBERFEDER')
MISCANTHUS SINENSIS 'STRICTUS'
MISCANTHUS SINENSIS 'VARIEGATUS'
MOLINIA CAERULEA SUBSP. ARUNDINACEA
NARCISSUS 'CARLTON'
NARCISSUS 'FORTUNE'
NARCISSUS 'HERA'
NARCISSUS 'LOCH FYNE'
NARCISSUS 'MOONMIST'
NARCISSUS 'MRS. ERNST H. KRELAGE'
NARCISSUS 'PEEPING TOM'
NARCISSUS 'POMONA'
NARCISSUS 'QUEEN OF SPAIN'
NARCISSUS 'TREVITHIAN'
NARCISSUS JONQUILLA
NARCISSUS PSEUDONARCISSUS SUBSP. OBVALLARIS
NYSSA SYLVATICA
ONOPORDUM ACANTHIUM
OXYDENDRUM ARBOREUM
PANICUM VIRGATUM 'STRICTUM'
PENNISETUM ALOPECUROIDES
PEROVSKIA ABROTANOIDES X P. ATRIPLICIFOLIA
PETASITES FRAGRANS
PHILADELPHUS CORONARIUS
PHILADELPHUS X FALCONERI
PHLOMIS RUSSELIANA
PHLOX PILOSA SUBSP. OZARKANA
PICEA ORIENTALIS
PINUS BUNGEANA
PINUS DENSIFLORA 'UMBRACULIFERA'
PINUS PARVIFLORA 'GLAUCA'
PINUS VIRGINIANA
PLATANUS OCCIDENTALIS
PRUNUS 'HALLY JOLIVETTE'
PRUNUS CERASIFERA 'THUNDERCLOUD'
PRUNUS SUBHIRTELLA 'AUTUMNALIS'
RHEUM PALMATUM 'RUBRUM'
RHODODENDRON (GABLE HYBRIDS)
RHODODENDRON ARBORESCENS

RHODODENDRON ATLANTICUM
RHODODENDRON SCHLIPPENBACHII
RHODODENDRON VASEYI
RHODODENDRON X GANDAVENSE 'COCCINEA SPECIOSA'
RHODODENDRON X GANDAVENSE 'DAVIESII'
RHODOTYPOS SCANDENS
RIBES ODORATUM
ROSA 'DOORENBOS SELECTION'
ROSA (GALLICA) 'CHARLES DE MILLS'
ROSA (POLYANTHA) 'THE FAIRY'
ROSA (SHRUB) 'LILLIAN GIBSON'
ROSA (SHRUB) 'SEA FOAM'
ROSA CAROLINA
ROSA EGLANTERIA
ROSA VIRGINIANA
RUBUS COCKBURNIANUS
SAGINA SUBULATA
SALIX 'HAKURO'
SALIX ACUTIFOLIA 'LONGIFOLIA'
SALIX CHAENOMELOIDES
SALIX DAPHNOIDES 'AGLAIA'
SALIX GRACILISTYLA
SALIX GRACILISTYLA 'MELANOSTACHYS'
SALIX X RUBRA 'EUGENEI'
SASSAFRAS ALBIDUM
SEDUM 'VERA JAMISON'
SEDUM FLORIFERUM 'WEIHANSTEPHANER GOLD'
SPIRAEA PRUNIFOLIA
STEPHANANDRA INCISA 'CRISPA'
STERNBERGIA LUTEA
STOKESIA LAEVIS 'BLUE DANUBE'
SYMPHORICARPOS X CHENAULTII 'HANCOCK'
SYMPHYTUM X UPLANDICUM
SYRINGA LACINIATA
SYRINGA RETICULATA
TAXUS BACCATA 'ADPRESSA FOWLE'
TAXUS BACCATA 'REPANDENS'
TAXUS X MEDIA 'SENTINALIS'
THUJA PLICATA 'ATROVIRENS'
THYMUS 'CLEAR GOLD'
THYMUS PSEUDOLANUGINOSUS
VALERIANA OFFICINALIS
VERBASCUM OLYMPICUM
VIBURNUM DILATATUM 'MICHAEL DODGE'
VIBURNUM FARRERI 'CANDIDISSIMUM'
VIBURNUM FARRERI 'NANUM'
VIBURNUM PLICATUM FORMA TOMENTOSUM
VIBURNUM SIEBOLDII 'SENECA'
WISTERIA FLORIBUNDA
XANTHORHIZA SIMPLICISSIMA

6
ABELIA X GRANDIFLORA
ACER PALMATUM 'EVER RED'
ACER PALMATUM VAR. DISSECTUM OR A. P. 'WATERFALL'
ACORUS GRAMINEUS 'OGON'
ADINA RUBELLA
AESCULUS SPLENDENS
ARUM ITALICUM 'PICTUM'
ARUNDO DONAX
BERBERIS JULIANAE 'NANA'
BERBERIS WISLEYENSIS (SYN. B. TRIACANTHOPHORA)
BIGNONIA CAPREOLATA
BUXUS SEMPERVIRENS 'SUFFRUTICOSA'
CALLICARPA DICHOTOMA

ZONE	LATIN NAME
	CALOCEDRUS DECURRENS
	CERATOSTIGMA PLUMBAGINOIDES
	CERCIS CHINENSIS
	CHAMAECYPARIS OBTUSA 'CRIPPSII'
	CLETHRA BARBINERVIS
	COTONEASTER ADPRESSUS VAR. PRAECOX
	COTONEASTER SALICIFOLIUS VAR. FLOCCOSUS
	CROCOSMIA 'LUCIFER'
	CROCOSMIA POTTSII
	CROCOSMIA X CROCOSMIIFLORA
	CRUCIANELLA STYLOSA
	CYTISUS SCOPARIUS
	CYTISUS X PRAECOX 'LUTEUS'
	ENKIANTHUS PERULATUS
	EUONYMUS FORTUNEI 'SILVER QUEEN'
	EUPATORIUM COELESTINUM
	FORSYTHIA VIRIDISSIMA 'BRONXENSIS'
	FORSYTHIA X INTERMEDIA 'SPRING GLORY'
	FRANKLINIA ALATAMAHA
	GALTONIA CANDICANS
	HEDERA HELIX 'BALTICA'
	HEDERA HELIX 'BUTTERCUP'
	HEDERA HELIX 'GOLD HEART'
	HYDRANGEA MACROPHYLLA 'BLUE BILLOW'
	ILEX CRENATA 'HELLERI'
	ILEX CRENATA 'MICROPHYLLA'
	ILEX OPACA 'ARDEN'
	ILEX OPACA 'XANTHOCARPA'
	IMPERATA CYLINDRICA 'RED BARON'
	ITEA VIRGINICA 'HENRY'S GARNET'
	JASMINUM NUDIFLORUM
	JUNIPERUS CHINENSIS 'KAIZUKA'
	LESPEDEZA THUNBERGII 'ALBIFLORA'
	MAGNOLIA 'SUSAN'
	MAGNOLIA DENUDATA (SYN. M. HEPTAPETA)
	MAGNOLIA MACROPHYLLA
	MAHONIA BEALEI
	PAEONIA 'BLACK PIRATE'
	PAEONIA—WOODY HYBRIDS
	PARONYCHIA KAPELA SUBSP. SERPYLLIFOLIA
	PAULOWNIA TOMENTOSA
	PHYLLOSTACHYS AUREOSULCATA
	PINUS THUNBERGIANA
	PINUS THUNBERGIANA 'OCULUS-DRACONIS'
	PONCIRUS TRIFOLIATA
	PRUNUS SUBHIRTELLA 'PENDULA'
	PRUNUS YEDOENSIS
	PSEUDOLARIX KAEMPFERI
	QUERCUS PHELLOS
	RHODODENDRON (GLENN DALE HYBRIDS)
	RHODODENDRON (KNAP HILL HYBRID) 'TUNIS'
	RHODODENDRON (KURUME HYBRIDS)
	RHODODENDRON X ERIOCARPUM AND R. X NAKAHARAI CULTIVARS AND HYBRIDS
	ROSA ROXBURGHII
	RUBUS IDAEUS 'AUREUS'
	SALVIA ARGENTEA
	SCIADOPITYS VERTICILLATA
	SOPHORA JAPONICA 'REGENT'
	STEWARTIA KOREANA
	STRANVAESIA DAVIDIANA VAR. UNDULATA 'PROSTRATA'
	STYRAX JAPONICUS

ZONE	LATIN NAME
	STYRAX JAPONICUS 'CARILLON'
	TAXODIUM DISTICHUM VAR. NUTANS 'PRAIRIE SENTINEL'
	VIBURNUM ICHANGENSE
	VIBURNUM NUDUM 'WINTERTHUR'
	VIBURNUM SETIGERUM
	VITEX AGNUS-CASTUS 'LATIFOLIA'
	VITEX AGNUS-CASTUS 'SILVER SPIRE'
	ZELKOVA SERRATA 'GREEN VASE'
7	BERBERIS WILSONIAE VAR. STAPFIANA
	BUXUS MICROPHYLLA 'COMPACTA'
	CEDRUS ATLANTICA 'GLAUCA'
	CHIMONANTHUS PRAECOX
	CLERODENDRUM TRICHOTOMUM
	DIOSPYROS KAKI
	ELAEAGNUS PUNGENS 'FRUITLANDII'
	ELAEAGNUS PUNGENS 'MACULATA'
	GENISTA SYLVESTRIS 'LYDIA'
	HEDERA COLCHICA 'DENTATA'
	HEDERA HELIX 'ERECTA'
	PYRACANTHA COCCINEA 'AUREA'
	SASA VEITCHII
	VIBURNUM MACROCEPHALUM FORMA MACROCEPHALUM
8	COTULA SQUALIDA
T	ACIDANTHERA BICOLOR
	CANNA X GENERALIS 'MOHAWK'
	CESTRUM NOCTURNUM
	DATURA INOXIA SUBSP. QUINQUECUSPIDA
	KOCHIA SCOPARIA FORMA TRICHOPHYLLA 'CHILDSII'
	POLIANTHES TUBEROSA
	RICINUS COMMUNIS
	RICINUS COMMUNIS 'ZANZIBARENSIS'

PARTIAL SHADE

ZONE	LATIN NAME
2	ASTER PUNICEUS
	BERGENIA 'PERFECTA'
	BERGENIA 'SUNNINGDALE'
	DICENTRA SPECTABILIS
	PAEONIA—HERBACEOUS HYBRIDS
	SAPONARIA OFFICINALIS
3	AEGOPODIUM PODAGRARIA 'VARIEGATUM'
	ALCHEMILLA VULGARIS
	AMELANCHIER ARBOREA (SYN. A. CANADENSIS)
	AMSONIA TABERNAEMONTANA
	ARUNCUS DIOICUS
	BETULA PENDULA 'GRACILIS'
	BETULA PENDULA 'YOUNGII'
	BRUNNERA MACROPHYLLA
	BUPHTHALUM SALICIFOLIUM
	CAMPANULA RAPUNCULOIDES
	CHELONE LYONII
	CIMICIFUGA RACEMOSA
	CLEMATIS HERACLEIFOLIA VAR. DAVIDIANA
	CORNUS ALBA 'ELEGANTISSIMA'
	CORNUS ALBA 'SPAETHII'
	CORNUS RACEMOSA
	CORNUS RACEMOSA (DWARF)
	DENNSTAEDTIA PUNCTILOBULA
	DICENTRA 'LUXURIANT'

ZONE	LATIN NAME
	DICENTRA EXIMIA 'PURITY'
	ECHINACEA PURPUREA
	EUPHORBIA COROLLATA
	FILIPENDULA ULMARIA 'AUREA'
	GERANIUM 'JOHNSON'S BLUE'
	GERANIUM MACRORRHIZUM
	GERANIUM SANGUINEUM
	HELLEBORUS NIGER
	HEMEROCALLIS LILIOASPHODELUS
	HOSTA 'KABITAN'
	HOSTA PLANTAGINEA
	HOSTA SIEBOLDIANA 'ELEGANS'
	HOSTA UNDULATA
	HOSTA VENTRICOSA
	INULA HELENIUM
	LYSIMACHIA CLETHROIDES
	LYTHRUM SALICARIA 'DROPMORE PURPLE'
	MACLEAYA CORDATA
	PHYSOSTEGIA VIRGINIANA
	PHYSOSTEGIA VIRGINIANA 'SUMMER SNOW'
	POLYSTICHUM ACROSTICHOIDES
	PTERIDIUM AQUILINUM VAR. LATIUSCULUM
	PULMONARIA ANGUSTIFOLIA
	PULMONARIA SACCHARATA 'MARGERY FISH'
	PULMONARIA SACCHARATA 'SISSINGHURST WHITE'
	SEDUM 'AUTUMN JOY'
	SEDUM ELLACOMBIANUM
	SEDUM SARMENTOSUM
	SEDUM SPURIUM
	SEDUM SPURIUM 'BRONZE CARPET'
	SORBARIA SORBIFOLIA
	THYMUS SERPYLLUM
	TIARELLA CORDIFOLIA VAR. COLLINA
	TSUGA CANADENSIS
	TSUGA CANADENSIS 'BENNETT'
	TSUGA CANADENSIS 'COLE'S PROSTRATE'
	TSUGA CANADENSIS 'PENDULA'
	VERONICA INCANA
	VIBURNUM ACERIFOLIUM
	VIBURNUM PRUNIFOLIUM
4	ACANTHOPANAX SIEBOLDIANUS
	AJUGA REPTANS
	AJUGA REPTANS 'BRONZE BEAUTY'
	AJUGA REPTANS (GIANT FORM)
	ANEMONE VITIFOLIA 'ROBUSTISSIMA'
	ARABIS PROCURRENS
	ARALIA SPINOSA
	ARENARIA VERNA
	ARUNCUS AETHUSIFOLIUS
	ASTILBE X ARENDSII CULTIVARS
	CEPHALANTHUS OCCIDENTALIS
	CLEMATIS 'MRS. CHOLMONDELEY'
	CLEMATIS 'PRINS HENDRIK'
	CLEMATIS 'RAMONA'
	CLEMATIS X JACKMANII
	CONVALLARIA MAJALIS
	CORNUS ALTERNIFOLIA
	EUONYMUS ALATA
	GAULTHERIA PROCUMBENS
	HAMAMELIS VIRGINIANA
	HELIOPSIS HELIANTHOIDES SUBSP. SCABRA 'KARAT'
	HELLEBORUS ORIENTALIS HYBRIDS
	HEUCHERA 'PALACE PURPLE' STRAIN
	MICROBIOTA DECUSSATA
	MONARDA DIDYMA

ZONE	LATIN NAME
	OSMUNDA CINNAMOMEA
	OSMUNDA CLAYTONIANA
	PACHYSANDRA PROCUMBENS
	PAEONIA TENUIFOLIA
	PAXISTIMA CANBYI
	PETASITES JAPONICUS
	PHALARIS ARUNDINACEA VAR. PICTA
	POLYGONATUM ODORATUM 'VARIEGATUM'
	RHODODENDRON (CATAWBIENSE HYBRIDS)
	RHODODENDRON MAXIMUM
	RHODODENDRON VISCOSUM
	RODGERSIA AESCULIFOLIA
	RODGERSIA PODOPHYLLA
	RODGERSIA TABULARIS
	SEDUM POPULIFOLIUM
	SEDUM TERNATUM
	TAXUS CUSPIDATA 'NANA'
	TAXUS CUSPIDATA (CAPITATA SELECTION)
	TYPHA ANGUSTIFOLIA
	VACCINIUM CORYMBOSUM
	VERONICA 'SUNNY BORDER BLUE'
	VERONICA LONGIFOLIA 'SUBSESSILIS'
	VINCA MINOR 'BOWLESII'
	VINCA MINOR 'VARIEGATA'
	VIOLA LABRADORICA
	WALDSTEINIA TERNATA
5	ACER PALMATUM 'BLOODGOOD'
	AESCULUS PARVIFLORA
	ALLIUM ZEBDANENSE
	ANEMONE BLANDA 'ATROCAERULEA'
	ANEMONE X HYBRIDA 'QUEEN CHARLOTTE'
	ARUNDINARIA VIRIDISTRIATA
	ASARUM EUROPAEUM
	ASTER CORDIFOLIUS
	ASTER X FRIKARTII 'MONCH'
	ATHYRIUM GOERINGIANUM 'PICTUM'
	BUXUS 'GREEN GEM'
	BUXUS SINICA VAR. INSULARIS 'TIDE HILL'
	BUXUS SINICA VAR. INSULARIS 'WINTERGREEN' (OHIO CULTIVAR)
	CALYCANTHUS FLORIDUS 'EDITH WILDER'
	CEPHALOTAXUS HARRINGTONIA VAR. PEDUNCULATA
	CHIONODOXA GIGANTEA 'ALBA'
	CHIONODOXA LUCILIAE
	CHIONODOXA SARDENSIS
	COLCHICUM 'AUTUMN QUEEN'
	COLCHICUM 'THE GIANT'
	CORNUS FLORIDA
	CORNUS FLORIDA 'HOHMAN'S GOLDEN'
	CORNUS MAS
	CORNUS OFFICINALIS
	CORYLOPSIS PLATYPETALA
	CRAMBE CORDIFOLIA
	CROCUS ANCYRENSIS 'GOLDEN BUNCH'
	CROCUS SIEBERI
	CROCUS TOMASINIANUS
	CYCLAMEN HEDERIFOLIUM
	DAPHNE CAUCASICA
	DEUTZIA GRACILIS
	DIPLAZIUM CONILII
	ENDYMION HISPANICUS 'EXCELSIOR' (SYN. SCILLA CAMPANULATA 'EXCELSIOR')

ZONE	LATIN NAME
	ENKIANTHUS CAMPANULATUS
	EPIMEDIUM PINNATUM SUBSP. COLCHICUM
	EPIMEDIUM X YOUNGIANUM 'NIVEUM'
	ERANTHIS HYEMALIS
	ERANTHIS X TUBERGENII
	EUONYMUS FORTUNEI 'GRACILIS'
	FILIPENDULA PURPUREA 'NANA'
	FOTHERGILLA GARDENII
	GALANTHUS NIVALIS
	GALIUM ODORATUM
	HALESIA TETRAPTERA
	HAMAMELIS MOLLIS 'PALLIDA'
	HAMAMELIS X INTERMEDIA 'DIANE'
	HAMAMELIS X INTERMEDIA 'JELENA'
	HAMAMELIS X INTERMEDIA 'PRIMAVERA'
	HEDERA HELIX 'BULGARIA'
	HEDERA HELIX 'OGALALLA'
	HELICTOTRICHON SEMPERVIRENS
	HEMEROCALLIS 'HYPERION'
	HEMEROCALLIS FULVA 'EUROPA'
	HOUTTUYNIA CORDATA 'CHAMELEON'
	HYDRANGEA ANOMALA SUBSP. PETIOLARIS 'SKYLANDS GIANT'
	HYDRANGEA QUERCIFOLIA
	ILEX X AQUIPERNYI 'SAN JOSE'
	INDIGOFERA INCARNATA 'ALBA'
	IRIS CRISTATA
	IRIS TECTORUM
	KALMIA LATIFOLIA
	KERRIA JAPONICA
	KIRENGESHOMA PALMATA
	LAMIASTRUM GALEOBDOLON 'VARIEGATUM'
	LAMIUM MACULATUM 'WHITE NANCY'
	LATHYRUS VERNUS
	LEUCOJUM VERNUM
	LEUCOTHOE FONTANESIANA
	LEUCOTHOE FONTANESIANA 'NANA'
	LIGUSTRUM QUIHOUI
	LILIUM 'BLACK DRAGON'
	LILIUM SPECIES AND HYBRIDS
	LYCORIS SPRENGERI
	LYCORIS SQUAMIGERA
	LYSICHITON AMERICANUM
	LYSICHITON CAMTSCHATCENSE
	LYSIMACHIA PUNCTATA
	MERTENSIA VIRGINICA
	MISCANTHUS SINENSIS 'CABARET'
	MISCANTHUS SINENSIS 'GRACILLIMUS'
	MISCANTHUS SINENSIS 'MORNING LIGHT'
	MISCANTHUS SINENSIS 'STRICTUS'
	MISCANTHUS SINENSIS 'VARIEGATUS'
	MUSCARI AZUREUM 'ALBUM'
	MUSCARI BOTRYOIDES 'ALBUM'
	MUSCARI TUBERGENIANUM
	NARCISSUS 'CARLTON'
	NARCISSUS 'FORTUNE'
	NARCISSUS 'HERA'
	NARCISSUS 'LOCH FYNE'
	NARCISSUS 'MOONMIST'
	NARCISSUS 'MRS. ERNST H. KRELAGE'
	NARCISSUS 'PEEPING TOM'
	NARCISSUS 'POMONA'
	NARCISSUS 'QUEEN OF SPAIN'
	NARCISSUS 'TREVITHIAN'
	NARCISSUS JONQUILLA
	NARCISSUS PSEUDONARCISSUS SUBSP. OBVALLARIS
	OMPHALODES VERNA

ZONE	LATIN NAME
	PACHYSANDRA TERMINALIS
	PETASITES FRAGRANS
	PHILADELPHUS CORONARIUS
	PHILADELPHUS X FALCONERI
	PHLOX PILOSA SUBSP. OZARKANA
	PHLOX STOLONIFERA 'ALBA'
	PHLOX STOLONIFERA 'BLUE RIDGE'
	PHLOX STOLONIFERA 'SHERWOOD PURPLE'
	POLYSTICHUM TRIPTERON
	RHEUM PALMATUM 'RUBRUM'
	RHODODENDRON (GABLE HYBRIDS)
	RHODODENDRON ARBORESCENS
	RHODODENDRON MUCRONULATUM
	RHODODENDRON SCHLIPPENBACHII
	RHODODENDRON VASEYI
	RHODODENDRON X GANDAVENSE 'COCCINEA SPECIOSA'
	RHODODENDRON X GANDAVENSE 'DAVIESII'
	RHODOTYPOS SCANDENS
	SAGINA SUBULATA
	SCILLA SIBERICA 'SPRING BEAUTY'
	SEDUM FLORIFERUM 'WEIHANSTEPHANER GOLD'
	SPIRAEA PRUNIFOLIA
	STEPHANANDRA INCISA 'CRISPA'
	SYMPHORICARPOS X CHENAULTII 'HANCOCK'
	SYMPHYTUM X UPLANDICUM
	TAXUS BACCATA 'REPANDENS'
	THALICTRUM ROCHEBRUNIANUM
	THELYPTERIS HEXAGONOPTERA
	THELYPTERIS NOVEBORACENSIS
	THELYPTERIS PHEGOPTERIS
	THYMUS 'CLEAR GOLD'
	THYMUS PSEUDOLANUGINOSUS
	VIBURNUM DILATATUM 'MICHAEL DODGE'
	VIBURNUM FARRERI 'CANDIDISSIMUM'
	VIBURNUM FARRERI 'NANUM'
	VIBURNUM PLICATUM FORMA TOMENTOSUM
	XANTHORHIZA SIMPLICISSIMA
6	ABELIA X GRANDIFLORA
	ACER PALMATUM 'EVER RED'
	ACER PALMATUM VAR. DISSECTUM OR A. P. 'WATERFALL'
	ACORUS GRAMINEUS 'OGON'
	ADINA RUBELLA
	ARUM ITALICUM 'PICTUM'
	BEGONIA GRANDIS
	BERBERIS JULIANAE 'NANA'
	BUXUS SEMPERVIRENS 'SUFFRUTICOSA'
	CERATOSTIGMA PLUMBAGINOIDES
	CHAMAECYPARIS OBTUSA 'CRIPPSII'
	CRUCIANELLA STYLOSA
	ENKIANTHUS PERULATUS
	EUONYMUS FORTUNEI 'SILVER QUEEN'
	EUPATORIUM COELESTINUM
	FILIPENDULA PURPUREA 'ELEGANS'
	HEDERA HELIX 'BALTICA'
	HEDERA HELIX 'BUTTERCUP'
	HEDERA HELIX 'GOLD HEART'
	HYDRANGEA MACROPHYLLA 'BLUE BILLOW'
	ILEX CRENATA 'HELLERI'
	ILEX CRENATA 'MICROPHYLLA'
	ITEA VIRGINICA 'HENRY'S GARNET'
	LIRIOPE MUSCARI (BIG BLUE SELECTION)
	LIRIOPE MUSCARI 'MONROE WHITE'

LIRIOPE MUSCARI 'VARIEGATA'
LUZULA SYLVATICA 'MARGINATA'
MAHONIA BEALEI
PAEONIA 'BLACK PIRATE'
PAEONIA—WOODY HYBRIDS
PIERIS JAPONICA
RHODODENDRON (GLENN DALE
    HYBRIDS)
RHODODENDRON (KAEMPFERI
    HYBRIDS)
RHODODENDRON (KNAP HILL HYBRID)
    'TUNIS'
RHODODENDRON (KURUME HYBRIDS)
RHODODENDRON X ERIOCARPUM
    AND R. X NAKAHARAI CULTIVARS
    AND HYBRIDS
SAXIFRAGA STOLONIFERA
TRACHYSTEMON ORIENTALIS
VIBURNUM RHYTIDOPHYLLUM

7
BUXUS MICROPHYLLA 'COMPACTA'
CHIMONANTHUS PRAECOX
HEDERA COLCHICA 'DENTATA'
HEDERA HELIX 'ERECTA'
HYDRANGEA ASPERA SUBSP.
    SARGENTIANA
OPHIOPOGON JAPONICUS 'NANUS'
RHODODENDRON CANESCENS
SASA VEITCHII
SKIMMIA REEVESIANA

8
COTULA SQUALIDA

T
CESTRUM NOCTURNUM

SHADE

ZONE	LATIN NAME
2	DICENTRA SPECTABILIS

3
ADIANTUM PEDATUM
AEGOPODIUM PODAGRARIA
    'VARIEGATUM'
CIMICIFUGA RACEMOSA
DENNSTAEDTIA PUNCTILOBULA
DICENTRA EXIMIA 'PURITY'
FILIPENDULA ULMARIA 'AUREA'
GERANIUM MACRORRHIZUM
HOSTA 'KABITAN'
HOSTA PLANTAGINEA
HOSTA SIEBOLDIANA 'ELEGANS'
HOSTA UNDULATA
HOSTA VENTRICOSA
OSMUNDA REGALIS
POLYSTICHUM ACROSTICHOIDES
PULMONARIA ANGUSTIFOLIA
PULMONARIA SACCHARATA 'MARGERY
    FISH'
PULMONARIA SACCHARATA
    'SISSINGHURST WHITE'
VIBURNUM ACERIFOLIUM

4
ACANTHOPANAX SIEBOLDIANUS
CONVALLARIA MAJALIS
GAULTHERIA PROCUMBENS
MICROBIOTA DECUSSATA
OSMUNDA CINNAMOMEA
OSMUNDA CLAYTONIANA
PACHYSANDRA PROCUMBENS

PETASITES JAPONICUS
POLYGONATUM ODORATUM
    'VARIEGATUM'
RHODODENDRON MAXIMUM
RODGERSIA AESCULIFOLIA
SEDUM TERNATUM
VINCA MINOR 'BOWLESII'
VINCA MINOR 'VARIEGATA'

5
ASARUM EUROPAEUM
ATHYRIUM GOERINGIANUM 'PICTUM'
DIPLAZIUM CONILII
EPIMEDIUM PINNATUM SUBSP.
    COLCHICUM
EPIMEDIUM X YOUNGIANUM 'NIVEUM'
GALIUM ODORATUM
HOUTTUYNIA CORDATA 'CHAMELEON'
INDIGOFERA INCARNATA 'ALBA'
LAMIASTRUM GALEOBDOLON
    'VARIEGATUM'
LAMIUM MACULATUM 'WHITE
    NANCY'
LEUCOTHOE FONTANESIANA
LEUCOTHOE FONTANESIANA 'NANA'
PACHYSANDRA TERMINALIS
PACHYSANDRA TERMINALIS 'GREEN
    CARPET'
PACHYSANDRA TERMINALIS
    'VARIEGATA' OR 'SILVER EDGE'
PETASITES FRAGRANS
PHLOX STOLONIFERA 'ALBA'
PHLOX STOLONIFERA 'BLUE RIDGE'
PHLOX STOLONIFERA 'SHERWOOD
    PURPLE'
POLYSTICHUM TRIPTERON
RHODOTYPOS SCANDENS
THELYPTERIS HEXAGONOPTERA
THELYPTERIS PHEGOPTERIS

6
BEGONIA GRANDIS
LUZULA SYLVATICA 'MARGINATA'
TRACHYSTEMON ORIENTALIS

APPENDIX 6
Plant Listing by Tolerance of Wind

In many gardens, windy conditions
limit which plants can be grown. Those
on the following list are good at
surviving windy sites, and many of the
larger plants can be used in windbreak
plantings to provide shelter for plants
that are less tolerant of wind.

The list has been divided by
hardiness zone.

Further information about all the
following plants is summarized in the
Master Lists, Appendices 1A and 1B.

ZONE	LATIN NAME
2	ACHILLEA MILLEFOLIUM 'ROSEA' ARTEMESIA STELLERIANA

3
ACER SACCHARUM
ASCLEPIAS TUBEROSA
BAPTISIA AUSTRALIS

COREOPSIS 'MOONBEAM'
CORNUS RACEMOSA
CORNUS RACEMOSA (DWARF)
CORNUS SERICEA
CORNUS SERICEA 'FLAVIRAMEA'
HIPPOPHAE RHAMNOIDES
JUNIPERUS HORIZONTALIS 'WILTONII'
JUNIPERUS VIRGINIANA
PHLOX SUBULATA
PICEA ABIES 'NIDIFORMIS'
PICEA PUNGENS 'HOOPSII'
PINUS MUGO VAR. MUGO
PSEUDOTSUGA MENZIESII
RHUS TYPHINA
RHUS TYPHINA 'LACINIATA'
ROSA RUGOSA AND HYBRIDS
SEDUM ELLACOMBIANUM
SEDUM SARMENTOSUM
SEDUM SPURIUM
SEDUM SPURIUM 'BRONZE CARPET'

4
ACANTHOPANAX SIEBOLDIANUS
ARTEMESIA LUDOVICIANA 'SILVER
    QUEEN'
BERBERIS THUNBERGII 'ATROPURPUREA'
CARYA OVATA
CARYOPTERIS X CLANDONENSIS 'BLUE
    MIST'
CEPHALANTHUS OCCIDENTALIS
CHAENOMELES JAPONICA VAR. ALPINA
CHAENOMELES X SUPERBA 'JET TRAIL'
CRATAEGUS NITIDA
CRATAEGUS PHAENOPYRUM
DIERVILLA SESSILIFOLIA
EUONYMUS ALATA
GINKGO BILOBA, STAMINATE
GLEDITSIA TRIACANTHOS VAR.
    INERMIS 'SHADEMASTER'
GYMNOCLADUS DIOICA
HAMAMELIS VIRGINIANA
JUNIPERUS SABINA 'TAMARISCIFOLIA'
JUNIPERUS X MEDIA 'PFITZERIANA
    COMPACTA'
MALUS FLORIBUNDA
MALUS SARGENTII
MYRICA PENSYLVANICA
PHLOX BIFIDA
PINUS FLEXILIS
PINUS KORAIENSIS
QUERCUS ALBA
QUERCUS MACROCARPA
ROSA NITIDA
SALIX REPENS VAR. ARGENTEA
STACHYS BYZANTINA
SYRINGA PATULA
    (SYN. S. PALIBINIANA, S.
    MICROPHYLLA 'INGWERSEN'S
    DWARF')
SYRINGA X CHINENSIS
TAMARIX RAMOSISSIMA
VACCINIUM CORYMBOSUM
YUCCA FLACCIDA 'GOLDEN SWORD'
YUCCA GLAUCA
YUCCA SMALLIANA

5
ABIES NORDMANNIANA
ALLIUM CERNUUM
AMSONIA HUBRICHTII
ARTEMESIA VERSICOLOR
ARUNDINARIA VIRIDISTRIATA
CALAMAGROSTIS X ACUTIFLORA
    'KARL FOERSTER'
    (SYN. C. EPIGEOUS 'HORTORUM')

ZONE	LATIN NAME
	CATALPA BIGNONIOIDES
	CEDRUS LIBANI VAR. STENOCOMA
	CERCIS CANADENSIS 'FOREST PANSY'
	CHAENOMELES X SUPERBA CULTIVARS
	COLUTEA X MEDIA
	CORNUS FLORIDA
	CORNUS FLORIDA 'HOHMAN'S GOLDEN'
	CORNUS MAS
	CORNUS OFFICINALIS
	CRATAEGUS VIRIDIS 'WINTER KING'
	FORSYTHIA SUSPENSA
	HEMEROCALLIS 'HYPERION'
	ILEX X MESERVEAE BLUE MAID ® 'MESID'
	ILEX X MESERVEAE BLUE STALLION ® 'MESAN'
	JUNIPERUS SCOPULORUM 'SKY ROCKET'
	JUNIPERUS X MEDIA 'OLD GOLD'
	LESPEDEZA THUNBERGII
	LIGUSTRUM QUIHOUI
	MISCANTHUS SINENSIS 'GRACILLIMUS'
	NARCISSUS 'CARLTON'
	NARCISSUS JONQUILLA
	PACHYSANDRA TERMINALIS
	PACHYSANDRA TERMINALIS 'GREEN CARPET'
	PACHYSANDRA TERMINALIS 'VARIEGATA' OR 'SILVER EDGE'
	PENNISETUM ALOPECUROIDES
	PINUS BUNGEANA
	PINUS VIRGINIANA
	ROSA CAROLINA
	ROSA EGLANTERIA
	SALIX ACUTIFOLIA 'LONGIFOLIA'
	SASSAFRAS ALBIDUM
	SEDUM 'VERA JAMISON'
	SEDUM FLORIFERUM 'WEIHANSTEPHANER GOLD'
	STEPHANANDRA INCISA 'CRISPA'
	SYRINGA LACINIATA
	SYRINGA RETICULATA
	VERBASCUM OLYMPICUM
	VIBURNUM SIEBOLDII 'SENECA'
	WISTERIA FLORIBUNDA
6	CERATOSTIGMA PLUMBAGINOIDES
	COTONEASTER ADPRESSUS VAR. PRAECOX
	CYTISUS SCOPARIUS
	EUPATORIUM COELESTINUM
	ILEX OPACA 'ARDEN'
	ILEX OPACA 'XANTHOCARPA'
	JUNIPERUS CHINENSIS 'KAIZUKA'
	PINUS THUNBERGIANA
7	ELAEAGNUS PUNGENS 'FRUITLANDII'
	ELAEAGNUS PUNGENS 'MACULATA'

APPENDIX 7
Plant Listing by Tolerance of Poor Air Drainage

In hilly parts of the country, valley bottoms often have poor air circulation, and fences and closely spaced houses create a similar situation in some urban areas. Under such conditions certain plants are particularly prone to disease, and, because low temperatures linger longer in locales with poor air circulation, early and late frosts pose a special problem. The plants in the following list are particularly tolerant of such conditions.

The list has been divided by hardiness zone.

The letter *T* under the heading "Zone" indicates a plant that is tender, not tolerant of frost.

Further information about all the following plants is summarized in the Master Lists, Appendices 1A and 1B.

ZONE	LATIN NAME
2	ACHILLEA MILLEFOLIUM 'ROSEA'
3	AEGOPODIUM PODAGRARIA 'VARIEGATUM'
	ALCHEMILLA VULGARIS
	AMSONIA TABERNAEMONTANA
	ASCLEPIAS TUBEROSA
	BRUNNERA MACROPHYLLA
	COREOPSIS 'MOONBEAM'
	CORNUS RACEMOSA
	CORNUS RACEMOSA (DWARF)
	CORNUS SERICEA
	CORNUS SERICEA 'FLAVIRAMEA'
	DICENTRA 'LUXURIANT'
	DICENTRA EXIMIA 'PURITY'
	EUPHORBIA COROLLATA
	GERANIUM 'JOHNSON'S BLUE'
	GERANIUM MACRORRHIZUM
	HELLEBORUS NIGER
	HIPPOPHAE RHAMNOIDES
	HOSTA 'KABITAN'
	HOSTA PLANTAGINEA
	HOSTA UNDULATA
	HOSTA VENTRICOSA
	IRIS SIBIRICA CULTIVARS
	JUNIPERUS HORIZONTALIS 'WILTONII'
	JUNIPERUS VIRGINIANA
	LYTHRUM SALICARIA 'DROPMORE PURPLE'
	MALUS 'RED JADE'
	OSMUNDA REGALIS
	PAPAVER ORIENTALE
	PHLOX SUBULATA
	PHYSOSTEGIA VIRGINIANA
	PHYSOSTEGIA VIRGINIANA 'SUMMER SNOW'
	PICEA ABIES 'NIDIFORMIS'
	POLYSTICHUM ACROSTICHOIDES
	PULMONARIA ANGUSTIFOLIA
	QUERCUS RUBRA
	RHUS AROMATICA 'GRO-LOW'
	RHUS TYPHINA
	RHUS TYPHINA 'LACINIATA'
	SEDUM ELLACOMBIANUM
	SEDUM SARMENTOSUM

ZONE	LATIN NAME
	SEDUM SPURIUM
	SEDUM SPURIUM 'BRONZE CARPET'
	THUJA OCCIDENTALIS 'NIGRA'
	THYMUS SERPYLLUM
	TSUGA CANADENSIS 'COLE'S PROSTRATE'
	VIBURNUM ACERIFOLIUM
4	ACANTHOPANAX SIEBOLDIANUS
	ACER RUBRUM
	AJUGA REPTANS 'BRONZE BEAUTY'
	AJUGA REPTANS (GIANT FORM)
	ALLIUM TUBEROSUM
	ARALIA SPINOSA
	ARTEMESIA LUDOVICIANA 'SILVER QUEEN'
	ARUNCUS AETHUSIFOLIUS
	ASTILBE X ARENDSII CULTIVARS
	BACCHARIS HALIMIFOLIA, PISTILLATE
	BERBERIS THUNBERGII 'CRIMSON PYGMY'
	BETULA LENTA
	BETULA NIGRA
	CARYA OVATA
	CORYLUS AVELLANA 'CONTORTA'
	CORYLUS AVELLANA 'PENDULA'
	CRATAEGUS NITIDA
	CRATAEGUS PHAENOPYRUM
	EUONYMUS ALATA
	GLEDITSIA TRIACANTHOS VAR. INERMIS 'SHADEMASTER'
	GYMNOCLADUS DIOICA
	HAMAMELIS VIRGINIANA
	HELIOPSIS HELIANTHOIDES SUBSP. SCABRA 'KARAT'
	HELLEBORUS ORIENTALIS HYBRIDS
	HYDRANGEA PANICULATA
	ILEX VERTICILLATA
	ILEX VERTICILLATA 'WINTER RED'
	JUNIPERUS X MEDIA 'PFITZERIANA COMPACTA'
	MALUS FLORIBUNDA
	MALUS SARGENTII
	MONARDA DIDYMA
	MYRICA PENSYLVANICA
	OSMUNDA CINNAMOMEA
	OSMUNDA CLAYTONIANA
	PHLOX BIFIDA
	PINUS FLEXILIS
	PINUS KORAIENSIS
	POLYGONATUM ODORATUM 'VARIEGATUM'
	QUERCUS ALBA
	RHODODENDRON MAXIMUM
	RHODODENDRON VISCOSUM
	ROBINIA HISPIDA
	ROSA NITIDA
	SYRINGA PATULA (SYN. S. PALIBINIANA, S. MICROPHYLLA 'INGWERSEN'S DWARF')
	SYRINGA X CHINENSIS
	TAXUS CUSPIDATA 'NANA'
	TAXUS CUSPIDATA (CAPITATA SELECTION)
	TYPHA ANGUSTIFOLIA
	VACCINIUM CORYMBOSUM
	VERNONIA NOVEBORACENSIS
	VINCA MINOR 'BOWLESII'
	VINCA MINOR 'VARIEGATA'
	YUCCA FLACCIDA 'GOLDEN SWORD'
	YUCCA GLAUCA
	YUCCA SMALLIANA

ZONE	LATIN NAME
5	ACER GRISEUM
	ALLIUM CERNUUM
	ALLIUM ZEBDANENSE
	AMSONIA HUBRICHTII
	ANEMONE BLANDA 'ATROCAERULEA'
	ARTEMESIA VERSICOLOR
	ARUNDINARIA VIRIDISTRIATA
	ASARUM EUROPAEUM
	ASPHODELINE LUTEA
	ATHYRIUM GOERINGIANUM 'PICTUM'
	BUDDLEIA DAVIDII 'BLACK KNIGHT'
	BUDDLEIA DAVIDII 'OPERA'
	BUDDLEIA DAVIDII 'PURPLE PRINCE'
	CALAMAGROSTIS X ACUTIFLORA 'KARL FOERSTER' (SYN. C. EPIGEOUS 'HORTORUM')
	CAMPSIS X TAGLIABUANA 'MADAME GALEN'
	CATALPA BIGNONIOIDES
	CEDRUS LIBANI VAR. STENOCOMA
	CHAMAECYPARIS OBTUSA 'NANA GRACILIS'
	CHIONANTHUS VIRGINICUS
	CHIONODOXA GIGANTEA 'ALBA'
	CHIONODOXA LUCILIAE
	CHIONODOXA SARDENSIS
	CLETHRA ALNIFOLIA
	COLCHICUM 'AUTUMN QUEEN'
	COLCHICUM 'THE GIANT'
	COLUTEA X MEDIA
	CORNUS FLORIDA
	CORNUS FLORIDA 'HOHMAN'S GOLDEN'
	CORNUS MAS
	CORNUS OFFICINALIS
	COTINUS COGGYGRIA 'PURPUREUS'
	CRAMBE CORDIFOLIA
	CRATAEGUS VIRIDIS 'WINTER KING'
	CROCUS ANCYRENSIS 'GOLDEN BUNCH'
	CROCUS SIEBERI
	CROCUS TOMASINIANUS
	DAPHNE CAUCASICA
	DEUTZIA GRACILIS
	ENDYMION HISPANICUS 'EXCELSIOR' (SYN. SCILLA CAMPANULATA 'EXCELSIOR')
	EPIMEDIUM PINNATUM SUBSP. COLCHICUM
	EPIMEDIUM X YOUNGIANUM 'NIVEUM'
	ERANTHIS HYEMALIS
	ERANTHIS X TUBERGENII
	FORSYTHIA SUSPENSA
	FOTHERGILLA GARDENII
	GALANTHUS ELWESII
	GALANTHUS NIVALIS
	HEDERA HELIX 'BULGARIA'
	HEDERA HELIX 'OGALALLA'
	HEMEROCALLIS 'HYPERION'
	HIBISCUS SYRIACUS 'BLUEBIRD'
	HIBISCUS SYRIACUS 'DIANA'
	HYDRANGEA QUERCIFOLIA
	ILEX CHINA BOY ® 'MESDOB'
	ILEX CHINA GIRL ® 'MESOG'
	ILEX GLABRA 'DENSA'
	ILEX X AQUIPERNYI 'SAN JOSE'
	ILEX X MESERVEAE BLUE MAID ® 'MESID'
	ILEX X MESERVEAE BLUE STALLION ® 'MESAN'
	INDIGOFERA INCARNATA 'ALBA'
	IRIS CRISTATA
	JUNIPERUS SCOPULORUM 'SKY ROCKET'
	JUNIPERUS X MEDIA 'OLD GOLD'
	KERRIA JAPONICA
	KOELREUTERIA PANICULATA
	KOLKWITZIA AMABILIS
	LAMIASTRUM GALEOBDOLON 'VARIEGATUM'
	LESPEDEZA THUNBERGII
	LEUCOJUM VERNUM
	LIGUSTRUM QUIHOUI
	LILIUM 'BLACK DRAGON'
	LIQUIDAMBAR STYRACIFLUA
	LONICERA FRAGRANTISSIMA
	LYCORIS SPRENGERI
	LYCORIS SQUAMIGERA
	MAGNOLIA 'ELIZABETH'
	MAGNOLIA VIRGINIANA
	MERTENSIA VIRGINICA
	MISCANTHUS 'GIGANTEUS'
	MISCANTHUS SINENSIS 'CABARET'
	MISCANTHUS SINENSIS 'GRACILLIMUS'
	MISCANTHUS SINENSIS 'MORNING LIGHT'
	MISCANTHUS SINENSIS 'SILVER FEATHER' (= 'SILBERFEDER')
	MISCANTHUS SINENSIS 'STRICTUS'
	MISCANTHUS SINENSIS 'VARIEGATUS'
	MOLINIA CAERULEA SUBSP. ARUNDINACEA
	MUSCARI AZUREUM 'ALBUM'
	MUSCARI BOTRYOIDES 'ALBUM'
	MUSCARI TUBERGENIANUM
	NARCISSUS 'FORTUNE'
	NARCISSUS 'HERA'
	NARCISSUS 'LOCH FYNE'
	NARCISSUS 'MOONMIST'
	NARCISSUS 'MRS. ERNST H. KRELAGE'
	NARCISSUS 'PEEPING TOM'
	NARCISSUS 'POMONA'
	NARCISSUS 'QUEEN OF SPAIN'
	NARCISSUS 'TREVITHIAN'
	NARCISSUS PSEUDONARCISSUS SUBSP. OBVALLARIS
	NYSSA SYLVATICA
	PACHYSANDRA TERMINALIS
	PACHYSANDRA TERMINALIS 'GREEN CARPET'
	PACHYSANDRA TERMINALIS 'VARIEGATA' OR 'SILVER EDGE'
	PANICUM VIRGATUM 'STRICTUM'
	PENNISETUM ALOPECUROIDES
	PHILADELPHUS CORONARIUS
	PHILADELPHUS X FALCONERI
	PHLOX PILOSA SUBSP. OZARKANA
	PICEA ORIENTALIS
	PINUS PARVIFLORA 'GLAUCA'
	PINUS VIRGINIANA
	PLATANUS OCCIDENTALIS
	POLYSTICHUM TRIPTERON
	PRUNUS CERASIFERA 'THUNDERCLOUD'
	RHODODENDRON (GABLE HYBRIDS)
	RHODODENDRON ARBORESCENS
	RHODODENDRON MUCRONULATUM
	RHODODENDRON SCHLIPPENBACHII
	RHODODENDRON VASEYI
	RHODODENDRON X GANDAVENSE 'COCCINEA SPECIOSA'
	RHODODENDRON X GANDAVENSE 'DAVIESII'
	RHODOTYPOS SCANDENS
	ROSA (SHRUB) 'LILLIAN GIBSON'
	ROSA CAROLINA
	ROSA VIRGINIANA
	RUBUS COCKBURNIANUS
	SASSAFRAS ALBIDUM
	SCILLA SIBERICA 'SPRING BEAUTY'
	SEDUM 'VERA JAMISON'
	SEDUM FLORIFERUM 'WEIHANSTEPHANER GOLD'
	SPIRAEA PRUNIFOLIA
	SYMPHORICARPOS X CHENAULTII 'HANCOCK'
	SYMPHYTUM X UPLANDICUM
	SYRINGA RETICULATA
	TAXUS BACCATA 'ADPRESSA FOWLE'
	TAXUS X MEDIA 'SENTINALIS'
	THYMUS 'CLEAR GOLD'
	THYMUS PSEUDOLANUGINOSUS
	VERBASCUM OLYMPICUM
	VIBURNUM PLICATUM FORMA TOMENTOSUM
	VIBURNUM SIEBOLDII 'SENECA'
	WISTERIA FLORIBUNDA
	XANTHORHIZA SIMPLICISSIMA
6	ARUM ITALICUM 'PICTUM'
	BEGONIA GRANDIS
	BIGNONIA CAPREOLATA
	CALLICARPA DICHOTOMA
	CERATOSTIGMA PLUMBAGINOIDES
	CLETHRA BARBINERVIS
	COTONEASTER ADPRESSUS VAR. PRAECOX
	CROCOSMIA 'LUCIFER'
	CROCOSMIA POTTSII
	CROCOSMIA X CROCOSMIIFLORA
	CYTISUS SCOPARIUS
	EUPATORIUM COELESTINUM
	FORSYTHIA X INTERMEDIA 'SPRING GLORY'
	GALTONIA CANDICANS
	HEDERA HELIX 'BALTICA'
	ILEX CRENATA 'HELLERI'
	ILEX CRENATA 'MICROPHYLLA'
	ILEX OPACA 'ARDEN'
	ILEX OPACA 'XANTHOCARPA'
	ITEA VIRGINICA 'HENRY'S GARNET'
	JUNIPERUS CHINENSIS 'KAIZUKA'
	LESPEDEZA THUNBERGII 'ALBIFLORA'
	LIRIOPE MUSCARI (BIG BLUE SELECTION)
	LIRIOPE MUSCARI 'MONROE WHITE'
	LIRIOPE MUSCARI 'VARIEGATA'
	MAHONIA BEALEI
	RHODODENDRON (KAEMPFERI HYBRIDS)
	RHODODENDRON (KURUME HYBRIDS)
	ROSA ROXBURGHII
	SOPHORA JAPONICA 'REGENT'
	TRACHYSTEMON ORIENTALIS
	VITEX AGNUS-CASTUS 'LATIFOLIA'
	VITEX AGNUS-CASTUS 'SILVER SPIRE'
7	CHIMONANTHUS PRAECOX
	ELAEAGNUS PUNGENS 'FRUITLANDII'
	ELAEAGNUS PUNGENS 'MACULATA'
	PYRACANTHA COCCINEA 'AUREA'
	SASA VEITCHII
	VIBURNUM MACROCEPHALUM FORMA MACROCEPHALUM
T	ACIDANTHERA BICOLOR
	CANNA X GENERALIS 'MOHAWK'
	CESTRUM NOCTURNUM

ZONE	LATIN NAME
	DATURA INOXIA SUBSP. QUINQUECUSPIDA
	KOCHIA SCOPARIA FORMA TRICHOPHYLLA 'CHILDSII'
	RICINUS COMMUNIS
	RICINUS COMMUNIS 'ZANZIBARENSIS'

APPENDIX 8
Plant Listing by Tolerance of Low Fertility

Far too often in the construction of new houses, topsoil disappears and the homeowner is left with a less desirable growing medium. In addition to using various techniques to improve the soil structure and provide additional nutrients, the gardener can consider plants such as those listed below, which are especially tolerant of low fertility.

The list is divided by hardiness zone.

Further information about all the following plants is summarized in the Master Lists, Appendices 1A and 1B.

ZONE	LATIN NAME
2	ACHILLEA MILLEFOLIUM 'ROSEA'
	ARTEMESIA STELLERIANA
	POTENTILLA TRIDENTATA
	SAPONARIA OFFICINALIS
3	ACHILLEA 'MOONSHINE'
	AEGOPODIUM PODAGRARIA 'VARIEGATUM'
	ARTEMISIA ABSINTHIUM 'LAMBROOK SILVER'
	ASCLEPIAS TUBEROSA
	BAPTISIA AUSTRALIS
	BUPHTHALUM SALICIFOLIUM
	COREOPSIS 'MOONBEAM'
	EUPHORBIA COROLLATA
	HIPPOPHAE RHAMNOIDES
	JUNIPERUS VIRGINIANA
	LIATRIS SPICATA 'KOBOLD'
	LYTHRUM SALICARIA 'DROPMORE PURPLE'
	NEPETA X FAASSENII
	PHLOX SUBULATA
	RHUS AROMATICA 'GRO-LOW'
	RHUS TYPHINA
	RHUS TYPHINA 'LACINIATA'
	RUDBECKIA FULGIDA VAR. SULLIVANTII 'GOLDSTURM'
	SEDUM 'AUTUMN JOY'
	SEDUM ELLACOMBIANUM
	SEDUM SARMENTOSUM
	SEDUM SPURIUM
	SEDUM SPURIUM 'BRONZE CARPET'
	SORBARIA SORBIFOLIA
	THYMUS SERPYLLUM
4	ACANTHOPANAX SIEBOLDIANUS
	AJUGA REPTANS
	AJUGA REPTANS 'BRONZE BEAUTY'
	AJUGA REPTANS (GIANT FORM)
	ALLIUM TUBEROSUM

ZONE	LATIN NAME
	ARALIA SPINOSA
	ARTEMESIA LUDOVICIANA 'SILVER QUEEN'
	BERBERIS THUNBERGII 'ATROPURPUREA'
	BERBERIS THUNBERGII 'CRIMSON PYGMY'
	BUDDLEIA ALTERNIFOLIA
	COMPTONIA PEREGRINA
	CORYLUS AVELLANA 'CONTORTA'
	CORYLUS AVELLANA 'PENDULA'
	CRATAEGUS NITIDA
	CRATAEGUS PHAENOPYRUM
	EUONYMUS ALATA
	EUPHORBIA CYPARISSIAS
	EUPHORBIA EPITHYMOIDES
	HELIOPSIS HELIANTHOIDES SUBSP. SCABRA 'KARAT'
	JUNIPERUS SABINA 'TAMARISCIFOLIA'
	MYRICA PENSYLVANICA
	ROBINIA HISPIDA
	ROSA NITIDA
	SEDUM POPULIFOLIUM
	STACHYS BYZANTINA
	YUCCA FLACCIDA 'GOLDEN SWORD'
	YUCCA GLAUCA
	YUCCA SMALLIANA
5	AMSONIA HUBRICHTII
	ARTEMESIA VERSICOLOR
	ARUNDINARIA VIRIDISTRIATA
	CATALPA BIGNONIOIDES
	CERCIS CANADENSIS 'FOREST PANSY'
	CLETHRA ALNIFOLIA
	COLUTEA X MEDIA
	COTINUS COGGYGRIA 'PURPUREUS'
	CRATAEGUS VIRIDIS 'WINTER KING'
	DAPHNE X BURKWOODII 'CAROL MACKIE'
	EPIMEDIUM PINNATUM SUBSP. COLCHICUM
	EPIMEDIUM X YOUNGIANUM 'NIVEUM'
	FORSYTHIA SUSPENSA
	HEMEROCALLIS FULVA 'EUROPA'
	IRIS TECTORUM
	LAMIASTRUM GALEOBDOLON 'VARIEGATUM'
	LESPEDEZA THUNBERGII
	NARCISSUS 'LOCH FYNE'
	PACHYSANDRA TERMINALIS
	PHILADELPHUS CORONARIUS
	PINUS VIRGINIANA
	ROSA CAROLINA
	SAGINA SUBULATA
	SASSAFRAS ALBIDUM
	SEDUM 'VERA JAMISON'
	SEDUM FLORIFERUM 'WEIHANSTEPHANER GOLD'
	SYMPHORICARPOS X CHENAULTII 'HANCOCK'
	THYMUS 'CLEAR GOLD'
	THYMUS PSEUDOLANUGINOSUS
	VERBASCUM OLYMPICUM
6	FORSYTHIA X INTERMEDIA 'SPRING GLORY'
	SALVIA ARGENTEA
	VITEX AGNUS-CASTUS 'LATIFOLIA'
	VITEX AGNUS-CASTUS 'SILVER SPIRE'

APPENDIX 9
Plant Listing by Tolerance of Drought

One of the crosses that gardeners in the mid-Atlantic states have to bear is an unpredictable natural water supply during the growing season. Droughts during June, July, and August—prime gardening time—are frequent and devastating. The plants in the following list have some degree of drought tolerance.

The list has been divided by hardiness zone.

The letter *T* under the heading "Zone" indicates a plant that is tender, not tolerant of frost.

Further information about all the following plants is summarized in the Master Lists, Appendices 1A and 1B.

ZONE	LATIN NAME
2	ACHILLEA MILLEFOLIUM 'ROSEA'
	ARTEMESIA STELLERIANA
	POTENTILLA TRIDENTATA
3	ACHILLEA 'CORONATION GOLD'
	ACHILLEA 'MOONSHINE'
	AEGOPODIUM PODAGRARIA 'VARIEGATUM'
	ARTEMISIA ABSINTHIUM 'LAMBROOK SILVER'
	ASCLEPIAS TUBEROSA
	ASTER AMELLUS 'NOCTURNE'
	ASTER TATARICUS
	BAPTISIA AUSTRALIS
	COREOPSIS 'MOONBEAM'
	CORNUS RACEMOSA
	CORNUS RACEMOSA (DWARF)
	DICENTRA 'LUXURIANT'
	ECHINACEA PURPUREA
	EUPHORBIA COROLLATA
	HIPPOPHAE RHAMNOIDES
	IRIS SIBIRICA CULTIVARS
	JUNIPERUS HORIZONTALIS 'WILTONII'
	JUNIPERUS VIRGINIANA
	LIATRIS SCARIOSA 'WHITE SPIRE'
	LIATRIS SPICATA 'KOBOLD'
	NEPETA X FAASSENII
	PAPAVER ORIENTALE
	PHLOX SUBULATA
	PHYSOSTEGIA VIRGINIANA
	PHYSOSTEGIA VIRGINIANA 'SUMMER SNOW'
	PINUS MUGO VAR. MUGO
	POLYSTICHUM ACROSTICHOIDES
	PRUNUS X CISTENA
	PTERIDIUM AQUILINUM VAR. LATIUSCULUM
	PULMONARIA ANGUSTIFOLIA
	QUERCUS RUBRA
	RHUS AROMATICA 'GRO-LOW'
	RHUS TYPHINA
	RHUS TYPHINA 'LACINIATA'
	ROSA RUGOSA AND HYBRIDS
	SEDUM 'AUTUMN JOY'
	SEDUM ELLACOMBIANUM
	SEDUM SARMENTOSUM
	SEDUM SPURIUM
	SEDUM SPURIUM 'BRONZE CARPET'

ZONE	LATIN NAME

ZONE	LATIN NAME

SPIRAEA X VANHOUTTEI
THERMOPSIS CAROLINIANA
THUJA OCCIDENTALIS 'NIGRA'
THYMUS SERPYLLUM
VIBURNUM ACERIFOLIUM
VIBURNUM PRUNIFOLIUM

4
ACANTHOPANAX SIEBOLDIANUS
AJUGA REPTANS
AJUGA REPTANS 'BRONZE BEAUTY'
AJUGA REPTANS (GIANT FORM)
ALLIUM TUBEROSUM
ANEMONE VITIFOLIA 'ROBUSTISSIMA'
ARALIA SPINOSA
ARTEMESIA LUDOVICIANA 'SILVER
   QUEEN'
ARUNCUS AETHUSIFOLIUS
BACCHARIS HALIMIFOLIA, PISTILLATE
BERBERIS THUNBERGII 'ATROPURPUREA'
BERBERIS THUNBERGII 'CRIMSON
   PYGMY'
CARYA OVATA
CHAENOMELES JAPONICA VAR. ALPINA
CHAENOMELES X SUPERBA 'JET TRAIL'
CHAMAEMELUM NOBILE
COMPTONIA PEREGRINA
CORYLUS AVELLANA 'CONTORTA'
CORYLUS AVELLANA 'PENDULA'
CRATAEGUS NITIDA
CRATAEGUS PHAENOPYRUM
DIERVILLA SESSILIFOLIA
EUONYMUS ALATA
EUPHORBIA CYPARISSIAS
GINKGO BILOBA, STAMINATE
GLEDITSIA TRIACANTHOS VAR.
   INERMIS 'SHADEMASTER'
GYMNOCLADUS DIOICA
HAMAMELIS VIRGINIANA
HELIOPSIS HELIANTHOIDES SUBSP.
   SCABRA 'KARAT'
HYDRANGEA PANICULATA
HYPERICUM KALMIANUM
JUNIPERUS SABINA 'TAMARISCIFOLIA'
JUNIPERUS X MEDIA 'PFITZERIANA
   COMPACTA'
MYRICA PENSYLVANICA
PACHYSANDRA PROCUMBENS
PHELLODENDRON AMURENSE
PHLOX BIFIDA
PINUS FLEXILIS
PINUS KORAIENSIS
POLYGONATUM ODORATUM
   'VARIEGATUM'
QUERCUS MACROCARPA
ROBINIA HISPIDA
ROSA NITIDA
SEDUM POPULIFOLIUM
STACHYS BYZANTINA
SYRINGA PATULA
   (SYN. S. PALIBINIANA, S.
   MICROPHYLLA 'INGWERSEN'S
   DWARF')
SYRINGA X CHINENSIS
VINCA MINOR 'BOWLESII'
YUCCA FLACCIDA 'GOLDEN SWORD'
YUCCA GLAUCA
YUCCA SMALLIANA

5
AESCULUS PARVIFLORA
ALLIUM CERNUUM
ALLIUM ZEBDANENSE
AMSONIA HUBRICHTII
ARTEMESIA VERSICOLOR

ARUNDINARIA VIRIDISTRIATA
ASARUM EUROPAEUM
ASPHODELINE LUTEA
ASTER CORDIFOLIUS
BUDDLEIA DAVIDII 'BLACK KNIGHT'
BUDDLEIA DAVIDII 'OPERA'
BUDDLEIA DAVIDII 'PURPLE PRINCE'
CAMPSIS X TAGLIABUANA 'MADAME
   GALEN'
CATALPA BIGNONIOIDES
CHAENOMELES X SUPERBA CULTIVARS
COLUTEA X MEDIA
CORNUS MAS
CORNUS OFFICINALIS
CORYLUS COLURNA
COTINUS COGGYGRIA 'PURPUREUS'
COTONEASTER ADPRESSUS 'LITTLE
   GEM'
CRAMBE CORDIFOLIA
CRATAEGUS VIRIDIS 'WINTER KING'
DIOSPYROS VIRGINIANA
EPIMEDIUM PINNATUM SUBSP.
   COLCHICUM
EPIMEDIUM X YOUNGIANUM 'NIVEUM'
FORSYTHIA SUSPENSA
HEMEROCALLIS 'HYPERION'
HYPERICUM FRONDOSUM
ILEX X AQUIPERNYI 'SAN JOSE'
INDIGOFERA INCARNATA 'ALBA'
IRIS CRISTATA
JUNIPERUS SCOPULORUM 'SKY
   ROCKET'
JUNIPERUS X MEDIA 'OLD GOLD'
KOELREUTERIA PANICULATA
KOLKWITZIA AMABILIS
LAMIASTRUM GALEOBDOLON
   'VARIEGATUM'
LESPEDEZA THUNBERGII
LIGUSTRUM QUIHOUI
LONICERA FRAGRANTISSIMA
LYSIMACHIA PUNCTATA
MISCANTHUS SINENSIS 'CABARET'
MISCANTHUS SINENSIS 'GRACILLIMUS'
MISCANTHUS SINENSIS 'MORNING
   LIGHT'
MISCANTHUS SINENSIS 'SILVER
   FEATHER' (='SILBERFEDER')
MISCANTHUS SINENSIS 'STRICTUS'
MISCANTHUS SINENSIS 'VARIEGATUS'
ONOPORDUM ACANTHIUM
PACHYSANDRA TERMINALIS
PACHYSANDRA TERMINALIS 'GREEN
   CARPET'
PACHYSANDRA TERMINALIS
   'VARIEGATA' OR 'SILVER EDGE'
PHILADELPHUS CORONARIUS
PHILADELPHUS X FALCONERI
PHLOMIS RUSSELIANA
PHLOX PILOSA SUBSP. OZARKANA
PINUS BUNGEANA
PINUS VIRGINIANA
PRUNUS CERASIFERA
   'THUNDERCLOUD'
RHODOTYPOS SCANDENS
ROSA 'DOORENBOS SELECTION'
ROSA (POLYANTHA) 'THE FAIRY'
ROSA CAROLINA
ROSA VIRGINIANA
RUBUS COCKBURNIANUS
SASSAFRAS ALBIDUM
SEDUM 'VERA JAMISON'
SEDUM FLORIFERUM
   'WEIHANSTEPHANER GOLD'

ZONE	LATIN NAME

SPIRAEA PRUNIFOLIA
STERNBERGIA LUTEA
STOKESIA LAEVIS 'BLUE DANUBE'
SYMPHORICARPOS X CHENAULTII
   'HANCOCK'
SYMPHYTUM X UPLANDICUM
SYRINGA RETICULATA
THELYPTERIS HEXAGONOPTERA
THELYPTERIS PHEGOPTERIS
THYMUS 'CLEAR GOLD'
THYMUS PSEUDOLANUGINOSUS
VERBASCUM OLYMPICUM
VIBURNUM SIEBOLDII 'SENECA'
WISTERIA FLORIBUNDA

6
BIGNONIA CAPREOLATA
CALLICARPA DICHOTOMA
CERATOSTIGMA PLUMBAGINOIDES
COTONEASTER ADPRESSUS VAR.
   PRAECOX
CYTISUS SCOPARIUS
EUONYMUS FORTUNEI 'SILVER QUEEN'
EUPATORIUM COELESTINUM
FORSYTHIA X INTERMEDIA 'SPRING
   GLORY'
ILEX OPACA 'ARDEN'
ILEX OPACA 'XANTHOCARPA'
JUNIPERUS CHINENSIS 'KAIZUKA'
LESPEDEZA THUNBERGII 'ALBIFLORA'
LUZULA SYLVATICA 'MARGINATA'
PAEONIA 'BLACK PIRATE'
PAEONIA—WOODY HYBRIDS
PONCIRUS TRIFOLIATA
SALVIA ARGENTEA
SOPHORA JAPONICA 'REGENT'
VITEX AGNUS-CASTUS 'LATIFOLIA'
VITEX AGNUS-CASTUS 'SILVER SPIRE'

7
ELAEAGNUS PUNGENS 'FRUITLANDII'
ELAEAGNUS PUNGENS 'MACULATA'
GENISTA SYLVESTRIS 'LYDIA'
PYRACANTHA COCCINEA 'AUREA'

T
KOCHIA SCOPARIA FORMA
   TRICHOPHYLLA 'CHILDSII'

APPENDIX 10
Plant Listing by Tolerance of Shallow Soil

There are situations in which, because of rock ledges or underground structures of one sort or another, the soil available for plant growth is not very deep. Fortunately, the following plants are good at surviving such conditions.

The list is divided by hardiness zone.

Further information about all the following plants is summarized in the Master Lists, Appendices 1A and 1B.

ZONE	LATIN NAME
2	ACHILLEA MILLEFOLIUM 'ROSEA'
	POTENTILLA TRIDENTATA
3	CORNUS RACEMOSA
	CORNUS RACEMOSA (DWARF)
	RHUS TYPHINA 'LACINIATA'
	THYMUS SERPYLLUM
4	ACANTHOPANAX SIEBOLDIANUS
	ARTEMESIA LUDOVICIANA 'SILVER QUEEN'
	EUONYMUS ALATA
	MYRICA PENSYLVANICA
	PHLOX BIFIDA
	VACCINIUM CORYMBOSUM
5	ARTEMESIA VERSICOLOR
	ROSA (POLYANTHA) 'THE FAIRY'
	ROSA (SHRUB) 'SEA FOAM'
	ROSA CAROLINA
	SYMPHORICARPOS X CHENAULTII 'HANCOCK'
	THYMUS 'CLEAR GOLD'
	THYMUS PSEUDOLANUGINOSUS

APPENDIX 11
Plant Listing by Tolerance of High pH

Where I live, in Hockessin, Delaware, the soil is generally on the acid side, pH 6 and lower. In other parts of the United States and Canada and in occasional pockets within acid regions the soil is alkaline (that is, it has a high pH). If you are not sure of your soil pH you can have it tested at the office of the Cooperative Extension Service, School of Agriculture, at your nearest land grant university. The plants in the following list are tolerant of high pH.

The list has been divided by hardiness zone.

Further information about all the following plants is summarized in the Master Lists, Appendices 1A and 1B.

ZONE	LATIN NAME
2	BERGENIA 'PERFECTA'
	BERGENIA 'SUNNINGDALE'
3	ADIANTUM PEDATUM
	AMELANCHIER ARBOREA (SYN. A. CANADENSIS)
	BUPHTHALUM SALICIFOLIUM
	CHELONE LYONII
	CORNUS RACEMOSA
	CORNUS RACEMOSA (DWARF)
	DIANTHUS DELTOIDES
	GERANIUM SANGUINEUM
	JUNIPERUS HORIZONTALIS 'WILTONII'
	JUNIPERUS VIRGINIANA
	MALUS 'RED JADE'
	PICEA PUNGENS 'HOOPSII'
	PINUS MUGO VAR. MUGO
	PINUS STROBUS
	PINUS STROBUS 'FASTIGIATA'
	PRUNUS X CISTENA
	PSEUDOTSUGA MENZIESII
	QUERCUS RUBRA
	SORBARIA SORBIFOLIA
	SPIRAEA X VANHOUTTEI
	SYRINGA VULGARIS 'ALBA'
	SYRINGA VULGARIS HYBRIDS
	TELEKIA SPECIOSA
	TILIA CORDATA
	VERONICASTRUM VIRGINICUM
	VIBURNUM PRUNIFOLIUM
4	ACER PLATANOIDES 'CRIMSON KING'
	BACCHARIS HALIMIFOLIA, PISTILLATE
	BERBERIS THUNBERGII 'ATROPURPUREA'
	CARYA OVATA
	CARYOPTERIS X CLANDONENSIS 'BLUE MIST'
	CEPHALANTHUS OCCIDENTALIS
	CLADRASTIS LUTEA
	CLEMATIS 'MRS. CHOLMONDELEY'
	CLEMATIS 'PRINS HENDRIK'
	CLEMATIS 'RAMONA'
	CLEMATIS MAXIMOWICZIANA
	CLEMATIS X JACKMANII
	CRATAEGUS NITIDA
	CRATAEGUS PHAENOPYRUM
	DIERVILLA SESSILIFOLIA

ZONE	LATIN NAME
	EUONYMUS FORTUNEI VAR. RADICANS
	GINKGO BILOBA, STAMINATE
	GLEDITSIA TRIACANTHOS VAR. INERMIS 'SHADEMASTER'
	GYMNOCLADUS DIOICA
	HAMAMELIS VIRGINIANA
	HYDRANGEA PANICULATA
	MALUS FLORIBUNDA
	MALUS HUPEHENSIS
	MALUS SARGENTII
	PHALARIS ARUNDINACEA VAR. PICTA
	PHELLODENDRON AMURENSE
	PINUS FLEXILIS
	PINUS KORAIENSIS
	QUERCUS ALBA
	QUERCUS MACROCARPA
	ROBINIA HISPIDA
	SALIX ALBA VAR. TRISTIS
	SYRINGA X CHINENSIS
	TAMARIX RAMOSISSIMA
	THUJA OCCIDENTALIS 'HETZ' WINTERGREEN'
	VIBURNUM CARLESII
5	ACER GRISEUM
	ACER PALMATUM 'BLOODGOOD'
	AESCULUS PARVIFLORA
	CAMPSIS X TAGLIABUANA 'MADAME GALEN'
	CATALPA BIGNONIOIDES
	CERCIDIPHYLLUM JAPONICUM
	CERCIS CANADENSIS 'FOREST PANSY'
	CHIONANTHUS VIRGINICUS
	CORNUS OFFICINALIS
	CORYLUS COLURNA
	CRATAEGUS VIRIDIS 'WINTER KING'
	DIOSPYROS VIRGINIANA
	ERANTHIS HYEMALIS
	ERANTHIS X TUBERGENII
	GALANTHUS ELWESII
	GALANTHUS NIVALIS
	HELIANTHEMUM APENNINUM VAR. ROSEUM
	HYDRANGEA ANOMALA SUBSP. PETIOLARIS 'SKYLANDS GIANT'
	JUNIPERUS SCOPULORUM 'SKY ROCKET'
	JUNIPERUS X MEDIA 'OLD GOLD'
	KERRIA JAPONICA
	KOELREUTERIA PANICULATA
	KOLKWITZIA AMABILIS
	LESPEDEZA THUNBERGII
	LIGUSTRUM QUIHOUI
	LONICERA FRAGRANTISSIMA
	MAGNOLIA 'ELIZABETH'
	MAGNOLIA VIRGINIANA
	MAGNOLIA X LOEBNERI
	MAGNOLIA X SOULANGIANA 'VERBANICA'
	METASEQUOIA GLYPTOSTROBOIDES
	PHLOX PILOSA SUBSP. OZARKANA
	PHLOX STOLONIFERA 'ALBA'
	PHLOX STOLONIFERA 'BLUE RIDGE'
	PHLOX STOLONIFERA 'SHERWOOD PURPLE'
	PICEA ORIENTALIS
	PINUS BUNGEANA
	PINUS PARVIFLORA 'GLAUCA'
	PINUS VIRGINIANA
	PLATANUS OCCIDENTALIS
	PRUNUS CERASIFERA 'THUNDERCLOUD'
	SASSAFRAS ALBIDUM

ZONE	LATIN NAME
	STERNBERGIA LUTEA
	SYMPHORICARPOS X CHENAULTII 'HANCOCK'
	SYRINGA LACINIATA
	VIBURNUM FARRERI 'CANDIDISSIMUM'
	VIBURNUM SIEBOLDII 'SENECA'
6	ACER PALMATUM 'EVER RED'
	ACER PALMATUM VAR. DISSECTUM OR A. P. 'WATERFALL'
	CERCIS CHINENSIS
	HEDERA HELIX 'BUTTERCUP'
	HEDERA HELIX 'GOLD HEART'
	IMPERATA CYLINDRICA 'RED BARON'
	JUNIPERUS CHINENSIS 'KAIZUKA'
	MAGNOLIA 'SUSAN'
	MAGNOLIA DENUDATA (SYN. M. HEPTAPETA)
	MAGNOLIA MACROPHYLLA
	MAHONIA BEALEI
	PAULOWNIA TOMENTOSA
	PINUS THUNBERGIANA
	PINUS THUNBERGIANA 'OCULUS-DRACONIS'
	SOPHORA JAPONICA 'REGENT'
	TAXODIUM DISTICHUM VAR. NUTANS 'PRAIRIE SENTINEL'
	VIBURNUM RHYTIDOPHYLLUM
	ZELKOVA SERRATA 'GREEN VASE'
7	DIOSPYROS KAKI
	ELAEAGNUS PUNGENS 'FRUITLANDII'
	ELAEAGNUS PUNGENS 'MACULATA'

APPENDIX 12
Plant Listing by Tolerance of Hot, Muggy Summers

In addition to frequent summer droughts in the mid-Atlantic states, we are routinely afflicted with high humidity. Not only does humidity deplete the energy of gardeners, but it causes many plants that in other ways are solid citizens to simply collapse and cease being of ornamental interest. The plants in the following list are more tolerant than most of this adversity.

The list has been divided by hardiness zone.

The letter *T* under the heading "Zone" indicates a plant that is tender, not tolerant of frost.

Further information about all the following plants is summarized in the Master Lists, Appendices 1A and 1B.

ZONE	LATIN NAME
2	ARTEMESIA STELLERIANA
	POTENTILLA TRIDENTATA
3	AEGOPODIUM PODAGRARIA 'VARIEGATUM'
	ALCHEMILLA VULGARIS
	AMSONIA TABERNAEMONTANA
	ARTEMESIA ABSINTHIUM 'LAMBROOK SILVER'

ZONE	LATIN NAME
	ASCLEPIAS TUBEROSA
	ASTER AMELLUS 'NOCTURNE'
	ASTER TATARICUS
	BAPTISIA AUSTRALIS
	BRUNNERA MACROPHYLLA
	COREOPSIS 'MOONBEAM'
	CORNUS RACEMOSA
	CORNUS RACEMOSA (DWARF)
	CORNUS SERICEA
	CORNUS SERICEA 'FLAVIRAMEA'
	DICENTRA 'LUXURIANT'
	ECHINACEA PURPUREA
	EUPHORBIA COROLLATA
	GERANIUM 'JOHNSON'S BLUE'
	GERANIUM MACRORRHIZUM
	HELLEBORUS NIGER
	HIPPOPHAE RHAMNOIDES
	HOSTA 'KABITAN'
	HOSTA PLANTAGINEA
	HOSTA UNDULATA
	HOSTA VENTRICOSA
	IRIS SIBIRICA CULTIVARS
	JUNIPERUS HORIZONTALIS 'WILTONII'
	JUNIPERUS VIRGINIANA
	LYTHRUM SALICARIA 'DROPMORE PURPLE'
	MALUS 'RED JADE'
	NEPETA X FAASSENII
	OSMUNDA REGALIS
	PAPAVER ORIENTALE
	PHLOX SUBULATA
	PHYSOSTEGIA VIRGINIANA
	PHYSOSTEGIA VIRGINIANA 'SUMMER SNOW'
	PICEA ABIES 'NIDIFORMIS'
	POLYSTICHUM ACROSTICHOIDES
	PRUNUS X CISTENA
	PULMONARIA ANGUSTIFOLIA
	QUERCUS RUBRA
	RHUS AROMATICA 'GRO-LOW'
	RHUS TYPHINA
	RHUS TYPHINA 'LACINIATA'
	SEDUM 'AUTUMN JOY'
	SEDUM ELLACOMBIANUM
	SEDUM SARMENTOSUM
	SEDUM SPURIUM
	SEDUM SPURIUM 'BRONZE CARPET'
	THUJA OCCIDENTALIS 'NIGRA'
	THYMUS SERPYLLUM
	TSUGA CANADENSIS 'COLE'S PROSTRATE'
	VIBURNUM ACERIFOLIUM
4	ACANTHOPANAX SIEBOLDIANUS
	ACER RUBRUM
	AJUGA REPTANS 'BRONZE BEAUTY'
	AJUGA REPTANS (GIANT FORM)
	ALLIUM TUBEROSUM
	ARALIA SPINOSA
	ARTEMESIA LUDOVICIANA 'SILVER QUEEN'
	ARUNCUS AETHUSIFOLIUS
	ASTILBE X ARENDSII CULTIVARS
	BACCHARIS HALIMIFOLIA, PISTILLATE
	BERBERIS THUNBERGII 'CRIMSON PYGMY'
	BETULA LENTA
	BETULA NIGRA
	CARYA OVATA
	CORYLUS AVELLANA 'CONTORTA'
	CORYLUS AVELLANA 'PENDULA'
	CRATAEGUS NITIDA
	CRATAEGUS PHAENOPYRUM

ZONE	LATIN NAME
	EUONYMUS ALATA
	GLEDITSIA TRIACANTHOS VAR. INERMIS 'SHADEMASTER'
	GYMNOCLADUS DIOICA
	HAMAMELIS VIRGINIANA
	HELIOPSIS HELIANTHOIDES SUBSP. SCABRA 'KARAT'
	HELLEBORUS ORIENTALIS HYBRIDS
	HYDRANGEA PANICULATA
	ILEX VERTICILLATA
	ILEX VERTICILLATA 'WINTER RED'
	JUNIPERUS X MEDIA 'PFITZERIANA COMPACTA'
	MALUS FLORIBUNDA
	MALUS SARGENTII
	MONARDA DIDYMA
	MYRICA PENSYLVANICA
	OSMUNDA CINNAMOMEA
	OSMUNDA CLAYTONIANA
	PHLOX BIFIDA
	PINUS FLEXILIS
	PINUS KORAIENSIS
	POLYGONATUM ODORATUM 'VARIEGATUM'
	QUERCUS ALBA
	RHODODENDRON MAXIMUM
	RHODODENDRON VISCOSUM
	ROBINIA HISPIDA
	ROSA NITIDA
	SEDUM POPULIFOLIUM
	STACHYS BYZANTINA
	SYRINGA PATULA (SYN. S. PALIBINIANA, S. MICROPHYLLA 'INGWERSEN'S DWARF')
	SYRINGA X CHINENSIS
	TAXUS CUSPIDATA 'NANA'
	TAXUS CUSPIDATA (CAPITATA SELECTION)
	TYPHA ANGUSTIFOLIA
	VACCINIUM CORYMBOSUM
	VERNONIA NOVEBORACENSIS
	VINCA MINOR 'BOWLESII'
	VINCA MINOR 'VARIEGATA'
	YUCCA FLACCIDA 'GOLDEN SWORD'
	YUCCA GLAUCA
	YUCCA SMALLIANA
5	ACER GRISEUM
	ALLIUM CERNUUM
	ALLIUM ZEBDANENSE
	AMSONIA HUBRICHTII
	ANEMONE BLANDA 'ATROCAERULEA'
	ARTEMESIA VERSICOLOR
	ARUNDINARIA VIRIDISTRIATA
	ASARUM EUROPAEUM
	ASPHODELINE LUTEA
	ATHYRIUM GOERINGIANUM 'PICTUM'
	BUDDLEIA DAVIDII 'BLACK KNIGHT'
	BUDDLEIA DAVIDII 'OPERA'
	BUDDLEIA DAVIDII 'PURPLE PRINCE'
	CALAMAGROSTIS X ACUTIFLORA 'KARL FOERSTER' (SYN. C. EPIGEOUS 'HORTORUM')
	CAMPSIS X TAGLIABUANA 'MADAME GALEN'
	CATALPA BIGNONIOIDES
	CEDRUS LIBANI VAR. STENOCOMA
	CHAMAECYPARIS OBTUSA 'NANA GRACILIS'
	CHIONANTHUS VIRGINICUS
	CHIONODOXA GIGANTEA 'ALBA'
	CHIONODOXA LUCILIAE

ZONE	LATIN NAME
	CHIONODOXA SARDENSIS
	CLETHRA ALNIFOLIA
	COLCHICUM 'AUTUMN QUEEN'
	COLCHICUM 'THE GIANT'
	COLUTEA X MEDIA
	CORNUS FLORIDA
	CORNUS FLORIDA 'HOHMAN'S GOLDEN'
	CORNUS MAS
	CORNUS OFFICINALIS
	COTINUS COGGYGRIA 'PURPUREUS'
	CRAMBE CORDIFOLIA
	CRATAEGUS VIRIDIS 'WINTER KING'
	CROCUS ANCYRENSIS 'GOLDEN BUNCH'
	CROCUS SIEBERI
	CROCUS TOMASINIANUS
	DEUTZIA GRACILIS
	ENDYMION HISPANICUS 'EXCELSIOR' (SYN. SCILLA CAMPANULATA 'EXCELSIOR')
	EPIMEDIUM PINNATUM SUBSP. COLCHICUM
	EPIMEDIUM X YOUNGIANUM 'NIVEUM'
	ERANTHIS HYEMALIS
	ERANTHIS X TUBERGENII
	FORSYTHIA SUSPENSA
	FOTHERGILLA GARDENII
	GALANTHUS ELWESII
	GALANTHUS NIVALIS
	HEDERA HELIX 'BULGARIA'
	HEDERA HELIX 'OGALALLA'
	HEMEROCALLIS 'HYPERION'
	HIBISCUS SYRIACUS 'BLUEBIRD'
	HIBISCUS SYRIACUS 'DIANA'
	HYDRANGEA QUERCIFOLIA
	ILEX CHINA BOY ® 'MESDOB'
	ILEX CHINA GIRL ® 'MESOG'
	ILEX GLABRA 'DENSA'
	ILEX X AQUIPERNYI 'SAN JOSE'
	ILEX X MESERVEAE BLUE MAID ® 'MESID'
	ILEX X MESERVEAE BLUE STALLION ® 'MESAN'
	INDIGOFERA INCARNATA 'ALBA'
	IRIS CRISTATA
	JUNIPERUS SCOPULORUM 'SKY ROCKET'
	JUNIPERUS X MEDIA 'OLD GOLD'
	KERRIA JAPONICA
	KOELREUTERIA PANICULATA
	KOLKWITZIA AMABILIS
	LAMIASTRUM GALEOBDOLON 'VARIEGATUM'
	LESPEDEZA THUNBERGII
	LEUCOJUM VERNUM
	LIGUSTRUM QUIHOUI
	LILIUM 'BLACK DRAGON'
	LIQUIDAMBAR STYRACIFLUA
	LONICERA FRAGRANTISSIMA
	LYCORIS SPRENGERI
	LYCORIS SQUAMIGERA
	MAGNOLIA 'ELIZABETH'
	MAGNOLIA VIRGINIANA
	MERTENSIA VIRGINICA
	MISCANTHUS 'GIGANTEUS'
	MISCANTHUS SINENSIS 'CABARET'
	MISCANTHUS SINENSIS 'GRACILLIMUS'
	MISCANTHUS SINENSIS 'MORNING LIGHT'
	MISCANTHUS SINENSIS 'SILVER FEATHER' (='SILBERFEDER')
	MISCANTHUS SINENSIS 'STRICTUS'

ZONE	LATIN NAME
	MISCANTHUS SINENSIS 'VARIEGATUS'
	MOLINIA CAERULEA SUBSP. ARUNDINACEA
	MUSCARI AZUREUM 'ALBUM'
	MUSCARI BOTRYOIDES 'ALBUM'
	MUSCARI TUBERGENIANUM
	NARCISSUS 'CARLTON'
	NARCISSUS 'FORTUNE'
	NARCISSUS 'HERA'
	NARCISSUS 'LOCH FYNE'
	NARCISSUS 'MOONMIST'
	NARCISSUS 'MRS. ERNST H. KRELAGE'
	NARCISSUS 'PEEPING TOM'
	NARCISSUS 'POMONA'
	NARCISSUS 'QUEEN OF SPAIN'
	NARCISSUS 'TREVITHIAN'
	NARCISSUS JONQUILLA
	NARCISSUS PSEUDONARCISSUS SUBSP. OBVALLARIS
	NYSSA SYLVATICA
	PACHYSANDRA TERMINALIS
	PACHYSANDRA TERMINALIS 'GREEN CARPET'
	PACHYSANDRA TERMINALIS 'VARIEGATA' OR 'SILVER EDGE'
	PANICUM VIRGATUM 'STRICTUM'
	PENNISETUM ALOPECUROIDES
	PHILADELPHUS CORONARIUS
	PHILADELPHUS X FALCONERI
	PHLOMIS RUSSELIANA
	PHLOX PILOSA SUBSP. OZARKANA
	PICEA ORIENTALIS
	PINUS PARVIFLORA 'GLAUCA'
	PINUS VIRGINIANA
	PLATANUS OCCIDENTALIS
	POLYSTICHUM TRIPTERON
	PRUNUS CERASIFERA 'THUNDERCLOUD'
	RHODODENDRON (GABLE HYBRIDS)
	RHODODENDRON ARBORESCENS
	RHODODENDRON MUCRONULATUM
	RHODODENDRON SCHLIPPENBACHII
	RHODODENDRON VASEYI
	RHODODENDRON X GANDAVENSE 'COCCINEA SPECIOSA'
	RHODODENDRON X GANDAVENSE 'DAVIESII'
	RHODOTYPOS SCANDENS
	ROSA (SHRUB) 'LILLIAN GIBSON'
	ROSA CAROLINA
	ROSA VIRGINIANA
	RUBUS COCKBURNIANUS
	SASSAFRAS ALBIDUM
	SCILLA SIBERICA 'SPRING BEAUTY'
	SEDUM 'VERA JAMISON'
	SEDUM FLORIFERUM 'WEIHANSTEPHANER GOLD'
	SPIRAEA PRUNIFOLIA
	SYMPHORICARPOS X CHENAULTII 'HANCOCK'
	SYMPHYTUM X UPLANDICUM
	SYRINGA RETICULATA
	TAXUS BACCATA 'ADPRESSA FOWLE'
	TAXUS X MEDIA 'SENTINALIS'
	THYMUS 'CLEAR GOLD'
	THYMUS PSEUDOLANUGINOSUS
	VERBASCUM OLYMPICUM
	VIBURNUM PLICATUM FORMA TOMENTOSUM
	VIBURNUM SIEBOLDII 'SENECA'
	WISTERIA FLORIBUNDA
	XANTHORHIZA SIMPLICISSIMA

ZONE	LATIN NAME
6	ABELIA X GRANDIFLORA
	ARUM ITALICUM 'PICTUM'
	BIGNONIA CAPREOLATA
	CALLICARPA DICHOTOMA
	CERATOSTIGMA PLUMBAGINOIDES
	CLETHRA BARBINERVIS
	COTONEASTER ADPRESSUS VAR. PRAECOX
	CROCOSMIA 'LUCIFER'
	CROCOSMIA POTTSII
	CROCOSMIA X CROCOSMIIFLORA
	CYTISUS SCOPARIUS
	EUPATORIUM COELESTINUM
	FORSYTHIA X INTERMEDIA 'SPRING GLORY'
	GALTONIA CANDICANS
	HEDERA HELIX 'BALTICA'
	ILEX CRENATA 'HELLERI'
	ILEX CRENATA 'MICROPHYLLA'
	ILEX OPACA 'ARDEN'
	ILEX OPACA 'XANTHOCARPA'
	IMPERATA CYLINDRICA 'RED BARON'
	ITEA VIRGINICA 'HENRY'S GARNET'
	JUNIPERUS CHINENSIS 'KAIZUKA'
	LESPEDEZA THUNBERGII 'ALBIFLORA'
	LIRIOPE MUSCARI (BIG BLUE SELECTION)
	LIRIOPE MUSCARI 'MONROE WHITE'
	LIRIOPE MUSCARI 'VARIEGATA'
	MAHONIA BEALEI
	RHODODENDRON (KAEMPFERI HYBRIDS)
	RHODODENDRON (KURUME HYBRIDS)
	ROSA ROXBURGHII
	SOPHORA JAPONICA 'REGENT'
	TRACHYSTEMON ORIENTALIS
	VITEX AGNUS-CASTUS 'LATIFOLIA'
	VITEX AGNUS-CASTUS 'SILVER SPIRE'
7	CHIMONANTHUS PRAECOX
	ELAEAGNUS PUNGENS 'FRUITLANDII'
	ELAEAGNUS PUNGENS 'MACULATA'
	GENISTA SYLVESTRIS 'LYDIA'
	PYRACANTHA COCCINEA 'AUREA'
	SASA VEITCHII
	VIBURNUM MACROCEPHALUM FORMA MACROCEPHALUM
T	ACIDANTHERA BICOLOR
	CANNA X GENERALIS 'MOHAWK'
	CESTRUM NOCTURNUM
	DATURA INOXIA SUBSP. QUINQUECUSPIDA
	KOCHIA SCOPARIA FORMA TRICHOPHYLLA 'CHILDSII'
	RICINUS COMMUNIS
	RICINUS COMMUNIS 'ZANZIBARENSIS'

APPENDIX 13
Plant Listing by Seasonal Interest—Flower

Grouped together in this appendix and arranged by month are all of the plants that I have selected for flower effect. As the listing indicates, it is possible to have flowers in your garden twelve months of the year.

The choice is, of course, limited during the winter; the list for November shows 2 plants; December, 3 plants; January, 7 plants; February, 12 plants; and March, 30 plants. This contrasts sharply with a peak of 143 in May. These winter-flowering plants are therefore especially significant.

The wide palette of plants for April (99), May (143), and June (120) presents you with the necessity and challenge, on the other hand, of making choices to suit your own very specific design requirements.

Bloom dates are for my area and will, of course, vary outside Hockessin, Delaware.

The list is subdivided by hardiness zone.

The letter *T* under the heading "Zone" indicates a plant that is tender, not tolerant of frost.

Further information about all the following plants is summarized in the Master Lists, Appendices 1A and 1B.

JANUARY

ZONE	LATIN NAME
4	CORYLUS AVELLANA 'CONTORTA'
	CORYLUS AVELLANA 'PENDULA'
5	CORYLUS COLURNA
	HAMAMELIS MOLLIS 'PALLIDA'
	SALIX ACUTIFOLIA 'LONGIFOLIA'
	SALIX DAPHNOIDES 'AGLAIA'
7	CHIMONANTHUS PRAECOX

FEBRUARY

ZONE	LATIN NAME
4	CORYLUS AVELLANA 'CONTORTA'
	CORYLUS AVELLANA 'PENDULA'
5	CORYLUS COLURNA
	HAMAMELIS MOLLIS 'PALLIDA'
	HAMAMELIS X INTERMEDIA 'DIANE'
	HAMAMELIS X INTERMEDIA 'JELENA'
	HAMAMELIS X INTERMEDIA 'PRIMAVERA'
	LONICERA FRAGRANTISSIMA
	SALIX ACUTIFOLIA 'LONGIFOLIA'
	SALIX DAPHNOIDES 'AGLAIA'
6	JASMINUM NUDIFLORUM

ZONE	LATIN NAME
7	CHIMONANTHUS PRAECOX

MARCH

ZONE	LATIN NAME
3	HELLEBORUS NIGER
4	CORYLUS AVELLANA 'CONTORTA'
	CORYLUS AVELLANA 'PENDULA'
	HELLEBORUS ORIENTALIS HYBRIDS
5	CORNUS MAS
	CORNUS OFFICINALIS
	CORYLUS COLURNA
	CROCUS ANCYRENSIS 'GOLDEN BUNCH'
	CROCUS SIEBERI
	CROCUS TOMASINIANUS
	ERANTHIS HYEMALIS
	ERANTHIS X TUBERGENII
	GALANTHUS ELWESII
	GALANTHUS NIVALIS
	HAMAMELIS MOLLIS 'PALLIDA'
	HAMAMELIS X INTERMEDIA 'DIANE'
	HAMAMELIS X INTERMEDIA 'JELENA'
	HAMAMELIS X INTERMEDIA 'PRIMAVERA'
	LEUCOJUM VERNUM
	LONICERA FRAGRANTISSIMA
	SALIX ACUTIFOLIA 'LONGIFOLIA'
	SALIX CHAENOMELOIDES
	SALIX DAPHNOIDES 'AGLAIA'
	SALIX GRACILISTYLA
	SALIX GRACILISTYLA 'MELANOSTACHYS'
	SCILLA SIBERICA 'SPRING BEAUTY'
	VIBURNUM FARRERI 'CANDIDISSIMUM'
	VIBURNUM FARRERI 'NANUM'
6	JASMINUM NUDIFLORUM
	PIERIS JAPONICA

APRIL

ZONE	LATIN NAME
2	BERGENIA 'PERFECTA'
	BERGENIA 'SUNNINGDALE'
3	AMELANCHIER ARBOREA (SYN. A. CANADENSIS)
	BRUNNERA MACROPHYLLA
	HELLEBORUS NIGER
	PHLOX SUBULATA
	PULMONARIA ANGUSTIFOLIA
	PULMONARIA SACCHARATA 'MARGERY FISH'
	PULMONARIA SACCHARATA 'SISSINGHURST WHITE'
	RHUS AROMATICA 'GRO-LOW'
4	ACER RUBRUM
	BERBERIS THUNBERGII 'ATROPURPUREA'
	BERBERIS THUNBERGII 'CRIMSON PYGMY'
	CHAENOMELES JAPONICA VAR. ALPINA
	CHAENOMELES SPECIOSA CULTIVARS
	CHAENOMELES X SUPERBA 'JET TRAIL'

ZONE	LATIN NAME
	CORYLUS AVELLANA 'CONTORTA'
	CORYLUS AVELLANA 'PENDULA'
	EUPHORBIA CYPARISSIAS
	EUPHORBIA EPITHYMOIDES
	HELLEBORUS ORIENTALIS HYBRIDS
	PETASITES JAPONICUS
	PHLOX BIFIDA
	SALIX REPENS VAR. ARGENTEA
	SPIRAEA THUNBERGII
	VIBURNUM CARLESII
5	ALLIUM ZEBDANENSE
	ANEMONE BLANDA 'ATROCAERULEA'
	CERCIS CANADENSIS 'FOREST PANSY'
	CHAENOMELES X SUPERBA CULTIVARS
	CHIONODOXA GIGANTEA 'ALBA'
	CHIONODOXA LUCILIAE
	CHIONODOXA SARDENSIS
	CORNUS MAS
	CORNUS OFFICINALIS
	CORYLOPSIS PLATYPETALA
	CORYLUS COLURNA
	CROCUS TOMASINIANUS
	DAPHNE X BURKWOODII 'CAROL MACKIE'
	EPIMEDIUM PINNATUM SUBSP. COLCHICUM
	EPIMEDIUM X YOUNGIANUM 'NIVEUM'
	FORSYTHIA SUSPENSA
	FOTHERGILLA GARDENII
	HAMAMELIS MOLLIS 'PALLIDA'
	HAMAMELIS X INTERMEDIA 'DIANE'
	HAMAMELIS X INTERMEDIA 'JELENA'
	HAMAMELIS X INTERMEDIA 'PRIMAVERA'
	LATHYRUS VERNUS
	LONICERA FRAGRANTISSIMA
	LYSICHITON AMERICANUM
	LYSICHITON CAMTSCHATCENSE
	MAGNOLIA 'ELIZABETH'
	MAGNOLIA X LOEBNERI
	MAGNOLIA X SOULANGIANA 'VERBANICA'
	MERTENSIA VIRGINICA
	MUSCARI AZUREUM 'ALBUM'
	MUSCARI BOTRYOIDES 'ALBUM'
	MUSCARI TUBERGENIANUM
	NARCISSUS 'CARLTON'
	NARCISSUS 'FORTUNE'
	NARCISSUS 'HERA'
	NARCISSUS 'LOCH FYNE'
	NARCISSUS 'MOONMIST'
	NARCISSUS 'MRS. ERNST H. KRELAGE'
	NARCISSUS 'PEEPING TOM'
	NARCISSUS 'POMONA'
	NARCISSUS 'QUEEN OF SPAIN'
	NARCISSUS 'TREVITHIAN'
	NARCISSUS JONQUILLA
	NARCISSUS PSEUDONARCISSUS SUBSP. OBVALLARIS
	OMPHALODES VERNA
	PETASITES FRAGRANS
	PRUNUS 'HALLY JOLIVETTE'
	PRUNUS SUBHIRTELLA 'AUTUMNALIS'
	RHODODENDRON MUCRONULATUM
	RIBES ODORATUM
	SALIX ACUTIFOLIA 'LONGIFOLIA'
	SALIX CHAENOMELOIDES
	SALIX DAPHNOIDES 'AGLAIA'
	SALIX GRACILISTYLA
	SALIX GRACILISTYLA 'MELANOSTACHYS'
	SALIX X RUBRA 'EUGENEI'

ZONE	LATIN NAME
	SASSAFRAS ALBIDUM
	SCILLA SIBERICA 'SPRING BEAUTY'
	VIBURNUM FARRERI 'CANDIDISSIMUM'
	VIBURNUM FARRERI 'NANUM'
	XANTHORHIZA SIMPLICISSIMA
6	ENKIANTHUS PERULATUS
	FORSYTHIA VIRIDISSIMA 'BRONXENSIS'
	FORSYTHIA X INTERMEDIA 'SPRING GLORY'
	MAGNOLIA 'SUSAN'
	MAGNOLIA DENUDATA (SYN. M. HEPTAPETA)
	MAHONIA BEALEI
	PIERIS JAPONICA
	PONCIRUS TRIFOLIATA
	PRUNUS SUBHIRTELLA 'PENDULA'
	PRUNUS YEDOENSIS
	TRACHYSTEMON ORIENTALIS
7	VIBURNUM MACROCEPHALUM FORMA MACROCEPHALUM

MAY

ZONE	LATIN NAME
2	BERGENIA 'PERFECTA'
	BERGENIA 'SUNNINGDALE'
	DICENTRA SPECTABILIS
	PAEONIA—HERBACEOUS HYBRIDS
	POTENTILLA TRIDENTATA
3	ALCHEMILLA VULGARIS
	AMELANCHIER ARBOREA (SYN. A. CANADENSIS)
	AMSONIA TABERNAEMONTANA
	BAPTISIA AUSTRALIS
	BRUNNERA MACROPHYLLA
	DIANTHUS DELTOIDES
	DICENTRA 'LUXURIANT'
	DICENTRA EXIMIA 'PURITY'
	GERANIUM 'JOHNSON'S BLUE'
	GERANIUM MACRORRHIZUM
	GERANIUM SANGUINEUM
	HEMEROCALLIS LILIOASPHODELUS
	HOSTA SIEBOLDIANA 'ELEGANS'
	MALUS 'RED JADE'
	OSMUNDA REGALIS
	PAPAVER ORIENTALE
	PRUNUS X CISTENA
	RHODODENDRON PRINOPHYLLUM
	SEDUM SPURIUM
	SPIRAEA X VANHOUTTEI
	SYRINGA VULGARIS 'ALBA'
	SYRINGA VULGARIS HYBRIDS
	THERMOPSIS CAROLINIANA
	TIARELLA CORDIFOLIA VAR. COLLINA
	VIBURNUM PRUNIFOLIUM
4	ACANTHOPANAX SIEBOLDIANUS
	ACER PLATANOIDES 'CRIMSON KING'
	AJUGA REPTANS
	AJUGA REPTANS 'BRONZE BEAUTY'
	AJUGA REPTANS (GIANT FORM)
	ARABIS PROCURRENS
	ARUNCUS AETHUSIFOLIUS
	BUDDLEIA ALTERNIFOLIA
	CONVALLARIA MAJALIS
	CORNUS ALTERNIFOLIA
	CRATAEGUS NITIDA

ZONE	LATIN NAME
	CRATAEGUS PHAENOPYRUM
	EUPHORBIA EPITHYMOIDES
	GAULTHERIA PROCUMBENS
	HEDYOTIS CAERULEA
	MALUS FLORIBUNDA
	MALUS HUPEHENSIS
	MALUS SARGENTII
	OSMUNDA CINNAMOMEA
	OSMUNDA CLAYTONIANA
	PAEONIA TENUIFOLIA
	PHLOX BIFIDA
	POLYGONATUM ODORATUM 'VARIEGATUM'
	RHODODENDRON (CATAWBIENSE HYBRIDS)
	ROBINIA HISPIDA
	RODGERSIA AESCULIFOLIA
	RODGERSIA PODOPHYLLA
	RODGERSIA TABULARIS
	SEDUM TERNATUM
	SYRINGA PATULA (SYN. S. PALIBINIANA, S. MICROPHYLLA 'INGWERSEN'S DWARF')
	SYRINGA X CHINENSIS
	VACCINIUM CORYMBOSUM
	VINCA MINOR 'BOWLESII'
	VINCA MINOR 'VARIEGATA'
	WALDSTEINIA TERNATA
5	ALLIUM ZEBDANENSE
	AMSONIA HUBRICHTII
	ASPHODELINE LUTEA
	CALYCANTHUS FLORIDUS 'EDITH WILDER'
	CERCIS CANADENSIS 'FOREST PANSY'
	CHIONANTHUS VIRGINICUS
	CORNUS FLORIDA
	CORNUS FLORIDA 'HOHMAN'S GOLDEN'
	CORNUS KOUSA
	COTONEASTER APICULATUS
	COTONEASTER HORIZONTALIS
	CRAMBE CORDIFOLIA
	CRATAEGUS VIRIDIS 'WINTER KING'
	DAPHNE X BURKWOODII 'CAROL MACKIE'
	DEUTZIA GRACILIS
	ENDYMION HISPANICUS 'EXCELSIOR' (SYN. SCILLA CAMPANULATA 'EXCELSIOR')
	ENKIANTHUS CAMPANULATUS
	EXOCHORDA GIRALDII VAR. WILSONII
	FOTHERGILLA GARDENII
	GALIUM ODORATUM
	HALESIA TETRAPTERA
	IRIS CRISTATA
	IRIS GRAMINEA
	IRIS PSEUDACORUS
	IRIS TECTORUM
	KERRIA JAPONICA
	KOLKWITZIA AMABILIS
	LAMIASTRUM GALEOBDOLON 'VARIEGATUM'
	LAMIUM MACULATUM 'WHITE NANCY'
	LATHYRUS VERNUS
	LEUCOTHOE FONTANESIANA
	LEUCOTHOE FONTANESIANA 'NANA'
	LYSICHITON AMERICANUM
	LYSICHITON CAMTSCHATCENSE
	MAGNOLIA 'ELIZABETH'
	MERTENSIA VIRGINICA

ZONE	LATIN NAME
	NARCISSUS 'TREVITHIAN'
	OMPHALODES VERNA
	PHILADELPHUS X FALCONERI
	PHLOX PILOSA SUBSP. OZARKANA
	PHLOX STOLONIFERA 'ALBA'
	PHLOX STOLONIFERA 'BLUE RIDGE'
	PHLOX STOLONIFERA 'SHERWOOD PURPLE'
	PRUNUS CERASIFERA 'THUNDERCLOUD'
	RHEUM PALMATUM 'RUBRUM'
	RHODODENDRON (GABLE HYBRIDS)
	RHODODENDRON ATLANTICUM
	RHODODENDRON SCHLIPPENBACHII
	RHODODENDRON VASEYI
	RHODODENDRON X GANDAVENSE 'COCCINEA SPECIOSA'
	RHODODENDRON X GANDAVENSE 'DAVIESII'
	RHODOTYPOS SCANDENS
	ROSA 'DOORENBOS SELECTION'
	ROSA EGLANTERIA
	SEDUM FLORIFERUM 'WEIHANSTEPHANER GOLD'
	SPIRAEA PRUNIFOLIA
	SYMPHYTUM X UPLANDICUM
	SYRINGA LACINIATA
	VALERIANA OFFICINALIS
	VIBURNUM PLICATUM FORMA TOMENTOSUM
	WISTERIA FLORIBUNDA
6	ARUM ITALICUM 'PICTUM'
	BERBERIS JULIANAE 'NANA'
	BIGNONIA CAPREOLATA
	CERCIS CHINENSIS
	COTONEASTER ADPRESSUS VAR. PRAECOX
	CRUCIANELLA STYLOSA
	CYTISUS X PRAECOX 'LUTEUS'
	PAEONIA 'BLACK PIRATE'
	PAEONIA—WOODY HYBRIDS
	PAULOWNIA TOMENTOSA
	RHODODENDRON (GLENN DALE HYBRIDS)
	RHODODENDRON (KAEMPFERI HYBRIDS)
	RHODODENDRON (KNAP HILL HYBRID) 'TUNIS'
	RHODODENDRON (KURUME HYBRIDS)
7	RHODODENDRON CANESCENS
	SKIMMIA REEVESIANA
	VIBURNUM MACROCEPHALUM FORMA MACROCEPHALUM

JUNE

ZONE	LATIN NAME
2	ACHILLEA MILLEFOLIUM 'ROSEA'
	SAPONARIA OFFICINALIS
3	ACHILLEA 'CORONATION GOLD'
	ACHILLEA 'MOONSHINE'
	ALCHEMILLA VULGARIS
	ARUNCUS DIOICUS
	BAPTISIA AUSTRALIS
	BUPHTHALUM SALICIFOLIUM
	CAMPANULA RAPUNCULOIDES
	CIMICIFUGA RACEMOSA
	COREOPSIS 'MOONBEAM'

ZONE	LATIN NAME
	DIANTHUS DELTOIDES
	ECHINACEA PURPUREA
	GERANIUM MACRORRHIZUM
	GERANIUM SANGUINEUM
	HOSTA VENTRICOSA
	INULA HELENIUM
	IRIS SIBIRICA CULTIVARS
	LIATRIS SCARIOSA 'WHITE SPIRE'
	LIATRIS SPICATA 'KOBOLD'
	LYTHRUM SALICARIA 'DROPMORE PURPLE'
	MACLEAYA CORDATA
	NEPETA X FAASSENII
	RHODODENDRON PRINOPHYLLUM
	ROSA RUGOSA AND HYBRIDS
	SEDUM ELLACOMBIANUM
	SEDUM SARMENTOSUM
	SEDUM SPURIUM
	SEDUM SPURIUM 'BRONZE CARPET'
	SORBARIA SORBIFOLIA
	TELEKIA SPECIOSA
	THERMOPSIS CAROLINIANA
	THYMUS SERPYLLUM
4	ASTILBE X ARENDSII CULTIVARS
	CEPHALANTHUS OCCIDENTALIS
	CLADRASTIS LUTEA
	CLEMATIS 'MRS. CHOLMONDELEY'
	CLEMATIS 'PRINS HENDRIK'
	CLEMATIS 'RAMONA'
	CLEMATIS X JACKMANII
	DIERVILLA SESSILIFOLIA
	GYMNOCLADUS DIOICA
	HELIOPSIS HELIANTHOIDES SUBSP. SCABRA 'KARAT'
	MONARDA DIDYMA
	RHODODENDRON MAXIMUM
	RHODODENDRON VISCOSUM
	ROBINIA HISPIDA
	ROSA NITIDA
	STACHYS BYZANTINA
	TAMARIX RAMOSISSIMA
	WALDSTEINIA TERNATA
	YUCCA FLACCIDA 'GOLDEN SWORD'
	YUCCA GLAUCA
	YUCCA SMALLIANA
5	AESCULUS PARVIFLORA
	ALLIUM CERNUUM
	ASPHODELINE LUTEA
	CALAMAGROSTIS X ACUTIFLORA 'KARL FOERSTER' (SYN. C. EPIGEOUS 'HORTORUM')
	CATALPA BIGNONIOIDES
	CORNUS KOUSA
	CRAMBE CORDIFOLIA
	HELIANTHEMUM APENNINUM VAR. ROSEUM
	HELICTOTRICHON SEMPERVIRENS
	HEMEROCALLIS 'HYPERION'
	HEMEROCALLIS FULVA 'EUROPA'
	HERACLEUM MANTEGAZZIANUM
	HOUTTUYNIA CORDATA 'CHAMELEON'
	HYDRANGEA ANOMALA SUBSP. PETIOLARIS 'SKYLANDS GIANT'
	HYDRANGEA QUERCIFOLIA
	INDIGOFERA INCARNATA 'ALBA'
	IRIS TECTORUM
	KALMIA LATIFOLIA
	KOELREUTERIA PANICULATA
	LILIUM 'BLACK DRAGON'
	LILIUM SPECIES AND HYBRIDS
	LYSIMACHIA PUNCTATA

ZONE	LATIN NAME
	MAGNOLIA VIRGINIANA
	ONOPORDUM ACANTHIUM
	PHILADELPHUS X FALCONERI
	PHLOMIS RUSSELIANA
	PHLOX PILOSA SUBSP. OZARKANA
	RHEUM PALMATUM 'RUBRUM'
	RHODODENDRON ARBORESCENS
	ROSA 'DOORENBOS SELECTION'
	ROSA (GALLICA) 'CHARLES DE MILLS'
	ROSA (POLYANTHA) 'THE FAIRY'
	ROSA (SHRUB) 'LILLIAN GIBSON'
	ROSA (SHRUB) 'SEA FOAM'
	ROSA CAROLINA
	ROSA EGLANTERIA
	ROSA VIRGINIANA
	SEDUM FLORIFERUM 'WEIHANSTEPHANER GOLD'
	STEPHANANDRA INCISA 'CRISPA'
	SYMPHYTUM X UPLANDICUM
	SYRINGA RETICULATA
	THALICTRUM ROCHEBRUNIANUM
	THYMUS 'CLEAR GOLD'
	VALERIANA OFFICINALIS
	VERBASCUM OLYMPICUM
6	AESCULUS SPLENDENS
	ARUM ITALICUM 'PICTUM'
	BIGNONIA CAPREOLATA
	CROCOSMIA 'LUCIFER'
	CRUCIANELLA STYLOSA
	CYTISUS SCOPARIUS
	FILIPENDULA PURPUREA 'ELEGANS'
	GALTONIA CANDICANS
	HYDRANGEA MACROPHYLLA 'BLUE BILLOW'
	ITEA VIRGINICA 'HENRY'S GARNET'
	RHODODENDRON X ERIOCARPUM AND R. X NAKAHARAI CULTIVARS AND HYBRIDS
	ROSA ROXBURGHII
	SALVIA ARGENTEA
	SAXIFRAGA STOLONIFERA
	SOPHORA JAPONICA 'REGENT'
	STEWARTIA KOREANA
	STRANVAESIA DAVIDIANA VAR. UNDULATA 'PROSTRATA'
	STYRAX JAPONICUS
	STYRAX JAPONICUS 'CARILLON'
7	GENISTA SYLVESTRIS 'LYDIA'
T	DATURA INOXIA SUBSP. QUINQUECUSPIDA

JULY

ZONE	LATIN NAME
2	SAPONARIA OFFICINALIS
3	ACHILLEA 'CORONATION GOLD'
	ACHILLEA 'MOONSHINE'
	ASCLEPIAS TUBEROSA
	ASTER AMELLUS 'NOCTURNE'
	BUPHTHALUM SALICIFOLIUM
	CAMPANULA RAPUNCULOIDES
	CIMICIFUGA RACEMOSA
	CLEMATIS HERACLEIFOLIA VAR. DAVIDIANA
	COREOPSIS 'MOONBEAM'
	ECHINACEA PURPUREA
	ECHINOPS RITRO

ZONE	LATIN NAME
	EUPHORBIA COROLLATA
	HOSTA VENTRICOSA
	INULA HELENIUM
	LIATRIS SCARIOSA 'WHITE SPIRE'
	LIATRIS SPICATA 'KOBOLD'
	LYSIMACHIA CLETHROIDES
	LYTHRUM SALICARIA 'DROPMORE PURPLE'
	MACLEAYA CORDATA
	NEPETA X FAASSENII
	RHUS TYPHINA
	RHUS TYPHINA 'LACINIATA'
	RUDBECKIA FULGIDA VAR. SULLIVANTII 'GOLDSTURM'
	SORBARIA SORBIFOLIA
4	ARALIA SPINOSA
	CEPHALANTHUS OCCIDENTALIS
	HELIOPSIS HELIANTHOIDES SUBSP. SCABRA 'KARAT'
	HYPERICUM KALMIANUM
	MONARDA DIDYMA
	RHODODENDRON VISCOSUM
	TAMARIX RAMOSISSIMA
	VERONICA 'SUNNY BORDER BLUE'
	VERONICA LONGIFOLIA 'SUBSESSILIS'
5	BUDDLEIA DAVIDII 'BLACK KNIGHT'
	BUDDLEIA DAVIDII 'PURPLE PRINCE'
	CAMPSIS X TAGLIABUANA 'MADAME GALEN'
	CLETHRA ALNIFOLIA
	COLUTEA X MEDIA
	FILIPENDULA PURPUREA 'NANA'
	HEMEROCALLIS 'HYPERION'
	HEMEROCALLIS FULVA 'EUROPA'
	HOUTTUYNIA CORDATA 'CHAMELEON'
	HYPERICUM FRONDOSUM
	LIGUSTRUM QUIHOUI
	LILIUM 'BLACK DRAGON'
	LILIUM SPECIES AND HYBRIDS
	LYSIMACHIA PUNCTATA
	MAGNOLIA VIRGINIANA
	ONOPORDUM ACANTHIUM
	OXYDENDRUM ARBOREUM
	PEROVSKIA ABROTANOIDES X P. ATRIPLICIFOLIA
	ROSA (POLYANTHA) 'THE FAIRY'
	ROSA (SHRUB) 'SEA FOAM'
	STOKESIA LAEVIS 'BLUE DANUBE'
	SYMPHORICARPOS X CHENAULTII 'HANCOCK'
	THALICTRUM ROCHEBRUNIANUM
	VIBURNUM SIEBOLDII 'SENECA'
6	ABELIA X GRANDIFLORA
	CLETHRA BARBINERVIS
	CROCOSMIA POTTSII
	GALTONIA CANDICANS
	HYDRANGEA MACROPHYLLA 'BLUE BILLOW'
	SALVIA ARGENTEA
	SAXIFRAGA STOLONIFERA
	SOPHORA JAPONICA 'REGENT'
	VITEX AGNUS-CASTUS 'LATIFOLIA'
	VITEX AGNUS-CASTUS 'SILVER SPIRE'
7	HYDRANGEA ASPERA SUBSP. SARGENTIANA
T	CANNA X GENERALIS 'MOHAWK'
	DATURA INOXIA SUBSP. QUINQUECUSPIDA
	POLIANTHES TUBEROSA

AUGUST

ZONE	LATIN NAME
2	SAPONARIA OFFICINALIS
3	ASCLEPIAS TUBEROSA
	ASTER AMELLUS 'NOCTURNE'
	CHELONE LYONII
	CLEMATIS HERACLEIFOLIA VAR. DAVIDIANA
	COREOPSIS 'MOONBEAM'
	ECHINACEA PURPUREA
	ECHINOPS RITRO
	EUPHORBIA COROLLATA
	HOSTA 'KABITAN'
	HOSTA PLANTAGINEA
	HOSTA UNDULATA
	LYSIMACHIA CLETHROIDES
	PHYSOSTEGIA VIRGINIANA
	PHYSOSTEGIA VIRGINIANA 'SUMMER SNOW'
	RUDBECKIA FULGIDA VAR. SULLIVANTII 'GOLDSTURM'
	VERONICA INCANA
	VERONICASTRUM VIRGINICUM
4	ALLIUM TUBEROSUM
	ANEMONE VITIFOLIA 'ROBUSTISSIMA'
	ARALIA SPINOSA
	CARYOPTERIS X CLANDONENSIS 'BLUE MIST'
	CHAMAEMELUM NOBILE
	CLEMATIS MAXIMOWICZIANA
	HYDRANGEA PANICULATA
	HYPERICUM KALMIANUM
	VERNONIA NOVEBORACENSIS
	VERONICA 'SUNNY BORDER BLUE'
	VERONICA LONGIFOLIA 'SUBSESSILIS'
5	ANEMONE X HYBRIDA 'QUEEN CHARLOTTE'
	ASTER CORDIFOLIUS
	ASTER X FRIKARTII 'MONCH'
	BUDDLEIA DAVIDII 'BLACK KNIGHT'
	BUDDLEIA DAVIDII 'PURPLE PRINCE'
	CAMPSIS X TAGLIABUANA 'MADAME GALEN'
	CLETHRA ALNIFOLIA
	FILIPENDULA PURPUREA 'NANA'
	HIBISCUS SYRIACUS 'BLUEBIRD'
	HIBISCUS SYRIACUS 'DIANA'
	HYPERICUM FRONDOSUM
	PANICUM VIRGATUM 'STRICTUM'
	PENNISETUM ALOPECUROIDES
	PEROVSKIA ABROTANOIDES X P. ATRIPLICIFOLIA
	ROSA (POLYANTHA) 'THE FAIRY'
	ROSA (SHRUB) 'SEA FOAM'
	SEDUM 'VERA JAMISON'
	STOKESIA LAEVIS 'BLUE DANUBE'
	SYMPHORICARPOS X CHENAULTII 'HANCOCK'
	THALICTRUM ROCHEBRUNIANUM
6	ABELIA X GRANDIFLORA
	ADINA RUBELLA
	BEGONIA GRANDIS
	CERATOSTIGMA PLUMBAGINOIDES
	CLETHRA BARBINERVIS
	CROCOSMIA X CROCOSMIIFLORA
	FRANKLINIA ALATAMAHA
	LIRIOPE MUSCARI (BIG BLUE SELECTION)

ZONE	LATIN NAME
	LIRIOPE MUSCARI 'MONROE WHITE'
	LIRIOPE MUSCARI 'VARIEGATA'
	VITEX AGNUS-CASTUS 'LATIFOLIA'
	VITEX AGNUS-CASTUS 'SILVER SPIRE'
7	CLERODENDRUM TRICHOTOMUM
T	CANNA X GENERALIS 'MOHAWK'
	DATURA INOXIA SUBSP. QUINQUECUSPIDA
	POLIANTHES TUBEROSA

SEPTEMBER

ZONE	LATIN NAME
2	ASTER PUNICEUS
3	ASTER TATARICUS
	BOLTONIA ASTEROIDES 'SNOWBANK'
	CHELONE LYONII
	CLEMATIS HERACLEIFOLIA VAR. DAVIDIANA
	COREOPSIS 'MOONBEAM'
	HOSTA PLANTAGINEA
	PHYSOSTEGIA VIRGINIANA
	PHYSOSTEGIA VIRGINIANA 'SUMMER SNOW'
	SEDUM 'AUTUMN JOY'
4	ALLIUM TUBEROSUM
	BACCHARIS HALIMIFOLIA, PISTILLATE
	CARYOPTERIS X CLANDONENSIS 'BLUE MIST'
	CHAMAEMELUM NOBILE
	CLEMATIS MAXIMOWICZIANA
	HYDRANGEA PANICULATA
	VERNONIA NOVEBORACENSIS
5	ANEMONE X HYBRIDA 'QUEEN CHARLOTTE'
	ASTER CORDIFOLIUS
	ASTER NOVAE-ANGLIAE 'HARRINGTON'S PINK'
	ASTER X FRIKARTII 'MONCH'
	CHRYSANTHEMUM WEYRICHII 'WHITE BOMB'
	COLCHICUM 'AUTUMN QUEEN'
	COLCHICUM 'THE GIANT'
	ERIANTHUS RAVENNAE
	HELIANTHUS SALICIFOLIUS
	HIBISCUS SYRIACUS 'BLUEBIRD'
	HIBISCUS SYRIACUS 'DIANA'
	KIRENGESHOMA PALMATA
	LESPEDEZA THUNBERGII
	LYCORIS SPRENGERI
	LYCORIS SQUAMIGERA
	MISCANTHUS 'GIGANTEUS'
	MISCANTHUS SINENSIS 'CABARET'
	MISCANTHUS SINENSIS 'GRACILLIMUS'
	MISCANTHUS SINENSIS 'MORNING LIGHT'
	MISCANTHUS SINENSIS 'SILVER FEATHER' (='SILBERFEDER')
	MISCANTHUS SINENSIS 'VARIEGATUS'
	MOLINIA CAERULEA SUBSP. ARUNDINACEA
	PANICUM VIRGATUM 'STRICTUM'

ZONE	LATIN NAME
6	ABELIA X GRANDIFLORA
	ARUNDO DONAX
	BEGONIA GRANDIS
	CERATOSTIGMA PLUMBAGINOIDES
	EUPATORIUM COELESTINUM
	FRANKLINIA ALATAMAHA
	IMPERATA CYLINDRICA 'RED BARON'
	LESPEDEZA THUNBERGII 'ALBIFLORA'
7	CLERODENDRUM TRICHOTOMUM
	ELAEAGNUS PUNGENS 'FRUITLANDII'
T	CANNA X GENERALIS 'MOHAWK'

OCTOBER

ZONE	LATIN NAME
2	ASTER PUNICEUS
3	ASTER TATARICUS
	BOLTONIA ASTEROIDES 'SNOWBANK'
	COREOPSIS 'MOONBEAM'
4	HAMAMELIS VIRGINIANA
5	ASTER CORDIFOLIUS
	ASTER NOVAE-ANGLIAE 'HARRINGTON'S PINK'
	CHRYSANTHEMUM WEYRICHII 'WHITE BOMB'
	COLCHICUM 'AUTUMN QUEEN'
	COLCHICUM 'THE GIANT'
	CYCLAMEN HEDERIFOLIUM
	ERIANTHUS RAVENNAE
	HELIANTHUS SALICIFOLIUS
	MISCANTHUS 'GIGANTEUS'
	MISCANTHUS SINENSIS 'CABARET'
	MISCANTHUS SINENSIS 'MORNING LIGHT'
	MISCANTHUS SINENSIS 'SILVER FEATHER' (='SILBERFEDER')
	MISCANTHUS SINENSIS 'VARIEGATUS'
	MOLINIA CAERULEA SUBSP. ARUNDINACEA
	STERNBERGIA LUTEA
6	ARUNDO DONAX
	CERATOSTIGMA PLUMBAGINOIDES
	EUPATORIUM COELESTINUM
7	ELAEAGNUS PUNGENS 'FRUITLANDII'

NOVEMBER

ZONE	LATIN NAME
4	HAMAMELIS VIRGINIANA
5	PRUNUS SUBHIRTELLA 'AUTUMNALIS'

DECEMBER

ZONE	LATIN NAME
5	PRUNUS SUBHIRTELLA 'AUTUMNALIS'
	SALIX ACUTIFOLIA 'LONGIFOLIA'
	SALIX DAPHNOIDES 'AGLAIA'

APPENDIX 14
Plant Listing by Seasonal Interest—Fruit and Seed Heads

The plants in this appendix are of interest for their ornamental fruits or seed heads. They are listed by the month of their greatest interest in my area, Hockessin, Delaware. There are listings for every month of the year, but the numbers per month between January and June are small. Obviously, the season during which to capitalize on these characteristics is July through December, October being the peak month.

The list has been divided by hardiness zone.

Further information about all of the following plants is summarized in the Master Lists, Appendices 1A and 1B.

JANUARY

ZONE	LATIN NAME
4	CRATAEGUS NITIDA
	CRATAEGUS PHAENOPYRUM
	ILEX VERTICILLATA
	ILEX VERTICILLATA 'WINTER RED'
	MYRICA PENSYLVANICA
5	CRATAEGUS VIRIDIS 'WINTER KING'
	ILEX X AQUIPERNYI 'SAN JOSE'
	ROSA CAROLINA
	ROSA VIRGINIANA
6	ILEX OPACA 'ARDEN'
	ILEX OPACA 'XANTHOCARPA'

FEBRUARY

ZONE	LATIN NAME
4	CRATAEGUS NITIDA
	CRATAEGUS PHAENOPYRUM
	MYRICA PENSYLVANICA
5	CRATAEGUS VIRIDIS 'WINTER KING'
	ILEX X AQUIPERNYI 'SAN JOSE'
	ROSA CAROLINA
	ROSA VIRGINIANA
6	ILEX OPACA 'ARDEN'
	ILEX OPACA 'XANTHOCARPA'

MARCH

ZONE	LATIN NAME
4	CRATAEGUS NITIDA
5	ILEX X AQUIPERNYI 'SAN JOSE'
	ROSA CAROLINA
	ROSA VIRGINIANA

APRIL

ZONE	LATIN NAME
5	ILEX X AQUIPERNYI 'SAN JOSE'

MAY

ZONE	LATIN NAME
6	MAHONIA BEALEI

JUNE

ZONE	LATIN NAME
3	AMELANCHIER ARBOREA (SYN. A. CANADENSIS)
5	CHIONANTHUS VIRGINICUS

JULY

ZONE	LATIN NAME
3	AMELANCHIER ARBOREA (SYN. A. CANADENSIS)
	CORNUS RACEMOSA
	CORNUS RACEMOSA (DWARF)
	CORNUS SERICEA
	CORNUS SERICEA 'FLAVIRAMEA'
	HIPPOPHAE RHAMNOIDES
	MACLEAYA CORDATA
4	TYPHA ANGUSTIFOLIA
	VACCINIUM CORYMBOSUM
5	CALAMAGROSTIS X ACUTIFLORA 'KARL FOERSTER' (SYN. C. EPIGEOUS 'HORTORUM')
	CHIONANTHUS VIRGINICUS
	KOELREUTERIA PANICULATA
6	ARUM ITALICUM 'PICTUM'
	SOPHORA JAPONICA 'REGENT'

AUGUST

ZONE	LATIN NAME
3	CORNUS RACEMOSA
	CORNUS RACEMOSA (DWARF)
	CORNUS SERICEA
	CORNUS SERICEA 'FLAVIRAMEA'
	HIPPOPHAE RHAMNOIDES
	MACLEAYA CORDATA
	RHUS TYPHINA
	RHUS TYPHINA 'LACINIATA'
4	ARALIA SPINOSA
	GYMNOCLADUS DIOICA
	ROSA NITIDA
	TYPHA ANGUSTIFOLIA
	VACCINIUM CORYMBOSUM
5	CALAMAGROSTIS X ACUTIFLORA 'KARL FOERSTER' (SYN. C. EPIGEOUS 'HORTORUM')
	CORNUS MAS

ZONE	LATIN NAME
	CORNUS OFFICINALIS
	COTONEASTER APICULATUS
	KOELREUTERIA PANICULATA
	MAGNOLIA VIRGINIANA
	SASSAFRAS ALBIDUM
	VIBURNUM SIEBOLDII 'SENECA'
6	COTONEASTER ADPRESSUS VAR. PRAECOX
	SOPHORA JAPONICA 'REGENT'

SEPTEMBER

ZONE	LATIN NAME
3	JUNIPERUS VIRGINIANA
	RHUS TYPHINA
	RHUS TYPHINA 'LACINIATA'
	RUDBECKIA FULGIDA VAR. SULLIVANTII 'GOLDSTURM'
	VIBURNUM PRUNIFOLIUM
4	ARALIA SPINOSA
	BACCHARIS HALIMIFOLIA, PISTILLATE
	CORNUS ALTERNIFOLIA
	GAULTHERIA PROCUMBENS
	GYMNOCLADUS DIOICA
	PHELLODENDRON AMURENSE
	ROSA NITIDA
	TYPHA ANGUSTIFOLIA
5	CALAMAGROSTIS X ACUTIFLORA 'KARL FOERSTER' (SYN. C. EPIGEOUS 'HORTORUM')
	CALLICARPA JAPONICA
	CLETHRA ALNIFOLIA
	CORNUS FLORIDA
	CORNUS FLORIDA 'HOHMAN'S GOLDEN'
	CORNUS KOUSA
	CORNUS MAS
	CORNUS OFFICINALIS
	COTONEASTER APICULATUS
	COTONEASTER HORIZONTALIS
	LIGUSTRUM QUIHOUI
	MAGNOLIA VIRGINIANA
	PANICUM VIRGATUM 'STRICTUM'
	PENNISETUM ALOPECUROIDES
	RHODOTYPOS SCANDENS
	SASSAFRAS ALBIDUM
	SYMPHORICARPOS X CHENAULTII 'HANCOCK'
6	COTONEASTER ADPRESSUS VAR. PRAECOX
	LIRIOPE MUSCARI (BIG BLUE SELECTION)
	LIRIOPE MUSCARI 'MONROE WHITE'
	SOPHORA JAPONICA 'REGENT'
	VIBURNUM NUDUM 'WINTERTHUR'
	VIBURNUM SETIGERUM
7	CLERODENDRUM TRICHOTOMUM
	PYRACANTHA COCCINEA 'AUREA'

OCTOBER

ZONE	LATIN NAME
3	JUNIPERUS VIRGINIANA
	MALUS 'RED JADE'
	RHUS TYPHINA
	RHUS TYPHINA 'LACINIATA'
	ROSA RUGOSA AND HYBRIDS
	RUDBECKIA FULGIDA VAR.
	SULLIVANTII 'GOLDSTURM'
	SEDUM 'AUTUMN JOY'
	VIBURNUM ACERIFOLIUM
	VIBURNUM PRUNIFOLIUM
4	ARONIA ARBUTIFOLIA
	'BRILLIANTISSIMA'
	BACCHARIS HALIMIFOLIA, PISTILLATE
	CHAENOMELES JAPONICA VAR. ALPINA
	CHAENOMELES SPECIOSA CULTIVARS
	CHAENOMELES X SUPERBA 'JET TRAIL'
	CORNUS ALTERNIFOLIA
	GAULTHERIA PROCUMBENS
	GYMNOCLADUS DIOICA
	MALUS FLORIBUNDA
	MALUS HUPEHENSIS
	MALUS SARGENTII
	MYRICA PENSYLVANICA
	PHELLODENDRON AMURENSE
	ROSA NITIDA
	TYPHA ANGUSTIFOLIA
5	CALAMAGROSTIS X ACUTIFLORA
	'KARL FOERSTER'
	(SYN. C. EPIGEOUS 'HORTORUM')
	CALLICARPA JAPONICA
	CHAENOMELES X SUPERBA CULTIVARS
	CORNUS FLORIDA
	CORNUS FLORIDA 'HOHMAN'S
	GOLDEN'
	COTONEASTER HORIZONTALIS
	ERIANTHUS RAVENNAE
	ILEX GLABRA 'DENSA'
	LIGUSTRUM QUIHOUI
	MISCANTHUS 'GIGANTEUS'
	MISCANTHUS SINENSIS 'CABARET'
	MISCANTHUS SINENSIS 'GRACILLIMUS'
	MISCANTHUS SINENSIS 'MORNING
	LIGHT'
	MISCANTHUS SINENSIS 'SILVER
	FEATHER' (='SILBERFEDER')
	MISCANTHUS SINENSIS 'STRICTUS'
	MISCANTHUS SINENSIS 'VARIEGATUS'
	MOLINIA CAERULEA SUBSP.
	ARUNDINACEA
	PANICUM VIRGATUM 'STRICTUM'
	PENNISETUM ALOPECUROIDES
	RHODOTYPOS SCANDENS
	ROSA CAROLINA
	SYMPHORICARPOS X CHENAULTII
	'HANCOCK'
	VIBURNUM DILATATUM 'MICHAEL
	DODGE'
6	ARUNDO DONAX
	CALLICARPA DICHOTOMA
	COTONEASTER SALICIFOLIUS VAR.
	FLOCCOSUS
	IMPERATA CYLINDRICA 'RED BARON'
	LIRIOPE MUSCARI (BIG BLUE
	SELECTION)
	LIRIOPE MUSCARI 'MONROE WHITE'
	PONCIRUS TRIFOLIATA

ZONE	LATIN NAME
	STRANVAESIA DAVIDIANA VAR.
	UNDULATA 'PROSTRATA'
	VIBURNUM ICHANGENSE
	VIBURNUM NUDUM 'WINTERTHUR'
	VIBURNUM SETIGERUM
7	CEDRUS ATLANTICA 'GLAUCA'
	CLERODENDRUM TRICHOTOMUM
	DIOSPYROS KAKI
	PYRACANTHA COCCINEA 'AUREA'
	SKIMMIA REEVESIANA

NOVEMBER

ZONE	LATIN NAME
3	JUNIPERUS VIRGINIANA
	MALUS 'RED JADE'
	RHUS TYPHINA
	RHUS TYPHINA 'LACINIATA'
	ROSA RUGOSA AND HYBRIDS
	VIBURNUM ACERIFOLIUM
	VIBURNUM PRUNIFOLIUM
4	ARONIA ARBUTIFOLIA
	'BRILLIANTISSIMA'
	BACCHARIS HALIMIFOLIA, PISTILLATE
	CHAENOMELES JAPONICA VAR. ALPINA
	CHAENOMELES SPECIOSA CULTIVARS
	CHAENOMELES X SUPERBA 'JET TRAIL'
	CRATAEGUS NITIDA
	CRATAEGUS PHAENOPYRUM
	EUONYMUS ALATA
	GYMNOCLADUS DIOICA
	ILEX VERTICILLATA
	ILEX VERTICILLATA 'WINTER RED'
	MALUS FLORIBUNDA
	MALUS HUPEHENSIS
	MALUS SARGENTII
	MYRICA PENSYLVANICA
	PHELLODENDRON AMURENSE
	TYPHA ANGUSTIFOLIA
5	CALLICARPA JAPONICA
	CHAENOMELES X SUPERBA CULTIVARS
	CRATAEGUS VIRIDIS 'WINTER KING'
	ERIANTHUS RAVENNAE
	ILEX GLABRA 'DENSA'
	ILEX X AQUIPERNYI 'SAN JOSE'
	MISCANTHUS 'GIGANTEUS'
	MISCANTHUS SINENSIS 'CABARET'
	MISCANTHUS SINENSIS 'GRACILLIMUS'
	MISCANTHUS SINENSIS 'MORNING
	LIGHT'
	MISCANTHUS SINENSIS 'SILVER
	FEATHER' (='SILBERFEDER')
	MISCANTHUS SINENSIS 'STRICTUS'
	MISCANTHUS SINENSIS 'VARIEGATUS'
	MOLINIA CAERULEA SUBSP.
	ARUNDINACEA
	ROSA CAROLINA
	ROSA VIRGINIANA
	SYMPHORICARPOS X CHENAULTII
	'HANCOCK'
	VIBURNUM DILATATUM 'MICHAEL
	DODGE'
6	ARUNDO DONAX
	CALLICARPA DICHOTOMA
	COTONEASTER SALICIFOLIUS VAR.
	FLOCCOSUS
	ILEX OPACA 'ARDEN'

ZONE	LATIN NAME
	ILEX OPACA 'XANTHOCARPA'
	IMPERATA CYLINDRICA 'RED BARON'
	STRANVAESIA DAVIDIANA VAR.
	UNDULATA 'PROSTRATA'
	VIBURNUM ICHANGENSE
	VIBURNUM NUDUM 'WINTERTHUR'
	VIBURNUM SETIGERUM
7	CEDRUS ATLANTICA 'GLAUCA'
	DIOSPYROS KAKI
	PYRACANTHA COCCINEA 'AUREA'
	SKIMMIA REEVESIANA

DECEMBER

ZONE	LATIN NAME
3	JUNIPERUS VIRGINIANA
	MALUS 'RED JADE'
	ROSA RUGOSA AND HYBRIDS
4	ARONIA ARBUTIFOLIA
	'BRILLIANTISSIMA'
	CRATAEGUS NITIDA
	CRATAEGUS PHAENOPYRUM
	EUONYMUS ALATA
	GYMNOCLADUS DIOICA
	ILEX VERTICILLATA
	ILEX VERTICILLATA 'WINTER RED'
	MALUS SARGENTII
	MYRICA PENSYLVANICA
	TYPHA ANGUSTIFOLIA
5	CRATAEGUS VIRIDIS 'WINTER KING'
	ERIANTHUS RAVENNAE
	ILEX GLABRA 'DENSA'
	ILEX X AQUIPERNYI 'SAN JOSE'
	MISCANTHUS 'GIGANTEUS'
	MISCANTHUS SINENSIS 'CABARET'
	MISCANTHUS SINENSIS 'GRACILLIMUS'
	MISCANTHUS SINENSIS 'MORNING
	LIGHT'
	MISCANTHUS SINENSIS 'SILVER
	FEATHER' (='SILBERFEDER')
	MISCANTHUS SINENSIS 'STRICTUS'
	MISCANTHUS SINENSIS 'VARIEGATUS'
	MOLINIA CAERULEA SUBSP.
	ARUNDINACEA
	ROSA CAROLINA
	ROSA VIRGINIANA
	SYMPHORICARPOS X CHENAULTII
	'HANCOCK'
	VIBURNUM DILATATUM 'MICHAEL
	DODGE'
6	CALLICARPA DICHOTOMA
	COTONEASTER SALICIFOLIUS VAR.
	FLOCCOSUS
	ILEX OPACA 'ARDEN'
	ILEX OPACA 'XANTHOCARPA'
	IMPERATA CYLINDRICA 'RED BARON'
	STRANVAESIA DAVIDIANA VAR.
	UNDULATA 'PROSTRATA'
7	CEDRUS ATLANTICA 'GLAUCA'

Plant Listing by Structuring Qualities

Plants in this list are divided as follows:

Vertical
Horizontal
Mound
Ball on a Stick
Vase
Weeping
Irregular, Sculptural
Multistemmed
Climbing

I have included a few guidelines, beneath the headings, for some of the above categories. Those categories without any text below the headings are ones I considered self-explanatory.

Each of the sections is subdivided by hardiness zone.

The letter *T* under the heading "Zone" indicates a plant that is tender, not tolerant of frost.

Further information about all of the following plants is summarized in the Master Lists, Appendices 1A and 1B.

VERTICAL

The following are particularly useful for providing vertical structure to a plant composition.

ZONE	LATIN NAME
3	CIMICIFUGA RACEMOSA
	IRIS SIBIRICA CULTIVARS
	JUNIPERUS VIRGINIANA
	LIATRIS SCARIOSA 'WHITE SPIRE'
	LIATRIS SPICATA 'KOBOLD'
	OSMUNDA REGALIS
	PICEA PUNGENS 'HOOPSII'
	PINUS STROBUS 'FASTIGIATA'
	PSEUDOTSUGA MENZIESII
	SALIX ALBA 'REGALIS'
	THUJA OCCIDENTALIS 'NIGRA'
	TSUGA CANADENSIS
4	OSMUNDA CINNAMOMEA
	OSMUNDA CLAYTONIANA
	TAXUS CUSPIDATA (CAPITATA SELECTION)
	THUJA OCCIDENTALIS 'HETZ' WINTERGREEN'
	TYPHA ANGUSTIFOLIA
	YUCCA FLACCIDA 'GOLDEN SWORD'
	YUCCA GLAUCA
	YUCCA SMALLIANA
5	ABIES NORDMANNIANA
	ASPHODELINE LUTEA
	CALAMAGROSTIS X ACUTIFLORA 'KARL FOERSTER' (SYN. C. EPIGEOUS 'HORTORUM')
	CEDRUS LIBANI VAR. STENOCOMA
	EQUISETUM HYEMALE
	ERIANTHUS RAVENNAE
	ILEX X AQUIPERNYI 'SAN JOSE'

ZONE	LATIN NAME
	IRIS GRAMINEA
	IRIS PSEUDACORUS
	JUNIPERUS SCOPULORUM 'SKY ROCKET'
	METASEQUOIA GLYPTOSTROBOIDES
	MISCANTHUS 'GIGANTEUS'
	MISCANTHUS SINENSIS 'SILVER FEATHER' (='SILBERFEDER')
	ONOPORDUM ACANTHIUM
	PHLOMIS RUSSELIANA
	PICEA ORIENTALIS
	SALIX X RUBRA 'EUGENEI'
	TAXUS X MEDIA 'SENTINALIS'
	THUJA PLICATA 'ATROVIRENS'
	VERBASCUM OLYMPICUM
6	ARUNDO DONAX
	CALOCEDRUS DECURRENS
	CHAMAECYPARIS OBTUSA 'CRIPPSII'
	GALTONIA CANDICANS
	ILEX OPACA 'ARDEN'
	ILEX OPACA 'XANTHOCARPA'
	IMPERATA CYLINDRICA 'RED BARON'
	PHYLLOSTACHYS AUREOSULCATA
	PSEUDOLARIX KAEMPFERI
	SCIADOPITYS VERTICILLATA
	STEWARTIA KOREANA
	TAXODIUM DISTICHUM VAR. NUTANS 'PRAIRIE SENTINEL'
7	CEDRUS ATLANTICA 'GLAUCA'
T	ACIDANTHERA BICOLOR
	CANNA X GENERALIS 'MOHAWK'

HORIZONTAL

Plants on this list either have horizontal characteristics in their basic structure (the letter "*H*" precedes the name) or their principal recommended usage as a ground cover creates a horizontal line in a planting design.

See also Appendix 32, another approach to horizontality in plant composition.

ZONE	LATIN NAME
2	ACHILLEA MILLEFOLIUM 'ROSEA'
	ARTEMESIA STELLERIANA
	POTENTILLA TRIDENTATA
	SAPONARIA OFFICINALIS
3	ACHILLEA 'MOONSHINE'
	ADIANTUM PEDATUM
	AEGOPODIUM PODAGRARIA 'VARIEGATUM'
	ALCHEMILLA VULGARIS
	BRUNNERA MACROPHYLLA
	DENNSTAEDTIA PUNCTILOBULA
	DIANTHUS DELTOIDES
	DICENTRA 'LUXURIANT'
	DICENTRA EXIMIA 'PURITY'
	GERANIUM MACRORRHIZUM
	GERANIUM SANGUINEUM
	HELLEBORUS NIGER
	HOSTA 'KABITAN'
	HOSTA PLANTAGINEA
	HOSTA SIEBOLDIANA 'ELEGANS'
	HOSTA UNDULATA
	HOSTA VENTRICOSA

ZONE	LATIN NAME
H	JUNIPERUS HORIZONTALIS 'WILTONII'
	PHLOX SUBULATA
H	PICEA ABIES 'NIDIFORMIS'
	PINUS MUGO VAR. MUGO
	PINUS STROBUS
	POLYSTICHUM ACROSTICHOIDES
	PTERIDIUM AQUILINUM VAR. LATIUSCULUM
	PULMONARIA ANGUSTIFOLIA
	PULMONARIA SACCHARATA 'MARGERY FISH'
	PULMONARIA SACCHARATA 'SISSINGHURST WHITE'
	RHUS AROMATICA 'GRO-LOW'
	SEDUM ELLACOMBIANUM
	SEDUM SARMENTOSUM
	SEDUM SPURIUM
	SEDUM SPURIUM 'BRONZE CARPET'
	THYMUS SERPYLLUM
	TIARELLA CORDIFOLIA VAR. COLLINA
H	TSUGA CANADENSIS 'BENNETT'
H	TSUGA CANADENSIS 'COLE'S PROSTRATE'
	VERONICA INCANA
H	VIBURNUM PRUNIFOLIUM
4	AJUGA REPTANS
	AJUGA REPTANS 'BRONZE BEAUTY'
	AJUGA REPTANS (GIANT FORM)
	ARABIS PROCURRENS
H	ARALIA SPINOSA
	ARENARIA VERNA
	ARUNCUS AETHUSIFOLIUS
	BERBERIS THUNBERGII 'CRIMSON PYGMY'
	CHAENOMELES JAPONICA VAR. ALPINA
	CHAENOMELES X SUPERBA 'JET TRAIL'
	CHAMAEMELUM NOBILE
	COMPTONIA PEREGRINA
	CONVALLARIA MAJALIS
H	CORNUS ALTERNIFOLIA
H	CRATAEGUS NITIDA
H	CRATAEGUS PHAENOPYRUM
H	EUONYMUS ALATA
	EUONYMUS FORTUNEI 'COLORATA'
	EUONYMUS FORTUNEI VAR. RADICANS
H	FAGUS GRANDIFOLIA
	GAULTHERIA PROCUMBENS
H	HAMAMELIS VIRGINIANA
	HEDYOTIS CAERULEA
	HELLEBORUS ORIENTALIS HYBRIDS
H	JUNIPERUS X MEDIA 'PFITZERIANA COMPACTA'
H	MALUS FLORIBUNDA
H	MALUS SARGENTII
	MICROBIOTA DECUSSATA
	MONARDA DIDYMA
	PACHYSANDRA PROCUMBENS
	PAXISTIMA CANBYI
	PETASITES JAPONICUS
	PHALARIS ARUNDINACEA VAR. PICTA
H	PHELLODENDRON AMURENSE
	PHLOX BIFIDA
H	QUERCUS ALBA
H	QUERCUS MACROCARPA
	SALIX REPENS VAR. ARGENTEA
	SEDUM POPULIFOLIUM
	SEDUM TERNATUM
	STACHYS BYZANTINA
H	TAXUS CUSPIDATA 'NANA'
	VINCA MINOR 'BOWLESII'
	VINCA MINOR 'VARIEGATA'
	WALDSTEINIA TERNATA

ZONE	LATIN NAME
5 H	ACER PALMATUM 'BLOODGOOD'
	ALLIUM ZEBDANENSE
	ANEMONE BLANDA 'ATROCAERULEA'
	ARUNDINARIA VIRIDISTRIATA
	ASARUM EUROPAEUM
	ATHYRIUM GOERINGIANUM 'PICTUM'
H	CARPINUS BETULUS
H	CATALPA BIGNONIOIDES
H	CEPHALOTAXUS HARRINGTONIA VAR. PEDUNCULATA
	CHIONODOXA GIGANTEA 'ALBA'
	CHIONODOXA LUCILIAE
	CHIONODOXA SARDENSIS
	CHRYSANTHEMUM WEYRICHII 'WHITE BOMB'
H	CORNUS FLORIDA
H	CORNUS FLORIDA 'HOHMAN'S GOLDEN'
H	CORNUS KOUSA
H	CORNUS MAS
H	CORNUS OFFICINALIS
	COTONEASTER ADPRESSUS 'LITTLE GEM'
H	COTONEASTER HORIZONTALIS
	CRATAEGUS VIRIDIS 'WINTER KING'
	DIPLAZIUM CONILII
	EPIMEDIUM PINNATUM SUBSP. COLCHICUM
	EPIMEDIUM X YOUNGIANUM 'NIVEUM'
	ERANTHIS HYEMALIS
	ERANTHIS X TUBERGENII
	EUONYMUS FORTUNEI 'GRACILIS'
	EUONYMUS FORTUNEI 'MINIMA'
H	FAGUS SYLVATICA 'LACINIATA'
	GALANTHUS ELWESII
	GALANTHUS NIVALIS
	GALIUM ODORATUM
H	HALESIA TETRAPTERA
	HEDERA HELIX 'BULGARIA'
	HEDERA HELIX 'OGALALLA'
	HELIANTHEMUM APENNINUM VAR. ROSEUM
	HEMEROCALLIS 'HYPERION'
	HEMEROCALLIS FULVA 'EUROPA'
	HOUTTUYNIA CORDATA 'CHAMELEON'
	INDIGOFERA INCARNATA 'ALBA'
	IRIS CRISTATA
	IRIS TECTORUM
H	JUNIPERUS X MEDIA 'OLD GOLD'
	LAMIASTRUM GALEOBDOLON 'VARIEGATUM'
	LAMIUM MACULATUM 'WHITE NANCY'
	LEUCOJUM VERNUM
H	NYSSA SYLVATICA
	OMPHALODES VERNA
	PACHYSANDRA TERMINALIS
	PACHYSANDRA TERMINALIS 'GREEN CARPET'
	PACHYSANDRA TERMINALIS 'VARIEGATA' OR 'SILVER EDGE'
	PHLOX STOLONIFERA 'ALBA'
	PHLOX STOLONIFERA 'BLUE RIDGE'
	PHLOX STOLONIFERA 'SHERWOOD PURPLE'
H	PINUS DENSIFLORA 'UMBRACULIFERA'
H	PINUS PARVIFLORA 'GLAUCA'
H	PINUS VIRGINIANA
	POLYSTICHUM TRIPTERON
H	PRUNUS SUBHIRTELLA 'AUTUMNALIS'
	RHODODENDRON ATLANTICUM
	ROSA 'DOORENBOS SELECTION'
	ROSA (POLYANTHA) 'THE FAIRY'

ZONE	LATIN NAME
	SAGINA SUBULATA
H	SASSAFRAS ALBIDUM
	SCILLA SIBERICA 'SPRING BEAUTY'
	STERNBERGIA LUTEA
	SYMPHORICARPOS X CHENAULTII 'HANCOCK'
	TAXUS BACCATA 'REPANDENS'
	THELYPTERIS HEXAGONOPTERA
	THELYPTERIS NOVEBORACENSIS
	THELYPTERIS PHEGOPTERIS
	THYMUS 'CLEAR GOLD'
	THYMUS PSEUDOLANUGINOSUS
H	VIBURNUM PLICATUM FORMA TOMENTOSUM
	XANTHORHIZA SIMPLICISSIMA
6	BEGONIA GRANDIS
	CERATOSTIGMA PLUMBAGINOIDES
	EUONYMUS FORTUNEI 'SILVER QUEEN'
	FORSYTHIA VIRIDISSIMA 'BRONXENSIS'
	HEDERA HELIX 'BALTICA'
	LIRIOPE MUSCARI (BIG BLUE SELECTION)
	LIRIOPE MUSCARI 'MONROE WHITE'
	LIRIOPE MUSCARI 'VARIEGATA'
	PARONYCHIA KAPELA SUBSP. SERPYLLIFOLIA
H	PAULOWNIA TOMENTOSA
H	PRUNUS YEDOENSIS
H	PSEUDOLARIX KAEMPFERI
	RHODODENDRON X ERIOCARPUM AND R. X NAKAHARAI CULTIVARS AND HYBRIDS
	RUBUS IDAEUS 'AUREUS'
	SAXIFRAGA STOLONIFERA
	STRANVAESIA DAVIDIANA VAR. UNDULATA 'PROSTRATA'
H	STYRAX JAPONICUS
7	GENISTA SYLVESTRIS 'LYDIA'
	HEDERA COLCHICA 'DENTATA'
	HEDERA HELIX 'ERECTA'
	SASA VEITCHII
8	COTULA SQUALIDA

MOUND

ZONE	LATIN NAME
2	ACHILLEA MILLEFOLIUM 'ROSEA'
	BERGENIA 'PERFECTA'
	BERGENIA 'SUNNINGDALE'
	PAEONIA—HERBACEOUS HYBRIDS
3	ALCHEMILLA VULGARIS
	ASCLEPIAS TUBEROSA
	BAPTISIA AUSTRALIS
	BRUNNERA MACROPHYLLA
	COREOPSIS 'MOONBEAM'
	CORNUS RACEMOSA
	CORNUS RACEMOSA (DWARF)
	CORNUS SERICEA
	CORNUS SERICEA 'FLAVIRAMEA'
	DIANTHUS DELTOIDES
	DICENTRA 'LUXURIANT'
	DICENTRA EXIMIA 'PURITY'
	ECHINACEA PURPUREA
	FILIPENDULA ULMARIA 'AUREA'
	GERANIUM MACRORRHIZUM
	GERANIUM SANGUINEUM

ZONE	LATIN NAME
	HELLEBORUS NIGER
	HOSTA 'KABITAN'
	HOSTA PLANTAGINEA
	HOSTA SIEBOLDIANA 'ELEGANS'
	HOSTA UNDULATA
	HOSTA VENTRICOSA
	NEPETA X FAASSENII
	OSMUNDA REGALIS
	PINUS MUGO VAR. MUGO
	PRUNUS X CISTENA
	RHUS AROMATICA 'GRO-LOW'
	ROSA RUGOSA AND HYBRIDS
	RUDBECKIA FULGIDA VAR. SULLIVANTII 'GOLDSTURM'
	SEDUM 'AUTUMN JOY'
	SORBARIA SORBIFOLIA
	SPIRAEA X VANHOUTTEI
	THERMOPSIS CAROLINIANA
	VIBURNUM ACERIFOLIUM
	VIBURNUM PRUNIFOLIUM
4	ACANTHOPANAX SIEBOLDIANUS
	ALLIUM TUBEROSUM
	ASTILBE X ARENDSII CULTIVARS
	BACCHARIS HALIMIFOLIA, PISTILLATE
	BERBERIS THUNBERGII 'ATROPURPUREA'
	BERBERIS THUNBERGII 'CRIMSON PYGMY'
	BUDDLEIA ALTERNIFOLIA
	CARYOPTERIS X CLANDONENSIS 'BLUE MIST'
	CEPHALANTHUS OCCIDENTALIS
	COMPTONIA PEREGRINA
	DIERVILLA SESSILIFOLIA
	EUPHORBIA EPITHYMOIDES
	FAGUS GRANDIFOLIA
	HELIOPSIS HELIANTHOIDES SUBSP. SCABRA 'KARAT'
	HELLEBORUS ORIENTALIS HYBRIDS
	HYDRANGEA PANICULATA
	HYPERICUM KALMIANUM
	MALUS FLORIBUNDA
	MYRICA PENSYLVANICA
	PAEONIA TENUIFOLIA
	PHALARIS ARUNDINACEA VAR. PICTA
	RHODODENDRON (CATAWBIENSE HYBRIDS)
	RHODODENDRON MAXIMUM
	RODGERSIA AESCULIFOLIA
	RODGERSIA PODOPHYLLA
	RODGERSIA TABULARIS
	SALIX ELAEAGNOS
	SPIRAEA THUNBERGII
	SYRINGA PATULA (SYN. S. PALIBINIANA, S. MICROPHYLLA 'INGWERSEN'S DWARF')
	SYRINGA X CHINENSIS
	VACCINIUM CORYMBOSUM
	VIBURNUM CARLESII
5	ASTER X FRIKARTII 'MONCH'
	BUXUS 'GREEN GEM'
	BUXUS SINICA VAR. INSULARIS 'TIDE HILL'
	BUXUS SINICA VAR. INSULARIS 'WINTERGREEN' (OHIO CULTIVAR)
	CHAMAECYPARIS OBTUSA 'NANA'
	CHAMAECYPARIS PISIFERA 'GOLD SPANGLE'
	CORNUS MAS
	CORNUS OFFICINALIS
	CORYLOPSIS PLATYPETALA

ZONE	LATIN NAME
	COTINUS COGGYGRIA 'PURPUREUS'
	COTONEASTER ADPRESSUS 'LITTLE GEM'
	COTONEASTER APICULATUS
	DAPHNE CAUCASICA
	DAPHNE X BURKWOODII 'CAROL MACKIE'
	DEUTZIA GRACILIS
	ERIANTHUS RAVENNAE
	FAGUS SYLVATICA 'LACINIATA'
	FAGUS SYLVATICA 'RIVERSII'
	HELICTOTRICHON SEMPERVIRENS
	HYDRANGEA QUERCIFOLIA
	HYPERICUM FRONDOSUM
	ILEX CHINA BOY ® 'MESDOB'
	ILEX CHINA GIRL ® 'MESOG'
	ILEX GLABRA 'DENSA'
	ILEX X MESERVEAE BLUE MAID ® 'MESID'
	ILEX X MESERVEAE BLUE STALLION ® 'MESAN'
	KERRIA JAPONICA
	LEUCOTHOE FONTANESIANA
	LEUCOTHOE FONTANESIANA 'NANA'
	LONICERA FRAGRANTISSIMA
	MISCANTHUS SINENSIS 'CABARET'
	MISCANTHUS SINENSIS 'GRACILLIMUS'
	MISCANTHUS SINENSIS 'MORNING LIGHT'
	MISCANTHUS SINENSIS 'SILVER FEATHER' (='SILBERFEDER')
	MISCANTHUS SINENSIS 'VARIEGATUS'
	OMPHALODES VERNA
	PENNISETUM ALOPECUROIDES
	PETASITES FRAGRANS
	PHILADELPHUS CORONARIUS
	PHILADELPHUS X FALCONERI
	SALIX CHAENOMELOIDES
	SALIX GRACILISTYLA
	SALIX GRACILISTYLA 'MELANOSTACHYS'
	STEPHANANDRA INCISA 'CRISPA'
	STOKESIA LAEVIS 'BLUE DANUBE'
	SYRINGA LACINIATA
	TAXUS BACCATA 'REPANDENS'
	VIBURNUM FARRERI 'NANUM'
6	ABELIA X GRANDIFLORA
	ACER PALMATUM 'EVER RED'
	ACER PALMATUM VAR. DISSECTUM OR A. P. 'WATERFALL'
	ADINA RUBELLA
	BUXUS SEMPERVIRENS 'SUFFRUTICOSA'
	COTONEASTER ADPRESSUS VAR. PRAECOX
	COTONEASTER SALICIFOLIUS VAR. FLOCCOSUS
	ENKIANTHUS PERULATUS
	FORSYTHIA VIRIDISSIMA 'BRONXENSIS'
	FORSYTHIA X INTERMEDIA 'SPRING GLORY'
	HYDRANGEA MACROPHYLLA 'BLUE BILLOW'
	ILEX CRENATA 'HELLERI'
	ITEA VIRGINICA 'HENRY'S GARNET'
	PAEONIA 'BLACK PIRATE'
	PAEONIA—WOODY HYBRIDS
	PELTIPHYLLUM PELTATUM
	RHODODENDRON (GLENN DALE HYBRIDS)
	RHODODENDRON (KAEMPFERI HYBRIDS)
	RHODODENDRON (KURUME HYBRIDS)

ZONE	LATIN NAME
	ROSA ROXBURGHII
	STYRAX JAPONICUS 'CARILLON'
7	BERBERIS WILSONIAE VAR. STAPFIANA
	ELAEAGNUS PUNGENS 'FRUITLANDII'
	ELAEAGNUS PUNGENS 'MACULATA'
	GENISTA SYLVESTRIS 'LYDIA'
	PYRACANTHA COCCINEA 'AUREA'
	SKIMMIA REEVESIANA

BALL ON A STICK

These are basically round-headed plants that are normally used with lower branches absent. For plants trainable into topiary standards, see Appendix 33.

ZONE	LATIN NAME
3	ACER SACCHARUM
	AMELANCHIER ARBOREA (SYN. A. CANADENSIS)
	QUERCUS RUBRA
	TILIA CORDATA
4	ACER PLATANOIDES 'CRIMSON KING'
	ACER RUBRUM
	BETULA LENTA
	BUDDLEIA ALTERNIFOLIA
	QUERCUS MACROCARPA
5	ACER GRISEUM
	CARPINUS BETULUS
	CRATAEGUS VIRIDIS 'WINTER KING'
	KOELREUTERIA PANICULATA
	PLATANUS OCCIDENTALIS
	PRUNUS CERASIFERA 'THUNDERCLOUD'
6	AESCULUS SPLENDENS
	FRANKLINIA ALATAMAHA
	PAULOWNIA TOMENTOSA
	QUERCUS PHELLOS

VASE

The classic vase-shaped plant is the American elm. This form is very useful for framing views.

ZONE	LATIN NAME
2	BETULA PAPYRIFERA
4	ARALIA SPINOSA
	BETULA NIGRA
	CARYA OVATA
	GLEDITSIA TRIACANTHOS VAR. INERMIS 'SHADEMASTER'
	GYMNOCLADUS DIOICA
	HAMAMELIS VIRGINIANA
	MALUS HUPEHENSIS
5	ACER PALMATUM 'SANGOKAKU'
	CERCIS CANADENSIS 'FOREST PANSY'
	CORNUS KOUSA
	HAMAMELIS MOLLIS 'PALLIDA'
	HAMAMELIS X INTERMEDIA 'DIANE'
	HAMAMELIS X INTERMEDIA 'JELENA'

ZONE	LATIN NAME
	HAMAMELIS X INTERMEDIA 'PRIMAVERA'
	KOLKWITZIA AMABILIS
	PINUS DENSIFLORA 'UMBRACULIFERA'
	PRUNUS 'HALLY JOLIVETTE'
6	VIBURNUM SETIGERUM
	ZELKOVA SERRATA 'GREEN VASE'

WEEPING

ZONE	LATIN NAME
3	BETULA PENDULA 'GRACILIS'
	BETULA PENDULA 'YOUNGII'
	MALUS 'RED JADE'
	SPIRAEA X VANHOUTTEI
	TSUGA CANADENSIS 'COLE'S PROSTRATE'
	TSUGA CANADENSIS 'PENDULA'
	VIBURNUM ACERIFOLIUM
4	BUDDLEIA ALTERNIFOLIA
	CORYLUS AVELLANA 'PENDULA'
	POLYGONATUM ODORATUM 'VARIEGATUM'
	SALIX ALBA VAR. TRISTIS
5	ALLIUM CERNUUM
	FAGUS SYLVATICA 'PENDULA'
	FORSYTHIA SUSPENSA
	KIRENGESHOMA PALMATA
	LEUCOTHOE FONTANESIANA
	LEUCOTHOE FONTANESIANA 'NANA'
	MISCANTHUS 'GIGANTEUS'
	OXYDENDRUM ARBOREUM
	PHILADELPHUS CORONARIUS
	RIBES ODORATUM
	ROSA (SHRUB) 'LILLIAN GIBSON'
	RUBUS COCKBURNIANUS
	SYMPHORICARPOS X CHENAULTII 'HANCOCK'
	TAXUS BACCATA 'REPANDENS'
6	BEGONIA GRANDIS
	COTONEASTER SALICIFOLIUS VAR. FLOCCOSUS
	JASMINUM NUDIFLORUM
	PRUNUS SUBHIRTELLA 'PENDULA'
	STYRAX JAPONICUS 'CARILLON'
	VIBURNUM SETIGERUM
7	DIOSPYROS KAKI

IRREGULAR, SCULPTURAL

ZONE	LATIN NAME
3	AMELANCHIER ARBOREA (SYN. A. CANADENSIS)
	ASTER TATARICUS
	BETULA PENDULA 'YOUNGII'
	CLEMATIS HERACLEIFOLIA VAR. DAVIDIANA
	ECHINOPS RITRO
	HIPPOPHAE RHAMNOIDES
	INULA HELENIUM
	IRIS SIBIRICA CULTIVARS
	MACLEAYA CORDATA
	MALUS 'RED JADE'

ZONE	LATIN NAME
	PAPAVER ORIENTALE
	RHUS TYPHINA
	RHUS TYPHINA 'LACINIATA'
	ROSA RUGOSA AND HYBRIDS
	THERMOPSIS CAROLINIANA
4	CARYA OVATA
	CHAENOMELES SPECIOSA CULTIVARS
	CORYLUS AVELLANA 'CONTORTA'
	CORYLUS AVELLANA 'PENDULA'
	GINKGO BILOBA, STAMINATE
	GYMNOCLADUS DIOICA
	MALUS SARGENTII
	MYRICA PENSYLVANICA
	PINUS FLEXILIS
	ROBINIA HISPIDA
	TAMARIX RAMOSISSIMA
	TYPHA ANGUSTIFOLIA
	VACCINIUM CORYMBOSUM
	YUCCA FLACCIDA 'GOLDEN SWORD'
	YUCCA GLAUCA
	YUCCA SMALLIANA
5	ACER GRISEUM
	ACER PALMATUM 'SANGOKAKU'
	ASPHODELINE LUTEA
	CAMPSIS X TAGLIABUANA 'MADAME GALEN'
	CERCIS CANADENSIS 'FOREST PANSY'
	CHAMAECYPARIS OBTUSA 'NANA GRACILIS'
	CHAMAECYPARIS OBTUSA VAR. BREVIRAMEA
	CHAMAECYPARIS PISIFERA 'SQUARROSA'
	COTINUS COGGYGRIA 'PURPUREUS'
	CRAMBE CORDIFOLIA
	DIOSPYROS VIRGINIANA
	ENKIANTHUS CAMPANULATUS
	EQUISETUM HYEMALE
	ERIANTHUS RAVENNAE
	FAGUS SYLVATICA 'PENDULA'
	HELIANTHUS SALICIFOLIUS
	HERACLEUM MANTEGAZZIANUM
	HYDRANGEA ANOMALA SUBSP. PETIOLARIS 'SKYLANDS GIANT'
	IRIS PSEUDACORUS
	KALMIA LATIFOLIA
	LILIUM 'BLACK DRAGON'
	LILIUM SPECIES AND HYBRIDS
	MAGNOLIA VIRGINIANA
	MAGNOLIA X SOULANGIANA 'VERBANICA'
	MISCANTHUS 'GIGANTEUS'
	MISCANTHUS SINENSIS 'CABARET'
	MISCANTHUS SINENSIS 'MORNING LIGHT'
	MISCANTHUS SINENSIS 'SILVER FEATHER' (='SILBERFEDER')
	MISCANTHUS SINENSIS 'STRICTUS'
	MISCANTHUS SINENSIS 'VARIEGATUS'
	MOLINIA CAERULEA SUBSP. ARUNDINACEA
	NYSSA SYLVATICA
	ONOPORDUM ACANTHIUM
	OXYDENDRUM ARBOREUM
	PANICUM VIRGATUM 'STRICTUM'
	PHLOMIS RUSSELIANA
	PINUS DENSIFLORA 'UMBRACULIFERA'
	PINUS PARVIFLORA 'GLAUCA'
	PINUS VIRGINIANA
	RHEUM PALMATUM 'RUBRUM'
	RHODODENDRON ARBORESCENS

ZONE	LATIN NAME
	RHODODENDRON MUCRONULATUM
	RHODODENDRON SCHLIPPENBACHII
	RHODODENDRON VASEYI
	RHODODENDRON X GANDAVENSE 'COCCINEA SPECIOSA'
	RHODODENDRON X GANDAVENSE 'DAVIESII'
	SALIX ACUTIFOLIA 'LONGIFOLIA'
	SALIX DAPHNOIDES 'AGLAIA'
	SASSAFRAS ALBIDUM
	THALICTRUM ROCHEBRUNIANUM
	VALERIANA OFFICINALIS
	VERBASCUM OLYMPICUM
	VIBURNUM FARRERI 'CANDIDISSIMUM'
	WISTERIA FLORIBUNDA
6	ACER PALMATUM 'EVER RED'
	ACER PALMATUM VAR. DISSECTUM OR A. P. 'WATERFALL'
	ARUNDO DONAX
	FRANKLINIA ALATAMAHA
	HEDERA HELIX 'BUTTERCUP'
	JUNIPERUS CHINENSIS 'KAIZUKA'
	MAGNOLIA DENUDATA (SYN. M. HEPTAPETA)
	MAHONIA BEALEI
	PINUS THUNBERGIANA
	PINUS THUNBERGIANA 'OCULUS-DRACONIS'
	PONCIRUS TRIFOLIATA
	RHODODENDRON (KAEMPFERI HYBRIDS)
	RHODODENDRON (KNAP HILL HYBRID) 'TUNIS'
	SALVIA ARGENTEA
7	CEDRUS ATLANTICA 'GLAUCA'
	DIOSPYROS KAKI
	HEDERA HELIX 'ERECTA'
	RHODODENDRON CANESCENS
T	CANNA X GENERALIS 'MOHAWK'
	RICINUS COMMUNIS
	RICINUS COMMUNIS 'ZANZIBARENSIS'

MULTISTEMMED

ZONE	LATIN NAME
2	BETULA PAPYRIFERA
3	AMELANCHIER ARBOREA (SYN. A. CANADENSIS)
	RHUS TYPHINA
	RHUS TYPHINA 'LACINIATA'
	SORBARIA SORBIFOLIA
	SYRINGA VULGARIS 'ALBA'
	SYRINGA VULGARIS HYBRIDS
4	ARALIA SPINOSA
	BETULA NIGRA
5	CERCIDIPHYLLUM JAPONICUM
	CHIONANTHUS VIRGINICUS
	CLETHRA ALNIFOLIA
	ENKIANTHUS CAMPANULATUS
	KALMIA LATIFOLIA
	MAGNOLIA VIRGINIANA
	PINUS BUNGEANA
	PINUS DENSIFLORA 'UMBRACULIFERA'
	SYRINGA RETICULATA
6	CERCIS CHINENSIS
	CLETHRA BARBINERVIS
	PHYLLOSTACHYS AUREOSULCATA

CLIMBING

ZONE	LATIN NAME
4	CLEMATIS 'MRS. CHOLMONDELEY'
	CLEMATIS 'PRINS HENDRIK'
	CLEMATIS 'RAMONA'
	CLEMATIS MAXIMOWICZIANA
	CLEMATIS X JACKMANII
5	CAMPSIS X TAGLIABUANA 'MADAME GALEN'
	HYDRANGEA ANOMALA SUBSP. PETIOLARIS 'SKYLANDS GIANT'
6	BIGNONIA CAPREOLATA
	HEDERA HELIX 'BUTTERCUP'
	HEDERA HELIX 'GOLD HEART'
7	HEDERA COLCHICA 'DENTATA'

APPENDIX 16
Plant Listing by Seasonal Interest—Fragrance

The plants in this appendix have fragrant blossoms, except those marked

F = Fragrant Foliage
FRT = Fragrant Fruit
BK = Fragrant Bark

These plants are arranged by the month in which the fragrance occurs. Following these monthly lists, I have included two other lists, one of those plants with evergreen foliage, and one of those with especially long seasons of interest (two months or more).

The list is subdivided by hardiness zone.

The letter *T* under the heading "Zone" indicates a plant that is tender, not tolerant of frost.

Further information about all of the following plants is summarized in the Master Lists, Appendices 1A and 1B.

JANUARY

ZONE	LATIN NAME	
3	GERANIUM MACRORRHIZUM	F
4	MYRICA PENSYLVANICA	F, FRT, BK
5	HAMAMELIS MOLLIS 'PALLIDA'	
	SASSAFRAS ALBIDUM	BK
7	CHIMONANTHUS PRAECOX	

FEBRUARY

ZONE	LATIN NAME	
4	MYRICA PENSYLVANICA	F, FRT, BK
5	HAMAMELIS MOLLIS 'PALLIDA'	
	LONICERA FRAGRANTISSIMA	
	SASSAFRAS ALBIDUM	BK
7	CHIMONANTHUS PRAECOX	

MARCH

ZONE	LATIN NAME	
5	GALANTHUS ELWESII	
	GALANTHUS NIVALIS	
	HAMAMELIS MOLLIS 'PALLIDA'	
	LEUCOJUM VERNUM	
	LONICERA FRAGRANTISSIMA	
	SASSAFRAS ALBIDUM	BK
	VIBURNUM FARRERI 'CANDIDISSIMUM'	
	VIBURNUM FARRERI 'NANUM'	
7	CHIMONANTHUS PRAECOX	

APRIL

ZONE	LATIN NAME	
4	PETASITES JAPONICUS	
	VIBURNUM CARLESII	
5	CORYLOPSIS PLATYPETALA	
	DAPHNE X BURKWOODII 'CAROL MACKIE'	
	HAMAMELIS MOLLIS 'PALLIDA'	
	LONICERA FRAGRANTISSIMA	
	MAGNOLIA 'ELIZABETH'	
	MAGNOLIA X LOEBNERI	
	MAGNOLIA X SOULANGIANA 'VERBANICA'	
	MUSCARI AZUREUM 'ALBUM'	
	MUSCARI BOTRYOIDES 'ALBUM'	
	MUSCARI TUBERGENIANUM	
	NARCISSUS 'TREVITHIAN'	
	NARCISSUS JONQUILLA	
	PETASITES FRAGRANS	
	RIBES ODORATUM	
	VIBURNUM FARRERI 'CANDIDISSIMUM'	
	VIBURNUM FARRERI 'NANUM'	
6	MAGNOLIA 'SUSAN'	
	MAGNOLIA DENUDATA (SYN. M. HEPTAPETA)	
	MAHONIA BEALEI	
	PONCIRUS TRIFOLIATA	
	PRUNUS YEDOENSIS	

MAY

ZONE	LATIN NAME	
3	DENNSTAEDTIA PUNCTILOBULA	F
	GERANIUM MACRORRHIZUM	F
	HEMEROCALLIS LILIOASPHODELUS	
	RHODODENDRON PRINOPHYLLUM	
	SYRINGA VULGARIS 'ALBA'	
	SYRINGA VULGARIS HYBRIDS	
4	CHAMAEMELUM NOBILE	F
	COMPTONIA PEREGRINA	F
	CONVALLARIA MAJALIS	
	GAULTHERIA PROCUMBENS	F
	MALUS FLORIBUNDA	
	MALUS SARGENTII	
5	ASPHODELINE LUTEA	
	CALYCANTHUS FLORIDUS 'EDITH WILDER'	
	CHIONANTHUS VIRGINICUS	
	DAPHNE X BURKWOODII 'CAROL MACKIE'	
	GALIUM ODORATUM	F
	IRIS GRAMINEA	
	MAGNOLIA 'ELIZABETH'	
	PHILADELPHUS CORONARIUS	
	PHILADELPHUS X FALCONERI	
	RHODODENDRON ATLANTICUM	
	RHODODENDRON SCHLIPPENBACHII	
	RHODODENDRON X GANDAVENSE 'DAVIESII'	
	ROSA EGLANTERIA	
	VALERIANA OFFICINALIS	
	WISTERIA FLORIBUNDA	
6	PAULOWNIA TOMENTOSA	
7	RHODODENDRON CANESCENS	

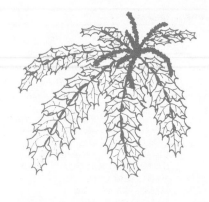

JUNE

ZONE	LATIN NAME	
3	DENNSTAEDTIA PUNCTILOBULA	F
	GERANIUM MACRORRHIZUM	F
	RHODODENDRON PRINOPHYLLUM	
	THYMUS SERPYLLUM	F
4	CHAMAEMELUM NOBILE	F
	CLADRASTIS LUTEA	
	COMPTONIA PEREGRINA	F
	CONVALLARIA MAJALIS	
	GAULTHERIA PROCUMBENS	F
	RHODODENDRON VISCOSUM	
5	ASPHODELINE LUTEA	
	CHIONANTHUS VIRGINICUS	
	GALIUM ODORATUM	
	HOUTTUYNIA CORDATA 'CHAMELEON'	F
	LILIUM 'BLACK DRAGON'	
	MAGNOLIA VIRGINIANA	
	PHILADELPHUS CORONARIUS	
	PHILADELPHUS X FALCONERI	
	RHODODENDRON ARBORESCENS	
	ROSA (GALLICA) 'CHARLES DE MILLS'	
	ROSA EGLANTERIA	
	THYMUS 'CLEAR GOLD'	F
	THYMUS PSEUDOLANUGINOSUS	F
	VALERIANA OFFICINALIS	
6	GALTONIA CANDICANS	
	ITEA VIRGINICA 'HENRY'S GARNET'	
	STYRAX JAPONICUS	
	STYRAX JAPONICUS 'CARILLON'	
T	CESTRUM NOCTURNUM	

JULY

ZONE	LATIN NAME	
3	CLEMATIS HERACLEIFOLIA VAR. DAVIDIANA	
	DENNSTAEDTIA PUNCTILOBULA	F
	GERANIUM MACRORRHIZUM	F
	THYMUS SERPYLLUM	F
4	CHAMAEMELUM NOBILE	F
	COMPTONIA PEREGRINA	F
	GAULTHERIA PROCUMBENS	F
5	CLETHRA ALNIFOLIA	
	HOUTTUYNIA CORDATA 'CHAMELEON'	F

ZONE	LATIN NAME	
	MAGNOLIA VIRGINIANA	
	THYMUS 'CLEAR GOLD'	F
	THYMUS PSEUDOLANUGINOSUS	F
6	GALTONIA CANDICANS	
T	CESTRUM NOCTURNUM	
	POLIANTHES TUBEROSA	

AUGUST

ZONE	LATIN NAME	
3	CLEMATIS HERACLEIFOLIA VAR. DAVIDIANA	
	DENNSTAEDTIA PUNCTILOBULA	
	GERANIUM MACRORRHIZUM	F
	HOSTA PLANTAGINEA	
	THYMUS SERPYLLUM	F
4	CHAMAEMELUM NOBILE	F
	CLEMATIS MAXIMOWICZIANA	
	COMPTONIA PEREGRINA	F
	GAULTHERIA PROCUMBENS	F
5	CLETHRA ALNIFOLIA	
	HOUTTUYNIA CORDATA 'CHAMELEON'	F
	THYMUS 'CLEAR GOLD'	F
	THYMUS PSEUDOLANUGINOSUS	F
6	ADINA RUBELLA	
7	CLERODENDRUM TRICHOTOMUM	
T	CESTRUM NOCTURNUM	
	POLIANTHES TUBEROSA	

SEPTEMBER

ZONE	LATIN NAME	
3	CLEMATIS HERACLEIFOLIA VAR. DAVIDIANA	
	DENNSTAEDTIA PUNCTILOBULA	F
	GERANIUM MACRORRHIZUM	F
	HOSTA PLANTAGINEA	
	THYMUS SERPYLLUM	F
4	CHAMAEMELUM NOBILE	F
	CLEMATIS MAXIMOWICZIANA	
	COMPTONIA PEREGRINA	F
	GAULTHERIA PROCUMBENS	F
5	HOUTTUYNIA CORDATA 'CHAMELEON'	F
	LYCORIS SQUAMIGERA	
	THYMUS 'CLEAR GOLD'	F
	THYMUS PSEUDOLANUGINOSUS	F
7	CLERODENDRUM TRICHOTOMUM	
	ELAEAGNUS PUNGENS 'FRUITLANDII'	
	ELAEAGNUS PUNGENS 'MACULATA'	
T	ACIDANTHERA BICOLOR	
	CESTRUM NOCTURNUM	

OCTOBER

ZONE	LATIN NAME	
3	GERANIUM MACRORRHIZUM	F
4	CHAMAEMELUM NOBILE	F
	CLEMATIS MAXIMOWICZIANA	
	COMPTONIA PEREGRINA	F
	GAULTHERIA PROCUMBENS	F
	HAMAMELIS VIRGINIANA	
	MYRICA PENSYLVANICA	F, FRT, BK
7	CLERODENDRUM TRICHOTOMUM	
	ELAEAGNUS PUNGENS 'FRUITLANDII'	
	ELAEAGNUS PUNGENS 'MACULATA'	

NOVEMBER

ZONE	LATIN NAME	
3	GERANIUM MACRORRHIZUM	F
4	CHAMAEMELUM NOBILE	F
	COMPTONIA PEREGRINA	F
	HAMAMELIS VIRGINIANA	
	MYRICA PENSYLVANICA	F, FRT, BK
7	ELAEAGNUS PUNGENS 'MACULATA'	

DECEMBER

ZONE	LATIN NAME	
3	GERANIUM MACRORRHIZUM	F
4	MYRICA PENSYLVANICA	F, FRT, BK
5	SASSAFRAS ALBIDUM	BK

EVERGREEN

ZONE	LATIN NAME	
6	BUXUS SEMPERVIRENS 'SUFFRUTICOSA'	F
	CALOCEDRUS DECURRENS	F, BK

LONG PERIOD OF INTEREST

ZONE	LATIN NAME	
3	DENNSTAEDTIA PUNCTILOBULA	F
	GERANIUM MACRORRHIZUM	F
	THYMUS SERPYLLUM	F
4	CHAMAEMELUM NOBILE	F
	COMPTONIA PEREGRINA	F
5	HAMAMELIS MOLLIS 'PALLIDA'	
	HOUTTUYNIA CORDATA 'CHAMELEON'	F
	THYMUS 'CLEAR GOLD'	F
	THYMUS PSEUDOLANUGINOSUS	F

APPENDIX 17
Plant Listing by Seasonal Interest—Bird Attractors

The plants in this appendix either have fruits that are attractive to a wide variety of birds or flowers that are specifically attractive to hummingbirds (these latter are preceded by the abbreviation *HB*.) All of the plants are arranged by the month or months during which the fruits are available or the flowers occur. (The reader will note that there are no plants listed for April, simply because there are none with available fruits at that time and because hummingbirds do not arrive then in Delaware to enjoy the flowers we have.)

From the monthly lists two additional lists have been assembled: one of plants with evergreen foliage, the other of those with an especially long season of interest (two months or more).

The lists have been subdivided by hardiness zone.

Further information about all of the following plants is summarized in the Master Lists, Appendices 1A and 1B.

JANUARY

ZONE	LATIN NAME	
4	CRATAEGUS NITIDA	
	CRATAEGUS PHAENOPYRUM	
	ILEX VERTICILLATA	
	ILEX VERTICILLATA 'WINTER RED'	
5	CRATAEGUS VIRIDIS 'WINTER KING'	
	ILEX X AQUIPERNYI 'SAN JOSE'	
	ROSA CAROLINA	
	ROSA VIRGINIANA	
6	ILEX OPACA 'ARDEN'	
	ILEX OPACA 'XANTHOCARPA'	

FEBRUARY

ZONE	LATIN NAME	
4	CRATAEGUS NITIDA	
	CRATAEGUS PHAENOPYRUM	
5	CRATAEGUS VIRIDIS 'WINTER KING'	
	ILEX X AQUIPERNYI 'SAN JOSE'	
	ROSA CAROLINA	
	ROSA VIRGINIANA	
6	ILEX OPACA 'ARDEN'	
	ILEX OPACA 'XANTHOCARPA'	

MARCH

ZONE	LATIN NAME	
5	CRATAEGUS VIRIDIS 'WINTER KING'	
	ILEX X AQUIPERNYI 'SAN JOSE'	

MAY

ZONE		LATIN NAME
3	HB	HEMEROCALLIS LILIOASPHODELUS
5	HB	ASPHODELINE LUTEA
	HB	KOLKWITZIA AMABILIS
6	HB	BIGNONIA CAPREOLATA

JUNE

ZONE		LATIN NAME
3		AMELANCHIER ARBOREA (SYN. A. CANADENSIS)
5	HB	CATALPA BIGNONIOIDES
	HB	HEMEROCALLIS 'HYPERION'
	HB	HEMEROCALLIS FULVA 'EUROPA'
6	HB	BIGNONIA CAPREOLATA

JULY

ZONE		LATIN NAME
3		AMELANCHIER ARBOREA (SYN. A. CANADENSIS)
		CORNUS RACEMOSA
		CORNUS RACEMOSA (DWARF)
		HIPPOPHAE RHAMNOIDES
	HB	HOSTA 'KABITAN'
	HB	HOSTA UNDULATA
	HB	HOSTA VENTRICOSA
4		VACCINIUM CORYMBOSUM
5	HB	CAMPSIS X TAGLIABUANA 'MADAME GALEN'
	HB	HEMEROCALLIS 'HYPERION'
	HB	HEMEROCALLIS FULVA 'EUROPA'
		MAGNOLIA VIRGINIANA
		SYMPHORICARPOS X CHENAULTII 'HANCOCK'
		VIBURNUM SIEBOLDII 'SENECA'
6	HB	ABELIA X GRANDIFLORA
	HB	SALVIA ARGENTEA

AUGUST

ZONE		LATIN NAME
3		CORNUS RACEMOSA
		CORNUS RACEMOSA (DWARF)
		HIPPOPHAE RHAMNOIDES
	HB	HOSTA 'KABITAN'
	HB	HOSTA PLANTAGINEA
	HB	HOSTA UNDULATA
	HB	HOSTA VENTRICOSA
4	HB	CARYOPTERIS X CLANDONENSIS 'BLUE MIST'
		VACCINIUM CORYMBOSUM
5	HB	CAMPSIS X TAGLIABUANA 'MADAME GALEN'
		CORNUS MAS

ZONE		LATIN NAME
		CORNUS OFFICINALIS
	HB	HEMEROCALLIS 'HYPERION'
	HB	HIBISCUS SYRIACUS 'BLUEBIRD'
	HB	HIBISCUS SYRIACUS 'DIANA'
		MAGNOLIA VIRGINIANA
		SASSAFRAS ALBIDUM
		SYMPHORICARPOS X CHENAULTII 'HANCOCK'
		VIBURNUM SIEBOLDII 'SENECA'
6	HB	ABELIA X GRANDIFLORA
	HB	SALVIA ARGENTEA

SEPTEMBER

ZONE		LATIN NAME
3	HB	HOSTA PLANTAGINEA
		VIBURNUM PRUNIFOLIUM
4	HB	CARYOPTERIS X CLANDONENSIS 'BLUE MIST'
		ROSA NITIDA
5		CORNUS FLORIDA
		CORNUS FLORIDA 'HOHMAN'S GOLDEN'
		CORNUS KOUSA
		CORNUS MAS
		CORNUS OFFICINALIS
	HB	HIBISCUS SYRIACUS 'BLUEBIRD'
	HB	HIBISCUS SYRIACUS 'DIANA'
		MAGNOLIA VIRGINIANA
		NYSSA SYLVATICA
		SASSAFRAS ALBIDUM
		SYMPHORICARPOS X CHENAULTII 'HANCOCK'
6	HB	ABELIA X GRANDIFLORA
		VIBURNUM NUDUM 'WINTERTHUR'
7		PYRACANTHA COCCINEA 'AUREA'

OCTOBER

ZONE		LATIN NAME
3		VIBURNUM PRUNIFOLIUM
4		ARONIA ARBUTIFOLIA 'BRILLIANTISSIMA'
		EUONYMUS ALATA
		MALUS HUPEHENSIS
		ROSA NITIDA
5		CORNUS FLORIDA
		CORNUS FLORIDA 'HOHMAN'S GOLDEN'
		NYSSA SYLVATICA
		ROSA CAROLINA
		ROSA VIRGINIANA
		SYMPHORICARPOS X CHENAULTII 'HANCOCK'
		VIBURNUM DILATATUM 'MICHAEL DODGE'
6		VIBURNUM ICHANGENSE
		VIBURNUM NUDUM 'WINTERTHUR'
7		PYRACANTHA COCCINEA 'AUREA'

NOVEMBER

ZONE		LATIN NAME
3		VIBURNUM PRUNIFOLIUM
4		ARONIA ARBUTIFOLIA 'BRILLIANTISSIMA'
		CRATAEGUS NITIDA
		CRATAEGUS PHAENOPYRUM
		EUONYMUS ALATA
		ILEX VERTICILLATA
		ILEX VERTICILLATA 'WINTER RED'
		MALUS HUPEHENSIS
5		CRATAEGUS VIRIDIS 'WINTER KING'
		ILEX X AQUIPERNYI 'SAN JOSE'
		NYSSA SYLVATICA
		ROSA CAROLINA
		ROSA VIRGINIANA
		SYMPHORICARPOS X CHENAULTII 'HANCOCK'
		VIBURNUM DILATATUM 'MICHAEL DODGE'
6		ILEX OPACA 'ARDEN'
		ILEX OPACA 'XANTHOCARPA'
		VIBURNUM ICHANGENSE
		VIBURNUM NUDUM 'WINTERTHUR'
7		PYRACANTHA COCCINEA 'AUREA'

DECEMBER

ZONE		LATIN NAME
4		CRATAEGUS NITIDA
		CRATAEGUS PHAENOPYRUM
		EUONYMUS ALATA
		ILEX VERTICILLATA
		ILEX VERTICILLATA 'WINTER RED'
5		CRATAEGUS VIRIDIS 'WINTER KING'
		ILEX X AQUIPERNYI 'SAN JOSE'
		ROSA CAROLINA
		ROSA VIRGINIANA
		SYMPHORICARPOS X CHENAULTII 'HANCOCK'
		VIBURNUM DILATATUM 'MICHAEL DODGE'
6		ILEX OPACA 'ARDEN'
		ILEX OPACA 'XANTHOCARPA'

EVERGREEN

ZONE		LATIN NAME
3		JUNIPERUS VIRGINIANA
5		ILEX X AQUIPERNYI 'SAN JOSE'
6	HB	BIGNONIA CAPREOLATA
		ILEX OPACA 'ARDEN'
		ILEX OPACA 'XANTHOCARPA'

LONG PERIOD OF INTEREST

ZONE		LATIN NAME
4		CRATAEGUS PHAENOPYRUM
		EUONYMUS ALATA
5		CRATAEGUS VIRIDIS 'WINTER KING'
		HEMEROCALLIS 'HYPERION'
		ILEX X AQUIPERNYI 'SAN JOSE'
6	HB	ABELIA X GRANDIFLORA

APPENDIX 18

Plant Listing by Seasonal Interest—Butterfly Attractors

Although I have observed and enjoyed butterflies in my own garden, I am not an authority on attracting them. From various readings I have assembled the following list of plants with significant garden value that are also butterfly attractors.

It is interesting that the list is predominantly herbaceous (70 percent) and is heavily loaded with plants from the families Compositae (Sunflower) and Leguminosae (Pea). Also of note is the fact that *Coreopsis* 'Moonbeam' (Sunflower family) has the longest season of bloom.

Plants are arranged according to the month in which they bloom. The lists are subdivided by hardiness zone.

The following abbreviations, which precede the plant's Latin name, are used in this appendix:

W = woody (as opposed to herbaceous)
E = evergreen foliage
C = Compositae
L = Leguminosae

Further information about all the following plants is summarized in the Master Lists, Appendices 1A and 1B.

APRIL

ZONE		LATIN NAME
3	E	PHLOX SUBULATA
4	E	PHLOX BIFIDA
5		MUSCARI AZUREUM 'ALBUM'
		MUSCARI BOTRYOIDES 'ALBUM'
		MUSCARI TUBERGENIANUM
6	W,E	MAHONIA BEALEI

MAY

ZONE		LATIN NAME
3		BAPTISIA AUSTRALIS
		SEDUM SPURIUM
	L	THERMOPSIS CAROLINIANA
4	W	BUDDLEIA ALTERNIFOLIA
	W,L	GLEDITSIA TRIACANTHOS VAR. INERMIS 'SHADEMASTER'
	E	PHLOX BIFIDA
	W,L	ROBINIA HISPIDA
		SEDUM POPULIFOLIUM
		SEDUM TERNATUM
5	W,L	CERCIS CANADENSIS 'FOREST PANSY'
	W	PHILADELPHUS CORONARIUS
	W	PHILADELPHUS X FALCONERI
		PHLOX STOLONIFERA 'ALBA'
		PHLOX STOLONIFERA 'BLUE RIDGE'
		PHLOX STOLONIFERA 'SHERWOOD PURPLE'
		SEDUM FLORIFERUM 'WEIHANSTEPHANER GOLD'
	W,L	WISTERIA FLORIBUNDA
6	W,L	CERCIS CHINENSIS
	W,E,L	CYTISUS X PRAECOX 'LUTEUS'

JUNE

ZONE		LATIN NAME
2	C	ACHILLEA MILLEFOLIUM 'ROSEA'
3	C	ACHILLEA 'CORONATION GOLD'
	C	ACHILLEA 'MOONSHINE'
		BAPTISIA AUSTRALIS
	C	BUPHTHALUM SALICIFOLIUM
	C	COREOPSIS 'MOONBEAM'
	C	LIATRIS SCARIOSA 'WHITE SPIRE'
	C	LIATRIS SPICATA 'KOBOLD'
		SEDUM ELLACOMBIANUM
	E	SEDUM SARMENTOSUM
		SEDUM SPURIUM
		SEDUM SPURIUM 'BRONZE CARPET'
	C	TELEKIA SPECIOSA
	L	THERMOPSIS CAROLINIANA
4	W,L	CLADRASTIS LUTEA
	W,L	GLEDITSIA TRIACANTHOS VAR. INERMIS 'SHADEMASTER'
	W,L	GYMNOCLADUS DIOICA
	C	HELIOPSIS HELIANTHOIDES SUBSP. SCABRA 'KARAT'
	W,L	ROBINIA HISPIDA
		SEDUM POPULIFOLIUM
		SEDUM TERNATUM
	W,E	YUCCA FLACCIDA 'GOLDEN SWORD'
	W,E	YUCCA GLAUCA
	W,E	YUCCA SMALLIANA
5	W,L	COLUTEA X MEDIA
	W,L	INDIGOFERA INCARNATA 'ALBA'
	C	ONOPORDUM ACANTHIUM
	W	PHILADELPHUS CORONARIUS
	W	PHILADELPHUS X FALCONERI
	E	PHLOX PILOSA SUBSP. OZARKANA
		SEDUM FLORIFERUM 'WEIHANSTEPHANER GOLD'

ZONE		LATIN NAME
6	W	AESCULUS SPLENDENS
	W,E,L	CYTISUS SCOPARIUS
	W,L	SOPHORA JAPONICA 'REGENT'
7	W,L	GENISTA SYLVESTRIS 'LYDIA'

JULY

ZONE		LATIN NAME
3	C	ACHILLEA 'CORONATION GOLD'
	C	ACHILLEA 'MOONSHINE'
		ASCLEPIAS TUBEROSA
	C	ASTER AMELLUS 'NOCTURNE'
	C	BUPHTHALUM SALICIFOLIUM
	C	COREOPSIS 'MOONBEAM'
	C	ECHINACEA PURPUREA
	C	ECHINOPS RITRO
	C	INULA HELENIUM
	C	LIATRIS SCARIOSA 'WHITE SPIRE'
	C	LIATRIS SPICATA 'KOBOLD'
	C	RUDBECKIA FULGIDA VAR. SULLIVANTII 'GOLDSTURM'
		SEDUM ELLACOMBIANUM
		SEDUM SPURIUM
		SEDUM SPURIUM 'BRONZE CARPET'
4	W	CEPHALANTHUS OCCIDENTALIS
	C	HELIOPSIS HELIANTHOIDES SUBSP. SCABRA 'KARAT'
		SEDUM POPULIFOLIUM
5	W	AESCULUS PARVIFLORA
	W	BUDDLEIA DAVIDII 'BLACK KNIGHT'
	W	BUDDLEIA DAVIDII 'OPERA'
	W	BUDDLEIA DAVIDII 'PURPLE PRINCE'
	W,L	COLUTEA X MEDIA
		SEDUM FLORIFERUM 'WEIHANSTEPHANER GOLD'
	C	STOKESIA LAEVIS 'BLUE DANUBE'
6	W	ABELIA X GRANDIFLORA
	W,L	SOPHORA JAPONICA 'REGENT'

AUGUST

ZONE		LATIN NAME
3	C	ACHILLEA 'MOONSHINE'
		ASCLEPIAS TUBEROSA
	C	ASTER AMELLUS 'NOCTURNE'
	C	COREOPSIS 'MOONBEAM'
	C	ECHINACEA PURPUREA
	C	ECHINOPS RITRO
4	W	CARYOPTERIS X CLANDONENSIS 'BLUE MIST'
	C	CHAMAEMELUM NOBILE
	C	VERNONIA NOVEBORACENSIS
5	C	ASTER CORDIFOLIUS
	C	ASTER X FRIKARTII 'MONCH'
	W	BUDDLEIA DAVIDII 'BLACK KNIGHT'
	W	BUDDLEIA DAVIDII 'OPERA'
	W	BUDDLEIA DAVIDII 'PURPLE PRINCE'
		SEDUM 'VERA JAMISON'
	C	STOKESIA LAEVIS 'BLUE DANUBE'
6	W	ABELIA X GRANDIFLORA

ZONE		LATIN NAME
2	C	ASTER PUNICEUS
3	C	ASTER TATARICUS
	C	BOLTONIA ASTEROIDES 'SNOWBANK'
	C	COREOPSIS 'MOONBEAM'
		SEDUM 'AUTUMN JOY'
4	W,C	BACCHARIS HALIMIFOLIA, PISTILLATE
	W	CARYOPTERIS X CLANDONENSIS 'BLUE MIST'
	C	CHAMAEMELUM NOBILE
		VERNONIA NOVEBORACENSIS
5	C	ASTER CORDIFOLIUS
	C	ASTER NOVAE-ANGLIAE 'HARRINGTON'S PINK'
	C	ASTER X FRIKARTII 'MONCH'
	C	HELIANTHUS SALICIFOLIUS
	W,L	LESPEDEZA THUNBERGII
6	W	ABELIA X GRANDIFLORA
	C	EUPATORIUM COELESTINUM

OCTOBER

ZONE		LATIN NAME
3	C	ASTER TATARICUS
	C	BOLTONIA ASTEROIDES 'SNOWBANK'
	C	COREOPSIS 'MOONBEAM'
4	W,C	BACCHARIS HALIMIFOLIA, PISTILLATE
5	C	ASTER CORDIFOLIUS
	C	HELIANTHUS SALICIFOLIUS
	W,L	LESPEDEZA THUNBERGII
6	C	EUPATORIUM COELESTINUM

APPENDIX 19
Plant Listing by Texture—Foliage

In the planning of plant combinations, contrast of textures presents a great opportunity for enrichment (see pages 40–42 and 98).

This appendix lists first those plants whose foliage has a particularly attractive fine texture, and then those with foliage of particularly attractive broad texture.

The appendix is organized as follows:

FOLIAGE TEXTURE—FINE DETAIL

- Narrow, linear foliage—needle (i.e., Hemlock [*Tsuga*])

- Narrow, linear foliage—blade (i.e., *Iris* or *Miscanthus*)

- Small, rounded foliage, often part of a compound leaf structure (i.e., *Adiantum pedatum* [Maidenhair Fern])

- Miscellaneous other leaf shapes finely divided in a variety of ways (i.e., *Acer palmatum* 'Ever Red' [Red Cutleaf Japanese Maple], *Dennstaedtia punctilobula* [Hay-Scented Fern], *Potentilla tridentata* [Three-Toothed Cinquefoil])

FOLIAGE TEXTURE—BROAD

- Particularly dramatic foliage, due to both largeness and strong design impact

- Foliage useful for ground cover massing

The section of the appendix that focuses on broad foliage is a selection of plants from a much larger group that technically have "broad" texture. This editorial liberty was taken in order to focus on the two groups outlined above, those with strong design impact and those appropriate for ground cover massing.

The first group includes those plants that are especially dramatic because their broad foliage is not only large but has a special design characteristic: i.e., shiny, coarse, dramatically compound. These plants are the designer's most useful pickings for structuring a planting and providing a dramatic background, an exotic atmosphere, or a focal point.

The second group consists of plants that are especially useful when used in mass as ground cover. Because of their broad texture they possess light-reflective qualities that make them useful in tying compositions together and/or providing interesting contrast to more complex textural and flower groupings.

Each list within the appendix is subdivided by hardiness zone.

The letter *T* under the heading "Zone" indicates a plant that is tender, not tolerant of frost.

ZONE	LATIN NAME

The abbreviation *E* indicates evergreen foliage.

Further information about all of the following plants is summarized in the Master Lists, Appendices 1A and 1B.

FOLIAGE TEXTURE—FINE DETAIL
Narrow, Linear—Needle

ZONE		LATIN NAME
3		BUPHTHALUM SALICIFOLIUM
		COREOPSIS 'MOONBEAM'
		DIANTHUS DELTOIDES
		EUPHORBIA COROLLATA
		HIPPOPHAE RHAMNOIDES
	E	JUNIPERUS HORIZONTALIS 'WILTONII'
	E	JUNIPERUS VIRGINIANA
		LIATRIS SCARIOSA 'WHITE SPIRE'
		LIATRIS SPICATA 'KOBOLD'
	E	PHLOX SUBULATA
	E	PICEA ABIES 'NIDIFORMIS'
	E	PICEA PUNGENS 'HOOPSII'
	E	PINUS MUGO VAR. MUGO
	E	PINUS STROBUS
	E	PINUS STROBUS 'FASTIGIATA'
	E	PSEUDOTSUGA MENZIESII
	E	SEDUM SARMENTOSUM
		THYMUS SERPYLLUM
	E	TSUGA CANADENSIS
	E	TSUGA CANADENSIS 'BENNETT'
	E	TSUGA CANADENSIS 'COLE'S PROSTRATE'
	E	TSUGA CANADENSIS 'PENDULA'
4		CHAMAEMELUM NOBILE
		EUPHORBIA CYPARISSIAS
	E	JUNIPERUS SABINA 'TAMARISCIFOLIA'
	E	JUNIPERUS X MEDIA 'PFITZERIANA COMPACTA'
	E	MICROBIOTA DECUSSATA
		PAEONIA TENUIFOLIA
	E	PAXISTIMA CANBYI
	E	PHLOX BIFIDA
	E	PINUS FLEXILIS
	E	PINUS KORAIENSIS
		SALIX ELAEAGNOS
		SPIRAEA THUNBERGII
		TAMARIX RAMOSISSIMA
	E	TAXUS CUSPIDATA 'NANA'
	E	TAXUS CUSPIDATA (CAPITATA SELECTION)
	E	THUJA OCCIDENTALIS 'HETZ' WINTERGREEN'
5	E	ABIES NORDMANNIANA
		AMSONIA HUBRICHTII
	E	CEDRUS LIBANI VAR. STENOCOMA
	E	CEPHALOTAXUS HARRINGTONIA VAR. PEDUNCULATA
	E	CHAMAECYPARIS OBTUSA 'FILICOIDES'
	E	CHAMAECYPARIS OBTUSA 'NANA GRACILIS'
	E	CHAMAECYPARIS OBTUSA 'NANA'
	E	CHAMAECYPARIS OBTUSA VAR. BREVIRAMEA
	E	CHAMAECYPARIS PISIFERA 'GOLD SPANGLE'
	E	CHAMAECYPARIS PISIFERA 'SQUARROSA'

ZONE	LATIN NAME
	DAPHNE X BURKWOODII 'CAROL MACKIE'
	GALIUM ODORATUM
E	JUNIPERUS SCOPULORUM 'SKY ROCKET'
E	JUNIPERUS X MEDIA 'OLD GOLD'
	METASEQUOIA GLYPTOSTROBOIDES
E	PICEA ORIENTALIS
E	PINUS BUNGEANA
E	PINUS DENSIFLORA 'UMBRACULIFERA'
E	PINUS PARVIFLORA 'GLAUCA'
E	PINUS VIRGINIANA
E	TAXUS BACCATA 'ADPRESSA FOWLE'
E	TAXUS BACCATA 'REPANDENS'
E	TAXUS X MEDIA 'SENTINALIS'
E	THUJA PLICATA 'ATROVIRENS'
	THYMUS 'CLEAR GOLD'
6	E BERBERIS WISLEYENSIS (SYN. BERBERIS TRIACANTHOPHORA)
	E CALOCEDRUS DECURRENS
	E CHAMAECYPARIS OBTUSA 'CRIPPSII'
	CRUCIANELLA STYLOSA
	E JUNIPERUS CHINENSIS 'KAIZUKA'
	PARONYCHIA KAPELA SUBSP. SERPYLLIFOLIA
	E PINUS THUNBERGIANA
	E PINUS THUNBERGIANA 'OCULUS-DRACONIS'
	PSEUDOLARIX KAEMPFERI
	QUERCUS PHELLOS
	E SCIADOPITYS VERTICILLATA
	TAXODIUM DISTICHUM VAR. NUTANS 'PRAIRIE SENTINEL'
7	E CEDRUS ATLANTICA 'GLAUCA'
T	KOCHIA SCOPARIA FORMA TRICHOPHYLLA 'CHILDSII'

FOLIAGE TEXTURE—FINE DETAIL
Narrow, Linear—Blade

ZONE	LATIN NAME
3	HEMEROCALLIS LILIOASPHODELUS
	IRIS SIBIRICA CULTIVARS
	SALIX ALBA 'SERICEA'
4	ALLIUM TUBEROSUM
	CARYOPTERIS X CLANDONENSIS 'BLUE MIST'
	EUPHORBIA EPITHYMOIDES
	PHALARIS ARUNDINACEA VAR. PICTA
	SALIX ALBA VAR. TRISTIS
	TYPHA ANGUSTIFOLIA
	E YUCCA GLAUCA
5	ALLIUM CERNUUM
	ALLIUM ZEBDANENSE
	ASPHODELINE LUTEA
	CALAMAGROSTIS X ACUTIFLORA 'KARL FOERSTER' (SYN. C. EPIGEOUS 'HORTORUM')
	EPIMEDIUM X YOUNGIANUM 'NIVEUM'
	EQUISETUM HYEMALE
	ERIANTHUS RAVENNAE
	HELIANTHUS SALICIFOLIUS
	HELICTOTRICHON SEMPERVIRENS

ZONE	LATIN NAME
	HEMEROCALLIS 'HYPERION'
	HEMEROCALLIS FULVA 'EUROPA'
	IRIS CRISTATA
	IRIS PSEUDACORUS
	IRIS TECTORUM
	LILIUM 'BLACK DRAGON'
	LILIUM SPECIES AND HYBRIDS
	MISCANTHUS 'GIGANTEUS'
	MISCANTHUS SINENSIS 'GRACILLIMUS'
	MISCANTHUS SINENSIS 'SILVER FEATHER' (='SILBERFEDER')
	MISCANTHUS SINENSIS 'STRICTUS'
	MISCANTHUS SINENSIS 'VARIEGATUS'
	MOLINIA CAERULEA SUBSP. ARUNDINACEA
	PANICUM VIRGATUM 'STRICTUM'
	PENNISETUM ALOPECUROIDES
	E PHLOX PILOSA SUBSP. OZARKANA
	STERNBERGIA LUTEA
	SYMPHORICARPOS X CHENAULTII 'HANCOCK'
6	ACORUS GRAMINEUS 'OGON'
	IMPERATA CYLINDRICA 'RED BARON'
	E LIRIOPE MUSCARI (BIG BLUE SELECTION)
	E LIRIOPE MUSCARI 'MONROE WHITE'
	E LIRIOPE MUSCARI 'VARIEGATA'
	PHYLLOSTACHYS AUREOSULCATA

FOLIAGE TEXTURE—FINE DETAIL
Small, Rounded

ZONE	LATIN NAME
3	ADIANTUM PEDATUM
	OSMUNDA REGALIS
4	GLEDITSIA TRIACANTHOS VAR. INERMIS 'SHADEMASTER'
5	E BUXUS SINICA VAR. INSULARIS 'TIDE HILL'
	CYCLAMEN HEDERIFOLIUM
	E EUONYMUS FORTUNEI 'MINIMA'
	HELIANTHEMUM APENNINUM VAR. ROSEUM
	LESPEDEZA THUNBERGII
	PHLOX STOLONIFERA 'ALBA'
	PHLOX STOLONIFERA 'BLUE RIDGE'
	PHLOX STOLONIFERA 'SHERWOOD PURPLE'
	ROSA 'DOORENBOS SELECTION'
	THALICTRUM ROCHEBRUNIANUM
6	CYTISUS SCOPARIUS
	CYTISUS X PRAECOX 'LUTEUS'
	JASMINUM NUDIFLORUM
	ROSA ROXBURGHII
	SOPHORA JAPONICA 'REGENT'
7	BERBERIS WILSONIAE VAR. STAPFIANA
	GENISTA SYLVESTRIS 'LYDIA'

FOLIAGE TEXTURE—FINE DETAIL
Other Leaf Shapes

ZONE	LATIN NAME
2	ACHILLEA MILLEFOLIUM 'ROSEA'
	ARTEMESIA STELLERIANA
	E POTENTILLA TRIDENTATA
3	ACHILLEA 'CORONATION GOLD'
	ACHILLEA 'MOONSHINE'
	ARUNCUS DIOICUS
	BETULA PENDULA 'GRACILIS'
	DENNSTAEDTIA PUNCTILOBULA
	DICENTRA 'LUXURIANT'
	DICENTRA EXIMIA 'PURITY'
	GERANIUM SANGUINEUM
	PTERIDIUM AQUILINUM VAR. LATIUSCULUM
	RHUS TYPHINA 'LACINIATA'
4	ACANTHOPANAX SIEBOLDIANUS
	ARTEMESIA LUDOVICIANA 'SILVER QUEEN'
	ARUNCUS AETHUSIFOLIUS
	ASTILBE X ARENDSII CULTIVARS
	COMPTONIA PEREGRINA
	OSMUNDA CINNAMOMEA
	OSMUNDA CLAYTONIANA
	SEDUM POPULIFOLIUM
	E WALDSTEINIA TERNATA
5	ACER PALMATUM 'BLOODGOOD'
	ARTEMESIA VERSICOLOR
	ATHYRIUM GOERINGIANUM 'PICTUM'
	DIPLAZIUM CONILII
	FAGUS SYLVATICA 'LACINIATA'
	PEROVSKIA ABROTANOIDES X P. ATRIPLICIFOLIA
	POLYSTICHUM TRIPTERON
	RIBES ODORATUM
	SEDUM FLORIFERUM 'WEIHANSTEPHANER GOLD'
	STEPHANANDRA INCISA 'CRISPA'
	SYRINGA LACINIATA
	THELYPTERIS HEXAGONOPTERA
	THELYPTERIS NOVEBORACENSIS
	THELYPTERIS PHEGOPTERIS
	VALERIANA OFFICINALIS
6	ACER PALMATUM 'EVER RED'
	ACER PALMATUM VAR. DISSECTUM OR A. P. 'WATERFALL'
8	COTULA SQUALIDA

FOLIAGE TEXTURE—BROAD
Strong Design Impact

ZONE	LATIN NAME
2	E BERGENIA 'PERFECTA'
	E BERGENIA 'SUNNINGDALE'
3	E HELLEBORUS NIGER
	HOSTA PLANTAGINEA
	HOSTA SIEBOLDIANA 'ELEGANS'
	HOSTA VENTRICOSA
	MACLEAYA CORDATA
	RHUS TYPHINA
	SORBARIA SORBIFOLIA

ZONE	LATIN NAME
4	ACER PLATANOIDES 'CRIMSON KING'
	ARALIA SPINOSA
	CARYA OVATA
	GYMNOCLADUS DIOICA
E	HELLEBORUS ORIENTALIS HYBRIDS
	PETASITES JAPONICUS
	PHELLODENDRON AMURENSE
E	RHODODENDRON (CATAWBIENSE HYBRIDS)
E	RHODODENDRON MAXIMUM
	RODGERSIA AESCULIFOLIA
	RODGERSIA PODOPHYLLA
	RODGERSIA TABULARIS
E	YUCCA FLACCIDA 'GOLDEN SWORD'
E	YUCCA SMALLIANA
5	AESCULUS PARVIFLORA
	ARUNDINARIA VIRIDISTRIATA
	CAMPSIS X TAGLIABUANA 'MADAME GALEN'
	CATALPA BIGNONIOIDES
	CRAMBE CORDIFOLIA
	HERACLEUM MANTEGAZZIANUM
E	ILEX X MESERVEAE BLUE MAID ® 'MESID'
E	ILEX X MESERVEAE BLUE STALLION ® 'MESAN'
	KOELREUTERIA PANICULATA
	LIQUIDAMBAR STYRACIFLUA
	PETASITES FRAGRANS
	RHEUM PALMATUM 'RUBRUM'
	VIBURNUM SIEBOLDII 'SENECA'
	WISTERIA FLORIBUNDA
6	AESCULUS·SPLENDENS
E	ARUM ITALICUM 'PICTUM'
	ARUNDO DONAX
E	MAHONIA BEALEI
	PAEONIA 'BLACK PIRATE'
	PAEONIA—WOODY HYBRIDS
	PAULOWNIA TOMENTOSA
	PELTIPHYLLUM PELTATUM
7	CLERODENDRUM TRICHOTOMUM
E	HEDERA COLCHICA 'DENTATA'
	HYDRANGEA ASPERA SUBSP. SARGENTIANA
E	SASA VEITCHII
T	CANNA X GENERALIS 'MOHAWK'
	RICINUS COMMUNIS 'ZANZIBARENSIS'

FOLIAGE TEXTURE—BROAD
For Ground Cover Massing

ZONE	LATIN NAME
2	E BERGENIA 'PERFECTA'
	E BERGENIA 'SUNNINGDALE'
3	BRUNNERA MACROPHYLLA
	GERANIUM MACRORRHIZUM
	E HELLEBORUS NIGER
	HOSTA 'KABITAN'
	HOSTA PLANTAGINEA
	HOSTA SIEBOLDIANA 'ELEGANS'
	HOSTA UNDULATA
	HOSTA VENTRICOSA
	E POLYSTICHUM ACROSTICHOIDES
	PULMONARIA ANGUSTIFOLIA

ZONE	LATIN NAME
	PULMONARIA SACCHARATA 'MARGERY FISH'
	SEDUM 'AUTUMN JOY'
	SEDUM ELLACOMBIANUM
	SEDUM SPURIUM
	SEDUM SPURIUM 'BRONZE CARPET'
4	AJUGA REPTANS
	AJUGA REPTANS 'BRONZE BEAUTY'
	AJUGA REPTANS (GIANT FORM)
E	EUONYMUS FORTUNEI 'COLORATA'
E	EUONYMUS FORTUNEI VAR. RADICANS
	GAULTHERIA PROCUMBENS
E	HELLEBORUS ORIENTALIS HYBRIDS
	HEUCHERA 'PALACE PURPLE' STRAIN
	PETASITES JAPONICUS
	RODGERSIA AESCULIFOLIA
	RODGERSIA PODOPHYLLA
	RODGERSIA TABULARIS
	STACHYS BYZANTINA
E	VINCA MINOR 'BOWLESII'
E	VINCA MINOR 'VARIEGATA'
E	YUCCA FLACCIDA 'GOLDEN SWORD'
E	YUCCA SMALLIANA
5	ARUNDINARIA VIRIDISTRIATA
E	ASARUM EUROPAEUM
	EPIMEDIUM PINNATUM SUBSP. COLCHICUM
E	EUONYMUS FORTUNEI 'GRACILIS'
	FILIPENDULA PURPUREA 'NANA'
E	HEDERA HELIX 'BULGARIA'
E	HEDERA HELIX 'OGALALLA'
	HOUTTUYNIA CORDATA 'CHAMELEON'
E	LEUCOTHOE FONTANESIANA
E	LEUCOTHOE FONTANESIANA 'NANA'
E	PACHYSANDRA TERMINALIS
E	PACHYSANDRA TERMINALIS 'GREEN CARPET'
E	PACHYSANDRA TERMINALIS 'VARIEGATA' OR 'SILVER EDGE'
	PETASITES FRAGRANS
	SEDUM 'VERA JAMISON'
6	E ARUM ITALICUM 'PICTUM'
	EUONYMUS FORTUNEI 'SILVER QUEEN'
	E HEDERA HELIX 'BALTICA'
	HEDERA HELIX 'BUTTERCUP'
	HEDERA HELIX 'GOLD HEART'
	SALVIA ARGENTEA
	SAXIFRAGA STOLONIFERA
	TRACHYSTEMON ORIENTALIS
7	E HEDERA COLCHICA 'DENTATA'
	E HEDERA HELIX 'ERECTA'
	E SASA VEITCHII
	E SKIMMIA REEVESIANA

APPENDIX 20
Plant Listing by Texture—Flower

The texture of individual blossoms and total inflorescences can have as much effect on a plant composition as plant structure itself and the texture of foliage and bark.

Flower texture is divided here into the following categories:

Projecting Landscape Effect: Spikes, Cones, Wands, and Spraylike Heads
Pendulous Landscape Effect
Daisylike Landscape Effect
Flat-Top Landscape Effect
Ball-like Landscape Effect
Irregular and/or Complex Landscape Effect

Blossoms included under "Spikes" et al. are projecting in nature and hence can be used to add structure to any composition. Pendulous inflorescences are useful in directing eye movement downward. Plants with daisylike and flat-top inflorescences generally have horizontal characteristics and exert a stabilizing influence on the composition. Those flowers that are ball-like and irregular and/or complex generally do not rock the boat but add great richness to the composition. Developing a happy balance between individuals and/or masses from any one category, and representations of the six categories, is the key to a harmonious picture.

Each list is subdivided by month of flowering.

Further information about all the following plants is summarized in the Master Lists, Appendices 1A and 1B.

FLOWER TEXTURE
Projecting Landscape Effect: Spikes, Cones, Wands, and Spraylike Heads

The inflorescences of the plants in this category are projecting forms, as opposed to the contained forms of daisylike and ball-like blooms.

MONTH	LATIN NAME
APR.	FOTHERGILLA GARDENII
	LYSICHITON AMERICANUM
	LYSICHITON CAMTSCHATCENSE
	MAHONIA BEALEI
	MUSCARI AZUREUM 'ALBUM'
	MUSCARI BOTRYOIDES 'ALBUM'
	MUSCARI TUBERGENIANUM
	RHUS AROMATICA 'GRO-LOW'
MAY	AJUGA REPTANS
	AJUGA REPTANS 'BRONZE BEAUTY'
	AJUGA REPTANS (GIANT FORM)
	ARUM ITALICUM 'PICTUM'
	ARUNCUS AETHUSIFOLIUS
	ASPHODELINE LUTEA

BAPTISIA AUSTRALIS
BUDDLEIA ALTERNIFOLIA
DICENTRA 'LUXURIANT'
DICENTRA EXIMIA 'PURITY'
ENDYMION HISPANICUS 'EXCELSIOR'
  (SYN. SCILLA CAMPANULATA
  'EXCELSIOR')
FOTHERGILLA GARDENII
HOSTA SIEBOLDIANA 'ELEGANS'
LAMIUM MACULATUM 'WHITE
  NANCY'
LYSICHITON AMERICANUM
LYSICHITON CAMTSCHATCENSE
OSMUNDA CINNAMOMEA*
OSMUNDA CLAYTONIANA*
OSMUNDA REGALIS*
PAULOWNIA TOMENTOSA
RHEUM PALMATUM 'RUBRUM'
RODGERSIA AESCULIFOLIA
RODGERSIA PODOPHYLLA
RODGERSIA TABULARIS
SPIRAEA PRUNIFOLIA
SYRINGA LACINIATA
SYRINGA PATULA
  (SYN. S. PALIBINIANA, S.
  MICROPHYLLA 'INGWERSEN'S
  DWARF')
SYRINGA VULGARIS 'ALBA'
SYRINGA VULGARIS HYBRIDS
SYRINGA X CHINENSIS
THERMOPSIS CAROLINIANA
TIARELLA CORDIFOLIA VAR. COLLINA

JUN.
AESCULUS PARVIFLORA
AESCULUS SPLENDENS
ARUM ITALICUM 'PICTUM'
ARUNCUS DIOICUS
ASPHODELINE LUTEA
ASTILBE X ARENDSII CULTIVARS
BAPTISIA AUSTRALIS
CALAMAGROSTIS X ACUTIFLORA
  'KARL FOERSTER'
  (SYN. C. EPIGEOUS 'HORTORUM')
CATALPA BIGNONIOIDES
CIMICIFUGA RACEMOSA
CROCOSMIA 'LUCIFER'
GALTONIA CANDICANS
HELICTOTRICHON SEMPERVIRENS
HOSTA VENTRICOSA
HYDRANGEA QUERCIFOLIA
INDIGOFERA INCARNATA 'ALBA'
ITEA VIRGINICA 'HENRY'S GARNET'
LIATRIS SCARIOSA 'WHITE SPIRE'
LIATRIS SPICATA 'KOBOLD'
LYTHRUM SALICARIA 'DROPMORE
  PURPLE'
MACLEAYA CORDATA
NEPETA X FAASSENII
PHLOMIS RUSSELIANA
RHEUM PALMATUM 'RUBRUM'
SALVIA ARGENTEA
SORBARIA SORBIFOLIA
TAMARIX RAMOSISSIMA
THALICTRUM ROCHEBRUNIANUM
THERMOPSIS CAROLINIANA
VERBASCUM OLYMPICUM
YUCCA FLACCIDA 'GOLDEN SWORD'

* This fern has reproductive fronds
that, although not technically flowers,
create the same landscape effect as
flowers.

YUCCA GLAUCA
YUCCA SMALLIANA

JUL.
ARALIA SPINOSA
BUDDLEIA DAVIDII 'BLACK KNIGHT'
BUDDLEIA DAVIDII 'PURPLE PRINCE'
CANNA X GENERALIS 'MOHAWK'
CIMICIFUGA RACEMOSA
CLEMATIS HERACLEIFOLIA VAR.
  DAVIDIANA
CLETHRA ALNIFOLIA
CROCOSMIA POTTSII
GALTONIA CANDICANS
HOSTA VENTRICOSA
LIATRIS SCARIOSA 'WHITE SPIRE'
LIATRIS SPICATA 'KOBOLD'
LIGUSTRUM QUIHOUI
LYTHRUM SALICARIA 'DROPMORE
  PURPLE'
MACLEAYA CORDATA
NEPETA X FAASSENII
PEROVSKIA ABROTANOIDES X P.
  ATRIPLICIFOLIA
POLIANTHES TUBEROSA
RHUS TYPHINA
RHUS TYPHINA 'LACINIATA'
SALVIA ARGENTEA
SORBARIA SORBIFOLIA
TAMARIX RAMOSISSIMA
THALICTRUM ROCHEBRUNIANUM
VERONICA 'SUNNY BORDER BLUE'
VERONICA LONGIFOLIA 'SUBSESSILIS'
VITEX AGNUS-CASTUS 'LATIFOLIA'
VITEX AGNUS-CASTUS 'SILVER SPIRE'

AUG.
ARALIA SPINOSA
BUDDLEIA DAVIDII 'BLACK KNIGHT'
BUDDLEIA DAVIDII 'PURPLE PRINCE'
CANNA X GENERALIS 'MOHAWK'
CHELONE LYONII
CLEMATIS HERACLEIFOLIA VAR.
  DAVIDIANA
CLETHRA ALNIFOLIA
CROCOSMIA X CROCOSMIIFLORA
HOSTA 'KABITAN'
HOSTA PLANTAGINEA
HOSTA UNDULATA
HYDRANGEA PANICULATA
LIRIOPE MUSCARI (BIG BLUE
  SELECTION)
LIRIOPE MUSCARI 'MONROE WHITE'
LIRIOPE MUSCARI 'VARIEGATA'
PANICUM VIRGATUM 'STRICTUM'
PENNISETUM ALOPECUROIDES
PEROVSKIA ABROTANOIDES X P.
  ATRIPLICIFOLIA
PHYSOSTEGIA VIRGINIANA
PHYSOSTEGIA VIRGINIANA 'SUMMER
  SNOW'
POLIANTHES TUBEROSA
THALICTRUM ROCHEBRUNIANUM
VERONICA 'SUNNY BORDER BLUE'
VERONICA INCANA
VERONICA LONGIFOLIA 'SUBSESSILIS'
VERONICASTRUM VIRGINICUM
VITEX AGNUS-CASTUS 'LATIFOLIA'
VITEX AGNUS-CASTUS 'SILVER SPIRE'

SEP.
ARUNDO DONAX
CANNA X GENERALIS 'MOHAWK'
CHELONE LYONII
CLEMATIS HERACLEIFOLIA VAR.
  DAVIDIANA
ERIANTHUS RAVENNAE
HOSTA PLANTAGINEA
HYDRANGEA PANICULATA
LYCORIS SPRENGERI
LYCORIS SQUAMIGERA
MISCANTHUS 'GIGANTEUS'
MISCANTHUS SINENSIS 'CABARET'
MISCANTHUS SINENSIS 'GRACILLIMUS'
MISCANTHUS SINENSIS 'MORNING
  LIGHT'
MISCANTHUS SINENSIS 'SILVER
  FEATHER' (='SILBERFEDER')
MISCANTHUS SINENSIS 'VARIEGATUS'
MOLINIA CAERULEA SUBSP.
  ARUNDINACEA
PANICUM VIRGATUM 'STRICTUM'
PHYSOSTEGIA VIRGINIANA
PHYSOSTEGIA VIRGINIANA 'SUMMER
  SNOW'

OCT.
ARUNDO DONAX
ERIANTHUS RAVENNAE
MISCANTHUS 'GIGANTEUS'
MISCANTHUS SINENSIS 'CABARET'
MISCANTHUS SINENSIS 'MORNING
  LIGHT'
MISCANTHUS SINENSIS 'SILVER
  FEATHER' (='SILBERFEDER')
MISCANTHUS SINENSIS 'VARIEGATUS'
MOLINIA CAERULEA SUBSP.
  ARUNDINACEA

FLOWER TEXTURE
Pendulous Landscape Effect

Either the total inflorescence is
pendulous or flowers within the
inflorescence are pendant.

MONTH	LATIN NAME

JAN.
CORYLUS AVELLANA 'CONTORTA'
CORYLUS AVELLANA 'PENDULA'

FEB.
CORYLUS AVELLANA 'CONTORTA'
CORYLUS AVELLANA 'PENDULA'

MAR.
CORYLUS AVELLANA 'CONTORTA'
CORYLUS AVELLANA 'PENDULA'
GALANTHUS ELWESII
GALANTHUS NIVALIS
LEUCOJUM VERNUM
PIERIS JAPONICA
SCILLA SIBERICA 'SPRING BEAUTY'

APR.
AMELANCHIER ARBOREA
  (SYN. A. CANADENSIS)
CORYLOPSIS PLATYPETALA
CORYLUS AVELLANA 'CONTORTA'
CORYLUS AVELLANA 'PENDULA'
MERTENSIA VIRGINICA
PIERIS JAPONICA
SCILLA SIBERICA 'SPRING BEAUTY'

MONTH	LATIN NAME
MAY	AMELANCHIER ARBOREA (SYN. A. CANADENSIS)
	BUDDLEIA ALTERNIFOLIA
	CHIONANTIIUS VIRGINICUS
	CONVALLARIA MAJALIS
	DICENTRA 'LUXURIANT'
	DICENTRA EXIMIA 'PURITY'
	DICENTRA SPECTABILIS
	ENKIANTHUS CAMPANULATUS
	EXOCHORDA GIRALDII VAR. WILSONII
	HALESIA TETRAPTERA
	MERTENSIA VIRGINICA
	POLYGONATUM ODORATUM 'VARIEGATUM'
	ROBINIA HISPIDA
	SYMPHYTUM X UPLANDICUM
	VACCINIUM CORYMBOSUM
	WISTERIA FLORIBUNDA
JUN.	CAMPANULA RAPUNCULOIDES
	CLADRASTIS LUTEA
	GYMNOCLADUS DIOICA
	ROBINIA HISPIDA
	STYRAX JAPONICUS
	STYRAX JAPONICUS 'CARILLON'
	SYMPHYTUM X UPLANDICUM
	YUCCA FLACCIDA 'GOLDEN SWORD'
	YUCCA GLAUCA
	YUCCA SMALLIANA
JUL.	ABELIA X GRANDIFLORA
	CAMPANULA RAPUNCULOIDES
	CLETHRA BARBINERVIS
	LYSIMACHIA CLETHROIDES
	OXYDENDRUM ARBOREUM
AUG.	ABELIA X GRANDIFLORA
	BEGONIA GRANDIS
	CLETHRA BARBINERVIS
	LYSIMACHIA CLETHROIDES
	PENNISETUM ALOPECUROIDES
SEP.	ABELIA X GRANDIFLORA
	BEGONIA GRANDIS
	KIRENGESHOMA PALMATA
	LESPEDEZA THUNBERGII 'ALBIFLORA'

FLOWER TEXTURE
Daisylike Landscape Effect

Open faced, radially symmetric.

MONTH	LATIN NAME
JAN.	CHIMONANTHUS PRAECOX
FEB.	CHIMONANTHUS PRAECOX
MAR.	ERANTHIS HYEMALIS
	ERANTHIS X TUBERGENII
	HELLEBORUS NIGER
	HELLEBORUS ORIENTALIS HYBRIDS
APR.	ANEMONE BLANDA 'ATROCAERULEA'
	CHAENOMELES JAPONICA VAR. ALPINA
	CHAENOMELES SPECIOSA CULTIVARS
	CHIONODOXA GIGANTEA 'ALBA'
	CHIONODOXA LUCILIAE
	CHIONODOXA SARDENSIS
	HELLEBORUS NIGER

MONTH	LATIN NAME
	HELLEBORUS ORIENTALIS HYBRIDS
	PONCIRUS TRIFOLIATA
MAY	ARABIS PROCURRENS
	CORNUS FLORIDA
	CORNUS FLORIDA 'HOHMAN'S GOLDEN'
	CORNUS KOUSA
	DIANTHUS DELTOIDES
	GERANIUM MACRORRHIZUM
	GERANIUM SANGUINEUM
	KERRIA JAPONICA
	MALUS 'RED JADE'
	MALUS SARGENTII
	PAEONIA TENUIFOLIA
	PHILADELPHUS X FALCONERI
	PHLOX PILOSA SUBSP. OZARKANA
	PHLOX STOLONIFERA 'ALBA'
	PHLOX STOLONIFERA 'BLUE RIDGE'
	PHLOX STOLONIFERA 'SHERWOOD PURPLE'
	POTENTILLA TRIDENTATA
	ROSA 'DOORENBOS SELECTION'
	VINCA MINOR 'BOWLESII'
	VINCA MINOR 'VARIEGATA'
	WALDSTEINIA TERNATA
JUN.	BUPHTHALUM SALICIFOLIUM
	CLEMATIS 'MRS. CHOLMONDELEY'
	CLEMATIS 'PRINS HENDRIK'
	CLEMATIS 'RAMONA'
	CLEMATIS X JACKMANII
	COREOPSIS 'MOONBEAM'
	CORNUS KOUSA
	DIANTHUS DELTOIDES
	ECHINACEA PURPUREA
	GERANIUM MACRORRHIZUM
	GERANIUM SANGUINEUM
	HELIANTHEMUM APENNINUM VAR. ROSEUM
	HELIOPSIS HELIANTHOIDES SUBSP. SCABRA 'KARAT'
	HOUTTUYNIA CORDATA 'CHAMELEON'
	INULA HELENIUM
	LYSIMACHIA PUNCTATA
	MAGNOLIA VIRGINIANA
	PHILADELPHUS X FALCONERI
	PHLOX PILOSA SUBSP. OZARKANA
	ROSA 'DOORENBOS SELECTION'
	ROSA (GALLICA) 'CHARLES DE MILLS'
	ROSA (SHRUB) 'LILLIAN GIBSON'
	ROSA NITIDA
	ROSA ROXBURGHII
	ROSA RUGOSA AND HYBRIDS
	ROSA VIRGINIANA
	STEWARTIA KOREANA
	TELEKIA SPECIOSA
	WALDSTEINIA TERNATA
JUL.	ASTER AMELLUS 'NOCTURNE'
	BUPHTHALUM SALICIFOLIUM
	COREOPSIS 'MOONBEAM'
	ECHINACEA PURPUREA
	EUPHORBIA COROLLATA
	HELIOPSIS HELIANTHOIDES SUBSP. SCABRA 'KARAT'
	HOUTTUYNIA CORDATA 'CHAMELEON'
	INULA HELENIUM
	LYSIMACHIA PUNCTATA
	MAGNOLIA VIRGINIANA
	RUDBECKIA FULGIDA VAR. SULLIVANTII 'GOLDSTURM'
	STOKESIA LAEVIS 'BLUE DANUBE'

MONTH	LATIN NAME
AUG.	ANEMONE VITIFOLIA 'ROBUSTISSIMA'
	ANEMONE X HYBRIDA 'QUEEN CHARLOTTE'
	ASTER AMELLUS 'NOCTURNE'
	ASTER CORDIFOLIUS
	ASTER X FRIKARTII 'MONCH'
	CLEMATIS MAXIMOWICZIANA
	COREOPSIS 'MOONBEAM'
	ECHINACEA PURPUREA
	EUPHORBIA COROLLATA
	FRANKLINIA ALATAMAHA
	HIBISCUS SYRIACUS 'BLUEBIRD'
	HIBISCUS SYRIACUS 'DIANA'
	RUDBECKIA FULGIDA VAR. SULLIVANTII 'GOLDSTURM'
	STOKESIA LAEVIS 'BLUE DANUBE'
SEP.	ANEMONE X HYBRIDA 'QUEEN CHARLOTTE'
	ASTER CORDIFOLIUS
	ASTER NOVAE-ANGLIAE 'HARRINGTON'S PINK'
	ASTER PUNICEUS
	ASTER TATARICUS
	ASTER X FRIKARTII 'MONCH'
	BOLTONIA ASTEROIDES 'SNOWBANK'
	CHRYSANTHEMUM WEYRICHII 'WHITE BOMB'
	CLEMATIS MAXIMOWICZIANA
	COREOPSIS 'MOONBEAM'
	FRANKLINIA ALATAMAHA
	HELIANTHUS SALICIFOLIUS
	HIBISCUS SYRIACUS 'BLUEBIRD'
	HIBISCUS SYRIACUS 'DIANA'
OCT.	ASTER CORDIFOLIUS
	ASTER NOVAE-ANGLIAE 'HARRINGTON'S PINK'
	ASTER PUNICEUS
	ASTER TATARICUS
	BOLTONIA ASTEROIDES 'SNOWBANK'
	CHRYSANTHEMUM WEYRICHII 'WHITE BOMB'
	COREOPSIS 'MOONBEAM'
	HELIANTHUS SALICIFOLIUS

FLOWER TEXTURE
Flat-Top Landscape Effect

Horizontal to slightly domed, these inflorescences generally contribute to a horizontal design effect.

MONTH	LATIN NAME
MAR.	VIBURNUM FARRERI 'CANDIDISSIMUM'
APR.	EUPHORBIA CYPARISSIAS
	EUPHORBIA EPITHYMOIDES
	VIBURNUM FARRERI 'CANDIDISSIMUM'
MAY	CORNUS ALTERNIFOLIA
	CRATAEGUS NITIDA
	CRATAEGUS PHAENOPYRUM
	CRATAEGUS VIRIDIS 'WINTER KING'
	EUPHORBIA EPITHYMOIDES
	SEDUM FLORIFERUM 'WEIHANSTEPHANER GOLD'
	SEDUM SPURIUM
	VALERIANA OFFICINALIS

MONTH	LATIN NAME
	VIBURNUM PLICATUM FORMA TOMENTOSUM
	VIBURNUM PRUNIFOLIUM
JUN.	ACHILLEA 'CORONATION GOLD'
	ACHILLEA 'MOONSHINE'
	ACHILLEA MILLEFOLIUM 'ROSEA'
	HERACLEUM MANTEGAZZIANUM
	HYDRANGEA ANOMALA SUBSP. PETIOLARIS 'SKYLANDS GIANT'
	HYDRANGEA MACROPHYLLA 'BLUE BILLOW'
	SEDUM ELLACOMBIANUM
	SEDUM FLORIFERUM 'WEIHANSTEPHANER GOLD'
	SEDUM SARMENTOSUM
	SEDUM SPURIUM
	SEDUM SPURIUM 'BRONZE CARPET'
	VALERIANA OFFICINALIS
JUL.	ACHILLEA 'CORONATION GOLD'
	ACHILLEA 'MOONSHINE'
	ASCLEPIAS TUBEROSA
	HYDRANGEA ASPERA SUBSP. SARGENTIANA
	HYDRANGEA MACROPHYLLA 'BLUE BILLOW'
	VIBURNUM SIEBOLDII 'SENECA'
AUG.	ASCLEPIAS TUBEROSA
	CLERODENDRUM TRICHOTOMUM
	SEDUM 'VERA JAMISON'
SEP.	CLERODENDRUM TRICHOTOMUM
	EUPATORIUM COELESTINUM
	SEDUM 'AUTUMN JOY'
OCT.	EUPATORIUM COELESTINUM

FLOWER TEXTURE
Ball-like Landscape Effect

Overall shape of inflorescence (flowers, single or multiple) is rounded, like a cup or dome.

MONTH	LATIN NAME
MAR.	CORNUS MAS
	CORNUS OFFICINALIS
APR.	ALLIUM ZEBDANENSE
	CORNUS MAS
	CORNUS OFFICINALIS
	MAGNOLIA 'ELIZABETH'
	MAGNOLIA 'SUSAN'
	MAGNOLIA DENUDATA (SYN. M. HEPTAPETA)
	MAGNOLIA X LOEBNERI
	MAGNOLIA X SOULANGIANA 'VERBANICA'
MAY	ACER PLATANOIDES 'CRIMSON KING'
	ALLIUM ZEBDANENSE
	CRUCIANELLA STYLOSA
	MAGNOLIA 'ELIZABETH'
	PAEONIA—HERBACEOUS HYBRIDS
	RHODODENDRON (CATAWBIENSE HYBRIDS)

MONTH	LATIN NAME
JUN.	ALLIUM CERNUUM
	CRUCIANELLA STYLOSA
	KALMIA LATIFOLIA
	ONOPORDUM ACANTHIUM
	RHODODENDRON MAXIMUM
JUL.	ECHINOPS RITRO
	ONOPORDUM ACANTHIUM
AUG.	ALLIUM TUBEROSUM
	ECHINOPS RITRO
SEP.	ALLIUM TUBEROSUM
	COLCHICUM 'AUTUMN QUEEN'
	COLCHICUM 'THE GIANT'
OCT.	COLCHICUM 'AUTUMN QUEEN'
	COLCHICUM 'THE GIANT'
	STERNBERGIA LUTEA

FLOWER TEXTURE
Irregular and/or Complex Landscape Effect

For purposes of simplificaton, this listing includes flowers that do not fit the previous textural categories. This section could be further subdivided. The flowers below are either not symmetrical or are not simple and do not open full-out flat. Included are tubular (*Bignonia*) and trumpet-shaped (*Lilium*) flowers, and members of the Iridaceae (Iris), Leguminosae (Pea), and Saxifragaceae (Saxifrage) families.

MONTH	LATIN NAME
JAN.	HAMAMELIS MOLLIS 'PALLIDA'
FEB.	HAMAMELIS MOLLIS 'PALLIDA'
	HAMAMELIS X INTERMEDIA 'DIANE'
	HAMAMELIS X INTERMEDIA 'JELENA'
	HAMAMELIS X INTERMEDIA 'PRIMAVERA'
	LONICERA FRAGRANTISSIMA
MAR.	HAMAMELIS MOLLIS 'PALLIDA'
	HAMAMELIS X INTERMEDIA 'DIANE'
	HAMAMELIS X INTERMEDIA 'JELENA'
	HAMAMELIS X INTERMEDIA 'PRIMAVERA'
	LONICERA FRAGRANTISSIMA
APR.	AMELANCHIER ARBOREA (SYN. A. CANADENSIS)
	BERGENIA 'PERFECTA'
	BERGENIA 'SUNNINGDALE'
	BRUNNERA MACROPHYLLA
	CERCIS CANADENSIS 'FOREST PANSY'
	EPIMEDIUM PINNATUM SUBSP. COLCHICUM
	EPIMEDIUM X YOUNGIANUM 'NIVEUM'
	FORSYTHIA X INTERMEDIA 'SPRING GLORY'
	HAMAMELIS MOLLIS 'PALLIDA'
	HAMAMELIS X INTERMEDIA 'DIANE'
	HAMAMELIS X INTERMEDIA 'JELENA'
	HAMAMELIS X INTERMEDIA 'PRIMAVERA'
	LONICERA FRAGRANTISSIMA

MONTH	LATIN NAME
	NARCISSUS 'CARLTON'
	NARCISSUS 'FORTUNE'
	NARCISSUS 'HERA'
	NARCISSUS 'LOCH FYNE'
	NARCISSUS 'MOONMIST'
	NARCISSUS 'MRS. ERNST H. KRELAGE'
	NARCISSUS 'PEEPING TOM'
	NARCISSUS 'POMONA'
	NARCISSUS 'QUEEN OF SPAIN'
	NARCISSUS 'TREVITHIAN'
	NARCISSUS PSEUDONARCISSUS SUBSP. OBVALLARIS
	PRUNUS 'HALLY JOLIVETTE'
	PRUNUS SUBHIRTELLA 'AUTUMNALIS'
	PRUNUS SUBHIRTELLA 'PENDULA'
	PRUNUS YEDOENSIS
	PULMONARIA ANGUSTIFOLIA
	PULMONARIA SACCHARATA 'MARGERY FISH'
	RHODODENDRON MUCRONULATUM
	RIBES ODORATUM
	TRACHYSTEMON ORIENTALIS
MAY	ALCHEMILLA VULGARIS
	AMELANCHIER ARBOREA (SYN. A. CANADENSIS)
	AMSONIA HUBRICHTII
	AMSONIA TABERNAEMONTANA
	BERGENIA 'PERFECTA'
	BERGENIA 'SUNNINGDALE'
	BIGNONIA CAPREOLATA
	BRUNNERA MACROPHYLLA
	CALYCANTHUS FLORIDUS 'EDITH WILDER'
	CERCIS CANADENSIS 'FOREST PANSY'
	CERCIS CHINENSIS
	CRAMBE CORDIFOLIA
	CYTISUS X PRAECOX 'LUTEUS'
	DEUTZIA GRACILIS
	HEMEROCALLIS LILIOASPHODELUS
	IRIS CRISTATA
	IRIS PSEUDACORUS
	IRIS TECTORUM
	KOLKWITZIA AMABILIS
	NARCISSUS 'TREVITHIAN'
	PRUNUS CERASIFERA 'THUNDERCLOUD'
	PRUNUS X CISTENA
	RHODODENDRON (GABLE HYBRIDS)
	RHODODENDRON (GLENN DALE HYBRIDS)
	RHODODENDRON (KAEMPFERI HYBRIDS)
	RHODODENDRON (KNAP HILL HYBRID) 'TUNIS'
	RHODODENDRON (KURUME HYBRIDS)
	RHODODENDRON ATLANTICUM
	RHODODENDRON CANESCENS
	RHODODENDRON PRINOPHYLLUM
	RHODODENDRON SCHLIPPENBACHII
	RHODODENDRON VASEYI
	RHODODENDRON X GANDAVENSE 'COCCINEA SPECIOSA'
	RHODODENDRON X GANDAVENSE 'DAVIESII'
JUN.	ALCHEMILLA VULGARIS
	BIGNONIA CAPREOLATA
	CRAMBE CORDIFOLIA
	CYTISUS SCOPARIUS
	FILIPENDULA PURPUREA 'ELEGANS'
	HEMEROCALLIS 'HYPERION'
	HEMEROCALLIS FULVA 'EUROPA'

MONTH	LATIN NAME
	IRIS SIBIRICA CULTIVARS
	IRIS TECTORUM
	LILIUM 'BLACK DRAGON'
	LILIUM SPECIES AND HYBRIDS
	MONARDA DIDYMA
	RHODODENDRON ARBORESCENS
	RHODODENDRON PRINOPHYLLUM
	RHODODENDRON VISCOSUM
	RHODODENDRON X ERIOCARPUM AND R. X NAKAHARAI CULTIVARS AND HYBRIDS
	ROSA (POLYANTHA) 'THE FAIRY'
	ROSA (SHRUB) 'SEA FOAM'
	SAXIFRAGA STOLONIFERA
JUL.	CAMPSIS X TAGLIABUANA 'MADAME GALEN'
	COLUTEA X MEDIA
	FILIPENDULA PURPUREA 'NANA'
	HEMEROCALLIS 'HYPERION'
	HEMEROCALLIS FULVA 'EUROPA'
	LILIUM 'BLACK DRAGON'
	LILIUM SPECIES AND HYBRIDS
	MONARDA DIDYMA
	RHODODENDRON VISCOSUM
	ROSA (POLYANTHA) 'THE FAIRY'
	ROSA (SHRUB) 'SEA FOAM'
	SAXIFRAGA STOLONIFERA
AUG.	CAMPSIS X TAGLIABUANA 'MADAME GALEN'
	CARYOPTERIS X CLANDONENSIS 'BLUE MIST'
	CERATOSTIGMA PLUMBAGINOIDES
	FILIPENDULA PURPUREA 'NANA'
	ROSA (POLYANTHA) 'THE FAIRY'
	ROSA (SHRUB) 'SEA FOAM'
	VERNONIA NOVEBORACENSIS
SEP.	CARYOPTERIS X CLANDONENSIS 'BLUE MIST'
	CERATOSTIGMA PLUMBAGINOIDES
	ELAEAGNUS PUNGENS 'FRUITLANDII'
	LESPEDEZA THUNBERGII
	LYCORIS SPRENGERI
	LYCORIS SQUAMIGERA
	VERNONIA NOVEBORACENSIS
OCT.	CERATOSTIGMA PLUMBAGINOIDES
	ELAEAGNUS PUNGENS 'FRUITLANDII'
	HAMAMELIS VIRGINIANA
NOV.	HAMAMELIS VIRGINIANA
	PRUNUS SUBHIRTELLA 'AUTUMNALIS'
DEC.	PRUNUS SUBHIRTELLA 'AUTUMNALIS'

APPENDIX 21
Plant Listing by Texture— Bark

The texture of the bark or stem of the plants listed below catches or reflects light to such a degree that it becomes a useful design tool.

The list is divided by hardiness zone.

Further information about all of the following plants is summarized in the Master Lists, Appendices 1A and 1B.

ZONE	LATIN NAME
3	RHUS TYPHINA—velvety, hairy twigs
	RHUS TYPHINA 'LACINIATA'—velvety, hairy twigs
4	ACANTHOPANAX SIEBOLDIANUS—spines
	BETULA LENTA—smooth, cherrylike, with lenticles
	BETULA NIGRA—peeling and exfoliating (curling) bark
	CARYA OVATA—shredding plates of bark
	CLADRASTIS LUTEA—smooth
	EUONYMUS ALATA—corky wings or ridges on twigs
	GINKGO BILOBA, STAMINATE—spurlike side shoots
	GYMNOCLADUS DIOICA—textured bark and coarse, stubby branches
	HYPERICUM KALMIANUM—peeling bark
	PHELLODENDRON AMURENSE—corky and heavily furrowed bark
	QUERCUS ALBA—slightly shaggy bark on a rugged framework
	QUERCUS MACROCARPA—unusually thick, heavily furrowed bark on trunk; irregularly ridged on branches
	ROBINIA HISPIDA—young twigs, densely bristled
	SPIRAEA THUNBERGII—significant overall textural effect provided by quantity, fineness, and grace of twigs

ZONE	LATIN NAME
5	ACER GRISEUM—sometimes exfoliating, sometimes highly polished
	CAMPSIS X TAGLIABUANA 'MADAME GALEN'—gnarly, longitudinally fissured
	CARPINUS BETULUS—smooth
	CHAMAECYPARIS OBTUSA VAR. BREVIRAMEA—fissured
	CORNUS OFFICINALIS—flaking bark
	CORYLUS COLURNA—roughly corky
	DIOSPYROS VIRGINIANA—deeply and regularly fissured
	EQUISETUM HYEMALE—colonies of these leafless, small-diameter stems, banded by internodes, provide a rich textural effect
	FAGUS SYLVATICA 'LACINIATA'—smooth
	FAGUS SYLVATICA 'PENDULA'—smooth
	FAGUS SYLVATICA 'RIVERSII'—smooth
	HYDRANGEA ANOMALA SUBSP. PETIOLARIS 'SKYLANDS GIANT'—flaky bark and interesting aerial rootlets
	HYDRANGEA QUERCIFOLIA—new twig growth covered with short hairs; exfoliating bark on old stems
	HYPERICUM FRONDOSUM—peeling bark
	KOLKWITZIA AMABILIS—bark that peels off in large strips and patches
	METASEQUOIA GLYPTOSTROBOIDES—fissured, shredding bark and interesting buttressed trunk
	NYSSA SYLVATICA—strongly patterned bark on old trees
	ONOPORDUN ACANTHIUM—winged stem and branches
	PINUS BUNGEANA—flaking bark (irregular rounded patches)
	PLATANUS OCCIDENTALIS—bark that exfoliates in large flakes
	RUBUS COCKBURNIANUS—smooth bark covered with white bloom
	STEPHANANDRA INCISA 'CRISPA'—mild exfoliation on branches, which have a dramatic zigzag habit
6	ADINA RUBELLA—cherrylike, with lenticels
	PONCIRUS TRIFOLIATA—dramatically angled branches with spectacular thorns
	ROSA ROXBURGHII—peeling bark
	TAXODIUM DISTICHUM VAR. NUTANS 'PRAIRIE SENTINEL'—vertically textured bark, buttressed base to trunk, plus "knees"

APPENDIX 22
Plant Listing by Color of Foliage—Spring and Summer

Plants in this appendix are divided as follows:

Blue-Green
Gray-Green
Green and White Variegated
Yellow-Green
Green and Gold Variegated
Pink and Red

Green is, of course, our most valuable background foliage color. There are shades of green other than those listed above that occur in spring and summer foliage and that are extremely useful. The lists here simply dramatize some that are particularly dynamic.

Included below some of the headings for the above categories are a few guidelines. Those categories without any text below the headings are ones I considered self-explanatory.

Each of the lists has been subdivided by hardiness zone.

The letter *T* under the heading "Zone" indicates a plant that is tender, not tolerant of frost.

Further information about all of the following plants is summarized in the Master Lists, Appendices 1A and 1B.

BLUE-GREEN

ZONE	LATIN NAME
3	ADIANTUM PEDATUM
	BAPTISIA AUSTRALIS
	EUPHORBIA COROLLATA
	GERANIUM MACRORRHIZUM
	HOSTA SIEBOLDIANA 'ELEGANS'
	JUNIPERUS HORIZONTALIS 'WILTONII'
	MACLEAYA CORDATA
	PICEA PUNGENS 'HOOPSII'
	PINUS STROBUS
	PINUS STROBUS 'FASTIGIATA'
	PSEUDOTSUGA MENZIESII
	RHODODENDRON PRINOPHYLLUM
	SEDUM 'AUTUMN JOY'
	SPIRAEA X VANHOUTTEI
	SYRINGA VULGARIS 'ALBA'
	SYRINGA VULGARIS HYBRIDS
	THERMOPSIS CAROLINIANA
4	EUPHORBIA CYPARISSIAS
	EUPHORBIA EPITHYMOIDES
	GYMNOCLADUS DIOICA
	PINUS FLEXILIS
	PINUS KORAIENSIS
	TAMARIX RAMOSISSIMA
5	COLUTEA X MEDIA
	EPIMEDIUM PINNATUM SUBSP. COLCHICUM
	EXOCHORDA GIRALDII VAR. WILSONII
	HELICTOTRICHON SEMPERVIRENS

ZONE	LATIN NAME
	JUNIPERUS SCOPULORUM 'SKY ROCKET'
	LONICERA FRAGRANTISSIMA
	MERTENSIA VIRGINICA
	PINUS PARVIFLORA 'GLAUCA'
	RHODODENDRON ATLANTICUM
	SALIX X RUBRA 'EUGENEI'
	THALICTRUM ROCHEBRUNIANUM
	THYMUS PSEUDOLANUGINOSUS
6	MAHONIA BEALEI
	PAEONIA 'BLACK PIRATE'
7	BERBERIS WILSONIAE VAR. STAPFIANA
	CEDRUS ATLANTICA 'GLAUCA'

GRAY-GREEN

ZONE	LATIN NAME
2	ARTEMESIA STELLERIANA
3	ACHILLEA 'MOONSHINE'
	ALCHEMILLA VULGARIS
	ARTEMESIA ABSINTHIUM 'LAMBROOK SILVER'
	DICENTRA 'LUXURIANT'
	DICENTRA EXIMIA 'PURITY'
	ECHINOPS RITRO
	HIPPOPHAE RHAMNOIDES
	PSEUDOTSUGA MENZIESII
	SALIX ALBA 'REGALIS'
	SALIX ALBA 'SERICEA'
	THYMUS SERPYLLUM
	VERONICA INCANA
4	ARTEMESIA LUDOVICIANA 'SILVER QUEEN'
	CARYOPTERIS X CLANDONENSIS 'BLUE MIST'
	JUNIPERUS SABINA 'TAMARISCIFOLIA'
	SALIX ELAEAGNOS
	SALIX REPENS VAR. ARGENTEA
	STACHYS BYZANTINA
	YUCCA GLAUCA
	YUCCA SMALLIANA
5	ARTEMESIA VERSICOLOR
	ASPHODELINE LUTEA
	ATHYRIUM GOERINGIANUM 'PICTUM'
	CHAMAECYPARIS PISIFERA 'SQUARROSA'
	ERIANTHUS RAVENNAE
	HELIANTHEMUM APENNINUM VAR. ROSEUM
	ONOPORDUM ACANTHIUM
	PEROVSKIA ABROTANOIDES X P. ATRIPLICIFOLIA
	RUBUS COCKBURNIANUS
	SEDUM 'VERA JAMISON'
	VERBASCUM OLYMPICUM
6	ARUNDO DONAX
	SALVIA ARGENTEA
	SAXIFRAGA STOLONIFERA
7	ELAEAGNUS PUNGENS 'FRUITLANDII'

GREEN AND WHITE VARIEGATED

Plants in this category, when used in mass in a landscape, generally read as gray when seen from a distance.

ZONE	LATIN NAME
3	AEGOPODIUM PODAGRARIA 'VARIEGATUM'
	CORNUS ALBA 'ELEGANTISSIMA'
	CORNUS ALBA 'SPAETHII'
	PULMONARIA SACCHARATA 'MARGERY FISH'
4	PHALARIS ARUNDINACEA VAR. PICTA
5	DAPHNE X BURKWOODII 'CAROL MACKIE'
	EUONYMUS FORTUNEI 'GRACILIS'
	LAMIASTRUM GALEOBDOLON 'VARIEGATUM'
	LAMIUM MACULATUM 'WHITE NANCY'
	MISCANTHUS SINENSIS 'CABARET'
	MISCANTHUS SINENSIS 'MORNING LIGHT'
	MISCANTHUS SINENSIS 'VARIEGATUS'
	PACHYSANDRA TERMINALIS 'VARIEGATA' OR 'SILVER EDGE'
6	EUONYMUS FORTUNEI 'SILVER QUEEN'

YELLOW-GREEN

Yellow-greens, when used with other shades of green, tend to liven up compositions. When used in mass, they serve as blenders for other colors.

ZONE	LATIN NAME
3	DENNSTAEDTIA PUNCTILOBULA
	HOSTA PLANTAGINEA
	SEDUM ELLACOMBIANUM
	SEDUM SARMENTOSUM
	TIARELLA CORDIFOLIA VAR. COLLINA
4	ACANTHOPANAX SIEBOLDIANUS
	SEDUM TERNATUM
	SPIRAEA THUNBERGII
5	AMSONIA HUBRICHTII
	CALAMAGROSTIS X ACUTIFLORA 'KARL FOERSTER' (SYN. C. EPIGEOUS 'HORTORUM')
	CATALPA BIGNONIOIDES
	EPIMEDIUM X YOUNGIANUM 'NIVEUM'
	EQUISETUM HYEMALE
	HEMEROCALLIS FULVA 'EUROPA'
	ILEX CHINA BOY ® 'MESDOB'
	ILEX CHINA GIRL ® 'MESOG'
	KERRIA JAPONICA
	LYSICHITON AMERICANUM
	METASEQUOIA GLYPTOSTROBOIDES
	PHLOMIS RUSSELIANA
	PINUS BUNGEANA
	PINUS DENSIFLORA 'UMBRACULIFERA'
	PINUS VIRGINIANA
	SEDUM FLORIFERUM 'WEIHANSTEPHANER GOLD'
	THELYPTERIS HEXAGONOPTERA
	THELYPTERIS NOVEBORACENSIS
	XANTHORHIZA SIMPLICISSIMA

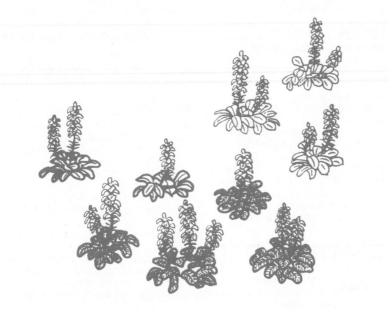

Plants in this appendix are divided as follows:

Orange
Yellow
Red
Wine

Each list is subdivided by hardiness zone.

The letter *T* under the heading "Zone" indicates a plant that is tender, not tolerant of frost.

Further information about all of the following plants is summarized in the Master Lists, Appendices 1A and 1B.

ORANGE

ZONE	LATIN NAME
3	ACER SACCHARUM
	GERANIUM MACRORRHIZUM
	RHUS AROMATICA 'GRO-LOW'
	RHUS TYPHINA
	RHUS TYPHINA 'LACINIATA'
	ROSA RUGOSA AND HYBRIDS
	VIBURNUM ACERIFOLIUM
4	CARYA OVATA
	CLADRASTIS LUTEA
	CRATAEGUS NITIDA
	CRATAEGUS PHAENOPYRUM
	RODGERSIA PODOPHYLLA
	SPIRAEA THUNBERGII
	VACCINIUM CORYMBOSUM
	VIBURNUM CARLESII
5	ACER GRISEUM
	BUDDLEIA DAVIDII 'BLACK KNIGHT'
	BUDDLEIA DAVIDII 'OPERA'
	BUDDLEIA DAVIDII 'PURPLE PRINCE'
	CALAMAGROSTIS X ACUTIFLORA 'KARL FOERSTER' (SYN. C. EPIGEOUS 'HORTORUM')
	CLETHRA ALNIFOLIA
	DIOSPYROS VIRGINIANA
	FOTHERGILLA GARDENII
	HYDRANGEA QUERCIFOLIA
	KOELREUTERIA PANICULATA
	METASEQUOIA GLYPTOSTROBOIDES
	NYSSA SYLVATICA
	RHODODENDRON (GABLE HYBRIDS)
	RHODODENDRON SCHLIPPENBACHII
	ROSA CAROLINA
	ROSA VIRGINIANA
	SASSAFRAS ALBIDUM
	SPIRAEA PRUNIFOLIA
	THELYPTERIS NOVEBORACENSIS
	XANTHORHIZA SIMPLICISSIMA
6	ACER PALMATUM VAR. DISSECTUM OR A. P. 'WATERFALL'
	BERBERIS JULIANAE 'NANA'
	BERBERIS WISLEYENSIS (SYN. B. TRIACANTHOPHORA)
	CROCOSMIA POTTSII
	CROCOSMIA X CROCOSMIIFLORA

ZONE	LATIN NAME
6	ACER PALMATUM VAR. DISSECTUM OR A. P. 'WATERFALL'
	BERBERIS JULIANAE 'NANA'
	BERBERIS WISLEYENSIS (SYN. B. TRIACANTHOPHORA)
	CRUCIANELLA STYLOSA
	EUPATORIUM COELESTINUM
	FORSYTHIA VIRIDISSIMA 'BRONXENSIS'
	JUNIPERUS CHINENSIS 'KAIZUKA'
	PHYLLOSTACHYS AUREOSULCATA
	PSEUDOLARIX KAEMPFERI
	TAXODIUM DISTICHUM VAR. NUTANS 'PRAIRIE SENTINEL'
7	CLERODENDRUM TRICHOTOMUM
T	KOCHIA SCOPARIA FORMA TRICHOPHYLLA 'CHILDSII'

GREEN AND GOLD VARIEGATED

Plants in this category, when used with other shades of green, tend to liven up any composition. When used in mass, most read as chartreuse, a color that blends well with other colors.

ZONE	LATIN NAME
3	FILIPENDULA ULMARIA 'AUREA'
	HOSTA 'KABITAN'
4	POLYGONATUM ODORATUM 'VARIEGATUM'
	VINCA MINOR 'VARIEGATA'
	YUCCA FLACCIDA 'GOLDEN SWORD'
5	ARUNDINARIA VIRIDISTRIATA
	CHAMAECYPARIS PISIFERA 'GOLD SPANGLE'
	CORNUS FLORIDA 'HOHMAN'S GOLDEN'
	JUNIPERUS X MEDIA 'OLD GOLD'
	MISCANTHUS SINENSIS 'STRICTUS'
	SALIX 'HAKURO'
	THYMUS 'CLEAR GOLD'

ZONE	LATIN NAME
6	ACORUS GRAMINEUS 'OGON'
	CHAMAECYPARIS OBTUSA 'CRIPPSII'
	HEDERA HELIX 'BUTTERCUP'
	HEDERA HELIX 'GOLD HEART'
	LIRIOPE MUSCARI 'VARIEGATA'
	PINUS THUNBERGIANA 'OCULUS-DRACONIS'
	RUBUS IDAEUS 'AUREUS'
7	ELAEAGNUS PUNGENS 'MACULATA'

PINK AND RED

ZONE	LATIN NAME
3	PRUNUS X CISTENA
	SEDUM SPURIUM 'BRONZE CARPET'
4	ACER PLATANOIDES 'CRIMSON KING'
	AJUGA REPTANS 'BRONZE BEAUTY'
	BERBERIS THUNBERGII 'ATROPURPUREA'
	BERBERIS THUNBERGII 'CRIMSON PYGMY'
	HEUCHERA 'PALACE PURPLE' STRAIN
	RODGERSIA AESCULIFOLIA
	RODGERSIA PODOPHYLLA
	VIOLA LABRADORICA
5	ACER PALMATUM 'BLOODGOOD'
	CERCIS CANADENSIS 'FOREST PANSY'
	COTINUS COGGYGRIA 'PURPUREUS'
	FAGUS SYLVATICA 'RIVERSII'
	HOUTTUYNIA CORDATA 'CHAMELEON'
	PRUNUS CERASIFERA 'THUNDERCLOUD'
6	ACER PALMATUM 'EVER RED'
	ADINA RUBELLA
	IMPERATA CYLINDRICA 'RED BARON'
8	COTULA SQUALIDA
T	CANNA X GENERALIS 'MOHAWK'
	RICINUS COMMUNIS 'ZANZIBARENSIS'

ZONE	LATIN NAME
	ENKIANTHUS PERULATUS
	RHODODENDRON (KAEMPFERI HYBRIDS)
	STEWARTIA KOREANA
	TAXODIUM DISTICHUM VAR. NUTANS 'PRAIRIE SENTINEL'
	ZELKOVA SERRATA 'GREEN VASE'
8	COTULA SQUALIDA

YELLOW

ZONE	LATIN NAME
2	BETULA PAPYRIFERA
3	ACER SACCHARUM
	AMELANCHIER ARBOREA (SYN. A. CANADENSIS)
	BETULA PENDULA 'GRACILIS'
	BETULA PENDULA 'YOUNGII'
	GERANIUM MACRORRHIZUM
	LYSIMACHIA CLETHROIDES
	RHUS TYPHINA
	RHUS TYPHINA 'LACINIATA'
	ROSA RUGOSA AND HYBRIDS
4	ACER RUBRUM
	BETULA LENTA
	BETULA NIGRA
	CLADRASTIS LUTEA
	CONVALLARIA MAJALIS
	FAGUS GRANDIFOLIA
	GINKGO BILOBA, STAMINATE
	GLEDITSIA TRIACANTHOS VAR. INERMIS 'SHADEMASTER'
	HAMAMELIS VIRGINIANA
	HELIOPSIS HELIANTHOIDES SUBSP. SCABRA 'KARAT'
	ILEX VERTICILLATA
	ILEX VERTICILLATA 'WINTER RED'
	PHELLODENDRON AMURENSE
	SPIRAEA THUNBERGII
	VIBURNUM CARLESII
5	ACER GRISEUM
	AMSONIA HUBRICHTII
	CALLICARPA JAPONICA
	CALYCANTHUS FLORIDUS 'EDITH WILDER'
	CERCIDIPHYLLUM JAPONICUM
	CHAMAECYPARIS PISIFERA 'GOLD SPANGLE'
	CHIONANTHUS VIRGINICUS
	CLETHRA ALNIFOLIA
	CORNUS FLORIDA 'HOHMAN'S GOLDEN'
	DIOSPYROS VIRGINIANA
	FOTHERGILLA GARDENII
	HALESIA TETRAPTERA
	HAMAMELIS MOLLIS 'PALLIDA'
	HAMAMELIS X INTERMEDIA 'DIANE'
	HAMAMELIS X INTERMEDIA 'JELENA'
	HAMAMELIS X INTERMEDIA 'PRIMAVERA'
	IRIS CRISTATA
	KERRIA JAPONICA
	LIQUIDAMBAR STYRACIFLUA
	RHODODENDRON (GABLE HYBRIDS)
	RHODODENDRON MUCRONULATUM
	RHODODENDRON SCHLIPPENBACHII

ZONE	LATIN NAME
	SASSAFRAS ALBIDUM
	THELYPTERIS NOVEBORACENSIS
	VERBASCUM OLYMPICUM
	WISTERIA FLORIBUNDA
	XANTHORHIZA SIMPLICISSIMA
6	ACER PALMATUM VAR. DISSECTUM OR A. P. 'WATERFALL'
	BERBERIS WISLEYENSIS (SYN. B. TRIACANTHOPHORA)
	BIGNONIA CAPREOLATA
	CERCIS CHINENSIS
	PONCIRUS TRIFOLIATA
	PSEUDOLARIX KAEMPFERI
	QUERCUS PHELLOS
	RHODODENDRON (KAEMPFERI HYBRIDS)
	RUBUS IDAEUS 'AUREUS'
	STEWARTIA KOREANA
	STYRAX JAPONICUS

RED

ZONE	LATIN NAME
3	ACER SACCHARUM
	AMELANCHIER ARBOREA (SYN. A. CANADENSIS)
	GERANIUM MACRORRHIZUM
	PRUNUS X CISTENA
	QUERCUS RUBRA
	RHUS AROMATICA 'GRO-LOW'
	RHUS TYPHINA
	RHUS TYPHINA 'LACINIATA'
	VIBURNUM ACERIFOLIUM
4	ACER RUBRUM
	AJUGA REPTANS 'BRONZE BEAUTY'
	ARALIA SPINOSA
	ARONIA ARBUTIFOLIA 'BRILLIANTISSIMA'
	BERBERIS THUNBERGII 'ATROPURPUREA'
	DIERVILLA SESSILIFOLIA
	EUONYMUS ALATA
	EUONYMUS FORTUNEI 'COLORATA'
	GAULTHERIA PROCUMBENS
	ROSA NITIDA
	VACCINIUM CORYMBOSUM
5	ACER GRISEUM
	ACER PALMATUM 'BLOODGOOD'
	CERCIDIPHYLLUM JAPONICUM
	CORNUS FLORIDA
	CORNUS FLORIDA 'HOHMAN'S GOLDEN'
	CORNUS KOUSA
	COTINUS COGGYGRIA 'PURPUREUS'
	ENKIANTHUS CAMPANULATUS
	KOLKWITZIA AMABILIS
	LEUCOTHOE FONTANESIANA
	LEUCOTHOE FONTANESIANA 'NANA'
	LIQUIDAMBAR STYRACIFLUA
	NYSSA SYLVATICA
	OXYDENDRUM ARBOREUM
	PRUNUS CERASIFERA 'THUNDERCLOUD'
	RHODODENDRON ARBORESCENS
	RHODODENDRON MUCRONULATUM
	RHODODENDRON SCHLIPPENBACHII
	RHODODENDRON VASEYI
	RIBES ODORATUM

ZONE	LATIN NAME
	ROSA CAROLINA
	ROSA VIRGINIANA
	SASSAFRAS ALBIDUM
	SPIRAEA PRUNIFOLIA
	VIBURNUM DILATATUM 'MICHAEL DODGE'
	VIBURNUM FARRERI 'CANDIDISSIMUM'
	VIBURNUM FARRERI 'NANUM'
6	BERBERIS JULIANAE 'NANA'
	BIGNONIA CAPREOLATA
	ENKIANTHUS PERULATUS
	IMPERATA CYLINDRICA 'RED BARON'
	ITEA VIRGINICA 'HENRY'S GARNET'
	RHODODENDRON (KURUME HYBRIDS)
	STEWARTIA KOREANA
7	BERBERIS WILSONIAE VAR. STAPFIANA
	DIOSPYROS KAKI
T	KOCHIA SCOPARIA FORMA TRICHOPHYLLA 'CHILDSII'
	RICINUS COMMUNIS 'ZANZIBARENSIS'

WINE

ZONE	LATIN NAME
2	BERGENIA 'PERFECTA'
	BERGENIA 'SUNNINGDALE'
3	CORNUS RACEMOSA
	CORNUS RACEMOSA (DWARF)
	VIBURNUM ACERIFOLIUM
	VIBURNUM PRUNIFOLIUM
4	HEUCHERA 'PALACE PURPLE' STRAIN
5	CERCIDIPHYLLUM JAPONICUM
	CORNUS FLORIDA 'HOHMAN'S GOLDEN'
	COTINUS COGGYGRIA 'PURPUREUS'
	HYDRANGEA QUERCIFOLIA
	LEUCOTHOE FONTANESIANA
	LEUCOTHOE FONTANESIANA 'NANA'
	LIQUIDAMBAR STYRACIFLUA
	METASEQUOIA GLYPTOSTROBOIDES
	OXYDENDRUM ARBOREUM
	PRUNUS CERASIFERA 'THUNDERCLOUD'
	RHODODENDRON MUCRONULATUM
	STEPHANANDRA INCISA 'CRISPA'
6	ABELIA X GRANDIFLORA
	ACER PALMATUM 'EVER RED'
	BIGNONIA CAPREOLATA
	CERATOSTIGMA PLUMBAGINOIDES
	COTONEASTER SALICIFOLIUS VAR. FLOCCOSUS
	FILIPENDULA PURPUREA 'ELEGANS'
	FORSYTHIA VIRIDISSIMA 'BRONXENSIS'
	FRANKLINIA ALATAMAHA
	ITEA VIRGINICA 'HENRY'S GARNET'
	VIBURNUM NUDUM 'WINTERTHUR'

APPENDIX 24
Plant Listing by Color of Flower

Plants in this appendix are divided as follows:

Yellow
Orange
Apricot
Red
Pink
Purple
Violet
Blue
Chartreuse
White

    Each of these categories is subdivided by the month in which the plant flowers.

    Further information about these plants is summarized in the Master Lists, Appendices 1A and 1B.

YELLOW

MONTH	LATIN NAME
JAN.	CHIMONANTHUS PRAECOX
	CORYLUS COLURNA
	HAMAMELIS MOLLIS 'PALLIDA'
FEB.	CHIMONANTHUS PRAECOX
	CORYLUS COLURNA
	HAMAMELIS MOLLIS 'PALLIDA'
	HAMAMELIS X INTERMEDIA 'PRIMAVERA'
	JASMINUM NUDIFLORUM
MAR.	CORNUS MAS
	CORNUS OFFICINALIS
	CORYLUS COLURNA
	CROCUS ANCYRENSIS 'GOLDEN BUNCH'
	ERANTHIS HYEMALIS
	ERANTHIS X TUBERGENII
	HAMAMELIS MOLLIS 'PALLIDA'
	HAMAMELIS X INTERMEDIA 'PRIMAVERA'
	JASMINUM NUDIFLORUM
	SALIX GRACILISTYLA 'MELANOSTACHYS'
APR.	BERBERIS THUNBERGII 'ATROPURPUREA'
	BERBERIS THUNBERGII 'CRIMSON PYGMY'
	CORNUS MAS
	CORNUS OFFICINALIS
	CORYLOPSIS PLATYPETALA
	CORYLUS COLURNA
	EPIMEDIUM PINNATUM SUBSP. COLCHICUM
	EUPHORBIA CYPARISSIAS
	EUPHORBIA EPITHYMOIDES
	FORSYTHIA SUSPENSA
	FORSYTHIA VIRIDISSIMA 'BRONXENSIS'
	FORSYTHIA X INTERMEDIA 'SPRING GLORY'
	HAMAMELIS MOLLIS 'PALLIDA'
	HAMAMELIS X INTERMEDIA 'PRIMAVERA'

MONTH	LATIN NAME
	LYSICHITON AMERICANUM
	MAGNOLIA 'ELIZABETH'
	MAHONIA BEALEI
	NARCISSUS 'CARLTON'
	NARCISSUS 'FORTUNE'
	NARCISSUS 'MOONMIST'
	NARCISSUS 'PEEPING TOM'
	NARCISSUS 'QUEEN OF SPAIN'
	NARCISSUS 'TREVITHIAN'
	NARCISSUS JONQUILLA
	NARCISSUS PSEUDONARCISSUS SUBSP. OBVALLARIS
	PETASITES JAPONICUS
	RHUS AROMATICA 'GRO-LOW'
	RIBES ODORATUM
	SALIX GRACILISTYLA 'MELANOSTACHYS'
MAY	ARUM ITALICUM 'PICTUM'
	ASPHODELINE LUTEA
	BERBERIS JULIANAE 'NANA'
	BIGNONIA CAPREOLATA
	CYTISUS X PRAECOX 'LUTEUS'
	ENKIANTHUS CAMPANULATUS
	EUPHORBIA EPITHYMOIDES
	HEMEROCALLIS LILIOASPHODELUS
	IRIS PSEUDACORUS
	KERRIA JAPONICA
	LAMIASTRUM GALEOBDOLON 'VARIEGATUM'
	LYSICHITON AMERICANUM
	MAGNOLIA 'ELIZABETH'
	NARCISSUS 'TREVITHIAN'
	PAEONIA—WOODY HYBRIDS
	RHODODENDRON X GANDAVENSE 'DAVIESII'
	SEDUM FLORIFERUM 'WEIHANSTEPHANER GOLD'
	THERMOPSIS CAROLINIANA
	WALDSTEINIA TERNATA
JUN.	ACHILLEA 'CORONATION GOLD'
	ACHILLEA 'MOONSHINE'
	ARUM ITALICUM 'PICTUM'
	ASPHODELINE LUTEA
	BIGNONIA CAPREOLATA
	BUPHTHALUM SALICIFOLIUM
	COREOPSIS 'MOONBEAM'
	CYTISUS SCOPARIUS
	DIERVILLA SESSILIFOLIA
	GENISTA SYLVESTRIS 'LYDIA'
	HEMEROCALLIS 'HYPERION'
	INULA HELENIUM
	KOELREUTERIA PANICULATA
	LILIUM SPECIES AND HYBRIDS
	LYSIMACHIA PUNCTATA
	PHLOMIS RUSSELIANA
	SEDUM ELLACOMBIANUM
	SEDUM FLORIFERUM 'WEIHANSTEPHANER GOLD'
	SEDUM SARMENTOSUM
	SOPHORA JAPONICA 'REGENT'
	TELEKIA SPECIOSA
	THERMOPSIS CAROLINIANA
	WALDSTEINIA TERNATA
JUL.	ACHILLEA 'CORONATION GOLD'
	ACHILLEA 'MOONSHINE'
	ASCLEPIAS TUBEROSA
	BUPHTHALUM SALICIFOLIUM
	COREOPSIS 'MOONBEAM'
	CROCOSMIA POTTSII
	HEMEROCALLIS 'HYPERION'

MONTH	LATIN NAME
	HYPERICUM FRONDOSUM
	HYPERICUM KALMIANUM
	INULA HELENIUM
	LILIUM SPECIES AND HYBRIDS
	LYSIMACHIA PUNCTATA
	SOPHORA JAPONICA 'REGENT'
AUG.	ASCLEPIAS TUBEROSA
	COREOPSIS 'MOONBEAM'
	HYPERICUM FRONDOSUM
	HYPERICUM KALMIANUM
SEP.	COREOPSIS 'MOONBEAM'
	HELIANTHUS SALICIFOLIUS
	KIRENGESHOMA PALMATA
OCT.	COREOPSIS 'MOONBEAM'
	HAMAMELIS VIRGINIANA
	HELIANTHUS SALICIFOLIUS
	STERNBERGIA LUTEA
NOV.	HAMAMELIS VIRGINIANA

ORANGE

MONTH	LATIN NAME
FEB.	HAMAMELIS X INTERMEDIA 'JELENA'
MAR.	HAMAMELIS X INTERMEDIA 'JELENA'
APR.	CHAENOMELES JAPONICA VAR. ALPINA
	CHAENOMELES SPECIOSA CULTIVARS
	CHAENOMELES X SUPERBA CULTIVARS
	HAMAMELIS X INTERMEDIA 'JELENA'
	NARCISSUS 'FORTUNE'
	NARCISSUS 'LOCH FYNE'
	NARCISSUS 'POMONA'
MAY	BIGNONIA CAPREOLATA
	PAPAVER ORIENTALE
	RHODODENDRON (KNAP HILL HYBRID) 'TUNIS'
	RHODODENDRON X GANDAVENSE 'COCCINEA SPECIOSA'
JUN.	BIGNONIA CAPREOLATA
	ECHINACEA PURPUREA
	HELICTOTRICHON SEMPERVIRENS
	HEMEROCALLIS FULVA 'EUROPA'
	LILIUM SPECIES AND HYBRIDS
JUL.	ASCLEPIAS TUBEROSA
	CAMPSIS X TAGLIABUANA 'MADAME GALEN'
	CROCOSMIA POTTSII
	ECHINACEA PURPUREA
	HEMEROCALLIS FULVA 'EUROPA'
	LILIUM SPECIES AND HYBRIDS
	RUDBECKIA FULGIDA VAR. SULLIVANTII 'GOLDSTURM'
AUG.	ASCLEPIAS TUBEROSA
	CAMPSIS X TAGLIABUANA 'MADAME GALEN'
	CROCOSMIA X CROCOSMIIFLORA
	ECHINACEA PURPUREA
	RUDBECKIA FULGIDA VAR. SULLIVANTII 'GOLDSTURM'

APRICOT

RED

PINK

MONTH	LATIN NAME
AUG.	ABELIA X GRANDIFLORA
	ANEMONE VITIFOLIA 'ROBUSTISSIMA'
	ANEMONE X HYBRIDA 'QUEEN CHARLOTTE'
	BEGONIA GRANDIS
	CHELONE LYONII
	ECHINACEA PURPUREA
	FILIPENDULA PURPUREA 'NANA'
	PENNISETUM ALOPECUROIDES
	PHYSOSTEGIA VIRGINIANA
	ROSA (POLYANTHA) 'THE FAIRY'
	SAPONARIA OFFICINALIS
	SEDUM 'VERA JAMISON'
	SYMPHORICARPOS X CHENAULTII 'HANCOCK'
	THALICTRUM ROCHEBRUNIANUM
	VERONICASTRUM VIRGINICUM
SEP.	ABELIA X GRANDIFLORA
	ANEMONE X HYBRIDA 'QUEEN CHARLOTTE'
	ASTER NOVAE-ANGLIAE 'HARRINGTON'S PINK'
	BEGONIA GRANDIS
	CHELONE LYONII
	LESPEDEZA THUNBERGII
	LESPEDEZA THUNBERGII 'ALBIFLORA'
	LYCORIS SPRENGERI
	MISCANTHUS SINENSIS 'CABARET'
	MISCANTHUS SINENSIS 'GRACILLIMUS'
	MISCANTHUS SINENSIS 'MORNING LIGHT'
	MISCANTHUS SINENSIS 'VARIEGATUS'
	PHYSOSTEGIA VIRGINIANA
	SEDUM 'AUTUMN JOY'
OCT.	ASTER NOVAE-ANGLIAE 'HARRINGTON'S PINK'
	CYCLAMEN HEDERIFOLIUM
	MISCANTHUS SINENSIS 'CABARET'
	MISCANTHUS SINENSIS 'MORNING LIGHT'
	MISCANTHUS SINENSIS 'VARIEGATUS'
NOV.	PRUNUS SUBHIRTELLA 'AUTUMNALIS'
DEC.	PRUNUS SUBHIRTELLA 'AUTUMNALIS'

PURPLE

MONTH	LATIN NAME
MAR.	CROCUS SIEBERI
	SALIX CHAENOMELOIDES
	SALIX GRACILISTYLA 'MELANOSTACHYS'
APR.	CERCIS CANADENSIS 'FOREST PANSY'
	LATHYRUS VERNUS
	MAGNOLIA 'SUSAN'
	PETASITES FRAGRANS
	PHLOX SUBULATA
	RHODODENDRON MUCRONULATUM
	SALIX CHAENOMELOIDES
	SALIX GRACILISTYLA 'MELANOSTACHYS'
MAY	CALYCANTHUS FLORIDUS 'EDITH WILDER'
	CERCIS CANADENSIS 'FOREST PANSY'
	CERCIS CHINENSIS

MONTH	LATIN NAME
	GERANIUM SANGUINEUM
	IRIS GRAMINEA
	LATHYRUS VERNUS
	PAULOWNIA TOMENTOSA
	PHLOX STOLONIFERA 'SHERWOOD PURPLE'
	RHODODENDRON (CATAWBIENSE HYBRIDS)
	RHODODENDRON (GABLE HYBRIDS)
	RHODODENDRON (GLENN DALE HYBRIDS)
	RHODODENDRON (KURUME HYBRIDS)
	SYRINGA LACINIATA
	SYRINGA PATULA (SYN. S. PALIBINIANA, S. MICROPHYLLA 'INGWERSEN'S DWARF')
	SYRINGA VULGARIS HYBRIDS
	WISTERIA FLORIBUNDA
JUN.	ASTILBE X ARENDSII CULTIVARS
	CLEMATIS 'RAMONA'
	CLEMATIS X JACKMANII
	GERANIUM SANGUINEUM
	HOSTA VENTRICOSA
	IRIS SIBIRICA CULTIVARS
	LIATRIS SPICATA 'KOBOLD'
	LILIUM SPECIES AND HYBRIDS
	ONOPORDUM ACANTHIUM
	ROSA CAROLINA
	ROSA RUGOSA AND HYBRIDS
	ROSA VIRGINIANA
	THYMUS SERPYLLUM
JUL.	BUDDLEIA DAVIDII 'BLACK KNIGHT'
	BUDDLEIA DAVIDII 'PURPLE PRINCE'
	HOSTA VENTRICOSA
	LIATRIS SPICATA 'KOBOLD'
	LILIUM SPECIES AND HYBRIDS
	ONOPORDUM ACANTHIUM
AUG.	BUDDLEIA DAVIDII 'BLACK KNIGHT'
	BUDDLEIA DAVIDII 'PURPLE PRINCE'
	CHELONE LYONII
	HOSTA UNDULATA
	VERNONIA NOVEBORACENSIS
SEP.	ASTER TATARICUS
	CHELONE LYONII
	COLCHICUM 'AUTUMN QUEEN'
	COLCHICUM 'THE GIANT'
	LESPEDEZA THUNBERGII
	LESPEDEZA THUNBERGII 'ALBIFLORA'
	LYCORIS SPRENGERI
	VERNONIA NOVEBORACENSIS
OCT.	ASTER TATARICUS
	COLCHICUM 'AUTUMN QUEEN'
	COLCHICUM 'THE GIANT'

VIOLET

MONTH	LATIN NAME
MAR.	CROCUS SIEBERI
	CROCUS TOMASINIANUS
APR.	CROCUS TOMASINIANUS
	PETASITES FRAGRANS
	PHLOX SUBULATA
	RHODODENDRON MUCRONULATUM

MONTH	LATIN NAME
	SALIX REPENS VAR. ARGENTEA
	TRACHYSTEMON ORIENTALIS
MAY	AJUGA REPTANS
	BAPTISIA AUSTRALIS
	BUDDLEIA ALTERNIFOLIA
	HEDYOTIS CAERULEA
	PAPAVER ORIENTALE
	PAULOWNIA TOMENTOSA
	RHODODENDRON (CATAWBIENSE HYBRIDS)
	RHODODENDRON (GABLE HYBRIDS)
	RHODODENDRON (GLENN DALE HYBRIDS)
	RHODODENDRON (KURUME HYBRIDS)
	ROBINIA HISPIDA
	SYRINGA LACINIATA
	SYRINGA PATULA (SYN. S. PALIBINIANA, S. MICROPHYLLA 'INGWERSEN'S DWARF')
	SYRINGA VULGARIS HYBRIDS
	SYRINGA X CHINENSIS
JUN.	ASTILBE X ARENDSII CULTIVARS
	BAPTISIA AUSTRALIS
	ECHINACEA PURPUREA
	IRIS SIBIRICA CULTIVARS
	LILIUM SPECIES AND HYBRIDS
	ROBINIA HISPIDA
	ROSA ROXBURGHII
	SALVIA ARGENTEA
	STACHYS BYZANTINA
	THALICTRUM ROCHEBRUNIANUM
JUL.	ASTER AMELLUS 'NOCTURNE'
	ECHINACEA PURPUREA
	HYDRANGEA ASPERA SUBSP. SARGENTIANA
	LILIUM SPECIES AND HYBRIDS
	PEROVSKIA ABROTANOIDES X P. ATRIPLICIFOLIA
	SALVIA ARGENTEA
	THALICTRUM ROCHEBRUNIANUM
	VITEX AGNUS-CASTUS 'LATIFOLIA'
AUG.	ASTER AMELLUS 'NOCTURNE'
	ASTER CORDIFOLIUS
	ASTER X FRIKARTII 'MONCH'
	ECHINACEA PURPUREA
	HOSTA 'KABITAN'
	HOSTA UNDULATA
	LIRIOPE MUSCARI (BIG BLUE SELECTION)
	LIRIOPE MUSCARI 'VARIEGATA'
	PEROVSKIA ABROTANOIDES X P. ATRIPLICIFOLIA
	THALICTRUM ROCHEBRUNIANUM
	VITEX AGNUS-CASTUS 'LATIFOLIA'
SEP.	ASTER CORDIFOLIUS
	ASTER PUNICEUS
	ASTER TATARICUS
	ASTER X FRIKARTII 'MONCH'
	COLCHICUM 'AUTUMN QUEEN'
	COLCHICUM 'THE GIANT'
	LESPEDEZA THUNBERGII
OCT.	ASTER CORDIFOLIUS
	ASTER PUNICEUS
	ASTER TATARICUS
	COLCHICUM 'AUTUMN QUEEN'
	COLCHICUM 'THE GIANT'

BLUE

MONTH	LATIN NAME
MAR.	SCILLA SIBERICA 'SPRING BEAUTY'
APR.	ANEMONE BLANDA 'ATROCAERULEA' BRUNNERA MACROPHYLLA CHIONODOXA LUCILIAE CHIONODOXA SARDENSIS MERTENSIA VIRGINICA MUSCARI TUBERGENIANUM OMPHALODES VERNA PHLOX BIFIDA PHLOX SUBULATA PULMONARIA ANGUSTIFOLIA PULMONARIA SACCHARATA 'MARGERY FISH' SCILLA SIBERICA 'SPRING BEAUTY' TRACHYSTEMON ORIENTALIS
MAY	AJUGA REPTANS AJUGA REPTANS 'BRONZE BEAUTY' AJUGA REPTANS (GIANT FORM) AMSONIA HUBRICHTII AMSONIA TABERNAEMONTANA BAPTISIA AUSTRALIS BRUNNERA MACROPHYLLA ENDYMION HISPANICUS 'EXCELSIOR' (SYN. SCILLA CAMPANULATA 'EXCELSIOR') HEDYOTIS CAERULEA IRIS CRISTATA IRIS TECTORUM MERTENSIA VIRGINICA OMPHALODES VERNA PHLOX BIFIDA PHLOX STOLONIFERA 'BLUE RIDGE' SYMPHYTUM X UPLANDICUM SYRINGA VULGARIS HYBRIDS VINCA MINOR 'BOWLESII' VINCA MINOR 'VARIEGATA'
JUN.	BAPTISIA AUSTRALIS CAMPANULA RAPUNCULOIDES CLEMATIS 'MRS. CHOLMONDELEY' CLEMATIS 'PRINS HENDRIK' CLEMATIS 'RAMONA' HOSTA VENTRICOSA HYDRANGEA MACROPHYLLA 'BLUE BILLOW' IRIS SIBIRICA CULTIVARS IRIS TECTORUM NEPETA X FAASSENII SYMPHYTUM X UPLANDICUM
JUL.	ASTER AMELLUS 'NOCTURNE' CAMPANULA RAPUNCULOIDES CLEMATIS HERACLEIFOLIA VAR. DAVIDIANA ECHINOPS RITRO HOSTA VENTRICOSA HYDRANGEA MACROPHYLLA 'BLUE BILLOW' NEPETA X FAASSENII PEROVSKIA ABROTANOIDES X P. ATRIPLICIFOLIA STOKESIA LAEVIS 'BLUE DANUBE' VERONICA 'SUNNY BORDER BLUE' VITEX AGNUS-CASTUS 'LATIFOLIA'
AUG.	ASTER AMELLUS 'NOCTURNE' ASTER CORDIFOLIUS ASTER X FRIKARTII 'MONCH'

MONTH	LATIN NAME
	CARYOPTERIS X CLANDONENSIS 'BLUE MIST' CERATOSTIGMA PLUMBAGINOIDES CLEMATIS HERACLEIFOLIA VAR. DAVIDIANA ECHINOPS RITRO HIBISCUS SYRIACUS 'BLUEBIRD' LIRIOPE MUSCARI (BIG BLUE SELECTION) LIRIOPE MUSCARI 'VARIEGATA' PEROVSKIA ABROTANOIDES X P. ATRIPLICIFOLIA STOKESIA LAEVIS 'BLUE DANUBE' VERONICA 'SUNNY BORDER BLUE' VERONICA INCANA VERONICASTRUM VIRGINICUM VITEX AGNUS-CASTUS 'LATIFOLIA'
SEP.	ASTER CORDIFOLIUS ASTER PUNICEUS ASTER TATARICUS ASTER X FRIKARTII 'MONCH' CARYOPTERIS X CLANDONENSIS 'BLUE MIST' CERATOSTIGMA PLUMBAGINOIDES CLEMATIS HERACLEIFOLIA VAR. DAVIDIANA EUPATORIUM COELESTINUM HIBISCUS SYRIACUS 'BLUEBIRD' LYCORIS SPRENGERI
OCT.	ASTER CORDIFOLIUS ASTER PUNICEUS ASTER TATARICUS CERATOSTIGMA PLUMBAGINOIDES EUPATORIUM COELESTINUM

CHARTREUSE

MONTH	LATIN NAME
JAN.	CORYLUS AVELLANA 'CONTORTA' CORYLUS AVELLANA 'PENDULA' CORYLUS COLURNA
FEB.	CORYLUS AVELLANA 'CONTORTA' CORYLUS AVELLANA 'PENDULA' CORYLUS COLURNA
MAR.	CORYLUS AVELLANA 'CONTORTA' CORYLUS AVELLANA 'PENDULA' CORYLUS COLURNA HELLEBORUS ORIENTALIS HYBRIDS LEUCOJUM VERNUM
APR.	CORYLUS AVELLANA 'CONTORTA' CORYLUS AVELLANA 'PENDULA' CORYLUS COLURNA EUPHORBIA EPITHYMOIDES HELLEBORUS ORIENTALIS HYBRIDS LYSICHITON AMERICANUM RHUS AROMATICA 'GRO-LOW' SASSAFRAS ALBIDUM VIBURNUM MACROCEPHALUM FORMA MACROCEPHALUM
MAY	ACANTHOPANAX SIEBOLDIANUS ALCHEMILLA VULGARIS ARUM ITALICUM 'PICTUM' EUPHORBIA EPITHYMOIDES LYSICHITON AMERICANUM

MONTH	LATIN NAME
	RHODODENDRON VASEYI VIBURNUM MACROCEPHALUM FORMA MACROCEPHALUM
JUN.	ALCHEMILLA VULGARIS ARUM ITALICUM 'PICTUM' LILIUM SPECIES AND HYBRIDS STEPHANANDRA INCISA 'CRISPA'
JUL.	LILIUM SPECIES AND HYBRIDS OXYDENDRUM ARBOREUM RHUS TYPHINA RHUS TYPHINA 'LACINIATA'
SEP.	MISCANTHUS 'GIGANTEUS'
OCT.	MISCANTHUS 'GIGANTEUS'

WHITE

MONTH	LATIN NAME
JAN.	SALIX ACUTIFOLIA 'LONGIFOLIA' SALIX DAPHNOIDES 'AGLAIA'
FEB.	LONICERA FRAGRANTISSIMA SALIX ACUTIFOLIA 'LONGIFOLIA' SALIX DAPHNOIDES 'AGLAIA'
MAR.	GALANTHUS ELWESII GALANTHUS NIVALIS HELLEBORUS NIGER HELLEBORUS ORIENTALIS HYBRIDS LEUCOJUM VERNUM LONICERA FRAGRANTISSIMA PIERIS JAPONICA SALIX ACUTIFOLIA 'LONGIFOLIA' SALIX CHAENOMELOIDES SALIX DAPHNOIDES 'AGLAIA' SALIX GRACILISTYLA VIBURNUM FARRERI 'CANDIDISSIMUM' VIBURNUM FARRERI 'NANUM'
APR.	ALLIUM ZEBDANENSE AMELANCHIER ARBOREA (SYN. A. CANADENSIS) CHAENOMELES SPECIOSA CULTIVARS CHAENOMELES X SUPERBA 'JET TRAIL' CHAENOMELES X SUPERBA CULTIVARS CHIONODOXA GIGANTEA 'ALBA' CHIONODOXA SARDENSIS DAPHNE X BURKWOODII 'CAROL MACKIE' ENKIANTHUS PERULATUS EPIMEDIUM X YOUNGIANUM 'NIVEUM' FOTHERGILLA GARDENII HELLEBORUS NIGER HELLEBORUS ORIENTALIS HYBRIDS LONICERA FRAGRANTISSIMA LYSICHITON CAMTSCHATCENSE MAGNOLIA DENUDATA (SYN. M. HEPTAPETA) MAGNOLIA X LOEBNERI MUSCARI AZUREUM 'ALBUM' MUSCARI BOTRYOIDES 'ALBUM' NARCISSUS 'HERA' NARCISSUS 'LOCH FYNE' NARCISSUS 'MRS. ERNST H. KRELAGE' NARCISSUS 'POMONA' OMPHALODES VERNA PIERIS JAPONICA

MONTH	LATIN NAME
	PONCIRUS TRIFOLIATA
	PRUNUS 'HALLY JOLIVETTE'
	PRUNUS YEDOENSIS
	PULMONARIA SACCHARATA 'SISSINGHURST WHITE'
	SALIX ACUTIFOLIA 'LONGIFOLIA'
	SALIX CHAENOMELOIDES
	SALIX DAPHNOIDES 'AGLAIA'
	SALIX GRACILISTYLA
	SALIX REPENS VAR. ARGENTEA
	SALIX X RUBRA 'EUGENEI'
	SPIRAEA THUNBERGII
	VIBURNUM CARLESII
	VIBURNUM FARRERI 'CANDIDISSIMUM'
	VIBURNUM FARRERI 'NANUM'
	VIBURNUM MACROCEPHALUM FORMA MACROCEPHALUM
MAY	ALLIUM ZEBDANENSE
	AMELANCHIER ARBOREA (SYN. A. CANADENSIS)
	ARABIS PROCURRENS
	ARUNCUS AETHUSIFOLIUS
	CHIONANTHUS VIRGINICUS
	CONVALLARIA MAJALIS
	CORNUS ALTERNIFOLIA
	CORNUS FLORIDA
	CORNUS FLORIDA 'HOHMAN'S GOLDEN'
	CORNUS KOUSA
	CRAMBE CORDIFOLIA
	CRATAEGUS NITIDA
	CRATAEGUS PHAENOPYRUM
	CRATAEGUS VIRIDIS 'WINTER KING'
	DAPHNE X BURKWOODII 'CAROL MACKIE'
	DEUTZIA GRACILIS
	DICENTRA EXIMIA 'PURITY'
	EXOCHORDA GIRALDII VAR. WILSONII
	FOTHERGILLA GARDENII
	GALIUM ODORATUM
	GAULTHERIA PROCUMBENS
	HALESIA TETRAPTERA
	HOSTA SIEBOLDIANA 'ELEGANS'
	LAMIUM MACULATUM 'WHITE NANCY'
	LEUCOTHOE FONTANESIANA
	LEUCOTHOE FONTANESIANA 'NANA'
	LYSICHITON CAMTSCHATCENSE
	MALUS 'RED JADE'
	MALUS FLORIBUNDA
	MALUS HUPEHENSIS
	MALUS SARGENTII
	OMPHALODES VERNA
	PAEONIA—HERBACEOUS HYBRIDS
	PAEONIA—WOODY HYBRIDS
	PHILADELPHUS X FALCONERI
	PHLOX STOLONIFERA 'ALBA'
	POLYGONATUM ODORATUM 'VARIEGATUM'
	POTENTILLA TRIDENTATA
	PRUNUS X CISTENA
	RHODODENDRON (CATAWBIENSE HYBRIDS)
	RHODODENDRON (GABLE HYBRIDS)
	RHODODENDRON (KURUME HYBRIDS)
	RHODODENDRON ATLANTICUM
	RHODODENDRON SCHLIPPENBACHII
	RHODODENDRON X GANDAVENSE 'DAVIESII'
	RHODOTYPOS SCANDENS
	RODGERSIA AESCULIFOLIA

MONTH	LATIN NAME
	RODGERSIA PODOPHYLLA
	RODGERSIA TABULARIS
	SEDUM SPURIUM
	SEDUM TERNATUM
	SKIMMIA REEVESIANA
	SPIRAEA PRUNIFOLIA
	SPIRAEA X VANHOUTTEI
	SYRINGA VULGARIS 'ALBA'
	SYRINGA VULGARIS HYBRIDS
	TIARELLA CORDIFOLIA VAR. COLLINA
	VACCINIUM CORYMBOSUM
	VALERIANA OFFICINALIS
	VIBURNUM MACROCEPHALUM FORMA MACROCEPHALUM
	VIBURNUM PLICATUM FORMA TOMENTOSUM
	VIBURNUM PRUNIFOLIUM
	WISTERIA FLORIBUNDA
JUN.	AESCULUS PARVIFLORA
	ARUNCUS DIOICUS
	ASTILBE X ARENDSII CULTIVARS
	CATALPA BIGNONIOIDES
	CEPHALANTHUS OCCIDENTALIS
	CIMICIFUGA RACEMOSA
	CLADRASTIS LUTEA
	CORNUS KOUSA
	CRAMBE CORDIFOLIA
	DATURA INOXIA SUBSP. QUINQUECUSPIDA
	GALTONIA CANDICANS
	HERACLEUM MANTEGAZZIANUM
	HOUTTUYNIA CORDATA 'CHAMELEON'
	HYDRANGEA ANOMALA SUBSP. PETIOLARIS 'SKYLANDS GIANT'
	HYDRANGEA QUERCIFOLIA
	INDIGOFERA INCARNATA 'ALBA'
	IRIS SIBIRICA CULTIVARS
	ITEA VIRGINICA 'HENRY'S GARNET'
	KALMIA LATIFOLIA
	LIATRIS SCARIOSA 'WHITE SPIRE'
	LILIUM 'BLACK DRAGON'
	LILIUM SPECIES AND HYBRIDS
	MAGNOLIA VIRGINIANA
	PHILADELPHUS X FALCONERI
	RHODODENDRON ARBORESCENS
	RHODODENDRON MAXIMUM
	RHODODENDRON VISCOSUM
	RHODODENDRON X ERIOCARPUM AND R. X NAKAHARAI CULTIVARS AND HYBRIDS
	ROSA (SHRUB) 'SEA FOAM'
	ROSA RUGOSA AND HYBRIDS
	SAPONARIA OFFICINALIS
	SAXIFRAGA STOLONIFERA
	SEDUM SPURIUM
	SEDUM SPURIUM 'BRONZE CARPET'
	SORBARIA SORBIFOLIA
	STEWARTIA KOREANA
	STRANVAESIA DAVIDIANA VAR. UNDULATA 'PROSTRATA'
	STYRAX JAPONICUS
	STYRAX JAPONICUS 'CARILLON'
	SYRINGA RETICULATA
	VALERIANA OFFICINALIS
	YUCCA FLACCIDA 'GOLDEN SWORD'
	YUCCA GLAUCA
	YUCCA SMALLIANA
JUL.	ABELIA X GRANDIFLORA
	ARALIA SPINOSA
	CEPHALANTHUS OCCIDENTALIS
	CIMICIFUGA RACEMOSA

MONTH	LATIN NAME
	CLETHRA ALNIFOLIA
	CLETHRA BARBINERVIS
	DATURA INOXIA SUBSP. QUINQUECUSPIDA
	EUPHORBIA COROLLATA
	GALTONIA CANDICANS
	HOUTTUYNIA CORDATA 'CHAMELEON'
	HYDRANGEA ASPERA SUBSP. SARGENTIANA
	LIATRIS SCARIOSA 'WHITE SPIRE'
	LIGUSTRUM QUIHOUI
	LILIUM 'BLACK DRAGON'
	LILIUM SPECIES AND HYBRIDS
	LYSIMACHIA CLETHROIDES
	MAGNOLIA VIRGINIANA
	OXYDENDRUM ARBOREUM
	POLIANTHES TUBEROSA
	RHODODENDRON VISCOSUM
	ROSA (SHRUB) 'SEA FOAM'
	SAPONARIA OFFICINALIS
	SAXIFRAGA STOLONIFERA
	SORBARIA SORBIFOLIA
	VIBURNUM SIEBOLDII 'SENECA'
	VITEX AGNUS-CASTUS 'SILVER SPIRE'
AUG.	ABELIA X GRANDIFLORA
	ADINA RUBELLA
	ALLIUM TUBEROSUM
	ARALIA SPINOSA
	ASTER CORDIFOLIUS
	CHAMAEMELUM NOBILE
	CLEMATIS MAXIMOWICZIANA
	CLERODENDRUM TRICHOTOMUM
	CLETHRA ALNIFOLIA
	CLETHRA BARBINERVIS
	DATURA INOXIA SUBSP. QUINQUECUSPIDA
	EUPHORBIA COROLLATA
	FRANKLINIA ALATAMAHA
	HIBISCUS SYRIACUS 'DIANA'
	HOSTA PLANTAGINEA
	HYDRANGEA PANICULATA
	LIRIOPE MUSCARI 'MONROE WHITE'
	LYSIMACHIA CLETHROIDES
	PHYSOSTEGIA VIRGINIANA 'SUMMER SNOW'
	POLIANTHES TUBEROSA
	ROSA (SHRUB) 'SEA FOAM'
	SAPONARIA OFFICINALIS
	VERONICASTRUM VIRGINICUM
	VITEX AGNUS-CASTUS 'SILVER SPIRE'
SEP.	ABELIA X GRANDIFLORA
	ALLIUM TUBEROSUM
	ARUNDO DONAX
	ASTER CORDIFOLIUS
	BACCHARIS HALIMIFOLIA, PISTILLATE
	BOLTONIA ASTEROIDES 'SNOWBANK'
	CHAMAEMELUM NOBILE
	CHRYSANTHEMUM WEYRICHII 'WHITE BOMB'
	CLEMATIS MAXIMOWICZIANA
	CLERODENDRUM TRICHOTOMUM
	ELAEAGNUS PUNGENS 'FRUITLANDII'
	ERIANTHUS RAVENNAE
	FRANKLINIA ALATAMAHA
	HIBISCUS SYRIACUS 'DIANA'
	HOSTA PLANTAGINEA
	HYDRANGEA PANICULATA
	MISCANTHUS 'GIGANTEUS'
	MISCANTHUS SINENSIS 'SILVER FEATHER' (='SILBERFEDER')

MONTH	LATIN NAME
	MISCANTHUS SINENSIS 'VARIEGATUS'
	PHYSOSTEGIA VIRGINIANA 'SUMMER SNOW'
OCT.	ARUNDO DONAX
	ASTER CORDIFOLIUS
	BOLTONIA ASTEROIDES 'SNOWBANK'
	CHRYSANTHEMUM WEYRICHII 'WHITE BOMB'
	ELAEAGNUS PUNGENS 'FRUITLANDII'
	ERIANTHUS RAVENNAE
	MISCANTHUS 'GIGANTEUS'
	MISCANTHUS SINENSIS 'SILVER FEATHER' (='SILBERFEDER')
	MISCANTHUS SINENSIS 'VARIEGATUS'
DEC.	SALIX ACUTIFOLIA 'LONGIFOLIA'
	SALIX DAPHNOIDES 'AGLAIA'

APPENDIX 25
Plant Listing by Color of Fruit or Seed Head

The plants in this appendix are divided as follows:

Yellow
Orange and Brown
Red
Purple-Black
Blue
White-Silver

Each of these categories is subdivided by the month in which the plant bears fruit.

Further information about all the following plants is summarized in the Master Lists, Appendices 1A and 1B.

YELLOW

MONTH	LATIN NAME
JAN.	ILEX OPACA 'XANTHOCARPA'
FEB.	ILEX OPACA 'XANTHOCARPA'
JUL.	KOELREUTERIA PANICULATA
	SOPHORA JAPONICA 'REGENT'
AUG.	KOELREUTERIA PANICULATA
	SOPHORA JAPONICA 'REGENT'
SEP.	PYRACANTHA COCCINEA 'AUREA'
	SOPHORA JAPONICA 'REGENT'
OCT.	CHAENOMELES JAPONICA VAR. ALPINA
	CHAENOMELES SPECIOSA CULTIVARS
	CHAENOMELES X SUPERBA 'JET TRAIL'
	CHAENOMELES X SUPERBA CULTIVARS
	MALUS FLORIBUNDA
	MALUS HUPEHENSIS
	PONCIRUS TRIFOLIATA
	PYRACANTHA COCCINEA 'AUREA'
	VIBURNUM DILATATUM 'MICHAEL DODGE'

MONTH	LATIN NAME
NOV.	CHAENOMELES JAPONICA VAR. ALPINA
	CHAENOMELES SPECIOSA CULTIVARS
	CHAENOMELES X SUPERBA 'JET TRAIL'
	CHAENOMELES X SUPERBA CULTIVARS
	ILEX OPACA 'XANTHOCARPA'
	MALUS FLORIBUNDA
	MALUS HUPEHENSIS
	PYRACANTHA COCCINEA 'AUREA'
	VIBURNUM DILATATUM 'MICHAEL DODGE'
DEC.	ILEX OPACA 'XANTHOCARPA'
	VIBURNUM DILATATUM 'MICHAEL DODGE'

ORANGE AND BROWN

MONTH	LATIN NAME
JAN.	CRATAEGUS VIRIDIS 'WINTER KING'
FEB.	CRATAEGUS VIRIDIS 'WINTER KING'
JUL.	CALAMAGROSTIS X ACUTIFLORA 'KARL FOERSTER' (SYN. C. EPIGEOUS 'HORTORUM')
	HIPPOPHAE RHAMNOIDES
	TYPHA ANGUSTIFOLIA
AUG.	CALAMAGROSTIS X ACUTIFLORA 'KARL FOERSTER' (SYN. C. EPIGEOUS 'HORTORUM')
	HIPPOPHAE RHAMNOIDES
	TYPHA ANGUSTIFOLIA
SEP.	CALAMAGROSTIS X ACUTIFLORA 'KARL FOERSTER' (SYN. C. EPIGEOUS 'HORTORUM')
	TYPHA ANGUSTIFOLIA
	VIBURNUM SETIGERUM
OCT.	CALAMAGROSTIS X ACUTIFLORA 'KARL FOERSTER' (SYN. C. EPIGEOUS 'HORTORUM')
	DIOSPYROS KAKI
	MISCANTHUS SINENSIS 'GRACILLIMUS'
	ROSA RUGOSA AND HYBRIDS
	SEDUM 'AUTUMN JOY'
	TYPHA ANGUSTIFOLIA
	VIBURNUM SETIGERUM
NOV.	CRATAEGUS VIRIDIS 'WINTER KING'
	DIOSPYROS KAKI
	MISCANTHUS SINENSIS 'GRACILLIMUS'
	ROSA RUGOSA AND HYBRIDS
	TYPHA ANGUSTIFOLIA
	VIBURNUM SETIGERUM
DEC.	CRATAEGUS VIRIDIS 'WINTER KING'
	MISCANTHUS SINENSIS 'GRACILLIMUS'
	ROSA RUGOSA AND HYBRIDS
	TYPHA ANGUSTIFOLIA

RED

MONTH	LATIN NAME
JAN.	CRATAEGUS NITIDA
	CRATAEGUS PHAENOPYRUM
	CRATAEGUS VIRIDIS 'WINTER KING'
	ILEX OPACA 'ARDEN'
	ILEX VERTICILLATA
	ILEX VERTICILLATA 'WINTER RED'
	ILEX X AQUIPERNYI 'SAN JOSE'
	ROSA CAROLINA
	ROSA VIRGINIANA
FEB.	CRATAEGUS NITIDA
	CRATAEGUS PHAENOPYRUM
	CRATAEGUS VIRIDIS 'WINTER KING'
	ILEX OPACA 'ARDEN'
	ILEX X AQUIPERNYI 'SAN JOSE'
	ROSA CAROLINA
	ROSA VIRGINIANA
MAR.	CRATAEGUS NITIDA
	ILEX X AQUIPERNYI 'SAN JOSE'
	ROSA CAROLINA
	ROSA VIRGINIANA
APR.	ILEX X AQUIPERNYI 'SAN JOSE'
JUN.	AMELANCHIER ARBOREA (SYN. A. CANADENSIS)
JUL.	AMELANCHIER ARBOREA (SYN. A. CANADENSIS)
	ARUM ITALICUM 'PICTUM'
	CORNUS RACEMOSA
	CORNUS RACEMOSA (DWARF)
AUG.	ARALIA SPINOSA
	CORNUS MAS
	CORNUS OFFICINALIS
	CORNUS RACEMOSA
	CORNUS RACEMOSA (DWARF)
	COTONEASTER ADPRESSUS VAR. PRAECOX
	COTONEASTER APICULATUS
	MAGNOLIA VIRGINIANA
	RHUS TYPHINA
	RHUS TYPHINA 'LACINIATA'
	ROSA NITIDA
	SASSAFRAS ALBIDUM
	VIBURNUM SIEBOLDII 'SENECA'
SEP.	ARALIA SPINOSA
	CORNUS ALTERNIFOLIA
	CORNUS FLORIDA
	CORNUS FLORIDA 'HOHMAN'S GOLDEN'
	CORNUS KOUSA
	CORNUS MAS
	CORNUS OFFICINALIS
	COTONEASTER ADPRESSUS VAR. PRAECOX
	COTONEASTER APICULATUS
	COTONEASTER HORIZONTALIS
	GAULTHERIA PROCUMBENS
	MAGNOLIA VIRGINIANA
	RHUS TYPHINA
	RHUS TYPHINA 'LACINIATA'
	ROSA NITIDA
	SASSAFRAS ALBIDUM
	SYMPHORICARPOS X CHENAULTII 'HANCOCK'

MONTH	LATIN NAME
	VIBURNUM NUDUM 'WINTERTHUR'
	VIBURNUM SETIGERUM
OCT.	ARONIA ARBUTIFOLIA 'BRILLIANTISSIMA'
	CORNUS ALTERNIFOLIA
	CORNUS FLORIDA
	CORNUS FLORIDA 'HOHMAN'S GOLDEN'
	COTONEASTER HORIZONTALIS
	COTONEASTER SALICIFOLIUS VAR. FLOCCOSUS
	GAULTHERIA PROCUMBENS
	MALUS 'RED JADE'
	MALUS HUPEHENSIS
	MALUS SARGENTII
	RHUS AROMATICA 'GRO-LOW'
	RHUS TYPHINA
	RHUS TYPHINA 'LACINIATA'
	ROSA CAROLINA
	ROSA NITIDA
	ROSA RUGOSA AND HYBRIDS
	SEDUM 'AUTUMN JOY'
	SKIMMIA REEVESIANA
	STRANVAESIA DAVIDIANA VAR. UNDULATA 'PROSTRATA'
	SYMPHORICARPOS X CHENAULTII 'HANCOCK'
	VIBURNUM ICHANGENSE
	VIBURNUM NUDUM 'WINTERTHUR'
	VIBURNUM SETIGERUM
NOV.	ARONIA ARBUTIFOLIA 'BRILLIANTISSIMA'
	COTONEASTER SALICIFOLIUS VAR. FLOCCOSUS
	CRATAEGUS NITIDA
	CRATAEGUS PHAENOPYRUM
	CRATAEGUS VIRIDIS 'WINTER KING'
	ILEX OPACA 'ARDEN'
	ILEX VERTICILLATA
	ILEX VERTICILLATA 'WINTER RED'
	ILEX X AQUIPERNYI 'SAN JOSE'
	MALUS 'RED JADE'
	MALUS HUPEHENSIS
	MALUS SARGENTII
	RHUS AROMATICA 'GRO-LOW'
	RHUS TYPHINA
	RHUS TYPHINA 'LACINIATA'
	ROSA CAROLINA
	ROSA RUGOSA AND HYBRIDS
	ROSA VIRGINIANA
	SKIMMIA REEVESIANA
	STRANVAESIA DAVIDIANA VAR. UNDULATA 'PROSTRATA'
	SYMPHORICARPOS X CHENAULTII 'HANCOCK'
	VIBURNUM ICHANGENSE
	VIBURNUM NUDUM 'WINTERTHUR'
	VIBURNUM SETIGERUM
DEC.	ARONIA ARBUTIFOLIA 'BRILLIANTISSIMA'
	COTONEASTER SALICIFOLIUS VAR. FLOCCOSUS
	CRATAEGUS NITIDA
	CRATAEGUS PHAENOPYRUM
	CRATAEGUS VIRIDIS 'WINTER KING'
	ILEX OPACA 'ARDEN'
	ILEX VERTICILLATA
	ILEX VERTICILLATA 'WINTER RED'
	ILEX X AQUIPERNYI 'SAN JOSE'
	MALUS 'RED JADE'

MONTH	LATIN NAME
	MALUS SARGENTII
	ROSA CAROLINA
	ROSA RUGOSA AND HYBRIDS
	ROSA VIRGINIANA
	STRANVAESIA DAVIDIANA VAR. UNDULATA 'PROSTRATA'
	SYMPHORICARPOS X CHENAULTII 'HANCOCK'

PURPLE-BLACK

MONTH	LATIN NAME
JAN.	MYRICA PENSYLVANICA
FEB.	MYRICA PENSYLVANICA
JUN.	AMELANCHIER ARBOREA (SYN. A. CANADENSIS)
	CHIONANTHUS VIRGINICUS
JUL.	AMELANCHIER ARBOREA (SYN. A. CANADENSIS)
	CHIONANTHUS VIRGINICUS
AUG.	ARALIA SPINOSA
	GYMNOCLADUS DIOICA
	SASSAFRAS ALBIDUM
SEP.	ARALIA SPINOSA
	CALLICARPA JAPONICA
	CLETHRA ALNIFOLIA
	CORNUS ALTERNIFOLIA
	GYMNOCLADUS DIOICA
	LIGUSTRUM QUIHOUI
	LIRIOPE MUSCARI (BIG BLUE SELECTION)
	LIRIOPE MUSCARI 'MONROE WHITE'
	PANICUM VIRGATUM 'STRICTUM'
	PENNISETUM ALOPECUROIDES
	PHELLODENDRON AMURENSE
	RHODOTYPOS SCANDENS
	RUDBECKIA FULGIDA VAR. SULLIVANTII 'GOLDSTURM'
	SASSAFRAS ALBIDUM
	VIBURNUM PRUNIFOLIUM
OCT.	CALLICARPA DICHOTOMA
	CALLICARPA JAPONICA
	CORNUS ALTERNIFOLIA
	GYMNOCLADUS DIOICA
	ILEX GLABRA 'DENSA'
	LIGUSTRUM QUIHOUI
	LIRIOPE MUSCARI (BIG BLUE SELECTION)
	LIRIOPE MUSCARI 'MONROE WHITE'
	MISCANTHUS SINENSIS 'GRACILLIMUS'
	MOLINIA CAERULEA SUBSP. ARUNDINACEA
	MYRICA PENSYLVANICA
	PANICUM VIRGATUM 'STRICTUM'
	PENNISETUM ALOPECUROIDES
	PHELLODENDRON AMURENSE
	RHODOTYPOS SCANDENS
	RUDBECKIA FULGIDA VAR. SULLIVANTII 'GOLDSTURM'
	VIBURNUM ACERIFOLIUM
	VIBURNUM PRUNIFOLIUM

MONTH	LATIN NAME
NOV.	CALLICARPA DICHOTOMA
	CALLICARPA JAPONICA
	GYMNOCLADUS DIOICA
	ILEX GLABRA 'DENSA'
	MISCANTHUS SINENSIS 'GRACILLIMUS'
	MOLINIA CAERULEA SUBSP. ARUNDINACEA
	MYRICA PENSYLVANICA
	PHELLODENDRON AMURENSE
	VIBURNUM ACERIFOLIUM
	VIBURNUM PRUNIFOLIUM
DEC.	CALLICARPA DICHOTOMA
	GYMNOCLADUS DIOICA
	ILEX GLABRA 'DENSA'
	MISCANTHUS SINENSIS 'GRACILLIMUS'
	MOLINIA CAERULEA SUBSP. ARUNDINACEA
	MYRICA PENSYLVANICA

BLUE

MONTH	LATIN NAME
JAN.	MYRICA PENSYLVANICA
FEB.	MYRICA PENSYLVANICA
MAY	MAHONIA BEALEI
JUL.	CORNUS SERICEA
	CORNUS SERICEA 'FLAVIRAMEA'
	VACCINIUM CORYMBOSUM
AUG.	CORNUS SERICEA
	CORNUS SERICEA 'FLAVIRAMEA'
	SASSAFRAS ALBIDUM
	VACCINIUM CORYMBOSUM
SEP.	CLERODENDRUM TRICHOTOMUM
	CORNUS ALTERNIFOLIA
	JUNIPERUS VIRGINIANA
	SASSAFRAS ALBIDUM
	VIBURNUM NUDUM 'WINTERTHUR'
	VIBURNUM PRUNIFOLIUM
OCT.	CLERODENDRUM TRICHOTOMUM
	CORNUS ALTERNIFOLIA
	JUNIPERUS VIRGINIANA
	MYRICA PENSYLVANICA
	VIBURNUM NUDUM 'WINTERTHUR'
	VIBURNUM PRUNIFOLIUM
NOV.	JUNIPERUS VIRGINIANA
	MYRICA PENSYLVANICA
	VIBURNUM NUDUM 'WINTERTHUR'
	VIBURNUM PRUNIFOLIUM
DEC.	JUNIPERUS VIRGINIANA
	MYRICA PENSYLVANICA

WHITE-SILVER

MONTH	LATIN NAME
JAN.	MYRICA PENSYLVANICA
FEB.	MYRICA PENSYLVANICA

MONTH	LATIN NAME
JUL.	CORNUS RACEMOSA
	CORNUS RACEMOSA (DWARF)
	CORNUS SERICEA
	CORNUS SERICEA 'FLAVIRAMEA'
AUG.	CORNUS RACEMOSA
	CORNUS RACEMOSA (DWARF)
	CORNUS SERICEA
	CORNUS SERICEA 'FLAVIRAMEA'
SEP.	BACCHARIS HALIMIFOLIA, PISTILLATE
OCT.	ARUNDO DONAX
	BACCHARIS HALIMIFOLIA, PISTILLATE
	CEDRUS ATLANTICA 'GLAUCA'
	ERIANTHUS RAVENNAE
	MISCANTHUS 'GIGANTEUS'
	MISCANTHUS SINENSIS 'SILVER FEATHER' (='SILBERFEDER')
	MYRICA PENSYLVANICA
NOV.	ARUNDO DONAX
	BACCHARIS HALIMIFOLIA, PISTILLATE
	CEDRUS ATLANTICA 'GLAUCA'
	ERIANTHUS RAVENNAE
	MISCANTHUS 'GIGANTEUS'
	MISCANTHUS SINENSIS 'SILVER FEATHER' (='SILBERFEDER')
	MYRICA PENSYLVANICA
DEC.	CEDRUS ATLANTICA 'GLAUCA'
	ERIANTHUS RAVENNAE
	MISCANTHUS 'GIGANTEUS'
	MISCANTHUS SINENSIS 'SILVER FEATHER' (='SILBERFEDER')
	MYRICA PENSYLVANICA

APPENDIX 26
Plant Listing by Color of Bark

Plants in this appendix are divided as follows:

Yellow
Orange-Cherry
Red
Purple
Green
Gray
White

Some plants are listed in more than one category because their bark provides multiple hues; e.g., *Acer griseum* (Orange-Cherry, Purple) and *Stewartia koreana* (Orange-Cherry, Green, White).

The category "White" contains plants whose bark is completely white as well as those whose bark has white blooms or markings.

Each of the categories is subdivided by hardiness zone.

Further information about all of the following plants is summarized in the Master Lists, Appendices 1A and 1B.

YELLOW

ZONE	LATIN NAME
3	CORNUS SERICEA 'FLAVIRAMEA'
	SALIX ALBA 'KALMTHOUT'
4	SALIX ALBA VAR. TRISTIS

ORANGE-CHERRY

ZONE	LATIN NAME
4	BETULA NIGRA
	GINKGO BILOBA, STAMINATE
	HYPERICUM KALMIANUM
	MICROBIOTA DECUSSATA
	SPIRAEA THUNBERGII
	TAMARIX RAMOSISSIMA
5	ACER GRISEUM
	CORNUS MAS
	CORNUS OFFICINALIS
	HYDRANGEA ANOMALA SUBSP. PETIOLARIS 'SKYLANDS GIANT'
	HYDRANGEA QUERCIFOLIA
	HYPERICUM FRONDOSUM
	KOLKWITZIA AMABILIS
	METASEQUOIA GLYPTOSTROBOIDES
	PINUS DENSIFLORA 'UMBRACULIFERA'
	PLATANUS OCCIDENTALIS
	PRUNUS SUBHIRTELLA 'AUTUMNALIS'
	SYRINGA RETICULATA
6	CALOCEDRUS DECURRENS
	CLETHRA BARBINERVIS
	PRUNUS SUBHIRTELLA 'PENDULA'
	PRUNUS YEDOENSIS
	ROSA ROXBURGHII
	STEWARTIA KOREANA
	ZELKOVA SERRATA 'GREEN VASE'

RED

ZONE	LATIN NAME
3	CORNUS ALBA 'ELEGANTISSIMA'
	CORNUS ALBA 'SPAETHII'
	CORNUS RACEMOSA
	CORNUS RACEMOSA (DWARF)
	CORNUS SERICEA
	RHUS TYPHINA
	RHUS TYPHINA 'LACINIATA'
4	BETULA LENTA
	BETULA NIGRA
	ROBINIA HISPIDA
	VACCINIUM CORYMBOSUM
5	ACER PALMATUM 'BLOODGOOD'
	ACER PALMATUM 'SANGOKAKU'
	ROSA CAROLINA
	ROSA VIRGINIANA
	STEPHANANDRA INCISA 'CRISPA'
6	ACER PALMATUM 'EVER RED'

PURPLE

ZONE	LATIN NAME
3	AMELANCHIER ARBOREA (SYN. A. CANADENSIS)
4	BETULA LENTA
5	ACER GRISEUM
	ACER PALMATUM 'BLOODGOOD'
	SALIX CHAENOMELOIDES
	SALIX DAPHNOIDES 'AGLAIA'
6	ACER PALMATUM 'EVER RED'

GREEN

ZONE	LATIN NAME
4	CORNUS ALTERNIFOLIA
	PINUS FLEXILIS
5	EQUISETUM HYEMALE
	KERRIA JAPONICA
	OXYDENDRUM ARBOREUM
	PINUS BUNGEANA
	SALIX X RUBRA 'EUGENEI'
	SASSAFRAS ALBIDUM
6	ACER PALMATUM VAR. DISSECTUM OR A. P. 'WATERFALL'
	CYTISUS SCOPARIUS
	CYTISUS X PRAECOX 'LUTEUS'
	JASMINUM NUDIFLORUM
	PHYLLOSTACHYS AUREOSULCATA
	PONCIRUS TRIFOLIATA
	SOPHORA JAPONICA 'REGENT'
	STEWARTIA KOREANA
7	GENISTA SYLVESTRIS 'LYDIA'

GRAY

ZONE	LATIN NAME
3	AMELANCHIER ARBOREA (SYN. A. CANADENSIS)
	CORNUS RACEMOSA
	PINUS STROBUS
4	ACER RUBRUM
	CARYA OVATA
	CLADRASTIS LUTEA
	CRATAEGUS NITIDA
	CRATAEGUS PHAENOPYRUM
	EUONYMUS ALATA
	FAGUS GRANDIFOLIA
	GYMNOCLADUS DIOICA
	PINUS FLEXILIS
	QUERCUS ALBA
	QUERCUS MACROCARPA
5	ABIES NORDMANNIANA
	ACER PALMATUM 'BLOODGOOD'
	CAMPSIS X TAGLIABUANA 'MADAME GALEN'
	CARPINUS BETULUS
	CHIONANTHUS VIRGINICUS
	CORNUS FLORIDA

ZONE	LATIN NAME
	CORNUS FLORIDA 'HOHMAN'S GOLDEN'
	CORYLUS COLURNA
	CRATAEGUS VIRIDIS 'WINTER KING'
	FAGUS SYLVATICA 'LACINIATA'
	FAGUS SYLVATICA 'PENDULA'
	FAGUS SYLVATICA 'RIVERSII'
	HALESIA TETRAPTERA
	LIQUIDAMBAR STYRACIFLUA
	MAGNOLIA 'ELIZABETH'
	MAGNOLIA VIRGINIANA
	MAGNOLIA X LOEBNERI
	MAGNOLIA X SOULANGIANA 'VERBANICA'
	ONOPORDUM ACANTHIUM
	PINUS BUNGEANA
	PLATANUS OCCIDENTALIS
	SALIX GRACILISTYLA
	WISTERIA FLORIBUNDA
6	ACER PALMATUM 'EVER RED'
	ACER PALMATUM VAR. DISSECTUM OR A. P. 'WATERFALL'
	FRANKLINIA ALATAMAHA
	MAGNOLIA 'SUSAN'
	MAGNOLIA DENUDATA (SYN. M. HEPTAPETA)
	ROSA ROXBURGHII
	STYRAX JAPONICUS
	STYRAX JAPONICUS 'CARILLON'
7	VIBURNUM MACROCEPHALUM FORMA MACROCEPHALUM

WHITE

ZONE	LATIN NAME
2	BETULA PAPYRIFERA
3	BETULA PENDULA 'GRACILIS'
	BETULA PENDULA 'YOUNGII'
5	HALESIA TETRAPTERA
	ONOPORDUM ACANTHIUM
	PINUS BUNGEANA
	PLATANUS OCCIDENTALIS
	RUBUS COCKBURNIANUS
	SALIX ACUTIFOLIA 'LONGIFOLIA'
	SALIX DAPHNOIDES 'AGLAIA'
6	STEWARTIA KOREANA

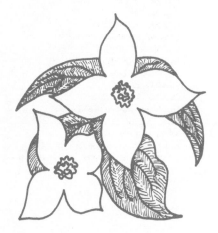

Plants Recommended as Ground Covers

Special effort has been taken to make this section on ground covers as comprehensive as possible. The importance of ground covers to successful garden design cannot be overrated:

- Successful ground cover plantings cover the soil and minimize the opportunity for weed growth.
- They help define spaces, thus giving form to a garden design.
- They tie together groupings of taller plants, thus giving a flow and unity to a design that might otherwise be uneven or jumpy.
- They enable us to make strong color and textural statements, which can in themselves provide structure to the composition.

In these listings of ground covers you will find that plant sizes range from the height of moss up to twenty-five feet. Please throw away any preconceived notions you may have about ground covers being the height of Baltic Ivy (*Hedera helix* 'Baltica') or *Pachysandra*. Think of a garden as a three-dimensional painting and of ground covers as a flow of paint on the artist's canvas that ties together other elements in the painting. If the garden is small, small-scale ground covers will be in order. If the garden is large, larger-scale ground covers will be needed to give bolder effects.

The following listings include more than 230 plants. They are broken down according to:

Size
Hardiness Zone
Soil Preference
Moisture Preference
Light Preference

Each of these sections is subdivided by plant type:

Herbaceous, Clump
Herbaceous, Mat-Forming
Herbaceous, Rampers
Herbaceous, Invasive
Woody, Rounded
Woody, Horizontal Branchers
Woody, Carpet-Forming
Woody, Sprawlers
Woody, Spread by Underground Stem or Root

The final section of the appendix is a summary, in chart form, of all the above information about plant type, with plants listed alphabetically by Latin name.

Further information about all of the following plants is summarized in the Master Lists, Appendices 1A and 1B.

GROUND COVER BY SIZE
Herbaceous, Clump

The following plants expand slowly and may never form a solid mat. With mulch and/or filter fabric, they make a satisfactory ground cover.

SIZE	LATIN NAME
LESS THAN 6 INCHES	ARTEMESIA VERSICOLOR
	DIANTHUS DELTOIDES
	SAXIFRAGA STOLONIFERA
	VIOLA LABRADORICA
6–12 INCHES	ACHILLEA 'MOONSHINE'
	ARABIS PROCURRENS
	ARTEMESIA STELLERIANA
	ARUNCUS AETHUSIFOLIUS
	ATHYRIUM GOERINGIANUM 'PICTUM'
	GERANIUM SANGUINEUM
	HELIANTHEMUM APENNINUM VAR. ROSEUM
	HELLEBORUS NIGER
	HOSTA UNDULATA
	IRIS CRISTATA
	IRIS TECTORUM
	OMPHALODES VERNA
	SEDUM POPULIFOLIUM
	VERONICA INCANA
12–18 INCHES	ALCHEMILLA VULGARIS
	BRUNNERA MACROPHYLLA
	COREOPSIS 'MOONBEAM'
	DICENTRA 'LUXURIANT'
	DICENTRA EXIMIA 'PURITY'
	FILIPENDULA PURPUREA 'NANA'
	HELLEBORUS ORIENTALIS HYBRIDS
	HOSTA 'KABITAN'
	POLYSTICHUM ACROSTICHOIDES
	POLYSTICHUM TRIPTERON
18 INCHES– 3 FEET	ACHILLEA MILLEFOLIUM 'ROSEA'
	ADIANTUM PEDATUM
	AMSONIA HUBRICHTII
	ANEMONE VITIFOLIA 'ROBUSTISSIMA'
	ASTILBE X ARENDSII CULTIVARS
	BEGONIA GRANDIS
	CRUCIANELLA STYLOSA
	HOSTA PLANTAGINEA
	HOSTA SIEBOLDIANA 'ELEGANS'
	HOSTA VENTRICOSA
	PENNISETUM ALOPECUROIDES
	POLYGONATUM ODORATUM 'VARIEGATUM'
	RODGERSIA AESCULIFOLIA
	RODGERSIA PODOPHYLLA
	RODGERSIA TABULARIS
3.0–6.5 FEET	AMSONIA TABERNAEMONTANA
	ANEMONE X HYBRIDA 'QUEEN CHARLOTTE'
	HELIOPSIS HELIANTHOIDES SUBSP. SCABRA 'KARAT'
	HEMEROCALLIS 'HYPERION'
	OSMUNDA CINNAMOMEA
	OSMUNDA CLAYTONIANA
	OSMUNDA REGALIS
	SYMPHYTUM X UPLANDICUM
	TELEKIA SPECIOSA
6.5–13.0 FEET	CIMICIFUGA RACEMOSA

GROUND COVER BY SIZE
Herbaceous, Mat-Forming

These plants expand by clump expansion, by spreading and rooting stems, or by underground stolons or roots.

SIZE	LATIN NAME
LESS THAN 6 INCHES	AJUGA REPTANS
	AJUGA REPTANS 'BRONZE BEAUTY'
	AJUGA REPTANS (GIANT FORM)
	ARENARIA VERNA
	ASARUM EUROPAEUM
	CHAMAEMELUM NOBILE
	COTULA SQUALIDA
	OPHIOPOGON JAPONICUS 'NANUS'
	PARONYCHIA KAPELA SUBSP. SERPYLLIFOLIA
	PHLOX STOLONIFERA 'ALBA'
	PHLOX STOLONIFERA 'BLUE RIDGE'
	PHLOX STOLONIFERA 'SHERWOOD PURPLE'
	PHLOX SUBULATA
	SAGINA SUBULATA
	SEDUM ELLACOMBIANUM
	SEDUM FLORIFERUM 'WEIHANSTEPHANER GOLD'
	SEDUM SARMENTOSUM
	SEDUM SPURIUM
	SEDUM TERNATUM
	THYMUS 'CLEAR GOLD'
	THYMUS PSEUDOLANUGINOSUS
	THYMUS SERPYLLUM
	WALDSTEINIA TERNATA
6–12 INCHES	CERATOSTIGMA PLUMBAGINOIDES
	CHRYSANTHEMUM WEYRICHII 'WHITE BOMB'
	CONVALLARIA MAJALIS
	EPIMEDIUM PINNATUM SUBSP. COLCHICUM
	EPIMEDIUM X YOUNGIANUM 'NIVEUM'
	EUPHORBIA CYPARISSIAS
	FILIPENDULA ULMARIA 'AUREA'
	GALIUM ODORATUM
	PACHYSANDRA PROCUMBENS
	PETASITES FRAGRANS
	PHLOX BIFIDA
	PHLOX PILOSA SUBSP. OZARKANA
	POTENTILLA TRIDENTATA
	PULMONARIA ANGUSTIFOLIA
	PULMONARIA SACCHARATA 'MARGERY FISH'
	PULMONARIA SACCHARATA 'SISSINGHURST WHITE'
	SEDUM SPURIUM 'BRONZE CARPET'
	TIARELLA CORDIFOLIA VAR. COLLINA
12–18 INCHES	DIPLAZIUM CONILII
	EUPATORIUM COELESTINUM
	GERANIUM MACRORRHIZUM
	HOUTTUYNIA CORDATA 'CHAMELEON'
	NEPETA X FAASSENII
	STACHYS BYZANTINA
	THELYPTERIS HEXAGONOPTERA
	THELYPTERIS NOVEBORACENSIS
	THELYPTERIS PHEGOPTERIS
18 INCHES– 3 FEET	ARTEMESIA LUDOVICIANA 'SILVER QUEEN'
	CAMPANULA RAPUNCULOIDES
	DENNSTAEDTIA PUNCTILOBULA
	LUZULA SYLVATICA 'MARGINATA'

SIZE	LATIN NAME
	LYSIMACHIA CLETHROIDES
	LYSIMACHIA PUNCTATA
	MONARDA DIDYMA
	PELTIPHYLLUM PELTATUM
	PETASITES JAPONICUS
	RUDBECKIA FULGIDA VAR. SULLIVANTII 'GOLDSTURM'
	SAPONARIA OFFICINALIS
	TRACHYSTEMON ORIENTALIS
3.0–6.5 FEET	ARTEMESIA ABSINTHIUM 'LAMBROOK SILVER'
	FILIPENDULA PURPUREA 'ELEGANS'
	HEMEROCALLIS FULVA 'EUROPA'
	LYTHRUM SALICARIA 'DROPMORE PURPLE'
	PHALARIS ARUNDINACEA VAR. PICTA
	PHYSOSTEGIA VIRGINIANA
	PHYSOSTEGIA VIRGINIANA 'SUMMER SNOW'
	PTERIDIUM AQUILINUM VAR. LATIUSCULUM

GROUND COVER BY SIZE
Herbaceous, Rampers

The following make a cover as effective as those of the mat formers when foliage is piled up.

SIZE	LATIN NAME
6–12 INCHES	LAMIUM MACULATUM 'WHITE NANCY'
18 INCHES– 3 FEET	LAMIASTRUM GALEOBDOLON 'VARIEGATUM'

GROUND COVER BY SIZE
Herbaceous, Invasive

The following suggestions for ground covers, selected from the three preceding herbaceous categories, represent those herbaceous plants that will compete aggressively with plants milder in nature. They are very useful in tough situations where nothing else will grow.

SIZE	LATIN NAME
6–12 INCHES	AEGOPODIUM PODAGRARIA 'VARIEGATUM'
	PETASITES FRAGRANS
18 INCHES– 3 FEET	CAMPANULA RAPUNCULOIDES
	DENNSTAEDTIA PUNCTILOBULA
	LYSIMACHIA CLETHROIDES
	LYSIMACHIA PUNCTATA
	PETASITES JAPONICUS
	SAPONARIA OFFICINALIS
3.0–6.5 FEET	PHALARIS ARUNDINACEA VAR. PICTA
	PHYSOSTEGIA VIRGINIANA
	PHYSOSTEGIA VIRGINIANA 'SUMMER SNOW'
	PTERIDIUM AQUILINUM VAR. LATIUSCULUM

GROUND COVER BY SIZE
Woody, Rounded

These plants are generally rounded (to oval) and typically "well dressed," with foliage to the ground. When spaced in such a way that foliage will touch and overlap slightly at maturity, they make very satisfactory ground covers.

SIZE	LATIN NAME
LESS THAN 6 INCHES	COTONEASTER ADPRESSUS 'LITTLE GEM'
6–12 INCHES	BUXUS MICROPHYLLA 'COMPACTA'
12–18 INCHES	BUXUS SINICA VAR. INSULARIS 'TIDE HILL'
	FORSYTHIA VIRIDISSIMA 'BRONXENSIS'
18 INCHES– 3 FEET	BERBERIS THUNBERGII 'CRIMSON PYGMY'
	BUXUS SINICA VAR. INSULARIS 'WINTERGREEN' (OHIO CULTIVAR)
	CARYOPTERIS X CLANDONENSIS 'BLUE MIST'
	CHAENOMELES JAPONICA VAR. ALPINA
	COTONEASTER ADPRESSUS VAR. PRAECOX
	COTONEASTER APICULATUS
	DEUTZIA GRACILIS
	EUONYMUS FORTUNEI 'SILVER QUEEN'
	GENISTA SYLVESTRIS 'LYDIA'
	HYPERICUM KALMIANUM
	ROSA (POLYANTHA) 'THE FAIRY'
	ROSA (SHRUB) 'SEA FOAM'
	STEPHANANDRA INCISA 'CRISPA'
3.0–6.5 FEET	BERBERIS WILSONIAE VAR. STAPFIANA
	CALLICARPA DICHOTOMA
	CHAENOMELES X SUPERBA CULTIVARS
	DAPHNE X BURKWOODII 'CAROL MACKIE'
	ENKIANTHUS PERULATUS
	FOTHERGILLA GARDENII
	HYPERICUM FRONDOSUM
	ILEX CRENATA 'HELLERI'
	RHODODENDRON (GABLE HYBRIDS)
	RHODODENDRON (GLENN DALE HYBRIDS)
	RHODODENDRON (KURUME HYBRIDS)
	RHODOTYPOS SCANDENS
	ROSA RUGOSA AND HYBRIDS
	ROSA VIRGINIANA
	SPIRAEA THUNBERGII
	SYRINGA LACINIATA
	SYRINGA PATULA (SYN. S. PALIBINIANA, S. MICROPHYLLA 'INGWERSEN'S DWARF')
6.5–13.0 FEET	ACANTHOPANAX SIEBOLDIANUS
	CALLICARPA JAPONICA
	FORSYTHIA SUSPENSA
	FORSYTHIA X INTERMEDIA 'SPRING GLORY'
	HYDRANGEA QUERCIFOLIA
	ILEX GLABRA 'DENSA'
	MYRICA PENSYLVANICA
	PHILADELPHUS X FALCONERI
	RHODODENDRON PRINOPHYLLUM

SIZE	LATIN NAME
	ROSA (SHRUB) 'LILLIAN GIBSON'
	ROSA ROXBURGHII
	SYRINGA X CHINENSIS
	VIBURNUM NUDUM 'WINTERTHUR'

GROUND COVER BY SIZE
Woody, Horizontal Branchers

These plants are "well dressed" to the ground, with foliage on horizontal branches. They are most effective in combating weed growth and forming taller ground cover masses that have a nicely unified aspect.

SIZE	LATIN NAME
18 INCHES– 3 FEET	JUNIPERUS X MEDIA 'OLD GOLD' JUNIPERUS X MEDIA 'PFITZERIANA COMPACTA'
3.0–6.5 FEET	TSUGA CANADENSIS 'BENNETT' TSUGA CANADENSIS 'COLE'S PROSTRATE'
6.5–13.0 FEET	EUONYMUS ALATA
13–26 FEET	CORNUS MAS CORNUS OFFICINALIS VIBURNUM PRUNIFOLIUM

GROUND COVER BY SIZE
Woody, Carpet-Forming

The plants in this group form low carpets by clump expansion, by aboveground roots, or by means of stems that root when they touch the soil. They generally form dense mats that compete successfully with weeds.

SIZE	LATIN NAME
LESS THAN 6 INCHES	EUONYMUS FORTUNEI 'MINIMA' GAULTHERIA PROCUMBENS HEDERA HELIX 'BALTICA' HEDERA HELIX 'BULGARIA' HEDERA HELIX 'OGALALLA' VINCA MINOR 'BOWLESII' VINCA MINOR 'VARIEGATA'
6–12 INCHES	EUONYMUS FORTUNEI 'COLORATA' EUONYMUS FORTUNEI 'GRACILIS' EUONYMUS FORTUNEI VAR. RADICANS JUNIPERUS HORIZONTALIS 'WILTONII' LIRIOPE MUSCARI (BIG BLUE SELECTION) LIRIOPE MUSCARI 'MONROE WHITE' LIRIOPE MUSCARI 'VARIEGATA' MICROBIOTA DECUSSATA
12–18 INCHES	JUNIPERUS SABINA 'TAMARISCIFOLIA' RHODODENDRON X ERIOCARPUM AND R. X NAKAHARAI CULTIVARS AND HYBRIDS

GROUND COVER BY SIZE
Woody, Sprawlers

These plants expand in an irregular way and make thick enough mats of foliage to compete with most weeds.

SIZE	LATIN NAME
6–12 INCHES	EUONYMUS FORTUNEI 'GRACILIS'
18 INCHES– 3 FEET	CHAENOMELES X SUPERBA 'JET TRAIL' COTONEASTER HORIZONTALIS JASMINUM NUDIFLORUM
3.0–6.5 FEET	CEPHALOTAXUS HARRINGTONIA VAR. PEDUNCULATA SALIX REPENS VAR. ARGENTEA TAXUS BACCATA 'REPANDENS'

GROUND COVER BY SIZE
Woody, Spread by Underground Stem or Root

The following plants, in addition to shading out weeds, provide tight root masses useful in holding soil that might otherwise be washed away. They should be used only in conjunction with other plants that will not suffer from the surface root competition.

SIZE	LATIN NAME
6–12 INCHES	PACHYSANDRA TERMINALIS PACHYSANDRA TERMINALIS 'GREEN CARPET' PACHYSANDRA TERMINALIS 'VARIEGATA' OR 'SILVER EDGE' PAXISTIMA CANBYI
12–18 INCHES	CORNUS RACEMOSA (DWARF) INDIGOFERA INCARNATA 'ALBA' XANTHORHIZA SIMPLICISSIMA
18 INCHES– 3 FEET	ARUNDINARIA VIRIDISTRIATA RHODODENDRON ATLANTICUM RHUS AROMATICA 'GRO-LOW' ROSA 'DOORENBOS SELECTION' SASA VEITCHII
3.0–6.5 FEET	COMPTONIA PEREGRINA CORNUS SERICEA CORNUS SERICEA 'FLAVIRAMEA' DIERVILLA SESSILIFOLIA ITEA VIRGINICA 'HENRY'S GARNET' KERRIA JAPONICA LEUCOTHOE FONTANESIANA ROBINIA HISPIDA ROSA CAROLINA ROSA NITIDA SORBARIA SORBIFOLIA SYMPHORICARPOS X CHENAULTII 'HANCOCK' VIBURNUM ACERIFOLIUM
6.5–13.0 FEET	AESCULUS PARVIFLORA ARONIA ARBUTIFOLIA 'BRILLIANTISSIMA' CLETHRA ALNIFOLIA CORNUS RACEMOSA RHODODENDRON VISCOSUM

GROUND COVER BY HARDINESS ZONE
Herbaceous, Clump

The following plants expand slowly and may never form a solid mat. With mulch and/or filter fabric, they make a satisfactory ground cover.

ZONE	LATIN NAME
2	ACHILLEA MILLEFOLIUM 'ROSEA' ARTEMESIA STELLERIANA
3	ACHILLEA 'MOONSHINE' ADIANTUM PEDATUM ALCHEMILLA VULGARIS AMSONIA TABERNAEMONTANA BRUNNERA MACROPHYLLA CIMICIFUGA RACEMOSA COREOPSIS 'MOONBEAM' DIANTHUS DELTOIDES DICENTRA 'LUXURIANT' DICENTRA EXIMIA 'PURITY' GERANIUM SANGUINEUM HELLEBORUS NIGER HOSTA 'KABITAN' HOSTA PLANTAGINEA HOSTA SIEBOLDIANA 'ELEGANS' HOSTA UNDULATA HOSTA VENTRICOSA OSMUNDA REGALIS POLYSTICHUM ACROSTICHOIDES TELEKIA SPECIOSA VERONICA INCANA
4	ANEMONE VITIFOLIA 'ROBUSTISSIMA' ARABIS PROCURRENS ARUNCUS AETHUSIFOLIUS ASTILBE X ARENDSII CULTIVARS HELIOPSIS HELIANTHOIDES SUBSP. SCABRA 'KARAT' HELLEBORUS ORIENTALIS HYBRIDS OSMUNDA CINNAMOMEA OSMUNDA CLAYTONIANA POLYGONATUM ODORATUM 'VARIEGATUM' RODGERSIA AESCULIFOLIA RODGERSIA PODOPHYLLA RODGERSIA TABULARIS SEDUM POPULIFOLIUM VIOLA LABRADORICA
5	AMSONIA HUBRICHTII ANEMONE X HYBRIDA 'QUEEN CHARLOTTE' ARTEMESIA VERSICOLOR ATHYRIUM GOERINGIANUM 'PICTUM' FILIPENDULA PURPUREA 'NANA' HELIANTHEMUM APENNINUM VAR. ROSEUM HEMEROCALLIS 'HYPERION' IRIS CRISTATA IRIS TECTORUM OMPHALODES VERNA PENNISETUM ALOPECUROIDES POLYSTICHUM TRIPTERON SYMPHYTUM X UPLANDICUM
6	BEGONIA GRANDIS CRUCIANELLA STYLOSA SAXIFRAGA STOLONIFERA

GROUND COVER BY HARDINESS ZONE
Herbaceous, Mat-Forming

These plants expand by clump expansion, by spreading and rooting stems, or by underground stolons or roots.

ZONE	LATIN NAME
2	POTENTILLA TRIDENTATA
	SAPONARIA OFFICINALIS
3	ARTEMESIA ABSINTHIUM 'LAMBROOK SILVER'
	CAMPANULA RAPUNCULOIDES
	DENNSTAEDTIA PUNCTILOBULA
	FILIPENDULA ULMARIA 'AUREA'
	GERANIUM MACRORRHIZUM
	LYSIMACHIA CLETHROIDES
	LYTHRUM SALICARIA 'DROPMORE PURPLE'
	NEPETA X FAASSENII
	PHLOX SUBULATA
	PHYSOSTEGIA VIRGINIANA
	PHYSOSTEGIA VIRGINIANA 'SUMMER SNOW'
	PTERIDIUM AQUILINUM VAR. LATIUSCULUM
	PULMONARIA ANGUSTIFOLIA
	PULMONARIA SACCHARATA 'MARGERY FISH'
	PULMONARIA SACCHARATA 'SISSINGHURST WHITE'
	RUDBECKIA FULGIDA VAR. SULLIVANTII 'GOLDSTURM'
	SEDUM ELLACOMBIANUM
	SEDUM SARMENTOSUM
	SEDUM SPURIUM
	SEDUM SPURIUM 'BRONZE CARPET'
	THYMUS SERPYLLUM
	TIARELLA CORDIFOLIA VAR. COLLINA
4	AJUGA REPTANS
	AJUGA REPTANS 'BRONZE BEAUTY'
	AJUGA REPTANS (GIANT FORM)
	ARENARIA VERNA
	ARTEMESIA LUDOVICIANA 'SILVER QUEEN'
	CHAMAEMELUM NOBILE
	CONVALLARIA MAJALIS
	EUPHORBIA CYPARISSIAS
	MONARDA DIDYMA
	PACHYSANDRA PROCUMBENS
	PETASITES JAPONICUS
	PHALARIS ARUNDINACEA VAR. PICTA
	PHLOX BIFIDA
	SEDUM TERNATUM
	STACHYS BYZANTINA
	WALDSTEINIA TERNATA
5	ASARUM EUROPAEUM
	CHRYSANTHEMUM WEYRICHII 'WHITE BOMB'
	DIPLAZIUM CONILII
	EPIMEDIUM PINNATUM SUBSP. COLCHICUM
	EPIMEDIUM X YOUNGIANUM 'NIVEUM'
	GALIUM ODORATUM
	HEMEROCALLIS FULVA 'EUROPA'
	HOUTTUYNIA CORDATA 'CHAMELEON'
	LYSIMACHIA PUNCTATA
	PETASITES FRAGRANS

ZONE	LATIN NAME
	PHLOX PILOSA SUBSP. OZARKANA
	PHLOX STOLONIFERA 'ALBA'
	PHLOX STOLONIFERA 'BLUE RIDGE'
	PHLOX STOLONIFERA 'SHERWOOD PURPLE'
	SAGINA SUBULATA
	SEDUM FLORIFERUM 'WEIHANSTEPHANER GOLD'
	THELYPTERIS HEXAGONOPTERA
	THELYPTERIS NOVEBORACENSIS
	THELYPTERIS PHEGOPTERIS
	THYMUS 'CLEAR GOLD'
	THYMUS PSEUDOLANUGINOSUS
6	CERATOSTIGMA PLUMBAGINOIDES
	EUPATORIUM COELESTINUM
	FILIPENDULA PURPUREA 'ELEGANS'
	LUZULA SYLVATICA 'MARGINATA'
	PARONYCHIA KAPELA SUBSP. SERPYLLIFOLIA
	PELTIPHYLLUM PELTATUM
	TRACHYSTEMON ORIENTALIS
7	OPHIOPOGON JAPONICUS 'NANUS'
8	COTULA SQUALIDA

GROUND COVER BY HARDINESS ZONE
Herbaceous, Rampers

The following make a cover as effective as those of the mat formers when foliage is piled up.

ZONE	LATIN NAME
5	LAMIASTRUM GALEOBDOLON 'VARIEGATUM'
	LAMIUM MACULATUM 'WHITE NANCY'

GROUND COVER BY HARDINESS ZONE
Herbaceous, Invasive

The following suggestions for ground covers, selected from the three preceding herbaceous categories, represent those herbaceous plants that will compete aggressively with plants milder in nature. They are very useful in tough situations where nothing else will grow.

ZONE	LATIN NAME
2	SAPONARIA OFFICINALIS
3	AEGOPODIUM PODAGRARIA 'VARIEGATUM'
	CAMPANULA RAPUNCULOIDES
	DENNSTAEDTIA PUNCTILOBULA
	LYSIMACHIA CLETHROIDES
	PHYSOSTEGIA VIRGINIANA
	PHYSOSTEGIA VIRGINIANA 'SUMMER SNOW'
	PTERIDIUM AQUILINUM VAR. LATIUSCULUM

ZONE	LATIN NAME
4	PETASITES JAPONICUS
	PHALARIS ARUNDINACEA VAR. PICTA
5	LYSIMACHIA PUNCTATA
	PETASITES FRAGRANS

GROUND COVER BY HARDINESS ZONE
Woody, Rounded

These plants are generally rounded (to oval) and typically "well dressed," with foliage to the ground. When spaced in such a way that foliage will touch and overlap slightly at maturity, they make very satisfactory ground covers.

ZONE	LATIN NAME
3	RHODODENDRON PRINOPHYLLUM
	ROSA RUGOSA AND HYBRIDS
4	ACANTHOPANAX SIEBOLDIANUS
	BERBERIS THUNBERGII 'CRIMSON PYGMY'
	CARYOPTERIS X CLANDONENSIS 'BLUE MIST'
	CHAENOMELES JAPONICA VAR. ALPINA
	HYPERICUM KALMIANUM
	MYRICA PENSYLVANICA
	SPIRAEA THUNBERGII
	SYRINGA PATULA (SYN. S. PALIBINIANA, S. MICROPHYLLA 'INGWERSEN'S DWARF')
	SYRINGA X CHINENSIS
5	BUXUS SINICA VAR. INSULARIS 'TIDE HILL'
	BUXUS SINICA VAR. INSULARIS 'WINTERGREEN' (OHIO CULTIVAR)
	CALLICARPA JAPONICA
	CHAENOMELES X SUPERBA CULTIVARS
	COTONEASTER ADPRESSUS 'LITTLE GEM'
	COTONEASTER APICULATUS
	DAPHNE X BURKWOODII 'CAROL MACKIE'
	DEUTZIA GRACILIS
	FORSYTHIA SUSPENSA
	FOTHERGILLA GARDENII
	HYDRANGEA QUERCIFOLIA
	HYPERICUM FRONDOSUM
	ILEX GLABRA 'DENSA'
	PHILADELPHUS X FALCONERI
	RHODODENDRON (GABLE HYBRIDS)
	RHODOTYPOS SCANDENS
	ROSA (POLYANTHA) 'THE FAIRY'
	ROSA (SHRUB) 'LILLIAN GIBSON'
	ROSA (SHRUB) 'SEA FOAM'
	ROSA VIRGINIANA
	STEPHANANDRA INCISA 'CRISPA'
	SYRINGA LACINIATA
6	CALLICARPA DICHOTOMA
	COTONEASTER ADPRESSUS VAR. PRAECOX
	ENKIANTHUS PERULATUS
	EUONYMUS FORTUNEI 'SILVER QUEEN'
	FORSYTHIA VIRIDISSIMA 'BRONXENSIS'

ZONE	LATIN NAME
	FORSYTHIA X INTERMEDIA 'SPRING GLORY'
	ILEX CRENATA 'HELLERI'
	RHODODENDRON (GLENN DALE HYBRIDS)
	RHODODENDRON (KURUME HYBRIDS)
	ROSA ROXBURGHII
	VIBURNUM NUDUM 'WINTERTHUR'
7	BERBERIS WILSONIAE VAR. STAPFIANA
	BUXUS MICROPHYLLA 'COMPACTA'
	GENISTA SYLVESTRIS 'LYDIA'

GROUND COVER BY HARDINESS ZONE
Woody, Horizontal Branchers

These plants are "well dressed" to the ground, with foliage on horizontal branches. They are most effective in combating weed growth and forming taller ground cover masses that have a nicely unified aspect.

ZONE	LATIN NAME
3	TSUGA CANADENSIS 'BENNETT'
	TSUGA CANADENSIS 'COLE'S PROSTRATE'
	VIBURNUM PRUNIFOLIUM
4	EUONYMUS ALATA
	JUNIPERUS X MEDIA 'PFITZERIANA COMPACTA'
5	CORNUS MAS
	CORNUS OFFICINALIS
	JUNIPERUS X MEDIA 'OLD GOLD'

GROUND COVER BY HARDINESS ZONE
Woody, Carpet-Forming

The plants in this group form low carpets by clump expansion, by aboveground roots, or by means of stems that root when they touch the soil. They generally form dense mats that compete successfully with weeds.

ZONE	LATIN NAME
3	JUNIPERUS HORIZONTALIS 'WILTONII'
4	EUONYMUS FORTUNEI 'COLORATA'
	EUONYMUS FORTUNEI VAR. RADICANS
	GAULTHERIA PROCUMBENS
	JUNIPERUS SABINA 'TAMARISCIFOLIA'
	MICROBIOTA DECUSSATA
	VINCA MINOR 'BOWLESII'
	VINCA MINOR 'VARIEGATA'
5	EUONYMUS FORTUNEI 'GRACILIS'
	EUONYMUS FORTUNEI 'MINIMA'
	HEDERA HELIX 'BULGARIA'
	HEDERA HELIX 'OGALALLA'
6	HEDERA HELIX 'BALTICA'
	LIRIOPE MUSCARI (BIG BLUE SELECTION)

ZONE	LATIN NAME
	LIRIOPE MUSCARI 'MONROE WHITE'
	LIRIOPE MUSCARI 'VARIEGATA'
	RHODODENDRON X ERIOCARPUM AND R. X NAKAHARAI CULTIVARS AND HYBRIDS

GROUND COVER BY HARDINESS ZONE
Woody, Sprawlers

These plants expand in an irregular way and make thick enough mats of foliage to compete with most weeds.

ZONE	LATIN NAME
4	CHAENOMELES X SUPERBA 'JET TRAIL'
	SALIX REPENS VAR. ARGENTEA
5	CEPHALOTAXUS HARRINGTONIA VAR. PEDUNCULATA
	COTONEASTER HORIZONTALIS
	EUONYMUS FORTUNEI 'GRACILIS'
	TAXUS BACCATA 'REPANDENS'
6	JASMINUM NUDIFLORUM

GROUND COVER BY HARDINESS ZONE
Woody, Spread by Underground Stem or Root

The following plants, in addition to shading out weeds, provide tight root masses useful in holding soil that might otherwise be washed away. They should be used only in conjunction with other plants that will not suffer from the surface root competition.

ZONE	LATIN NAME
3	CORNUS RACEMOSA
	CORNUS RACEMOSA (DWARF)
	CORNUS SERICEA
	CORNUS SERICEA 'FLAVIRAMEA'
	RHUS AROMATICA 'GRO-LOW'
	SORBARIA SORBIFOLIA
	VIBURNUM ACERIFOLIUM
4	ARONIA ARBUTIFOLIA 'BRILLIANTISSIMA'
	COMPTONIA PEREGRINA
	DIERVILLA SESSILIFOLIA
	PAXISTIMA CANBYI
	RHODODENDRON VISCOSUM
	ROBINIA HISPIDA
	ROSA NITIDA
5	AESCULUS PARVIFLORA
	ARUNDINARIA VIRIDISTRIATA
	CLETHRA ALNIFOLIA
	INDIGOFERA INCARNATA 'ALBA'
	KERRIA JAPONICA
	LEUCOTHOE FONTANESIANA
	PACHYSANDRA TERMINALIS
	PACHYSANDRA TERMINALIS 'GREEN CARPET'
	PACHYSANDRA TERMINALIS 'VARIEGATA' OR 'SILVER EDGE'
	RHODODENDRON ATLANTICUM

ZONE	LATIN NAME
	ROSA 'DOORENBOS SELECTION'
	ROSA CAROLINA
	SYMPHORICARPOS X CHENAULTII 'HANCOCK'
	XANTHORHIZA SIMPLICISSIMA
6	ITEA VIRGINICA 'HENRY'S GARNET'
7	SASA VEITCHII

GROUND COVER BY SOIL PREFERENCE
Herbaceous, Clump

The following plants expand slowly and may never form a solid mat. With mulch and/or filter fabric, they make a satisfactory ground cover.

SOIL	LATIN NAME
CLAY AND CLAY LOAM	ACHILLEA 'MOONSHINE'
	ACHILLEA MILLEFOLIUM 'ROSEA'
	AMSONIA HUBRICHTII
	AMSONIA TABERNAEMONTANA
	HELIOPSIS HELIANTHOIDES SUBSP. SCABRA 'KARAT'
	HEMEROCALLIS 'HYPERION'
	SYMPHYTUM X UPLANDICUM
ORGANIC LOAM	ACHILLEA 'MOONSHINE'
	ACHILLEA MILLEFOLIUM 'ROSEA'
	ADIANTUM PEDATUM
	ALCHEMILLA VULGARIS
	AMSONIA HUBRICHTII
	AMSONIA TABERNAEMONTANA
	ANEMONE VITIFOLIA 'ROBUSTISSIMA'
	ANEMONE X HYBRIDA 'QUEEN CHARLOTTE'
	ARABIS PROCURRENS
	ARTEMESIA VERSICOLOR
	ARUNCUS AETHUSIFOLIUS
	ASTILBE X ARENDSII CULTIVARS
	ATHYRIUM GOERINGIANUM 'PICTUM'
	BEGONIA GRANDIS
	BRUNNERA MACROPHYLLA
	CIMICIFUGA RACEMOSA
	COREOPSIS 'MOONBEAM'
	CRUCIANELLA STYLOSA
	DICENTRA 'LUXURIANT'
	DICENTRA EXIMIA 'PURITY'
	FILIPENDULA PURPUREA 'NANA'
	GERANIUM SANGUINEUM
	HELIOPSIS HELIANTHOIDES SUBSP. SCABRA 'KARAT'
	HELLEBORUS NIGER
	HELLEBORUS ORIENTALIS HYBRIDS
	HEMEROCALLIS 'HYPERION'
	HOSTA 'KABITAN'
	HOSTA PLANTAGINEA
	HOSTA SIEBOLDIANA 'ELEGANS'
	HOSTA UNDULATA
	HOSTA VENTRICOSA
	IRIS CRISTATA
	OMPHALODES VERNA
	OSMUNDA CINNAMOMEA
	OSMUNDA CLAYTONIANA
	OSMUNDA REGALIS
	PENNISETUM ALOPECUROIDES
	POLYGONATUM ODORATUM 'VARIEGATUM'
	POLYSTICHUM ACROSTICHOIDES

SOIL	LATIN NAME
	POLYSTICHUM TRIPTERON
	RODGERSIA AESCULIFOLIA
	RODGERSIA PODOPHYLLA
	RODGERSIA TABULARIS
	SAXIFRAGA STOLONIFERA
	SEDUM POPULIFOLIUM
	SYMPHYTUM X UPLANDICUM
	TELEKIA SPECIOSA
	VERONICA INCANA
	VIOLA LABRADORICA
SANDY LOAM	ACHILLEA 'MOONSHINE'
	ACHILLEA MILLEFOLIUM 'ROSEA'
	ARABIS PROCURRENS
	ARTEMESIA STELLERIANA
	ARTEMESIA VERSICOLOR
	COREOPSIS 'MOONBEAM'
	DIANTHUS DELTOIDES
	HELIANTHEMUM APENNINUM VAR. ROSEUM
	HELIOPSIS HELIANTHOIDES SUBSP. SCABRA 'KARAT'
	HEMEROCALLIS 'HYPERION'
	IRIS TECTORUM
	SEDUM POPULIFOLIUM
	SYMPHYTUM X UPLANDICUM
STONY, GRAV-ELLY	ACHILLEA 'MOONSHINE'
	HELIANTHEMUM APENNINUM VAR. ROSEUM
	HELIOPSIS HELIANTHOIDES SUBSP. SCABRA 'KARAT'
	IRIS TECTORUM

GROUND COVER BY SOIL PREFERENCE
Herbaceous, Mat-Forming

These plants expand by clump expansion, by spreading and rooting stems, or by underground stolons or roots.

SOIL	LATIN NAME
CLAY AND CLAY LOAM	DENNSTAEDTIA PUNCTILOBULA
	EUPATORIUM COELESTINUM
	EUPHORBIA CYPARISSIAS
	GERANIUM MACRORRHIZUM
	HEMEROCALLIS FULVA 'EUROPA'
	LYTHRUM SALICARIA 'DROPMORE PURPLE'
	PETASITES FRAGRANS
	PHALARIS ARUNDINACEA VAR. PICTA
	PHYSOSTEGIA VIRGINIANA
	PHYSOSTEGIA VIRGINIANA 'SUMMER SNOW'
	RUDBECKIA FULGIDA VAR. SULLIVANTII 'GOLDSTURM'
	SEDUM ELLACOMBIANUM
	SEDUM FLORIFERUM 'WEIHANSTEPHANER GOLD'
	SEDUM SARMENTOSUM
	SEDUM SPURIUM
	SEDUM SPURIUM 'BRONZE CARPET'
	TRACHYSTEMON ORIENTALIS
ORGANIC LOAM	AJUGA REPTANS
	AJUGA REPTANS 'BRONZE BEAUTY'
	AJUGA REPTANS (GIANT FORM)
	ARTEMESIA ABSINTHIUM 'LAMBROOK SILVER'

SOIL	LATIN NAME
	ARTEMESIA LUDOVICIANA 'SILVER QUEEN'
	ASARUM EUROPAEUM
	CAMPANULA RAPUNCULOIDES
	CERATOSTIGMA PLUMBAGINOIDES
	CHAMAEMELUM NOBILE
	CHRYSANTHEMUM WEYRICHII 'WHITE BOMB'
	CONVALLARIA MAJALIS
	COTULA SQUALIDA
	DENNSTAEDTIA PUNCTILOBULA
	DIPLAZIUM CONILII
	EPIMEDIUM PINNATUM SUBSP. COLCHICUM
	EPIMEDIUM X YOUNGIANUM 'NIVEUM'
	EUPATORIUM COELESTINUM
	FILIPENDULA PURPUREA 'ELEGANS'
	FILIPENDULA ULMARIA 'AUREA'
	GALIUM ODORATUM
	GERANIUM MACRORRHIZUM
	HEMEROCALLIS FULVA 'EUROPA'
	HOUTTUYNIA CORDATA 'CHAMELEON'
	LUZULA SYLVATICA 'MARGINATA'
	LYSIMACHIA CLETHROIDES
	LYSIMACHIA PUNCTATA
	LYTHRUM SALICARIA 'DROPMORE PURPLE'
	MONARDA DIDYMA
	NEPETA X FAASSENII
	OPHIOPOGON JAPONICUS 'NANUS'
	PACHYSANDRA PROCUMBENS
	PARONYCHIA KAPELA SUBSP. SERPYLLIFOLIA
	PELTIPHYLLUM PELTATUM
	PETASITES JAPONICUS
	PHALARIS ARUNDINACEA VAR. PICTA
	PHLOX PILOSA SUBSP. OZARKANA
	PHLOX STOLONIFERA 'ALBA'
	PHLOX STOLONIFERA 'BLUE RIDGE'
	PHLOX STOLONIFERA 'SHERWOOD PURPLE'
	PHYSOSTEGIA VIRGINIANA
	PHYSOSTEGIA VIRGINIANA 'SUMMER SNOW'
	POTENTILLA TRIDENTATA
	PULMONARIA ANGUSTIFOLIA
	PULMONARIA SACCHARATA 'MARGERY FISH'
	PULMONARIA SACCHARATA 'SISSINGHURST WHITE'
	RUDBECKIA FULGIDA VAR. SULLIVANTII 'GOLDSTURM'
	SAPONARIA OFFICINALIS
	SEDUM ELLACOMBIANUM
	SEDUM FLORIFERUM 'WEIHANSTEPHANER GOLD'
	SEDUM SARMENTOSUM
	SEDUM SPURIUM
	SEDUM SPURIUM 'BRONZE CARPET'
	SEDUM TERNATUM
	THELYPTERIS HEXAGONOPTERA
	THELYPTERIS NOVEBORACENSIS
	THELYPTERIS PHEGOPTERIS
	THYMUS 'CLEAR GOLD'
	THYMUS PSEUDOLANUGINOSUS
	THYMUS SERPYLLUM
	TIARELLA CORDIFOLIA VAR. COLLINA
	TRACHYSTEMON ORIENTALIS
	WALDSTEINIA TERNATA
SANDY LOAM	AJUGA REPTANS
	AJUGA REPTANS 'BRONZE BEAUTY'
	AJUGA REPTANS (GIANT FORM)

SOIL	LATIN NAME
	ARENARIA VERNA
	ARTEMESIA ABSINTHIUM 'LAMBROOK SILVER'
	ARTEMESIA LUDOVICIANA 'SILVER QUEEN'
	CAMPANULA RAPUNCULOIDES
	CERATOSTIGMA PLUMBAGINOIDES
	DENNSTAEDTIA PUNCTILOBULA
	HOUTTUYNIA CORDATA 'CHAMELEON'
	LYTHRUM SALICARIA 'DROPMORE PURPLE'
	PARONYCHIA KAPELA SUBSP. SERPYLLIFOLIA
	PHALARIS ARUNDINACEA VAR. PICTA
	PHLOX BIFIDA
	PHLOX SUBULATA
	PHYSOSTEGIA VIRGINIANA
	PHYSOSTEGIA VIRGINIANA 'SUMMER SNOW'
	POTENTILLA TRIDENTATA
	PTERIDIUM AQUILINUM VAR. LATIUSCULUM
	RUDBECKIA FULGIDA VAR. SULLIVANTII 'GOLDSTURM'
	SAGINA SUBULATA
	SAPONARIA OFFICINALIS
	SEDUM ELLACOMBIANUM
	SEDUM FLORIFERUM 'WEIHANSTEPHANER GOLD'
	SEDUM SARMENTOSUM
	SEDUM SPURIUM
	SEDUM SPURIUM 'BRONZE CARPET'
	STACHYS BYZANTINA
	THYMUS 'CLEAR GOLD'
	THYMUS PSEUDOLANUGINOSUS
	THYMUS SERPYLLUM
STONY, GRAV-ELLY	ARENARIA VERNA
	EUPHORBIA CYPARISSIAS
	PARONYCHIA KAPELA SUBSP. SERPYLLIFOLIA
	PHLOX BIFIDA
	PTERIDIUM AQUILINUM VAR. LATIUSCULUM
	SAGINA SUBULATA
	SEDUM ELLACOMBIANUM
	SEDUM FLORIFERUM 'WEIHANSTEPHANER GOLD'
	SEDUM SARMENTOSUM
	SEDUM SPURIUM
	SEDUM SPURIUM 'BRONZE CARPET'
	SEDUM TERNATUM
	THYMUS 'CLEAR GOLD'
	THYMUS PSEUDOLANUGINOSUS
	THYMUS SERPYLLUM

GROUND COVER BY SOIL PREFERENCE
Herbaceous, Rampers

The following make a cover as effective as those of the mat formers when foliage is piled up.

SOIL	LATIN NAME
CLAY AND CLAY LOAM	LAMIASTRUM GALEOBDOLON 'VARIEGATUM'

SOIL	LATIN NAME
ORGANIC LOAM	LAMIASTRUM GALEOBDOLON 'VARIEGATUM'
	LAMIUM MACULATUM 'WHITE NANCY'
STONY, GRAV-ELLY	LAMIASTRUM GALEOBDOLON 'VARIEGATUM'

GROUND COVER BY SOIL PREFERENCE
Herbaceous, Invasive

The following suggestions for ground covers, selected from the three preceding herbaceous categories, represent those herbaceous plants that will compete aggressively with plants milder in nature. They are very useful in tough situations where nothing else will grow.

SOIL	LATIN NAME
CLAY AND CLAY LOAM	AEGOPODIUM PODAGRARIA 'VARIEGATUM'
	DENNSTAEDTIA PUNCTILOBULA
	PETASITES FRAGRANS
	PHALARIS ARUNDINACEA VAR. PICTA
	PHYSOSTEGIA VIRGINIANA
	PHYSOSTEGIA VIRGINIANA 'SUMMER SNOW'
ORGANIC LOAM	AEGOPODIUM PODAGRARIA 'VARIEGATUM'
	CAMPANULA RAPUNCULOIDES
	DENNSTAEDTIA PUNCTILOBULA
	LYSIMACHIA CLETHROIDES
	LYSIMACHIA PUNCTATA
	PETASITES JAPONICUS
	PHALARIS ARUNDINACEA VAR. PICTA
	PHYSOSTEGIA VIRGINIANA
	PHYSOSTEGIA VIRGINIANA 'SUMMER SNOW'
	SAPONARIA OFFICINALIS
SANDY LOAM	AEGOPODIUM PODAGRARIA 'VARIEGATUM'
	CAMPANULA RAPUNCULOIDES
	DENNSTAEDTIA PUNCTILOBULA
	PHALARIS ARUNDINACEA VAR. PICTA
	PHYSOSTEGIA VIRGINIANA
	PHYSOSTEGIA VIRGINIANA 'SUMMER SNOW'
	PTERIDIUM AQUILINUM VAR. LATIUSCULUM
	SAPONARIA OFFICINALIS
STONY, GRAV-ELLY	PTERIDIUM AQUILINUM VAR. LATIUSCULUM

GROUND COVER BY SOIL PREFERENCE
Woody, Rounded

These plants are generally rounded (to oval) and typically "well dressed," with foliage to the ground. When spaced in such a way that foliage will touch and overlap slightly at maturity, they make very satisfactory ground covers.

SOIL	LATIN NAME
CLAY AND CLAY LOAM	ACANTHOPANAX SIEBOLDIANUS
	BERBERIS THUNBERGII 'CRIMSON PYGMY'
	BERBERIS WILSONIAE VAR. STAPFIANA
	BUXUS SINICA VAR. INSULARIS 'TIDE HILL'
	CALLICARPA DICHOTOMA
	CALLICARPA JAPONICA
	CHAENOMELES JAPONICA VAR. ALPINA
	CHAENOMELES X SUPERBA CULTIVARS
	EUONYMUS FORTUNEI 'SILVER QUEEN'
	FORSYTHIA SUSPENSA
	FORSYTHIA VIRIDISSIMA 'BRONXENSIS'
	FORSYTHIA X INTERMEDIA 'SPRING GLORY'
	HYDRANGEA QUERCIFOLIA
	HYPERICUM FRONDOSUM
	HYPERICUM KALMIANUM
	ILEX GLABRA 'DENSA'
	MYRICA PENSYLVANICA
	PHILADELPHUS X FALCONERI
	RHODOTYPOS SCANDENS
	ROSA (POLYANTHA) 'THE FAIRY'
	ROSA (SHRUB) 'LILLIAN GIBSON'
	ROSA ROXBURGHII
	ROSA RUGOSA AND HYBRIDS
	ROSA VIRGINIANA
	SPIRAEA THUNBERGII
	STEPHANANDRA INCISA 'CRISPA'
	SYRINGA LACINIATA
	SYRINGA PATULA (SYN. S. PALIBINIANA, S. MICROPHYLLA 'INGWERSEN'S DWARF')
	SYRINGA X CHINENSIS
ORGANIC LOAM	ACANTHOPANAX SIEBOLDIANUS
	BERBERIS THUNBERGII 'CRIMSON PYGMY'
	BERBERIS WILSONIAE VAR. STAPFIANA
	BUXUS MICROPHYLLA 'COMPACTA'
	BUXUS SINICA VAR. INSULARIS 'TIDE HILL'
	BUXUS SINICA VAR. INSULARIS 'WINTERGREEN' (OHIO CULTIVAR)
	CALLICARPA DICHOTOMA
	CALLICARPA JAPONICA
	CARYOPTERIS X CLANDONENSIS 'BLUE MIST'
	CHAENOMELES JAPONICA VAR. ALPINA
	CHAENOMELES X SUPERBA CULTIVARS
	COTONEASTER ADPRESSUS 'LITTLE GEM'
	COTONEASTER ADPRESSUS VAR. PRAECOX
	COTONEASTER APICULATUS
	DAPHNE X BURKWOODII 'CAROL MACKIE'
	DEUTZIA GRACILIS
	ENKIANTHUS PERULATUS
	EUONYMUS FORTUNEI 'SILVER QUEEN'
	FORSYTHIA SUSPENSA
	FORSYTHIA VIRIDISSIMA 'BRONXENSIS'
	FORSYTHIA X INTERMEDIA 'SPRING GLORY'
	FOTHERGILLA GARDENII
	GENISTA SYLVESTRIS 'LYDIA'
	HYDRANGEA QUERCIFOLIA
	HYPERICUM FRONDOSUM
	HYPERICUM KALMIANUM
	ILEX CRENATA 'HELLERI'
	ILEX GLABRA 'DENSA'
	MYRICA PENSYLVANICA

SOIL	LATIN NAME
	PHILADELPHUS X FALCONERI
	RHODODENDRON (GABLE HYBRIDS)
	RHODODENDRON (GLENN DALE HYBRIDS)
	RHODODENDRON (KURUME HYBRIDS)
	RHODODENDRON PRINOPHYLLUM
	RHODOTYPOS SCANDENS
	ROSA (POLYANTHA) 'THE FAIRY'
	ROSA (SHRUB) 'LILLIAN GIBSON'
	ROSA (SHRUB) 'SEA FOAM'
	ROSA ROXBURGHII
	ROSA RUGOSA AND HYBRIDS
	ROSA VIRGINIANA
	SPIRAEA THUNBERGII
	STEPHANANDRA INCISA 'CRISPA'
	SYRINGA LACINIATA
	SYRINGA PATULA (SYN. S. PALIBINIANA, S. MICROPHYLLA 'INGWERSEN'S DWARF')
	SYRINGA X CHINENSIS
	VIBURNUM NUDUM 'WINTERTHUR'
SANDY LOAM	ACANTHOPANAX SIEBOLDIANUS
	BERBERIS THUNBERGII 'CRIMSON PYGMY'
	BERBERIS WILSONIAE VAR. STAPFIANA
	BUXUS SINICA VAR. INSULARIS 'TIDE HILL'
	BUXUS SINICA VAR. INSULARIS 'WINTERGREEN' (OHIO CULTIVAR)
	CALLICARPA DICHOTOMA
	CALLICARPA JAPONICA
	CARYOPTERIS X CLANDONENSIS 'BLUE MIST'
	DAPHNE X BURKWOODII 'CAROL MACKIE'
	FORSYTHIA X INTERMEDIA 'SPRING GLORY'
	GENISTA SYLVESTRIS 'LYDIA'
	HYPERICUM KALMIANUM
	MYRICA PENSYLVANICA
	ROSA RUGOSA AND HYBRIDS
	ROSA VIRGINIANA
STONY, GRAV-ELLY	ACANTHOPANAX SIEBOLDIANUS
	BERBERIS THUNBERGII 'CRIMSON PYGMY'
	CALLICARPA DICHOTOMA
	CARYOPTERIS X CLANDONENSIS 'BLUE MIST'
	CHAENOMELES JAPONICA VAR. ALPINA
	CHAENOMELES X SUPERBA CULTIVARS
	EUONYMUS FORTUNEI 'SILVER QUEEN'
	GENISTA SYLVESTRIS 'LYDIA'
	HYPERICUM KALMIANUM
	MYRICA PENSYLVANICA
	ROSA (POLYANTHA) 'THE FAIRY'
	ROSA (SHRUB) 'SEA FOAM'
	ROSA RUGOSA AND HYBRIDS

GROUND COVER BY SOIL PREFERENCE
Woody, Horizontal Branchers

These plants are "well dressed" to the ground, with foliage on horizontal branches. They are most effective in combating weed growth and forming taller ground cover masses that have a nicely unified aspect.

SOIL	LATIN NAME
CLAY AND CLAY LOAM	CORNUS MAS
	CORNUS OFFICINALIS
	EUONYMUS ALATA
	JUNIPERUS X MEDIA 'OLD GOLD'
	JUNIPERUS X MEDIA 'PFITZERIANA COMPACTA'
	TSUGA CANADENSIS 'BENNETT'
	TSUGA CANADENSIS 'COLE'S PROSTRATE'
	VIBURNUM PRUNIFOLIUM
ORGANIC LOAM	CORNUS MAS
	CORNUS OFFICINALIS
	EUONYMUS ALATA
	JUNIPERUS X MEDIA 'OLD GOLD'
	JUNIPERUS X MEDIA 'PFITZERIANA COMPACTA'
	TSUGA CANADENSIS 'BENNETT'
	TSUGA CANADENSIS 'COLE'S PROSTRATE'
	VIBURNUM PRUNIFOLIUM
SANDY LOAM	JUNIPERUS X MEDIA 'OLD GOLD'
	JUNIPERUS X MEDIA 'PFITZERIANA COMPACTA'
STONY, GRAV-ELLY	JUNIPERUS X MEDIA 'OLD GOLD'
	JUNIPERUS X MEDIA 'PFITZERIANA COMPACTA'

GROUND COVER BY SOIL PREFERENCE
Woody, Carpet-Forming

The plants in this group form low carpets by clump expansion, by aboveground roots, or by means of stems that root when they touch the soil. They generally form dense mats that compete successfully with weeds.

SOIL	LATIN NAME
CLAY AND CLAY LOAM	EUONYMUS FORTUNEI 'COLORATA'
	EUONYMUS FORTUNEI 'GRACILIS'
	EUONYMUS FORTUNEI 'MINIMA'
	JUNIPERUS HORIZONTALIS 'WILTONII'
	JUNIPERUS SABINA 'TAMARISCIFOLIA'
	MICROBIOTA DECUSSATA
ORGANIC LOAM	EUONYMUS FORTUNEI 'COLORATA'
	EUONYMUS FORTUNEI 'GRACILIS'
	EUONYMUS FORTUNEI 'MINIMA'
	EUONYMUS FORTUNEI VAR. RADICANS
	GAULTHERIA PROCUMBENS
	HEDERA HELIX 'BALTICA'
	HEDERA HELIX 'BULGARIA'
	HEDERA HELIX 'OGALALLA'
	JUNIPERUS HORIZONTALIS 'WILTONII'
	JUNIPERUS SABINA 'TAMARISCIFOLIA'
	LIRIOPE MUSCARI (BIG BLUE SELECTION)
	LIRIOPE MUSCARI 'MONROE WHITE'
	LIRIOPE MUSCARI 'VARIEGATA'
	MICROBIOTA DECUSSATA
	RHODODENDRON X ERIOCARPUM AND R. X NAKAHARAI CULTIVARS AND HYBRIDS
	VINCA MINOR 'BOWLESII'
	VINCA MINOR 'VARIEGATA'

SOIL	LATIN NAME
SANDY LOAM	GAULTHERIA PROCUMBENS
	JUNIPERUS HORIZONTALIS 'WILTONII'
STONY, GRAV-ELLY	HEDERA HELIX 'BALTICA'
	JUNIPERUS HORIZONTALIS 'WILTONII'

GROUND COVER BY SOIL PREFERENCE
Woody, Sprawlers

These expand in an irregular way and make thick enough mats of foliage to compete with most weeds.

SOIL	LATIN NAME
CLAY AND CLAY LOAM	CHAENOMELES X SUPERBA 'JET TRAIL'
	EUONYMUS FORTUNEI 'GRACILIS'
ORGANIC LOAM	CEPHALOTAXUS HARRINGTONIA VAR. PEDUNCULATA
	CHAENOMELES X SUPERBA 'JET TRAIL'
	COTONEASTER HORIZONTALIS
	EUONYMUS FORTUNEI 'GRACILIS'
	JASMINUM NUDIFLORUM
	SALIX REPENS VAR. ARGENTEA
	TAXUS BACCATA 'REPANDENS'
SANDY LOAM	CEPHALOTAXUS HARRINGTONIA VAR. PEDUNCULATA
	SALIX REPENS VAR. ARGENTEA
STONY, GRAV-ELLY	CHAENOMELES X SUPERBA 'JET TRAIL'
	COTONEASTER HORIZONTALIS

GROUND COVER BY SOIL PREFERENCE
Woody, Spread by Underground Stem or Root

The following plants, in addition to shading out weeds, provide tight root masses useful in holding soil that might otherwise be washed away. They should be used only in conjunction with other plants that will not suffer from the surface root competition.

SOIL	LATIN NAME
CLAY AND CLAY LOAM	ARUNDINARIA VIRIDISTRIATA
	CLETHRA ALNIFOLIA
	DIERVILLA SESSILIFOLIA
	RHUS AROMATICA 'GRO-LOW'
	ROBINIA HISPIDA
	ROSA 'DOORENBOS SELECTION'
	ROSA CAROLINA
	ROSA NITIDA
	SYMPHORICARPOS X CHENAULTII 'HANCOCK'
ORGANIC LOAM	AESCULUS PARVIFLORA
	ARONIA ARBUTIFOLIA 'BRILLIANTISSIMA'
	ARUNDINARIA VIRIDISTRIATA
	CLETHRA ALNIFOLIA

SOIL	LATIN NAME
	COMPTONIA PEREGRINA
	CORNUS RACEMOSA
	CORNUS RACEMOSA (DWARF)
	CORNUS SERICEA
	CORNUS SERICEA 'FLAVIRAMEA'
	DIERVILLA SESSILIFOLIA
	INDIGOFERA INCARNATA 'ALBA'
	ITEA VIRGINICA 'HENRY'S GARNET'
	KERRIA JAPONICA
	LEUCOTHOE FONTANESIANA
	PACHYSANDRA TERMINALIS
	PACHYSANDRA TERMINALIS 'GREEN CARPET'
	PACHYSANDRA TERMINALIS 'VARIEGATA' OR 'SILVER EDGE'
	PAXISTIMA CANBYI
	RHODODENDRON ATLANTICUM
	RHODODENDRON VISCOSUM
	RHUS AROMATICA 'GRO-LOW'
	ROBINIA HISPIDA
	ROSA 'DOORENBOS SELECTION'
	ROSA CAROLINA
	ROSA NITIDA
	SASA VEITCHII
	SORBARIA SORBIFOLIA
	SYMPHORICARPOS X CHENAULTII 'HANCOCK'
	VIBURNUM ACERIFOLIUM
	XANTHORHIZA SIMPLICISSIMA
SANDY LOAM	COMPTONIA PEREGRINA
	DIERVILLA SESSILIFOLIA
	RHODODENDRON ATLANTICUM
	RHODODENDRON VISCOSUM
	ROBINIA HISPIDA
	ROSA 'DOORENBOS SELECTION'
	ROSA CAROLINA
	ROSA NITIDA
	XANTHORHIZA SIMPLICISSIMA
STONY, GRAV-ELLY	CORNUS RACEMOSA
	CORNUS RACEMOSA (DWARF)
	RHUS AROMATICA 'GRO-LOW'
	ROBINIA HISPIDA
	ROSA CAROLINA
	SYMPHORICARPOS X CHENAULTII 'HANCOCK'
	VIBURNUM ACERIFOLIUM

GROUND COVER BY MOISTURE PREFERENCE
Herbaceous, Clump

The following plants expand slowly and may never form a solid mat. With mulch and/or filter fabric, they make a satisfactory ground cover.

MOIS-TURE	LATIN NAME
BOG OR STAND-ING WATER	RODGERSIA AESCULIFOLIA
	RODGERSIA PODOPHYLLA
	RODGERSIA TABULARIS
WATER'S EDGE	ASTILBE X ARENDSII CULTIVARS
	FILIPENDULA PURPUREA 'NANA'
	OSMUNDA CINNAMOMEA
	OSMUNDA CLAYTONIANA
	OSMUNDA REGALIS
	RODGERSIA AESCULIFOLIA

MOIS-TURE	LATIN NAME
	RODGERSIA PODOPHYLLA
	RODGERSIA TABULARIS
	TELEKIA SPECIOSA
CONSIS-TENTLY MOIST, NOT BOGGY	ADIANTUM PEDATUM
	ALCHEMILLA VULGARIS
	ANEMONE X HYBRIDA 'QUEEN CHARLOTTE'
	ARABIS PROCURRENS
	ARUNCUS AETHUSIFOLIUS
	ASTILBE X ARENDSII CULTIVARS
	ATHYRIUM GOERINGIANUM 'PICTUM'
	BEGONIA GRANDIS
	BRUNNERA MACROPHYLLA
	CIMICIFUGA RACEMOSA
	DICENTRA 'LUXURIANT'
	DICENTRA EXIMIA 'PURITY'
	FILIPENDULA PURPUREA 'NANA'
	GERANIUM SANGUINEUM
	HELLEBORUS NIGER
	HELLEBORUS ORIENTALIS HYBRIDS
	HOSTA 'KABITAN'
	HOSTA PLANTAGINEA
	HOSTA SIEBOLDIANA 'ELEGANS'
	HOSTA UNDULATA
	HOSTA VENTRICOSA
	IRIS CRISTATA
	IRIS TECTORUM
	OSMUNDA CINNAMOMEA
	OSMUNDA CLAYTONIANA
	OSMUNDA REGALIS
	POLYGONATUM ODORATUM 'VARIEGATUM'
	POLYSTICHUM TRIPTERON
	RODGERSIA AESCULIFOLIA
	RODGERSIA PODOPHYLLA
	RODGERSIA TABULARIS
	SAXIFRAGA STOLONIFERA
	SYMPHYTUM X UPLANDICUM
	TELEKIA SPECIOSA
AVER-AGE, DRY BETWEEN RAINS	ACHILLEA 'MOONSHINE'
	ACHILLEA MILLEFOLIUM 'ROSEA'
	ALCHEMILLA VULGARIS
	AMSONIA HUBRICHTII
	AMSONIA TABERNAEMONTANA
	ANEMONE VITIFOLIA 'ROBUSTISSIMA'
	ARABIS PROCURRENS
	ARTEMESIA STELLERIANA
	ARTEMESIA VERSICOLOR
	ARUNCUS AETHUSIFOLIUS
	ATHYRIUM GOERINGIANUM 'PICTUM'
	BEGONIA GRANDIS
	BRUNNERA MACROPHYLLA
	CIMICIFUGA RACEMOSA
	COREOPSIS 'MOONBEAM'
	CRUCIANELLA STYLOSA
	DIANTHUS DELTOIDES
	DICENTRA 'LUXURIANT'
	DICENTRA EXIMIA 'PURITY'
	FILIPENDULA PURPUREA 'NANA'
	GERANIUM SANGUINEUM
	HELIANTHEMUM APENNINUM VAR. ROSEUM
	HELIOPSIS HELIANTHOIDES SUBSP. SCABRA 'KARAT'
	HELLEBORUS NIGER
	HELLEBORUS ORIENTALIS HYBRIDS
	HEMEROCALLIS 'HYPERION'
	HOSTA 'KABITAN'
	HOSTA PLANTAGINEA

MOIS-TURE	LATIN NAME
	HOSTA SIEBOLDIANA 'ELEGANS'
	HOSTA UNDULATA
	HOSTA VENTRICOSA
	IRIS CRISTATA
	OSMUNDA CINNAMOMEA
	PENNISETUM ALOPECUROIDES
	POLYGONATUM ODORATUM 'VARIEGATUM'
	POLYSTICHUM ACROSTICHOIDES
	POLYSTICHUM TRIPTERON
	SAXIFRAGA STOLONIFERA
	SEDUM POPULIFOLIUM
	SYMPHYTUM X UPLANDICUM
	TELEKIA SPECIOSA
	VERONICA INCANA
	VIOLA LABRADORICA
DRY	ACHILLEA 'MOONSHINE'
	ACHILLEA MILLEFOLIUM 'ROSEA'
	AMSONIA HUBRICHTII
	AMSONIA TABERNAEMONTANA
	ARTEMESIA STELLERIANA
	ARTEMESIA VERSICOLOR
	BRUNNERA MACROPHYLLA
	COREOPSIS 'MOONBEAM'
	HELIOPSIS HELIANTHOIDES SUBSP. SCABRA 'KARAT'
FAST-DRAIN-ING	ACHILLEA 'MOONSHINE'
	ACHILLEA MILLEFOLIUM 'ROSEA'
	ADIANTUM PEDATUM
	ANEMONE X HYBRIDA 'QUEEN CHARLOTTE'
	ARABIS PROCURRENS
	ARTEMESIA STELLERIANA
	ARTEMESIA VERSICOLOR
	COREOPSIS 'MOONBEAM'
	CRUCIANELLA STYLOSA
	DIANTHUS DELTOIDES
	GERANIUM SANGUINEUM
	HELIANTHEMUM APENNINUM VAR. ROSEUM
	HELIOPSIS HELIANTHOIDES SUBSP. SCABRA 'KARAT'
	HEMEROCALLIS 'HYPERION'
	POLYGONATUM ODORATUM 'VARIEGATUM'
	VERONICA INCANA

GROUND COVER BY MOISTURE PREFERENCE
Herbaceous, Mat-Forming

These plants expand by clump expansion, by spreading and rooting stems, or by underground stolons or roots.

MOIS-TURE	LATIN NAME
BOG OR STAND-ING WATER	HOUTTUYNIA CORDATA 'CHAMELEON'
	LYTHRUM SALICARIA 'DROPMORE PURPLE'
	PELTIPHYLLUM PELTATUM
WATER'S EDGE	FILIPENDULA PURPUREA 'ELEGANS'
	FILIPENDULA ULMARIA 'AUREA'
	HOUTTUYNIA CORDATA 'CHAMELEON'
	LYSIMACHIA CLETHROIDES
	LYSIMACHIA PUNCTATA

MOIS-TURE	LATIN NAME
	LYTHRUM SALICARIA 'DROPMORE PURPLE'
	MONARDA DIDYMA
	PELTIPHYLLUM PELTATUM
	PETASITES FRAGRANS
	PETASITES JAPONICUS
	PHALARIS ARUNDINACEA VAR. PICTA
CONSIS-TENTLY MOIST, NOT BOGGY	ARENARIA VERNA
	ASARUM EUROPAEUM
	CAMPANULA RAPUNCULOIDES
	CONVALLARIA MAJALIS
	COTULA SQUALIDA
	DENNSTAEDTIA PUNCTILOBULA
	EPIMEDIUM PINNATUM SUBSP. COLCHICUM
	EPIMEDIUM X YOUNGIANUM 'NIVEUM'
	EUPATORIUM COELESTINUM
	FILIPENDULA PURPUREA 'ELEGANS'
	FILIPENDULA ULMARIA 'AUREA'
	GALIUM ODORATUM
	GERANIUM MACRORRHIZUM
	HEMEROCALLIS FULVA 'EUROPA'
	HOUTTUYNIA CORDATA 'CHAMELEON'
	LUZULA SYLVATICA 'MARGINATA'
	LYSIMACHIA CLETHROIDES
	LYSIMACHIA PUNCTATA
	LYTHRUM SALICARIA 'DROPMORE PURPLE'
	MONARDA DIDYMA
	NEPETA X FAASSENII
	PACHYSANDRA PROCUMBENS
	PETASITES FRAGRANS
	PETASITES JAPONICUS
	PHALARIS ARUNDINACEA VAR. PICTA
	PHLOX PILOSA SUBSP. OZARKANA
	PHLOX STOLONIFERA 'ALBA'
	PHLOX STOLONIFERA 'BLUE RIDGE'
	PHLOX STOLONIFERA 'SHERWOOD PURPLE'
	PHYSOSTEGIA VIRGINIANA
	PHYSOSTEGIA VIRGINIANA 'SUMMER SNOW'
	PTERIDIUM AQUILINUM VAR. LATIUSCULUM
	PULMONARIA ANGUSTIFOLIA
	PULMONARIA SACCHARATA 'MARGERY FISH'
	RUDBECKIA FULGIDA VAR. SULLIVANTII 'GOLDSTURM'
	SAGINA SUBULATA
	SEDUM TERNATUM
	THELYPTERIS HEXAGONOPTERA
	THELYPTERIS NOVEBORACENSIS
	THELYPTERIS PHEGOPTERIS
	TIARELLA CORDIFOLIA VAR. COLLINA
	TRACHYSTEMON ORIENTALIS
	WALDSTEINIA TERNATA
AVER-AGE, DRY BETWEEN RAINS	AJUGA REPTANS
	AJUGA REPTANS 'BRONZE BEAUTY'
	AJUGA REPTANS (GIANT FORM)
	ARTEMESIA ABSINTHIUM 'LAMBROOK SILVER'
	ARTEMESIA LUDOVICIANA 'SILVER QUEEN'
	ASARUM EUROPAEUM
	CERATOSTIGMA PLUMBAGINOIDES
	CHAMAEMELUM NOBILE
	CHRYSANTHEMUM WEYRICHII 'WHITE BOMB'
	CONVALLARIA MAJALIS

MOIS-TURE	LATIN NAME
	COTULA SQUALIDA
	DENNSTAEDTIA PUNCTILOBULA
	DIPLAZIUM CONILII
	EPIMEDIUM PINNATUM SUBSP. COLCHICUM
	EPIMEDIUM X YOUNGIANUM 'NIVEUM'
	EUPATORIUM COELESTINUM
	EUPHORBIA CYPARISSIAS
	GERANIUM MACRORRHIZUM
	HEMEROCALLIS FULVA 'EUROPA'
	LUZULA SYLVATICA 'MARGINATA'
	LYSIMACHIA CLETHROIDES
	LYSIMACHIA PUNCTATA
	LYTHRUM SALICARIA 'DROPMORE PURPLE'
	NEPETA X FAASSENII
	OPHIOPOGON JAPONICUS 'NANUS'
	PACHYSANDRA PROCUMBENS
	PARONYCHIA KAPELA SUBSP. SERPYLLIFOLIA
	PETASITES FRAGRANS
	PHALARIS ARUNDINACEA VAR. PICTA
	PHLOX BIFIDA
	PHLOX PILOSA SUBSP. OZARKANA
	PHLOX STOLONIFERA 'ALBA'
	PHLOX STOLONIFERA 'BLUE RIDGE'
	PHLOX STOLONIFERA 'SHERWOOD PURPLE'
	PHLOX SUBULATA
	PHYSOSTEGIA VIRGINIANA
	PHYSOSTEGIA VIRGINIANA 'SUMMER SNOW'
	PTERIDIUM AQUILINUM VAR. LATIUSCULUM
	PULMONARIA ANGUSTIFOLIA
	PULMONARIA SACCHARATA 'MARGERY FISH'
	PULMONARIA SACCHARATA 'SISSINGHURST WHITE'
	RUDBECKIA FULGIDA VAR. SULLIVANTII 'GOLDSTURM'
	SAGINA SUBULATA
	SEDUM ELLACOMBIANUM
	SEDUM FLORIFERUM 'WEIHANSTEPHANER GOLD'
	SEDUM SARMENTOSUM
	SEDUM SPURIUM
	SEDUM SPURIUM 'BRONZE CARPET'
	SEDUM TERNATUM
	STACHYS BYZANTINA
	THYMUS 'CLEAR GOLD'
	THYMUS PSEUDOLANUGINOSUS
	TIARELLA CORDIFOLIA VAR. COLLINA
	TRACHYSTEMON ORIENTALIS
	WALDSTEINIA TERNATA
DRY	ARTEMESIA ABSINTHIUM 'LAMBROOK SILVER'
	ARTEMESIA LUDOVICIANA 'SILVER QUEEN'
	EPIMEDIUM PINNATUM SUBSP. COLCHICUM
	EPIMEDIUM X YOUNGIANUM 'NIVEUM'
	EUPATORIUM COELESTINUM
	EUPHORBIA CYPARISSIAS
	GERANIUM MACRORRHIZUM
	HEMEROCALLIS FULVA 'EUROPA'
	LYTHRUM SALICARIA 'DROPMORE PURPLE'
	NEPETA X FAASSENII
	POTENTILLA TRIDENTATA

MOIS-TURE	LATIN NAME
	PTERIDIUM AQUILINUM VAR. LATIUSCULUM
	SEDUM ELLACOMBIANUM
	SEDUM FLORIFERUM 'WEIHANSTEPHANER GOLD'
	SEDUM SARMENTOSUM
	SEDUM SPURIUM
	SEDUM SPURIUM 'BRONZE CARPET'
	STACHYS BYZANTINA
	THYMUS 'CLEAR GOLD'
	THYMUS PSEUDOLANUGINOSUS
	THYMUS SERPYLLUM
	WALDSTEINIA TERNATA
FAST-DRAIN-ING	ARTEMESIA ABSINTHIUM 'LAMBROOK SILVER'
	ARTEMESIA LUDOVICIANA 'SILVER QUEEN'
	CERATOSTIGMA PLUMBAGINOIDES
	CHAMAEMELUM NOBILE
	DENNSTAEDTIA PUNCTILOBULA
	EUPATORIUM COELESTINUM
	EUPHORBIA CYPARISSIAS
	GALIUM ODORATUM
	GERANIUM MACRORRHIZUM
	LUZULA SYLVATICA 'MARGINATA'
	NEPETA X FAASSENII
	PARONYCHIA KAPELA SUBSP. SERPYLLIFOLIA
	PHLOX BIFIDA
	PHLOX STOLONIFERA 'ALBA'
	PHLOX STOLONIFERA 'BLUE RIDGE'
	PHLOX STOLONIFERA 'SHERWOOD PURPLE'
	PHLOX SUBULATA
	PHYSOSTEGIA VIRGINIANA
	PHYSOSTEGIA VIRGINIANA 'SUMMER SNOW'
	POTENTILLA TRIDENTATA
	PTERIDIUM AQUILINUM VAR. LATIUSCULUM
	SAPONARIA OFFICINALIS
	SEDUM ELLACOMBIANUM
	SEDUM FLORIFERUM 'WEIHANSTEPHANER GOLD'
	SEDUM SARMENTOSUM
	SEDUM SPURIUM
	SEDUM SPURIUM 'BRONZE CARPET'
	STACHYS BYZANTINA
	THELYPTERIS HEXAGONOPTERA
	THELYPTERIS NOVEBORACENSIS
	THELYPTERIS PHEGOPTERIS
	THYMUS 'CLEAR GOLD'
	THYMUS PSEUDOLANUGINOSUS
	THYMUS SERPYLLUM
	WALDSTEINIA TERNATA

GROUND COVER BY SOIL MOISTURE
Herbaceous, Rampers

The following make a cover as effective as those of the mat formers when foliage is piled up.

MOIS-TURE	LATIN NAME
CONSIS-TENTLY MOIST, NOT BOGGY	LAMIUM MACULATUM 'WHITE NANCY'
AVER-AGE, DRY BETWEEN RAINS	LAMIASTRUM GALEOBDOLON 'VARIEGATUM'
	LAMIUM MACULATUM 'WHITE NANCY'
DRY	LAMIASTRUM GALEOBDOLON 'VARIEGATUM'
FAST-DRAIN-ING	LAMIASTRUM GALEOBDOLON 'VARIEGATUM'

GROUND COVER BY SOIL MOISTURE
Herbaceous, Invasive

The following suggestions for ground covers, selected from the three preceding herbaceous categories, represent those herbaceous plants that will compete aggressively with plants milder in nature. They are very useful in tough situations where nothing else will grow.

MOIS-TURE	LATIN NAME
WATER'S EDGE	LYSIMACHIA CLETHROIDES
	LYSIMACHIA PUNCTATA
	PETASITES FRAGRANS
	PETASITES JAPONICUS
	PHALARIS ARUNDINACEA VAR. PICTA
CONSIS-TENTLY MOIST, NOT BOGGY	AEGOPODIUM PODAGRARIA 'VARIEGATUM'
	CAMPANULA RAPUNCULOIDES
	DENNSTAEDTIA PUNCTILOBULA
	LYSIMACHIA CLETHROIDES
	LYSIMACHIA PUNCTATA
	PETASITES FRAGRANS
	PETASITES JAPONICUS
	PHALARIS ARUNDINACEA VAR. PICTA
	PHYSOSTEGIA VIRGINIANA
	PHYSOSTEGIA VIRGINIANA 'SUMMER SNOW'
	PTERIDIUM AQUILINUM VAR. LATIUSCULUM
AVER-AGE, DRY BETWEEN RAINS	AEGOPODIUM PODAGRARIA 'VARIEGATUM'
	DENNSTAEDTIA PUNCTILOBULA
	LYSIMACHIA CLETHROIDES
	LYSIMACHIA PUNCTATA
	PETASITES FRAGRANS
	PHALARIS ARUNDINACEA VAR. PICTA

MOIS-TURE	LATIN NAME
	PHYSOSTEGIA VIRGINIANA
	PHYSOSTEGIA VIRGINIANA 'SUMMER SNOW'
	PTERIDIUM AQUILINUM VAR. LATIUSCULUM
DRY	AEGOPODIUM PODAGRARIA 'VARIEGATUM'
	PTERIDIUM AQUILINUM VAR. LATIUSCULUM
FAST-DRAIN-ING	AEGOPODIUM PODAGRARIA 'VARIEGATUM'
	DENNSTAEDTIA PUNCTILOBULA
	PHYSOSTEGIA VIRGINIANA
	PHYSOSTEGIA VIRGINIANA 'SUMMER SNOW'
	PTERIDIUM AQUILINUM VAR. LATIUSCULUM
	SAPONARIA OFFICINALIS

GROUND COVER BY SOIL MOISTURE
Woody, Rounded

These plants are generally rounded (to oval) and typically "well dressed," with foliage to the ground. When spaced in such a way that foliage will touch and overlap slightly at maturity, they make very satisfactory ground covers.

MOIS-TURE	LATIN NAME
WATER'S EDGE	ENKIANTHUS PERULATUS
	MYRICA PENSYLVANICA
	ROSA VIRGINIANA
CONSIS-TENTLY MOIST, NOT BOGGY	CALLICARPA JAPONICA
	ENKIANTHUS PERULATUS
	FOTHERGILLA GARDENII
	ILEX GLABRA 'DENSA'
	MYRICA PENSYLVANICA
	ROSA VIRGINIANA
	VIBURNUM NUDUM 'WINTERTHUR'
AVER-AGE, DRY BETWEEN RAINS	ACANTHOPANAX SIEBOLDIANUS
	BERBERIS THUNBERGII 'CRIMSON PYGMY'
	BERBERIS WILSONIAE VAR. STAPFIANA
	BUXUS MICROPHYLLA 'COMPACTA'
	BUXUS SINICA VAR. INSULARIS 'TIDE HILL'
	BUXUS SINICA VAR. INSULARIS 'WINTERGREEN' (OHIO CULTIVAR)
	CALLICARPA DICHOTOMA
	CALLICARPA JAPONICA
	CARYOPTERIS X CLANDONENSIS 'BLUE MIST'
	CHAENOMELES JAPONICA VAR. ALPINA
	CHAENOMELES X SUPERBA CULTIVARS
	COTONEASTER ADPRESSUS 'LITTLE GEM'
	COTONEASTER ADPRESSUS VAR. PRAECOX
	COTONEASTER APICULATUS
	DAPHNE X BURKWOODII 'CAROL MACKIE'
	DEUTZIA GRACILIS
	ENKIANTHUS PERULATUS

MOIS-TURE	LATIN NAME
	EUONYMUS FORTUNEI 'SILVER QUEEN'
	FORSYTHIA SUSPENSA
	FORSYTHIA VIRIDISSIMA 'BRONXENSIS'
	FORSYTHIA X INTERMEDIA 'SPRING GLORY'
	FOTHERGILLA GARDENII
	GENISTA SYLVESTRIS 'LYDIA'
	HYDRANGEA QUERCIFOLIA
	HYPERICUM FRONDOSUM
	HYPERICUM KALMIANUM
	ILEX CRENATA 'HELLERI'
	ILEX GLABRA 'DENSA'
	MYRICA PENSYLVANICA
	PHILADELPHUS X FALCONERI
	RHODODENDRON (GABLE HYBRIDS)
	RHODODENDRON (GLENN DALE HYBRIDS)
	RHODODENDRON (KURUME HYBRIDS)
	RHODODENDRON PRINOPHYLLUM
	RHODOTYPOS SCANDENS
	ROSA (POLYANTHA) 'THE FAIRY'
	ROSA (SHRUB) 'LILLIAN GIBSON'
	ROSA (SHRUB) 'SEA FOAM'
	ROSA ROXBURGHII
	ROSA RUGOSA AND HYBRIDS
	ROSA VIRGINIANA
	SPIRAEA THUNBERGII
	STEPHANANDRA INCISA 'CRISPA'
	SYRINGA LACINIATA
	SYRINGA PATULA (SYN. S. PALIBINIANA, S. MICROPHYLLA 'INGWERSEN'S DWARF')
	SYRINGA X CHINENSIS
	VIBURNUM NUDUM 'WINTERTHUR'
DRY	ACANTHOPANAX SIEBOLDIANUS
	BERBERIS THUNBERGII 'CRIMSON PYGMY'
	BUXUS MICROPHYLLA 'COMPACTA'
	BUXUS SINICA VAR. INSULARIS 'TIDE HILL'
	CALLICARPA DICHOTOMA
	CHAENOMELES JAPONICA VAR. ALPINA
	CHAENOMELES X SUPERBA CULTIVARS
	COTONEASTER ADPRESSUS 'LITTLE GEM'
	COTONEASTER ADPRESSUS VAR. PRAECOX
	COTONEASTER APICULATUS
	EUONYMUS FORTUNEI 'SILVER QUEEN'
	FORSYTHIA SUSPENSA
	FORSYTHIA VIRIDISSIMA 'BRONXENSIS'
	FORSYTHIA X INTERMEDIA 'SPRING GLORY'
	GENISTA SYLVESTRIS 'LYDIA'
	HYPERICUM FRONDOSUM
	HYPERICUM KALMIANUM
	ILEX GLABRA 'DENSA'
	MYRICA PENSYLVANICA
	PHILADELPHUS X FALCONERI
	RHODOTYPOS SCANDENS
	ROSA (POLYANTHA) 'THE FAIRY'
	ROSA (SHRUB) 'SEA FOAM'
	ROSA RUGOSA AND HYBRIDS
	ROSA VIRGINIANA
	STEPHANANDRA INCISA 'CRISPA'
	SYRINGA LACINIATA
	SYRINGA PATULA (SYN. S. PALIBINIANA, S. MICROPHYLLA 'INGWERSEN'S DWARF')
	SYRINGA X CHINENSIS

MOIS-TURE	LATIN NAME
FAST-DRAIN-ING	ACANTHOPANAX SIEBOLDIANUS
	BERBERIS THUNBERGII 'CRIMSON PYGMY'
	BUXUS MICROPHYLLA 'COMPACTA'
	BUXUS SINICA VAR. INSULARIS 'TIDE HILL'
	CALLICARPA DICHOTOMA
	CARYOPTERIS X CLANDONENSIS 'BLUE MIST'
	CHAENOMELES JAPONICA VAR. ALPINA
	CHAENOMELES X SUPERBA CULTIVARS
	COTONEASTER ADPRESSUS 'LITTLE GEM'
	COTONEASTER ADPRESSUS VAR. PRAECOX
	COTONEASTER APICULATUS
	DAPHNE X BURKWOODII 'CAROL MACKIE'
	EUONYMUS FORTUNEI 'SILVER QUEEN'
	FORSYTHIA SUSPENSA
	FORSYTHIA VIRIDISSIMA 'BRONXENSIS'
	FORSYTHIA X INTERMEDIA 'SPRING GLORY'
	GENISTA SYLVESTRIS 'LYDIA'
	HYPERICUM FRONDOSUM
	HYPERICUM KALMIANUM
	ILEX GLABRA 'DENSA'
	MYRICA PENSYLVANICA
	PHILADELPHUS X FALCONERI
	RHODOTYPOS SCANDENS
	ROSA (POLYANTHA) 'THE FAIRY'
	ROSA (SHRUB) 'SEA FOAM'
	ROSA RUGOSA AND HYBRIDS
	ROSA VIRGINIANA
	SPIRAEA THUNBERGII
	STEPHANANDRA INCISA 'CRISPA'
	SYRINGA LACINIATA
	SYRINGA PATULA (SYN. S. PALIBINIANA, S. MICROPHYLLA 'INGWERSEN'S DWARF')
	SYRINGA X CHINENSIS

GROUND COVER BY SOIL MOISTURE
Woody, Horizontal Branchers

These plants are "well dressed" to the ground, with foliage on horizontal branches. They are most effective in combating weed growth and forming taller ground cover masses that have a nicely unified aspect.

MOIS-TURE	LATIN NAME
AVER-AGE, DRY BETWEEN RAINS	CORNUS MAS
	CORNUS OFFICINALIS
	EUONYMUS ALATA
	JUNIPERUS X MEDIA 'OLD GOLD'
	JUNIPERUS X MEDIA 'PFITZERIANA COMPACTA'
	TSUGA CANADENSIS 'BENNETT'
	TSUGA CANADENSIS 'COLE'S PROSTRATE'
	VIBURNUM PRUNIFOLIUM
DRY	EUONYMUS ALATA
	JUNIPERUS X MEDIA 'OLD GOLD'
	JUNIPERUS X MEDIA 'PFITZERIANA COMPACTA'
	VIBURNUM PRUNIFOLIUM

MOIS-TURE	LATIN NAME
FAST-DRAIN-ING	CORNUS MAS
	CORNUS OFFICINALIS
	EUONYMUS ALATA
	JUNIPERUS X MEDIA 'OLD GOLD'
	JUNIPERUS X MEDIA 'PFITZERIANA COMPACTA'

GROUND COVER BY SOIL MOISTURE
Woody, Carpet-Forming

The plants in this group form low carpets by clump expansion, by aboveground roots, or by means of stems that root when they touch the soil. They generally form dense mats that compete successfully with weeds.

MOIS-TURE	LATIN NAME
WATER'S EDGE	GAULTHERIA PROCUMBENS
CONSIS-TENTLY MOIST, NOT BOGGY	GAULTHERIA PROCUMBENS
AVER-AGE, DRY BETWEEN RAINS	EUONYMUS FORTUNEI 'COLORATA'
	EUONYMUS FORTUNEI 'GRACILIS'
	EUONYMUS FORTUNEI 'MINIMA'
	EUONYMUS FORTUNEI VAR. RADICANS
	HEDERA HELIX 'BALTICA'
	HEDERA HELIX 'BULGARIA'
	HEDERA HELIX 'OGALALLA'
	JUNIPERUS HORIZONTALIS 'WILTONII'
	JUNIPERUS SABINA 'TAMARISCIFOLIA'
	LIRIOPE MUSCARI (BIG BLUE SELECTION)
	LIRIOPE MUSCARI 'MONROE WHITE'
	LIRIOPE MUSCARI 'VARIEGATA'
	MICROBIOTA DECUSSATA
	RHODODENDRON X ERIOCARPUM AND R. X NAKAHARAI CULTIVARS AND HYBRIDS
	VINCA MINOR 'BOWLESII'
	VINCA MINOR 'VARIEGATA'
DRY	EUONYMUS FORTUNEI 'COLORATA'
	EUONYMUS FORTUNEI 'GRACILIS'
	EUONYMUS FORTUNEI 'MINIMA'
	JUNIPERUS HORIZONTALIS 'WILTONII'
	JUNIPERUS SABINA 'TAMARISCIFOLIA'
	MICROBIOTA DECUSSATA
FAST-DRAIN-ING	EUONYMUS FORTUNEI 'COLORATA'
	EUONYMUS FORTUNEI 'GRACILIS'
	EUONYMUS FORTUNEI 'MINIMA'
	GAULTHERIA PROCUMBENS
	HEDERA HELIX 'BALTICA'
	JUNIPERUS HORIZONTALIS 'WILTONII'
	JUNIPERUS SABINA 'TAMARISCIFOLIA'
	MICROBIOTA DECUSSATA

GROUND COVER BY SOIL MOISTURE
Woody, Sprawlers

These expand in an irregular way and make thick enough mats of foliage to compete with most weeds.

MOIS-TURE	LATIN NAME
WATER'S EDGE	SALIX REPENS VAR. ARGENTEA
CONSIS-TENTLY MOIST, NOT BOGGY	CEPHALOTAXUS HARRINGTONIA VAR. PEDUNCULATA
	SALIX REPENS VAR. ARGENTEA
AVER-AGE, DRY BETWEEN RAINS	CEPHALOTAXUS HARRINGTONIA VAR. PEDUNCULATA
	CHAENOMELES X SUPERBA 'JET TRAIL'
	COTONEASTER HORIZONTALIS
	EUONYMUS FORTUNEI 'GRACILIS'
	JASMINUM NUDIFLORUM
	SALIX REPENS VAR. ARGENTEA
	TAXUS BACCATA 'REPANDENS'
DRY	CHAENOMELES X SUPERBA 'JET TRAIL'
	COTONEASTER HORIZONTALIS
	EUONYMUS FORTUNEI 'GRACILIS'
FAST-DRAIN-ING	CEPHALOTAXUS HARRINGTONIA VAR. PEDUNCULATA
	CHAENOMELES X SUPERBA 'JET TRAIL'
	COTONEASTER HORIZONTALIS
	EUONYMUS FORTUNEI 'GRACILIS'
	TAXUS BACCATA 'REPANDENS'

GROUND COVER BY SOIL MOISTURE
Woody, Spread by Underground Stem or Root

The following plants, in addition to shading out weeds, provide tight root masses useful in holding soil that might otherwise be washed away. They should be used only in conjunction with other plants that will not suffer from the surface root competition.

MOIS-TURE	LATIN NAME
BOG OR STAND-ING WATER	CLETHRA ALNIFOLIA
WATER'S EDGE	CLETHRA ALNIFOLIA
	CORNUS RACEMOSA
	CORNUS RACEMOSA (DWARF)
	CORNUS SERICEA
	CORNUS SERICEA 'FLAVIRAMEA'
	ITEA VIRGINICA 'HENRY'S GARNET'
	LEUCOTHOE FONTANESIANA
	RHODODENDRON VISCOSUM

MOIS-TURE	LATIN NAME
CONSIS-TENTLY MOIST, NOT BOGGY	ARONIA ARBUTIFOLIA 'BRILLIANTISSIMA'
	ARUNDINARIA VIRIDISTRIATA
	CLETHRA ALNIFOLIA
	CORNUS RACEMOSA
	CORNUS RACEMOSA (DWARF)
	CORNUS SERICEA
	CORNUS SERICEA 'FLAVIRAMEA'
	ITEA VIRGINICA 'HENRY'S GARNET'
	LEUCOTHOE FONTANESIANA
	RHODODENDRON ATLANTICUM
	RHODODENDRON VISCOSUM
	XANTHORHIZA SIMPLICISSIMA
AVER-AGE, DRY BETWEEN RAINS	AESCULUS PARVIFLORA
	ARONIA ARBUTIFOLIA 'BRILLIANTISSIMA'
	ARUNDINARIA VIRIDISTRIATA
	CLETHRA ALNIFOLIA
	COMPTONIA PEREGRINA
	CORNUS RACEMOSA
	CORNUS RACEMOSA (DWARF)
	CORNUS SERICEA
	CORNUS SERICEA 'FLAVIRAMEA'
	DIERVILLA SESSILIFOLIA
	INDIGOFERA INCARNATA 'ALBA'
	ITEA VIRGINICA 'HENRY'S GARNET'
	KERRIA JAPONICA
	LEUCOTHOE FONTANESIANA
	PACHYSANDRA TERMINALIS
	PACHYSANDRA TERMINALIS 'GREEN CARPET'
	PACHYSANDRA TERMINALIS 'VARIEGATA' OR 'SILVER EDGE'
	PAXISTIMA CANBYI
	RHODODENDRON ATLANTICUM
	RHODODENDRON VISCOSUM
	RHUS AROMATICA 'GRO-LOW'
	ROBINIA HISPIDA
	ROSA 'DOORENBOS SELECTION'
	ROSA CAROLINA
	ROSA NITIDA
	SASA VEITCHII
	SORBARIA SORBIFOLIA
	SYMPHORICARPOS X CHENAULTII 'HANCOCK'
	VIBURNUM ACERIFOLIUM
	XANTHORHIZA SIMPLICISSIMA
DRY	ARUNDINARIA VIRIDISTRIATA
	COMPTONIA PEREGRINA
	CORNUS RACEMOSA
	RHUS AROMATICA 'GRO-LOW'
	ROBINIA HISPIDA
	ROSA 'DOORENBOS SELECTION'
	ROSA CAROLINA
	ROSA NITIDA
	SYMPHORICARPOS X CHENAULTII 'HANCOCK'
	VIBURNUM ACERIFOLIUM
FAST-DRAIN-ING	ARUNDINARIA VIRIDISTRIATA
	COMPTONIA PEREGRINA
	CORNUS RACEMOSA
	CORNUS RACEMOSA (DWARF)
	DIERVILLA SESSILIFOLIA
	LEUCOTHOE FONTANESIANA
	PAXISTIMA CANBYI
	RHODODENDRON ATLANTICUM
	RHUS AROMATICA 'GRO-LOW'
	ROBINIA HISPIDA

MOIS-TURE	LATIN NAME
	ROSA 'DOORENBOS SELECTION'
	ROSA CAROLINA
	ROSA NITIDA
	SYMPHORICARPOS X CHENAULTII 'HANCOCK'
	VIBURNUM ACERIFOLIUM

GROUND COVER BY LIGHT PREFERENCE
Herbaceous, Clump

The following plants expand slowly and may never form a solid mat. With mulch and/or filter fabric, they make a satisfactory ground cover.

LIGHT	LATIN NAME
FULL SUN	ACHILLEA 'MOONSHINE'
	ACHILLEA MILLEFOLIUM 'ROSEA'
	AMSONIA HUBRICHTII
	AMSONIA TABERNAEMONTANA
	ANEMONE VITIFOLIA 'ROBUSTISSIMA'
	ANEMONE X HYBRIDA 'QUEEN CHARLOTTE'
	ARABIS PROCURRENS
	ARTEMESIA STELLERIANA
	ARTEMESIA VERSICOLOR
	ARUNCUS AETHUSIFOLIUS
	ASTILBE X ARENDSII CULTIVARS
	COREOPSIS 'MOONBEAM'
	CRUCIANELLA STYLOSA
	DIANTHUS DELTOIDES
	FILIPENDULA PURPUREA 'NANA'
	GERANIUM SANGUINEUM
	HELIANTHEMUM APENNINUM VAR. ROSEUM
	HELIOPSIS HELIANTHOIDES SUBSP. SCABRA 'KARAT'
	HEMEROCALLIS 'HYPERION'
	IRIS TECTORUM
	PENNISETUM ALOPECUROIDES
	RODGERSIA PODOPHYLLA
	RODGERSIA TABULARIS
	SEDUM POPULIFOLIUM
	SYMPHYTUM X UPLANDICUM
	TELEKIA SPECIOSA
	VERONICA INCANA
PARTIAL SHADE	ALCHEMILLA VULGARIS
	AMSONIA TABERNAEMONTANA
	ANEMONE VITIFOLIA 'ROBUSTISSIMA'
	ANEMONE X HYBRIDA 'QUEEN CHARLOTTE'
	ARABIS PROCURRENS
	ARUNCUS AETHUSIFOLIUS
	ASTILBE X ARENDSII CULTIVARS
	ATHYRIUM GOERINGIANUM 'PICTUM'
	BEGONIA GRANDIS
	BRUNNERA MACROPHYLLA
	CIMICIFUGA RACEMOSA
	CRUCIANELLA STYLOSA
	DICENTRA 'LUXURIANT'
	DICENTRA EXIMIA 'PURITY'
	FILIPENDULA PURPUREA 'NANA'
	GERANIUM SANGUINEUM
	HELIOPSIS HELIANTHOIDES SUBSP. SCABRA 'KARAT'
	HELLEBORUS NIGER
	HELLEBORUS ORIENTALIS HYBRIDS
	HEMEROCALLIS 'HYPERION'

LIGHT	LATIN NAME
	HOSTA 'KABITAN'
	HOSTA PLANTAGINEA
	HOSTA SIEBOLDIANA 'ELEGANS'
	HOSTA UNDULATA
	HOSTA VENTRICOSA
	IRIS CRISTATA
	IRIS TECTORUM
	OMPHALODES VERNA
	OSMUNDA CINNAMOMEA
	OSMUNDA CLAYTONIANA
	POLYGONATUM ODORATUM 'VARIEGATUM'
	POLYSTICHUM ACROSTICHOIDES
	POLYSTICHUM TRIPTERON
	RODGERSIA AESCULIFOLIA
	RODGERSIA PODOPHYLLA
	RODGERSIA TABULARIS
	SAXIFRAGA STOLONIFERA
	SEDUM POPULIFOLIUM
	SYMPHYTUM X UPLANDICUM
	VERONICA INCANA
	VIOLA LABRADORICA
SHADE	ADIANTUM PEDATUM
	ATHYRIUM GOERINGIANUM 'PICTUM'
	BEGONIA GRANDIS
	CIMICIFUGA RACEMOSA
	DICENTRA EXIMIA 'PURITY'
	HOSTA 'KABITAN'
	HOSTA PLANTAGINEA
	HOSTA SIEBOLDIANA 'ELEGANS'
	HOSTA UNDULATA
	HOSTA VENTRICOSA
	OSMUNDA CINNAMOMEA
	OSMUNDA CLAYTONIANA
	OSMUNDA REGALIS
	POLYGONATUM ODORATUM 'VARIEGATUM'
	POLYSTICHUM ACROSTICHOIDES
	POLYSTICHUM TRIPTERON
	RODGERSIA AESCULIFOLIA

GROUND COVER BY LIGHT PREFERENCE
Herbaceous, Mat-Forming

These plants expand by clump expansion, by spreading and rooting stems, or by underground stolons or roots.

LIGHT	LATIN NAME
FULL SUN	AJUGA REPTANS
	AJUGA REPTANS 'BRONZE BEAUTY'
	AJUGA REPTANS (GIANT FORM)
	ARTEMESIA ABSINTHIUM 'LAMBROOK SILVER'
	ARTEMESIA LUDOVICIANA 'SILVER QUEEN'
	CERATOSTIGMA PLUMBAGINOIDES
	CHAMAEMELUM NOBILE
	CHRYSANTHEMUM WEYRICHII 'WHITE BOMB'
	COTULA SQUALIDA
	DENNSTAEDTIA PUNCTILOBULA
	EUPATORIUM COELESTINUM
	EUPHORBIA CYPARISSIAS
	GALIUM ODORATUM
	HEMEROCALLIS FULVA 'EUROPA'
	LYSIMACHIA CLETHROIDES
	LYSIMACHIA PUNCTATA

LIGHT	LATIN NAME
	LYTHRUM SALICARIA 'DROPMORE PURPLE'
	MONARDA DIDYMA
	NEPETA X FAASSENII
	PARONYCHIA KAPELA SUBSP. SERPYLLIFOLIA
	PETASITES FRAGRANS
	PHALARIS ARUNDINACEA VAR. PICTA
	PHLOX BIFIDA
	PHLOX PILOSA SUBSP. OZARKANA
	PHLOX SUBULATA
	PHYSOSTEGIA VIRGINIANA
	PHYSOSTEGIA VIRGINIANA 'SUMMER SNOW'
	POTENTILLA TRIDENTATA
	PTERIDIUM AQUILINUM VAR. LATIUSCULUM
	RUDBECKIA FULGIDA VAR. SULLIVANTII 'GOLDSTURM'
	SAGINA SUBULATA
	SAPONARIA OFFICINALIS
	SEDUM ELLACOMBIANUM
	SEDUM FLORIFERUM 'WEIHANSTEPHANER GOLD'
	SEDUM SARMENTOSUM
	SEDUM SPURIUM
	SEDUM SPURIUM 'BRONZE CARPET'
	STACHYS BYZANTINA
	THYMUS 'CLEAR GOLD'
	THYMUS PSEUDOLANUGINOSUS
	THYMUS SERPYLLUM
	WALDSTEINIA TERNATA
PARTIAL SHADE	AJUGA REPTANS
	AJUGA REPTANS 'BRONZE BEAUTY'
	AJUGA REPTANS (GIANT FORM)
	ARENARIA VERNA
	ASARUM EUROPAEUM
	CAMPANULA RAPUNCULOIDES
	CERATOSTIGMA PLUMBAGINOIDES
	CONVALLARIA MAJALIS
	COTULA SQUALIDA
	DENNSTAEDTIA PUNCTILOBULA
	DIPLAZIUM CONILII
	EPIMEDIUM PINNATUM SUBSP. COLCHICUM
	EPIMEDIUM X YOUNGIANUM 'NIVEUM'
	EUPATORIUM COELESTINUM
	FILIPENDULA PURPUREA 'ELEGANS'
	FILIPENDULA ULMARIA 'AUREA'
	GALIUM ODORATUM
	GERANIUM MACRORRHIZUM
	HEMEROCALLIS FULVA 'EUROPA'
	HOUTTUYNIA CORDATA 'CHAMELEON'
	LUZULA SYLVATICA 'MARGINATA'
	LYSIMACHIA CLETHROIDES
	LYSIMACHIA PUNCTATA
	LYTHRUM SALICARIA 'DROPMORE PURPLE'
	MONARDA DIDYMA
	OPHIOPOGON JAPONICUS 'NANUS'
	PACHYSANDRA PROCUMBENS
	PETASITES FRAGRANS
	PETASITES JAPONICUS
	PHALARIS ARUNDINACEA VAR. PICTA
	PHLOX PILOSA SUBSP. OZARKANA
	PHLOX STOLONIFERA 'ALBA'
	PHLOX STOLONIFERA 'BLUE RIDGE'
	PHLOX STOLONIFERA 'SHERWOOD PURPLE'
	PHYSOSTEGIA VIRGINIANA
	PHYSOSTEGIA VIRGINIANA 'SUMMER SNOW'

LIGHT	LATIN NAME
	PTERIDIUM AQUILINUM VAR. LATIUSCULUM
	PULMONARIA ANGUSTIFOLIA
	PULMONARIA SACCHARATA 'MARGERY FISH'
	PULMONARIA SACCHARATA 'SISSINGHURST WHITE'
	SAGINA SUBULATA
	SAPONARIA OFFICINALIS
	SEDUM ELLACOMBIANUM
	SEDUM FLORIFERUM 'WEIHANSTEPHANER GOLD'
	SEDUM SARMENTOSUM
	SEDUM SPURIUM
	SEDUM SPURIUM 'BRONZE CARPET'
	SEDUM TERNATUM
	THELYPTERIS HEXAGONOPTERA
	THELYPTERIS NOVEBORACENSIS
	THELYPTERIS PHEGOPTERIS
	THYMUS 'CLEAR GOLD'
	THYMUS PSEUDOLANUGINOSUS
	THYMUS SERPYLLUM
	TIARELLA CORDIFOLIA VAR. COLLINA
	TRACHYSTEMON ORIENTALIS
	WALDSTEINIA TERNATA
SHADE	ASARUM EUROPAEUM
	CONVALLARIA MAJALIS
	DENNSTAEDTIA PUNCTILOBULA
	DIPLAZIUM CONILII
	EPIMEDIUM PINNATUM SUBSP. COLCHICUM
	EPIMEDIUM X YOUNGIANUM 'NIVEUM'
	FILIPENDULA ULMARIA 'AUREA'
	GALIUM ODORATUM
	GERANIUM MACRORRHIZUM
	HOUTTUYNIA CORDATA 'CHAMELEON'
	LUZULA SYLVATICA 'MARGINATA'
	PACHYSANDRA PROCUMBENS
	PETASITES FRAGRANS
	PETASITES JAPONICUS
	PHLOX STOLONIFERA 'ALBA'
	PHLOX STOLONIFERA 'BLUE RIDGE'
	PHLOX STOLONIFERA 'SHERWOOD PURPLE'
	PULMONARIA ANGUSTIFOLIA
	PULMONARIA SACCHARATA 'MARGERY FISH'
	PULMONARIA SACCHARATA 'SISSINGHURST WHITE'
	SEDUM TERNATUM
	THELYPTERIS HEXAGONOPTERA
	THELYPTERIS PHEGOPTERIS
	TRACHYSTEMON ORIENTALIS

GROUND COVER BY LIGHT PREFERENCE
Herbaceous, Rampers

The following make a cover as effective as those of the mat formers when foliage is piled up.

LIGHT	LATIN NAME
FULL SUN	LAMIUM MACULATUM 'WHITE NANCY'
PARTIAL SHADE	LAMIASTRUM GALEOBDOLON 'VARIEGATUM'
	LAMIUM MACULATUM 'WHITE NANCY'
SHADE	LAMIASTRUM GALEOBDOLON 'VARIEGATUM'
	LAMIUM MACULATUM 'WHITE NANCY'

GROUND COVER BY LIGHT PREFERENCE
Herbaceous, Invasive

The following suggestions for ground covers, selected from the three preceding herbaceous categories, represent those herbaceous plants that will compete aggressively with plants milder in nature. They are very useful in tough situations where nothing else will grow.

LIGHT	LATIN NAME
FULL SUN	DENNSTAEDTIA PUNCTILOBULA
	LYSIMACHIA CLETHROIDES
	LYSIMACHIA PUNCTATA
	PETASITES FRAGRANS
	PHALARIS ARUNDINACEA VAR. PICTA
	PHYSOSTEGIA VIRGINIANA
	PHYSOSTEGIA VIRGINIANA 'SUMMER SNOW'
	PTERIDIUM AQUILINUM VAR. LATIUSCULUM
	SAPONARIA OFFICINALIS
PARTIAL SHADE	AEGOPODIUM PODAGRARIA 'VARIEGATUM'
	CAMPANULA RAPUNCULOIDES
	DENNSTAEDTIA PUNCTILOBULA
	LYSIMACHIA CLETHROIDES
	LYSIMACHIA PUNCTATA
	PETASITES FRAGRANS
	PETASITES JAPONICUS
	PHALARIS ARUNDINACEA VAR. PICTA
	PHYSOSTEGIA VIRGINIANA
	PHYSOSTEGIA VIRGINIANA 'SUMMER SNOW'
	PTERIDIUM AQUILINUM VAR. LATIUSCULUM
	SAPONARIA OFFICINALIS
SHADE	AEGOPODIUM PODAGRARIA 'VARIEGATUM'
	DENNSTAEDTIA PUNCTILOBULA
	PETASITES FRAGRANS
	PETASITES JAPONICUS

GROUND COVER BY LIGHT PREFERENCE
Woody, Rounded

These plants are generally rounded (to oval) and typically "well dressed," with foliage to the ground. When spaced in such a way that foliage will touch and overlap slightly at maturity, they make very satisfactory ground covers.

LIGHT	LATIN NAME
FULL SUN	ACANTHOPANAX SIEBOLDIANUS
	BERBERIS THUNBERGII 'CRIMSON PYGMY'
	BERBERIS WILSONIAE VAR. STAPFIANA
	BUXUS MICROPHYLLA 'COMPACTA'
	BUXUS SINICA VAR. INSULARIS 'TIDE HILL'
	BUXUS SINICA VAR. INSULARIS 'WINTERGREEN' (OHIO CULTIVAR)
	CALLICARPA DICHOTOMA
	CALLICARPA JAPONICA
	CARYOPTERIS X CLANDONENSIS 'BLUE MIST'
	CHAENOMELES JAPONICA VAR. ALPINA
	CHAENOMELES X SUPERBA CULTIVARS
	COTONEASTER ADPRESSUS 'LITTLE GEM'
	COTONEASTER ADPRESSUS VAR. PRAECOX
	COTONEASTER APICULATUS
	DAPHNE X BURKWOODII 'CAROL MACKIE'
	DEUTZIA GRACILIS
	ENKIANTHUS PERULATUS
	EUONYMUS FORTUNEI 'SILVER QUEEN'
	FORSYTHIA SUSPENSA
	FORSYTHIA VIRIDISSIMA 'BRONXENSIS'
	FORSYTHIA X INTERMEDIA 'SPRING GLORY'
	FOTHERGILLA GARDENII
	GENISTA SYLVESTRIS 'LYDIA'
	HYDRANGEA QUERCIFOLIA
	HYPERICUM FRONDOSUM
	HYPERICUM KALMIANUM
	ILEX CRENATA 'HELLERI'
	ILEX GLABRA 'DENSA'
	MYRICA PENSYLVANICA
	PHILADELPHUS X FALCONERI
	RHODODENDRON (GABLE HYBRIDS)
	RHODODENDRON (GLENN DALE HYBRIDS)
	RHODODENDRON (KURUME HYBRIDS)
	RHODODENDRON PRINOPHYLLUM
	RHODOTYPOS SCANDENS
	ROSA (POLYANTHA) 'THE FAIRY'
	ROSA (SHRUB) 'LILLIAN GIBSON'
	ROSA (SHRUB) 'SEA FOAM'
	ROSA ROXBURGHII
	ROSA RUGOSA AND HYBRIDS
	ROSA VIRGINIANA
	SPIRAEA THUNBERGII
	STEPHANANDRA INCISA 'CRISPA'
	SYRINGA LACINIATA
	SYRINGA PATULA (SYN. S. PALIBINIANA, S. MICROPHYLLA 'INGWERSEN'S DWARF')
	SYRINGA X CHINENSIS
	VIBURNUM NUDUM 'WINTERTHUR'

LIGHT	LATIN NAME
PARTIAL SHADE	ACANTHOPANAX SIEBOLDIANUS
	BUXUS MICROPHYLLA 'COMPACTA'
	BUXUS SINICA VAR. INSULARIS 'TIDE HILL'
	BUXUS SINICA VAR. INSULARIS 'WINTERGREEN' (OHIO CULTIVAR)
	DEUTZIA GRACILIS
	ENKIANTHUS PERULATUS
	EUONYMUS FORTUNEI 'SILVER QUEEN'
	FOTHERGILLA GARDENII
	HYDRANGEA QUERCIFOLIA
	ILEX CRENATA 'HELLERI'
	PHILADELPHUS X FALCONERI
	RHODODENDRON (GABLE HYBRIDS)
	RHODODENDRON (GLENN DALE HYBRIDS)
	RHODODENDRON (KURUME HYBRIDS)
	RHODOTYPOS SCANDENS
	STEPHANANDRA INCISA 'CRISPA'
SHADE	ACANTHOPANAX SIEBOLDIANUS
	RHODOTYPOS SCANDENS

GROUND COVER BY LIGHT PREFERENCE
Woody, Horizontal Branchers

These plants are "well dressed" to the ground, with foliage on horizontal branches. They are most effective in combating weed growth and forming taller ground cover masses that have a nicely unified aspect.

LIGHT	LATIN NAME
FULL SUN	CORNUS MAS
	CORNUS OFFICINALIS
	EUONYMUS ALATA
	JUNIPERUS X MEDIA 'OLD GOLD'
	JUNIPERUS X MEDIA 'PFITZERIANA COMPACTA'
	TSUGA CANADENSIS 'BENNETT'
	TSUGA CANADENSIS 'COLE'S PROSTRATE'
	VIBURNUM PRUNIFOLIUM
PARTIAL SHADE	CORNUS MAS
	CORNUS OFFICINALIS
	EUONYMUS ALATA
	TSUGA CANADENSIS 'BENNETT'
	TSUGA CANADENSIS 'COLE'S PROSTRATE'
	VIBURNUM PRUNIFOLIUM

GROUND COVER BY LIGHT PREFERENCE
Woody, Carpet-Forming

The plants in this group form low carpets by clump expansion, by above-ground roots, or by means of stems that root when they touch the soil. They generally form dense mats that compete successfully with weeds.

LIGHT	LATIN NAME
FULL SUN	EUONYMUS FORTUNEI 'COLORATA'
	EUONYMUS FORTUNEI 'GRACILIS'
	EUONYMUS FORTUNEI 'MINIMA'
	EUONYMUS FORTUNEI VAR. RADICANS
	HEDERA HELIX 'BALTICA'
	HEDERA HELIX 'BULGARIA'
	HEDERA HELIX 'OGALALLA'
	JUNIPERUS HORIZONTALIS 'WILTONII'
	JUNIPERUS SABINA 'TAMARISCIFOLIA'
	MICROBIOTA DECUSSATA
	RHODODENDRON X ERIOCARPUM AND R. X NAKAHARAI CULTIVARS AND HYBRIDS
	VINCA MINOR 'BOWLESII'
	VINCA MINOR 'VARIEGATA'
PARTIAL SHADE	EUONYMUS FORTUNEI 'GRACILIS'
	GAULTHERIA PROCUMBENS
	HEDERA HELIX 'BALTICA'
	HEDERA HELIX 'BULGARIA'
	HEDERA HELIX 'OGALALLA'
	LIRIOPE MUSCARI (BIG BLUE SELECTION)
	LIRIOPE MUSCARI 'MONROE WHITE'
	LIRIOPE MUSCARI 'VARIEGATA'
	MICROBIOTA DECUSSATA
	RHODODENDRON X ERIOCARPUM AND R. X NAKAHARAI CULTIVARS AND HYBRIDS
	VINCA MINOR 'BOWLESII'
	VINCA MINOR 'VARIEGATA'
SHADE	GAULTHERIA PROCUMBENS
	MICROBIOTA DECUSSATA
	VINCA MINOR 'BOWLESII'
	VINCA MINOR 'VARIEGATA'

GROUND COVER BY LIGHT PREFERENCE
Woody, Sprawlers

These expand in an irregular way and make thick enough mats of foliage to compete with most weeds.

LIGHT	LATIN NAME
FULL SUN	CHAENOMELES X SUPERBA 'JET TRAIL'
	COTONEASTER HORIZONTALIS
	EUONYMUS FORTUNEI 'GRACILIS'
	JASMINUM NUDIFLORUM
	SALIX REPENS VAR. ARGENTEA
	TAXUS BACCATA 'REPANDENS'
PARTIAL SHADE	CEPHALOTAXUS HARRINGTONIA VAR. PEDUNCULATA
	EUONYMUS FORTUNEI 'GRACILIS'
	TAXUS BACCATA 'REPANDENS'

GROUND COVER BY LIGHT PREFERENCE
Woody, Spread by Underground Stem or Root

The following plants, in addition to shading out weeds, provide tight root masses useful in holding soil that might otherwise be washed away. They should be used only in conjunction with other plants that will not suffer from the surface root competition.

LIGHT	LATIN NAME
FULL SUN	AESCULUS PARVIFLORA
	ARONIA ARBUTIFOLIA 'BRILLIANTISSIMA'
	ARUNDINARIA VIRIDISTRIATA
	CLETHRA ALNIFOLIA
	COMPTONIA PEREGRINA
	CORNUS RACEMOSA
	CORNUS RACEMOSA (DWARF)
	CORNUS SERICEA
	CORNUS SERICEA 'FLAVIRAMEA'
	DIERVILLA SESSILIFOLIA
	INDIGOFERA INCARNATA 'ALBA'
	ITEA VIRGINICA 'HENRY'S GARNET'
	KERRIA JAPONICA
	LEUCOTHOE FONTANESIANA
	RHODODENDRON ATLANTICUM
	RHODODENDRON VISCOSUM
	RHUS AROMATICA 'GRO-LOW'
	ROBINIA HISPIDA
	ROSA 'DOORENBOS SELECTION'
	ROSA CAROLINA
	ROSA NITIDA
	SASA VEITCHII
	SORBARIA SORBIFOLIA
	SYMPHORICARPOS X CHENAULTII 'HANCOCK'
	XANTHORHIZA SIMPLICISSIMA
PARTIAL SHADE	AESCULUS PARVIFLORA
	ARUNDINARIA VIRIDISTRIATA
	CORNUS RACEMOSA
	CORNUS RACEMOSA (DWARF)
	INDIGOFERA INCARNATA 'ALBA'
	ITEA VIRGINICA 'HENRY'S GARNET'
	KERRIA JAPONICA
	LEUCOTHOE FONTANESIANA
	PACHYSANDRA TERMINALIS
	PAXISTIMA CANBYI
	RHODODENDRON VISCOSUM
	SASA VEITCHII
	SORBARIA SORBIFOLIA
	SYMPHORICARPOS X CHENAULTII 'HANCOCK'
	VIBURNUM ACERIFOLIUM
	XANTHORHIZA SIMPLICISSIMA
SHADE	INDIGOFERA INCARNATA 'ALBA'
	LEUCOTHOE FONTANESIANA
	PACHYSANDRA TERMINALIS
	PACHYSANDRA TERMINALIS 'GREEN CARPET'
	PACHYSANDRA TERMINALIS 'VARIEGATA' OR 'SILVER EDGE'
	VIBURNUM ACERIFOLIUM

SUMMARY OF GROUND COVERS BY PLANT TYPE

NAME	HERBACEOUS				WOODY				
	CLUMP	MAT-FORMING	RAMPER	INVASIVE	ROUNDED	HORIZONTAL BRANCHER	CARPET-FORMING	SPRAWLER	SPREAD BY UNDERGROUND STEM OR ROOT
ACANTHOPANAX SIEBOLDIANUS FIVELEAF-ARALIA					X				
ACHILLEA 'MOONSHINE' HYBRID YARROW	X								
ACHILLEA MILLEFOLIUM 'ROSEA' PINK COMMON YARROW	X								
ADIANTUM PEDATUM MAIDENHAIR FERN	X								
AEGOPODIUM PODAGRARIA 'VARIEGATUM' VARIEGATED GOUTWEED				X					
AESCULUS PARVIFLORA BOTTLEBRUSH BUCKEYE									X
AJUGA REPTANS CARPET BUGLEWEED		X							
AJUGA REPTANS 'BRONZE BEAUTY' CARPET BUGLEWEED (BRONZE FOLIAGE)		X							
AJUGA REPTANS (GIANT FORM) BUGLEWEED		X							
ALCHEMILLA VULGARIS LADY'S-MANTLE	X								
AMSONIA HUBRICHTII BLUESTAR (NARROWLEAF)	X								
AMSONIA TABERNAEMONTANA BLUE STAR	X								
ANEMONE VITIFOLIA 'ROBUSTISSIMA'	X								
ANEMONE X HYBRIDA 'QUEEN CHARLOTTE' JAPANESE ANEMONE (HYBRID, PINK)	X								
ARABIS PROCURRENS ROCKCRESS	X								
ARENARIA VERNA IRISH MOSS		X							
ARONIA ARBUTIFOLIA 'BRILLIANTISSIMA' RED CHOKEBERRY									X
ARTEMESIA ABSINTHIUM 'LAMBROOK SILVER'		X							
ARTEMESIA LUDOVICIANA 'SILVER QUEEN'		X							
ARTEMESIA STELLERIANA BEACH WORMWOOD	X								
ARTEMESIA VERSICOLOR MUGWORT	X								
ARUNCUS AETHUSIFOLIUS GOAT'S BEARD (KOREAN)	X								
ARUNDINARIA VIRIDISTRIATA BAMBOO (YELLOW VARIEGATED)									X
ASARUM EUROPAEUM EUROPEAN WILD-GINGER		X							
ASTILBE X ARENDSII CULTIVARS	X								
ATHYRIUM GOERINGIANUM 'PICTUM' JAPANESE SILVER FERN	X								
BEGONIA GRANDIS HARDY BEGONIA	X								
BERBERIS THUNBERGII 'CRIMSON PYGMY' CRIMSON PYGMY BARBERRY					X				
BERBERIS WILSONIAE VAR. STAPFIANA WILSON'S BARBERRY					X				
BRUNNERA MACROPHYLLA SIBERIAN BUGLOSS	X								
BUXUS MICROPHYLLA 'COMPACTA' KINGSVILLE LITTLELEAF BOXWOOD					X				
BUXUS SINICA VAR. INSULARIS 'TIDE HILL' TIDE HILL KOREAN BOXWOOD					X				

NAME	HERBACEOUS				WOODY				
	CLUMP	MAT-FORMING	RAMPER	INVASIVE	ROUNDED	HORIZONTAL BRANCHER	CARPET-FORMING	SPRAWLER	SPREAD BY UNDERGROUND STEM OR ROOT
BUXUS SINICA VAR. INSULARIS 'WINTERGREEN' (OHIO CULTIVAR) WINTERGREEN KOREAN BOXWOOD					X				
CALLICARPA DICHOTOMA CHINESE BEAUTYBERRY					X				
CALLICARPA JAPONICA JAPANESE BEAUTYBERRY					X				
CAMPANULA RAPUNCULOIDES CREEPING BELLFLOWER		X		X					
CARYOPTERIS X CLANDONENSIS 'BLUE MIST' BLUEBEARD					X				
CEPHALOTAXUS HARRINGTONIA VAR. PEDUNCULATA PLUM YEW (SPREADING)								X	
CERATOSTIGMA PLUMBAGINOIDES PLUMBAGO		X							
CHAENOMELES JAPONICA VAR. ALPINA ALPINE JAPANESE FLOWERING QUINCE					X				
CHAENOMELES X SUPERBA 'JET TRAIL' HYBRID FLOWERING QUINCE (SPREADING, WHITE-FLOWERED)								X	
CHAENOMELES X SUPERBA CULTIVARS HYBRID FLOWERING QUINCE					X				
CHAMAEMELUM NOBILE CHAMOMILE		X							
CHRYSANTHEMUM WEYRICHII 'WHITE BOMB'		X							
CIMICIFUGA RACEMOSA BLACK SNAKEROOT	X								
CLETHRA ALNIFOLIA SWEET PEPPERBUSH									X
COMPTONIA PEREGRINA SWEET-FERN									X
CONVALLARIA MAJALIS LILY-OF-THE-VALLEY		X							
COREOPSIS 'MOONBEAM'	X								
CORNUS MAS CORNELIAN-CHERRY						X			
CORNUS OFFICINALIS JAPANESE CORNELIAN-CHERRY						X			
CORNUS RACEMOSA GRAY DOGWOOD									X
CORNUS RACEMOSA (DWARF) DWARF GRAY DOGWOOD									X
CORNUS SERICEA RED-TWIG DOGWOOD									X
CORNUS SERICEA 'FLAVIRAMEA' YELLOW-TWIG DOGWOOD									X
COTONEASTER ADPRESSUS 'LITTLE GEM' CREEPING COTONEASTER (DWARF)					X				
COTONEASTER ADPRESSUS VAR. PRAECOX CREEPING COTONEASTER					X				
COTONEASTER APICULATUS CRANBERRY COTONEASTER					X				
COTONEASTER HORIZONTALIS ROCKSPRAY COTONEASTER								X	
COTULA SQUALIDA NEW ZEALAND BRASS-BUTTONS		X							
CRUCIANELLA STYLOSA CROSSWORT	X								

NAME	HERBACEOUS				WOODY				
	CLUMP	MAT-FORMING	RAMPER	INVASIVE	ROUNDED	HORIZONTAL BRANCHER	CARPET-FORMING	SPRAWLER	SPREAD BY UNDERGROUND STEM OR ROOT
DAPHNE X BURKWOODII 'CAROL MACKIE'					X				
DENNSTAEDTIA PUNCTILOBULA HAY-SCENTED FERN		X		X					
DEUTZIA GRACILIS SLENDER DEUTZIA					X				
DIANTHUS DELTOIDES MAIDEN PINK	X								
DICENTRA 'LUXURIANT' BLEEDING-HEART (HYBRID)	X								
DICENTRA EXIMIA 'PURITY' WILD BLEEDING-HEART (WHTE)	X								
DIERVILLA SESSILIFOLIA SOUTHERN BUSH-HONEYSUCKLE									X
DIPLAZIUM CONILII		X							
ENKIANTHUS PERULATUS WHITE ENKIANTHUS					X				
EPIMEDIUM PINNATUM SUBSP. COLCHICUM		X							
EPIMEDIUM X YOUNGIANUM 'NIVEUM'		X							
EUONYMUS ALATA WINGED EUONYMUS, BURNING BUSH						X			
EUONYMUS FORTUNEI 'COLORATA' PURPLELEAF WINTERCREEPER							X		
EUONYMUS FORTUNEI 'GRACILIS' WINTERCREEPER (WHITE VARIEGATED)							X	X	
EUONYMUS FORTUNEI 'MINIMA' LITTLELEAF WINTERCREEPER							X		
EUONYMUS FORTUNEI 'SILVER QUEEN' SILVER QUEEN WINTERCREEPER					X				
EUONYMUS FORTUNEI VAR. RADICANS WINTERCREEPER (SPREADING)							X		
EUPATORIUM COELESTINUM HARDY AGERATUM		X							
EUPHORBIA CYPARISSIAS CYPRESS SPURGE		X							
FILIPENDULA PURPUREA 'ELEGANS' SHOWY JAPANESE MEADOWSWEET		X							
FILIPENDULA PURPUREA 'NANA' DWARF JAPANESE MEADOWSWEET	X								
FILIPENDULA ULMARIA 'AUREA' GOLDEN QUEEN OF THE MEADOW		X							
FORSYTHIA SUSPENSA WEEPING FORSYTHIA					X				
FORSYTHIA VIRIDISSIMA 'BRONXENSIS' DWARF GREENSTEM FORSYTHIA					X				
FORSYTHIA X INTERMEDIA 'SPRING GLORY' SPRING GLORY FORSYTHIA					X				
FOTHERGILLA GARDENII DWARF FOTHERGILLA					X				
GALIUM ODORATUM SWEET WOODRUFF		X							
GAULTHERIA PROCUMBENS WINTERGREEN							X		
GENISTA SYLVESTRIS 'LYDIA' SPREADING BROOM					X				
GERANIUM MACRORRHIZUM BIGROOT CRANESBILL		X							
GERANIUM SANGUINEUM BLOODY CRANESBILL	X								

NAME	HERBACEOUS				WOODY				
	CLUMP	MAT-FORMING	RAMPER	INVASIVE	ROUNDED	HORIZONTAL BRANCHER	CARPET-FORMING	SPRAWLER	SPREAD BY UNDERGROUND STEM OR ROOT
HEDERA HELIX 'BALTICA' BALTIC IVY							X		
HEDERA HELIX 'BULGARIA' BULGARIAN IVY							X		
HEDERA HELIX 'OGALALLA' OGALALLA ENGLISH IVY							X		
HELIANTHEMUM APENNINUM VAR. ROSEUM SUN ROSE	X								
HELIOPSIS HELIANTHOIDES SUBSP. SCABRA 'KARAT'	X								
HELLEBORUS NIGER CHRISTMAS-ROSE	X								
HELLEBORUS ORIENTALIS HYBRIDS LENTEN-ROSE	X								
HEMEROCALLIS 'HYPERION' HYPERION DAYLILY	X								
HEMEROCALLIS FULVA 'EUROPA' ORANGE DAYLILY		X							
HOSTA 'KABITAN' PLANTAIN-LILY (YELLOW VARIEGATED)	X								
HOSTA PLANTAGINEA FRAGRANT PLANTAIN-LILY	X								
HOSTA SIEBOLDIANA 'ELEGANS' SIEBOLD PLANTAIN-LILY (BLUE, SEERSUCKER LEAVES)	X								
HOSTA UNDULATA WAVY-LEAVED PLANTAIN-LILY	X								
HOSTA VENTRICOSA BLUE PLANTAIN-LILY	X								
HOUTTUYNIA CORDATA 'CHAMELEON'		X							
HYDRANGEA QUERCIFOLIA OAKLEAF HYDRANGEA					X				
HYPERICUM FRONDOSUM GOLDEN ST.-JOHN'S-WORT					X				
HYPERICUM KALMIANUM KALM ST.-JOHN'S-WORT					X				
ILEX CRENATA 'HELLERI' HELLERI DWARF JAPANESE HOLLY					X				
ILEX GLABRA 'DENSA' DWARF INKBERRY HOLLY					X				
INDIGOFERA INCARNATA 'ALBA' CHINESE INDIGO (WHITE)									X
IRIS CRISTATA CRESTED IRIS	X								
IRIS TECTORUM ROOF IRIS	X								
ITEA VIRGINICA 'HENRY'S GARNET' VIRGINIA SWEETSPIRE									X
JASMINUM NUDIFLORUM WINTER JASMINE								X	
JUNIPERUS HORIZONTALIS 'WILTONII' BLUE RUG JUNIPER							X		
JUNIPERUS SABINA 'TAMARISCIFOLIA' TAMARIX JUNIPER							X		
JUNIPERUS X MEDIA 'OLD GOLD' OLD GOLD JUNIPER						X			
JUNIPERUS X MEDIA 'PFITZERIANA COMPACTA' NICK'S COMPACT JUNIPER						X			

NAME	HERBACEOUS				WOODY				
	CLUMP	MAT-FORMING	RAMPER	INVASIVE	ROUNDED	HORIZONTAL BRANCHER	CARPET-FORMING	SPRAWLER	SPREAD BY UNDERGROUND STEM OR ROOT
KERRIA JAPONICA KERRIA (SINGLE-FLOWERED)									X
LAMIASTRUM GALEOBDOLON 'VARIEGATUM' YELLOW-ARCHANGEL (WHITE VARIEGATED)			X						
LAMIUM MACULATUM 'WHITE NANCY' SPOTTED-DEAD-NETTLE (WHITE)			X						
LEUCOTHOE FONTANESIANA FOUNTAIN LEUCOTHOE									X
LIRIOPE MUSCARI (BIG BLUE SELECTION) BIG BLUE LILYTURF							X		
LIRIOPE MUSCARI 'MONROE WHITE' LILYTURF (WHITE)							X		
LIRIOPE MUSCARI 'VARIEGATA' LILYTURF (YELLOW VARIEGATED)							X		
LUZULA SYLVATICA 'MARGINATA' GREATER WOOD RUSH		X							
LYSIMACHIA CLETHROIDES GOOSENECK LOOSESTRIFE		X		X					
LYSIMACHIA PUNCTATA GARDEN LOOSESTRIFE		X		X					
LYTHRUM SALICARIA 'DROPMORE PURPLE' PURPLE LOOSESTRIFE		X							
MICROBIOTA DECUSSATA SIBERIAN-CYPRESS							X		
MONARDA DIDYMA BEE BALM		X							
MYRICA PENSYLVANICA BAYBERRY					X				
NEPETA X FAASSENII		X							
OMPHALODES VERNA BLUE-EYED MARY	X								
OPHIOPOGON JAPONICUS 'NANUS' DWARF MONDO GRASS		X							
OSMUNDA CINNAMOMEA CINNAMON FERN	X								
OSMUNDA CLAYTONIANA INTERRUPTED FERN	X								
OSMUNDA REGALIS ROYAL FERN	X								
PACHYSANDRA PROCUMBENS ALLEGHANY SPURGE		X							
PACHYSANDRA TERMINALIS JAPANESE SPURGE									X
PACHYSANDRA TERMINALIS 'GREEN CARPET' GREEN CARPET JAPANESE SPURGE									X
PACHYSANDRA TERMINALIS 'VARIEGATA' OR 'SILVER EDGE' JAPANESE SPURGE (WHITE VARIEGATED)									X
PARONYCHIA KAPELA SUBSP. SERPYLLIFOLIA CREEPING NAILWORT		X							
PAXISTIMA CANBYI									X
PELTIPHYLLUM PELTATUM UMBRELLA PLANT		X							
PENNISETUM ALOPECUROIDES HARDY FOUNTAIN GRASS	X								
PETASITES FRAGRANS WINTER HELIOTROPE		X		X					
PETASITES JAPONICUS JAPANESE BUTTERBUR		X		X					

NAME	HERBACEOUS				WOODY				
	CLUMP	MAT-FORMING	RAMPER	INVASIVE	ROUNDED	HORIZONTAL BRANCHER	CARPET-FORMING	SPRAWLER	SPREAD BY UNDERGROUND STEM OR ROOT
PHALARIS ARUNDINACEA VAR. PICTA RIBBON GRASS (WHITE VARIEGATED)		X		X					
PHILADELPHUS X FALCONERI FALCONER HYBRID MOCKORANGE					X				
PHLOX BIFIDA SAND PHLOX		X							
PHLOX PILOSA SUBSP. OZARKANA OZARK DOWNY PHLOX		X							
PHLOX STOLONIFERA 'ALBA' CREEPING PHLOX		X							
PHLOX STOLONIFERA 'BLUE RIDGE' CREEPING PHLOX		X							
PHLOX STOLONIFERA 'SHERWOOD PURPLE' CREEPING PHLOX		X							
PHLOX SUBULATA MOSS PHLOX		X							
PHYSOSTEGIA VIRGINIANA FALSE DRAGONHEAD		X		X					
PHYSOSTEGIA VIRGINIANA 'SUMMER SNOW' FALSE DRAGONHEAD (WHITE)		X		X					
POLYGONATUM ODORATUM 'VARIEGATUM' SOLOMON'S SEAL (WHITE VARIEGATED)	X								
POLYSTICHUM ACROSTICHOIDES CHRISTMAS FERN									
POLYSTICHUM TRIPTERON	X								
POTENTILLA TRIDENTATA THREE-TOOTHED CINQUEFOIL		X							
PTERIDIUM AQUILINUM VAR. LATIUSCULUM BRACKEN		X		X					
PULMONARIA ANGUSTIFOLIA LUNGWORT		X							
PULMONARIA SACCHARATA 'MARGERY FISH' BETHLEHEM LUNGWORT		X							
PULMONARIA SACCHARATA 'SISSINGHURST WHITE' BETHLEHEM LUNGWORT (WHITE)		X							
RHODODENDRON (GABLE HYBRIDS) GABLE HYBRID AZALEAS					X				
RHODODENDRON (GLENN DALE HYBRIDS) GLENN DALE HYBRID AZALEAS					X				
RHODODENDRON (KURUME HYBRIDS) KURUME HYBRID AZALEAS					X				
RHODODENDRON ATLANTICUM COAST AZALEA									X
RHODODENDRON PRINOPHYLLUM ROSESHELL AZALEA					X				
RHODODENDRON VISCOSUM SWAMP AZALEA									X
RHODODENDRON X ERIOCARPUM AND R. X NAKAHARAI CULTIVARS AND HYBRIDS							X		
RHODOTYPOS SCANDENS JETBEAD					X				
RHUS AROMATICA 'GRO-LOW' FRAGRANT SUMAC (DWARF)									X
ROBINIA HISPIDA ROSE-ACACIA									X
RODGERSIA AESCULIFOLIA RODGERSIA	X								

NAME	HERBACEOUS				WOODY				
	CLUMP	MAT-FORMING	RAMPER	INVASIVE	ROUNDED	HORIZONTAL BRANCHER	CARPET-FORMING	SPRAWLER	SPREAD BY UNDERGROUND STEM OR ROOT
RODGERSIA PODOPHYLLA BRONZELEAF RODGERSIA	X								
RODGERSIA TABULARIS SHIELDLEAF RODGERSIA	X								
ROSA 'DOORENBOS SELECTION' HYBRID SPINOSISSIMA ROSE									X
ROSA (POLYANTHA) 'THE FAIRY'					X				
ROSA (SHRUB) 'LILLIAN GIBSON'					X				
ROSA (SHRUB) 'SEA FOAM'					X				
ROSA CAROLINA PASTURE ROSE									X
ROSA NITIDA SHINING ROSE									X
ROSA ROXBURGHII CHESTNUT ROSE					X				
ROSA RUGOSA AND HYBRIDS					X				
ROSA VIRGINIANA VIRGINIA ROSE					X				
RUDBECKIA FULGIDA VAR. SULLIVANTII 'GOLDSTURM' GARDEN BLACK-EYED-SUSAN		X							
SAGINA SUBULATA CORSICAN PEARLWORT		X							
SALIX REPENS VAR. ARGENTEA PUSSY WILLOW (CREEPING)								X	
SAPONARIA OFFICINALIS BOUNCING BET		X		X					
SASA VEITCHII VEITCH BAMBOO									X
SAXIFRAGA STOLONIFERA STRAWBERRY-BEGONIA	X								
SEDUM ELLACOMBIANUM		X							
SEDUM FLORIFERUM 'WEIHANSTEPHANER GOLD'		X							
SEDUM POPULIFOLIUM POPLAR STONECROP	X								
SEDUM SARMENTOSUM STRINGY STONECROP		X							
SEDUM SPURIUM TWO ROW STONECROP		X							
SEDUM SPURIUM 'BRONZE CARPET' TWO ROW STONECROP (BRONZE FOLIAGE)		X							
SEDUM TERNATUM MOUNTAIN STONECROP		X							
SORBARIA SORBIFOLIA URAL FALSE SPIRAEA									X
SPIRAEA THUNBERGII					X				
STACHYS BYZANTINA LAMB'S-EARS		X							
STEPHANANDRA INCISA 'CRISPA' STEPHANANDRA (COMPACT CUTLEAF)					X				
SYMPHORICARPOS X CHENAULTII 'HANCOCK' HANCOCK CORALBERRY									X
SYMPHYTUM X UPLANDICUM RUSSIAN COMFREY	X								
SYRINGA LACINIATA CUT-LEAF LILAC					X				

NAME	HERBACEOUS				WOODY				
	CLUMP	MAT-FORMING	RAMPER	INVASIVE	ROUNDED	HORIZONTAL BRANCHER	CARPET-FORMING	SPRAWLER	SPREAD BY UNDERGROUND STEM OR ROOT
SYRINGA PATULA (SYN. S. PALIBINIANA, S. MICROPHYLLA 'INGWERSEN'S DWARF') LILAC (DWARF)					X				
SYRINGA X CHINENSIS CHINESE LILAC					X				
TAXUS BACCATA 'REPANDENS' WEEPING ENGLISH YEW								X	
TELEKIA SPECIOSA HEARTLEAF OXEYE	X								
THELYPTERIS HEXAGONOPTERA BROAD BEECH FERN		X							
THELYPTERIS NOVEBORACENSIS NEW YORK FERN		X							
THELYPTERIS PHEGOPTERIS NARROW BEECHFERN		X							
THYMUS 'CLEAR GOLD' HYBRID THYME (YELLOW LEAF)		X							
THYMUS PSEUDOLANUGINOSUS WOOLY THYME		X							
THYMUS SERPYLLUM WILD THYME		X							
TIARELLA CORDIFOLIA VAR. COLLINA WHERRY'S FOAM FLOWER		X							
TRACHYSTEMON ORIENTALIS		X							
TSUGA CANADENSIS 'BENNETT' BENNETT'S DWARF HEMLOCK						X			
TSUGA CANADENSIS 'COLE'S PROSTRATE' COLE'S PROSTRATE HEMLOCK						X			
VERONICA INCANA WOOLY SPEEDWELL	X								
VIBURNUM ACERIFOLIUM MAPLELEAF VIBURNUM									X
VIBURNUM NUDUM 'WINTERTHUR' SMOOTH WITHE-ROD (SUPERIOR SELECTION)					X				
VIBURNUM PRUNIFOLIUM BLACKHAW						X			
VINCA MINOR 'BOWLESII' BOWLES PERIWINKLE							X		
VINCA MINOR 'VARIEGATA' PERIWINKLE (GREEN AND YELLOW)							X		
VIOLA LABRADORICA	X								
WALDSTEINIA TERNATA		X							
XANTHORHIZA SIMPLICISSIMA YELLOWROOT									X

APPENDIX 28
Plants for Use Between Stepping-stones

Plantings in connection with stepping-stones provide an opportunity for intimate gardening; one tends to walk more slowly in such situations, looking down as one goes. There is the chance for both flower interest (*Pulmonaria* and *Ceratostigma*) and textural contrasts (fine texture, *Aruncus aethusifolius* and *Phlox bifida*; broadleaf texture; *Bergenia* and *Convallaria*). Generally speaking, it is advisable to use low plants that can stand the pressure of foot traffic along the center line of the pathway (*Thymus serpyllum* and *Chamaemelum nobile* are good examples; both provide fragrance when pressured by a foot) and to keep higher plants to the side.

The appendix is divided by hardiness zone.

Further information about all of the following plants is summarized in the Master Lists, Appendices 1A and 1B.

ZONE	LATIN NAME
2	BERGENIA 'PERFECTA'
	BERGENIA 'SUNNINGDALE'
	POTENTILLA TRIDENTATA
3	ACHILLEA 'MOONSHINE'
	COREOPSIS 'MOONBEAM'
	PHLOX SUBULATA
	PULMONARIA ANGUSTIFOLIA
	PULMONARIA SACCHARATA 'MARGERY FISH'
	PULMONARIA SACCHARATA 'SISSINGHURST WHITE'
	SEDUM SARMENTOSUM
	SEDUM SPURIUM
	SEDUM SPURIUM 'BRONZE CARPET'
	THYMUS SERPYLLUM
	VERONICA INCANA
4	AJUGA REPTANS
	AJUGA REPTANS 'BRONZE BEAUTY'
	AJUGA REPTANS (GIANT FORM)
	ARABIS PROCURRENS
	ARENARIA VERNA
	ARUNCUS AETHUSIFOLIUS
	CHAMAEMELUM NOBILE
	CONVALLARIA MAJALIS
	HEDYOTIS CAERULEA
	PHLOX BIFIDA
	STACHYS BYZANTINA
	VINCA MINOR 'BOWLESII'
	VINCA MINOR 'VARIEGATA'
	WALDSTEINIA TERNATA
5	ATHYRIUM GOERINGIANUM 'PICTUM'
	CHRYSANTHEMUM WEYRICHII 'WHITE BOMB'
	EPIMEDIUM X YOUNGIANUM 'NIVEUM'
	EUONYMUS FORTUNEI 'MINIMA'
	HELIANTHEMUM APENNINUM VAR. ROSEUM
	IRIS CRISTATA

ZONE	LATIN NAME
	PHLOX STOLONIFERA 'ALBA'
	PHLOX STOLONIFERA 'BLUE RIDGE'
	PHLOX STOLONIFERA 'SHERWOOD PURPLE'
	SAGINA SUBULATA
	SEDUM FLORIFERUM 'WEIHANSTEPHANER GOLD'
	THYMUS 'CLEAR GOLD'
6	CERATOSTIGMA PLUMBAGINOIDES
	PARONYCHIA KAPELA SUBSP. SERPYLLIFOLIA
8	COTULA SQUALIDA

APPENDIX 29
Plants to Give Mosslike Effect

The velvet texture of moss has wide appeal and many uses in garden design. Although it is not as hard to grow and maintain as is commonly believed, there are places where one must substitute for it. The following are very close to moss in height and in their ability to form a carpet, and they are tolerant of some of the conditions unacceptable to moss. For instance, most of these, including *Sedum sarmentosum* and *Thymus* 'Clear Gold,' will stand full sun.

The appendix is divided by hardiness zone.

Further information about all the following plants is summarized in the Master Lists, Appendices 1A and 1B.

ZONE	LATIN NAME
3	SEDUM SARMENTOSUM
	THYMUS SERPYLLUM
4	ARENARIA VERNA
	CHAMAEMELUM NOBILE
5	SAGINA SUBULATA
	THYMUS 'CLEAR GOLD'
6	PARONYCHIA KAPELA SUBSP. SERPYLLIFOLIA
7	OPHIOPOGON JAPONICUS 'NANUS'
8	COTULA SQUALIDA

APPENDIX 30
Ground Covers Useful over Spring-Flowering Bulbs

This appendix lists the two kinds of ground covers that are useful in connection with plantings of spring-blooming bulbs:

Lower Ground Covers
Taller Ground Covers

The first group contains those plants that are lower than the flowering bulbs and that complement the bulbs when in flower, either because their foliage serves as an attractive accent or contrast, or because they flower at the same time as the bulb and make for a happy color relationship.

Plants in the second group grow taller that the bulbs after bulb season, covering their unattractive dying foliage and providing a later period of foliage or bloom interest for that part of the garden.

Each of the two categories is subdivided by hardiness zone.

Further information about many of these plants can be found in Appendix 27.

LOWER GROUND COVERS

ZONE	LATIN NAME
3	BRUNNERA MACROPHYLLA
	PHLOX SUBULATA
	PULMONARIA ANGUSTIFOLIA
	PULMONARIA SACCHARATA 'MARGERY FISH'
	THYMUS SERPYLLUM
	TIARELLA CORDIFOLIA VAR. COLLINA
4	AJUGA REPTANS
	AJUGA REPTANS 'BRONZE BEAUTY'
	AJUGA REPTANS (GIANT FORM)
	ARABIS PROCURRENS
	ARENARIA VERNA
	CHAMAEMELUM NOBILE
	PHLOX BIFIDA
	VINCA MINOR 'BOWLESII'
	VINCA MINOR 'VARIEGATA'
5	EPIMEDIUM PINNATUM SUBSP. COLCHICUM
	EPIMEDIUM X YOUNGIANUM 'NIVEUM'
	GALIUM ODORATUM
	LAMIUM MACULATUM 'WHITE NANCY'
	OMPHALODES VERNA
	PHLOX STOLONIFERA 'ALBA'
	PHLOX STOLONIFERA 'BLUE RIDGE'
	PHLOX STOLONIFERA 'SHERWOOD PURPLE'
	SAGINA SUBULATA
	THYMUS 'CLEAR GOLD'

ZONE	LATIN NAME
6	PARONYCHIA KAPELA SUBSP. SERPYLLIFOLIA
8	COTULA SQUALIDA

TALLER GROUND COVERS

ZONE	LATIN NAME
3	CAMPANULA RAPUNCULOIDES
	COREOPSIS 'MOONBEAM'
	DENNSTAEDTIA PUNCTILOBULA
	HOSTA IN VARIETY
	NEPETA X FAASSENII
	PHYSOSTEGIA VIRGINIANA
	PHYSOSTEGIA VIRGINIANA 'SUMMER SNOW'
	PTERIDIUM AQUILINUM VAR. LATIUSCULUM
4	HEUCHERA 'PALACE PURPLE' STRAIN
	OSMUNDA CINNAMOMEA
	OSMUNDA CLAYTONIANA
5	ATHYRIUM GOERINGIANUM 'PICTUM'
	CHRYSANTHEMUM WEYRICHII 'WHITE BOMB'
	FILIPENDULA PURPUREA 'NANA'
	HEMEROCALLIS IN VARIETY
	HOUTTUYNIA CORDATA 'CHAMELEON'
	LAMIASTRUM GALEOBDOLON 'VARIEGATUM'
	PHLOX PILOSA SUBSP. OZARKANA
	THELYPTERIS NOVEBORACENSIS
6	BEGONIA GRANDIS
	CERATOSTIGMA PLUMBAGINOIDES
	EUPATORIUM COELESTINUM

APPENDIX 31
Old Shrub Roses

Old Shrub Roses, it must be noted, are a very different kettle of fish from the ubiquitous hybrid teas. It is a bit difficult to understand their appeal until you have grown some in your own garden and lived with them.

Hybrid teas bloom all season, are prized for their buds, are of recent hybridization (new ones are promoted annually), generally are without fragrance, are high-maintenance, and have branching habits without any grace. Old Shrub Roses, on the other hand, bloom but once (late May to early June, for two to three weeks), are grown for the fully opened blossom, in many cases (but not all) are of early origins and are survivors (requiring little or no spraying), are of captivating fragrance in the majority of instances, and are extremely graceful in habit (some to the point of being utterly lax, alas).

I suppose it is because of their fragrance, preciously short season, lush habit, and historical associations that an aura of romance surrounds them,

emotions run high among their devotees, and a veritable cult has grown up promoting them.

Their color and fragrance has hooked me. I am particularly fond of the purples, carmines, and mauves (what V. Sackville-West referred to as Ancien Regime colors; see *Rosa* [Gallica] 'Alain Blanchard' and *Rosa* [Gallica] 'Cardinal de Richelieu' below), and I use them in contrast to a very few light pinks.

Following are some of my favorite Old Shrub Roses, all outstandingly fragrant. This small list is entirely personal and is given only to show the romance of the names involved and the range of colors I use. For these reasons these plants (with the exception of *Rosa* (Gallica) 'Charles de Mills') are not included in the Master Lists, Appendices 1A and 1B.

Readers are encouraged to visit gardens where Old Shrub Roses are grown and to make their own choices at flowering time from among the immense number available. An excellent book on the subject is *The Old Shrub Roses*, by Graham Stuart Thomas, V.M.H. (London: J. M. Dent & Sons Ltd., 1957, with subsequent reprintings).

Descriptions are difficult, since the colors vary with moisture and temperature, whether the plant is in full sun or partial shade, and the age of the particular blossom. These dynamics of course further fuel the aura of romance surrounding Old Shrub Roses.

ROSA (GALLICA) 'ALAIN BLANCHARD'— Mauve blend
ROSA (GALLICA) 'ALICE VENA'—Mauve
ROSA (GALLICA) 'CARDINAL DE RICHELIEU'—Mauve
ROSA (MOSS) 'CRESTED MOSS,' ALSO CALLED 'CHAPEAU DE NAPOLEON'—Medium pink
ROSA (GALLICA) 'CHARLES DE MILLS'— Mauve
ROSA (MOSS) 'DEUIL DE PAUL FONTAINE'—Mauve, deep purple-pink
ROSA (MOSS) 'HENRI MARTIN'— Medium red, deep pink
ROSA (HYBRID BLANDA) 'LILLIAN GIBSON'—Medium pink
ROSA (BOURBON) 'MADAME ISAAC PERRIERE'—Deep pink, raspberry
ROSA (RUGOSA HYBRID) 'ROSERAIE DE L'HAY'—Dark red, mauve
ROSA (SPECIES) GLAUCA (SYN. R. RUBRIFOLIA)—Medium pink, single
ROSA (HYBRID PERPETUAL) 'SOUVENIR DU DOCTEUR JAMAIN'—Dark red, almost black
ROSA (CENTIFOLIA) 'THE BISHOP'— Mauve
ROSA (GALLICA) 'TUSCANY'—Dark maroon-crimson, yellow stamens; the old velvet rose
ROSA (BOURBON) 'VARIEGATA DI BOLOGNA'—Red blend
ROSA (DAMASCENA) 'YORK AND LANCASTER'—Pink blend

APPENDIX 32
Plants Useful for Hedges

The plants in this appendix are recommended because they will produce dense hedges that retain their lower branches.

Plants in this listing are divided into the following categories:

Evergreen—Needle
Evergreen—Broadleaf
Deciduous
Herbaceous

Each category is subdivided by hardiness zone, height of plant, and the following characteristics:

V   Tall and narrow by nature.

N   Naturally well clothed to the ground (shrubs and trees).

P   Performs well when trimmed to a cross-sectional form that is narrow at the top and broader at the base. Most work well because they have, at least to some extent, good horizontal branching characteristics.

T   Possesses thorns or spiny leaves, enhancing its usefulness as a barrier.

Note: Some plants in the lowest size ranges are useful for creating diminutive clipped hedges in ornamental patterns (similar to early needlework) on the ground. The practice is called embroiderie and is more traditionally done with herbaceous plants.

The letter *T* under the heading "Zone" indicates a plant that is tender, not tolerant of frost.

Further information about these plants is summarized in the Master Lists, Appendices 1A and 1B.

EVERGREEN—NEEDLE

ZONE		HEIGHT (FEET)/LATIN NAME
3		3.0–6.5
	N, P	PICEA ABIES 'NIDIFORMIS'
	N, P	TSUGA CANADENSIS 'BENNETT'
	N, P	TSUGA CANADENSIS 'COLE'S PROSTRATE'
		26–52
	V	THUJA OCCIDENTALIS 'NIGRA'
		52 +
	P	TSUGA CANADENSIS
4		1.5–3.0
	N	JUNIPERUS X MEDIA 'PFITZERIANA COMPACTA'
		6.5–13.0
	P	TAXUS CUSPIDATA (CAPITATA SELECTION)
	N, P	TAXUS CUSPIDATA 'NANA'

ZONE	LATIN NAME
5	**1.5–3.0**
P	TAXUS BACCATA 'ADPRESSA FOWLE'
	3.0–6.5
N	JUNIPERUS X MEDIA 'OLD GOLD'
N, P	TAXUS BACCATA 'REPANDENS'
	52 +
P	CHAMAECYPARIS PISIFERA 'SQUARROSA'
V	THUJA PLICATA 'ATROVIRENS'
6	**13–26**
P	CHAMAECYPARIS OBTUSA 'CRIPPSII'
7	**52 +**
P	CEDRUS ATLANTICA 'GLAUCA'

EVERGREEN—BROADLEAF

ZONE	HEIGHT (FEET)/LATIN NAME
5	**1.0–1.5**
N	BUXUS SINICA VAR. INSULARIS 'TIDE HILL'
	1.5–3.0
N	BUXUS SINICA VAR. INSULARIS 'WINTERGREEN' (OHIO CULTIVAR)
N	BUXUS 'GREEN GEM'
	3.0–6.5
N, P	ILEX X MESERVAE BLUE MAID ® 'MESID'
N, P	ILEX X MESERVAE BLUE STALLION ® 'MESAN'
N, P	ILEX CHINA BOY ® 'MESDOB'
N, P	ILEX CHINA GIRL ® 'MESOG'
	6.5–13.0
N	ILEX GLABRA 'DENSA'
	13–26
T, P	ILEX X AQUIPERNYI 'SAN JOSE'
6	**3.0–6.5**
N, P, T	BERBERIS JULIANAE 'NANA'
N, P, T	BERBERIS WISLEYENSIS (SYN. B. TRIACANTHOPHORA)
N	BUXUS SEMPERVIRENS 'SUFFRUTICOSA'
N, P	ILEX CRENATA 'HELLERI'
	6.5–13.0
N, P	ILEX CRENATA 'MICROPHYLLA'
	13–26
N, P, T	ILEX OPACA 'ARDEN'
7	**0.5–1.0**
N	BUXUS MICROPHYLLA 'COMPACTA'
	3.0–6.5
N, P, T	BERBERIS WILSONIAE VAR. STAPFIANA

DECIDUOUS

ZONE	HEIGHT (FEET)/LATIN NAME
3	**3.0–6.5**
N	SPIRAEA X VANHOUTTEI
	13–26
N, P	VIBURNUM PRUNIFOLIUM
4	**1.5–3.0**
N, P, T	BERBERIS THUNBERGII 'CRIMSON PYGMY'
	3.0–6.5
N, P, T	BERBERIS THUNBERGII 'ATROPURPUREA'
N, P	EUONYMUS ALATA 'COMPACTA'
N	SYRINGA PATULA (SYN. S. PALIBINIANA, S. MICROPHYLLA 'INGWERSEN'S DWARF')
N	SPIRAEA THUNBERGII
	6.5–13.0
N, P, T	ACANTHOPANAX SIEBOLDIANUS
N, P	EUONYMUS ALATA
N	MYRICA PENSYLVANICA
N	SYRINGA X CHINENSIS
	13–26
N, P, T	CRATAEGUS NITIDA
N, P, T	CRATAEGUS PHAENOPYRUM
	52 +
P	FAGUS GRANDIFOLIA
5	**3.0–6.5**
N	DAPHNE X BURKWOODII 'CAROL MACKIE'
N	SPIRAEA PRUNIFOLIA
	6.5–13.0
N, P	LONICERA FRAGRANTISSIMA
N, P	VIBURNUM PLICATUM FORMA TOMENTOSUM

ZONE	LATIN NAME
	13–26
P	ACER PALMATUM 'BLOODGOOD'
N, P	CORNUS MAS
N, P	CORNUS OFFICINALIS
	26–52
P	CARPINUS BETULUS
	52 +
P	FAGUS SYLVATICA 'LACINIATA'
P	FAGUS SYLVATICA 'RIVERSII'
N, P	METASEQUOIA GLYPTOSTROBOIDES
6	**0.5–1.5**
N	FORSYTHIA VIRIDISSIMA 'BRONXENSIS'
	3.0–6.5
N	ITEA VIRGINICA 'HENRY'S GARNET'
	6.5–13.0
N, P	FORSYTHIA X INTERMEDIA 'SPRING GLORY'
N, P, T	PONCIRUS TRIFOLIATA
	13–26
N	PHYLLOSTACHYS AUREOSULCATA (This bamboo is useful as a "hedge" only where it can be confined between two belowground barriers, such as masonry, 30 inches deep.)

HERBACEOUS

ZONE	HEIGHT (FEET)/LATIN NAME
3	**3.0–6.5**
N	BAPTISIA AUSTRALIS (Perennial; shrublike in effect, broadleaf.)
T	**3.0–6.5**
N	KOCHIA SCOPARIA FORMA TRICHOPHYLLA 'CHILDSII' (Tender bedding plant; shrublike with light green needle foliage, turning scarlet in the fall.)

APPENDIX 33
Plants Useful for Topiary Standards

The plants recommended in this appendix for use as topiary standards are divided into two categories:

Primarily for Foliage Effect
For Effect of Foliage, Flowers, and/or Fruit

Within each category the plants are arranged according to whether they are evergreen or deciduous (those in the second category are all deciduous) and are subdivided by hardiness zone. The letter *S* indicates a plant requiring the support of a permanent stake.

In the "Primarily for Foliage Effect" category, the plants listed can be made into closely sheared, traditional, ball-on-a-stick standards. Such standards meet the need for a strong architectural statement.

Of equal or greater delight are the standards or "trees" with blossoms or fruit on them during the gardening season, which can be formed with the plants given in the second category. These standards are necessarily less contained than those in the first category because severe clipping would keep them from blossoming and fruiting.

Further information about the following plants is summarized in the Master Lists, Appendices 1A and 1B.

PRIMARILY FOR FOLIAGE EFFECT
Evergreen

ZONE		LATIN NAME
6	S	ILEX CRENATA 'MICROPHYLLA'—Narrow, dark green leaves
		ILEX OPACA 'ARDEN'—Olive green foliage, typical holly shape; red berries
		ILEX OPACA 'XANTHOCARPA'—Olive green foliage, typical holly shape; yellow fruit

Deciduous

ZONE	LATIN NAME
5	CARPINUS BETULUS—Olive green foliage, gray bark
	PRUNUS CERASIFERA 'THUNDERCLOUD'—Wine-colored foliage

FOR EFFECT OF FOLIAGE, FLOWERS AND/OR FRUIT
Deciduous

ZONE	LATIN NAME
3	VIBURNUM PRUNIFOLIUM—Flat heads of creamy white blossoms, May;

foliage deep purple to scarlet in fall; fruit progresses from yellow-green in summer to blue-black in mid-autumn

ZONE		LATIN NAME
4	S	BUDDLEIA ALTERNIFOLIA—Wandlike sprays lined with clusters of lavender blossoms, May
		CRATAEGUS NITIDA—Lustrous leaves turn orange-red in fall; red to orange fruits effective October through most of winter
	S	SYRINGA PATULA (SYN. S. PALIBINIANA, S. MICROPHYLLA 'INGWERSEN'S DWARF')—Lavender blossoms, May
	S	SYRINGA X CHINENSIS—Erect panicles of lavender-to-red-purple florets, late May
5		CORNUS MAS —Clusters of cheerful yellow blossoms, April
	S	HIBISCUS SYRIACUS 'BLUEBIRD'—Blue blossoms with white flower parts, midsummer
	S	HIBISCUS SYRIACUS 'DIANA'—White blossoms, midsummer
		LIGUSTRUM QUIHOUI—Orderly foliage, spikes of showy white blossoms, June; repeat bloom, early fall
	S	SYRINGA LACINIATA—Deeply dissected leaves, pale lavender flowers, May
		VIBURNUM SIEBOLDII 'SENECA'—Lustrous, leathery, bright green foliage; red fruits persist for three months
	S	WISTERIA FLORIBUNDA —Dramatic compound foliage; pendulous inflorescenses of florets in white and pink and shades of lavender and purple, depending on which of many cultivars is selected, May
6		PONCIRUS TRIFOLIATA—Fragrant white blossoms, April; small yellow lemons, fall
7	S	CLERODENDRUM TRICHOTOMUM—Fragrant white blossoms held in red calyces (late summer), followed by bright blue berries; should be planted only where hardiness is assured
	S	PYRACANTHA COCCINEA 'AUREA'—Yellow fruit, fall

APPENDIX 34
Plants Useful for Espaliers

Because considerable investment of effort and time (pruning and tying in at least once annually) is involved in training an espalier, it seems to me desirable to select a subject that provides some special interest or delight at least once during the gardening year. From the large group of plants that lend themselves to espalier work, I have selected the following, largely because of their attractive flowers, fruit, bark, and/or foliage.

The plants in this appendix are divided into two categories:

Evergreen
Deciduous

Each category is subdivided by hardiness zone and then by height of plant. The letter *P* indicates that the plant lends itself to being trained in a more traditional, formal pattern, usually rectilinear in design. (The effectiveness of most of the others depends on carefully following, even exaggerating, the natural habit of the plant.)

Further information about these plants can be found in the Master Lists, Appendices 1A and 1B.

EVERGREEN

ZONE		HEIGHT (FEET)/LATIN NAME
4		6.5–13.0
		TAXUS CUSPIDATA 'NANA'—Stiff, needle-y, dark green foliage
5		3.0–6.5
		ILEX 'CHINA GIRL' ® 'MESOG'—Shiny, horned foliage and red berries
		TAXUS BACCATA 'REPANDENS'—Soft, dark green needles
6		3.0–6.5
		JUNIPERUS CHINENSIS 'KAIZUKA'—Bonsai-like habit
		6.5–13.0
	P	ILEX CRENATA 'MICROPHYLLA'—Boxwoodlike foliage
		13–26
	P	ILEX OPACA 'ARDEN'—Red berries, winter
	P	ILEX OPACA 'XANTHOCARPA'—Yellow berries, winter
7		6.5–13.0
		ELAEAGNUS PUNGENS 'MACULATA'—Gold-and-green-variegated foliage
		13–26
		ELAEAGNUS PUNGENS 'FRUITLANDII'—Gardenia-scented blossoms, October

ZONE	HEIGHT (FEET)/LATIN NAME
	52 +
	CEDRUS ATLANTICA 'GLAUCA'—Blue needle foliage

DECIDUOUS

ZONE	HEIGHT (FEET)/LATIN NAME
4	**3.0–6.5**

CHAENOMELES SPECIOSA CULTIVARS—Branching habit of great character; cultivars available with blossoms pale pink to brilliant red, April

VIBURNUM CARLESII—Charming informal habit; highly fragrant white blossoms, April

6.5–13.0

CORYLUS AVELLANA 'PENDULA'—Attractive pendulous catkins on male plants, late winter

EUONYMUS ALATA—Small red berries, fall; corky bark, winter

HYDRANGEA PANICULATA—Handsome cones of white, August–September

P MALUS SARGENTII—Low horizontal habit; pink buds, white blossoms, May, followed by red fruit, fall

13–26

P CRATAEGUS NITIDA—Orange-red fruits effective October through most of winter

P MALUS FLORIBUNDA—Quintessence of "apple tree": pink buds, white flowers, May, followed by small yellow fruit, fall

MALUS HUPEHENSIS—Striking, open vase shape; pink blossoms, May, followed by yellow and red fruit, fall

TAMARIX RAMOSISSIMA—Blue-green needle foliage; rosy pink blossom in midsummer

| **5** | **1.5–3.0** |

COTONEASTER HORIZONTALIS—Beautiful fanlike branching habit; red berries

6.5–13.0

FORSYTHIA SUSPENSA—Makes a waterfall of yellow, April

HIBISCUS SYRIACUS 'BLUE BIRD'—Blue blossoms with white flower parts, August

HIBISCUS SYRIACUS 'DIANA'—Large glossy white blossoms, August

P VIBURNUM PLICATUM FORMA TOMENTOSUM—Striking horizontal habit to branches and white blossoms, May

13–26

CORNUS KOUSA—Star-shaped white blossoms, late May–early June; multicolored bark, winter

CORNUS OFFICINALIS—Exfoliating bark, winter; clusters of cheerful yellow blossoms, early April

HAMAMELIS MOLLIS 'PALLIDA'—Spidery yellow blossoms, January–March

---

ZONE	HEIGHT (FEET)/LATIN NAME

HAMAMELIS X INTERMEDIA 'DIANE'—Spidery reddish blossoms, February–March

HAMAMELIS X INTERMEDIA 'JELENA'—Spidery orange blossoms, February–March

HAMAMELIS X INTERMEDIA 'PRIMAVERA'—Spidery clear yellow blossoms, February–March

MAGNOLIA X SOULANGIANA 'VERBANICA'—Gray bark, attractive winter flower buds; clear pink blossoms, April

P PRUNUS CERASIFERA 'THUNDERCLOUD'—Deep wine-colored foliage, all summer

PRUNUS 'HALLY JOLIVETTE'—Small tree with fine twigs, fat buds, pink opening to white, April

26–52

MAGNOLIA 'ELIZABETH'—Gray bark, attractive winter flower buds; green-yellow blossoms, May

MAGNOLIA VIRGINIANA—Sweetly scented waxy white blossoms, June, followed by small "cones" of red berries

| **6** | **3.0–6.5** |

ITEA VIRGINICA 'HENRY'S GARNET'—Nodding white panicles, June; foliage turns the color of port wine, fall

6.5–13.0

P PONCIRUS TRIFOLIATA—Spiny green twigs; orange-scented white blossoms, April; yellow lemons, fall

RHODODENDRON (KAEMPFERI HYBRIDS)—Attractive sympodial habit, making a handsome silhouette; cultivars in many shades of pink; foliage orange-yellow, fall

ROSA ROXBURGHII—Attractive small-scale foliage; single violet-pink blossoms, late May–June; flaking cherry-gray bark

13–26

MAGNOLIA 'SUSAN'—Compact form, gray bark, interesting flower buds, winter; purple-pink blossoms, April

STEWARTIA KOREANA—White camellialike flowers, June; bark patterned in cherry, green, and white

26–52

MAGNOLIA DENUDATA (SYN. M. HEPTAPETA)—Gray bark; waxy white cup-shaped blossoms, April

| **7** | **6.5–13.0** |

P PYRACANTHA COCCINEA 'AUREA'—Yellow berries, fall

13–26

P VIBURNUM MACROCEPHALUM FORMA MACROCEPHALUM—Snowball-like blossoms, chartreuse in April, white in May

---

APPENDIX 35
Plants Useful for Clipped Topiary

Before making a selection of a plant for clipped topiary, you should consider carefully the intended shape and size of the object to be portrayed (cone, spiral, pyramid, ball) and the natural shape of the plants recommended here. The closer the match, the more successful the result will be.

The plants in this appendix are divided into two categories:

Evergreen
Deciduous

Each category is subdivided by hardiness zone.

Further information about these plants is summarized in the Master Lists, Appendices 1A and 1B.

EVERGREEN

ZONE	LATIN NAME
3	THUJA OCCIDENTALIS 'NIGRA'
4	TAXUS CUSPIDATA (CAPITATA SELECTION)
5	ILEX CHINA BOY ® 'MESDOB'
	ILEX CHINA GIRL ® 'MESOG'
	ILEX X AQUIPERNYI 'SAN JOSE'
	ILEX X MESERVAE BLUE MAID ® 'MESID'
	ILEX X MESERVAE BLUE STALLION ® 'MESAN'
	TAXUS BACCATA 'ADPRESSA FOWLE'
	THUJA PLICATA 'ATROVIRENS'
6	CHAMAECYPARIS OBTUSA 'CRIPPSII'
	ILEX CRENATA 'MICROPHYLLA'
	ILEX OPACA 'ARDEN'
	ILEX OPACA 'XANTHOCARPA'

DECIDUOUS

ZONE	LATIN NAME
3	VIBURNUM PRUNIFOLIUM
4	ACANTHOPANAX SIEBOLDIANUS
	BERBERIS THUNBERGII 'ATROPURPUREA'
	CRATAEGUS NITIDA
	CRATAEGUS PHAENOPYRUM
	EUONYMUS ALATA
	EUONYMUS ALATA 'COMPACTA'
	FAGUS GRANDIFOLIA
5	CORNUS MAS
	CORNUS OFFICINALIS
	FAGUS SYLVATICA 'LACINIATA'
	FAGUS SYLVATICA 'RIVERSII'

APPENDIX 36
Bulbs for Naturalizing

The bulbs listed in this appendix are but a small sampling of those that can be naturalized in lawns and meadows. They have all performed well for me. In all cases, the area must not be mowed until the bulb foliage has died, in order for the bulbs to continue to bloom well in succeeding years. Bulbs will do best where grass roots are less vigorous and matlike (fescues are ideal) and where they receive an annual feeding.

The bulbs are listed by the month in which they bloom.

Further information about the following plants can be found in the Master Lists, Appendices 1A and 1B.

MONTH	LATIN NAME
MAR.	CROCUS ANCYRENSIS 'GOLDEN BUNCH'—Orange-yellow, style reddish orange
	CROCUS SIEBERI—Dark purple to white, throat orange, style orange-red
	CROCUS TOMASINIANUS—Lavender
	ERANTHIS HYEMALIS—Yellow
	GALANTHUS ELWESII (SUN)—White
	GALANTHUS NIVALIS (SHADE)—White
	LEUCOJUM VERNUM—White tipped with green
	SCILLA SIBIRICA 'SPRING BEAUTY'— Blue
APR.	ANEMONE BLANDA 'ATROCAERULEA'— Dark blue
	CHIONODOXA LUCILIAE—Bright blue with white center
	CHIONODOXA GIGANTEA 'ALBA'— White
	CHIONODOXA SARDENSIS—Sky blue, filaments white
	CROCUS TOMASINIANUS—Lavender
	MUSCARI AZUREUM 'ALBUM'—White
	MUSCARI BOTRYOIDES 'ALBUM'—White
	MUSCARI TUBERGENIANUM—Blue
	NARCISSUS 'CARLTON'—(Large Cup) Yellow
	NARCISSUS 'FORTUNE'—(Large Cup) Yellow, crown deep red-orange
	NARCISSUS 'HERA'—(Leedsi) White
	NARCISSUS 'LOCH FYNE'— (Incomparabilis) White, orange cup
	NARCISSUS 'MOONMIST'—Pale yellow
	NARCISSUS 'MRS. E.H. KRELAGE'— (Trumpet) White with lemon-white cup
	NARCISSUS 'PEEPING TOM'—(Long trumpet) Yellow early
	NARCISSUS ' POMONA'—(Barri) White flat cup, orange fading to apricot and green at center
	NARCISSUS 'TREVITHIAN'—(Barri) Yellow, small cup, very fragrant
	SCILLA SIBIRICA 'SPRING BEAUTY'— Blue
MAY	ENDYMION HISPANICUS 'EXCELSIOR' (SYN. SCILLA CAMPANULATA 'EXCELSIOR')—Blue

MONTH	LATIN NAME
	MERTENSIA VIRGINICA—Blue (not technically a bulb but behaves in a similar manner)
SEP.	COLCHICUM 'AUTUMN QUEEN'—Deep purple checks on a paler ground
	COLCHICUM 'THE GIANT'—Violet with a white base
	LYCORIS SPRENGERI—Rose, purple, carmine, and blue
	LYCORIS SQUAMIGERA—Rose lilac or pink
	STERNBERGIA LUTEA—Yellow
OCT.	CROCUS SPECIOUS—Blue-lavender
	COLCHICUM 'AUTUMN QUEEN'—Deep purple checks on paler ground
	COLCHICUM 'THE GIANT'—Violet with white base
	STERNBERGIA LUTEA—Yellow

APPENDIX 37
Plants for Meadow Effect

There are many situations in contemporary gardens where the close-mowed look is not desirable and that of an established meadow is. For the meadow effect to be as maintenance-free as possible, hardy perennials and biennial plants should be used rather than the annuals that predominate in many of the "meadow-in-a-can" seed mixes being advertised. To help nature along with this natural look, there is no reason that the showiest top performers and best cultivars among the perennials and biennials shouldn't be used. The following list gives some recommendations. Determine the soil and moisture conditions of your site and, after studying these plants in Appendix 1A, choose those that fit your conditions.

The area should be seeded with the less aggressive sorts of meadow grasses after you've prepared the soil. It is best to select grasses native to your own area and to use more than one kind. I recommend clump formers rather than mat formers. The former are less likely to crowd out the biennials and perennials. Examples are *Sporobolus heterolepis, Koeleria cristata, Schizachyrium scoparium*, and *Andropogon virginicus*. Allow the grasses to become established for a year before planting pot- or field-grown biennials and perennials.

The plants in this appendix are listed by time of landscape interest, which includes foliage (*Imperata cylindrica* 'Red Baron' in August; *Iris pseudacorus* in October) and seed heads (*Echinops ritro* in August; *Rudbeckia fulgida* var. *Sullivantii* 'Goldsturm' in September and October), as well as blossoms.

Further information about the following plants is summarized in the Master Lists, Appendices 1A and 1B.

MONTH	LATIN NAME
JUN.	ACHILLEA MILLEFOLIUM 'ROSEA'
	BAPTISIA AUSTRALIS
	CAMPANULA RAPUNCULOIDES
	CIMICIFUGA RACEMOSA
	FILIPENDULA PURPUREA 'ELEGANS'
	HELIOPSIS HELIANTHOIDES SUBSP. SCABRA 'KARAT'
	HEMEROCALLIS FULVA 'EUROPA'
	HEMEROCALLIS 'HYPERION'
	HERACLEUM MANTEGAZZIANUM
	IMPERATA CYLINDRICA 'RED BARON'
	IRIS PSEUDACOROUS
	IRIS SIBIRICA CULTIVARS
	LIATRIS SCARIOSA 'WHITE SPIRE'
	LIATRIS SPICATA 'KOBOLD'
	LILIUM 'BLACK DRAGON'
	LILIUM SPECIES AND HYBRIDS
	LYSIMACHIA PUNCTATA
	MISCANTHUS SINENSIS 'SILVER FEATHER' (='SILBERFEDER')
	MOLINIA CAERULEA SUBSP. ARUNDINACEA
	MONARDA DIDYMA
	PANICUM VIRGATUM 'STRICTUM'
	SAPONARIA OFFICINALIS
	SYMPHYTUM X UPLANDICUM
	TELEKIA SPECIOSA
	THALICTRUM ROCHEBRUNIANUM
	THERMOPSIS CAROLINIANA
JUL.	ASCLEPIAS TUBEROSA
	ASTER AMELLUS 'NOCTURNE'
	BUPHTHALUM SALICIFOLIUM
	CALAMAGROSTIS X ACUTIFLORA 'KARL FOERSTER' (SYN. C. EPIGEOUS 'HORTORUM')
	CAMPANULA RAPUNCULOIDES
	CIMICIFUGA RACEMOSA
	ECHINACEA PURPUREA
	ECHINOPS RITRO
	EUPHORBIA COROLLATA
	HELIOPSIS HELIANTHOIDES SUBSP. SCABRA 'KARAT'
	HEMEROCALLIS FULVA 'EUROPA'
	HEMEROCALLIS 'HYPERION'
	INULA HELENIUM
	IMPERATA CYLINDRICA 'RED BARON'
	IRIS PSEUDACOROUS
	LIATRIS SCARIOSA 'WHITE SPIRE'
	LIATRIS SPICATA 'KOBOLD'
	LILIUM 'BLACK DRAGON'
	LILIUM SPECIES AND HYBRIDS
	LYSIMACHIA PUNCTATA
	MISCANTHUS SINENSIS 'SILVER FEATHER' (='SILBERFEDER')
	MOLINIA CAERULEA SUBSP. ARUNDINACEA
	MONARDA DIDYMA
	NEPETA X FAASSENII
	PANICUM VIRGATUM 'STRICTUM'
	PEROVSKIA ABROTANOIDES X P. ATRIPLICIFOLIA
	RUDBECKIA FULGIDA VAR. SULLIVANTII 'GOLDSTURM'
	SAPONARIA OFFICINALIS
	THALICTRUM ROCHEBRUNIANUM
	VERONICA LONGIFOLIA 'SUBSESSILIS'

MONTH	LATIN NAME
AUG.	ASTER AMELLUS 'NOCTURNE'
	CALAMAGROSTIS X ACUTIFLORA
	'KARL FOERSTER'
	CHELONE LYONII
	ECHINACEA PURPUREA
	ECHINOPS RITRO
	IMPERATA CYLINDRICA 'RED BARON'
	IRIS PSEUDACOROUS
	LYSIMACHIA CLETHROIDES
	MISCANTHUS SINENSIS 'SILVER
	FEATHER' (='SILBERFEDER')
	MOLINIA CAERULEA SUBSP.
	ARUNDINACEA
	PANICUM VIRGATUM 'STRICTUM'
	PENNISETUM ALOPECUROIDES
	PEROVSKIA ABROTANOIDES X P.
	ATRIPLICIFOLIA
	PHYSOSTEGIA VIRGINIANA
	PHYSOSTEGIA VIRGINIANA 'SUMMER
	SNOW'
	RUDBECKIA FULGIDA VAR.
	SULLIVANTII 'GOLDSTURM'
	SAPONARIA OFFICINALIS
	THALICTRUM ROCHEBRUNIANUM
	VERNONIA NOVEBORACENSIS
	VERONICA LONGIFOLIA 'SUBSESSILIS'
	VERONICASTRUM VIRGINIANUM
SEP.	ASTER NOVAE-ANGLIAE
	'HARRINGTON'S PINK'
	ASTER PUNICEUS
	ASTER TATARICUS
	BOLTONIA ASTEROIDES 'SNOWBANK'
	CALAMAGROSTIS X ACUTIFLORA
	'KARL FOERSTER'
	(SYN. C. EPIGEOUS 'HORTORUM')
	CHELONE LYONII
	EUPATORIUM COELESTINUM
	HELIANTHUS SALICIFOLIUS
	IMPERATA CYLINDRICA 'RED BARON'
	IRIS PSEUDACOROUS
	MISCANTHUS SINENSIS 'SILVER
	FEATHER' (='SILBERFEDER')
	MOLINIA CAERULEA SUBSP.
	ARUNDINACEA
	PANICUM VIRGATUM 'STRICTUM'
	PENNISETUM ALOPECUROIDES
	PHYSOSTEGIA VIRGINIANA
	PHYSOSTEGIA VIRGINIANA 'SUMMER
	SNOW'
	RUDBECKIA FULGIDA VAR.
	SULLIVANTII 'GOLDSTURM'
	VERNONIA NOVEBORACENSIS
OCT.	ASTER NOVAE-ANGLIAE
	'HARRINGTON'S PINK'
	ASTER PUNICEUS
	ASTER TATARICUS
	BOLTONIA ASTEROIDES 'SNOWBANK'
	CALAMAGROSTIS X ACUTIFLORA
	'KARL FOERSTER'
	(SYN. C. EPIGEOUS 'HORTORUM')
	EUPATORIUM COELESTINUM
	HELIANTHUS SALICIFOLIUS
	IMPERATA CYLINDRICA 'RED BARON'
	IRIS PSEUDACOROUS
	MISCANTHUS SINENSIS 'SILVER
	FEATHER' (='SILBERFEDER')
	MOLINIA CAERULEA SUBSP.
	ARUNDINACEA
	PANICUM VIRGATUM 'STRICTUM'
	PENNISETUM ALOPECUROIDES
	RUDBECKIA FULGIDA VAR.
	SULLIVANTII 'GOLDSTURM'

APPENDIX 38
Some Favorite Plant Combinations

I have chosen to end the Appendices with this list of thirty plant combinations. Although lists of plants for various purposes may be valuable tools, it is important to remember that the combinations are the ultimate objective.

These combinations also serve to emphasize the fact that gardens can provide wonderfully rich experiences every month of the year. All we have to do is adapt the choreography to our needs and desires.

I have included combinations for those months when we are most likely to be outdoors. Whereas only one combination each is shown for January, February, March, November, and December, two are given for September and October, and three or more for April, May, June, July, and August.

The annual psychological peak of interest in gardening usually comes in early May. This enthusiasm begins building during the fall before and reaches fever pitch in March and April. Then, with the approach of vacation time and the dog days of summer, attention to gardening traditionally declines from mid-May through August. As the following lists show, such a decline is hardly justified, considering the many delightful effects that can be achieved during these months. Since the increasing popularity of the swimming pool has meant a growing trend toward outdoor living in summertime, the effects you can create during this season are particularly significant.

More than 225 plants are used in the following combinations. To demonstrate the diversity of plants available, I have used each plant only once during the course of the year—even though many plants do, of course, have more than one season of interest—and I have assumed that the gardener is interested in a display each month. As a matter of actual practice, some gardeners may prefer to have their garden remain passive during some seasons. Certainly there may be many fewer kinds of plants in any single garden than are shown here. This exercise is done to show maximum potential.

These combinations are not meant to be transferred literally into any one garden. My aim is simply to encourage the reader to study them as samples of the possibilities that are available. He or she will be best rewarded by deciding what works best under the given site conditions and in line with personal preferences. See the Master Lists, Appendices 1A and 1B, for more information about individual plants.

Please note how each combination features a plant or group of plants as a center of interest. The other plants in the combination are a sort of support system. Some structure the scheme; some provide contrasts of texture or assist in carrying out the color objective; and the ground covers reinforce the above and do the very important job of tying it all together. These principles are further elucidated in Chapters 1–5.

The figures given in parentheses after each Latin name indicate the number of each plant to be used.

All plant names are listed within each category by order of height (from tallest to lowest), with the exception of those in the category "Ground Cover," which are arranged alphabetically.

JANUARY

Structure:
   BETULA NIGRA (1)
   PINUS DENSIFLORA 'UMBRACULIFERA' (1)
   CYTISUS PRAECOX 'LUTEUS' (5)

Center of Interest:
   CHIMONANTHUS PRAECOX (1)

Texture, Broad:
   COTONEASTER SALICIFOLIUS VAR.
     FLOCCOSUS (3)
   LEUCOTHOE FONTANESIANA (25)

Texture, Fine:
   TSUGA CANADENSIS 'COLE'S PROSTRATE' (4)

Ground Cover:
   ARUM ITALICUM 'PICTUM' (9)
   PAXISTIMA CANBYI (300)

The fat jewellike buds of *Chimonanthus* become fragrant yellow flowers and open sequentially on warm days during January and February. They are borne on a plant of open airy form, featured here in a three-level ground cover planting of contrasting broadleaf (*Arum*) and needle (*Tsuga* and *Paxistima*) foliage texture. The rich background features rusty bark colors (*Betula* and *Pinus*), bronze foliage (*Cotoneaster* and *Leucothoe*), and bright green twigs (*Cytisus*).

FEBRUARY

Structure:
   PINUS THUNBERGIANA 'OCULUS
     DRACONIS' (3)
   ACER GRISEUM (1)
   ILEX X AQUIPERNYI 'SAN JOSE' (5)

Center of Interest:
   HAMAMELIS MOLLIS 'PALLIDA' (1)

Texture, Broad:
   SKIMMIA REEVESIANA (9)
   CORNUS SERICEA 'FLAVIRAMEA' (4)
   PONCIRUS TRIFOLIATA (3)

Texture, Fine:
   MICROBIOTA DECUSSATA (15)

Ground Cover:
   EUONYMUS FORTUNEI VAR. RADICANS
     (300)
   YUCCA FLACCIDA 'GOLDEN SWORD' (3)

Against a background of dark green (*Ilex*, foliage; *Skimmia*, foliage; *Poncirus*, twigs; and *Euonymus*, foliage) and rusty purple (*Acer*, bark; and *Microbiota*, foliage), the spidery yellow blossoms of this *Hamamelis* (our earliest-flowering Witch-hazel) alternately curl and uncurl, depending on the weather. In addition to the sparkle of red berries (*Ilex* and *Skimmia*), the picture is enhanced by repetition of yellow in the foliage variegation of the *Pinus* and *Yucca* and the twig color of the *Cornus*.

MARCH

Structure:
    CORYLUS COLURNA (3)

Center of Interest:
    HAMAMELIS X INTERMEDIA 'PRIMAVERA' (1)
    HAMAMELIS X INTERMEDIA 'JELENA' (3)
    HAMAMELIS X INTERMEDIA 'DIANE' (5)

Texture, Broad:
    SALIX GRACILISTYLA 'MELANOSTACHYS' (1)
    RUBUS COCKBURNIANUS (5)
    KERRIA JAPONICA (5)

Texture, Fine:
    TAXUS BACCATA 'REPANDENS' (7)

Ground Cover:
    JASMINUM NUDIFLORUM (12)
    VINCA MINOR 'BOWLESII' (1,000)
    Underplanted with:
        ADONIS AMURENSIS (12)
        CROCUS TOMASINIANUS (300)
        ERANTHIS HYEMALIS (50)
        GALANTHUS ELWESII (100)
        LEUCOJUM VERNUM (50)

Black catkins (*Salix*), gray bark (*Corylus*), and white (*Rubus*) and bright green twigs (*Kerria* and *Jasminum*), all combined with the dark green foliage of *Vinca* and *Taxus*, provide a delightfully offbeat background for a medley of clear yellow ('Primavera'), orange ('Jelena'), and rust red ('Diane') hybrid *Hamamelis* blossoms. Their color and fine detail are enhanced by a carpet of diminutive bulbs in white (*Galanthus* and *Leucojum*), yellow (*Eranthis* and *Adonis*), and silvery lavender (*Crocus*).

EARLY APRIL

Structure:
    SALIX X RUBRA 'EUGENEI' (5)
    CORNUS OFFICINALIS (7)

Center of Interest:
    MAGNOLIA DENUDATA (SYN. M.
        HEPTAPETA) (1)

Texture, Broad:
    SALIX CHAENOMELOIDES (1)
    SALIX GRACILISTYLA (3)
    MAHONIA BEALEI (7)

Texture, Fine:
    JUNIPERUS HORIZONTALIS 'WILTONII' (15)

Ground Cover:
    HELLEBORUS NIGER (300)
    Interplanted with:
        CHIONODOXA GIGANTEA 'ALBA' (300)
        TRACHYSTEMON ORIENTALE (25)
    Underplanted with:
        NARCISSUS 'PEEPING TOM' (12)

Magnolia denudata (Yulan Magnolia) becomes a large tree and bears incomparable waxy white blossoms, which are echoed by those of the *Helleborus*. The three *Salix* provide silvery catkins of varying shapes, which sparkle

in the breeze and contrast with the yellow blossoms of the *Cornus*, *Mahonia*, and *Narcissus*. The foliage of *Mahonia* and *Juniperus* and blossoms of *Trachystemon* pick up the beautiful blue of the spring sky.

LATE APRIL: A

Structure:
    PICEA ORIENTALIS (4)
    SALIX ALBA 'TRISTIS' (1)

Center of Interest:
    CERCIS CHINENSIS (3)

Texture, Broad:
    VIBURNUM MACROCEPHALUM FORMA
        MACROCEPHALUM (4)

Texture, Fine:
    CEPHALOTAXUS HARRINGTONIA VAR.
        PEDUNCULATA (3)

Ground Cover:
    HEMEROCALLIS FULVA 'EUROPA' (25)
    PULMONARIA ANGUSTIFOLIA (300)
    SALIX REPENS VAR. ARGENTEA (9)
    Underplanted with:
        MERTENSIA VIRGINICA (200)
        VIOLA LABRADORICA (150)
    Interplanted with:
        DICENTRA SPECTABILIS (3)

The dark green foliage of *Picea* and *Cephalotaxus*, combined with the light green foliage of *Salix alba* 'Tristis' and *Hemerocallis* and the chartreuse of the *Viburnum* blossoms, provides a perfect foil for the delightful, shocking mauve of the *Cercis*, with its related coterie of flowers: blue (*Pulmonaria* and *Mertensia*), pink (*Dicentra*), and purple (*Viola*) and silver (*Salix repens* var. *argentea*) catkins.

LATE APRIL: B

Structure:
    MAGNOLIA 'ELIZABETH' (1)

Center of Interest:
    CHAENOMELES X SUPERBA 'ROWALLANE' (3)

Texture, Broad:
    RIBES ODORATUM (5)

Texture, Fine:
    SPIRAEA THUNBERGII (15)

Ground Cover:
    EPIMEDIUM PINNATUM SUBSP. COLCHICUM
        (12)
    PHLOX BIFIDA (100)
    Underplanted with:
        MUSCARI TUBERGENIANUM (50)
        FRITILLARIA MELEAGRIS (50)
        NARCISSUS 'TREVITHIAN' (12)

The yellow flowers of *Magnolia* and *Ribes* and feathery white blossoms of *Spiraea* have been chosen as background for the orange-red blossoms of the *Chaenomeles*, strikingly displayed on zigzag branches. A rich ground cover of blue (*Phlox* and *Muscari*), wine (*Fritillaria*), and yellow (*Epimedium* and *Narcissus*) blossoms enhances the foreground.

EARLY MAY: A

Structure:
    CERCIDIPHYLLUM JAPONICUM (1)

Center of Interest:
    TULIPA 'QUEEN OF THE NIGHT' (30)

Texture, Broad:
    VIBURNUM CARLESII (5)

Texture, Fine:
    DENNSTAEDTIA PUNCTILOBULA (300)

Ground Cover:
    HOSTA 'KABITAN' (50)
    LATHYRUS VERNUS (25)

The boldness of these black-purple tulips is contrasted with a series of spring subtleties: the pink of tiny emerging leaves (*Cercidiphyllum*) and fragrant blossoms (*Viburnum*); the light green of fern fronds (*Dennstaedtia*) and young golden-variegated foliage (*Hosta*); and the remarkably wonderful blue-and-mauve-lavender bicolor blossoms of the *Lathyrus*.

EARLY MAY: B

Structure:
    AMELANCHIER ARBOREA (SYN. A.
        CANADENSIS) (3)

Center of Interest:
    RHODODENDRON SCHLIPPENBACHII (7)

Texture, Broad:
    VIBURNUM PLICATUM FORMA
        TOMENTOSUM (5)

Texture, Fine:
    OSMUNDA REGALIS (300)

Ground Cover:
    HOSTA UNDULATA 'ALBO-MARGINATA' (25)
    IRIS CRISTATA (300)

In a puddle of blue flowers (*Iris*), the elegantly structured *Rhododendron* carry large, soft pink blossoms featured against white and green: the green of fern fronds (*Osmunda*), the white blossoms of *Amelanchier* and *Viburnum*, amid the green and white foliage of *Hosta*.

MID-MAY: A

Structure:
    CHIONANTHUS VIRGINICUS (1)

Center of Interest:
    IRIS GERMANICA 'SABLE NIGHT' (12)

Texture, Broad:
    PAEONIA 'BLACK PIRATE' (5)

Texture, Fine:
    GALIUM ODORATUM (300)

Ground Cover:
    GERANIUM 'JOHNSON'S BLUE' (150)

Blue (*Geranium*) and maroon (*Paeonia*) blossoms and light green foliage (*Galium*) were chosen here to feature this especially handsome dark purple *Iris*. The white blossoms of the *Chionanthus* and *Galium* are unobtrusive but add sparkle to the scene.

MID-MAY: B

Structure:
    WISTERIA FLORIBUNDA 'MACROBOTRYS' (1)
    (trained as a tree)

Center of Interest:
    IRIS SIBIRICA 'FLIGHT OF BUTTERFLIES' (3)

Texture, Broad:
    COTINUS COGGYGRIA 'PURPUREUS' (3)
    SYRINGA PATULA (SYN. S. PALIBINIANA, S. MICROPHYLLA 'INGWERSEN'S DWARF') (7)

Texture, Fine:
    AMSONIA HUBRICHTII (25)

Ground Cover:
    BERBERIS THUNBERGII 'CRIMSON PYGMY' (10)

Groupings of maroon foliage (*Cotinus* and *Berberis*) and lavender (*Syringa*) and pale blue (*Amsonia*) blossoms are suggested to show off the clump of blue-veined *Iris* featured below the *Wisteria* (long, pendulous lavender blossoms).

LATE MAY–EARLY JUNE: A

Structure:
    CORNUS ALTERNIFOLIA (3)

Center of Interest:
    IRIS PSEUDACORUS (1)

Texture, Broad:
    RHEUM PALMATUM 'RUBRUM' (3)
    RODGERSIA AESCULIFOLIA (30)

Texture, Fine:
    TYPHA ANGUSTIFOLIA (5)

Ground Cover:
    CONVALLARIA MAJALIS (300)
    FILIPENDULA ULMARIA 'AUREA' (9)

For a water's-edge location. The vertical qualities of this elegant yellow-flowered *Iris* are echoed by the *Typha* and contrast with the *Cornus*. The yellow of the *Iris* blossoms is echoed by the *Filipendula* foliage and teased by the green-pink of the *Rheum* blossoms and the white-pink blossoms of the *Rodgersia*. The white of the *Cornus* blossoms is repeated by those of the *Convallaria*.

LATE MAY–EARLY JUNE: B

Structure:
    PRUNUS CERASIFERA 'THUNDERCLOUD' (3)

Center of Interest:
    ASPHODELINE LUTEA (5)

Texture, Broad:
    RHODODENDRON (KNAP HILL HYBRID) 'TUNIS' (10)

Texture, Fine:
    BERBERIS WISLEYENSIS (SYN. B. TRIACANTHOPHORA) (15)

Ground Cover:
    PARONYCHIA KAPELA SUBSP. SERPYLLIFOLIA (300)
    SEDUM SPURIUM 'BRONZE CARPET' (50)

Maroon-wine foliage (*Prunus* and *Sedum*), orange-flushed brick-red blossoms (*Rhododendron*), and light green foliage (*Berberis*) are grouped here to show off the dramatic yellow flower spike of *Asphodeline*. The narrow gray foliage of the Asphodel contrasts with the rounded foliage of the *Paronychia* (diminutive) and *Sedum* (larger).

LATE MAY–EARLY JUNE: C

Structure:
    CORNUS KOUSA (3)

Center of Interest:
    ONOPORDUM ACANTHIUM (1)

Texture, Broad:
    PHILADELPHUS CORONARIUS (5)
    CORNUS ALBA 'ELEGANTISSIMA' (4)

Texture, Fine:
    INDIGOFERA INCARNATA 'ALBA' (50)

Ground Cover:
    LAMIUM MACULATUM 'WHITE NANCY' (300)

This tour de force of white and gray features a silver-foliaged thistle, *Onopordum*, grown for the sculptural qualities of its form and spiny leaves. White blossoms are provided by the *Cornus kousa*, *Philadelphus*, *Indigofera*, and *Lamium*. Additional gray effects are produced by the green-and-white-variegated foliage of the *Lamium* and the *Cornus alba*.

LATE MAY–EARLY JUNE: D

Structure:
    CHAMAECYPARIS OBTUSA 'CRIPPSII' (3)

Center of Interest:
    HERACLEUM MANTEGAZZIANUM (1)

Texture, Broad:
    CORNUS ALBA 'SPAETHII' (3)
    ARUNDINARIA VIRIDISTRIATA (5)

Texture, Fine:
    CHAMAECYPARIS PISIFERA 'GOLD SPANGLE' (12)

Ground Cover:
    HEDERA HELIX 'BUTTERCUP' (300)
    INULA HELENIUM (7)

A medley of gold and green has been selected as a setting for one of the plant kingdom's finest pieces of sculpture: the white-flowered Giant Hogweed, *Heracleum mantegazzianum*. Golden yellow flowers of *Inula* are supplemented by the golden foliage of the *Chamaecyparis pisifera* and the green and golden foliage of *Chamaecyparis obtusa* and the *Cornus*, *Arundinaria*, and *Hedera*.

LATE MAY–EARLY JUNE: E

Structure:
    AESCULUS SPLENDENS (3)

Center of Interest:
    SALVIA PRAETENSIS 'INDIGO' (3)

Texture, Broad:
    PRUNUS X CISTENA (5)
    KOLKWITZIA AMABILIS (3)
    BAPTISIA AUSTRALIS (15)
    SYMPHYTUM X UPLANDICUM (12)

Texture, Fine:
    SOPHORA DAVIDII (7)

Ground Cover:
    HELIANTHEMUM APPENINUM VAR. ROSEUM (300)

The handsome lavender-blue spikes of this *Salvia* (echoed by those of the *Baptisia*) have been chosen as the centerpiece for an exuberant palette of pinks (*Aesculus, Kolkwitzia, Helianthemum*), maroons (*Prunus*) and blues (*Symphytum* and *Sophora*). Rich twists are added by the touches of apricot in the *Aesculus* and of yellow in the *Kolkwitzia* and by the grayed quality of the *Sophora* blue.

MID-JUNE: A

Structure:
 SALIX ELAEAGNOS (1)

Center of Interest:
 HYDRANGEA MACROPHYLLA 'BLUE BILLOW'
 (5)

Texture, Broad:
 POLYGONATUM ODORATUM 'VARIEGATA'
 (12)

Texture, Fine:
 OSMUNDA CLAYTONIANA (25)

Ground Cover:
 PACHYSANDRA TERMINALIS 'SILVER EDGE'
 (300)

The combination of gray and green has been selected as a foil for this unusually hardy, refreshingly rich blue lacecap Hydrangea. The gray of the narrow foliage of the Salix is picked up by the green and white foliages of the Polygonatum and Pachysandra. The green fern foliage (Osmunda) enhances the cooling effect of the blue hydrangea.

MID-JUNE: B

Structure:
 KOELREUTERIA PANICULATA (1)

Center of Interest:
 CIMICIFUGA RACEMOSA (3)

Texture, Broad:
 HYDRANGEA QUERCIFOLIA (12)
 TELEKIA SPECIOSA (9)

Texture, Fine:
 ACORUS GRAMINEUS 'OGON' (12)

Ground Cover:
 HOUTTUYNIA CORDATA 'CHAMELEON' (100)

The white spikes of Cimicifuga pick up on the heavy conelike white blossoms of the Hydrangea and add spice to this mid-June planting of yellow blossoms (Koelreuteria and Telekia) and gold and green foliage (Acorus and Houttuynia; the latter foliage also includes pink).

MID-JUNE: C

Structure:
 STEWARTIA KOREANA (3)

Center of Interest:
 LILIUM 'BLACK DRAGON' (5)

Texture, Broad:
 BUDDLEIA ALTERNIFOLIA (4)
 ECHINACEA PURPUREA (12)

Texture, Fine:
 THALICTRUM ROCHEBRUNIANUM (7)

Ground Cover:
 ARUNCUS AETHUSIFOLIUS (50)
 SAXIFRAGA STOLONIFERA (100)

The robust, white, highly scented Lilium 'Black Dragon' is featured with violet-lavender (Buddleia, Echinacea, and Thalictrum) and white (Stewartia, Aruncus, and Saxifraga) blossoms. The pink and orange overtones of the Echinacea, mistlike quality of the Thalictrum, and distinctly contrasting foliage textures of the ground covers add special charm.

JULY: A

Structure:
 METASEQUOIA GLYPTOSTROBOIDES (1)

Center of Interest:
 SORBARIA SORBIFOLIA (3)

Texture, Broad:
 HOSTA SIEBOLDIANA 'ELEGANS' (25)
 HYDRANGEA ASPERA SUBSP. SARGENTIANA
 (9)

Texture, Fine:
 ATHYRIUM GOERINGIANUM 'PICTUM' (300)
 BUPHTHALUM SALICIFOLIUM (50)

Ground Cover:
 ASARUM EUROPAEUM (500)

Plumes of white and dramatic dark green foliage characterize the Sorbaria, which is seen against the violet-flowered lacecap Hydrangea and light green needle foliage of Metasequoia. Blue (Hosta), gray (Athyrium), and dark green (Asarum) foliage and yellow flowers (Buphthalum) cover the ground in bold interlocking sweeps.

JULY: B

Structure:
 ARALIA SPINOSA (4)
 PAULOWNIA TOMENTOSA (1)

Center of Interest:
 ARUNDO DONAX (1)

Texture, Broad:
 PETASITES JAPONICUS (50)

Texture, Fine:
 MISCANTHUS SINENSIS 'STRICTUS' (10)

Ground Cover:
 LIRIOPE MUSCARI 'VARIEGATA' (500)

The giant, dramatic, cornlike grass Arundo is featured among contrasting foliage textures: rounded (Paulownia and Petasites), compound (Aralia), and linear (Miscanthus and Liriope). Gold spots, contrasted with the green of the Miscanthus foliage, and linear stripes of gold, contrasted with the green of the Liriope foliage, provide color liveliness.

JULY: C

Structure:
 BUDDLEIA DAVIDII 'BLACK KNIGHT' (3)
 BUDDLEIA DAVIDII 'OPERA' (1)
 BUDDLEIA DAVIDII 'PURPLE PRINCE' (2)

Center of Interest:
 LIATRIS SPICATA 'KOBOLD' (3)

Texture, Broad:
 ASCLEPIAS TUBEROSA (9)
 RUDBECKIA FULGIDA VAR. SULLIVANTII
 'GOLDSTURM' (15)

Texture, Fine:
 PEROVSKIA ABROTANOIDES X P.
 ATRIPLICIFOLIA (6)
 PANICUM VIRGATUM 'STRICTUM' (3)

Ground Cover:
 COREOPSIS 'MOONBEAM' (100)
 VERONICA 'SUNNY BORDER BLUE' (3)

A grouping of drought-tolerant, nodding, butterfly-clothed Buddleias surrounded by drifts of tough perennials seems appropriate for high summer. Spikes of mauve Liatris are the focal point, echoing the color of Buddleia davidii 'Opera.' The color scheme uses purple (the other two Buddleias and Panicum), orange (Asclepias), yellow (Rudbeckia and Coreopsis), and blue (Perovskia and Veronica) to complete the exuberance.

AUGUST: A

Structure:
 HIBISCUS SYRIACUS 'BLUEBIRD' (3)

Center of Interest:
 VITEX AGNUS-CASTUS 'LATIFOLIA' (1)

Texture, Broad:
 BERBERIS THUNBERGII 'ATROPURPUREA' (5)

Texture, Fine:
 INDIGOFERA GERARDIANA (25)
 CARYOPTERIS X CLANDONENSIS 'BLUE
 MIST' (7)

Ground Cover:
 ASTER FRIKARTI 'MONCH' (5)
 SEDUM 'VERA JAMISON' (100)

In a sea of pink (Indigofera and Sedum), violet-blue (Aster), and blue (Caryopteris), the blue spikes of Vitex are displayed against the wine foliage of the Berberis and the white-centered blue blossoms of the Hibiscus. The result is a refreshing picture on a hot day.

AUGUST: B

Structure:
 SALIX ALBA 'SERICEA' (1)

Center of Interest:
 VITEX AGNUS-CASTUS 'SILVER SPIRE' (1)

Texture, Broad:
 HYDRANGEA PANICULATA (3)
 HIBISCUS SYRIACUS 'DIANA' (5)

Texture, Fine:
 EUPHORBIA COROLLATA (12)
 CHAMAECYPARIS OBTUSA 'NANA GRACILIS'
 (4)
 MISCANTHUS SINENSIS 'CABARET' (3)

Ground Cover:
    ALLIUM TUBEROSUM (5)
    STACHYS BYZANTINA (300)

This subtle combination is of special charm in the low light of a summer evening. Silver (*Salix*), dark green (*Chamaecyparis*), green and white (*Miscanthus*), and gray (*Stachys*) foliages complement a rich collection of white flower forms (*Hydrangea*, *Hibiscus*, *Euphorbia*, and *Allium*), which reaches its finest moment in the spikes of *Vitex agnus-castus* 'Silver Spire.'

AUGUST: C

Structure:
    CLETHRA BARBINERVIS (1)

Center of Interest:
    HOSTA PLANTAGINEA (3)

Texture, Broad:
    BEGONIA GRANDIS (15)

Texture, Fine:
    POLYSTICHUM TRIPTERON (100)

Ground Cover:
    LIRIOPE MUSCARI 'BIG BLUE' (300)

Light green foliage and fragrant white flowers make this old-time *Hosta* a winner worth featuring in any late-summer garden. It reigns here beneath the pendulous white blossoms of the *Clethra* in a bed of contrasting foliages: oval (*Begonia*), fernlike (*Polystichum*), and linear (*Liriope*). Pink (*Begonia*) and blue (*Liriope*) blossoms sweeten the scene.

SEPTEMBER: A

Structure:
    COTINUS COGGYGRIA 'PURPUREUS' (1)

Center of Interest:
    LYCORIS SPRENGERI (12)

Texture, Broad:
    LESPEDEZA THUNBERGII (3)

Texture, Fine:
    PENNISETUM ALOPECUROIDES (12)
    IMPERATA CYLINDRICA 'RED BARON' (3)

Ground Cover:
    CERATOSTIGMA PLUMBAGINOIDES (300)
    COLCHICUM AUTUMNALE (15)

The striking purple, blue, and pink markings of the (bulbous) *Lycoris* flowers serve to pull together an unusual fall color scheme: mauve (*Lespedeza*), blue (*Ceratostigma*), lavender (*Colchicum*), and red (*Imperata*), all seen against the deep claret foliage of *Cotinus*.

SEPTEMBER: B

Structure:
    MISCANTHUS SINENSIS 'VARIEGATA' (3)

Center of Interest:
    EQUISETUM HYEMALE (3)

Texture, Broad:
    LESPEDEZA THUNBERGII 'ALBIFLORA' (7)

Texture, Fine:
    BOLTONIA ASTEROIDES 'SNOWBANK' (12)

Ground Cover:
    LIRIOPE MUSCARI 'MONROE WHITE' (300)

The green, black-banded, leafless stems of the 200-million-year-old Mesozoic Era Scouring Rush (*Equisetum hyemale*) are a mysterious and enchanting focal point for an all-white planting: green-and-white-variegated foliage (*Miscanthus*) and white flowers (*Lespedeza*, *Boltonia*, and *Liriope*).

OCTOBER: A

Structure:
    PONCIRUS TRIFOLIATA (3)

Center of Interest:
    HELIANTHUS SALICIFOLIUS (1)

Texture, Broad:
    VIBURNUM SETIGERUM (2)
    CALLICARPA DICHOTOMA (15)

Texture, Fine:
    MOLINIA CAERULEA SUBSP. ARUNDINACEA (5)

Ground Cover:
    CHRYSANTHEMUM WEYRICHII 'WHITE BOMB' (100)

Yellow (*Poncirus*), red (*Viburnum*), and purple (*Callicarpa*) fruits, highlighted by Purple Moor Grass (*Molinia*), provide a rich background for the sculptural *Helianthus*, whose wandlike branches, covered with yellow daisies, move gracefully in the breeze. The dark green foliage and white blossoms of the *Chrysanthemum* cover the ground below.

OCTOBER: B

Structure:
    PSEUDOLARIX KAEMPFERI (1)

Center of Interest:
    MISCANTHUS SINENSIS 'SILVER FEATHER' (='SILBERFEDER') (1)

Texture, Broad:
    ITEA VIRGINICA 'HENRY'S GARNET' (7)
    VIBURNUM DILATATUM 'MICHAEL DODGE' (5)

Texture, Fine:
    TAXUS CUSPIDATA 'NANA' (5)

Ground Cover:
    GERANIUM MACRORRHIZUM (100)
    VINCA MINOR 'VARIEGATA' (300)
    Underplanted with:
        CROCUS SPECIOSUS (100)
        STERNBERGIA LUTEA (50)

This planting capitalizes on the wonderful backlighting of October afternoons, which is so magnificently picked up by the plumes of the *Miscanthus sinensis* and which causes the *Pseudolarix* to glow with gold. Golden yellow is repeated with the *Viburnum* (berries), *Vinca* (foliage variegation), and *Sternbergia* (blossoms), while contrasting darker colors add depth and enrichment: dark green foliage (*Taxus*), burgundy foliage (*Itea* and *Geranium*), and blue blossoms (*Crocus*).

NOVEMBER

Structure:
    GINKGO BILOBA (1)
    CRATAEGUS VIRIDIS 'WINTER KING' (3)

Center of Interest:
    HAMAMELIS VIRGINIANA (1)

Texture, Broad:
    ILEX OPACA 'XANTHOCARPA' (5)

Texture, Fine:
    JUNIPERUS X MEDIA 'OLD GOLD' (12)

Ground Cover:
    CYCLAMEN HEDERIFOLIUM (36)
    POLYSTICHUM ACROSTICHOIDES (300)

The drama of leaf fall brings renewed appreciation for branch structure (broad-spreading *Ginkgo* and *Crataegus*) and the charm of mixing deciduous with evergreen (pyramidal *Ilex*, horizontal *Juniperus*, and *Polystichum* ground cover). Sparkle is added by yellow berries (*Ilex*), orange-red berries (*Crataegus*), and golden-variegated foliage (*Juniperus*). The central feature of this magic world is the delicate, fragrant blossoms of the Witch-hazel (*Hamamelis*), underplanted with rose-pink *Cyclamen*.

DECEMBER

Structure:
    SCIADOPITYS VERTICILLATA (5)

Center of Interest:
    SALIX ACUTIFOLIA 'LONGIFOLIA' (1)

Texture, Broad:
    ILEX X MESERVAE 'BLUE MAID' ® (MESID) (7)
    ILEX VERTICILLATA 'WINTER RED' (5)

Texture, Fine:
    CORNUS SERICEA (3)

Ground Cover:
    EUONYMUS FORTUNEI 'GRACILIS' (300)
    SASA VEITCHII (15)

Christmas colors in the garden will inspire you to decorate with those plants in the house. Dark green (*Sciadopitys* and *Ilex* x *meservae* foliage) and red (*Cornus*, stems; and *Ilex verticillata*, berries) take on an especially cheerful character when contrasted with the green and white variegation of the *Sasa* and *Euonymus* foliage. On slender branches, the first silvery *Salix* catkins of the year highlight the grouping.

A NOTE ABOUT RESOURCES

All of the plants discussed in these lists are available someplace in the United States, but not all of them will be at your local garden center. Although locating some will require a special effort on your part, this can become a challenging treasure hunt.

Your local garden center or landscape contractor may be helpful in locating and supplying hard-to-find varieties. Try to make your inquiry a season in advance of actual need.

Information centers at flower shows and horticultural societies can often be good sources. Members of horticultural societies also frequently have the privilege of advertising their needs in the society's publication.

Most public gardens, botanic gardens, and arboreta worth their salt can help in this regard as well. Currently in the libraries of most of these institutions are the following extremely useful publications, which list plant sources:

Andersen Horticultural Library's
Source List of Plants and Seeds
Minnesota Landscape Arboretum
3675 Arboretum Drive, Box 39
Chanhassen, MN 55317

Combined Rose List (current year)
Compiled and available from:
Beverly R. Dobson
215 Harriman Road
Irvington, NY 10533

The success of these publications of course depends on frequent updating. Ask for the most recent issue.

INDEX

Page references in **boldface** refer to illustrations